Śabdapramāṇa

Word and Knowledge as Testimony

Studies of Classical India

THE aim of this series is to publish fundamental studies concerning classical Indian civilization. It will conclude editions of texts, translations, specialized studies, and scholarly works of more general interest related to various fields of classical Indian culture such as philosophy, grammar, literature, religion, art and history.

In this context, the term 'Classical India', covers a vast area both historically and geographically, and embraces various religions and philosophical traditions, such as Buddhism, Jainism, and Hinduism, and many languages from Vedic and Epic Sanskrit to Pāli, Prākṛt and Apabhraṁśa. We believe that in a profoundly traditional society like India, the study of classical culture is always relevant and important.

Classical India presents an interesting record of deep human experience, thoughts, beliefs and myths, which have been a source of inspiration for countless generations. We are persuaded of its lasting value and relevance to modern man.

By using extensive and for the most part unexplored material with scientific rigor and modern methodology, the authors and editors of this series hope to stimulate and promote interest and research in a field that needs to be placed in its proper perspective.

Studies of Classical India, v. 10

Śabdapramāṇa
Word and Knowledge as Testimony
in Indian Philosophy

by
Purushottama Bilimoria

Foreword by
J. N. Mohanty

Pre-word by
K.T. Pandurangi

Prologue by
Stephen H. Phillips

D.K.Printworld (P) Ltd.
New Delhi

Cataloging in Publication Data — DK
[Courtesy: D.K. Agencies (P) Ltd. <docinfo@dkagencies.com>]

Bilimoria, Purushottama.
Śabdapramāṇa = Word and knowledge as testimony : in Indian philosophy / by Purushottama Bilimoria; foreword by J.N. Mohanty; pre-word by K.T. Pandurangi; prologue by Stephen H. Phillips.
p., cm.
Reprint. Originally published: Dordrecht : Kluwer Academic Publishers, 1988. (Studies of classical India ; v. 10)
Includes bibliographical references (p.)
Includes indexes.
ISBN 13: 9788124604328
ISBN 10: 8124604320

1. Knowledge, Theory of (Hinduism). 2. Language and languages — Philosophy. 3. Phenomenology. 4 Philosophy, Indic. I. Title. II. Title: Word and knowledge.

DDC 181.4 22

ISBN 13: 978-81-246-0432-8
ISBN 10: 81-246-0432-0
First Published in The Netherlands in 1988
Republished in India in 2008
with due permission and copyright release from Springer Verlag, Dordrecht.

Published and printed by:
D.K. Printworld (P) Ltd.
Regd. Office: 'Srikunj', F-52, Bali Nagar
Ramesh Nagar Metro Station
New Delhi-110 015
Phones: (011) 2545 3975; 2546 6019; *Fax*: (011) 2546 5926
E-mail: dkprintworld@vsnl.net
Website: www.dkprintworld.com

TABLE OF CONTENTS

FOREWORD

Dr Purusọttama Bilimoria's book on *śabdapramāṇa* is an important one, and so is likely to arouse much controversy. I am pleased to be able to write a Foreword to this book, at a stage in my philosophical thinking when my own interests have been turning towards the thesis of *śabdapramāṇa* as the basis of Hindu religious and philosophical tradition. Dr Bilimoria offers many novel interpretations of classical Hindu theories about language, meaning, understanding and knowing. These interpretations draw upon the conceptual resources of contemporary analytic and phenomenological philosophies, without sacrificing the authenticity that can arise only out of philologically grounded scholarship. He raises many issues, and claims to have resolved some of them. Certainly, he advances the overall discussion, and this is the best one could hope for in writing on a topic to which the best minds of antiquity and modern times have applied themselves.

In this Foreword, I wish to focus on one of the issues which I have raised on earlier occasions, and on which Dr Bilimoria has several important things to say. The issue is: is *śabdabodha eo ipso* a linguistic knowing, i.e., *śabdapramā*, or does *śabdabodha* amount to knowing only when certain specifiable conditions are satisfied. It the second alternative be accepted, these additional conditions could not be the same as the familiar *āsatti* (contiguity), *yogyatā* (semantic fitness), *ákāṅkṣā* (expectancy) and *tātparya* (intention), for these are, on the theory, conditions of *śabdabodha* itself. For these conditions, the reader should consult the text of this book. It should be noted that on the first alternative, all *śabdabodha* is *pramā*, i.e. true, so that a false (a-*pramā*) *śabdabodha* would be a contradiction in terms. And yet, in an intuitively clear sense, one does *understand* a false sentence. What then hearing a false sentence being uttered by a speaker taken to be competent generates in the hearer could not be knowledge. It can only be an understanding of the meaning of the sentence. From this, one could proceed to the more general thesis: in all cases – whether the sentence heard is true or false – there is a linguistic understanding. In the case of a true sentence, the understanding becomes a component of knowing. In the case of a false sentence, when the falsity is discovered (and so is the incompetency of the speaker), the knowledge claim is revoked, the underlying understanding stands all by itself.

Now this last picture is clearly rejected by the theories of *śabdabodha* in classical Indian philosophy (with the possible exception of the so-called grammarians). These theories, in fact, take (i) *śabdabodha* to be, by definition, true, (ii) and consequently have *no* interesting notion of linguistic *understanding*. A notion of understanding requires not only a concept of meaning, but also one that is different from that of reference. It is not necessary that this theory of meaning be as strongly Platonistic as the Fregean theory of sense; what is necessary is that it not be a purely referential theory. The Indian theories under consideration did subscribe to a purely referential theory. Words directly refer to their objects. A sentence directly refers to a complex relational object. Understanding a sentence is knowing this object, if the sentence is true i.e. if there is such an object. What happens if the sentence is false?

The Indian theories generally held the view that we do not have a *śabdabodha* of a false sentence. (Rather, what we have in such a case is a peculiar mental (*mānasa*) state.) Is this view counter-intuitive? It would be so, *only if* we construe *śabdabodha* as linguistic *understanding*. It is counter-intuitive to say that we do not understand the meaning of a false sentence. But the view is *not* counter-intuitive, if by *śabdabodha* is meant linguistic *knowledge*: we surely cannot be said to know, when the sentence heard is false.

Let me then take it as uncontroversial (1) that we do *understand* false sentences, but (2) do not have a *knowledge* upon hearing and understanding such a sentence. (1) entails a theory of understanding which the Indian theories do not have. (2) leaves the basic theory of *śabdabodha* intact: *śabdabodha* is intrinsically *pramā* (at least, with regard to *utpatti,* if not with regard to *jñapti* – i.e., it *is* true, to begin with, even if it is not known to be so).

But this would be an unsatisfactory solution, for (1) and (2) cannot be held together. A theory of understanding as is implied in (1) requires a theory of meaning – of meaning that is grasped in understanding a sentence, no matter if that sentence is true or false. But such a theory of meaning – which cannot be purely referential, for then (1) will have to be rejected – will undermine the claim made in (2). Nothing less than a purely referential theory can save (2), and yet a purely referential theory will undermine (1). That (2) needs a purely referential theory is corroborated by the passage, Dr Bilimoria cites from the late K.C. Bhattacharyya: a word qua sentence refers "directly to the thing, expresses the thing, *touches* it." (K.C. Bhattacharyya, *Studies in*

Philosophy, Vol. I, Ch. III, p. 83, cited in this book, p. 326, fn. 150). With a purely referential theory of meaning, understanding a false sentence becomes a 'mock-understanding' (as Arindam Chakraborty would have it using a Fregean locution).

Let me here turn to Arindam Chakraborty's paper 'Understanding Falsehoods: A Note on the Nyāya concept of Yogyatā' (*The Journal of the Asiatic Society,* XXVIII, 1986, pp. 10–20) in which he directly confronts the problem. Chakraborty recognizes that on the usual understanding of '*yogyatā*' as (semantic) compatibility or fitness, although sentences such as "Idleness is green" and "He is sprinkling with fire" are ruled out from generating *śabdabodha*, a false sentence such as "The jar is on the floor" is not, (when there actually is no jar on the floor referred to in the context of the utterance). Wishing to rule out this possibility, Chakraborty then interprets a suggestion from *Siddhāntamuktāvalī* as implying that a sentence '*a* is *F*' is characterised by fitness (*yogyatā*) only if *a* is *F* – which makes fitness collapse with 'truth'. Only true sentences are *fit* and so can generate *śabdabodha*. Not only contradictory sentences such as "The fireless hill has fire", but also consistent but semantically absurd sentences such as "Idleness is green" and even contingently false sentences such as "It is raining" (when it in fact is not) – all these cannot generate *śabdabodha*. They may generate "a mental state" consisting of *memories* of the referents of the component words, but they cannot generate a relational, qualificative cognition, for there *is* no such relational entity to know.

Now, this ingenuous interpretation of '*yogyatā*' is indistinguishable from 'truth', in fact, it is the same as that. It smacks of ruling out the possibility of understanding false sentences by stipulating by a fiat, as it were, that truth is a condition of sentence-understanding. Even if this anxiety is in some way alleviated, consider this interpretation of *yogyatā* together with the position that what is required for *śabdabodha* is not *yogyatā* itself but *awareness* of *yogyatā*, then a certain determination of truth is being built into the theory – which is in conflict with the thesis of *parataḥ-prāmāṇya*. The only way of obviating this is to weaken the sense of 'awareness of *yogyatā* (= truth)' to mean 'absence of firm disbelief in absence of *yogyatā* (i.e. in untruth)', but in that case when one believes a sentence (in fact false) to be true (and regards the speaker to be competent etc.) one must be understanding it, and since he is not knowing anything, *this* understanding has to find a place in a theory of *śabdabodha*. To say that in this and other cases of putative understanding of false sentences, what occurs is simply recalling of meanings of the component expressions but no integrated sentence meaning won't do for four reasons: first, to base this claim on the fact that there is no integrated 'featured individual' of the sort is precisely to beg the issue about what one grasps in understanding (as contrasted with knowing); secondly, one cannot distinguish phenomenologically the two experiences (i.e. understanding a false sentence when believed to be true and understanding a true sentence believed to be true); the matter gets – in the third place – more complicated, to the disadvantage of the proposal under consideration, when one considers true sentences taken to be false; and, finally, the way the distinction is sought to be drawn (namely, that in the case of true sentences there is a 'qualificative cognition' whereas in the case of false sentences there is merely memory of 'unrelated' substantial meanings) is compatible with the Prābhākara theory of *a-khyāti* rather than with the Nyāya theory of *anyathākhyāti*.

Let me now return to the sentence quoted from K.C. Bhattacharyya: 'The word *directly* refers to the thing, expresses the thing, *touches* it in a sense." Likewise, "The sentence at once refers to an objective relation." There are two things about K.C. Bhattacharyya's thesis (or interpreation of *śabdapramāṇa*) which deserve attention. For one thing, in the sentence just preceding the first-quoted one, he writes that *even in the case of a word* remembering is not understanding the meaning. This contrasts with the account we examined earlier: in the case of a false sentence, we do understand the meanings of words by way of remembering them, but that does not constitute self-understanding. K.C Bhattacharyya is, in fact, distinguishing between (let us not forget, he is interpreting the Vedānta, and not the Nyāya theory) the name, the concept and the objective reference, for he goes on to write: "The free concept not only requires the name for its support but is identical with it, though transcending it." Then, a little later, he continues: "the same determination of the self gives the name and the concept an identical object-reference." I take "the free concept" to mean "meaning" (as distinguished from objective reference). By "the determination of the self", I take it, following the editor's footnote at that place, to mean "the assertive function of the self". Read this together with what follows in the next paragraph (and this is the second thing to be attended to): "The primordial objective reference of a judgement is a provisional belief, a belief, it may be, with a certain general cautiousness induced by experience: if it is only *thought,* it is at any rate *continuous* with knowledge." And we are far removed from the Nyāya theory commented upon earlier. It is a theory of *direct* reference of sentence, *mediated by* provisional, uncontradicted belief, and also a theory of *direct* reference of words, again mediated by a concept that is *not distinguished from* the name. Let us remember that the locutions "direct" and "indirect" are ambiguous: one can ask, how direct? how indirect? You may have a concept of mediation by a sense-content (conceived as transparent, objectified only in reflection) which is compatible with a theory of direct reference. This is what I have been intending these critical remarks to point to.

At the end, I will raise another question about the idea of *śabda* as a means of *knowing*, as a *pramāṇa*. In what sense, one wonders, is linguistic knowing (*śabdajñāna*), a grasping (*grahaṇa*) of a relational ontological structure (or of a properly qualified individual)? Since one may *also* perceive the same individual (exactly as qualified as in the case of linguistic knowing), how is the purely linguistic grasping of the object different, qua grasping, from a perceptual grasping of it – especially from the sort of perceptual grasping that, according to both Nyāya and Mīmāṃsā, is shot through (*anuviddha*) with linguisticality, i.e. from the so-called *savikalpaka* percention? Of course, one may want to explain the cognitive difference by means of the different way each is *caused*, but what I am at present interested in is, how is the one cognition, *as a grasping,* different from the other when both are graspings of the same object. Perhaps, the distinction between 'direct' and 'indirect' ('*aparokṣa*' and '*parokṣa*') will help, but this distinction is hopelessly ambigiuous as already pointed out. Perhaps the locution of 'grasping' is misleading, when extended from perception to linguistic knowing. It may be that the Jaina distinction between '*viṣada*' and '*aviṣada*' ('clear' and 'not-clear') will help.

J. N. Mohanty,
Professor of Philosophy, Chair,
Department of Philosophy,
Temple University
Philadelphia
U.S.A.

Śabdapramāṇaka vayam, yac chabda āha tad asmākaṃ pramāṇam – we go by the authority of the word. What the word says is our authority.

---Patañjali (*Mahābhāṣya* on *Pāṇini* IV 1 3).

Vāc is the leg of the mind, for by its use the mind gives expression to what it has to communicate to another, much as a cow (arises) on its legs (to move) towards its destination.

---Śaṅkara (*Chāndogya Upaniṣad-bhāṣya* III.18)

anuviddhamiva jñānaṃ sarvaṃ śabdena bhāsate—
all knowledge shines, as though impregnated with the word.

--Bhartṛhari (*c*.350-500 C.E.), *Vākyapadīya* I.123 (115)

Language is an instrument. . . Its concepts are instruments.'

--Wittgenstein, *Philosophical Investigations* II.Xi

Pre-Word

Śabdapramāṇa has an important place in Indian philosophy. Two schools of Indian philosophy, Pūrva-Mīmāṁsā and Uttara Mīmāṁsā (Vedānta), entirely derive their doctrines from *śabdapramāṇa*, from the Brāhmaṇa portion of Veda and Upaniṣads respectively. These two consider *śabdapramāṇa* as the supreme authority. In contrast, the two schools of Vaiśeṣika and Prābhākara-Mīmāṁsā include it under inference. Prābhākaras accept *śabdapramāṇa* so far as Veda is concerned and include *pauruṣeya śabda* under inference.

In Indian philosophy the nature of *pramāṇa* in general, its classification, the nature of *śabda* in the case of *śabdapramāṇa*, the theories of word-meaning, the theories of sentence-meaning, and the theories of truth and error are discussed in detail.

Dr Purushottama Bilimoria analyses the Nyāya, Mīmāṁsā and Advaita views on these issues. His chief purpose is to give an exposition of the Advaita concept of *śabdapramāṇa*. He presents the relevant portion of the Sanskrit text of *Vedānta Paribhāṣā* and its English exposition with his comments.

The Definition of Pramāṇa

The expression *pramāṇa* conveys both valid cognition and the means of valid cognition. It is both *bhāvārtha* and *kāraṇārtha*. From the context it has to be ascertained whether it is used in the sense of valid cognition or the means of valid cognition. The expression *pramā* means valid cognition. Therefore it is preferable to use this word to convey valid cognition.

Vedānta Paribhāṣā defines *pramāṇa* as *pramākaraṇa* (means of valid cognition) and defines *pramā* as *anadhigata abādhita jñāna* (the cognition that is not already acquired, and not sublated, is valid cognition).

In this definition the clause *anadhigata* excludes *smṛti* (memory) and *anuvāda* (re-statement) from the scope of valid cognition. The clause *abādhita* (not sublated) excludes *viparyaya*, i.e. distorted cognition and doubt from the scope of the valid cognition. *Vedānta Paribhāṣā* is not particular about the exclusion of *smṛti* (memory) from the scope of valid cognition. Therefore, it is also stated that the clause *anadhigata* may be deleted from the definition of valid cognition. It may also be noted that Dvaita Vedānta considers *smṛti* (memory) as valid cognition. The ground for the validity of the cognition of an object is that it should reflect the time and place at which the object is cognized. This is true in the case of memory, since it does reflect the time and place wherein the object was first cognized. Further, memory is not produced by *saṁskāra*. It is produced by *manas*. *Saṁskāra* is only a *vyāpāra*, i.e. intermediary process.

Prābhākaras do not require the clause *abādhita* (not sublated) as all cognitions are valid according to their *ākhyāti* theory of truth and error.

Nyāya defines valid cognition as *tadvati tatprakārakam jñānam* — the cognition of an object as characterized by its own characteristic. In the case of distorted cognition the object is cognized as qualified by the characteristic of some other object. For instance, when *rajata* is cognized as characterized by *rajatattva*, it is valid cognition. On the contrary when *śukti* is cognized as characterized by *rajatattva,* it is distorted cognition.

The clause *abādhita* needs an explanation in Advaita. According to Advaita the entire world is sublated when *ātmaikya-jñāna* arises. Hence, the scope of *abādhita* should be limited to *saṁsāra* stage only. The cognition that is not sublated during *saṁsāra* stage is valid cognition. If it is sublated during *saṁsāra* stage it is not a valid cognition.

After discussing the definition of *pramāṇa* in general, the *Vedānta-Paribhāṣā* takes up the discussion of *pratyakṣa*, *anumāna* and *āgama.*

The theory of sentence-meaning constitutes *āgama pramāṇa* or *śabdapramāṇa*. Sentence is of the nature of relation of the word-meanings or the related word-meanings. The sentence of which the intended relation is not contradicted by any other *pramāṇa* leads to valid cognition.

> *yasya vākyasya tātparya viṣayībhūta saṁsargaḥ*
> *mānantareṇa na bādhyate tadvākyam pramāṇam* ।

Four Requirements of Sentence-Meaning

For the generation of the cognition by the sentence, there are four requirements: (1) *ākāṅkṣā*, i.e. mutual expectancy of the words that convey the agent, object and action, (2) *yogyatā*, i.e. non-contradiction of the intended relation of word meanings, (3) *sannidhi*, i.e. proximity, that is to say, the presentation of the meaning of the words in the sentence without any interruption; and (4) *tātparya* which is defined as *tatpratītijanana yogyatva* (the capacity of a sentence to generate the cognition intended by the sentence).

It should be noted that the intention stated here is not the intention of the speaker but the intention built into the in the structure of the sentence itself. This is important because there is no speaker in the case of the Veda. A sentence has an inbuilt capacity to convey its meaning. This is *tātparya* or *tatparatva*. This could be ascertained from the *prakaraṇa*, i.e. context, etc. in *laukika* statements and *upakrama, upasaṁhāra,* etc. criteria in the case of Vedic statements.

The Theories of Word Meaning

A word is a group of syllables that has a meaning. A single syllable also is a word if it has meaning.

There are two levels of denotative powers for words: (i) primary and (ii) secondary. These are designated as *śakti* and *lakṣaṇā*.

In respect of *śakti* —

(i) Bhāṭṭas hold the view that *jāti*, i.e. class characteristic, is conveyed by the primary denotative power. The *vyakti*, i.e. the object, is conveyed by *lakṣaṇā*.

(ii) Vaiśeṣikas hold the view that *jāti viśiṣṭa vyakti*, i.e. the object qualified by class characteristic, is conveyed.

(iii) Grammarians hold the view "in some cases *jāti* is conveyed, in others *vyakti* is conveyed."

(iv) Nyāya also holds the same view.

(v) Advaita holds the same view as that of Bhāṭṭa.

Lakṣaṇā, the secondary denotative power is of three types:

(i) *Jahallakṣaṇā*

(ii) *Ajahallakṣaṇā*

(iii) *Jahadajahallakṣaṇā*

Among these the third one plays a special role in Advaita.

Interpretation of Tat tvam asi

The statement *tat tvam asi* is interpreted adopting this *lakṣaṇā*. The word *tat* means *sarvajñatva viśiṣṭa caitanya* (*Brahman*); *tvam* means *alpajñatva viśiṣṭa caitanya* (*jīva*); *asi* states an identity between the two. There cannot be identity between *sarvajña* and *alpajña*. Hence these attributes have to be ignored and only the *caitanya* aspect of the two should be taken to work out the identity.

Vedānta Paribhāṣā explains this position followed by earlier writers but states that without even *lakṣaṇā*, the identity can be worked out.

When the identity between two qualified objects conveyed by primary denotative power is not possible, then the identity can be worked out between the objects while ignoring the qualification. There is no need of *lakṣaṇā* for this purpose:

> *viśiṣṭa vācaka padānām ekadeśa paratve na lakṣaṇā iśaktyupasthitayaḥ viśeṣyayoreva anvayā virodhāt*

Strictly speaking, the statement *tat tvam asi* leads to *nirvikalpaka pratyakṣa* of *śuddha caitanya Brahman* without involving any relation. This is technically designated as *akhaṇḍārtha*.

To arrive at such cognition through this statement *tātparya viṣayatva* constitutes the ground. The statement *sadeva saumya* at the commencement of the discourse and *tat tvam asi* at the end determine the *tātparya* in the identity. The term *akhaṇḍatva* is explained as *saṁsarganavagahi yathārtha jñāna*.

Apauruṣeyatva of Veda

Nyāya holds the view that the Vedas are composed by God. Mīmāṁsā considers the Veda as eternal. However, Advaita holds that the Vedas are created at the time of the creation of the world and continue in the same order until *pralaya*.

The *varṇa* (syllables) are also enduring from the time of *sṛṣṭi* to that of *pralaya*. This can be ascertained by the recognition of syllables in different utterences of words as the same syllable. When a word is uttered the syllables in it are manifested. These are not generated.

Vedas arising at the time of creation from God do not affect the *apauruṣeyatva* of Vedas. Recitation of Vedic texts in the same manner generation after generation is *apauruṣeyatva*. God also recites it exactly in the same manner in which it was recited in the earlier *kalpa*.

> *sargadyakāle parameśvaraḥ pūrva sarga siddha vedānupūrvī samanānupūrvikam vedam virucitvan na tu tad vijātīyam*

Intrinsic Validity of Cognition

Advaita considers the validity of cognition to be intrinsic and self-evident both in respect of its generation and comprehension. The means of generating the cognition are also the means of generating validity. When a cognition is generated its validity is also generated without any additional or external means. Similarly, the means of comprehending the cognition is also the means of comprehending its validity; no additional means is required for it. Thus both in respect of generation and comprehension validity of a cognition is intrinsic and self-evident. *Apramāṇya,* i.e. invalidity, is due to distortion of the means of cognition.

Nyāya holds the opposite view. According to Nyāya, *guṇa*, i.e. perfection in the application of the means of cognition, will ensure validity, while with *doṣa* certain drawbacks will lead to invalidity. Validity can be ascertained by a successful result, and the failure of a result will indicate invalidity. For instance, a person observes from a distance a lake-like object and thinks that there is water. On proceeding to that place if he finds water and is able to drink it his cognition is successful; on the contrary, if it is a mirage, he will not find water, and consequently his cognition results in failure and indicates the invalidity of the cognition.

This theory leads to *anavasthā,* i.e. infinite regress. Here the cognition of water is verified by the cognition of drinking the water and quenching the thirst. But this second cognition also has to be verified by another cognition to confirm its validity. This third cognition by one more results in infinite regress.

All these issues are discussed by Dr Purushottama Bilimoria within modern epistemological and linguistic perspectives.

Prof. K.T. Pandurangi
Hon. Director
Dvaita Vedanta Foundation, Bangalore

PROLOGUE*

READING Bilimoria's book after having read a review of it by Johannes Bronkhorst[1] prompted me to respond with a piece of a somewhat unusual cast. Here, a main concern of mine is the question of how it is possible for Bronkhorst and myself to have such different reactions, and appraisals, of Bilimoria's book. The gap in our responses may have to do with opposition between the goals and methods of Indology, on the one hand, and the nature of philosophical engagement on the other. I hope not. The two disciplines should be complementary, not antagonistic. I shall present reflections on this possible opposition, and in the process what I think about Bilimoria's book will become clear.

It is indisputable that there are, broadly, two distinct scholarly approaches to Sanskrit philosophical texts that we group as the Indological, which is philological and historical in orientation, and the philosophical, which is, at bottom, evaluative. There are, accordingly, two groups of scholars: professors of Indology and a motley crew of philosophers working on classical Sanskrit texts. Indological readings are attuned to questions of intellectual history, aimed toward an understanding of the Sanskrit text or texts within the relevant history of ideas and, sometimes, within a broader cultural context. Philosophical readings aim at evaluation, the deciding of what we should believe about specified topics and why — normally the very topics addressed by the Sanskrit text being studied. The philosophic approach makes the text party to contemporary philosophic discussions; the Indological approach typically does not. Bronkhorst's worst mistake appears to be a failure to appreciate the evaluative engagement in Bilimoria's writings.

Let me stress that in the review by Bronkhorst one finds such a cavalier attitude toward, in particular, Bilimoria's evaluative conclusions that one has to suspect a disrespect not just for Bilimoria's effort in this particular book, but for philosophic studies in general. *Śabda-pramāṇa* is an excellent example of a properly philosophic study. It is an outstanding example of philosophic engagement with classical Sanskrit texts, ranking with the best of the

* First published as a Book Review Response in *Philosophy East & West*, vol 45, no 2, April 1995, pp 273-79. Gratefully, with permissions of the author, Editor of *Philosophy and East & West*, and its publisher, the University of Hawaii Press, Honolulu.

1. Johannes Bronkhorst, review of Bilimoria's *Śabda-pramāṇa*, *Journal of Indian Philosophy* 21 (1) (March 1993): 103-05.

achievements of B. K. Matilal, Sibajiban Bhattacharyya, Kalidas Bhattacharyya, Karl Potter, J. N. Mohanty and a handful of others. Bilimoria urges us to think *with* the texts, and this book is the result of many years of his doing just that. It is telling that Bronkhorst intends to make his most biting remark — or one of his most biting remarks — in speculating about Bilimoria's intended audience. The answer, however, is obvious: philosophers, especially those (located primarily in India) familiar with classical Indian thinkers and schools. (Bilimoria says as much: "*Philosophy,* in a somewhat wider sense than the currently dominant approach, is where I would place this work" — p. 4). Bronkhorst's review shows that he is unfamiliar with issues of philosophy, and suggests that he only skimmed Bilimoria's book. My sense is that his criticisms reflect not so much conflicts between goals and methodologies as misappreciation of Bilimoria's project. Bronkhorst seems to have little respect for philosophy as such. But I do want to worry further about the question of possible antagonism between the two disciplines, and not myself be cavalier about Bronkhorst's appraisal. After first righting the record by taking up certain outright errors in the review, I shall address methodological questions.

According to Bronkhorst (p. 103), Bilimoria finds the claim that the Veda has no author *(apauruṣeya)* "preposterous". But in fact what Bilimoria says is, "This (the doctrine of *apauruṣeya*) appears, on the face of it, to be a preposterous claim" (p. 19). Surely, *apauruṣeya* does seem to be, prima facie, or at first blush, a preposterous claim. But to say this by way of introducing a careful exploration of the position is a far cry from judging it ultima facie a preposterous claim. In fact, Bilimoria comes around not so much to defending *apauruṣeya* but to using it as a "methodological device for the possibility of *understanding śruti"* (p. 21), a step on a ladder to appreciating Vedāntin and Mīmāṁsaka views, and, beyond that, a veritable defense of *śabda-pramāṇa* (see, in particular, pp. 307-09). Thus Bronkhorst's representation is, on its face, outrageous, given what Bilimoria actually says.[2]

In other words, Bronkhorst makes a not-so-subtle shift of perspective in purportedly describing Bilimoria's attitude, suggesting an insensitivity to what the classical advocates of *apauruṣeya* proposed. Bronkhorst then pretends indignation based on his misreading and says, "The very presence of an authoritative body of texts without author induced the

2. Has justice fled our small world? Soon after *Śabda-pramāṇa* came out, Bilimoria published "On the Idea of Authorless Revelation (*Apauruṣeya*)" — in *Indian Philosophy of Religion,* ed. Roy W. Perrett (Dordrecht: Kluwar, 1989). This piece *is* practically an outright defense of *apauruṣeya,* as well as another, even more sympathetic disclosure of its sense within Mīmāṁsaka views of language and the holy. It is by far the best essay on the subject that, at least in English (or French, etc.), has so far appeared.

Mimāṁsakas and the Vedāntins to accept that words by themselves — not spoiled by an unreliable or ignorant author, or by some other defect — constitute a means of valid cognition. This so-called *svataḥprāmāṇya* guarantees the validity of the words of the Veda, precisely because they have no author." Note Bronkhorst's expression "precisely because." His next sentence also contains a "because" ["Moreover, because they (the words of the Veda) deal with invisible things, they cannot conflict with any other means of valid cognition"], so I guess it is not *precisely,* or only, because of *apauruṣeya* that the Veda is to be regarded as having *svataḥprāmāṇya* (but also because the Veda deals with invisible things). In any case, *svataḥprāmāṇya* is not, according to Bronkhorst, an epistemic position, capturing in general the stance toward questions of justification, but, rather, it is itself justified — or is justified with respect to the words of the Veda — by the Veda's being without an author (and its being about invisible things). But of course Mīmāṁsakas and Vedāntins would say that *apauruṣeya* (and the Veda's being about invisible things) and indeed *svataḥprāmāṇya* itself are self-justified doctrines. Bronkhorst cavalierly speeds past deep issues, failing to identify *svataḥprāmāṇya* as an epistemological stance. He thus makes a sloppy reconstruction, a fault that a little patience with philosophy, and with Bilimoria's book in particular, might have led him to see, clean up, and put straight.

Instead of defending or elaborating his own interpretation, Bronkhorst proceeds to state flatly, "Bilimoria does not like it (the *svataḥprāmāṇya* doctrine," p. 104). What a misrepresentation! Bilimoria's exploration of this thesis is crucial to his conveying — as it is crucial to the views of many of the classical philosophers he examines — a hard-won and sympathetic appreciation! of "word" or testimony as a knowledge source.

The *svataḥprāmāṇya* thesis is close to what epistemologists call in English "negative coherentism," that is, the view that a claim, simply as cognized or understood, is to be regarded as justified, requiring no justification from anything outside itself, but is also defeatable by failing to cohere with a larger body of belief, or by being contradicted by a claim that coheres more tightly with a larger body of belief. The point of the *svataḥprāmāṇya* label is that innocence is the justificational default. Now the classical Indian thesis is not exactly this; for one thing, it is to apply to cognitions, *jñāna,* not prepositional dispositions. One must renounce the temptation to an easy mapping. But that's just what Bilimoria does, namely, painstakingly delivering this and, more broadly, classical views surrounding the *śabda-pramāṇa* thesis, in wide philosophic perspective, foregoing all easy correspondences. (His is a meticulous study.)

In accordance with the properly philosophic task of evaluation, Bilimoria finds merits and faults with a wide range of classical Indian epistemology, but he has not, contra Bronkhorst, tried to adjust or reinterpret to meet modern tastes. This is not the place to rehearse many details of Bilimoria's reflection; that would require a long essay, the result of an effort undisturbed by Bronkhorst's complaints and questions about philology. Bronkhorst focuses on only a few of Bilimoria's statements about *svataḥprāmāṇya* and so forth and shows that he, Bronkhorst, does not know what he is talking about. Then he has the audacity to generalize, condemning Bilimoria's scholarship, and that with words dripping with sarcasm and irony!

One general remark, that Bronkhorst makes, however, is on target. He is right that "philology necessarily precedes philosophy" (p. 104), at least in the sense that, in the case of reading a Sanskrit philosophical text, one has to know a lot of grammar as well as technical terms, and, usually, be practised in rendering long compounds. Let me not make light of what is required: there are many degrees of proficiency in Sanskrit. (Fortunately, with several exceptions — Dharmakīrti, Śrīharṣa, and poetry writers generally — philosophers tend to have small, if abstract and sometimes technical, vocabularies, and to use straightforward constructions.) But sound philology requires, in addition to Sanskrit ability, familiarity with intellectual context, as Bilimoria stresses (almost *ad nauseam*), since background theories, with any given text, are often elliptically alluded to or are otherwise relevant.

Furthermore, it would be just about as impossible to have at all an adequate understanding of a late text such as the *Vedānta-paribhāṣā* (Bilimoria's principal focus), or anything in Navya-Nyāya, without a sound appreciation of philosophy as a universal discipline, as it would be for a person blind from birth to know phenomenologically what *nīla* means. To cite a truism attributed to Ludwig Wittgenstein, understanding human speech requires participation in human forms of life: fundamentally, we know what the word 'blue' means by knowing English *and* by knowing the practice of correlating certain presentations of experience with use of the word — whether or not we also know how to talk about blue scientifically as a band of the visible spectrum, et cetera. People blind from birth do not know what 'blue' means phenomenologically, whatever be their mastery of science, I think there is something roughly parallel to the phenomenology of colour appreciation in appreciating issues of philosophy, at least with many issues (philosophy of religion may present the widest departure from the principle).

The parallel would seem to hold especially with issues of epistemology, and with those of ontology, I believe, as well. Usages of the Sanskrit word *nīla* in, say, the fourteenth century in Mithilā, may depart marginally from current uses of 'blue' in Melbourne.[3] Were Gaṅgeśa and a Melbourne local to survey

3. At the Ninth World Sanskrit Conference, Melbourne, January 1994, I read an earlier draft.

some one hundred coloured items, lets us imagine, there would probably be some slight discrepancy between those identified as blue and those identified as *nīla*. Similarly, the projects of epistemology influenced by the heritage of Plato, Aristotle, Descartes, and Hume depart from those shaped by Nāgārjuna, Gautama the *Nyāyasūtra-kāra,* Dharmakīrti, Udayana, Śrīharṣa, et alia.

But there is still an objectivity — attempts to track the facts — indeed both an objectivity in these and similar projects and an educational requirement. Education is required to become sensitive to epistemological issues and so forth, somewhat in the way education is required for one to be able to represent even a familiar musical theme, or to recognize a letter of a foreign alphabet that, in the physical sense, one has seen thousands of times. To know Bessie as a cow is not necessarily to realize that cowhood is a universal or natural kind, though it may well be that a universal does indeed ground identification of Bessie as the type of critter she is. There is universality in the projects of philosophy, especially those of epistemology and ontology (less, perhaps, in issues arising out of religion), although it may require training to be able to see what these are. The considerable variations of views presented in philosophy worldwide have to be seen in the context of roughly common concerns with truth, justification, what there is, value, the nature of ourselves as knowers and agents, and canons of argumentation. No mere philologist would be capable of understanding Gaṅgeśa, or Dharmarāja Adhvarīndra. Training in philosophy is required.

What kind of training? My *pūrvapakṣin* would urge that the training should be predominantly historical, that, to take the example of Gaṅgeśa, what one needs to know is the *Nyāyasūtra* and its commentaries, along with, in particular, the extracommentarial treatises of Udayana, as well as several Mīmāṁsaka texts, particularly those of Prabhākara, maybe some of Śrīharṣa's *Khaṇḍanakhaṇḍakhādya,* to appreciate the direction of Gaṅgeśa's arguments on such subjects as *tarka*. Well, no, one should not stop there. Before Gaṅgeśa comes Maṇikaṇṭha Miśra, a Naiyāyika who may have first formulated some of the definitions (of *vyāpti*, etc.) for which Gaṅgeśa became renowned. And renowned among whom? Does not one need to know the responses and commentaries by Raghunātha, Mathurānātha, and others really to understand the earlier Naiyāyika? Nyāya is a self-contained intellectual phenomenon, with a singular history and peculiar concerns, whose pertinent context, beyond its own texts, is the texts of Mīmāṁsā, Vedānta, and so on. Patient, focused Indology, not some vague universalist training, is what is required. According to sound philological method, fourteenth-century writings in Sanskrit in other genres are more relevant than some impossibly ahistorical discipline of philosophy. How else will one know the precise shade meant with Gaṅgeśa's famous example, *nīlo ghaṭaḥ*?

Well, probably neither I nor anyone these days knows precisely what shade Gaṅgeśa intended. Somehow, that seems irrelevant to appreciating his *nīlo ghaṭaḥ*. How, then, are canons of relevance to be established? Are these not determined historically? Well, sometimes, in some cases; it is difficult to generalize. But I dare say that an understanding of predicate logic, or of the realist ontology of Wittgenstein's *Tractatus*, or the reflections of Gottlieb Frege, or of Bertrand Russell on propositions would help a great deal more with Gaṅgeśa's *nīlo ghaṭaḥ* than the fourteenth-century poetry of Mithilā. (The repeated usage shows that Gaṅgeśa uses *nīlo ghaṭaḥ* to stand for any qualificative cognition, *viśiṣṭa-jñāna*, with *nīla* as something like a predicate variable.) Moreover, understanding Gaṅgeśa's reflections on *nīlo ghaṭaḥ* helps one to understand Frege, Wittgenstein, Russell, and the foundations of predicate logic.

Bilimoria and others trained in academia as professional philosophers have found that they share a deep affinity with traditional Naiyāyika and Mīmāṁsaka *paṇḍita*s in India, who, though with no university training, think like philosophers. Consider the contrast between (a) thinking ahistorically about *pramāṇa*, say, or almost any topic of philosophy, and (b) thinking historically, lining up the contributions to the classical Indian *pramāṇa* debate chronologically. Where would a traditionally trained Naiyāyika *paṇḍita* line up with respect to this contrast? Answer: he would line up with ahistorically minded philosophers. It is a commonplace that philosophers of the classical traditions were not much concerned with names and especially dates; they were concerned, and are concerned, with what we should believe or accept *(aṅgīkāra)* about certain issues and why. It is the approach of those with an exclusive concern with history that is alien to the classical traditions, not the approach of those who, like Bilimoria, are concerned, ultimately, with what we should believe about certain topics and why. Traditional Indology, as Bilimoria suggests, is often ethnocentric, unbending in its concerns and, unlike philosophers, unwilling to learn — in the sense of appropriate, take to heart — anything from the texts being inspected. Indology too often seems to have only an "other"; philosophy has a shared "we."

If at the heart of philology with respect to Indian *darśana, ānvīkṣikī,* and *tarka-śāstra* there is a concern with accurate intellectual history, than philologists have much to learn from philosophers such as Bilimoria, since without understanding the issues of philosophy it would be impossible to understand the direction of the intellectual developments. There is progress in philosophy. Considerations are taken into account and positions changed or refined. Gaṅgeśa and other Navya-Nyāya philosophers forge a response to Śrīharṣa's criticisms of Udayana, for example. Uddyotakara, Jayanta, and

Vācaspati refute the Buddhhist *apoha* theory of generality. Madhusudana Sarasvatī takes Gaṅgeśa's definition of *pramā,* veridical awareness, and uses it to shore up the Advaita epistemological stance. History requires focus — and judgment about what is valuable or relevant and what is not. Philosophers make such judgments in responding to their heritages, and anyone who would trace intellectual history in this area must be able to see how and why philosophers are moved.

All this is not to belittle patient scholarship with respect to names and dates — and texts. There are so many pages to turn, and I can understand why philologically oriented Indologists get impatient with philosophers' evaluative pronouncements. There are, after all, many subtle nuances of view and argument, and it is extremely difficult, in some cases, to bring hidden suppositions to light. Bilimoria, by the way, is well aware of the difficulties facing philosophic interpreters of classical Sanskrit texts. There is special irony in Bronkhorst's complaints because of the breadth of classical texts that Bilimoria brings to bear on the interpretation of a single work, the *Vedāntaparibhāṣā.* Patient philology has preceded philosophy with Bilimoria's book. Unfortunately, philologically oriented Indologists sometimes seem less appreciative of sound philosophical engagement.

The disciplines of intellectual history and of philosophy, even in its subfield of the history of philosophy, have distinct aims, the first descriptive, the second evaluative. But these goals are intertwined. There is mutual dependence. One should not pretend to evaluate what one does not understand; similarly, philosophic evaluation must direct intellectual history as well as be reflected by it. Thus, in particular, all of us should be sensitive to the evaluations expressed by the classical philosophers themselves.

Stephen H. Phillips
Professor of Philosophy and Asian Studies
Department of Philosophy
University of Texas at Austin
Austin (USA)

ACKNOWLEDGEMENTS

In preparing this book I have been greatly aided by the comments of Professors Bimal K. Matilal (Oxford), Karl Potter (Washington), and S. D. Joshi (Poona)—all of whom painstakingly read the two volume work initially prepared on this subject. Professor J. N. Mohanty (Oklahoma; now in Temple) made some incisive comments on a submitted draft which has added vastly to the improvement of this work. I had also the good pleasure of working closely on this book with Professor Matilal during a sabbatical in Oxford (1983). Professors Ninian Smart and Raimundo Panikkar also looked the work at its various stages and encouraged me with valuable comments and suggestions (particularly during two short visits to University of California, Santa Barbara). Professor Harold Coward (Calgary) also looked at the final draft and made some suggestions.

A number of scholars rendered me invaluable assistance while I worked on my doctoral dissertation on this subject, which was submitted to the Department of Philosophy, La Trobe University, Victoria, Australia. I take this opportunity to record my debt to all of them, in particular Drs G. V. Devasthali, V. N. Jha, Shiv Kumar, Professor S. S. Barlingay (all of University of Poona, Pune, where I spent two separate terms reading relevant texts).

Nearer to home, I owe much to (the late) Dr Ian Kesarcodi-Watson (who inspired me to commence this work but regrettably did not live to see this book in print), Professor Max Charlesworth, Mr Patrick Hutchings (both at Deakin), Dr Moshe Kroy (La Trobe), Dr Telwatte Rahula, Dr Robert Slonek (Monash), and Prof. Kalidas Bhattacharyya (with whom I was corresponding on this work just prior to his sudden death). But for Professors Alan Musgrave (Otago) and Brian Ellis (La Trobe) I may have never risked crossing the Tasman sea, nor beyond.

The Editors and Publisher are to be thanked for including this work in an important series; and I am grateful to Professor J. N. Mohanty for agreeing to pen a Foreword to this book. Dr Peter Fenner (Deakin) read through the manuscript and tendered helpful comments. A number of libraries came to my aid and provided essential service. The Borchardt Library in La Trobe University, Deakin University Library, Madras Government Manuscript Office, Adyar Research and Archive Centre, Bhandarkar Oriental Research Institute, the Centre for Advanced Studies in Sanskrit (Poona), the Indian Institute (Bodleian, Oxford) and the Philosophy departmental library (Oxford) helped give shape to this book. Poona University and All Souls (Oxford) are to be thanked for the facilities provided during the preparation of the thesis and manuscript respectively.

A La Trobe University postgraduate research scholarship, a British Council grant, and a Deakin University sabbatical program and several conference grants saw fruitfully to the continuity of the project, amidst other academic commitments. The secretarial assistance provided by the School of Humanities at Deakin also helped along the way. Mr Campbell McAdam's assistance with preparing the 'proofs' for publication proved to be invaluable beyond words.

I am grateful to the publishers of the following journals for use of my papers, in part or in full, in the present work -*Philosophy East and West* (Honolulu), *Journal of Indian Philosophy* (Dordrecht), *Indian Philosophical Quarterly* (Poona), *Journal of Dharma* (Bangalore), *Annals of the Bhandarkar Oriental Research Institute* (Poona), *Annali, dell'Istituto Universatario Orientale*, Napoli.

Last but not least, beside a number of friends and well-wishers whom I owe considerable gratitude, I am indebted to my dear friend and wife Dr Renuka Sharma, for her compassionate presence and support throughout. I have dedicated this effort to Sathyanarayana and Vishalakshi (lovers of *truth*, of sorts).

ABBREVIATIONS

For ease of reading, some titles and compounds have been broken up into the constituent terms—e.g. *Brahmansūtrabhāṣya* = *Brahma-sūtra-bhāṣya*; *bhaktiyoga* = *bhakti-yoga*.

*	indication of cognate philosophical concept or term
AS	*Advaita Siddhi* of Madhusūdana Sarasvatī
BG	*Bhagavadgītā*
BP	*Bhāṣā-Pariccheda* of Viśvanātha (see also *SM*)
Bṛh Up	*Bṛhadāraṇyaka Upaniṣad*
BSB	*Brahma-sūtra-bhāṣya* of Śaṅkara
Ch Up	*Chāndogya Upaniṣad*
EIP	*Encyclopaedia of Indian Philosophies* (Potter, ed)
ELG	*Epistemology, Logic and Grammar* (Matilal)
GTT	*Gaṅgeśa's Theory of Truth* (Mohanty)
IPQ(P)	*Indian Philosophical Quarterly* (Poona)
IPQ(F)	*International Philosophical Quarterly* (Fordham)
JIP	*Journal of Indian Philosophy* (Dordrecht)
JS	-see *MS*
MBh	*Mahābhāṣya* of Patañjali with *Kātyāyana-vārttika* (Kielhorn edn)
MS	*Mīmāṃsā-sūtras* (sometimes *JS*) of Jaimini
MSB	*Mīmāṃsā-sūtra-bhāṣya* of Śabara (= *Śābara-bhāṣya*)
NKM	*Nyāyakusumāñjali* of Udayana
NM	*Nyāyamañjarī* of Jayanta
NND	*Navya-nyāya Doctrine of Negation* (Matilal)
NS	*Nyāya-sūtras* of Gautama
NSB	*Nyāya-sūtra-bhāṣya* of Vātsyāyana
PS	*Pāṇini-sūtras* or *Aṣṭāthyāyī* of Pāṇini
RS	*Readings in Semantics* (Zabeeh *et at* eds.)
RSG	*A Reader on Sanskrit Grammarians*
SB	*Siddhānta-bindu* of Madhusūdana Sarasvatī
SDS	*Sarvadarśanasaṃgraha* of Mādhava
TV	*Tantravārttika* of Kumārila Bhaṭṭa
SD	*Śāstradīpikā* of Pārthasārathi Miśra
SM	*Siddhānta-muktāvalī* of Viśvanātha on *BP*
SV	*Ślokavārttika* of Kumārila Bhaṭṭa
SSP	*Śabdaśaktiprakāśikā* of Jagadīśa
TB	*Tarkabhāṣā* of Keśava Miśra
TC	*Tattvacintāmaṇi* of Gaṅgeśa
TS	*Tarkasaṃgraha* of Annaṃbhaṭṭa
TS(D)	*Tarkasaṃgraha-dīpikā* of Annaṃbhaṭṭa
VKP	*Vākyapadīya* of Bhartṛhari

VP	*Vedānta-paribhāṣā* of Dharmarājādhvarīndra
VC/Bm	*Bhāmatī* of Vācaspati Miśra
VC/Vr	*Nyāya-sūtra-vārttika* of Vācaspati Miśra
YS	*Yoga-sūtra* of Patañjali (no relation to *MBh*)

For full bibliographical details and abbreviations of other journals, periodicals, serials ,etc., see Appendix B.

Note on transliteration

Standard transliteration of Sanskrit texts has been used. However, for the sake of simplicity, in some places Sanskrit compounds have been broken up into constituent terms, and the English 's' added to indicate the plural (e.g. *doṣaḥ aprāmāṇya janakaḥ*; and, '*guṇas* are *dravyā-śritā*').

INTRODUCTION

The problem

This book makes an attempt at a systematic examination of a rather important problem in Indian philosophy – in particular, a thesis within Advaita Vedānta's theory of knowledge (but not restricted to Advaita, since this is a thesis that also concerns Nyāya, Pūrva Mīmāṃsā, Sāṃkhya and other schools). The thesis in question generally goes under the rubric of *śabdapramāṇa* [or '*śabda-pramāṇa*']: the derivation of knowledge from linguistic utterances or *words*. This work borders between epistemology and philosophy of language, but as such is not an exercise in linguistics, though its relevance in the context of the present discussion cannot be underrated. The problem itself is worthy of philosophical investigation as it has implications for theories of knowledge, language and 'revelation' – implications which should be of considerable interest to scholars and students of philosophy and religion, and of Indian thought and 'spirituality' at large.

The basic aim here is to make sense of the theoretical basis of the 'doctrine of the word', and to consider whether *śabdapramāṇa*, so understood, is a philosophically sound thesis. The traditional presentation of the thesis and of the grounds for its acceptance has often been dense and a difficult terrain, so to speak, for the uninitiate to wade through without loosing oneself in the plethora of arguments, counterarguments, analyses, criticisms and sometimes sheer polemics. Each of the three or four major schools of thought (*darśanas*) that accepts this particular *pramāṇa* or means of knowledge goes about justifying its respective stance in quite different ways. Attempts have been made to synthesise the various different approaches to this problem, but here again several significant issues have been left unattended or not dealt with adequately. In our own times, similar attempts, scarce as they are, have been hampered by, on the one hand, an excessive preoccupation with philological-historical analyses, and, on the other, over-indulgence in speculative 'metaphysic', albeit with a sectarian tinge to it.

It has been thought necessary, therefore, to re-state the thesis in more contemporary terms, while reconstructing the arguments and examining each of the steps in the appropriate contexts of the linguistic, cognitive and epistemic processes that supposedly render successful this particular *pramāṇa vis-à-vis* other means of knowledge. Consequently, what I attempt to develop here is a relatively broad epistemologically based theoretical framework for analysing, understanding and appraising the thesis. And although the source for the analysis was initially derived from works in Advaita Vedānta, the present investigation is by no means confined to Advaita epistemology. Rather, Nyāya arguments and, to an extent, (Pūrva) Mīmāṃsā understanding constitute strong and serious grounding for the present work. Reference to texts from all three schools, therefore, is profuse and varied. (It may be noted in passing that 'Vedānta' is itself regarded to be a version of Mīmāṃsā, namely Uttar Mīmāṃsā, presumably coming 'after', or being hermeneutically posterior to, the orthodox (Pūrva) Mīmāṃsā school.) The relevant views of the Grammarians are also considered, although not to the same extent as the Advaita-Nyāya views are.

In basing the examination largely on Sanskritic texts, I do not mean to deter the non-specialist from participating in this enterprise; rather, my aim has been to make the thesis equally accessible to the general reader who has some acquaintance with the sorts of philosophical issues we are concerned with here. It is for that reason that I have attempted to translate or explain each difficult term or notion used in the context of the discussion. A few pages later, some of the general terms of the doctrine are elucidated.

There should be interest here for religion and moral culture as well, which is derived from the consideration that *śabda*, in its varying forms, is one of the fundamental bases or sources for the sorts of experience and understanding that fall specifically within the domain of religious discourse and doctrinaire activities. The ramifications are enormous when we consider that *śabda* constituted by *śruti*, or the special class of sacrosanct scriptures of Hinduism, such as the Upaniṣads and certain other texts of the Vedas, is the basis for the authentication and acceptance of some very fundamental beliefs and ideas that are regarded to be central to the Hindu tradition. Thus it is that the notions of *authority* and *tradition* weigh heavily on the 'doctrine of the word'.

As such the doctrine is, in the words of Kalidas Bhattacharyya, 'critically relevant for all transcendental Indian philosophy, and also. . .for much of Indian ethics (life of action). That is why all forms of Vedānta, Yoga, Jainism and Mīmāṃsā. . .speak so much, and in such finest details, on *śabda-pramāṇa*, taking the scriptures (of various sorts) as (probably) the only anchorage for all that is transcendental and ethical.'[1]

To be sure, as Prof. J. N. Mohanty, in calling for a re-examination of the priorities and relative strengths and weaknesses of this doctrine, remarks: '[N]o other age since antiquity has been, sheerly on theoretical grounds, more congenial to the idea of recognising the centrality of linguistic texts in a culture's self-understanding and of language in cognitive, moral and religious lives.'[2]

Nevertheless, it is a doctrine that is also, as Kunhan Raja put it, 'the most misunderstood and most misrepresented in the entire range of Indian philosophy.'[3] It is an issue in Indian philosophy and religion generally that, according to Prof. Ninian Smart, has hitherto not received the systematic treatment it clearly deserves.[4] This point cannot be stressed more. The present work was undertaken with a view to rectifying these shortcomings in the current state of scholarship.

The approach

The work deals basically with a technical theory from one area of Indian philosophy in light of philosophical and epistemological issues in the context of recent developments. While I am taking into account recent development and thus, to that extent, am engaged in comparative philosophy, this is not the main concern here. The extremes in any 'comparativist' approach, as in the early movements in religious studies, are to be avoided. For, one danger is that the 'native' view, so to speak, can get overlaid with categories extrapolated from another alien tradition or system, and, in the process, lose its original meaning and function. And yet, at the same time, it is desirable to make intelligible the views of another system of tradition in terms accessible to another school or system, so that there is mutual appreciation, critical reflection—and self-reflection—and an enhancement of what must be, in the last resort, a common quest.

One cannot afford, however, to minimise the difficulties encountered in reading some of the abstruse texts of classical Indian philosophy, which require not only some acquaintance with the texts, written mostly in Sanskrit (perhaps also Pali, Tibetan, Hindi, Bengali, etc.), but also familiarity with the technical terminology of the philosophical and religious tracts that utilise that language and form of discourse. That understanding may require one to read widely *and* also to sit with traditional scholars and paṇḍits in order to appreciate the background texts and contexts against which some of the views were developed and have or had gained currency. Mastery of linguistic skills is one requirement, while insightful skills in the discourse is another, indispensible, requirement.

In other words, being proficient at reading texts is not sufficient; one also has to be able to *interpret* and critically appraise the *philosophic* intent that underscore the arguments. It is here that the real task of the philosopher/scholar begins; and at the same time one has to be sensitive to the totality of the contexts of the thought being studied, not shying away from the useful insights and assistance that relevant intellectual disciplines besides philosophy may have to offer. This, however, is not a plea as such for inter-disciplinarity (whose relevance in particular areas of inquiry is not being questioned), much less for the multi-disciplinary approach popular in some quarters.

Being wary of the works of grand generalisations and wild speculations (supposedly based on Indian philosophy and spirituality), on the one hand, and the formidably stringent approach expected by Indologists (and their predecessor Orientalists, preoccupied more with *philological* than with philosophical concerns), on the other hand, I have tried to steer clear of both extremes.[5] *Philosophy*, in a somewhat wider sense than the currently dominant approach would have it, is where I would place this work. I am guided, though, by the awareness that the method of philosophy is doubtless a tight and a disciplined one inspired by critical reflection and not one given to vain speculation or fanciful flights. Philosophy, indeed, begins with description and the clarification of one's understanding of some problem in relation to the views of others or other systems of thought. As Ludwig Wittgenstein put it: 'a philosophical work consists essentially of elucidation.'[6]

I have, accordingly, struggled to elucidate what I believe underlies an insight into a particular problem of knowing in a tradition of philosophy, bearing in mind developments in another. The abstruse nature of the subject matter apart, and notwithstanding Quine's principle of indeterminancy of translation (and, by extension, of interpretation), the material for this work has been drawn in main from Sanskrit, but also from Hindi and contemporary writing in the area, and has been worked at over some nine years.

Aim and objectives

I wish now to discuss the chief objectives of this work, which I will do in terms of the following: a) the *aim* of this inquiry in respect of the thesis being investigated; and, b) the central problems being examined, in the background of the major text (*Vedāntaparibhāṣā*) and the context relevant to this inquiry. I have already commented on the particular approach taken in this work with some perfunctory remarks in respect of the scope and limits in the context somewhat of comparative thought.

A. In general, my aim is to render intelligible the Advaita position on *śabdapramāṇa*, with critical cross-reference to the respective views in, specially,

Nyāya and Mīmāṃsā schools of Indian thought. The operative question is whether this is a philosophically defensible position based on sound epistemological grounds.

B. There are four major problems; stated briefly, they are:
(i) Whether *śabda* or a linguistic utterance is a valid means of knowing, and if so under what conditions? In other words, is a linguistic utterance a sufficient instrument (*karaṇa*) for generating valid (true) *śābdabodha* or linguistic cognition?

(ii) What is the logical status of the linguistically-generated *bodha* or cognition: is it *true* in and of itself, or does it depend for its truth on factors and conditions other than those necessary for the linguistic process (*vyāpāra*)? A related issue is whether the truth of a cognition is apprehended with the cognition itself, or whether it is apprehended *ab extra.*

(iii) Whether *śabdapramāṇa* is independent of other *pramāṇas* or means of knowing, and if not is the dependency contingent or a necessary one? Does the fact of the dependence detract from the validity and value of this particular means of knowing? What, if anything, is so unique about *śabdapramāṇa* that is not shared by, say, perception?
(iv) Whether the thesis and the ramifications thereof bear significance on the discussion of *śruti* (literally, 'heard word') or scriptural words as a possible source of understanding? What ramifications does this thesis have for a broader appreciation of the 'heard word', or the 'revealed word', as it may be termed in western theology. What are, broadly speaking, the religious ramifications of this thesis in the context of Indian spirituality?
(v) A further question is whether *śabdapramāṇa* has any significance on the wider discussion of a 'theory of knowledge' or *pramāṇaśāstra.*

Since problems *i-iii* are of crucial importance to the inquiry and to an intelligible presentation of the thesis under investigaton, these problems will occupy the entire pages to follow, while problems *iv* and *v*, although of considerable interest, will be touched upon only in passing, and problem *iv* in particular is best left for a more detailed treatment in a separate work.

The issues raised in problems *i-iii* can be broadly clustered under three general categories, viz. *linguistic, phenomenological,* and *logical truth.* In chapter one I weave the three categories in the argument central to the thesis and show how they bear on the thesis. Chapter two begins on a linguistic note and considers the claim that *śabda* or a linguistic unit (i.e. the word) is a *karaṇa* or essential instrument in the generation of *śābdabodha.* Chapter three deals with the connected problem of 'meaning' in terms of *śakti* or 'word-power' which is understood to be an attribute of words and which gives them the constructive form that results in the utterance of a sentence (*vākya*). In chapter four the larger problem of sentence and sentence-meaning in respect of the generation of linguistic cognition (*śābdabodhajanya)* is taken up. In five to six the analysis of *śābdabodha* is taken a step further to show how certain significant conditions, *kāraṇas,* are involved in *understanding* or comprehending sentence-meaning. If the *sense* of a sentence is different from its linguistically generated meaning then the specific conditions for its apprehension have also to be noted. Questions about the nature of the cognition generated and its relation to subjectivity are raised here as well. Chapter seven attempts to grapple with the problem of truth and falsity, and its relevance and impact in the context of the present discussion.

The general problem concerning the distinction (considered to be fundamental) between a cognition (*jñāna*) and a *true* cognition (*pramā*) is introduced in the discussion that follows shortly. The ramifications of the conclusion to be drawn from the analyses and the discussion in the chapters that follow are stated by way of remarks on the Indian notion of 'authoritative word', in the final chapter. The Appendix carries a transliteration of the complete chapter (on *'Āgama'* or *'Śabda'*) from Dharmarājādhvarīndra's work on which largely the argument presented and analysed in the following pages is based. A selection of works consulted and of relevance to the discussion is also appended in the bibliography. This also provides details omitted in the references in the Notes to each chapter.

The thesis and its background

Now I would like to make some comments about the historical scenario in terms of which we can fruitfully discuss the emergence and nourishment of the thesis under consideration. But while I draw upon some historical data to get as it were to the basic orientation and motives that led to the development of the particular doctrine, I am not restricted by this methodology. I thus eschew any attempt to draw historicist claims or to go into the diverse socio-cultural factors that may have moulded the views in the different schools. And while I do not deny the value of investigating the historical forces and the structural context that may have helped to shape such doctrines, particularly from the perspective of history of ideas, what commends to me most is the intrinsic worth of these doctrines. Accordingly, I am looking basically for the more refined and complete expression of the doctrine or thesis in the various schools. This I find to be expressed in terms of three basic concerns, shared largely by a number of Indian schools, namely:

(a) the notion of *pramāṇa* and its importance in classical thought;

(b) the authoritativeness of scriptural word or *śruti*;
(c) the 'power' of language (or, the medium with a message).

Pramāṇa

Our discussion of the notion of *pramāṇa* can only be brief here.[7] In the main, *pramāṇa* seeks to deal with the question of the possibility and grounds of the valid means of knowing. Questions such as 'how do we know?', 'how do we know what we know?', 'how do we know, or establish, the truth or falsity of what we claim to know?', 'how many ways of knowing are there?' and 'do they all lead to the same truth?', arise in this context. Sometimes, an existential dimension is added to these questions in asking what sorts of consequences does *knowing* have for the problem of *being* or for authentic living, and for whatever might be the 'ultimate concern', or the ultimate quest, of human endeavour.

Pramāṇa is defined in terms of the instruments (*kāraṇa-karaṇa*) and the concatenation of conditions and factors (*sāmagrī*) that are capable of bringing about a desired result, in this instance, a genuine piece of knowledge. The criteria for determining the truth or otherwise of this 'knowledge'—i.e. *prāmāṇyaniścaya*—is also given alongside the definition, Further, the sorts of criteria that are accepted, the relative emphasis on each, and the application of these in the context of different *pramāṇa* varies from school to school. Still, there is no gainsaying the fact these issues received prime attention in traditional Indian thought. Indeed, the larger *sūtra* and *bhāṣya* tradition, for example, that characterises the basic experience of each of the major philosophical systems, makes the issue of *pramāṇaśāstra* one of its very first concerns. This is expressed succinctly in one of earliest Nyāya maxims : 'To know the thing to be measured, one must first know the measure.'[8] The aim of philosophy (*ānvīkṣikī*) is explained by Vātsyāyana as having to do with the 'examination of 'objects' of knowledge by means of *pramāṇa*.'[9] Philosophy, apart from its overall quest for *truth (tattva)*, is in one sense *darśana* or 'seeing as', 'an outlook upon', 'a point of view', presumably based on firm grounds or evidence. But in another sense philosophy involves the describing, classifying, examining, questioning, scrutinising, and criticising of the 'objects' of knowledge—i.e. 'measuring' in accordance with certain logical procedures and assumptions. Overall, as M. Hiriyanna points out also,[10] there are three functions of *pramāṇa* that are basic to philosophy. Firstly, as *karaṇa*, the 'source' or 'sources' of knowledge, i.e. the means or instruments of knowing. Secondly, as a means for scrutinising, criticising and evaluating through the process of reasoning the knowledge derived through the 'source/s'. Thirdly, as *prāmāṇya*, the 'measurement' in terms of the criteria for 'truth' or 'falsity', characterised as the problem of validity.

Together, these constitute the *grounds* for the possibility of knowing: *pramāṇavāda*.

In regard to the first function above, the major question raised concerns the nature and number of means of knowing that could feasibly be accepted as being *legitimate*.[11] Experience, it would appear, shows us that perception (*pratyakṣa*), by which we principally mean visual 'seeing', is the first and perhaps the primary source of our knowledge, since sense-experience, of which 'seeing' is a part, is the most common means of awareness of the external world. Although this is not to say that the process of perception itself is a simple one by any means, nor that the configuration of our perception necessarily conforms to that of reality. Nevertheless, to borrow a Kantian parody, perception as it were begins us on the long and difficult road to knowledge, though it may not be seen to deliver the final goods.

Now, when the 'objects' of perceptual awareness are scrutinised and stand in need of appraisal – especially when they are mutually conflicting, or when doubt arises about their authenticity, or when attempt is made to relate them to some structure – *reasoning*, as a mode of ordered thinking, becomes imminent. The early name given for this process was *nyāya*, understood as the process of 'reasoning' or, more specifically, *anumāna*, roughly, 'inference'. It was obvious to Indian philosophers that the usefulness of *anumāna* lay not merely in its capacity to respond to doubt, or to convince oneself or another of the truth or falsity of some claim. For it also functioned as a formal process for deducing or inferring novel understanding from the interrelation of facts, objects or events perceived through such other sources as perception and so forth. 'Logic' is developed as an extension and an aid to the wider capabilities of *anumāna*. The status of this logical source of knowledge as a *pramāṇa* in its own right gave little cause for alarm to almost every school, with the exception of the Cārvāka or so-called Materialist school which accepted *pratyakṣa* or perception as the one and only legitimate means of knowing.

The other major source of knowledge accepted in traditional times was *āgama* or the 'word of tradition', where 'the word' is largely identified with inherited wisdom that is enshrined in the scriptures that are traditionally revered and sanctioned. Undoubtedly, a sense of *wisdom* has invariably been associated with *tradition*, not only in India, but in good many ancient civilisations. What is embedded in tradition is regarded to be valuable since it is backed by years of experience. The experience of the individual is complemented by the cumulative experience of tradition, for which the individual relies upon the 'testimony' either of scriptures or of others who are entrusted with the preservation of the received traditional wisdom. In this context, words become in a technical sense the media and the possibility of communication. The wider acceptance of this means caused little alarm to all except the Cārvāka school. Other schools developed the idea into a theory and articulated its justification in response to the opposition and censorship meted out by those who remained sceptical.

Prima facie, one cannot deny that tradition, whether in a culture or in a structure, functions as an important source of knowledge; it may even be part of the structure. The Indians wanted to argue for a more independent status of this source of understanding, with the concomitant recognition that not any and every bit of information, idea, ritual, behavioural disposition and accumulated wisdom needs to be seriously entertained as part of the tradition. Popular culture at any time is also a rich repository of human understanding and a wide range of knowledge, but not all of it is necessarily authoritative and worth preserving for future ocassions and subsequent generations. One usually looks for what is philosophically interesting and of perennial value among the accumulated body of knowledge, etc., before the question of authority is entertained. Thus begins the process of delimiting and restricting tradition, and thereby its scope and authority.

Hence, it is not tradition as such that becomes a distinct source of knowledge, but rather a tradition that has been systematised as a result of reasoned enquiry,[12] and which has specified a set of epistemological criteria. Examination, interpretation, evaluation and such functions of *pramāṇa* are brought to bear equally on tradition as a viable source of knowledge. Rigorous criteria were evolved to discern what is acceptable and what is to be rejected. A hermeneutics for interpreting the sentences of scriptures (*śruti*) was developed in particular by the Mīmāṃsā school for the purpose of deciding between those *śruti* texts which pertain to rituals or actions from those that concern themselves with knowledge or philosophic understanding. All this is by way of saying that the theoretical underpinning of *śabdapramāṇa*—as the more precise articulation of *āgama* or 'Tradition' came to be known—has its roots in the very early attempt to systematise and justify tradition as one but a legitimate and significant means of knowing. Hence, also, the preoccupation of the Indian philosophers with 'the word' (*śabda*) or linguistic utterance.

The uniqueness of *śabda* as a means of knowing, lay in its having the capacity to be a special instrument among an aggregate of conditions. In particular, it seemed that *śabda* has that capacity to elicit knowledge in contexts and conditions where the other means of knowing seemed to fall short or proved to be less adequate and not very informative. The possibilities of communication that words open up, so to speak, and their encapsulative power, were also reckoned to present certain advantages that most of the other sources clearly lacked.

But the question that haunted the minds of antagonists and protagonists alike was whether this seemingly unique character was sufficient to render *śabda* an independent *pramāṇa*? Intense debate ensued over this question, and several attempts were made by various thinkers to reduce or explain *śabdapramāṇa* in terms of the *pramāṇa* of perception, or of inferential reasoning (chs. 2, 7). The issue of the independence of *śabdapramāṇa* was raised with respect not only to the 'source' of the understanding but also its 'truth'. In other words, it was asked, does the independence of the *pramāṇa* in question cease with the delivery of the cognition (*śābdabodha*) whereafter it relies upon other *pramāṇas* to settle the problem of truth or falsity in respect of the cognition? Some responded to this in the affirmative and argued in support of this contention, while others disagreed vehemently and argued that, *in principle* at least, given that the instruments and operation deployed are not defective, the *śābdabodha* generated attests to its own validity. The process therefore does not need to depend on any other *pramāṇa*, except perhaps in an ancillary way. They may admit, however, that for pragmatic considerations other *pramāṇas* may indeed be utilised for corroborating the truth, or for manifesting the falsity, of the cognition generated. Thus a utilitarian distinction could be seen to be made between a 'theory of truth' and criteria for a 'test of truth'. In the latter, the other *pramāṇa/s* constitute, in part or full, the criteria.

If a moral could be drawn from the above discussion, it is that methodologically, one should be prepared to allow the claim to truth of any piece of knowledge, or authoritative testimony, to be subjected to the scrutiny of tests and countertests for its confirmation, or for its resistance to falsification. This would appear to apply equally well to the class of 'truths' believed to be 'infallible', such as those of the *śāstra* (scriptures), *ṛṣis* (sages or seers), *Īśvara* (*God), *ācārya* (pontiff), *guru* (*master or mentor), or *swāmī* (initiate of a renunciate order), and so forth.

Jñāna

Two concepts that arise in the discussion of *pramāṇa* and which are too often confused need to be placed in their epistemological context. They are *jñāna* and *pramā*. (For a more detailed discussion see ch. 7, and the writer's '*Jñāna and pramā*—the Logic of Knowing', 1985).

Jñāna is a mentalistic term (without presupposing a mentalistic ontology) that denotes any act of awareness, and by extension, 'ideation', 'cognition', 'judgement', 'belief', propositional apprehension' and, maybe, 'wondering'. Of course, there are other sorts of cognitive awareness, such as doubting, supposing, sensing, dreaming, inferring, remembering, guessing etc., that come under the rubric of 'cognitive acts'. But *jñāna* as such is that class of mental phenomena (act or event, temporaly though not spatially coordinated) that have objective content, that refer to actual 'objects', that are not borrowed from contents of another or other cognitions.[13] For example, in a reported cognition of 'hare's horn', *horn* is as though borrowed from, say, a cognition of a deer, and associated with the cognition of a hare. Only such mental modes whose contents are unborrowed, or are 'novel', are epistemically significant and therefore qualify for knowledge *(pramā)* as such, since they are said to have truth-value or contend to satisfy some truth condition. It could be said, though, that the significance of the cognition (*jñāna*) is equally in respect of its *content*-having (content-*ness*, *viṣayatā*), as it is in having truth-value. But it is the latter that constitutes the criterion for the qualification of a *pramā*, the equivalence of which in western epistemology would be 'knowledge', and only in exceptional circumstances, 'justified true belief'.

There are two further qualifications that apply to *pramā* that distinguish them from other sorts of cognitions. First, since cognitions are particular instances of apprehension or awareness, they require a special sort of instrumental cause (*karaṇa*) and process (*vyāpāra*) to bring them about. *Pramāṇa*, as we said earlier, is itself a cause or a set of causal conditions that is efficacious in generating *jñāna* that would, if certain other conditions are met, qualify for a *pramā*. Thus, while not being the only means for the generation of *jñāna*, of sorts, it is a special one since it includes in its set a distinctive *karaṇa* that is necessary, though perhaps not sufficient, for generating a *pramā*-qualifying *jñāna*. This distinctive *karaṇa* differs from one *pramāṇa* to another, and is usually in respect of the specific set of causal conditions (*sādhāraraṇakaraṇa*) that constitute it, with at least one extraordinary (*asādhāraṇakaraṇa*) instrumental condition. This 'extraordinary' causal condition is identified as the particular *pramāṇa* in operation, in conjunction with other *sādhāraṇa* causal conditions.

The second qualification, at least from the Nyāya point of view, is that those cognitive or episodic states that have objective content also have a qualificative structure, much as could be said of *propositional* attitudes or apprehensions. This is necessary in order for the disparate 'objects' and 'properties' in the apprehension to be appropriately related to each other. This condition thus requires there to be an awareness of a distinguishing property (*viśeṣaṇa*) of the object cognised (*viṣaya*) in each particular *jñāna*. Thus, if something, say, x is presented in my awareness, it is presented as qualified by a distinguishing property y. This 'propositional' awareness can be represented in the qualified-qualifier structure as follows:

where, x – qualificand, y – qualifier

$$Q(xy)$$

Thus when I sit at the kitchen table and an object, 'this', 'floats' into my awareness, and I further become aware that the distinguishing element in this object is its *cupness*, then my cognition is said to have the following structure:

Q(this, cupness)

If I then notice that in the cup there is some liquid which I recognise to be tea, then I have a further *jñāna*; thus:

Q(cup, tea)

Qualificative cognition (*savikalpa* or *viśiṣṭa*) is distinguished from *nirvikalpajñāna* or nonqualificative awareness in respect of the former having *viṣayatā*, objective content*ness*, which is characterised as its property of being 'intentional'—i.e. in being *of* or directed *to* or being *about* some 'object' or other (*saviṣayaktva*) in addition to having a relational structure in its 'intentional presentation' (to borrow a concept from Brentano). What gives *jñāna*, as an awareness-state, greater significance, for our purposes at least, is in its intentional content lending itself to linguistic expressibility, that is to say, to the representation of the components of the cognitive structure in verbal-logical terms, which links it to *śābdabodha* (the understanding derived from 'hearing' a linguistic expression or speech-act). Logically speaking, it should be possible for a *jñāna* of one person, conveyed through its linguistic representation, to evoke the same *jñāna qua* qualificative awareness in an audience, bearing in mind, however, as Professor B. K. Matilal points out, that 'the cognition that an audience will have after listening to and understanding these words or this utterance is not identical, although it may be harmonious, with the cognition which gave rise to the utterance.'[14] From the hearer's point of view at least, the difference may not be so obvious, and if this is the only source that will give him the particular understanding, difficult of attaining, then he can scarcely afford to be too concerned about the logical gap between his and the speaker's understanding upon which he has relied.

We should emphasise that *jñāna* is to be understood as particular instances of *episodic* understanding or apprehension, and not as propositions of logic; they are comparable neither to the empirical sentences of Quine ('true no matter what') nor to the 'true for all purposes' propositions and proto-type sentences logical-empiricists have been looking for. This does not mean, however, that *jñāna* is any less epistemically significant, for in so far as *jñāna* is qualificative it is amenable to analysis, and its content (which it must have) correlatable to some linguistic form, i.e. to some actual or possible utterance,[15] analysing which is tantamount to analysing the cognition itself. The objective content-*ness* is thereby rendered open for intersubjective evaluation and to the rigours of logical scrutiny.

Pramā

Pramāṇa, as we said, is one source of generating *jñāna*, though perhaps not the only source; the *jñāna* generated in this way is more likely than not to be *pramā*, provided that no vitiating factors or defects interfere with the operation. Thus, a cognitive state that has been achieved through a *pramāṇa* is more likely to be a *pramā*, a *true* (valid) cognition, than one achieved by some other means. Not all *jñānas* are either true or false. The *nirvikalpa* cognition, for instance, as a pure sensory apprehension is neither true nor false. But every qualificative *jñāna* is either true (valid) or false (invalid). The case of *doubt* may be an exception, for all one can say in this instance is that something appears not to be true but may well be true.

The criteria for the qualification of *jñāna* as a *pramā* is stated in terms of *prāmāṇya*, usually rendered as the condition under which a cognition is said to have truth-value. This is not necessarily to be taken as correspondence to a real object. Correspondence alone is not what is meant by this *prāmāṇya* criterion. In other words, the truth of a cognition is not defined totally as a function of the conditions under which it conforms with reality. A more acceptable approach would be to suggest the conditions under which a cognition would be *false*, and such other criteria as would either serve in place of the former or collaborate with it. According to Gaṅgeśa, a cognition would be false if its qualifier (*y*) is not actually related to the qualificand (*x*) of the objective content.[16] For instance, in the awareness '(this) gold is green', if the qualifier 'green' does not correlate to the actual colour of the object cognised, then the *jñāna* is said to be false; it is *apramā*. To take another instance, in the awareness 'hare's horn', there is complex of two *viṣayatās*, namely, 'hare' and 'horn'. Each of the *viṣayatā* is *real* in its own right, but in this instance their relation is at fault, with the consequence that the resulting *jñāna* lacks truth. Yet another instance, the awareness 'Devadatta is eating' would be falsified if Devadatta is seen to be running without any edibles in his hand, or if there is any doubt as to what he is really up to.

It follows that, if *jñāna* is to qualify for *pramā* it should be falsifiable, that is to say, it should be possible to state the conditions under which the *jñāna* would be false (invalid). The possibility of contradiction by *jñāna* achieved through some other *pramāṇa* would also be a serious consideration. The further qualification that an unfalsified *jñāna* would need in order for it to be accepted as a *pramā* include the following criteria:

i. that the information it provides is of something *new* – i.e. that it is a novel awareness;
ii. that it carries conviction (*niścaya*) or assuredness (*asaṃdigdha*);
iii. that it is not doubted;
iv. that it is productive in fulfilling the purposive goal or end it is directed toward (*pravṛtti-sāmarthya*).

When these criteria are meet then the *jñāna* is *pramā*. It is a standard argument in some schools that a *pramāṇa*, such as for instance perception, deployed in the most efficient manner possible, should as a matter of course fulfil the qualifications specified above, thereby giving rise to *jñāna* that is *pramā*.

We have, of course, given a rather cursory introduction to a distinction of much greater complexity, having ignored the differences in the views held in various schools (such as, e.g. between the early and later Nyāya, between Nyāya and Advaita). Nothing has been said also about the one exception Advaita makes in accepting a nonqualificative *jñāna*, that is, a particular sort of *jñāna* that lacks relational structure, as amongst the highest sort of *pramāṇa*. This is the identity-awareness generated by the *mahāvākyas* or 'great sentences' of *śruti* that attempt to convey understanding of that which admits of no division or distinction in itself, there being only *one* and one *only* of that.

Śabda

Śabda is a term that has had wide currency in Indian philosophical and linguistic speculations. Its sense is by no means always clear, as it could mean different things in different contexts. To begin with, however, *śabda* means, first and foremost, 'sound', in the sense of noise, made in the utterances of animals and humans. It is what leads to speech or, as we might say, verbal sound. In fact, the generality of *śabda* is analogous to the term 'verbal', which stretches from a sequence of articulated sounds to complex sentential structures as modes of expression. Likewise, as Madhav Deshpande notes, the term *śabda* is elastic enough to range from individual sounds to sentential sequences and from pronounced words [*padas*] to the communicative aspects of language.[17] As such, *śabda* would cover the spoken word and heard word, and would seem to include written word as a token of the spoken or heard word. 'Linguistic utterance', then, would be the broadest equivalence of *śabda* in linguistics, where the concern is presumably more with words and meanings than with the 'sounds' associated with these words. In the philosophical context, *śabda* would tend to stand for an expression or linguistic property that states a proposition, i.e. intends to convey meaning and truth-value. *Śabda* is distinguished from—although sometimes confused with—*pada* or 'a word' as a 'linguistic unit' that serves, as it were, as the building block of a linguistic utterance. We deal with this distinction in some detail in chapter two. When *śabda* is compounded with other terms that imply a linguistic property in the object or act referred to, *śabda* is taken to mean 'verbal' or, simply, 'linguistic'. For instance, *śābdabodha* is usually rendered 'verbal comprehension', or more precisely, as '*understanding (bodha)* derived from an expression or utterance', or even more succinctly, as 'linguistic cognition'.

In an even wider sense, *śabda* could be taken to stand for 'speech', which covers a broad spectrum of linguistic behaviour, such as making utterances, forming linguistic units, constructing grammatical complexes, conveying thoughts and ideas through verbal signs and ideograms, and performing speech-acts. The spoken word is the best example of speech, though as already indicated, we would want to include heard and written word. Speech implies a source that manifests verbal signs or expressions, but the immediate source need not always be a human or a personal source; purely 'textual' sources, such as of the scriptures, or *śruti*, literally the 'heard word', would be an instance. *Āgama*, as we saw earlier, stands for the 'authoritative word of tradition', without necessarily implying a personal authority. The scope of *śabda* is thus much wider in Indian thought than would at first appear.

Another peculiarity of *śabda* is that, as a generic term it may stand for the whole field or enterprise of speech and language. In this sense it is not restricted to any one part or unit of speech. Perhaps it was to emphasise the inter-connectedness of the different parts of speech in its wider linguistic structure that *śabda* has been used in this way. This is certainly how Bhartṛhari, the celebrated linguist-philosopher, took it to be. Bhartṛhari maintained that linguistic structure is a unitary phenomenon and cannot be divided, except perhaps for the expedience of grammatical description. He believed in the indivisibility (*akhaṇḍatva*) of language, and criticised those who believed that language is inherently broken up into the 'atomic bits' of words, meanings, relations and so on.[18]

Though Bhartṛhari's theory of language is based on a prior ontological commitment, its epistemological implications are significant and have some bearing on our analysis.

In a narrower sense, *śabda* is used to mean sentence, or any such well-formed composite expression, and sometimes even to stand for a 'word', by which we mean the 'atomic' meaning-bearing linguistic unit. The grammarians, though, may have been more specific in their choice of terms when they wished to talk about sentences and words as independent linguistic elements. '*Vākya*' was used for sentence, and *pada* for (a) word, and *artha* for 'meaning'. *Vākya* is taken for a composite expression which is constitituted of individual words that combine in a syntactic relation to yield a composite sense (*vākyārtha*). The comprehension of sentence-meaning is termed *vākyārthajñāna* or, more commonly and simply, *śābdabodha*—i.e. the *understanding (bodha)* that arises when the linguistic process is completed. Thus it is *śābda*, that which arises through *śabda*, or the 'linguistically-derived'. But we should note that *śabda* here stands for sentence, and is thus synonymous with *vākya*; it may stand for word, i.e. *pada*, as a linguistic item, if only one or a few words are used in loose combination, as in a phrase. But even when a word (*pada*) appears on its own, or is referred to individually as an inflected morpheme, *śabda* is sometimes used to indicate *the word*; likewise for a concatenation of words, and for a sentence (*vākya*). The use of *śabda* in these contexts is then considerably more specific, referring to some particular feature or features of speech as the parts that make for the 'whole' of speech. It would be rare, if ever, however, to come across the putative features themselves making reference to the whole of speech in its generic sense. For instance, *pada*, or *vākya*, are not used generically to stand for *speech*, except perhaps for speech-acts. By way of contrast, the common western equivalence, namely 'word'—or, more precisely, 'the word'—is used in this very sense (as should be obvious from the subtitle of this book).

Śabda, then, while standing for speech, covers the broad spectrum of linguistic items, such as *vākya* (sentence), *pada* (morpheme), *sphoṭa* (word-whole), *vāc* (sacred word), *dhvani* (sound-syllable), *varṇa* (letter), pronouncement, mystic syllables (such as '*Oṃ*'), and any speech-act. And even in respect of the comprehension of any one of these, *śabda*, it seems, is preferred in place, say, to *vākya* when talking about something as specific as understanding of sentence-meaning. Thus '*śabda*' in *śabdārthajñāna*, or simply *śābdabodha*, and '*śābdī*' in *śābdījñāna* stand for 'that which is derived from *śabda*'. The derivation and that from which it is derived are not necessarily identical, though they are causally related, as silk is to cocoon. Thus, at least *prima facie*, what is achieved from and through *śabda* is a distinct *understanding qua* a meaning-content, that may be quite different from a surface awareness of a sentence, for *śabda* conveys a deeper sense of the speech-act.

I do believe, however, that traditional writers have been rather loose in their univocal use of the term '*śabda*' for the many distinct and specific features in the broader spectrum of speech, for this only blurrs the specificity of the term and often creates confusion, particularly when more specific terms are available for their respective linguistic designation. (Indeed, this is an unpardonable paradox of a linguistic tradition.) The author of *Vedānta-paribhāṣā*, for instance, uses *śabda* interchangeably with *pada* for '(the) word' (IV.22, 24). We could afford to be more precise and use *pada* for '(the) word', *vākya* for 'sentence', and *śābda*, as in *śābdabodha*, as that which is linguistically derived, most often through the utterance of an expression or a sentence. And similarly, the term *śabda*, in the compound *śabdapramāṇa*, will mean the sentence as used for the expression of a statement or proposition, and which is of epistemic significance. By extension, *śabda* could also stand for speech or linguistic behaviour in a broader sense. But generally speaking, if *pramāṇa* stands for 'a valid means of knowledge', then, in this context, *śabdapramāṇa* will mean *'that means of knowledge which has for its source sentence or sentences (vākya).'*

On logical and traditional grounds, the application is extended to *āgama* ('word of tradition'), *śruti* ('heard word'—of scripture), and *vāc*, the sacred or inspired word (*Ṛg Veda* X.125). In any case, it is *śabda* which is the special causal condition for this source of understanding, whether profane or sacred. The source of the *śabda*, however, need not itself be another *śabda*, since the 'cognition which the utterer expresses by uttering a sentence may be perceptual, inferential, or something else',[19] but the cognition of the hearer is most definitely *śabda*, since this is all that he perceives, at least before his understanding deepens. Suffice it to say that, the statement about *śabda* as a 'special causal condition' (*asādhāraṇakāraṇa-karaṇa*) is a major step toward making a case for the functional independence of *śabda* as a legitimate means of knowing.

The grammarians in the tradition could also be said to have evolved a theory of *śabdapramāṇa*, not, however, in direct reference to the authority of scriptural words, but in their avowed recognition of the 'power', so to speak, of words as a significant medium for conveying information and sense. They articulated the importance of language as an instrument in human speech-behaviour and communication of cognitive understanding. Bhartṛhari (of whom we made mention a little earlier) was one such grammarian and a significant one from a philosopher's point of view.

Bhartṛhari raised the question of the relation between knowledge and language, and language and reality. He went so far as to identify *knowledge* with *language*, and *language* with *reality*, such that one's knowledge *qua* language is that of reality itself. Of course, this is a gross simplification of the rather more sophisticated 'holistic' theory that Bhartṛhari presents in his famed *Vākyapadīya*.[20]

The holistic analysis of language that Bhartṛhari advances, as a thorough master of the classical linguistic works of Patañjali *et al*, is a contribution that no serious student of Indian thought and linguistics can afford to ignore. Quite apart from the intriguing metaphysical underpinning of his theory—which cannot be our concern here—the numerous epistemological insights that he makes are illumining. And these too we can only touch on here, when rounding out the Advaita theory of language in the context of *śabdapramāṇa*.

It may be appropriate to mention here two salient features of his theory which I regard as important for an understanding of *śabda*. The first concerns his emphasis on the principal role of the *sentence (vākya)*. According to Bhartṛhari, what is permanent is the relation that sentence bears to its meaning.[21] The second concerns his notion of '*sphoṭa*'. If 'sentence' is the minimal *meaningful* speech-element, then there cannot be anything less than the sentence which could also be said to be a meaningful unit. But *sphoṭa* is sometimes taken to be discrete units of meaning, such as a word, a letter,or a particle, through which 'meaning', as it were, 'bursts forth'. But in Professor S.D. Joshi's understanding, *sphoṭa* is used in Bhartṛhari's analysis only in reference to holistic *sound* property constituted by a cluster of meaningless *varṇas* or 'phonemes'.[22] The reference, then, is not to any *meaning*-bearing element as such, unless the association is with a sentence. Bhartṛhari may, however, in certain circumstances, and for purposes of grammatical analysis, accept *pada* or word-unit to be *meaningful* independently of a sentence, but he would, it seems, deny meaningfulness to *varṇa* or 'phonematic unit' ('*letter*') in its own right, as Joshi points out. *Varṇas*, in Bhartṛhari's view, are basically discrete sound sequences through which a word is manifested, i.e. through which meaning is disclosed; they are, therefore, not units of meaning as such but they, as it were, embody meaning . The later grammarians, however, attempted to wed the notion of *varṇa* with *artha*, i.e. sound sequence with meaningfulness, and thus came up with a view about *varṇa* as being the discrete meaningful speech-element of language. J.Brough maintains that *sphoṭa qua varṇasphoṭa*—'syllable'—in Patañjali *is* a meaningful self-disclosing speech-element, and that this could be true of *varṇas* as much as of words and sentences.[23] The grammarians developed, in effect, an implication in Bhartṛhari's linguistics—i.e. that *varṇas* manifest meaning—by giving equal emphasis to the syllabic form as to words and sentences as the basic constituents of speech. It is through this theory of the minimally *meaningful* speech-element that we can make intelligible the sense of the Advaita and Mīmāṃsā theory of *śabda*, based on *varṇa*, reinforced, in some ways, by the Nyāya view of language. This we attempt briefly in chapter two.

Interesting as Bhartṛhari's theory is, we want to be able to avoid some of the metaphysical assumptions that are germain to his system—for instance, that there is an ontological identity between language, at its most subtle level, and reality, in its penultimate nature. Nor do we want to assume that the problem of the relation between knowledge and reality is reducible to the problem of the relation between knowledge and meaning and between language and reality. But, as in any analysis, I do make some assumptions which I cannot hope to justify here, and which are to be disavowed as soon as their elucidatory purpose has been served. For instance, I say nothing about the nature of the 'origin' of language. I assume that, by and large, language succeeds in functioning as a repository of the symbolic representation of the human's experiences and understandings, and which presumably accounts for the continuity of language. Also, that the human mind (*manas, antaḥkaraṇa* or *buddhi*) has the capacity to assimilate the operators of language, which are analysed in terms of words, meanings, sentences, or whatever other linguistic categories that are appropriate to a particular language.

Ideality of language

One other assumption made in Advaita and Mīmāṃsā theories of language concern the independence of language from 'personality'. This appears, on the face of it, to be a preposterous claim. Obviously, without persons there cannot be language. But what is being said, I believe, is that language as a presupposition of human communication is logically prior to its 'use' by persons, though it would be true to say, at the same time, that apart from its *use* there would be no significant impact of language, as felt in communication among persons. In other words, even if without use language would be as good as dead, it is not inconceivable that as a network of multi-linked concepts and meaning-structures that facilitate communication among persons, language is prior to the conventions that make possible its use. Unlike manufactured things, such as cars and houses, language can be looked upon as a phenomenon that man does not manufacture, but discovers with his own mental powers as he attempts to communicate with his fellow beings—and in so using language he also manifests it. That is to say, man discovers within his own consciousness the self-transcending *ground* for the possibility of communication in a medium of concepts and meaning-structures that are somehow 'there'. The resemblance to the Chomskian-Fodorian thesis of 'deep structure' of language should be obvious here. That there is this possibility of a 'deeper' linguistic basis or structure of meaning and concepts, prior to its use in speech, is what constitutes an argument for the independence of language from human production or 'personality'. This viewpoint, known as *apauruṣeya*, is a phenomenological and not necessarily, for Advaita at least, an ontological claim about the 'origin' of language.

This view bears strong resemblance to Husserl's thesis of the ideality of meaning. Husserl argues, in Professor J. N. Mohanty's words, that 'logical discourse requires that meanings retain an identity in the midst of varying contexts; secondly, meanings can be communicated by one person to another, and in that sense can be shared; further, in different speech acts and in different contexts, the same speaker or different speakers can always return to the same meaning. . .The theories that reduce meaning to the experiences of the speaker or hearer cannot explain how it is possible for private experiences (images, for example) of one to be communicated to, and shared by, another.'[24a]

Śruti

Śruti, literally, means 'the heard word', and is analogous to 'the revealed word' to which is attached some sanctity and authority. The relevance of *śruti* as an issue in this work is more by way of implication than a direct concern, though the ground-work prepared here should prove to be useful for a comprehensive work in progress presently.[24] But any discussion on *śruti* has to face some important issues. I consider the following to be some of them:

(a) what is *śruti*?
(b) in what respect specifically does *śruti* differ from words of ordinary utterances – i.e. is the distinction in respect of the structure of *śruti* sentences, or their contents, or their end-products?
(c) how do we understand the alleged *apauruṣeyatva* (non-personal 'origin') of *śruti*?
(d) how do we deal with the problem of communication, meaningfulness and interpretation of *śruti* utterances?
(e) what is the process of initiation into and instruction in the supposed wisdom of *śruti*, i.e. how is *śruti* disseminated and its continuity maintained?
(f) what sort of framework is provided for the structuring and analysis of the experiences resulting from the process (in *e*)? what sorts of methodological innovations are possible here?
(g) how is the question of truth or authenticity of the experience and the *understanding* derived from *śruti* dealt with, and what are the criteria proposed for evaluation of the same?
(h) finally, what are the ramifications of the analysis for philosophy of knowledge?

The 'dogma' of śruti : apauruṣeya

Traditionally, *śruti* has been identified as a corpus of scriptural words which have come down to us as the Vedas ('what is known'), from '*vid*, 'to know', cognate with the Greek *oida*, Latin *vidi*, and the English 'wisdom'. What it 'reveals' is said to be of perennial value (*philosophia perennis*) and *apauruṣeya* or 'not of personal origin'. Like *logos*, *śruti* is said to be revealed, since it allegedly embodies 'truths of ultimate value' (*paramārtha*), though its source cannot be attributed to any personal nature or agency, or authorship. Its authority, therefore, is characterised as being *apauruṣeya*, i.e. as essentially transpersonal.

Now, one way to make sense of this sort of a talk about 'text without an author'—which perhaps shares a family resemblance with the post-modern discourse of 'authorless text'—is to look upon it as an ontological claim, not about language, but about the *truths* conveyed through language. The argument is that, to talk about the timelessness and *apauruṣeyatva* of *śruti* is really to talk about the 'truths' represented in *śruti* more than to talk about the 'word' or *vāc* itself. Thus, for example, when the Veda calls *vāc* the 'first born of truth',[25] the suggestion is that *truth* is begining-less, although it needs the 'word' to manifest itself, for which purpose *vāc* is created. It is also assumed, in consonance with such a view of truth, that truths which are independent, as it were, of personality, being timeless and prior to the 'creation' of personal beings with powers of expression, are higher than truths that arise from personal experience or in the context of personhood. The reason being that the latter arise through the grasping of the mind or *buddhi*, the discriminating and reasoning faculty in the person, which have their own limitations and deficiencies.

Language, too, cannot be said to represent or embody these truths in their totality, as language deals with concepts and the truths are not necessarily conceptual, though they may come close to the conceptual structures, say, of certain cognitive understandings. Language may, however, succeed in *pointing* to these truths. Thus, it may be said, truths of the higher order outrun, as it were, language and grasping by person or persons. And yet, it is through a form of language that an attempt is made to disclose or 'reveal' the higher truths (*parāvidyā*): *śruti* thus assumes itself to be *one* with these truths, being able to embody some and point to others. And this assumption, as we said earlier, need only be taken as a methodological device for the possibility of *understanding śruti* rather than as a metaphysical assertion about *śruti* or the Vedas.

To this end, the framework made possible through an analysis of *śabdapramāṇa* should prove to be immensely helpful in responding to the methodological issues raised earlier. Thus also, when we are finished with *śruti* or the Vedas, or any scriptures, we should be able to discard them as the many steps on a ladder and not cling to them as the many dogmas.

Text and Author

The *(Advaita) Vedānta-paribhāṣā* was authored by one Dharmarājādhvarīndra, also known as Dharmarāja Dīksita, who lived around the middle of the seventeeth century. He was a native of Tanjore (Tanjavur, South India).[26] Burnell, in the catalogue of the Tanjore manuscripts (p90) fixes the date of the author around 1672 A.D.(Saṃvat 1728). Dharmarāja aligned himself closely with the school of thought promulgated by the great Advaita savant and thinker Śaṅkara (*c* 820 A.D.? Nakamura redate : 700-750), and systematised further by Padmapāda, a direct pupil and one of the foremost savant of the post-Śaṅkara Advaita tradition. Dharmarāja seemed to follow closely in the footsteps of Padmapāda in his rigorous analysis of and concern with problems of knowing, as distinct from the interests in metaphysical reconstruction, which some other pupils, in particular Sureśvara, concerned themselves with. Padmapāda was succeeded by Prakāśātman, also a significant 'light' (his name-sake), in the development of Advaita thought. It was the efforts of the latter two that could be said to have provided the foundations for further epistemological development in Vedānta circles in later periods, which reached its culmination in the dialecticism of Śrīharṣa and Citsukha.

The school of thought immediately after Śaṅkara became divided in its approach, due to some fundamental differences in the philosophical temperaments of two of the leading pupils of Śaṅkara, namely, Sureśvara and Maṇḍana Miśra (disregarding for now the claim of the alleged identity of the two). Maṇḍana Miśra was a convert to Śaṅkara Advaita from Mīmāṃsā, and could not reconcile himself completely with the idealistic monism as interpreted by Sureśvara and others. The school that grew around and after Sureśvara came to be known as *Vivaraṇa*, in view of its commitment to the unrealness of change *qua* strict causality. Padmapāda, and Dharmarāja after him, followed in the wake of this paradigm, and consequently drew a number of epistemological implications that were not countenanced favourably by the adherents in the rival school. Foremost among adversaries, after Maṇḍana, emerged in the versatile and erudite scholar of Vācaspati Miśra. Although eclectic and a prolific commentator on texts from a number of different schools, he remained committed to Vedānta and carried further the cause championed by Maṇḍana Miśra. His major treatise in this regard gave the name to this school within Śaṅkara Advaita – viz. *Bhāmatī*. To give some minor instances of the differences between Vivaraṇa and Bhāmatī, Vācaspati argued that *śruti* could never generate absolutely immediate apprehension; what it may do is to create a disposition that indirectly leads to the final intuition, but which itself is brought about by a distinct process that involves meditational reflection as one of its major components. And what is more, this final intuition is an episode within the mind (*manas*), which itself is said to be a *sense-organ* (rather like the penetration of the notion of the substitutable 'brain' in some versions of philosophical behaviourism).

The Bhāmatī school also maintained that the 'I-thou' distinction given in common sense experience of consciousness is not unreal as widely claimed in some Advaita circles,[27] since each monadic self (*jīvā*) is self-individuated and '*other*- conscious'. Of course, if this tenet were to be taken seriously and literally it would make it implausible to argue for a non-dualistic absolute, as Śaṅkara seemed to have wanted to. But since the Bhāmatī view is not averse to 'real change' continuum, it does not see any real difficulty in this position, provided that, in principle, the *absolute* is not any less itself, nor has an 'other' beside Itself.

In contradistinction, Vivaraṇa denied that *śruti* lacked direct efficiency in respect of the final intuition sought. *Śruti qua śabda*, they argued, is capable of generating direct awareness (*aparokṣānubhūti*) without the necessary intermediacy of the apparatus of the mental, which at any rate, is decidedly *not* a sense-organ (*indriya*). Such was the 'faith', one might say, in the 'power of the heard word' (*śrutiśakti*); which, incidentally, was elevated to the status of a goddess in the Veda, namely as *Vāc* (*cf.* *Ṛg Veda* 1.164.37-39; X.71; *Taittirīya Brāhmaṇa* II.8.8.5; *Śatapatha Brāhmaṇa* I.4.4.1; *Brahma-sūtra-bhāṣya* I.iii.28).

Vivaraṇa, however, pushed this argument only in the context of the *mahāvākyas* (literally, the 'great' or 'major' sentences of *śruti*), as did, for instance, Sureśvara in his celebrated *Naiṣkarmyasiddhi*, in taking the *śruti*: *tat tvam asi* (That you are) as the statement epitomising both the process and the product.[28] And as regards the issue of the identity of the self, Vivaraṇa argued for a more consistent, though ostensibly more difficult application and interpretation of Śaṅkara's nondualistic (*advaita*) ontology, namely that, the individuation process is itself causally neutral, although given a semblance of separable co-existence by a process called *upādhi* (association *ab extra*). Consequently, they argued that the apparently individual *jīvās* or selves have their collective identity in one cosmic self (*Īśvara*, much like Spinoza's God), who is responsible for mitigating dispensations accrued from actions, good and bad, in empirical living.

Dharmarāja went a little further and identified the 'one cosmic self' with the unindividuated 'self' of person or persons. This thereby rendered the notion of the 'Overself' *acosmic*, and made it more empirically and phenomenologically grounded than would otherwise suggest, since the 'larger', cosmic, self is given in and through the experience of the individual self. And therefore, it follows that the *transendentalism* of Advaita is a phenomenological concept within the bounds, as it were, of logic, and is not, as mistaken by many, a metaphysical construct susceptible to efferent mysticism.

One reading of Śaṅkara lends support to this contention, while, as it is clear, another reading, as in Bhāmatī, would not so typically.[29] Enough, though, by way of background to the 'metaphysical disquisitions', although the differences make for much fascinating debate in the branch of philosophy that generally goes under the rubric of *metaphysics.*

Cit: consciousness in the knowing process

Of interest also, from the point of view of the classical development of epistemology, is the view that emerges in some detail in the section on *pramāṇa*. It is that, cognition, as an episodic event, occurs through an intentional process of the delimitation of consciousness (*cit*) by the *antaḥkaraṇa* or 'inner vehicle of apperception'; the subjectivity constituted, in this way, is known as *pramātṛ*. The objective, or the 'given' of which it is an experience, likewise, is said to be a function of consciousness delimitation, albeit constituted extensionally by the 'object' of experience, which as such is known as *prameya*. The connectedness between the subjective and the objective is described as a *vṛtti* or modification (intentionality) of consciousness, which is yet another function of *cit* in which a quasi-identity (*tādātmya* or 'identity-with-difference') is established between the two polarities, so to speak, of experience. The subjective and the objective are said to be connected in the same instance of consciousness-modification (*vṛtti*), as a result of sense-organ contact (*indriyasannikarṣa*) or through some other input process (e.g. the *karaṇas* of a *pramāṇa*). Their connectedness is revealed in a subsequent reflection (*anuvyavasāya*), showing the components to be related in a qualificative structure, as, for example, in the cognitive affirmation: 'I'm seeing the chair'. We shall return to this later.[30]

Dharmarāja and Navya-nyāya

Such then was the background Dharmarājādhvarīndra inherited when he came to present his own formulation of the argument for *śabdapramāṇa*. For this, he largely followed Madhusūdana Sarasvatī (16th c), but also improved on him, particularly with regard to some logical issues in the analyses, for which he relied on his training in Nyāya. Being thoroughly versed in the works of the prominent Navya-nyāya thinkers (especially Gaṅgeśa), Dharmarāja was able to attend to several issues that had not been dealt with adequately by his Advaitin predecessors, within a Nyāya analytical style of philosophising.

It is clear that Dharmarāja was influenced by the Nyāya system of thought, in particular by Gaṅgeśa's '*navīna-nyāya*' or Navya-nyāya ('The New Logic', *vide VP* pp2-3), and he [as also his son] wrote critical subcommentaries on Nyāya works, the most famous of which is *Tarkacūḍāmaṇi* on Ruccidatta's *Prakāśa* on Gaṅgeśa's celebrated *Tattvacin-*

tāmaṇi; the other major commentary was on *Nyāyasiddhāntadīpa* (*EIP* I, p295). He also commented on *Pañcapādikā*, a classic in Advaita thought by Padmapāda. His use of Upaniṣadic material is also profuse. He states that the *Paribhāṣā* has been based on Vedāntic teachings (*VP* I.6), meaning specifically Advaita epistemology, within the general thrust we have already outlined, along perhaps with the ontological presuppositions inherited from the rich speculations of his predecessors. I myself have eschewed from committing the able author to the latter presuppositions in this work, though I am aware of them. I maintain that *śabdapramāṇa* as a thesis stands on its own linguistic and epistemological grounds. The author himself, for similar reasons I suppose, deals with the problem of the *pramāṇas* before he ventures into the metaphysical world of the *final* 'objects' of knowledge (*pāramārthika-viṣayam*) to deal with substantive ontological issues – which goes beyond the scope of the present work, anyway.

Vedānta-paribhāṣā is often commended for its lucidity and brevity of statement (notably by Dasgupta),[31] but it is not altogether without its faults and flaws. Though the author appears to follow closely the Vivaraṇa school (with a Nyāya bias), his strict realism, especially in the earlier parts, belies the metaphysical framework of neo-idealism of the Vivaraṇa school, and of much modern-day speculations in popularised versions of Advaita (Vedānta) thought and 'religion'. The realism, however, has not been developed to the rigour it could have been in Dharmarāja's work. That project has been taken up admirably by some modern writers.

While most commentators and scholars looking at the *Vedānta-paribhāṣā* have concentrated on the latter part of the book, which deals extensively with metaphysical and ontological problems of existence, only a few have paid attention to the richness of the epistemological treatise, and still fewer to the discussion of *śabda* in the chapter dedicated to this thesis. There is hardly a text in Advaita that could present its epistemological development in light of the interactions among the different schools of thought in more concise way than has been done in the *Āgama* chapter.

There is said to be one other work comparable to the *Vedānta-paribhāṣā*, namely, *Vedāntakaumudī* by Rāmādvaya (*c* 1320; published in 1955). After all this is said, it remains true, as Pandit S.S. Suryanarayana Sastri put it: 'As a compendious yet full treatment of the psychology and epistemology of Advaita Vedānta, the *Paribhāṣā* is unrivalled.'[32] The most notable commentary on the *Paribhāṣā* was written by Dharmarāja's son, Rāmakṛṣṇa Adhvarīndra, and it was called *Śikhāmaṇi*, also known as *Vedānta-cūḍāmaṇi*. He also commented on his father's *Tarkacūḍāmaṇi*. *Śikhāmaṇi*, with Amaradāsa's *Maṇiprabhā*, was published in 1901 (*EIP* I, p295).

Another useful commentary is *Arthadīpikā*, written by one Śrī Dhanapati Sūrisut Śivadatta. Two commentaries in Hindi are also quite popular, and have been consulted for this work. And a twentieth-century commentary in Sanskrit has been published, written by no less a scholar than Mm.N. S. Anantakṛṣṇa Śāstrī, called *Paribhāsā-prakāśikā* (Calcutta University).

The present work is also to be regarded as a commentary on the '*Āgama*' section of *VP*, albeit written in English closer to the tradition of philosophy in this part of the twentieth century. In due course it may be worth our while to render the present work in Sanskrit, and perhaps also in one or two of the modern Indian languages (such as Hindi and Bengali). And this in the interest of continuing dialogue between traditionally-trained *paṇḍits* and scholars of more modern ilk and, often, Western training. (It might also make a modest contribution to *modern* Sanskrit classics).

The *Vedānta-paribhāṣā* was first translated into English by Arthur Venis, which appeared in the issues of *The Paṇḍit*, from 1882-1885 (Benaras), but apparently never came out in book form. D. M. Datta, in his lucid, but now rather dated, *Six Ways of Knowing* (London; Calcutta) gives translations of parts of the text. Datta's book, however, is not based on the *Vedānta-paribhāṣā*. The better known editions and translations of the text have been two, both of which are useful for consultation. One is by S.S. Suryanarayana Sastri, published in 1942 (Adyar Library and Research Centre), which have been claimed by S. Radhakrishnan and K. Kunjunni Raja to be reliable.[33] The other is by Swami Mādhavānanda of Ramakrishna Mission, Belur, published in 1942, which, as we said, was commended by Dasgupta. The notes and clarification given in both volumes are encouraging and helpful. My own translation of the *pramāṇa* section has been aided by reference to the two volumes, but I have taken issue on points of interpretation with both scholars in several instances. I have not found Arthur Venis's translation to be very useful. Since to offer yet another translation is not part of the project I set for myself, I shall not pursue this matter any further. I have been more interested in reading the text and making it intelligible in terms of the sort of philosophical enquiry we are engaged in here. And this leads me to say the following.

Vedānta-paribhāṣā, when it is accompanied by a comprehensive commentary and critical appraisal in English, could prove to be a major sourcebook for an approach to Advaita epistemology, and an indispensable guide for a study of the *pramāṇas*, especially *śabdapramāṇa*, as I have found it to be. Significantly enough, the text has been a standard prescription for Master's degree coursework in some Indian universities, perhaps in recognition of the enormous benefit it presents to the student by drawing its sources and arguments from numerous different authorities and expressing them in a rather more systematic and concise style than many such treatises usually succeed in doing. (Again, *VP* owes this particular merit to Navya-nyāya.) It might be more profitable if each of the *pramāṇas* and major philosophical problem discussed in the text were given thorough and separate treatment in the context of cross-*darśana* and modern developments. Hence, partly to this end, this humble offering. I hope it stimulates comments. That alone will make this effort worthwhile.

NOTES TO INTRODUCTION

0. *Mānādhīnā meyasiddhir iti nyāyenapramāṇasya prathamamuddeśe (Akṣapāda)* in *Sarvadarśanasaṃgraha* by Mādhava (Vidyāsāgara ed. p112; also in Cowell and Gough, p. 162). For bibliographical details, where absent, see Bibliography in Appendix.

1. Kalidas Bhattacharyya, 'Traditional Indian Philosophy as a Modern Thinker Views It', in S. S. Rama Rao Pappu and R. Puligandla (edited), *Indian Philosophy: Past and Present* (Motilal Banarsidass, Delhi, 1982, pp171-224), p216, 217.

2. J. N. Mohanty, 'Indian Philosophy between Tradition and Modernity', in Pappu and Puligandla (edited) *op cit*, p250, *vide* p237ff. See also his 'Philosophy as Reflection on Experience', in *Indian Philosophy Today*, N. K. Devaraja (edited), (Motilal Banarsidass, Delhi. 1975, pp. 169-185).

3. Kunhan Raja, *Some Fundamental Problems in Indian Philosophy*, (Motilal Banarsidass, Delhi, 1974), p94ff.

4. In an introduction to a seminar (Santa Barbara). See his *Doctrine and Argument in Indian Philosophy* (Muirhead Library of Philosophy series, Humanities Press, N.J. 1964). *Cf.* Søren Kiekergaard, *On Revelation and Authority* (tr. and edited by Walter Lowrie, Harper, 1955).

5. See comments in *NND*, p10, 147, 167ff. Also, J. N. Mohanty, 'Phenomenology and Existentialism : Encounter with Indian Philosophy', and 'Subject and Person : Eastern and Western Modes of Thinking about Man' (details in bibl.). Also, *Recent Indian Philosophy*, Kalidas Bhattacharyya (edited), (Calcutta, 1963) 'Introduction'.

6. Ludwig Wittgenstein, *Tractatus* 4.112, p49. Not just erstwhile, of course, but also a time-honoured one at that. Wittgenstein of course was not showing any anti-philosophical tendencies, but rather a *new* way of going about the business of philosophising.

7. See my '*Pramāṇavāda (I)*, towards an Indian theory of knowledge. . .outline for a programme', *Darshana International* (Moradabad), April, 1980. Also, 'Perception *(pratyakṣa)* in Advaita Vedānta', *Philosophy East and West*, January 1980.

8. *Cf.* note 0 above; and Vātsāyaya's opening statement to *NS: pramāṇato 'rthapratipattau pravṛttisāmarthyāt arthavat pramāṇam*. (Discussion in ch 7 *infra*).

9. *Bhāṣya* on above *NS* I.i.1: *pratyakṣāgamāśritam anumāṇa; sā anvīkṣā; tayā pravartata ityāṇvīkṣikī nyāyavidyā nyāyaśāstram*.

10. M. Hiriyanna, *Outline of Indian Philosophy* p178

11. Concerning the etymological root of *pramāṇa* it may be noted that the suffix *ana* denotes an instrument, 'that by which'; but it may also denote *bhāva* (the meaning of the root itself), thus in this sense the term *pramāṇa* is used for (valid) knowledge itself. The number of *pramāṇas* accepted as being legitimate means of knowing, differ from school to school. The Cārvāka, as we said, recognise only perception (*pratyakṣa*); some Buddhist schools and Vaiśeṣika recognise two, namely, perception and inference (*anumāna*); the Sāṅkhya recognised three: the two above and *śabda* (verbal testimony); the Nyāya recognised four: the three above plus comparison (*upamāna*); the Prābhākara branch of Mīmāṃsā added to the above presumption (*arthāpatti*); the Bhāṭṭa branch included to the above non-apprehension (*anupalabdhi*) as the sixth *pramāṇa*. Some lesser known schools, like the Paurāṇika (Ancient thought) recognised the six above, adding necessary inclusion (*saṃbhava*) and traditional hearsay (*aitihya*) as the seventh and eighth *pramāṇas* respectively. Later schools discarded the last two and disputed over one or other of the six remaining. For a discussion see S. C. Chatterjee, *The Nyāya Theory of Knowledge*, ch. 3; and *EIP* II.

   In western philosophy, the problem of knowledge is some times put in a way similar to the *pramāṇas*. R. M. Chisholm. for instance, reports: 'One approach to the question 'How are we to decide, in any particular case, *whether* we know?' is to refer to the 'sources' of our knowledge and to say that an ostensible item of knowledge is genuine if, and only if, it is the product of a properly accredited source. Thus, it is traditional in Western philosophy to say that there are four such sources:

1. 'external perception'
2. memory
3. 'self-awareness' ('reflection' or 'inner consciousness')
4. reason (or 'reasoning').' R. M. Chisholm, *Theory of Knowledge*, p57.

12. K. N. Chatterjee, *Word and Meaning—a new perspective in light of Jagadīśa's Śabdaśaktiprakāśikā...* pxxiii.

13. B. K. Matilal, *NND*, p8ff.

14. *Ibid* p11. Of course it is not being said that there is any essential connection of the *savikalpajñāna* with linguistic expression, only that its intentional content is qualified in a certain way and is therefore amenable to 'description', and conversely that a linguistic expression may share the intentional content of the cognitive (mental) state that give rises to such speech. It may be noted also, that though Advaita would not insist that there has to be a *real* object in each instance of qualificative *jñāna*, still the content of *jñāna* has to be described as being *objective (viṣayībhūta, VP.* IV.1) just so far as there is some 'object' which is the *content* of the awareness-state, even if it is an abstract, or is self-referential. In other words, the *jñāna* has to be significant in epistemic terms. We shall ignore reference to the supposed exception to this qualification - viz. *Brahmavidyā*.

15. In *NND* p16, n31. More in next chapter, under *prāmāṇya* and note 20 therein.

16. Detailed discussion in the writer's '*Jñāna and pramā*: the logic of knowing, a critical appraisal', (*JIP* 13, #1 1985 pp. 73-102). Further critical discussion in ch. 7 (*infra*).

17. Madhav Deshpande, 'Sentence-cognition in Nyāya Epistemology', p219. cf. Bhartṛhari *Vākyapadīya (VKP)* II.41-42 (Limaye ed.).

18. Bhartṛhari, *Vākyapadīya (*=VKP), Book I (I.75ff). See also note after next.

19. I am grateful to Professor J. N. Mohanty for this comment.

20. *VKP, loc cit; cf*: 'If this eternal identity of knowledge and the word were to disappear, knowledge would cease to be knowledge; it is this identity which makes identification possible' (I.124; tr. K. A. Subramania Iyer, 1965, pp 110-111).

21. *Ibid. Cf.* Discussion in Kunjunni Raja, *Indian Theories of Meaning*, p197, n2.

22. See S. D. Joshi in his *The Sphoṭanirṇaya of Kauṇḍa Bhaṭṭa* (Ch XIV of *Vaiyākaraṇabhūṣaṇasāra*, ed. trans. with Intro. and notes), esp pp 29-47 and 48-59. See also ch. 2 (*infra*).

23. J. Brough ('General Linguistics'), *qv* ch. 2: 2.7, n18, n24 (*infra*)

24a. J. N. Mohanty, 'Husserl's Thesis of the Ideality of Meanings', in his (edited), *Readings on Edmund Husserl's Logical Investigations*, (pp76-82), p76.

24. Discussion of some preliminary work in *infra* ch. 7, n.125; see also writer's 'Renaissance reaction to *Śruti*' (*Annals of Bhandarkar Oriental Research Institute*, Poona, LXV, 1984, pp43-58), and [with reservations], '*Śruti and Apauruṣeya*: an approach to Scriptures and Revelation', *Journal of Dharma* (Bangalore), VII.3, 1982, pp275-91.

25. *Ṛg Veda* X. 164-37; *cf.* J. F. Staal, 'Ṛgveda 10.71 on the Origin of Language', in Coward and Sivaraman (ed.) *Revelation in Indian Thought*, pp3-14.

26. Dharmarāja [as we shall call the author] in his *maṅgalācaraṇam* (or invocatory passage in the introduction) pays tribute to his intellectual guru, one Veñkaṭanātha, resident of Velāṅgudi. Whether Dharmarāja also lived in Velāṅguḍi is not clear. S. S. Suryanarayana Sastri, in his edition of *VP* (pxiii), identifies Dharmarāja as a resident of the village Kandramanikkam, Tanjavur district, South India. (He refers us to the Tanjavur Library MSS, Intro. pxiii). Dharmarāja was a contemporary of Appayya Dīkṣita. A follower of Ṛg Veda, the author continued the systematisation of Advaita epistemology, with a strong leaning towards the Navya-nyāya method of analysis.

As such, the *VP* is more a work in neo-Advaita-Nyāya than in orthodox Vedānta scholasticism. Afterall, it was Gaṅgeśa who introduced the new style of arranging logical discourse under the category of the basic *pramāṇas* and *vādas* (which deal with a wider range of conceptual-philosophical enquiry). Ḍharmarāja seems to be the first of the Advaita writers to have followed this form. He would, therefore, have been better placed calling his work something like *Tarkaparibhāṣā*, or even *Tattvacūḍāmaṇi*, having already written *Tarkacūḍāmaṇi* (treating of the subject matter in Gaṅgeśa's *Tattvacintāmaṇi*), so as also to implicate his fortification with the resplendent logical sense of the Navya-nyāya ('New Logic') school. It may be mentioned in passing that in the *Tarkacūḍāmaṇi* Dharamarāja deals with *anumāna* (inference), *upamāna* (analogy) and *śabda khaṇḍas*, and he boasts to have incisively criticised ten previous commentaries on the *Tattvacintāmaṇi* in this work (*vide* Introduction in *VP*).

His son, Rāmakṛṣṇādhvarīndra, who exuded no less a critical acumen, retrospectively commented on the *pratyakṣa* (perception) *khaṇḍa*, which has been published in the Tirupati (1973) edition of *Tattvacintāmiṇi*, with Rucidatta's *Prakāśa* or *Dīdhiti*. V. Raghavan, in his Foreword to this edition, suggests that the works of these two South Indian scholars, when fully available, should furnish further invaluable historical and chronological information on the development of Navya-nyāya.

As explained in Appendix B (where a transliteration of the *Āgama* and some related text is given), the numeral ordering of the text in the *Vedānta-paribhāṣā* is adopted from the Adyar edition (S. S. Suryanarayana Sastri, 1942, 1971), though neither the text nor the translation therein are adopted. The purpose of adopting this numeral ordering is that it facilitates an easy and ready reference to the specific text (in the chapter on *Āgama* as well in other places). Fortunately or unfortunately, this particular edition of *VP* is also more readily available than most others are. (See Bibliography under Dharmarāja for the range of editions available and consulted.)

27. *vyavahārānāditayā tatkāraṇasyādhyāsasya*, (p15). It is also argued that without this distinction the empirical means of knowing and self-identification with knowledge so derived, as well as the functions of the senses and the body would be unintelligible (pp47-52). Also, even a brahmin has to take himself seriously as a brahmin if he wants to attain self-realisation by performing offerings incumbent upon a brahmin (p54): and an analogy: 'The rope-nature of the rope cannot be negated even by a thousand continuous apprehensions of a snake.' (Vācaspati, *Bhāmatī, Catussūtrī*, Sastri and Raja trs., Adyar, 1933, p61.)

28. *Cf.* Sureśvara's forceful remarks in his *Naiṣkarmyasiddhi* 1.90: 'When this consummation of knowledge, destructive of bondage can be attained as a matter of immediate perception, to speak of knowledge as being of no help as it is without any supporting injunction does not seem to us to be in accordance with any reason' (Raghavachar, tr. 1965, p41).

29. By elevating *Śruti* as a *pramāṇa* over and above the adjudication of perception and ratiocination, and in claiming for scriptural word a special power of identification, *Bhāmatī* could be said to border on mysticism.

30. *VP* I.55-57, 88 (on referencing convention for *VP*, see note 26 above, 2nd paragraph). Advaita and Nyāya differ on what *anuvyavasāya* involves; for Advaita the subjective self-identification with the awareness-state is more significant (thus, '*I* am aware of this *table*', 'I am happy'), while for Nyāya (at least with Gaṅgeśa), the affirmation of the bare intentional content (minus the relation) of awareness is more significant (thus, 'my awareness is of *this* as having *thisness* (qualificand) and *tableness* (qualifier)).' More in ch.7, see note 19 therein.

31. S. N. Dasgupta, foreword to Swami Mādhavānanda's translation of *VP*, Ramakrishna Math, Belur, 1942.

32. S. S. Suryanarayana Sastri, *op cit*, Adyar, pxv.

33. S. Radhakrishnan, in his foreword to Suryanarayana Sastri, *ibid*. Kunjunni Raja's comment was obtained in conversation.

I

OUTLINE OF THE ARGUMENT FOR ŚABDAPRAMĀṆA

1.0 In the Indian theory of knowledge, a properly accredited *pramāṇa* is fundamental to the production of true (valid) knowledge. Indeed, *pramāṇa* is an instrument for (valid) knowledge and therefore proves to be viable source of knowledge if properly executed. As we said in the Introduction, one such 'source' identified in the tradition is *śabdapramāṇa* or (the) word as a valid means of knowing.

The argument for *śabdapramāṇa* is presented in the *Vedānta-paribhāṣā* in a set of rather terse propositions which are then analysed and elucidated. The intention here is to follow a similar format, by first stating the condensed argument then unpacking it, as it were, into its many parts.

1.1 *The Statement (Text)*

> *athāgamo nirūpyate/ yasya vākyasya tātparya viṣayībhūtasaṃsargo mānāntareṇa na bādhyate tadvākyaṃ pramāṇam/ vākyajanye ca jñāne ākāṅkṣāyogyatāsattayas tātparyajñānaṃ ceti catvāri kāraṇāni* [1] :
>
> After that, follows an appraisal of *āgama* [i.e. *śabdapramāṇa*]. When it is the case that there is a sentence whose intentional content, relating to an objective state of affairs, is not falsified by any other evidence (*māna*), that sentence is [said to be] a *pramāṇa* [that generates *pramā* true (valid) knowledge]; and in the case of such sentence-generated knowledge there are four [basic] causal factors, namely, syntactic-expectancy (*ākāṅkṣā*), semantic competence (*yogyatā*), word-element contiguity (*āsatti*), and awareness of 'intentionality' (*tātparyajñāna*).

1.2 *Elucidation*

The text begins with 'after that', meaning after having examined the properly accredited *pramāṇas* of 'perception' (*pratyakṣa*), 'inference' (*anumāna*), it is now time to look at the fourth *pramāṇa*, accepted by Advaita and rejected by some, or accepted in either a modified or a stronger form such as Nyāya and Mīmāṃsā do respectively. This means of knowing is often called *āgama*, by traditional schools whose concern is mostly with the vindication of the 'words of tradition' or such authoritative source as the scriptures. *Āgama* is here taken to be synonymous with *śabdapramāṇa*, as that term commonly used in Nyāya, Sāṅkhya, Yoga and Vedānta schools. (See under *Śabda* in Introduction.) Sentence (*vākya*) is taken to be the basic linguistic unit in an utterance. It is taken in this view to be a viable and productive instrument for generating a certain sort of cognition (*jñāna*).

1.3 Two principles are deduced here.

i. The first concerns the content of the cognition in respect of that of which it is cognition. The cognition that arises as a result of hearing a sentence, and understanding its meaning, has a particular 'intentional content' that has a correlate objective structure (*viṣayībhūta* : literally, 'object'or thing apprehended or *about* which it is). The 'intentional content' is conveyed or given by the putative linguistic 'bits' and the relations (*saṃsarga*) that obtain *inter alia*, which are intended to yield a particular cognition, albeit linguistic cognition. This occurs when the composite sentence sense is comprehended by the audience in the relative context of the utterance.

ii. The second principle is in respect of the causally instrumental conditions, contingent upon the utterance of the sentence, that are efficacious in generating the cognition. The cognition-particular in the episodic sense is termed *śābdabodha*, linguistically derived apprehension. It requires for its production certain basic 'causes' which are intimately connected with the process of the comprehension of the 'meaning' of a sentence relative to the context in which its utterance occurs. In large part, these causal conditions make the distinctiveness of this *pramāṇa* in contrast to other means of knowing. The principal role that 'words' play in this respect is the first of the characteristics unique to this *pramāṇa*. After the perception of the word-elements, there is the recollection of the 'meanings' of the individual linguistic items, whether they be words or phrases. Then follows the process of the assimilation of the 'meanings' of the putative bits, until they are coalesced into a unified or composite 'significance'—i.e. the sentence-meaning plus the overall intended sense, which together we may call the 'propositional sense expressed' in making the utterance (allowing for different types of speech-acts and differing uses of the same sentence-type). The success of the process is contingent upon certain conditions obtaining in the hearer that causally affect ('create'—in the aesthetic sense—or 'reveal') the *significance* or unified understanding that has the content structure as described in principle **i**. These causal conditions, together with a number of auxiliary factors common to other *pramāṇas*, are considered to be indispensable for the successful emergence of *śābdabodha*, the cognition specific to this *pramāṇa*.

1.4 Very briefly, the four causal conditions (*kāraṇas*) are: *ākāṅkṣā* or the mutual expectancy that one word rouses for another in the absence of one of them; *yogyatā* or the semantic compatibility that two or more words must share if they are to be related meaningfully to yield a coherent sentence-meaning; *āsatti* or the proximity that words, and maybe word-meanings, in their juxtaposition must have for a unified sentence-meaning to arise; and *tātparyajñāna* or awareness of the intention with which the sentence is uttered or which the sentence-token is intended to convey, since the intended *sense* could differ from the literal meaning and could be different in different speech-acts or utterances of the same sentence-type. Thus, the awareness of 'meaning-*intention*' is a most important aspect of *śabdapramāṇa.*

There is a third, though salient, principle that concerns the derivation of the 'truth' of the cognition generated. What conditions must prevail for a cognition to be a 'true' cognition and not a *false* one? Particular criteria determine whether the truth-character obtains in a cognition-particular, one of which is mentioned in the quoted text as being the principle of falsification. That is to say, the *śābdabodha* generated should not be falsified or refuted by evidence from another source, *śabda* or otherwise. The list is extended to include other criteria, to which we shall return later. But the emphasis in the Advaita view is on the conditions internal and not on the conditions external (*ab extra*) to the collective set required for the generation of the *śābdabodha* provided that the process is effective and unerring.

The contention is that, if the principles, sketched in their broad generality here, are fulfilled, then the sentence whose utterance gave rise to the particular cognition is regarded to be a viable *pramāna.* Herein lie the rudiments of the vindication of *śabda* as a legitimate, accredited, *pramāṇa.*

1.5 *Analysis*

It is now time to unpack the argument further and analyse it in terms of some basic categories that would be seen to present an adequate and epistemologically complete account of *śabdapramāṇa.* I have chosen some seven categories. I have exercised some arbitrariness, yet have basically sought to expand upon the more limited number to be found in some traditional analysis. Gaṅgeśa's analysis of the problem in the *śabdakhaṇḍa* section, for instance, is presented by Vidyābhūṣaṇa in his lengthy preface to the first volume of *Tattvacintāmaṇi* in terms of the following four categories:[2]

śravaṇa—hearing (of words)
smaraṇa—recollection (of word-meanings)
saṃsargabodha— comprehension (via syntactical relation)
anuvyavasāya - subjective affirmation (of the cognition)

I believe that an intuitively more consistent and systematic approach, which will also be fairer to Gaṅgeśa, would need to involve several other categories that are crucial to the analysis, and which are quite clearly focused upon by Viśvanātha, a Navyanyāya logician.[3] *Śābdabodha* (follows *saṃsargabodha*), *vyavasāya* (which precedes *anuvyavasāya*) and *prāmāṇya* (which considers the logical status of the cognition) would appear to be at least three major additions to the above four. Analogous categories can be seen to be operative in the analysis of any *pramāṇa*, appropriately converted to reflect the relative process. Vidyābhūṣaṇa has only partly represented the *prayojakas* or categories that, on closer reading, one would also find in Gaṅgeśa. One would have thought, that what needs to be emphasised about *śravaṇa* and *smaraṇa* is the role the specific *kāraṇas* and the linguistic process (*vyāpāra*) play in order for the utterance to function as a principal *karaṇa* before a comprehension could take place. Further to this, *saṃsargabodha* involves the operation of the *kāraṇas* of *ākāṅkṣā*, *yogyatā*, and so on, which is more than a mere awareness of the syntactical relation obtaining among the linguistic elements.

These considerations call for a re-appraisal of the terms and categories in which the analysis of *śabdapramāṇa* has hitherto been presented. Not only in the case of *śabda*, but also with respect to other *pramāṇas*, the framework being suggested here should prove to be of much assistance.[4] Such an analysis aids our approach by looking at each category for their self-consistency, then examining them together for the coherency they lend as the many steps in the argument. This is just what I intend to do in the following chapters in looking at the argument in question. For now, we must continue with the task of expanding on the categories I have suggested here.

1.6 *Karaṇa*

Karaṇa is one of the most important categories in Indian theory of knowledge. It is defined as: *vyāpāravad asādhāraṇaṃ kāraṇaṃ karaṇam*,[5] i.e. that rather *special* cause (*karaṇa*) among the sum-total of causal conditions, which triggers off the process (*vyāpāra*) of apprehension aided by other relatively non-special (*sādhāraṇa*) causal conditions. For any desired result in any empirical act or event the efficiency of an appropriate *karaṇa* cannot be overstated. The definition of *karaṇa* specifies that the causal condition delineated here be *asādhāraṇa*, a special or extraordinary cause as distinct to *sādhāraṇa*, which is a general or ordinary causes. The former is the non-ordinary *efficient* or instrumental cause, while the latter is the more common and generally prevalent causal condition, or aggregate of conditions contingent to a process. Both are necessary and neither is sufficient in itself; yet the former marks off the special cause of the effect or class of effects desired for a particular but maybe not for other similar processes. The overall process no doubt largely depends on other, intermediate causal conditions – such as the *kāraṇas* as distinct to the *karaṇa* – and upon their cooperation in leading to the desired effect; but the intermediate process is itself a consequence of the immediate antecedent of the *asādhāraṇa-kāraṇa-karaṇa*.

Karaṇa, then, is that invariable and indispensable antecedent factor (or *ananyathāsiddha*)[6] without which the entire operation would not proceed in the manner desired: *kāryaniyatāvyavahitapūrvavṛtti ananyathāsiddhaṃ ca kāraṇam.*[7]

More pertinently, in later Indian analysis, *karaṇa* was defined as a *special* cause which is the most *necessary* among all the many conditions that go toward bringing about an effect; and conversely, in the absence of the *asādhāraṇa* cause, even though all the other *sādhāraṇa* causes may be present, the effect would not be achieved, or not generated successfully.[8]

Often, the instrumental function of a *karaṇa* is compared to that of an axe in the act of felling a tree: without an axe, or a similar cutting instrument, such as a saw, it would be well-nigh impossible to get the tree down (notwithstanding "acts of God"). Likewise, every *pramāṇa* is said to have a distinct *karaṇa* which has a unique function of relating the subject to some 'object' in a way another *pramāṇa* would not be capable of. It is this that accounts for the distinctiveness of the process and, consequently, for the end-result or the effect also, namely, the particular cognition yielded through the respective *pramāṇa*. But just an axe can become useful as an aid to, say, breaking open a hotel room door – where the appropriate key, unless lost, would have achieved the same – a *karaṇa* special to one *pramāṇa* can become a subsidiary link and aid in another *pramāṇa*. For instance, sense-experience, such as seeing and listening, though a special cause in the *pramāṇa* of perception, becomes relatively secondary but none-the-less necessary in *śabdapramāṇa* in so far as words have to be perceived in the process of understanding sentence-sense.

Obviously, then, what is unique to *śabdapramāṇa* is *words* themselves, for without an utterance, be it spoken, written or given through some other media, there would be no question of understanding or making sense of a sentence. If *śābdabodha* is the desired effect, it follows that the linguistic apprehension requires cognitive coalescing of linguistic elements with respect to their meanings and mutual relations. The compound '*śābdabodha*' itself indicates the combination of two elements – viz. cognitive (*bodha*) and linguistic (*śabda*). We cannot say that the former is uniquely peculiar to *śabdapramāṇa*, since it is incumbent upon each *pramāṇa* to generate cognition. But we can say that the latter (i.e. *śabda*) is peculiar and unique to this particular *pramāṇa*, since (a) it is not a necessary cause in other *pramāṇas*, and (b) without its efficiency there would be no *śābdabodha* as such.

1.7 The linguistic element taken to be basic in the analysis of *śabdapramāṇa,* as noted in 1.1, is *vākya* or sentence; although a sentence may not be the basic *unit* in linguistic analysis. The basic unit in linguistic analysis may be *pada*, roughly equivalent to (the) "word" in western understanding, or perhaps closer still to the *morpheme* of western linguistics.[9] The consideration, however, for regarding the sentence as the basic linguistic element in *śabdapramāṇa* is a logical one, for the understanding derived from grasping the meaning of a sentence is greater than the 'understanding' delivered by the words of the sentence, when taken independently. Thus, the *karaṇa* for *śabdapramāṇa* is *śabdajñāna* or, more specifically, *vākyajñāna—awareness of the sentence*—in which the *sentence* has the function of being the 'extraordinary' (*asādhāraṇa*) cause, and the cognition-particular distinctive to this *pramāṇa* is said to be *sentence-generated (vākyajanya)*. And that unique cognition is termed *śābdabodha.*

If this argument is valid, then it follows that *śabda qua vākya* or sentence is a legitimate source of knowing.

Before going any further, we should mention that the Nyāya position in respect of the *karaṇa* presents some difficulties. Some Naiyāyikas regard *padajñāna* or 'awareness of the word' as the *karaṇa* for *śābdabodha* : *padajñānaṃ tu karaṇam.*[10] While others, like Jayanta Bhaṭṭa, do not consider any one particular *karaṇa* or cause to be special and more important than any other cause or set of causes necessary in a the generation of cognition. They argue for the efficiency of the *aggregate* of causes, rather than of any one, in the process.

There seems, however, to be good reason to suggest that at least one *karaṇa* is involved in a significant and nontrivial way, so that this very first step differentiates the manner in which the subject comes in contact with the 'object' of which cognition is had. Each *pramāṇa* involves different means for this initial 'contact' between the knower (*pramātṛ*) and the known (*prameya*). For instance, the *fire* that one infers on a hill from the evidence of smoke bellowing above it, is neither initially nor finally presented to the subject as is the fire in the hearth he sits near. It must be obvious that the *karaṇa* operative in the two respective *pramāṇas*—namely, inference and perception—are quite distinct and not negotiable.

Similarly, in the case of *śābdabodha*, it would be correct to say that the initial contact the subject has is with the utterance, and although perception is used for an immediate acquaintance with the sentence uttered, there is neither any significant resemblance between the utterance and the fire (inferred or perceived), nor, as yet, any awareness of what is expressed or intended to be expressed by the utterance. In other words, the subject cannot claim to know or to have understood what the sentence conveys in terms of its meaning 'infra-structure.' His acquaintance is at best with the outward expression, what we might call the *statement*, but not with the *proposition* expressed therein. The function of perception as a *karaṇa*, albeit a *sādhāraṇa* or a general cause, ceases with this step. And unless we suppose that some other *karaṇa* continues to be effective one could not possibly make sense of the utterance, save repeat as does a parrot the utterance 'heard'.

An example may help to illustrate the point being made here. Someone asks a friend if he knows the meaning of the sentence 'our doors of perception are befogged'. If the friend goes no further than perception then obviously he would not respond to the question of the 'meaning', but he may say something like, 'I read that in Mr X's book'. Presuming that he attempts to respond to the question proper, but can only remember having read the sentence somewhere, he would say something like, 'I know that statement, but I don't know what it means or what Mr X was getting at', meaning that he has some acquaintance with the sentence but he cannot recall what it expresses or what the author intended to convey by making that particular utterance. He could, though, find out. The very investigation would require that he go beyond perception and take the sentence and its significant structure as his next step. Already, a particular and special *karaṇa* is being involved in the process. This goes to show that, while it is important to stress the cooperative process involving an aggregate of *karaṇas*, it is also important to emphasise the particularity of the *karaṇa* that stands out in the process as being the most significant and relevant. So the Advaita approach does a little better than some Nyāya alternatives in this regard.

Vyāpāra

1.8 The next category after *karaṇa* that needs to be defined in our stepwise analysis is *vyāpāra*, the operative process. *Vyāpāra* is defined as: *tajjanyaḥ tajjanyajanakaśca vyapārāḥ.*[11] That is to say, *vyāpāraḥ* is a process brought into operation by the *karaṇa* (i.e. special cause) and which is instrumental in producing the final effect. For instance, if the stick (*daṇḍa*) a potter holds is the *karaṇa*, which he uses to revolve the wheel and thereby shape the clay, then the rotation of the wheel is the *vyāpāra*, and the shaping of the clay another intermediary cause, which cooperate to produce the end-product, namely, the pot. *Vyāpāra* then is the necessary intermediate process that renders effective the instrumental cause or *karaṇa*. The process itself may need for its operation a number of causal links and intermediate effects before the final effect is achieved. To refer back to our example of felling the tree, *vyāpāra* is here comparable to the actual *striking* of the axe, or the sawing, through which the cutting occurs. Striking and cutting are two aspects of the same *vyāpāra*, we may say. But without the striking there would be no cutting, and without cutting no felling. Thus the *vyāpāra* delimits the function of the *karaṇa* by introducing a necessary operational factor without which it is not efficient, or possibly not quite as efficient. This is in much the same way as we would say that *formal* efficiency stands in need of being complemented by *material* efficiency.

1.9 In *śabdapramāṇa*, the *vyāpāra* is said to be *śabdārthajñāna*, or better still, *vākyārthajñāna* : 'awareness of sentence-meaning'. The operative steps preceding the achievement of *śābdabodha* is what is being referred to here. The process entails the 'raw' apprehension of meaning of the sentence in terms of its constituent word-elements, followed with a deepening of its intended sense relative to the context of the utterance. That is to say, the process involves the assimilation of the mutually related meanings of the 'bits' that constitute the sentence. The 'bits' in the analysis of *vyāpāra* begin with words, but may also be phrases, clauses, and even whole sentences and passages, as the categories of relation. The analysis of *vyāpāra* in these terms or categories gains strength as the relation of meaning becomes increasingly more complex at higher orders of expression, when it gets a bit cumbersome to break down the process into the putative minimal 'bits', such as words. The relation among 'wholes' is equally effective in generating *śābdabodha* in the broader sense of verbal understanding in more complex forms of discourse and communication. We shall take the lead of the traditional analysis and consider *vyāpāra* mostly at the level of *pada* or the 'word' (and word-meaning),[12] as an anchor for our own analysis.

1.10 *Vyāpāra* actually begins, as we said, with *padajñāna*, perception of words. This in turn leads to the apprehension of word-meanings, which is a necessary step prior to there being an awareness of the syntactical relation. Thus, *padārtha-jñāna-saṃsargabodha*. *Padajñāna* is not sufficient for this awareness-process either, for the essential 'power' of the word, in terms of the relation it has with the 'object' it signifies, lies in its meaning (*śaktaṃ padam*). Every word has a meaning whereby it is related to the 'object' it signifies in the sentence. Without the assimilation of the meanings of the individual words that make up the sentence the chances of comprehending the sentence meaning (and through it the relation the sentence as a whole has, to the 'object' or objective content signified) would be minimal. Awareness of the *meanings* of the words and their inter-relation then become necessary for the comprehension of the relational content of the sentence. The meanings of the words are apprehended through another aligned process which is considered to be one of the distinct functions of *vyāpāra* in Advaita view.[13]

1.10 There are, of course, problems with this analysis. What exactly is *pada* or (the) word? Does each and every word have 'meaning'? Is 'meaning' any one thing? What is the relation between word and meaning? and between 'meaning' and that of which it is supposed to be the meaning? Further, is the 'meaning' of a sentence the same as the 'meanings' of the words that make up the sentence? Or could we have a sentence whose meaning is not the sum total of the meanings of the words? The responses vary and there is usually quite a bit of controversy over these questions. A treatise on 'meaning' would occupy more than the space we can afford for the larger problem at hand. We can, though, begin to sketch the approach we shall take, and develop it further in the relevant chapter (i.e. 3).

Briefly, the general view in classical Indian linguistics is that every word has a particular significatory function, which is expressed in terms of the *power*, *śakti*, the word has. It is in virtue of this 'power' that a word is capable of expressing, indicating, or suggesting the meaning it does in a sentence. The word's capacity to convey its meaning, or the meaning associated with it in the context of its use, is also attributed to this power (*saktaṃ padam*). Just as an axe has its function determined by the inherent potency to *cut*, which determines its function, so also word has its potency in its meaning, capable of being conveyed in a psycho-linguistic process. The importance of this potency lies in its significatory function (*vṛtti*) through which the particular meaning, or 'sense', or an indirect but related meaning, (i.e. the 'connotative sense', *lakṣayārtha*) is made apparent. A prior acquaintance, not so much with the meaning as with the significatory function (*vṛtti*) is an essential factor for *vyāpāra* in bringing together the meanings of the words juxtaposed in the sentence. Once the outward verbal form is perceived, there follows the recollection (*smaraṇa*) of the meanings of the words. For this process memory, as a psychic function, is considered to be the auxiliary *vyāpāra*. Meaning, though, may vary from one context to another. This fact is recognised and expressed in terms of the dual significatory function that a word in principle has, namely, the expressive or primary (*śakti*) and the implied or 'indicative', or secondary (*lakṣaṇā*) function. Between these two arise a wide spectrum and range of meanings and senses. For instance, a word is said to express primarily, *qua śakti*, a universal (*jāti*) and only secondarily does it express, *qua lakṣaṇā*, a particular (*vyakti*), possibly indicated by the context of its occurrence.[14]

1.11 Two examples are given to illustrate the distinction between the two significatory functions. In the sentence 'The village (is) in the river', if one were to take river' in its primary expressive function, one would have to understand the sentence as saying that the village is actually *in* that river, amongst its rapid waters. But this is a physical impossibility, for, generally speaking, no village can last in the rapid flow of a river. One then has to relate the term 'river' to another, probable sense, and here the secondary significatory function becomes of use. Through *lakṣaṇā* one derives that since the river has some relation with its bank or banks, the bank therefore might be the probable locus of the village. Thus the sentence is understood to convey: "the village is on the bank (of the river)". In the second example, the sentence 'This cow is red' is given. Now, individually considered, the word 'cow' expresses a *cow*-universal, since it is conceivable that the term 'cow' could refer to the countless number of cows there are at any one time. But in the particular instance of its occurrence, the word 'cow' signifies or designates a particular animal which is an instance of the universal. For this to be possible, however, the word must be capable of such a signification, which in turn would depend upon some inherent function the word assumes in a particular utterance. This significatory function is identified as *lakṣaṇā*. Without a detailed analysis of 'word-power', the discussion of *vyāpāra* would not be complete. In chapter four we pursue this matter further.

1.12 *Kāraṇa*

Kāraṇa is the third category in the analysis of *śabdapramāṇa* that is of considerable interest. *Kāraṇa*, however, is to be distinguished from *karaṇa*, the first category we looked at. *Kāraṇa* is the condition or set of conditions that determine the causal nexus in the *vyāpāra* process. We noted the efficiency of the instrumental cause in 1.1., pointing out that this is one among the aggregate of the psycho-physical causes and conditions in the process that gives rise to *jñāna* (*bodhasvabhāvasāmagrī*). Other causes, though perhaps not as invariable and immediate as the *asādhāraṇa karaṇa*, are equally important and to a large extent indispensable (*ananyathāsiddha*). These are classed under *sādhāraṇakāraṇa karaṇa* or general causes. But in the case of *śabdapramāṇa* even these causes have crucial determinant roles to play in the generation of *śābdabodha*. They therefore command considerable attention, and feature significantly in Indian linguistic analysis.

The *kāraṇas* form a very relevant part of the *material* cause and contribute to the efficiency of the overall process. Logically, a *kāraṇa* is the antecedent condition that necessarily precedes an effect: *kāryaniyatāpūrvavṛtti-kāraṇam.*[15] But it must also be proximate and closely related to the production of the effect. By contrast, the act on the part of the donkey carrying the clay to the potter's workshop, though causally related to the production of the pot, is not a *kāraṇa* in the strict sense, for its connection with the effect is remote and contingent, and not a necessary one. It is *anyathāsiddha*, dispensable or superfluous, or perhaps negotiable with some other cause, such as the arrival of the clay on a truck-load: while the clay, the water used in the mixing, the potter's hands, and the stick for revolving the wheel are *fairly* immediate and largely indispensable causes in the process whose effect is the production of the ceramic. They are, as in Mill's system, the unconditional and invariable antecedents.

One of these is the special and efficient cause, distinguished from the rest by the classification '*asādhāraṇa-kāraṇa-karaṇa*'. Its pre-eminence, as we said, consists in its capacity to instigate the entire activity or efficiency necessary for the production of the final effect—*vyāpāratvakaraṇam*. Non-superfluous necessary antecedents (*ananyathāsiddha niyata*) could be few in number. It is useful sometimes to consider the *kāraṇas* in the context of *vyāpāra*, since the purpose of the *kāraṇas* is to aid the process towards its completion.

1.13 The *kāraṇas* pertain in particular to the *saṃsarga* aspect of the process described as '*padārthajñāna-saṃsarga-bodha* : the awareness of the relation of the word-meanings apprehended'. If we regard sentence as a complex linguistic structure in which word-meanings (*padārthas*) are juxtaposed in certain mutual relations to yield a combined sentence-sense, the conditions which contribute to the comprehension of these relations, and through these the combined sentence-sense, are known as the *kāraṇas*. They, indeed, 'cause' the comprehension by bringing about the appropriate awareness of the inter-relation of the word-meanings and the discrete linguistic elements that go to make the utterance. Non-linguistic factors are, of course, also involved in some utterances or speech-acts, and these too are taken care of by the *kāraṇas* or one amongst them, depending on their complexity. These causes are aided in the process by other auxiliary conditions (*sahakāri-kāraṇas*) which become operative when more complex relations are involved, such as, for example, between the expressive sense of one word with the indicative sense of another with which it is juxtaposed in a sentence. The function of the *kāraṇa* is then essential to the process of comprehending the sentence-sense.

There are four major *kāraṇas* discussed in most analyses, although there is considerable difference in the interpretation each receive, and there is some controversy about the fourth one. The controversy centres largely round the issue of whether there has to be a concomitant awareness of the *kāraṇa*, in this case of *tātparya* or intentionality, in the process of comprehending the sentence sense. Advaita requires awareness only in respect of *tātparya* but not of any other of the relevant *kāraṇas* whose function nonetheless contributes enormously to the *vyāpāra* which involves assimilating the syntactical relations (*saṃsarga*) that obtain in the sentence. We do not necessarily have to be aware of every bit of syntax to understand a sentence-utterance. Perhaps our awareness of such factors is unconscious, while we are often consciously aware of the intention with which an utterance has been made. When pressed, as in a linguistic exercise, we are able to point to the consistency or inconsistency of the use of syntax in a sentence.

The other importance of the *kāraṇas* is in their contribution to the awareness of the objective content through syntactical correlation in the sentence. The comprehension of sentence-sense entails at the same time the awareness of the 'objects' and their relations as represented in the linguistic elements of the sentence. *Viṣayībhūta-saṃsarga-bodha* implies, then, the cognition of the objective correlate *qua* the syntactical relation (*saṃsarga*) in the intentional mode.

1.14 In very simple terms, the four *kāraṇas* are described as follows. *Ākāṅkṣā* or mutual expectancy is the relation of expectation that obtains between two words, so that when one word is heard it gives cause to an expectancy for the other word, and thereby the word-meaning related to it, in order for there to be a completion of the whole meaning of the expression heard. For example, when the word 'close' is heard, one would expect something else to follow so as to complete the expression and its understanding. An expectation has been roused for another term, such as 'door', that would complete the understanding for the listener. Similarly, when one hears, say, the word 'bring', it is likely to rouse the expectancy : 'bring what?'. The action-word 'bring' requires another word, possibly one that denotes an object, to complete the pending sense of the utterance heard. There are many types of *ākāṅkṣā* that reflect the different, possible relations between words, or the relations between the word-meanings, that contribute toward the comprehension of the sentence sense.

1.15 *Yogyatā* is described as the competency or 'fitness' of one word to enter into relation so as to yield a semantically acceptable sentence sense. For example, the sentence '(he) sprinkles (the field) with fire' (*vahninā siñcati*) has two incompatible words in it, for the word 'sprinkle' is not competent (*yogyatva*) to be related to the word 'fire' as their attempted relation presents a logical difficulty. One sprinkles a field with water, not with fire which will result in the contrary effect to one desired. *Prima facie* this is the understanding that *yogyatā* functions to present. There may be exceptions and more specialised uses of the pair of terms in another expression; but then it would be the function not of *yogyatā* but of one of the other *kāraṇas*, in particular of *tātparya* or intentionality, to make this clear – as we shall explore in a later chapter . Thus the function of each *kāraṇa* gets exhausted and sometimes subsumed by that of another.

1.16 *Āsatti* is the third *kāraṇa* and is related to the contiguity or the proximity with which words require to be juxtaposed for their mutual relation to bear significance. It is argued that intervals between the presentation of words interfere with a consistent grasping of their related sense in the sentence. Indeed, Dharmarāja contends that the proximity ought to be between the word-meanings and not necessarily between words. Intervals between the utterances of words will not necessarily be an obstacle if the listener can recall their meanings and retain them in memory and relate them at a later stage. Some other writers take issue with this view.

1.17 *Tātparyajñāna* is the fourth *kāraṇa* in the analysis. We have rendered it 'intentionality', but it has much to do with the awareness of the intention, that is to say, the intention with which the utterance is made. The author of *VP* does not believe that intention consists in the *desire* or wish of the utterer to convey a particular sense by his utterance, rather it is the linguistic capacity of generating a particular understanding intended through the relation of the word-meanings. The purpose of formulating the *kāraṇa* in this way is to free, so to speak, intentionality from the necessity of assuming a *personal* intention, such as would be true, say, of certain textual 'utterances' whose author or authors are not known, and whose intentions are not accessible. Also, sometimes utterances are made, or repeated, without any particular wish to convey this or that sense. The priest in his recitation of some scriptural texts and the parrot imitating another's locution need have no idea of their own to convey; they intend nothing more than the 'texts' themselves do.

1.18 Apart from the *kāraṇas* there are other more secondary causes and ancillary aids that contribute to the process. An assurance of the absence of vitiating factors, defects in the operators and in the linguistic capacity of the audience is one among them. At a higher stage of confronting more complex utterances, such as those with deeper philosophical import, tradition recommends the assistance of some amount of intellectual and mental practice, which may involve contemplative concentration of the mind, quietitude and reflective meditation on, say, *śruti* utterances. One may be told to achieve a phenomenological appraisal of the substance, as it were, of the understanding derived, which would, in some cases, require an experiential dimension, possibly in the wider existential and social context of its relevance.

Śābdabodha

1.19 Given that the process is accomplished without hindrance, and the *karaṇa* with the *kāraṇas* function with success, then there should arise the *understanding* intended to be effected by the sentence-utterance. The co-operative functioning of the causes involved, successfully generates, it is said, *śābdabodha*. There is, however, no unanimity as regards the exact description of the overall process. There is a school that goes back to Bhartṛhari that does not consider the process as involving, first, the assimilation of word-meanings, then, the collective grasping of the sentence sense. Rather, the view here is that the process is essentially one of a holistic grasping in a 'flash' of intuition (*pratibhā*) upon hearing an utterance, without necessarily requiring the assimilation of the discrete words, their meanings and relations.[16]

The division into words, meanings and relations, in this view, is considered to be an artificial process, engaged in mostly by grammarians. On this view it does not reflect the process of understanding itself. Between the two extreme views are several variations, the more important of which we shall consider in chapter four.

Viṣayibhūta

The meaning of a sentence as its propositional content is said to be (intentionally) related to the state of affairs it signifies or 'represents'. In this respect, it could be said that *śābdabodha* corresponds more or less to the 'proposition' in Western philosophy.[17] There are, however, certain things one can say of propositions that would be incorrect to attribute to sentences, such as, for example, that a proposition is true or false—notwithstanding the Tarskian attempt to define truth in terms of the semantics of a sentence.[18] And in so far as Tarski also seeks to substitute logical symbols as synonyms for the particular sentence this differentiates his concept of a sentence from that essentially conceived as the context-specific speech-act for *śābdabodha*. In the Indian view, a sentence must be capable of the following (here invoking parts of Searle's catalogue):

i. telling the hearer that he is being told something (i.e. draw the attention of the audience);
ii. indicate that the message is being conveyed through a linguistic activity–i.e. that the telling is a locutionary act (- akin to Austin's -), that distinguishes it from noise and animal sound;
iii. intends that the hearer be involved in the speech-act;
iv. points to a certain state of affairs or object (*viṣaya*);
v. intends that the telling is exactly this;
vi. succeeds in producing the corresponding awareness of these in the hearer in accordance with certain rule-governed conventions of the speaker's and listener's linguistic community, and, where applicable;
vii. produces the desired effect in respect of what the speaker wants to achieve through the utterance, such as to follow an injunction, a rite or practice, or some purpose-directed goal.

Clearly, by laying stress on the hearer's involvement and participation, and requiring the awareness of intentionality, *śābdabodha* is distinguished from the more logical character of propositions. It is a little like what Searle had in mind when he remarked: 'On the speaker's side, saying something and meaning it are closely connected with intending to produce certain effects on the hearer. On the hearer's side, understanding the speaker's utterance is closely connected with recognising his intentions.'[19]

Śābdabodha, then, is a particular instantiation of an awareness (*jñāna*) that is related to and derived from the syntactic-semantic (and R) content of a sentence. What is 'intentionally' given or presented in the *śābdabodha* is the *viṣaya* or *viṣayībhūta*, literally, what has become the *object* of apprehension in a judgement – i.e. the state of affairs that 'satisfies' that *śābdabodha*. It is not, however, presumed that in each instance of a *bodha* *x* that has *y* as its *viṣaya* that *y* actually makes reference to some external *object* as such. In some cases the *viṣaya* is *vastu* ('thing' or some actual object), in others it is *vastuśūnya* (empty of actual object-ness). What does not follow also is a). that no property or properties can be predicated of *y qua viṣaya*, since otherwise it would be difficult to speak of relation among the relevant terms of the intentional content of cognitions (i.e. it is not content*less*), and b). that no truth-value can be attributed to the judgement in question. This brings us to the category of *prāmāṇya*.

1.20 *PRĀMĀṆYA: the problem of truth of a judgement*

In almost all systems of Indian thought *truth* is distinguished from error, and therefore from what is *false*. Truth is considered to be a 'character' of awareness (*jñāna*) which it is has when it is a 'true awareness', and falsity when the awareness is in error (*mithyājñāna, avidyā, viparyaya, bhrānti*, etc). A true cognition is comprised of an awareness that has the particular features of that of which it is an awareness: *tadvati tatprakāraka-jñānatvaṃ prāmāṇyam*.[20]

In giving this general definition we have avoided reference to 'real entity or object' of cognition, for though it requires conformity of the cognitive content or 'intentional essence' in its structure with its objective correlate, there can however be conformity between ideas, abstract entities, and between a concept and a picture, whether in whole or in parts.[21] Thus, it is not necessary to stipulate that the conformity be to a 'real entity' *if* what was causally efficacious in generating that cognition was not itself 'real entity or entities', as clearly is not the case in *śabda* generated *śābdabodha*. The conformity, then, in the latter case, must have to do with the relational content of the sentence in addition to the intentionality in uttering the sentence. No doubt, some elements in the relational content of the sentence would, or perhaps may, refer to real things, and in so far as they do, the awareness would have to be in accord to these and their inter-relation. But this reference need not become a necessary characteristic of each and every cognition. Indeed, sometimes, even though reference appears to be made to real things, the major purpose of the utterance is to point at the 'mood' of a state of affairs – e.g. at a funeral of a much beloved friend, or the sense of illusioriness at a party.

1.21 More importantly, however, the theory of truth being enunciated here is not exactly what is generally known as the 'correspondence theory of truth', though it is comparable to it. There are several reasons for this. One is that the 'comformity' is not a measure as such between, on the one hand, the cognition, and, on the other hand, that of which it is a cognition, since this would involve a process like introspection or some external means of comparing the cognition against the 'reality' of which it is supposed to be a representation, very much as one compares an image to its likeness. The principle is that, in the transparency, there is either conformity or there isn't: no question of 'awareness' of this conformity is implicated here—at least in the Nyāya view.[22] Thus, it could be said of *śābdabodha* in this connection, that it is *pramā* if, and only if, its intensional correlate is in conformity with the intentional-relational content of the sentence utterance. This is achieved, in the Nyāya view, if the cognition, over and above fulfilling the conditions of the particular *pramāṇa* has a *guṇa*, or mark of excellence. The *guṇa*, in this instance, could be the potentiality of the awareness to lead to some fruitful or productive outcome. As the 'ascertainment' of this mark or characteristic of truth would involve another cognition—such as 'there is productive outcome'—one could say that 'correspondence' also becomes a subsequent test for purposes of corroboration, just as some other marks, such as the reliability of the author, could become part of the criteria.

1.22 The Advaita view is not dissimilar to the Nyāya view, with the exception that the characteristic of 'excellence' (*guṇa*) is not directly sought after, although the pragmatic mark of fulfilling a purposive end or goal, is included in the criteria overall. Thus, rather than look for a direct conformity, the Advaita view places greater emphasis on the efficacious deployment, as it were, of the instruments of the *pramāṇa* in question. *Doubt*, or the suspicion of a falsification from another evidence or understanding, would be important factors in the final judgement.[23] The criteria that Advaita develops further require that the *jñāna* should tell us something significantly new, that it carry conviction (*niścaya*), that, in the case of *śabda*, its 'source' be authoritative and that it be not contradicted or falsified by what is already known or by the already accepted truth on the matter under inquiry.

Later, in chapter 7, we shall consider in detail the Advaita theory of truth under the following criteria which characterise an awareness if it is a *pramā*:

a. *tadvati tatprakārakatvam*—conformity of qualifier with the qualified in the cognition just as it is in the object;

b. *abādhita*—unfalsified by other knowledge;

c. *asaṃdighatva*—conviction, absence of doubt, tenacity
d. *anadhigatatva* (*apūrvatva*)—novelty of awareness, 'new', (like 'novel prediction');
e. *pravṛtti-sāmarthya*—condition of satisfaction, in terms of fulling a purposive goal or making it successful;
f. *āptoktajñāna*—reliability of 'source'.

In short, the Advaita view is that the conditions that generate the cognition are also the conditions that make it true, provided an appropriate *pramāṇa-karaṇa* is operative, and that if it is *true* it should be consistent with the above criteria. The theory of truth sketched here is called *svataḥ-prāmāṇyavāda*, 'truth self-established'. Distinction, however, has to be made between how truth is established and how truth is ascertained, and between how truth is checked and how its corroboration is achieved. The Nyāya thinkers were aware that it is not enough merely to say that the conditions that generate an awareness where a legitimate *pramāṇa* is operative are the conditions that make it true, since one could be mistaken in overlooking or disregarding errors in the process. Thus, steps have to be taken to ascertain that a cognition is actually true, and if a doubt arises then to seek corroboration of its truth. This is achieved by going through the characteristics outlined above.

Vyavasāya : 'illumination'

1.23 Before there is awareness of something hitherto not known, there is said to be an 'imposed condition' (*upādhi*) of ignorance that, as it were, conceals the particular object to be known. When this obscurring property is lifted or 'sublated' by another awareness then there is illumination of the object in awareness. This 'illumination' is called *vyavasāya* and constitutes an affirmation of the awareness. Suppose someone encounters a shining object but her awareness of it is rather oblique; all she can say is that there is something—'this'—here. As she comes closer she is able to identify that the object is an opal. Thus arises the awareness : 'this [is an] opal'. Presuming now that she could not identify the object for what it is, and so decides to take it to a geologist or a metallurgist to seek their testimony. She is told: 'This is an opal'. The awareness she has through the testimony of the experts is again the *vyavasāya* in respect of the object to be known. There is no *assertion* here of the awareness and its subjective relation to the object known; it is simply an affirmation of an awareness with a particular *contentual* structure.

Sanskrit provides a better way of representing an affirmation by omitting the use of the verbal connector 'to be'; thus the *vyavasāya* : *idaṃ śivadhātuḥ*—'this [is] opal'; *idam na rajatam*—'this [is] not silver'.

1.24 *Anuvyavasāya: 'reflexive affirmation'*

Finally, at least in the Nyāya view, there is *anuvyavasāya*, which roughly amounts to the appropriation of the *vyavasāya* as a conscious (intentional) property of the knowing subject. This itself is an affirmation of the preceding *vyavasāya* step, in awareness. But since this affirmation cannot be in the same awareness as that which unveils the object to be known, there has to be an additional awareness of which the *vyavasāya* is a subset. It is not always the case that there is self-consciousness of an awareness of the sort we exemplified earlier. In other words, the *vyavasāya* that I have, say, in respect of the opal, that 'this [is an] opal', does not necessarily carry with it an affirmation of *my* having this awareness. I may be quite unself-conscious when this awareness arises. But when there is a subjective affirmation of the awareness, which occurs when there is a subjective identification with the *vyavasāya*, then there is said to be an *anuvyavasāya*. For instance, when the "I" is identified with the *vyavasāya* of 'this [is an] opal', then there is the *anuvyavasāya* of 'I know *this [is an] opal*'. The awareness, then, while still being in respect of the object to be known, is related to the subject who has this awareness, and the affirmation of this is called *anuvyavasāya*.[24a]

The essentially phenomenological process involved here is often confused with introspection, or with reflection, which, however, involves a self-conscious effort to scan, or inspect, some internal state, be it mental, emotional or psychical, while in the case of *anuvyavasāya* no such self-conscious effort is implicated : the awareness arises as a matter of course. There is also no 'back-ward' going as 'reflection' implies, rather there is an instantaneous affirmation in as much as the *vyavasāya* throws itself, so to speak, into the 'self-awareness' of the subjective consciousness. There is also no separate *vyavasāya* once the *anuvyavasāya* has emerged; it is more a process of tranformation wherein one awareness is subsumed under another awareness of a different order.

Advaita borrows from Nyāya its account of *vyavasāya*, but does not consider *anuvyavasāya* to be crucial to the process. Once the awareness revealing the object to be known has emerged there is little need for a subjective self-affirmation of the awareness. What is more, Advaita sees a problem in such subjective self-affirmations, and poses the question of the affirmation not taking the form : 'I am the opal', or, 'I am the pot', since this is what would be expected when the subjective consciousness is identified with the objective content in consciousness.[24] All the same, we do make affirmations of the sort: 'I know this [is an] opal', and there must be some means to account for this. Advaita argues that the relation between the subjective and the objective is not simply one of identification, but one of 'identity-with-difference' (*tādātmya*).

Either way, *anuvyavasāya* represents the culmination of the subjective-objective relation (*viṣayī-viṣaya-sambandha*), commenced in the subject's encounter with the object to be known. On the basis of the understanding derived, one may wish to adopt a certain attitude or belief toward the object known and other things related to it. The knowledge one gains in this way may have a normative value for him, and may help mould his overall attitude toward life, and so forth. Such an extension from the pure epistemic to normative consideration is more marked in the case of *śabdapramāṇa* than with the other *pramāṇas*, since one of the major contributions *śabda* (and particularly *śruti*), is seen to make, is precisely in respect of such concerns.

NOTES TO CHAPTER ONE

1. *Vedānta-paribhāṣā* (= *VP*), '*Āgama*', 1 & 2. *Cf.* Jagadīśa in *Śabdaśaktiprakāśikā* #3.4ff.
2. Gaṅgeśa *Tattvacintāmaṇi* (=*TC*), vol I, with introduction by Mhn. S. C. Vidyabhusana, 1974, p 44-45. Text in vol. edited by Kāmākhyānātha Tarkavāgīśha, Bibliotheca Indica 98, 1888-1901, vol III, pt ii.
3. Namely, *Bhāṣā-Pariccheda* (= *BP*), with auto-commentary *Siddhāntamuktāvalī* (= *SM*), #81-2, #134-6, #58; better still, Gaṅgeśa's own *Prāmāṇyavāda* (*TC* V).
4. I call this breakdown 'the Prolegomena for *pramāṇa*', which is discussed in a paper by this title, with the heading '*Pramāṇavāda* II' (unpub).
5. *Tarkasaṃgraha*, and *Dīpikā* on same, by Annaṃbhaṭṭa, #37- p25. (Reference for *TS* is, unless otherwise specified, usually to the BORI edition, 1974, which is a reprint of the Bombay Sanskrit and Prakrit Series no. LV, edited by Y. V. Athalye, 1897). See also discussion by S. Kuppuswami Sastri in *A Primer of Indian Logic*, 1961, p152. *Cf. VP* Intro 3: *tatra pramākaraṇaṃ pramāṇam. Vide*, Bimal K. Matilal, *Logic, Language and Reality* (MB, Delhi, 1985), #5.1 'The Doctrine of *Karaṇa*', pp372ff.
6. *BP* #16; *TS* # 37ff, with *Dīpikā*; and Kuppuswami, p150.
7. *Ibid*; *cf TS-D* #37-41 #38, or note 5 next chp.
8. *Ibid.* See also *TS* (BORI) *loc cit; cf Tarkabhāṣā* (BORI, 1979), p28, p32.
9. See next chapter, Part B (2.7ff)
10. *BP* #81; also *SM*, and *Kiraṇāvalī* on same; see ch 4 (*infra*); *cf NND* p25.
11. *Tarkabhāṣā*, p33 (variant readings); *vide* Cinnambhaṭṭa comm. p121; and *TS-D* #41.
12. *dvaram tatra padārthadhīh BP* #81; with *SM*: *padajanyapadārthasmaraṇaṃ vyāpāraḥ* (KSS 212, Varanasi, re:1983, p291).
13. Which presently we shall assume to be consistent with the Nyāya view. *vide TS* #59 with *Dīpikā* for *saktaṃ padam*; also Gaṅgeśa (note 2 above). The competence of the relational binding is known as *saṃsargamaryādā* (see ch. 4). So important is this notion that without it Nyāya would not achieve a realist epistemology, because the relational structure in the sentence in terms of what we have called its 'intentional content' [some say 'intensional content'] correlates to *relations* that inhere between objects in the world. The world itself being a whole complex of objects in inter-relations. Thus *relations* take priority over and above 'facts' in Nyāya ontology. Any 'speech making', from the Nyāya point of view, must be sensitive to this notion of 'fit' that obtains between the *tātparyavṛtti* (intentional or propositional content) of a sentence and the state of affairs in the world that makes a *śābdabodha* successful.
14. Some aspects of the discussion is in a separate work, entitled 'Universals and Particulars in Indian thought' (being reworked).
15. *TS* #38; *cf. BP* #16
16. See *Vākyapadīya* I.73, II.55, 143-4; little more in chapters to follow.
17. See *NND* ch 2. See ch 7A (*infra*).
18. See Alfred Tarski, 'The Semantic Conception of Truth', *RS*, pp 677-711.
19. R. Searle, *Speech Acts: An Essay in the Philosophy of Language* , CUP, 1969. p45. See also his *Intentionality: An Essay in the Philosophy of Mind*, CUP, 1983. It is intriguing to observe that Searle began with his speech-act theory, and later came to his 'intentionality' theory, but insists that the *latter* is the foundation for the former, not vice versa. That is to say, in so far as speech-acts could be said to be characterised by Intentionality, it is 'derived Intentionality', derived from the fundamental and 'intrinsic' Intentionality of mental states. The Indian philosophers, who centuries earlier had worked out a theory of mind in terms of the intrinsic intentional properties of awareness-states,

were not *so* bewitched by language-behavior of humans as to have got the proper order of enquiry turned on its heard, so to speak. Thus, it is that discussion of *śabda* (more precisely, *śābdabodha*) comes after an examination of 'experience' (*anubhava*) and its structures. (See again, terminology section in our 'Introduction', and ch. 7 part A).

20. *VP* VII.1. *Cf. BP #135: tatprakāraṃ yajjñānaṃ tadvadviśeṣyakam.* (*TS* #35: *tadvati tatprakārakaḥ anubhavaḥ yathārthaḥ.)* Some may insist that the difference between the Nyāya and Advaita view is that Nyāya will insist upon the *real*-ness of the 'object of experience' (*yathārthaḥ*), while to Advaita a *viṣaya*, in terms of *vastu* or *viṣayībhūta* could be any 'fact' (real or ideal). Thus, a distinction might be licit between 'epistemic content' and 'objective content' (the latter alone answering to an ontological correlate), and in such a way that the latter cannot be re-defined in terms of some conceptual schema or some satisfaction condition as *purposive* goal or end. This issue is taken up in the main body of ch. 7. Meanwhile see *VP* on criterion of 'knowability', I.83-84ff. But Dharmarāja moves later to a more realist satisfaction-condition for a 'true' awareness or [valid] knowledge.

21. As H. H. Joachim states it: 'Two factors . . . 'correspond' when each constituent of the one stands in a one-one relation to a determinant constituent of the other', in his *The Nature of Truth*, OUP, 1939, p9. Different ways of construing the notion of 'correspondence' in different theories of truth under discussion will be looked at in ch. 7A.

22. The definitions in note 20 do not include an apprehension of the fact of the concomitant 'conformity' that is supposed to characterise a true awareness. Ideally, Nyāya could respond that the omniscient *Īśvara*, much like Bishop Berkeley's God, is invariably aware of each and every object and the relation they enter into with a subject. But in Nyāya epistemology, the awareness is categorically of the object, and not of, say, an 'idea' or sense-data 'representation' in the mind. In perceptual terms, one cannot make a distinction between the *viṣayatā* (the epistemic content) and the *viṣaya* (the object *qua* the ontological correlate) of an awareness-state. Thus, in real terms, *esse* does not depend upon *percepi*, but *percepi* depends upon *esse*.

23. Doubt (*saṃśaya*) is an issue of considerable interest in the Indian epistemological analysis. Since *doubt* is necessarily an extrinsic factor that brings into question the truth of the cognition, its source has to be detected and ascertained extrinsically. Likewise for falsity.

24a. As pointed out in note 30, previous chapter, there are differences in what Advaita and Nyāya understand by *anuvyavasāya*. For Advaita the subjective self-identification with the awareness-state (that occurs by virtue of the self-luminous consciousness illuming the 'I-sense' along with the awareness-state) is more significant. While for Nyāya, after Gaṅgeśa, the affirmation is of the substantive-property characterisation in the object of awareness – i.e. affirmation of the awareness of *this* as having *thisness* (as the *qualificand) and tableness* (as the qualifier). See note 19 ch. 7.

24. *VP* I.1, I.4, I.44, I.93 (*viṣaya-viṣayī-caitanyāvacchinna*), I.50, 52 for self-luminosity or self-evidentiality of *anuvyavasāya*. For further discussion, see my 'Perception (*pratyakṣa*)', and S. S. Barlingay's 'Awareness', in which he argues that there is a 'self-assertive reflection' involved here. (In *Belief, Reason and Reflection*, Poona, 1984, pp 85-98.)

2

ON WORDS

LINGUISTIC *KARAṆA* AND THE *WORD*

Part A: *Karaṇa*, causal instrument for *śābdabodha*
Part B: What is a *word?*

A. *Karaṇa*

2.0 In our discussion of *śābdabodha* we noted that in order for *śabda* (a 'word') to be *pramāṇa* it has to generate knowledge (*pramā*) whose truth is beyond doubt, and that this can be achieved when certain conditions, stated in terms of the categories(1.2-1.5)for a *pramāṇa*, have been properly satisfied. The cognitive result peculiar to *śabdapramāṇa* is described as *śābdabodha*, a particular sort of awareness or understanding generated when an utterance or 'speech' is 'heard' by the audience. The *understanding* in this sense may involve other linguistic and non-linguistic factors that affect the understanding. These may be related to the intention of the utterer, the context of the utterance, the specific use or usage made of the utterance, its time and place, and the peculiar 'licence' the expression may assume in some literary or philosophical context. The expression may also be used in non-indicative ways, for example, in issuing speech-acts, such as imperatives, commands, interrogations, censor, injunctions, orders for action, or for making promises or promisory assurances. For such wider significations one often has to look beyond, so to say, the more ostensible meaning of the sentence in the context of its utterance. One could, at least, start with the bare or raw sentence structure;[1] but the comprehensive understanding derived as the end-product would appear rather towards the end than during the beginning stages of *śabdapramāṇa*. For now, we should be more interested in the beginning stages than in the end-product. The distinction is analogous to the 'input-output' indicators in a computer program.[2]

The first thing to look at, therefore, are the early stages and the factors, both specific and general, that are involved in generating *śābdabodha*. We should say that here we are interested in the causal instruments (*kāraṇa-karaṇa*), as well as the process and the conditions of its successful operation (*vyāpāra*), and so forth. One distinct overall causal nexus in *śābdabodha* was identified as *śabdajñāna* (1.7), the stage of linguistic apprehension or the cognitive assimilation of linguistic elements in respect of their appearance, presentation, inter-relation and relative significations (*arthasaṃsargabodha*). The emphasis here is on the *linguistic* principle (1.9) we identified in the previous chapter. And this is the *sine qua non* for an analysis of the cognitive understanding process that follows in later chapters.

2.1 We can say, I believe, that *śabdajñāna* is at the *constructive* stage of *śābdabodha*, for without acquaintance with the verbal or linguistic elements and forms through which an audience is presented with an expression or sentence, one cannot begin to 'construct' the *meaning* of the expression. It is as though one desires to build a house but is not able to make a start without the necessary basic material, such as cement, timber, nails, steel and so forth. In language-behaviour, we identify speech as perhaps the most common form of such presentation, which basically proceeds in the form of utterances of expressions or sentences (let us for now not suppose any crucial distinction between the two). In the Indian analysis this would be *vākya*. *Śabdajñāna* would, then, indicate the apprehension or 'awareness' of *śabda* (in its widest sense) as the source for *śābdabodha*, and since the 'linguistic element' taken to be basic in the analysis of *śābdabodha* is *vākya* or sentence, we can understand *śabdajñāna* to indicate either 'the apprehension or awareness of sentence' or the 'awareness of words that constitute the sentence'. Sometimes we may even simply say that one has a knowledge of the words of the sentence uttered. The latter must also be a correct understanding of *śabdajñāna*, for without an awareness in some way of the words or 'linguistic bits' one cannot be made aware of the sentence constituted of these words. Once, however, the awareness of the sentence as a linguistic-whole arises, the awareness of the 'bits' as words may no longer be necessary. Further, because it is the *sentence* as distinct to any other linguistic element that is taken to be the principal instrument (*karaṇa*) or 'special cause' of *śābdabodha*, *śabdajñāna* is initially taken to indicate 'awareness of sentence'. But the awareness of the sentence in its surface linguistic structure does not necessarily lead one to any understanding of its *meaning*, and what other significance it may have in the context of its utterance. We could regard the 'meaning' or signification element of the linguistic-whole, which is a sentence, as the subtle structure of this element; and to grasp this, one has to become aware of other aspects of the sentence-construction, such as the meaning of its individual parts and their syntactic composition and so on.

At any rate, an awareness (or *comprehension*—to be more precise), of the meaning of the sentence as a linguistic-whole also has to arise in the process, and the 'comprehension of the meaning of words', for a knowledge of the meanings of the putative bits must precede the arising of the meaning of the 'whole' utterance. But the meaning of the 'word bits' do not yield sentence-meaning by virtue simply of being juxtaposed side-by-side. They have to be related and associated in a particular way or ways, and this relationship may be dependent upon certain grammatical rules and conditions that determine the consistent arising of a meaning-whole, such as that of a sentence: *śabdārthajñāna-saṃsarga*. And one therefore has to have some understanding of the factors that are causally linked to these relations, i.e. the conditions that determine the appropriateness of the specific relations that occur in any particular sentence: *śabdārthajñānasaṃsargabodha.*[3]

There are a few more steps to this process, and a few ancillary ones that we need not go into right away. The major factor that we need to take note of here is *karaṇa*. To this end there are two parts to this analysis. These will be our concern for the remainder of the chapter. The first part is an attempt to relate the *vākya* or sentence to its linguistic meaning-bearing units in the minimal form. These we shall identify as 'words' (taken roughly to be the equivalence of *padas*), and shall examine in some detail in the second part. Our other concern is to further identify the distinct *karaṇa* for *śābdabodha* in contradistinction to those that are appropriate to the other (accredited) *pramāṇas*. This latter issue is linked to the argument that *śabdapramāṇa* is not reducible to the *pramāṇa* of either *pratyakṣa* ('perception') or *anumāna* ('inference'), as these are understood in Indian epistemology, in spite of the fact that both, though the former in a more significant way than the latter, are involved in the *earlier* stages of the process.

2.2 *The word as karaṇa*

We saw *karaṇa* defined as that 'special cause' among the sum-total of causal conditions in a process that is instrumental in achieving an end-effect. Furthermore, it is 'special' or *extra-ordinary*, as distinct from the more general and ordinary causal conditions that function in the same process. It is the necessary antecedent factor (*ananyathāsiddhi*) without which the entire operation would not proceed in the desired manner. It is the instrumental cause *par excellence*. Now, though Nyāya and Advaita are not agreed on the exact location of the *karaṇa* for *pratyakṣa* ('perception')—an issue largely not of relevance here[4]—it lies somewhere between sense-organ contact (*indriyārthasannikarṣaḥ*), as one major movement in Nyāya maintains, and *antaḥkaraṇavṛtti*—the modification of the internal mental faculty—which accounts for the 'object-taking' (intentional content) of awareness in perceptual experience. But perceptual experience it must be and this accounts for the distinction between this and other *pramāṇas*. Therefore, both schools agree that the *karaṇa* as a linguistic experience *qua śābdabodha* that is given in *śabdapramāṇa* differs categorically from the *karaṇa* of perception. That is to say, the *karaṇa* for *śābdabodha*, and by extension of *śabdapramāṇa*, is neither to be located simply in sense-organ contact merely, nor, for that matter, in *antaḥkaraṇavṛtti* (mental modification), bearing in mind that these are distinct processes.[5]

What is claimed, however, is that the product of a particular type of perceptual process is what functions as the *karaṇa* in *śabdapramāṇa*, albeit in a restricted and qualified sense of perceptual product, for this item is intimately linked to a process which is an antecedent and contingent condition of *śābdabodha*. The perception involved is the perception of the sentence through hearing words (*śravaṇapratyakṣa*) or, better still, 'hearing the sentence'. By 'perception of the sentence' is meant much more than the mere contact and assimilation (or objectification) of sound or markings, such as scribbles, clusters of alphabetical letters and so forth, which convey the expression. But it means much less than what would be indicated by 'comprehending' or *understanding*, which effectively is the end-product of the process, in which perception undoubtedly is a factor, but only in the beginning stages of the process, as we earlier explained with the example of the utterance "the doors of perception are befogged". Let us explore this argument further.

2.3 *Hearing* words *and* 'hearing meaning'

When one first confronts a sentence, either in reading or hearing an utterance, there is at first a rather vague awareness that the expression just read or heard has a sentence in it, expressed in a sequence of what we shall take to be words. When it becomes a little clearer in the mind of the audience that a particular sentence with a particular form as a linguistic-whole of expression has been made, we say that he has become aware of the sentence expressed. That is to say, we consider that he has had a 'perception' or 'cognition', or perhaps we might even be able to say, an 'apprehension' of the sentence, for the process has been a *perceptual* apprehension. Our subject could have been reading off the words of the sentence much as he would have put names to objects drawn in ink on paper. In other words, perception is involved in apprehending the sentence in as much as one has to have a prior mental acquaintance with the surface-structure of the sentence before any attempt is made to apprehend or rather *comprehend* what the sentence has to or is intended to express with respect to its *meaning*-content. But for this 'acquaintance with the surface-structure' (*śabdajñāna*) there would not result processes subsequently required for understanding of the meaning of the sentence. However, the acquaintance with the surface-structure of the sentence is only at the perceptual level, where one *perceives* just that outer presentation which in itself is not tantamount to a *comprehension* of the sentence – in terms of its meaning-content – let alone the purpose or 'deeper intentions' with which the sentence was uttered.

There is obviously something more, indeed much more, involved in the latter stages of the process than what occurs at the earlier stages. This does not, however, mean that the earlier stage is any less important than the later stages; indeed, what it does mean is that the earlier stage is an antecedent condition that determines the later, and is therefore indispensable in the success of a *pramāṇa*. This then involves the perception of the 'surface- structure' of the expression, for this is all there could be a *perception* of, in as much as perception can only be of that which is presented to the *antaḥkaraṇa* through sense-organ contact.

Consider the following analogy. A man plans on building a timber house. What would be the chief instrument in effecting the end-product? Someone may say that it is labour or human agency. But human labour would be an agency for building any type of shelter, indeed for building much else besides shelters. The most important element in building a timber house would presumably be timber, for without timber there can be no timber house. A pool of human, or any other form of labour, may be of considerable importance to the project, but without timber even the robots would be expending their energies fruitlessly. Thus timber, in this rather trivial example, is said to be the *karaṇa* proper of a timber house. This is analogous to the sentence being the *karaṇa* of the desired result, namely, of *śābdabodha*. To acquire the timber, however, some preliminary operations become necessary. Timber is produced from felling trees in the forest. Now the process of *felling* the trees to produce the timber is a process distinct from *using the timber* as beams and wallboards in building the house, though the latter stage is causally related to the former. But in so far as the felling of the trees requires another *karaṇa*, namely, the instrument known as an 'axe', or a saw, we cannot say that this is the same *karaṇa* as deployed in building the house. The axe is the principal instrument or 'special cause' in felling the tree and the end-product of this process is not the planned house, but rather the timber. We then have to embark on another process, with factors and operations that are somewhat distinct from those utilised in felling the tree. In view of the distinctness of the latter process, i.e. the uniqueness of its operations and the factors and necessary instrumentation, it would be gratuitous to suggest that the *karaṇa* for building a house is identical to the *karaṇa* for the felling of trees, even though in the long term process the felling of trees was necessary for the house to be erected. But in so far as we recognise the distinctiveness of the processes involved at each stage of the overall operation, we would not confuse the more general causes with the relatively unique and non-ordinary causes, and yet be alert to the insufficiency of the non-ordinary causes with the necessary and contingent antecedents.

2.4 The implications of the above analogy for *śabdapramāṇa* should by now be clear. The *karaṇa* for *śābdabodha* is not considered to be effective without the necessary and contingent determinants; it is as if the *kāraṇa-karaṇa* lends sufficiency to the antecedent necessities in the process. This does not make the process any less collective, as Jayanta might fear. We shall now attempt to clarify some salient features of the process by considering another, more relevant, example. A child learns the letters of an alphabet by being able to associate a sound pattern to each of the different markings on paper corresponding to the letters of an alphabetical system, say the Roman system. Now, each time, what to the teacher is a word is presented to the child, the child may read off the letters he has learnt to recognise them in such constructions, but often without being able to pronounce the word as a composite sound-unit, and much less being able to state what it means or stands for. When, for instance, the teacher presents the child with the word 'water' (written on the board), the child reads it as "w", "a", "t", "e", "r", very much as he would identify the letters in an alphabetical table.

To take another example, when a person with a failing eye-sight is asked by the optician to read out those letters on the Letter Chart he can 'see', he would be 'seeing' the letters very much as the child could be said to be in the earlier example. In both cases, perception is used for identifying the 'letters' presented as several markings on the board. In a manner of speaking, we say the child and the eye-patient are 'seeing' or 'perceiving' the letters. Likewise, when the child comes to learn that the properly ordered aggregation of letters is a word which is pronounced as "water", then at some later time, when the word is again presented to him in writing, we would say that he 'sees' or 'perceives' the word 'water'. When he hears his brother later in the day utter the word "water", we would again say that he hears or 'perceives' the word 'water'. A little later he stumbles upon a dictionary and looks under "w", and there in one of the columns he recognises the ideogram 'water', presented here in the lexical form as *water.* It may not be until the next day or so that he would learn what water refers to, or is used for in utterances that include reference to the term 'water'. After he has learned that 'water' refers to the fluid that flows from the bath taps, that it is a fluid he drinks when he is thirsty, or what pours down as rain, he then understands when next he 'perceives' the words 'water' that someone is making reference to that fluid, even though he may not perceive the fluid at the same time, it being within his perceptual field. This same process also occurs in learning the use and referents of more difficult and 'foreign' words.

Transferring the above analogy to the situation where sentences are uttered or read, we can say that since a sentence consists of words, there first has to occur a 'perception' of the words as the units that constitute a sentence. Only after that, is there a possibility of the apprehension of the sentence-meaning as a unified relation among the word-meanings. It is the cognition of the sentence that precedes the recognition of sentence-form, just as the cognition of the sound-units precede the recognition of the ideogram 'water'. The recollection of the meanings of the individual words follow that. The next step involves the conceptual apprehension of the *relation* (***R***) between the components and units that constitute the sentence-whole. It is argued that this awareness of the relation(s) is what is novel in *śābdabodha vis-à-vis* a straightforward 'perception' of the sentence *qua* its 'surface-structure'. *Śabdārthasaṃsargabodha* or apprehension of the *relation* between the meanings of the linguistic units is not given or presented in and of itself, in an ordinary perceptual process (*pratyakṣa*).[6] If it is not given in a perceptual process then it could not be given in the perception of a sentence either. Its emergence must be due, then, to some factors other than those that generate perception, thus some *kāraṇa-karaṇa* distinct from that of perception itself. Up to this point, perception is considered a vital fabric, as it were, of the process; but after this point, perception exhausts its function and another process commences which involves other sorts of operators and causal conditions necessary for the efficiency of *śabdapramāṇa*.

2.5 *Hearing more meaning.*

Suppose the child, who we mentioned in the earlier example, is taught some months later the techniques of sentence formation, as distinct to word formations. The child has learnt to recognise word-forms when he 'perceives' a certain number of letters, and he is able to identify a good number of words as they appear in a sentence in his story book. In one paragraph, he notices some familiar words, and he reads them out aloud: "dog", "drink", "water".

On first appearance his perception of these words is no different to the perception of the same words in the lexicon or on the blackboard at different times over the last few weeks. Then the teacher explains that the three words are inter-related in more ways than could be conveyed by drawing pictures of a dog and a bowl of water in different corners of the board. The word 'drink', a word referring to an act of drinking, relates the dog to water. There is, in other words, a relationship between the 'dog' and 'water' in this sentence, expressed in terms of drinking. Thus the teacher may represent the sentence to the child not as he first 'saw' it (that is, as a collection of words with which he was familiar) but as language-whole in which the *meanings* of the words are *related* in a particular way. For example, as "dog-drinking-water". The child now should understand something about the words which he would not have, had the teacher not made the point about their being related in some special way. Likewise, someone learning another language may initially be able to read the words of a sentence he may never have come across before in the new language and may fail to grasp what the sentence as a new-language-whole means and through this refers to. He has as yet not learned to further apprehend the inter-relation between the lexical ideogram and the syntactic item, although he has cognition of the items themselves. He may even be able to identify the meaning of each of the words, though this itself may require another and a distinct process from that of percepting the words, and he may fail to apprehend the inter-relation of the disparate word-meanings. Hence, because the latter two stages require distinct processes, they cannot be reduced nor equated to the perceptual process that necessarily precedes them. Even in the case of word-meanings, perception of words, as a mental or sense-organ perception is not sufficient. One has to connect a word to its meaning, either through recollection of a previous awareness of such a connection, or by consulting a lexicon or some other source. We might say that apprehension of words is the *perceptive* connection in the emergence of word-meanings; and similarly, we could say, apprehension of a sentence—in terms of its ostensible surface-structure—is the *perceptive-connective* for the emergence of sentence-meaning. The further connections required are the *relation* between the words and their meanings. For instance, the most that perception could give us, to use the earlier example, is 'dog' + 'drink' + 'water', while what we want for the emergence of sentence-meaning cognition is 'dog' ***R*** 'drink' ***R*** 'water', or more simply, "dog [*r*] drinks [*r*] water". The relation could be one of the qualified-qualifier type, in which case one would have to apprehend which word qualifies which in the sentence, and which other word may be qualifying this one. We need not go into the details of the process at this stage, except to mention that such qualifying relations cannot be explicitly perceived, as their comprehension requires more subtle operations of the *antaḥkaraṇa*, which can be identified as distinct features of some psychological processes (which are best left for psycho-linguists to inform us further about).[7] In any case, the argument for *śābdabodha* cannot be reduced to that for perception, even though 'perception of sentence' as a cognitive process is the principal instrument in *vākyajanyajñāna* or understanding arising from the deliverance of a sentence.

2.6 It follows from the preceding argument that *śābdabodha* cannot be reduced to the *pramāṇa* of inference either. There are two major grounds for this claim. (*a*) Inference itself is dependent on perception for its 'material' content, whilst as a *formal* criterion of reasoning it may be sufficient in itself. But for the content provided by perception (or 'observation') for its 'material' content, its operation would be empty of substantial content. That is not to say, however, that inference does not provide valid and novel judgements. But where inferential cognition depends on perception, then its limitations are those of perception, which we have already noted in the case of *śabda*. (*b*) Each inferential cognition is based on a previous apprehension of the relation of concomitance (*vyāpti*) between the major term (*sādhya*) and the middle (*hetu*). But in the awareness of a novel sentence, which one may never have heard before, nor ever had an apprehension of the relation between the words in the sentence, there is still the contingency of the sentence-meaning being apprehended independently of such an inferential process. There has to be a recognition of the meanings associated with each word, possibly recollected from a previous experience of such associations. However, the interrelations between the word-meanings are not a matter of their having been invariably related (*vyāptau*) in the particular sequence and way they would be related in this sentence. Indeed, as Jagadīśa points out, the relation could be quite the converse of what one may have apprehended previously, and thus the same inference, if there were to be one, could not arise, in the awareness of the sentence-meaning and its relational content.[8] In some parts of the process inference may play a role, just as perception and memory do, but this role would be *sahakāri-kāraṇa*, i.e. an auxiliary function or even a fairly ordinary cause in any form of complex apprehension, but it is by no means necessary and sufficient for *śābdabodha*. We shall, in a later chapter, examine the significance that some Nyāya writers attach to inference, though admittedly not in a reductive fashion, since the function of inference is limited to ascertaining the *reliability* or trustfulness of the source of a sentence utterance. It is clear that the inference in this respect is not an inference of the *knowledge qua śābdabodha* as such that is conveyed in a unique way through the use of the sentence.

B.*What is a word'?*

In this part we will discuss the issue raised regarding the discrete and minimal unit of language from which sentences appear to be built. This links us to the notion of the 'word'. Now any linguistic analysis would be seen to break whole expressions into putative 'bits' or some such constituent elements and to identify these with whatever is regarded to be the more basic and fundamental elements of speech, be they 'words' (in some sense of the term), characters, phrases, sentences, syllables, letters, or maybe grammatical particles. Some Indian theories of language, as we remarked in the previous chapter, regard the basic linguistic unit – more fundamental than the sentence – to be *pada*, the 'atomic verbal element'. We also suggested that *pada* or *śabda* is not generally understood to be the 'word' but is rather closer to the 'morpheme' of Western linguistics[9]. We shall take the liberty, however, to interchange *pada* with the term 'word', except where we wish to be more specific. We may also remark that not all linguistic theories accept such a division of speech; some regard speech to be essentially undivisive (for example, Bhartṛhari *VKP* 1.75ff), while others identify the basic unit in different ways, for example the *sphoṭa* of the Indian grammarians.[10] We shall look further into the notion of the 'word' in a short while. It is interesting to note how some Nyāya writers consider *pada* to be the basic unit not only of linguistic analysis, but also of *śabdapramāṇa*, as Nyāya identifies the *jñāna* of *pada* – in contrast to the sentence (*vākya*) in Advaita – as the *karana* for *śābdabodha* : *padajñāna tu karaṇam.*[11] We could ask, though, whether or not Nyāya sees any difficulty in reducing sentence-whole to the putative 'bits' that constitute it, and to identifying these as *padas*. Presently, however, we are more interested in what *pada* means to both Nyāya and Advaita, so that we can derive a picture, so to say, of the role *pada* or the 'word' plays in *śabdajñāna* or sentence-awareness as the *karaṇa* for *śābdabodha*. We need, therefore, to explore further the notion of the 'word', and its significance in the fulfillment of the first category of a *pramāṇa*.

A tripartite theory of (the) 'word'

2.7 Advaita has not given us a very explicit account of its theory of language, but it has said a lot about language. *Śabdapramāṇa* is itself based implicitly on a theory of language that appears to be unique to Advaita.

Śaṅkara has argued against several conceptions of the 'word', particularly against the Sāṅkhya and the *sphoṭa*-based theories of the 'word'.[12] Śaṅkara himself suggested the adequacy of the 'letter', or better, 'syllable' theory of the word which is akin, though not identical to, the Mīmāṃsā theory. Other Advaita writers have argued for or against some theory of language prevalent in their times. Some – following Upavarṣa – have argued against the theory Śaṅkara accepted – viz. *varṇa eva śabdaḥ* : 'the word is a collection of letters'.[13] Given also that Śaṅkara followed Mīmāṃsā in regarding language to subsist at a subtle level somewhat independent of human convention, it must be the case that the 'stuff' (*dravya*) or the 'substantive entity' of speech could not be the manifest sound ostensibly produced when words are uttered, for the very reason that sound is a *product*, and is produced only 'when two things strike (or are struck)', in the words of Śabara (the renowned commentator on Mīmāṃsā).[14] In human speech, audible sound arises from the air striking the organs of speech, and could at best be the 'vehicle' (*varṇātmaka* or *abhivyañjaka* or simply *dhvani*) of speech, not the *dravya* ('substance') of speech itself.

The Mīmāṃsā, however, does claim that sound, in some sense, is all-pervasive and everlasting.[15] Though a distinction is made between 'sound' and 'noise' (*dhvani*), because 'sound' is regarded to be all-pervasive. Were it not, we would hear it all at once and altogether as a continuous uproar (*kolāhala*), much like the chatter of several performances in a gathering of acrobats or of various musical instrument in an orchestra.[16] But Mīmāṃsā makes it clear that what we hear ostensibly is only the audible sound that functions as an instrument for the manifestation of an implicit sound-element that resides in a subtler and less perceptible level but which is given with the hearing of the overt sound. It is perhaps better described as the *potentiality* of the subtle sound-element to manifest in a more ostensive form, just as the audible sound from the radio is a manifestation of the 'unseen' and implicit radio-wave.[17] Mīmāṃsā also regards the all-pervasive 'sound' to be broken up in speech into aggregates of sound-sequences, or what it calls *varṇas* : 'letters'. We shall take the *varṇa* or 'letter' to be an implicit form of *articulate* sound-element, analogous to the letters of the alphabet, but much more complex than these. The suggestion here is that the Mīmāṃsā theory of language is based on an understanding that, underlying the spoken word is the more subtle and imperceptibly discrete units of speech, called *varṇas* ('letters'), which evoke the audible sound manifested through their impact on the speech-organs. We wish to develop this theory further, taking *varṇa* as our starting point, while suggesting that the *varṇa* is more a 'syllable' than a 'letter', since the latter is conspicuous by its absence of an integral 'meaning-element', i.e. a *conceptual* basis, which we consider to be fundamental to the 'word', and more significant than any other aspect of that element of speech. (While at the same time, we do not commit ourselves to the distinction of type-token, meaning-reference, even though they are undoubtedly related). This recognition accounts partly for our disagreement with any theory that bases itself exclusively on some form of sound, on the one hand, or on a conceptual element unrelated to the manifesting *potential*, on the other. We shall develop this view, by combining the 'letter' of Mīmāṃsā with the 'morphemic' element (*pada*) of Nyāya, which together lean towards the *sphoṭa* of Patañjali (the grammarian[18]), in identifying an intermediary structure where the two elements are integrated. We shall begin with some general observations of the 'word'.

2.8 Now, in examining the structure of (human) speech, we shall approach the problem by looking at the elemental unit or 'building block', as it were, of language. Not all languages, however, as we said earlier, have the same form of elemental *unit*; nor do all theories of language admit such discrete units (e.g. in Bhartṛhari's 'holistic' theory, where the substantive unit is the sentence). Generally though, the words, in some form, are admitted as the basic linguistic units. But it has not been possible to arrive at a clear, nor a consensually agreed upon theory of the 'word'. Worries regarding the clear formulation of such a theory are no less well known in modern linguistics.[19] Some attempt, however, has been made in a few linguistic traditions. Lexicons used in translating one language into another do make a list of the words of one language and their equivalence in the other, in spite of the problems concerning the indeterminacy of translation. This, of course, is a concern particularly for logicians such as Quine. We shall assume for now that the equivalence is a *functional* one, in that it serves to shift the sign-elements mutually, and that there is no commitment in such cases to the exact correspondence of what is taken to be the 'word', or some other basic unit, in one language to that in another language, and so on. One may argue that the 'word' in one language has an equivalence in that part of the other language that has the same or similar linguistic function; that is to say, it has a functional equivalence which can be taken to be the 'word' in the latter language.

A picture of the 'word'

Hence, when looking in Indian linguistics for the equivalence of the notion of *word* as understood in Western linguistics, in Indian linguistics we have settled for *pada*, somewhat arbitrarily, since this is the closest notion one can find. Still, it only serves the functional purpose. In saying this we should bear in mind also that the separation of *pada* from its sentence is never quite admitted in Indian linguistics, nor for that matter totally accepted in Western linguistics. As Patañjali stated in 2nd century (B.C.): '. . .words are in each individual case generated (or come into existence) in accordance with the rules for their formation of grammatically correct speech, but their order (mutual connection) is free. . .'[20] Even Bhartṛhari, the extreme protagonist of the 'indivisibility of language' thesis, accepted the division of a sentence into *varṇa* ('phoneme') and *pada* for the purposes though only of grammatical analysis. He says that: 'Just as a single homogeneous picture is described (subsequently) in terms of differentiating (features) such as the blue colour which are of distinctive characteristics, similarly a sentence which is a single entity complete in all respects is subsequently described in terms of mutually expectant words which are different from (the indivisible sentence).'[21] He goes on to argue that: 'Just as in a given inflected word, the stem, the affix and so on, are isolated (subsequently through linguistic analysis), similar is the analytic extraction of individual words in a given sentence.'[22] But in so far as it is possible to analytically isolate words from a sentence, we can speak of words as the basic unit of linguistic analysis. It is here that the notion of the 'word' *qua pada* becomes useful. Still, the question remains, what do we understand the word 'word' to be?

2.9 We now need to look at some of the prominent theories that formed the background as it were in which the Advaita view was formulated and developed. Pāṇini, perhaps the earliest to put forth a theory (*circa* 400 B.C.), defined a word more in terms of a syntactic criterion in consonance with his grammatical analysis of (the Sanskrit) language—namely, as *suptiṅantaṃ padam* (*PS* 1.4.14).[23] He defined the 'word' as that which has either a verbal inflection or a nominal inflection. Pāṇini, it may be noted, has used a formal criterion.

Patañjali (circa 200 B.C.) developed the implications of Pāṇinian linguistics by adding a semantic structure to the Pāṇinian formulation, and analysed the structure in terms of a succession of *varṇas*, 'phonematic units' or 'letters'.[24] And Patañjali called this structure '*sphoṭa*', which, as J. Brough makes clear for us, is not the much misunderstood "hypostatisation of sound"[25] or some mysterious abstraction usually associated with Bhartṛhari's (later) conception of *sphoṭa*, but was to Patañjali the *minimal unit of meaning* comprehensible, and which would 'burst forth' in speech-sounds (*dhvani/nāda*) or in linguistic signs as the distinct element that occasions the *sphoṭa*.[26] (There is an interesting comparison here to be drawn with John Lyon's rendering of *lexeme* in linguistic analysis.) Sound, in this view, is merely an attribute of the real word. How is this so? Patañjali asks, and makes the following allegorical response: 'Like a drum-beat, when a drum is struck, one drum-beat may travel twenty feet, another thirty, another forty. But the *sphoṭa* is of precisely such and such a size, the increase in length is caused by the sound.'[27]

What Patañjali is saying is that the essential linguistic 'measure'—literally *pada* (step)—is not the sound, but the underlying *sphoṭa* or meaning-bearer.

Sphoṭa, in Patañjali's analysis, is simply the term for a fixed pattern of 'letters' or phoneme sequence in their meaning bearing aspect,[28] and is not quite what the later grammarians and philosophers took it to be.[29] It makes no reference to the 'vehicle' of sound nor to its referent. The sequence of fixed letters could be said to be comparable to the Mīmāṃsā formulation of *śabda* in terms of an aggregate of *varṇas*, on the one hand, and the Nyāya formulation of *pada* in terms of a morphemic element – the minimal meaning-bearing unit – on the other hand. But whilst to Patañjali the comprehension of *śabda*, the *word*, occurs in a 'bursting forth' of the whole *meaning* as a 'gestalt', in Mīmāṃsā and Nyāya analysis, the *varṇas* arrive, so to speak, and register themselves as discrete impressions left by the letters in the mind of the audience, and it is the last of the phonemic impressions that help the recollection of the preceding letter-impressions registered in the memory. Thus, *sphoṭa* is simply the *word* considered as a single meaningful symbol, distinct from the sound-vehicle (*dhvani* or *nāda*) that help to manifest it; it is comprised of a phoneme sequence (*varṇas*) which, though, to Patañjali was a *linguistic* abstraction and not the ostensible aspect of sound. It would perhaps be correct to say that the phomene sequence (*varṇas*) too in its more subtle and abstract aspect *qua sphoṭa* is the possibility (*śakti*, 'potency') for the ostensible realisation of the *sphoṭa* at, say, the phonological level, which is a less subtle level of linguistic abstraction.

In our view the *word qua varṇa-sphoṭa* is prior in all respects to the phonological structure, as we shall argue shortly, and prior to this is what we have called 'syllables' or the phoneme sequence *in consciousness*, that arises before its utterance in a speech-act, which reveals the *(varṇa)sphoṭa*.[30]

One other point to note is that Pāṇini and Patañjali would admit the existence of lexical items independent of language structures, such as the alphabet '*l*'. But in a word like '*lavaṇa*', "*l*" is a phoneme, a *varṇa*, and its meaning changes, because it is integrated with the *sphoṭa* which is not divisible as such into letters for its meaning-content; its divisibility is admitted only in so far as a sequence of *varṇas* is necessary for presenting the *sphoṭa* to the mind. Otherwise, the letters are organised *tout ensemble*; as individual items they are meaningless (*MBh* I p220).[31]

2.10 Now, the Nyāya began with a theory closer to Pāṇini's, but ended up, in the Navya-nyāya era, with a definition that moved away from Patañjali to one not too dissimilar to the more modern notion of *morpheme*.[32] Gautama provided the earlier impetus for a definition by regarding *pada* to be a sequence of phonemes (*varṇas*) ending in terminal inflection (*vibhakti*) : *te vibhaktyantāḥ padam*. The inflectional endings are said, by Vātsyāyana (commenting on Gautama), to be twofold : *nominal* ending and *verbal* ending, the example of which are given as *brāhmaṇaḥ* and *pacati.*[33] Indeclinables are excepted, but generally it is case that 'meaning is signified by an inflected word', as Vātsyāyana stressed. Among the 'indeclinables' (*avyaya*) are propositions, particles, and other terms with zero-inflections. Gautama's definition is a formal one and therefore reinforces Pāṇini's syntactical criterion. V. N. Jha asserts that 'Gautama has accepted the definition of *pada* given by Pāṇini.'[34] At any rate, the early Nyāya took the 'word' to be a grammatical unit, and regarded the 'grammatical word' to be the chief element in a linguistic structure, such as a sentence or a phrase.

Navya-nyāya definition of the *word*

2.11 In later Nyāya, the criterion shifted from a *formal* to a *semantic* one. The clearest statement of this is in Annaṃbhaṭṭa's famously cryptic formulation : *śaktaṃ padam*[35], that is to say the 'power' to signify, or have significatory function. Two types of word-power (*padaśakti*) were accepted: *abhidhā*, the expressive and primary significatory capacity, and *lakṣaṇā* or the secondary, 'indicative', capacity. Sometimes, as we shall see more of in the next chapter, a blanket term *vṛtti* is used to cover both the potentialities said to be inherent in words. Now a definition of *pada* in terms of *śakti* would be as follows: a (minimal) phoneme sequence (*varṇā*) which possesses *śakti* or significatory capacity. An atomic *pada* would then be the smallest meaning-bearing phoneme sequence; and as Matilal observes, according to this theory, even an *affix* or a *suffix* should be called a *pada* or 'word', provided one can assign some meaning to it.[36] Other linguistic categories this definition would cover are : stems, roots, indeclinables (like *na*, *evam*) and other classes of 'morphemic elements'.

Thus *gām*, which would be a single *pada*, consists (in Nyāya theory), of two *padas*, 'go' and 'am'. If the modern linguists' 'morphemes' [*'lexemes'* *pace* Lyons] are defined as classes of 'minimal meaning-bearing units'—e.g. 'thing', 'of', 'un-', 'ing', '-s'—then the Navya-nyāya concept of *pada* will be their nearest analogue.[37] In modern linguistics, generally—though not universally—the smaller grammatical units, such as 'sail-', '-ed', 'sea-', '-s', are referred to as *morphemes*; the morpheme here is the "minimal, indivisible or primitive unit; the word is merely one of a hierarchy of complex of non-minimal units, including the phrase, the clause, the sentence, and maybe others still larger".[38] This is somewhat different to Bloomfield's earlier notion of 'morpheme' for which he not only required the sameness of the meaning-bearing aspect, but also the sameness of the *form* in its recurrent utterance. But the forms may change even in such instances as difference of intonation, and when a word adapts to some grammatical variation in a compound; but on grounds of meaning and syntactic function, it may remain impeccable.

Notwithstanding this difference, Nyāya also describes a word such as 'unthinkable' to be a *function* of three *padas*, as it consists of three *minimal* morphemes, namely, 'un-', '-think-', and '-able'. What holds the morphemic items together is the feature of *ākāṅkṣā* or expectancy, a condition which applies as a syntactic rule in the formation of sentences from its component bits, as also to this rather minimally basic feature of any linguistic structure.[39]

It is, however, clear that *pada* is not, in such instances, quite what the 'word' is in Western linguistics, because while the *padas* identified here as the morphemic items as 'un-', '-think', and '-able' etc., are bound forms and do not stand free (even though they have significatory capacity, in sofar as they cannot stand free and independent of each other), they cannot be regarded as 'words' in the way 'unthinkable' is. If *pada* is to be taken as the 'word' it conflicts with Bloomfield's definition of word as a "minimum free form"[40]. This definition depends upon a prior distinction of "free" and "bound" forms in the following way: some linguistic forms, which we call *bound forms*, are never used as sentences. . .Forms which occur as sentences are free forms, as, for instance, *poor John*, or *John ran away* or *yes, Sir*, is a phrase. A free form which does not consist entirely of (two or more) lesser free forms. In brief, a word is a *minimum free form*.[41]

There is a problem, however, with the above definition, in that it is too restrictive. We may let go the objection that 'think' in the above word 'unthinkability' is not a free form; but what about an instance such as "waiting", does this not contain a free form 'wait' as well as being one itself? John Lyons[42] has pointed out that Bloomfield's criterion meets with more difficulty when we consider cases of words such as 'matchbox', 'blackbird', and we may add *śivānanda* and *bhagavadgītā*, which by Bloomfield's definition would only have one free form each, while each is shown to have two free forms: 'black' and 'bird', 'match' and 'box', *śiva* and *ānanda*, and *bhagavat* and *gītā*, none of which contain bound forms.

It may be observed that Bloomfield's definition is based on a phonological criterion rather than on a semantical criterion, and this accounts for its chief weakness and difference in contrast to other theories of the word based on the recognition of morpheme as a 'free form'.

2.12 Nevertheless, from another point of view, namely the grammatical one, it is useful to make a distinction between 'free' and 'bound' morphemes, as the significance of bound forms only become apparent in grammatical-type constructions and not when they attempt to stand on their own as free forms, except perhaps purely as lexical items. Unlike the later Nyāya, the early Nyāya, which to some extent makes the distinction between 'free' and 'bound' forms, takes into consideration the grammatical criterion. For them, inflectional items, such as suffixes and prefixes, are regarded as components that aid the completion of a word as a semantic whole, as distinct from regarding a morpheme as self-complete merely on the basis of its phonological form. This can be seen in the later Nyāya categorisation of 'un-' as a *pada* ('word'). The grammar of a word does not make it another word, though it might change its form, but brings to bear on the morphemic element certain determinants that govern its proper and acceptable use in language. It also makes clear the function it (the morpheme) has in terms of *śakti* or the potency of its phoneme sequence in some particular use or usage, which is determined by its relation to other words in the expression in which it occurs. Thus we surmise that the later, modified, definition of *pada* ('word') was too broad, as it did not pay sufficient attention to the formal criterion, which the earlier Nyāya did. But the useful contribution of the later Nyāya is precisely in respect of the *semantical* emphasis : *śaktaṃ padam*, which when combined with the formal aspect provides for a more complete and finished form of the word, and which brings *pada* nearer to the *word* in Western linguistics. From the critical discussion we have engaged in so far, we can extract an *integrated* definition in the following terms:

> The word is a minimum free and finished morphemic item, consisting of syllables, i.e. meaning-bearing sequence of phonemes (*varṇa-sphoṭas*), which normally does not need another phoneme for its semantic completeness, and which has the potentiality of manifesting itself through a symbolic vehicle' (such as an ideogram, a linguistic sign of *dhvani* or speech-sound, etc).

Like Patañjali's *varṇas* or letters, the 'syllables' in the above definition need not necessarily be organised into *sphoṭa*-like whole units in order for them to be semantically significant. Nothing much has been said in the definition about the aspect of language that makes the word ostensible and presents it to the mind of the audience. But something of the potentiality for overt manifestation has been suggested here in the inclusion of an integral *varṇasphoṭa* element as the meaning-bearing sequence of phonemes. We suggest that this element be understood as 'syllables', in contradistinction to the 'letters' of Nyāya and Mīmāṃsā—though we shall continue to use the term *varṇa* for syllables.

2.13 The definition arrived at still differs in one major respect from that of Patañjali's, which, as stated earlier, is defined in terms of the minimal unit of speech comprehensible as a uniform whole (of *sphoṭa*) – namely, in respect of the realness of the *varṇa* or *syllable*, as the minimal *meaning* bearing unit in speech (and not accepted merely for the purposes of analysis).[43] But in most other respects our definition is consistent with that of Patañjali. We do not, however, say that there is nothing to be gained from the Mīmāṃsā notion of *varṇa*, although we would not advocate a whole-sale adoption of this theory as Śaṅkara appeared to be doing in rejecting the *sphoṭa* doctrine as propounded by the grammarians (and Bhartṛhari also, one would presume).[44]

The Nyāya view of *varṇa*, then, is a good model but not an equivalence for the 'syllable' we make of *varṇasphoṭa*, since the Nyāya *varṇa* does not get to be any more subtle than *audible* articulate phoneme. *Sphoṭa* is a more subtle and implicit abstraction than the speech-sound that reveals it in an utterance. We should here dwell a little on the phenomenon of 'sound' and its treatment in some Indian theories.

Sound, in Nyāya view, is said to be of two types – *varṇa* and *dhvani* ; the latter is more a term for noise in contrast to the former, which stands for 'letter' or articulate sound.[45] But (*varṇa-)sphoṭa* need not be sound items, for the syllables constituted as a *pada* can be conveyed and used by dumb and deaf persons alike with the same significative function as a person with adequate hearing capacity can, using the same word. Further, it is said of *varṇa* that it is in its pristine form inarticulatable (*dhvani*), that it modifies, arises and disappears (being a property merely of *ākāśa* or 'ether'), while the essential word (*śabda*) does not as such arise and disappear with speech-sounds that more occasionally function as 'vehicles' for the abiding element(s) by which the same word is re-identifiable as the *same word*. It is admittedly difficult at times to dissociate the phonological form of a word from its meaning-bearing grammatical element, even when the word is presented in an orthographical or some ideographic form, for, as D. M. Datta has argued,[46] even the orthographical form is a minute transformation of the phonological which is a necessary antecedent for a word to be apprehended. But the case of the deaf who uses the Braille or some such implement falsifies the argument that the phonological aspect is an inherent element of the word, and not a convenient vehicle for manifesting the (*varṇa-)sphoṭa* or syllables, and which could be substituted by another similar vehicle capable of overt, or covert, manifestation. But their usability is in respect of some context, namely that of speech-act in its various forms.

2.14 Coming back to the distinction between *dhvani* and *varṇa*, it seems more the case that *dhvani* is sound, which we hear when two things are struck, and when speech-forms are uttered, while *varṇa*, in our terms, is a structure of the word that is more subtle and basic than the phonological structure. One might well say that sound is of two forms: articulate and inarticulate, and that it is the former that is associated with word. Such a distinction is made by the grammarians, such as Bhartṛhari and by Nārāyaṇa Bhaṭṭa[47]. The indefinite or inarticulate sound is the 'noise' produced by, say, the beating of a drum, whilst the inarticulate follows the pattern of syllables of a language. The point remains, however, that the distinction between articulate and inarticulate sound is not sufficient to account for the exact relation of sounds to words. Further, the articulate, as much as the inarticulate, arise and disappear with the utterance, yet words in their meaning-bearing grammatical element, at least, do not disappear as such, for if they did there would be nothing to account for their reappearance the next day in another speech-act, and in written, uttered or even Braille signs, that convey the same meaning and have the same function or 'job' as they did in the earlier utterance. It seems more the case that the articulate is an acoustic pattern determined as the phonological aspect which is distinct for each language (though there may be, indeed are, exceptions). The phonological structure in each individual language determines the functioning of the sound-units for words with particular meaning and function. When the same 'meaning-structure' is used in another language the phonological structure is likely to change, yet somehow it is possible to identify the 'meaning-structures' in both languages to be alike. By following merely the sound-pattern, or other orthographical signs and characters, such a task would be formidable. There is something more at the level of the so-called phoneme-sequence than an ordered pattern of sound. The latter is still in a sense *noise*, albeit an ordered and articulate one that we identified as *dhvani*,[48] the external acoustic aspect through which the more subtle levels of syllable (*varṇa*) are transmitted.

2.15 Mīmāṃsā makes a similar distinction between *dhvani* and *varṇa*[49] (as 'letters') and define the word (*śabda*) as a unitary aggregate of letters (*varṇas*). But *varṇa* in the Mīmāṃsā view, as discussed earlier (2.7), is eternal and all-pervasive. What distinguishes *varṇa* from *dhvani* in Mīmāṃsā is the potency on the part of the former to yield a composite pattern in mutual connection with each other, whilst the latter amounts to noise. But all sound, according to this view, is manifested or 'revealed' when two objects collide; the sound so produced becomes audible to the ear, but not otherwise. And its ordering agency or 'frequency', to use an analogy from wave-theory, lies beyond itself. Sound, in other words, is neither self-produced *nor* self-ordered.

Śabara, explaining the Mīmāṃsā position, goes on to talk about 'conjunctions' and 'disjunctions' of *varṇas* in making manifest the word, which, but for their conjunction and disjunction, would remain latent and unmanifest. Śabara elaborates thus: What happens is that the stagnant air particles disturbed by the (sound-provoking) stroke against the stagnant air particles produce *conjunctions* and *disjunctions* (i.e. ripples) on all sides, which go on spreading as long as the moments last; the *conjunction* and *disjunction* (ripples) are not perceived, because the air (of which they are ripples) is imperceptible; and as for the sound, it is heard so long and so far as the ripples do not cease, and after they have ceased, the sound is not heard. Thus there is no incongruity at all. It is for this same reason that the Sound is heard at a greater distance when the wind is favourable.[50]

Now here we have Śabara giving us a theory of 'sound' which appears to reduce it to sound at a fairly mundane level. If he still wants to maintain that the "sound" produced by ripples in the "air" is eternal, his argument would be gratuitous. But to even make an attempt to establish that the 'sound' *qua varṇa* is something more permanent than the fleeting sound of noise, he would have to tell us what the true characters of the 'conjunctions' and 'disjunctions' are, and whether they are prior to and in some way latent properties of the letters which begin to stir from their dormant state when the word is about to be uttered. And there is little doubt that Śabara (speaking for Mīmāṃsā) would want to give up their theory of the 'eternality of word' even though their theory of sound encounters considerable empirical difficulties.

But we do not believe that the problem cannot be resolved. In our opinion, there is another consideration that needs to be added to the notion of *varṇa*. This consideration would take *varṇa* as a linguistic abstraction at two levels deeper than the phonological one (which is only one of the 'vehicles', in the form of ostensible articulate sound-units) for some more subtle *varṇa*. It is these that we have called *syllables* or *varṇasphoṭa*, and which constitute the *śakti* in terms of being the potential meaning-bearers. And, as with the Mīmāṃsakas who regard the relation between *pada* and meaning to be permanent, this could be said to be *autpattika* (although not in the the sense of being eternal, though perhaps as relatively 'fixed').[51] We can continue to call the syllabic elements 'phonemes', since they are also the potential sound-sequence, although they do not manifest as such, until an articulate form attaches itself to the sequence. The *phonemes*, in our terms, are then the subtle syllabic structure of the smallest significant meaning-bearing segments of the word. And an aggregate of such *phonemes* (*varṇa-sphoṭa*) forms a *morpheme*—i.e. an 'atomic' *pada* or 'word'.

2.16 One can see that the theory as formulated is superior and goes one better than the Nyāya thesis, which poses several difficulties, and appears to be ambiguous, at least in Gautama's presentation.[52] For, if sound is said to disappear soon after arising, what then accounts for the continuity of the phonological pattern which is involved in a similar speech-act at a later time, or in another utterance at the same time? And what accounts for the recognition of a pattern of acoustic sound as being the 'acoustic *image*' or the phonological proto-type associated with a particular word?[53] What is more important to ask is, how does the hearing of a sequence of sound lead to the apprehension of a numerical whole? For there is presumably no one moment when the sound-units are grasped simultaneously: how then, it may be asked, is it possible for the word to be grasped as a whole? Is it the case that after hearing the last letter-sound one recollects the successive sequence *tout ensemble*? If the response is in the affirmative then we would have to assume that, for any given word, one has to apprehend every sound-bit that goes to make the aggregate, while at the same time being aware of the sequence in which the letters occur, and the pause between them that marks off adjacent aggregates. But how can one maintain a hold on the letters *qua* sounds, and their sequence and separation when the sounds themselves vanish as soon as they arise and reach the listener's ears? What is in that case retained, the sound-bits or the impressions they leave behind, or both?

Now, if it is the case that impressions were left behind then we should ask, whether the word consists of an aggregate of impressions *or* an aggregate of sound-bits? If the latter, then we would have to say that the word disappears with the disappearance of the sound-bits; nor can we say that the life-span of the former is any longer than the retention power of the memory of the auditor. Or the auditor may have written the word down on paper, in which case we cannot say that he has deposited the sound-bits or phonemes, nor his impressions on paper. The orthographic form may manifest the same word to him at a later time, or to another, but could we say in these instances that the same phonemes manifest themselves in the form of the word heard before? The point we are endeavouring to make is that whatever manifests, or aids in manifesting a structure, is not necessarily identical with the structure itself; it is an aspect of a complex linguistic structure.

The upshot of the above argument is that it is the *meaningful* syllable sequence that is the common structure underlying both the speech-sound and the written ideogram, both of which signal the syllables in segments of discrete letters, and vice versa. What we have argued for is what some

Indian linguists intended to convey by their thesis of *varṇasphoṭa*. (Nāgeśa Bhaṭṭa, we believe, was one among them.) *Varṇa* is basically a 'syllable' vibrant with meaning, which in an aggregate yields a composite syllabic construction. This aggregate has a potency for signifying, which makes it a *morphemic* item (*pada*). It also has the capacity to become manifest ostensibly once it attaches itself to the linguistic sign appropriate to the context of its occurrence, such a phonological 'token'. And more likely than not, the morphemic element will be a finished form.

The ostensible manifestation is not always in phonological structures; there are other forms and structures for manifestation. Thus, for example, for the utterance "cow", the phonological items , in their discrete letters, are **"c"**, **"o"**, **"w"**; its *phoneme sequence (varṇasphoṭa)* form in its syllables, are **"C"**, **"O"**, **"W"**, which as an aggregate combine to form the morphemic item: **COW**, which is relatively permanent, has significatory potency and a capacity to manifest itself through a 'vehicle'. It is, however, in virtue of the particular syllabic construction as the phonematic 'infra-structure', that enables a phonological or some other manifesting structure to be realised. Thus, non-uttered systems of signs and symbols, such as the various written scripts, Braille, computer encoding, indices and so on, can function as signals that disclose the representative syllabic base which then lead to the apprehension of the 'word' expressed through these signs in any language community.[54]

In principle, the point to be stressed is that the syllabic construction, which has significatory potency, is a more important and discrete element than the phonological or the orthographical structure. The most fundamental and necessary condition of any linguistic element to be a 'word' is that: (*a*) it be a morphemic item; *(b)* it have a basic syllabic construction which is its aggregate of *varṇas* or *phonemes*; *(c)* the syllabic feature be also the potential for its manifestation (as *pada*), or its realisation at a lesser abstract level, particularly in speech through the phonological structure. The orthographical and other systems of symbolisation may be added to this. A scale of the manifesting symbolic-vehicles, all of which eventually become related to the more basic syllabic construction. can be listed in a framework represented in a diagram that follows shortly.

2.17 The two diagrams presented below attempt to represent the modified integrated theory of the 'word', in which we have argued for an *integral meaningful syllable* form as the lowest denominator of what we now to be the 'word'. We finally make some suggestions as to how, in terms of this theory, the 'sameness' of words can be accounted for across different languages, when these words are identified to have the same signification and relatively similar functions in each of these languages. We realise the conjectural nature of these suggestions and admit that much more work would need to be done before definite conclusions could be drawn. But as some implications of the theory of the word we have been developing, they are certainly deserving of consideration.

2.18 Let us take the word 'water'. The level of the ostensive symbolic representation, whether written or spoken, we shall call *word(f)*. The same *word-form* (i.e. *word(f)* can be achieved). Though different signals, the most common representation being at the phonological level. For argument sake, we can take the phonological form to be the paradigm for *word(f)*. Now when we get to the more abtract syllabic level, the subtle *varṇas* underlying the phonological possibility, we have what we could call *word-unit*, or simply *word(v)*, which is the same for each of the different *word-forms* or terms used in expressing the same word. It is the *sameness* of the syllabic structure that accounts for the sameness of the *word* in various speech-acts. Underlying, as it were, the *varṇa* or phonematic level, we shall, for purposes of analysis, distinguish the *morphemic* element (*pada*) as the meaning-element in terms of the 'power of signification' (*sphoṭa qua śakti*) which is but a feature of the syllabic construction. This is the *word-power*, we shall call *word(p)*. In the case of the example with the word "water", we may say that the *word-power* is WATER. This is the fundamental 'measure', *pada* of the word. It is also grammatically finished, having incorporated the formal criterion at the morphemic level, in deference to the early Nyāya requirement, which was really Pāṇini's criterion. The last aspect represented by an '*f*' after '*word-power*' indicates that the formal criterion has been met, and hence the word is in a *finished form, free and self-standing*. But for all practical purposes, it will be assumed that *word-power* has in each case fulfilled the formal criterion.

To summarise, there are three aspects to the 'word'. At the primary level is its basic language-specific form with the capability of being realised (*qua* the symbolic token); at the secondary level is a more abstract syllabic construction, patterned as a phoneme sequence in consonance with the third, which is the *meaning* or significatory base, that is also fundamental to the 'word'. Thus:

i. word(f) or *word-form*:

typified in the ostensible manifesting structures in speech, such as the phonological (*dhvanivyañgya*).

ii. word(v) or *word-unit*:

second level abstraction as the *syllable* structure, comprising a *phoneme* or *varṇa* sequence, as the underlying potential for(i).

iii word(p) or *word-power*:

third level abstraction as the pure morphemic item, the significatory potency in terms of the meaning-bearing aspect, in a finished form.

Typology of the **'word'**

i

ii

iii

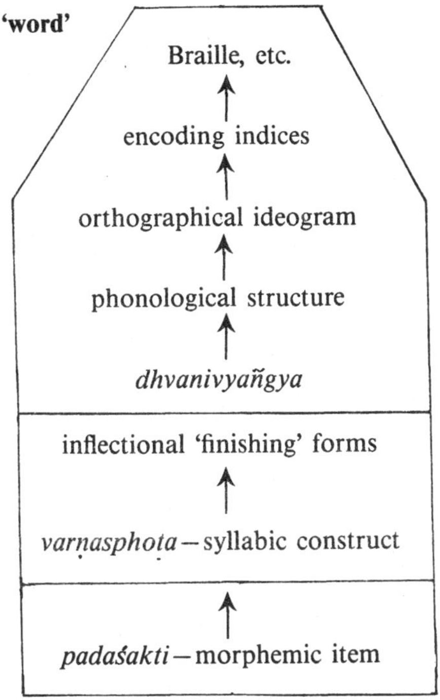

2.18 ***An example***

English	- water
German	- *Wasser*
Sanskrit	- *āpas*
Latin	- *aqua*
Amerindian	- *nipēw*
Hindi	- *pānī*
Telugu	- *nīru*
Japanese	- *mizu*

In the sense of *word(f)*, these are all different 'words', for as *word-forms* in their respective language community, they are distinct from each other. However, as their significatory function is the same in each of the languages is the same, there is in this case a common base of *meaning* that runs through, as it were, each of the words. That is to say, in the sense of *word(p)* they are the same because they each have a common *word-power.* Our argument has been that *word(v)* is a potency for signification, which as a category of linguistic capacity cannot subsist outside consciousness and on which the ostensive manifesting structures, such as the phonological, depend. This basic and implicit structure is identified as a subtle form of syllabic construction in which the *meaning* element inheres; this is the *word-unit*, e.g. **'w-a-t-e-r'**, underlying the different tokens or symbolic-vehicles in the same language, and underlying the different 'words' across the few languages, as exemplified above, as equivalences of the English word "water", or vice versa. Such then, is the nature of the 'word' (*śabda*), in our view.

In concluding this chapter it would be worthwhile to remark that the 'word', at least in some of the more prominent Indian theories of language, is less of a physical 'entity', and more a 'psychical entity'. Bhartṛhari himself points to this view : *śabda buddhisthaḥ*[55], whose chief 'revealer', as it were, is sound. The earlier thinkers in India also, as Kunjunni Raja points out, were very much given to the awareness that the 'word' is 'something more than the audible sounds uttered by the speaker and heard by the listener'.[56] Likewise, Vyāsa, commenting on the celebrated *Yoga-sūtras* asserts that the 'word' is apprehended in the mind, even though it is brought together by the sounds.[57]

Mīmāṃsā similarly recognised that there is much more to the word than the articulate sound that manifests it. They expressed this in terms of the sequence of subtle phonemes.[58]

Following on from the Mīmāṃsā account, Advaita considered the 'word' to be an aggregate of permanent 'letters' (*varṇas*) in a fixed order. Going a step further, we have attempted to incorporate the grammarian insight of the necessity of the meaning-element to be an integral part of the 'word', which we have located in the discrete phoneme sequence, thus giving rise to the notion of *varṇasphoṭa*. We could render *varṇasphoṭa* as the 'semanteme'. Integrating the phonemic structure to form the finished morphemic item or *lexeme* (*pada*) yields the *word (śabda)*.

NOTES TO CHAPTER TWO

1. We assume that the speaker and hearer, in the normal circumstances of worldly discourse, do share a common language, and also many of the conventions of speech.

2. What is basically at issue is whether our apprehension of the sentence in terms of its constituents can be separated from the *meaning* that is comprehended. The unput is the sentence, and the output, as it were, is the intentional content of the speech assimilated from the constituents of the sentence.

3. *padānām padārthabodhopakṣīṇatvād vyavahitatavācca padārthā eva svasaṃsargarūpaṃ vākyārthaṃ bodhayanti* : since the words are exhausted with conveying the meaning of the words, and are also remote, it is only the meaning of the words that convey the meaning of the sentence, which is in the form of a relation among themselves. *Mānameyodaya* of Nārāyaṇa Bhaṭṭa, IV.5 (*śabda* ch.) p95.

4. For Gautama and most earlier Naiyāyikas, it is clearly *indriyārthasannikarṣotpannam jñānam :* cognition produced through sense-organ coming into contact with an object' (*Nyāya-sūtras* I.1.4). Gaṅgeśa's modification of this rather restrictive definition removed the contingency of the sense-organ contact and redefined it as a 'direct form of apprehension'. *Cf.* Viśvanātha's very guarded words: *'indriyaṃ karaṇaṃ matam'* (*BP* #52, 58).

5 See *TS* #37–41, with analyses in *Dīpikā*. *Cf* pp43–5 previous chapter. The point is that the *understanding* via speech being unique, its content, *śābdabodha*, is qualificatively different from the 'graspings' of perception and other cognitive acts.

6 *na tu padārthānāṃ-upasthiti-mātram*, in *Śabdaśaktiprakāśikā*, p7. Gaṅgeśa in his *TC* gives a good illustration of the putative 'bits' we hear, but which would remain separated in meaning unless and until their meanings are mutually connected – thus words in speech (heard): *ghaṭa* + ḥ + as + ti ('there + is + a + pot'); after recollection of meaning of each part, and their mutual connection, there arises awareness of the 'pot' qualified by a number and a place of existence.

Or, to put it in another way, the inter-relation of objects signified by the sentence-components has an *a-R-b* structure, the important elements of this structure being *R*, the relation (for, as we remarked earlier, the Nyāya ontology is fundamentally rooted in relations). For a good discussion see Sibajiban Bhattacharyya, 'Some Indian Theories of Meaning', *The Journal of the Indian Academy of Philosophy*, vol XX111, no 2, 1984 pp25-41.

7. For instance, the now well-known works of Piaget and Chomsky and Fodor. See Chomsky, *Language and Mind*, New York, 1968.

8. Jagadīśa, *op cit* p. 17 (and see note 6 above).

9. In earlier 'Introduction' section, under *śabda*.

10. To be precise on the difference, for Bhartṛhari the *sphoṭa* was more the *word-principle, śabdatva*, inherent in the word, which partook of the Reality of the supreme Principle – viz. *Śabda-Brahman* (*VKP 1ff*). But the *sphoṭa* of the later grammarians was again different to Bhartṛhari's, since they allowed for a division within the basic word in terms of more discrete *sphoṭas*.

But here we are talking about the indivisibility of the utterance-unit (or unit of speech), not necessarily of the *unit of meaning*. On traditional theories of the indivisibility of the sentence, see Gaurinath Sastri, *The Philosophy of Word and Meaning*, 1959, pp83ff. Sastri uses Puṇyarāja's argument to show that Pāṇini and Patañjali also admit the reality of a sentence over and above that of words.

11. *BP* #81. The contrast to note is that Viśvanātha qualifies the *karaṇa* to be not mere 'word' but 'word-awareness', for, he argues, even one under the vow of silence can com-

municate effectively the meanings of a verse he may be reciting (or thinking) silently. My hunch is that the argument for telepathy, if the phenomenon is to be feasible, must tell us how the *varṇas* by-pass the ostensive revealing process, such as *śravaṇa-pratyakṣa* or hearing. Or how does it convey physical but non-verbal signals.

12. Śaṅkara engages in a lengthy dispute in his commentary on *BS* 1.iii.28. He spares nothing in his critique of the *sphoṭa* view. First, he summarises the *sphoṭa* doctrine, then gives his own objections to the charges that the word could not be an aggregate of 'letters' as letters are said to disappear no sooner than they are produced. Śaṅkara's response is that we do recognise the word *qua* the *letters* to be the same (each time they are produced anew). If the letters were not the same, he argues, this would not be possible; the same letters are recognised as often as they are produced through an external sound-element which does change with different speakers, but the inherent nature of letters do not. Perhaps he would also agree that for a certain number of 'letters' their continuous usage in a fixed succession enables them to be associated with meaning. Letters, as signifiers or signs, then are capable of being *vācaka*, significant, and recognised as such. *'varṇā eva tu śabdaḥ' iti bhagavānupavarṣaḥ. nanutpannapradhvaṃsitvaṃ varṇānāmukttam. tanna ta evati pratyabhijñānāt*. See *BS-Bhāṣya* 1 iii 28 (1863, part 1, p291). See note 44.

13. It is interesting to note that Maṇḍana Miśra did not follow Śaṅkara on this point. He believed in the power of the *sphoṭa*, (*cf.* his text called *Sphoṭasiddhi*). Maṇḍana Miśra maintained that there is something over and above the letters. It is not a mere aggregate of letters that arise in the same cognition, conveying a unified meaning. The letter-sounds do no more than manifest the *sphoṭa* which is within both the speaker and the hearer. The relation between *sphoṭa* or the *word-unit* and the *meaning* is that of *vācyavācakabhāva* or the expression and the expressed. Thus is unlike Patañjali's notion of *sphoṭa. cf Sphoṭasiddhi* #3. See also Gaurinath Sastri *(loc cit*, and *passim*), and D. M. Datta *op cit* p259ff, for an Advaita critique of *sphoṭa*.

Patañjali regards words to be eternal, whose essence (*śabdakṛti*) is never destroyed—*tadapi nityaṃ yasmistattvaṃ na vihanyate; Mahābhāṣya* 1.1.1 p7. Other classifications used by Patañjali include: *kūṭastha* (subtle), *avicāli* (motionless), *avikāri* (without modification), *anupajana* (without origin), *anapāya* (indestructible), and that sounds suggest words *qua* their respective *sphoṭa. Śabdānuśāna* is the sound that is expressive of sense in popular usage: *athvā pratītapadārthako loke dhvaniḥ śabdetyucyate (loc cit)*. It was is not as though Patañjali has no place for letters; he does recognise them, but only in so far as they are means for disclosing the *sphoṭa: kṛtavarṇaparigrahā. cf.* Śabara, note 18 below, and note 24.
Against this, Mīmāṃsā argues that the letters of the word or words one heard the day before hold good on this day also, thus we must admit to the reality of the *varnas* : *tāvatkālaṃ sthiraṃ cainaṃ kaḥ paścānnāśayiṣyati;—Ślokavārttika (ŚV) (śabdanityādhīkaraṇam* #366, p823, 1893 edn; p583, 1978 Varanasi edn. by Dvārikādāsa Śāstrī, Tara, Delhi.) Śaṅkara would go along with this view.

14. *Śābara-bhāṣya*, I.vi.13. See note 50 below.

15. *Ibid* (under I.vi.17); also *Mānameyodaya* #140, p289. See also *Jaimini-Mīmāṃsā-sūtras, I. i.12: samaṃ tu tatra darśanam*. Sure Sabara considers the view 'word is sound' (*tasmād dhvaniḥ śabdaḥ): śtrotragrahaṇe hi arthe loke śabdaśabdaḥ prasiddhaḥ* (on *MS* I.i 5 *autpattika-sūtra*), but rejects it in favour of a definition that gives primacy to *varṇas* or 'letters'. Hence he adopts the view attributed to Upavarṣa: *gaurityatra kaḥ śabdaḥ? gakāraukāravisarjanīyā iti bhagavānupavarṣaḥ* (1873 *edn*, p13).

16. This is a standard Nyāya objection, where a distinction is made between mere noise and meaning-conveying sound (i.e. we do not, as it were, "hear *meaning*" in all forms of sound). Viśvanātha makes this very clear: *śabdo dhvaniśca varṇaśca mṛdaṅgādibhavo dhvaniḥ*; *BP* #164. Thus, while Nyāya will want to say that sound, of any form, is produced, (and therefore that is an ostensibly empirical phenomenon, even though sound is not identified as such with significant letters, nor for that matter presupposed

by them), the Mīmāṃsā will want to argue that sound is presupposed (*prāgabhāva*) since it is required for the manifestation (*abhivyañjaka*) of *varṇas*. See *MS*. I.i.12 and *Ślokavārtika* #642, *Cf*, Bhartṛhari, for whom, apart from *sphoṭa*, a word consisted of the admixture of wind, discrete atoms and fire.

17. See *Mānameyodaya* 140 (p229) where a similar analogy is used: 'what is inferred in the sense of hearing alone can be apprehended; it is originated on the analogy of the motion of a wave of *kadambam* buds'. As we shall see shortly, Nyāya also had a 'wave-theory' of sound, albeit a temporal continuum, as it is neither there before the moment nor after the speech-utterance that conveys the *varṇas*, thus both sound and *varṇas* are produced (*kṛtaka*). See *Bhāṣya et Vārttika* on *NS II.2.12-13;* the 'wave-theory' is referred to as *vīcītaraṅganyāya, kadambagolakanyāya* (*ND*, 1936-44, p596), underwritten as a, non-metaphysical quality of ethereal vibrations in space. See also *BP* #166: *vīcitaraṅganyāyena tadutpattistu kīrtitā kadambagolakanyāyadutpattiḥ kaśyacinmate.*

But sound is not ether itself, nor atoms per se (*NS*. II.2.23); *cf TB: padaṃ ca varṇa samūhaḥ*. Each letter heard arises and disappears sequentially and the word is gathered in a retrospective flash: *pūrvapūrvavarṇānubhūyantyavarṇaśravaṇakāle pūrvapūrvavarṇānubhavajanita-saṃskārasahakṛtenāntyavarṇasambandena padavyutpādansamayagrahānugṛhītena śrotrendriyena* (*TB*, p18, 1953; p49, 1978).

18. The late J. Brough pointed out how the *sphoṭa* in Patañjali's view 'was a rather different conception to that found in the later grammarians'. It is not clear, as S. D. Joshi points out, whether Bhartṛhari intended *sound* to be excluded from his notion of *sphoṭa* (see 21, 30 below). But in Patañjali, *sphoṭa* is not a "hypostatisation of sound" as S. K. De would have it, but is primarily a *Bedeutung-sträger*—i.e. a meaning-bearer. It is *śabda*-as-expressing-meaning and is the abiding speech-aspect, *vācakam, cf.* J. Brough 'General Linguistics in the Sanskrit Grammarians', p404-405. *Cf Mahābhāṣya* on *PS* 1.1.70 (Kielhorn edn. p181).

19. The analogue of *pada* to the *morpheme* in Western linguistics is generally accepted by writers on Indian linguistics. However, we have attempted to restrict the scope of the analogue by reference to the so-called *phoneme* (yet another analogue) sequence, roughly in the way John Lyons has done with in respect of, what he calls, *lexeme* (see n41 *infra*). On the larger issue, I found helpful Ian Kesarcodi-Watson's 'Modern linguists and "the Word"', *Indian Journal of Linguistics*, 8(2) 1981: pp 1-12.

20. *saṃskṛtya saṃskṛtya padāny utsṛjyante teṣāṃ yatheṣṭam abhisaṃbandho bhavati (PS*, Kielhorn edn. I p39, lines 18-19 (re: 1962); also quoted in J. F. Staal *Word Order in Sanskrit and Universal Grammar*, p28. See also note 13 *supra.*

21. Bhartṛhari in *Vākyapadīya* II 8-9 (Limaye and Abhyankar eds, p21). A *varṇa* may be a vowel (*svara*) or consonant (*vyañjana*). To render *varṇa* as 'phoneme we have the authority of various scholars, notably Subramania Iyer, Kunjunni Raja (*Theories of Meaning*, section on *sphoṭa*), J. Brough (*loc cit), et al*, more as an abstraction of minute speech-unit as distinct from speech-sound (*dhvani*), though in some views sound is a quality of *varṇa* or a manifesting agent of the same. However, a few Indian linguists who use the term 'phoneme' point out that the Sanskrit equivalence is not always a purely *sound*-abstraction in the Saussurean sense, devoid utterly of meaning. When, for example, the *varṇa* is associated with *sphoṭa* in Patañjali's sense, what would be the 'bursting forth'? Would it not be of *meaning*, even if it is of sound as well? We use '*dhvani* to denote the pure sound-element devoid of meaning, yet which has an *expressive* function, and thus is one of the 'vehicles' for the phoneme.

22. *Vākyapadīya* II.10, see also II.31.

23. *Pāṇini-sūtras* (Kielhorn, *op cit*) p318. 'It may be noted here that Pāṇini also gave several definitions of *pada* in subsequent *sūtras*, e.g. *svādiṣv asarvarṇāmasthanesu:* 1.4.17'. from B. K. Matilal, 'Indian Theorists on the Nature of the Sentence', p379, n3. *Cf.*

S.D.Joshi: 'According to Pāṇini, the first constituent of a sentence is *pada* which consists of two or more than two morphemes (stems, suffixes and empty morphs). He did not attempt to define a phoneme or a morpheme but simply listed them in his first fourteen *sutras* and then listed the morphemes exhaustively. . .', in 'Two Methods of Interpreting Pāṇini', (Poona, 1965), p57.

24. J. Brough, *op cit* (see note 20 above). He points to two unique features of Patañjali's notion of *sphoṭa*: (a) that it 'consists of a fixed pattern of letters, with a long and short vowel', which can be analysed. He says, as 'a succession of phonematic units' (p407), and that, (b) *sphoṭa* is 'bursting', 'a splitting open' of meaning (p406), dispelling the common sense view that the word consists of actual sounds of instance (p405). Patañjali's response to his own rhetorical question: 'What then is this word (*śabda*) 'cow'?'. . . 'It is that by means of which, when uttered, there arises an *understanding* of creatures with dewlap, tail, hump, hooves, and horns' [italics added] *Mahābhāṣya* I: *atha gaur ity atra kaḥ śabdaḥ? . . yenoccāritena sāsnā-lāṅgūla-kakuda-khuraviṣāṇinām saṃpratyayo bhavati sa śabdaḥ*. (Also in J. Brough, *ibid*, 405, n17). *Cf.* Śabara's parody on the same question, note 15 above.

25. Brough, *ibid,* p406.

26. Brough: '. . . the essential nature of the meaning-bearer was not seen by Patañjali in the same light as it was by later thinkers. This is clear from the discussion of Pāṇini in *sūtra* 1 i 70 (*taparas tatkālasya*), where he explicitly distinguishes *speech-sound (dhvani)* and '*sphoṭa*' (*ibid*, p406). J. Brough is critical of cemmentators who have tended to interpret *sphoṭa* as some sort of a 'mysterious entity' (A. B. Keith), or as a 'somewhat mystical conception' (referring to S. K. De *Studies in the History of Sanskrit Poetics*, Vol ii p108), (*ibid*, p405). For contrasting views, see S. D. Joshi: *The Sphoṭa-nirṇaya*, Poona, 1967, p29ff; Bhartṛhari *Vākyapadīya* (I.77 : *sphoṭātmā tairna bhidyate*); Subramania Iyer, 'The Doctrine of Sphota', p134ff.

27. *Mahābhāṣya* on *PS* I.I.70 Kielhorn, p181; tr. Brough, (*loc cit*) p407.

28. Brough, *op cit*, p406.
See also note 18 above.

29. Bhartṛhari appeared to have made a similar distinction within the *dhvani* in terms of *prākṛta-dhvani* ('primary sound') and *vaikṛta-dhvani* ('secondary sound'). But this is too subtle a distinction and scholars are also not agreed as to the actual intent of Bhartṛhari – see. Subramania Iyer's criticism of J. Brough and Kunjunni Raja's reading of the same, 'Bhartṛhari on Dhvani', *op cit.* p62ff.

30. Because for Patañjali a *sphoṭa* is fundamentally a structure consisting of a succession of phonematic units, it becomes possible to talk of the *sphoṭa* of a single 'letter' (*varṇa*) or phoneme. Nāgeśa Bhaṭṭa in his *Sphoṭavāda* gives a classification of eight types of *sphotas* entitling his first chapter as '*sphoṭabhedāḥ*' (difference in *sphoṭas*). He begins with *varṇasphoṭas* (edited: V. Krishnamacharya, p5).

31. See Kunjunni Raja, *Indian Theories of Meaning*, p108, and n1. He reflects: 'On the one hand it may be said that letters are meaningful, since meaning can be understood from verbal roots, stems, suffixes and particles which consist of a single letter, and also since the substitution of a different letter can produce a difference of the meaning, while the absence of a letter may make it impossible to understand the meaning of a word. On the other hand it may also be said that letters are meaningless in themselves, since a meaning is not understood by the hearer from each letter separately. Here Patañjali was conscious of the role of letters in building up higher units which are full symbols with a meaning of their own. . .Unlike the Mīmāṃsaka-s, he emphasized the importance of the meaning-bearing aspect of words; but he did not explain it fully.'

32. This is clear from the definition of the later Nyāya school as the 'smallest meaning-bearing phoneme sequence' (see note below, and note 17 above); *Cf.* Matilal, *op cit*, p279ff; P. H. Matthews *Morphology* (CUP, 1974, p11).

33. *Nyāya-sūtras*, II.2.58 (57 in Banaras, 1920): *te vibhaktyantāḥ padam*; *vide* commentary of Vātsyāyana on same (*loc cit*). For discussion, see V. N. Jha in 'Naiyāyikas' Concept of Pada and Vākya', in S. D. Joshi (ed.), *Sentence-Meaning* (1980, Poona, pp 85-94), esp. 85-87.

34. V. N. Jha, *loc cit*; See also Matilal, *op cit*, p379.

35. Annaṃbhaṭṭa, *TS* #59 (BORI).

36. Matilal, *op cit*, p379.

37. *Cf.* Matthews, *op cit* (note 32 above).

38. *Ibid*, p12-13.

39. It is the same condition which applies in the larger context of the apprehension of word-meanings in relation to one another. See Ch. 4, section on *ākāṅkṣā*.

40. L. Bloomfield, *Language*, p178 (1935; 1964· Delhi)

41. John Lyons renders the passage in somewhat simpler terms: '(language) forms which never occur alone as whole utterances (in some normal situations) are bound forms; forms which may occur alone as utterances are *free* forms. Any free form is, by Bloomfield's definition, a word', in his *Introduction to Theoretical Linguistics* (Cambridge, 1968, p201). John Lyons' own analysis of the word in terms of *lexemes* is quite interesting, and bears some resemblance to the view being developed here; however, because Lyons bases much of his reliance on the lexical item for the 'paradigm' of any word, we hesitate to say anything further.

42. Lyons, *ibid*.

43. In other words, we are invoking Patañjali for shifting the meaning-bearing unit from whole-words to the letter-parts. As we said earlier, for Bhartṛhari such a division would be permissible only for the purposes of analysis, but otherwise there is no real separating of words from sentence and *varṇa* from word (*VKP* II.1; I.73).

44. The view of *sphoṭa* that Śaṅkara considers is this: 'the actual perception of the last letter combined with the impressions left by the preceding letters. . .is that which intimates the sense of the word; for that effect of the impressions—viz. the recollection of the entire word, is itself something that consists of parts which succeed each other in time. From all this it follows that the *sphoṭa* is the word. . .the *sphoṭa* presents itself in the *buddhi* all at once as the object of one mental act of apprehension.' Sankara takes exception to this view and argues that the sense of the word may be apprehended from the letters themselves which as an aggregate constitute the word, 'and not anything else'. But he does not depart too far from the Mīmāṃsā view of 'letters', and would not have the 'definite sense' associated with the letters. Thus, he denies the usefulness of the conception of *sphoṭa* at the discrete level as well.*Bhāṣya* on *BS* I.iii.28 (text in 1901, p22). (Thibaut tr. p206, 210.) See n12 above. *Cf Chāndogya Up-bhāṣya* III.18.

45. Vātsyāyana on *NS* II.2.40.*BP-SM* #164-165. Both forms of sounds are said to be transitory.

46. D. M. Datta, *Six Ways of Knowing*, p252ff.

47. *dhvani* and *nāda*, articulate and inarticulate; *Mānameyodaya* 140. p229: *vācaka*, *avācaka*. But, by contrast, we wish to retain the *vācaka* of Mīmāṃsā as the significant element of *varṇa*, while also wanting to revert to Patañjali's 'wave-reverberation' prior to the ostensible sound. It is also interesting to note what Kunhan Raja (the teacher of Kunjunni Raja) says on this point: 'All the systems of Indian though in ancient Indian have this one view in common that what is experienced as sound, as language, is not a phenomenon in the physical air, that it is an effect in the air originating from some phenomenon in a finer medium, and that both in origin and final cognition there is a point in some medium which is finer than the air through which it is transmitted as

waves.' *Some Fundamental Problems in Indian Philosophy* p73.

48. If we follow Bhartṛhari and make an even finer distinction within *dhvani*, then it moves away from being 'noise' to being much more refined and articulate sounds, such as polished speech or musical notes.

49. *Mānameyodaya* 140-141, p229, see note 16 above. cf. Śaṅkara, under I.iii.28: 'If, for instance, the word cow is pronounced twice, we think not that two different words have been pronounced, but that the same individual word has been repeated' (p207). cf Bhartrhari *VKP* I.71.

50. *Śābara-bhāṣya* under I.vi.13 (G.Jha, tr., p35; 1889 text, p26).

51. *autpattika sūtra* I.i.5 *MS* of Jaimini. The *autpattika sūtra* is not without its difficulties. The basic argument is that the relations we discover in our use of words, that are taught to us by our peers, were there from time immemorial. If we do not acknowledge this, then language, particularly historical records, would loose their force. Common sense is invoked to suggest that, the word 'cow' uttered yesterday has not really vanished beyond all reference in respect of both the sign (*signifiant*, ideogram, lexical item) and that which is signified (*signifié*). Although it is a wonder why, if there is this fixity of *signifiant-signifié* relation that the word 'razor', upon its utterance, does not slit the tongue! Kumārila's response is that the relation is with the expressiveness (the signification) and not with the expressed (referent). Thus the relation holds true with imperceptibles as well, by virtue of the signification competency of the word. Empirically, however, such a conclusion of its timeless fixity would be unacceptable on the grounds of the limited historical observations that the Mīmāṃsakas invoke. Problems of historicity and inductivism aside, the Mīmāṃsakas were not seeking to establish a thesis in this way, rather they were looking for evidence that would support a 'received view' in their tradition.

For Śabara *autpattika* stood for 'originary', 'self-sufficient', not depending on any other instrument. M. Biardieau has pointed out that the later Mīmāmsakas turned the idea of a temporaly-perceived permanency into an idea of eternality (*nityatva*). *Autpattika* need not be taken in the sense of eternality of the relation. (Biardeau, *Théorie de la Connaissance et Philosophie de la Parole dans le Brahmanisme classique,* Paris, 1964, pp68-100).

At any rate, the notion of the unity of *vācya-vācaka* bears certain resemblance to the relative permanency of the *signifiant-signifié* relation in de Saussure's *Cours de Linguistic générale* (tr. Wade Buskins, 1974). And more speculatively *autpattika* might be said to be making the sort of link of unity-in-difference that the coined '*differánce*' in Derrida is keen to make, for Derrida does want to say, it seems, that the *phone*, the signified substance *given to consciousness* is that which is most intimately tied to the thought of the signified concept (*Position*, tr. & notes by Allan Bass, The Athetone Press, London, 1972, p21). But the conclusions that Derrida goes on to draw from this about the nature of the *text* would not be acceptable to the Mīmāṃsakas. (I cannot go into the arguments here.)

As for its resemblance to the Platonic *Ideas*, Krishna Sivaraman rightly cautions us against taking the comparison to be more than an aesthetic resemblance, which got rather out of hand in T. R. V. Murti's remark : 'The eternality of words as propounded by the schools of Mīmāṃsā and Grammar is the Indian counterpart of the [Platonic] doctrine of Ideas.' Sivaraman, 'The Word as a Category of Revelation', in Coward and Sivaraman (eds.), *Revelation in Indian Thought*, pp45-64, p. 59-60, n9.

Cf. Heidegger: 'Our experience of language is that we receive it from others (and others from others. . .). We may make transpositions in what we have been given but we are far from creating language. . . language is the house of being.' M. Heidegger, *Poetry, Language and Thought*, (tr. & intro. by Albert Hofstader, New York, 1952).

52. see note 45 above.

53. 'Acoustic image' is analogous to Bhartṛhari's *prākṛta-dhvani*, the more abstract sound pattern which Kunjunni Raja aptly describes as 'the acoustic image of the normal expression or the expression in the mind keeping the time-order with it', and distinguishes this from the actual sounds, or the speech-instances, the *vaikṛta-dhvani*, as the 'engram' left behind by the former in *la langue* or the phonematic pattern or the acoustic images, which is accepted, he says, by modern linguists also. (*op cit*, p117-122).

54. S. C. Chatterjee, *Nyāya Theory of Knowledge*, pp 32-36.

55. *Vākyapadīya* I.46: *śabdo'pi buddhisthaḥ śrutīnāṃ kāraṇaṃ pṛthak*, p5 (Limaye ed).

56. Raja, *op cit, passim.*

57. On *Yoga-sūtras*, III.17: *padaṃ pūnarnādānusaṃhārabuddhinirgrāhyamiti; varṇā ekasamayāsaṃbhavitvāt-parasparaniranugrahātmānaste. . .pratyekemapadasvarūpā ucyante.*

58 *Cf.* Gardiner: 'As words exist in the possession of every individual (of a linguistic community), they are psychical entities, comprising on the one hand an area of *meaning*, and on the other hand the *image* of a particular *sound* susceptible of being *physically reproduced* whenever wanted.' *Speech and Language* p69.

3

ON MEANING

A. ***Some general remarks on 'meaning'.***
B. ***Indian theories of 'meaning'.***
C. ***The linguistic functions of 'meaning'***

A.

3.0 In terms of the theory of word evolved in the preceding chapter, the implications for *śabdapramāṇa* may be summed up thus:

(a) the meaning-bearing aspect means that the word has signification, i.e. a word has the capacity to *signify*, or in a general sense to stand for, refer to, name; describe, denote or intend. Through this capacity, the word succeeds in performing a particular *function* in speech, namely that of conveying *sense* (*artha*) and intention. This is possible in virtue of the *śakti* or 'power' of the word that relates it to its signification, and this *relation* can vary in different uses of the word;

(b) in virtue of the constituent meaning-syllables or *varṇas* there is an *abiding* aspect to the word that accounts for its re-emergence or repeatability—this ensemble of *varṇas* is the reservoir, as it were, of meaning (or the subtle *Bedeutungsträger*);[1] the subtle 'sound-essence' to which the *varṇas* are linked becomes 'exteriorised' in multi-symbolic levels by being associated with linguistic signs, and symbols as manifested and realised in speech-behaviour, or through other modes of comunication, enabling the word to transfer the sense immanent in it from one sentient being to another, and which also makes for synonyms and translation equivalences.

3.1 Now if *meaning* is the fundamental element of the word, we must arrive at a comprehensive understanding of its nature and function in respect of *śābdabodha*. If through the instrumental efficacy of *śabda qua meaning* certain desired or intended communications can be effected, then it is also through this that certain understandings and 'knowledge' are communicable or 'obtainable', from the point of view of the audience. Meaning, then, is integral to the analysis of *śābdabodha*. In this chapter we examine the different nuances of meaning, its role and related functions in the *vyāpāra* or operative process that results in valid knowledge. Before going any further, it would be appropriate to clarify our use of some difficult terminology.

We use 'meaning' and 'to mean' in a general way bearing in mind the different possible kinds of meaning (*artha*),[2] and 'signification' for a more specific sense of what a word essentially signifies *qua* word-essence. While 'significance', of which there could be more than one 'sense', is construed as a function of the *use* of the word in appropriate circumstances. The express or 'literal' meaning in respect of the latter is called *abhidhā* or *mukhyārtha*, the 'primary meaning', and the varying degrees of extended or metaphorical 'meanings' are the 'secondary' senses, i.e. 'implicative', 'suggestive', 'poetic' and so forth. *Śakti* is described as the essential 'word-power' in virtue of which a word has signification, but *śakti* is also one of the two basic functional relations (*vṛtti*) a word has with its 'meaning', the other functional relation being *lakṣaṇā*, i.e. the 'secondary signification function'.

Theory of meaning

3.2 Earlier on we suggested a distinction between the closing stages of the process, where the *material* causes have been effective, and the beginning stages of the process, where the *efficient* causes are effective. Having dealt with the beginning stages of the process in the earlier chapter, we now proceed to examine the intermediate stages. Neither *padajñāna* or word-awareness nor *vākyapramāṇarūpa* or sentence-form are the end-product of the overall process They, however, become efficient in generating a set of operations in the intermediate stages of the process, in which begins the *assimilation* of the meanings of the component parts of the sentence, that is, the meanings of words, and their *synthesis* into the composite sentence-meaning. This occurs through stages of awareness of the relation between the juxtaposed components, that is to say, the relation among the words, or to be more precise, among *word-meanings*[3]. But whether the comprehension of the sentence-meaning arises as a result of the awareness of word-meanings, or simply as the result of an awareness of the component words of the sentence as a holistic linguistic unit is an issue on which some schools are vehemently divided. This issue will concern us in a later chapter.

Presently, we want to concern ourselves with the problem of meaning. What is it for a word to have *meaning*? How is *meaning* related to the *word*? How is it that each word has its own meaning- capacity—or does it? How is meaning of a word known? Can a word mean more than one thing, that is to say, can a word have more than one meaning or 'sense', and how is that possible? These are some of the problems that concern any theory of meaning. Ours though, is a more limited concern and is related to the examination of the *vyāpāra* category, which basically involves 'the awareness (usually by recollection) of word-meanings through the (functional relation or) *vṛtti* of the words, either in their *express* function (*śakti*) or in their *implicative* function (*lakṣaṇā*)'. Generally though, the functional relation or *vṛtti* is identified with the *śakti* relation, but essentially the *vṛtti* of a word is the disjunction of the *śakti* and the *lakṣaṇā* relations respectively.

Relation of *word* and *meaning*: *pada-padārtha-sambandha*[4]

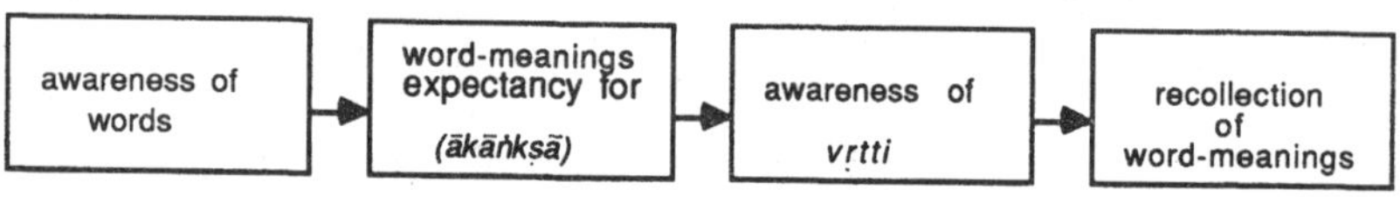

3.3 The above diagram[5] illustrates the functional process through which meaning is usually obtained from an initial awareness of words. Memory recollection plays a role where there has been prior acquaintance with the particular word. There are other ways of getting to the meaning of words, as we shall notice when we deal with some specific issues regarding the relation of word and meaning. For now, our interest is with the notion of 'meaning' itself. To have meaning presumably a word must have some significance, it must be capable of *signifying* 'something', or some function or relation, as with prepositions.[6] And that 'something' the word signifies is what the word stands for, indicates, denotes, points to, or connotes depending on the context of its use and occurrence.[7] Words sometimes *name*, without necessarily having any significance beyond naming.[8] Word *via* the meaning is also said to be used to designate, to imply, to refer to, and even *to mean*. But are these different signification functions of words, or are they aspects of the same signification function in terms of some broader 'significatory capacity' that the word may have? There are many aspects to any theory of 'meaning', none of which are without their own problems. We may consider some responses in terms of a few well known theories of meaning.

3.4 Most realist inclined systems proffer the 'referential' theory of meaning, which requires a word to be directly related to the 'thing' or 'event' the word stands for or denotes. Nyāya, and to an extent Mīmāṃsā, adhered to this view; and Russell amongst others gave voice to it in modern times. In the Indian context some schools identified meaning with the particular referent denoted by a word. Putting their case, R. C. Pandeya remarks: 'Meaning cannot hang in the air. Being a relation it has two terms on which it depends. One is the word, and the other is the referent.'[9] Mīmāṃsā looks for referents for adjectives and verbs as well – e.g. of 'whiteness', regarded to denote a class of white things, which manifests as a particular in instances such as that of a white jar. And in the case of verbs, the referents were the actions or the specific activity as an event in the world which lead to an accomplishment of certain identifiable ends. For example, 'bring' in 'bring the cow' is not only a command, but also a particular *act* referring to certain movements and behaviour on the part of an entity (viz. the human). A referent is assumed for every word, whether it denotes a particular or a class (*jāti*). This includes relations (*sambandha*) as well. The supersensibles (*apūrva*) were also "things" or "entities' referred to in the scriptures according to Mīmāṃsā.[10] So the referential theory identifies the meaning of an expression with the actual entity, class of entities, event, or class of events that the word (or expression) denotes, indicates, designates, stands for, or names.

3.5 But there are a few problems with the referential theory. First is the problem articulated by P. F. Strawson[11] in criticising Russell for identifying meaning with referring. Strawson pointed out rightly that we use expressions not always to refer to or mention objects, events and so forth (e.g. "the king" in the sentence 'the King of France is a wise man'). Besides, it is not in the use of expression that *the 'object' referred to is given – though it can be used* to make reference to that object – but it is in virtue of the *meaning* of the word or expression that it can be used in this way. I can, for instance, talk about 'my handkerchief', but I do not have to pull out the object I am referring to if you know what I mean, and the meaning of the expression 'my handkerchief' is certainly not something I can pull out of my pocket.

Second, is the problem of 'two senses' for one referent. Now two words or expressions may have the same *referent* without having the same *sense* in all respects. For example, 'sodium chloride' and "salt" designate one and the same substance, but while the former makes reference to its chemical constituents, the latter expresses the 'common *sense*' use. Frege pointed out that the two expressions, "the morning star" and "the evening star" designate the same referent – viz., the planet Venus, (the same 'thing-meant'), but yet, the two expressions do not have the *same sense* (*Sinn*).[12] For to those who are aware that the two expressions refer to one and the same planet, they would have a different meaning, and even to those who know their identity, the identity is not a linguistic matter, but a discovery of astronomy, while different senses would continue to be attached to the two expressions. An object is never referred to directly, according to Frege, without saying something about it.[13] In each of the two expressions, something is said about the same object, but in a different 'mode of presentation' or signification.[14] Likewise, in the case of 'sodium chloride' and 'salt', the same object is denoted (*Bedeutung*) but signified in different ways *qua* the senses (*Sinn*) in each expression. Thus, meaning, in one sense, cannot be identified with the 'thing-meant' (*vastu-nibandha*), the referent. A distinction, therefore, ought to be made between the *referent* (the 'thing-meant', *Bedeutung*) and the '*sense*' (the expressed significance presenting the referent; *Sinn*) which contains the mode or manner in which the referent is signified or presented. Nor is it necessary that for every word grammatically expressed, there has to be a referent, though its significance may not be denied in the expression.

Another way of elucidating the distinction made between the two expressions is to say that both have the same referent, but different 'cognitive contents' (*viṣayatās*).[15] The difference between the two expressions arise because the difference between the two corresponds to a difference in the 'mode of presentation' of the same object – i.e. a difference in their cognitive contents related to the two expressions, and this has partly to do with the meaning intended in any act of speech. The speaker presumably does not intend the conntctations of the laboratory use of the chemical to go along with his request for salt at the dinner table; but in an argument with his colleague over some issue relating to chemistry, he may well refer to the content in the salt-shaker as 'sodium chloride', particularly when he intends to stress some property it has as a chemical. The same referent then is susceptible to different modes of signification – i.e. 'sense' and the 'mode of signification' have nothing to do with the existence or reality of the 'object' referred to. A third person overhearing the conversation may not immediately grasp the two senses in which the 'same thing' is being spoken of. But when he learns *what* is referred to in using the second, he *learns* that both expressions have the 'same referent', which allows his friend to make the identity statement: 'Salt is sodium chloride'. The referent, however, though the same, does not stand out on its own: in both instances it has to be indicated through a certain expression (*abhidhāna*), corresponding to a sense or 'mode of presentation' or the cognitive content. As Bhartṛhari put it: 'The same person (at different times), and different persons (at the same or different times), understand the meaning of the word in different ways due to the changing conditions of understanding.'[16]

Bhartṛhari emphasised three things that occur upon hearing a word:

(i) the form of the word itself *(śabda-svarūpa)*, (ii) an intended meaning *(artha, vācya)*, (iii) an object *(viṣaya)* external to the (bodily) senses, are apprehended. (*Ibid*, I.52ff.)

These considerations, it should be noted, show how referential theory fails to give an adequate account of meaning. At best it helps to identify one function of meaning in so far as it is a sign standing for, or indicating another thing or object in the world. In the case of names or proper names, this function is given prominence over the meaning or 'sense' (significance) which a word also expresses. But to express meaning or sense, it is not necessary for there to be a correspondingly real object or referent which the word as a sign stands for, or refers to. As Frege remarked: 'In grasping a sense, one is not certainly assured of a reference.' And where there is reference, it may vary in different uses or usages of the same word.

3.6 A word or two needs to be said about the function of 'use'. Now it is not the case that 'meaning' can be unequivocally identified with the function of the use of words. The meaning of 'fortuitous', for instance, is *accidental*, and we may point to the meaning of 'fortuitous' by saying that the use of 'fortuitous' is *accidental.* Saying what the meaning of a word or expression is, does not just amount to saying what its use is, nor to saying that it has the same use as another word, or different use or usage on different occasions. Certainly, if we knew what the use of 'fortuitous' was, we would be in a better position to say what it means, and show this understanding by saying something like, 'it means *due to chance*'. But the converse is not necessarily guaranteed, for although we may know what a word means (by showing the understanding in the manner indicated above), we may yet not be in a position to adequately make use of the word – for the concept, or concepts which the word stands for, is independent of the contingencies of any specific speech-act.

Thus when Wittgenstein pronounces, 'Let the use of the words teach you their meaning',[17] he is not defining the meaning of a word or an expression in terms of its *use*, but is recommending that, if we were to look at a word or an expression in terms of its use in language, we would get a clearer picture of it than by looking at it abstractly, for it is the use that makes the meaning manifest. It is the determined relation of the word to its meaning that enables the word to have the *same use* in different occurrences, and so by observing the uses of the same word in different instances of its occurrence we can grasp the sameness of the concept-content it stands for in all these uses. The sameness of the *concept-content* points to the sameness of its *meaning*. But this power of the word to be related to the same specific meaning in its recurrent use does not belong to the fact of its *use* itself, but to 'the ability to be *put to* a certain use', which is intrinsic to the word, as its *śakti* or significatory capacity. It is this that enables the word to convey the *same meaning* through each use in language – i.e. it enables the word to 'be put to the same use', or with a similar function in different uses, or usages, of it. It needs to be stressed that this 'capacity' is not dependent on the *use* of the word, though what the meaning or 'sense' is in the particular occurrence may not be obvious without observing the use of the word and the specific meaning or 'sense' that is linked with it in that context. But the use of the word need not be taken as the sole determinant of the significance of the word, nor also the place where meaning is *invariably* – only more clearly – detected, though it is a place to look for *one* of its functions in operation, viz. the sense or senses *qua* the *meaning* manifested in that specific occurrence. But the meaning should not be confused with use, as meaning *qua concept-content* is independent of the contingencies of its occurrence in any specific act of speech, i.e. its actual use.

This should not be taken to mean, however, that we cannot use words quite communicably and successfully without actually knowing their meaning. This is especially true of children learning a language, and of adults learning a new language. We use them in the way we use coins of a foreign country while travelling in that land, without knowing its currency system. Much as in court, a lawyer directs his somewhat illiterate client to utter, 'No, your Honour', when he hears the words, 'Do you plead guilty, Mr. . .?'; and, 'Yes, your Honour', if he hears,'You do not plead guilty?'.

What is important, however, to note from the above example, is that the different uses of the words *presuppose* their having meaning, and a specific one in the particular context in which the word occurs. But someone using the word or expression in a particular utterance may not be aware of its specific meaning. Though it might be different with another hearing, who may not understand what is being said without being aware of the meaning of the word or expression used.

3.7 In sum, the importance of the notion of use, and usage, cannot be overlooked, since it attempts to describe the manner in which a word occurs, and therefore the way in which the word is put to use or usage in that context. Thus, the notion of use complements the primary signification of words, for certain words and expressions do not signify anything, nor connote some other 'thing' indirectly, but are used to give voice to feelings and wishes, evoke certain attitudes and responses in others, or to *perform* certain 'illocutionary' acts, such as promises, commands, injunctions, requests, curses, and so forth. Many utterances and written expressions have hidden implications and suggestions, which, though a part of the function of meaning, are only secondarily so. To discuss them is not fruitful unless they are brought under the notion of use[18]. The concept of use enables us to discover the precise implications and suggestions expressed in certain contexts of the utterance of words and complex expressions, such as phrases, sentences, etc. For example, when John's friend says, 'John is utterly and truly mad', he may be using this expression to imply that John is not thinking adequately, but he may not mean that John is afflicted with insanity or a mental disorder sufficient to warrant him psychiatric consultation. The sense of being "mad" here is indirectly presented, though it is dependent upon the direct significative function of *mad*, and is in fact an extension of it. But to grasp the manner in which it is *differently* presented, one has to look at the use it has in that context, or in other varying circumstances of its use[19]. Such linguistic manoeuvres appear sometimes in the scriptures when the philosopher or sage is not able to express his understanding, or 'intuition', easily in the available idioms of the language he has acquaintance with.

B. *Indian Theories of Meaning*

3.8 In view of the considerations discussed above, one of the first questions asked in the Indian linguistic tradition concerns the *relation* between word and meaning, its origin, nature and duration. The meaning-aspect of a word is recognised as perhaps the most essential characteristic of the word in as much as the word has some significance. It is this aspect of meaning that makes word, as the basic unit in language, a *significant* expression. If a word did not have this capacity it would fail to signify what it does signify in recurrent use of the word. We may say then that there is a sort of relation between word and its meaning that seems, at least *prima facie*, to be invariable and direct. Direct, because on uttering a word the hearer very often grasps the meaning of the word without the need of another word to point to the *meaning* or 'signification' of the word.

To reinforce the inherentness of the connection between word and its meaning *qua* signification, the Indian thinkers postulate a particular linguistic operation, called *śakti-vṛtti* which determines the functional relation between word and its signification. Such that, by virtue of this *vṛtti*, there is the possibility of understanding the meaning of the word through hearing the word itself (*tatrāpi vṛttyā padajanyatvaṃ bodhyam*).[20] The function of *vṛtti*, in other words, is to enable the preservation of the relation between a word and its meaning in each occurrence of the word, notwithstanding the variations the meaning may evince in such occurrences. Gaṅgeśa put the matter plainly, in stating that the special relation that exists between a word and what it signifies is called *vṛtti*.[21]

Gaṅgeśa, however, as is the case with the Nyāya school, has reduced the relation to a direct one between the word and the *object* it denotes—*pada padārtha sambandha*. This is understandable, for Nyāya, with its realist orientation,[22] subscribes to the 'name' theory of meaning—viz. *abhidheyatvaṃ padārthatvam*—according to which there could be no *padārtha* ('object', "fact") without a *name*; all words are related to some *object* or other—even 'sky-flower' as naming *sky* and *flower*.[23] Another reason why Nyāya insists on the direct relation between word and the object denoted is the persuasion that when, for example, a word such as 'pot' is uttered, because 'pot' is a word-sound (*śabda*) and because *śabda* is related to *akāśa* or the substratum of sound, one could easily mistake the word to be related to the configuration of *akāśa* that forms the word 'pot'. And in this way the word gets related to something like space, in which the sound inheres, instead of that which the word refers to, namely the object *pot*. A word always refers to something other than itself, it does not stand for itself (except for the term 'word');[24a]hence, what a word is related to is what it refers to, i.e. what it stands for, or denotes. The relation is then between the word ('word-form') and the 'thing-meant', the referent. Nyāya denies that there is a *concept-content* or 'concept' through which the relation between the word and that which it denotes is established, and which the Indian grammarians insist on. Advaita and Mīmāṃsā follow this explanation. The following diagramatic representation of the two positions illustrate the difference:

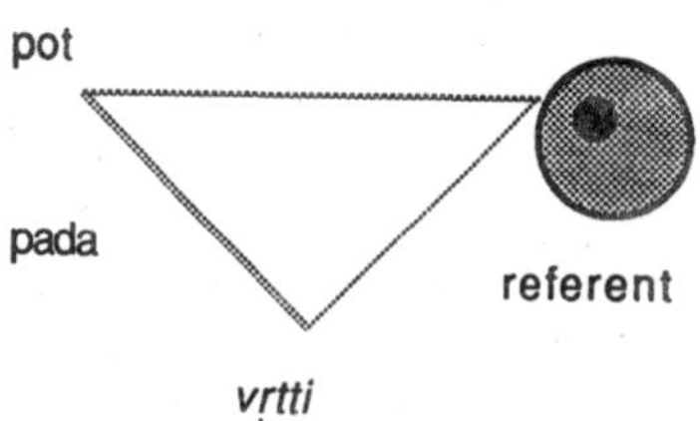

(NYĀYA)

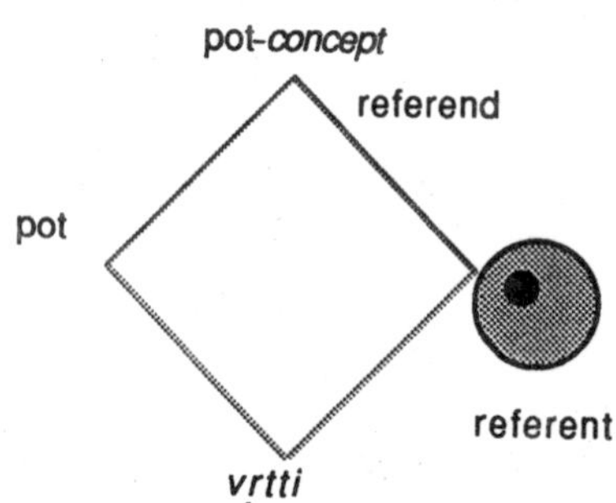

(MĪMĀṂSĀ)

Now this relation between word and meaning, in both the Mīmāṃsā or Nyāya thesis, is also considered as a 'power' inherent in the word: it is *śakti* or 'significatory power'—the "meaning-capacity" as we have noted earlier. It is this signification function in virtue of which the word signifies what other words, besides synonyms, do not signify in common speech. And this 'power' is of two sorts, *śakti* and *lakṣaṇā*.[24] Annaṃbhaṭṭa explains that a 'significant' word is a word that has the power to 'signify' something, and which helps in recalling the thing 'signified': 'signifying power' of a word consists in its *relation* between word and what it 'signifies'.

Annaṃbhaṭṭa further describes the relation as one which serves as 'the indirect determinant (*prayojaka*) of the recollection of the entity (denoted).'[25] As Gopinath Bhattacharya, elucidating this statement, makes the observation: '. . .it is a truism that memory of something depends on the previous cognition of that thing. The remembrance by a person of the *thing signified* is occasioned by his awareness of the *signifying word*. And that a person understands only a specific thing when he has the awareness of only a specific word is due not merely to the mere existence of the signifying relation but to his knowledge of that relation.'[26] *Śakti* or the signifying function of a word is then the indirect determinant of the understanding or recollection of what the word stands for. Its function is indirect in the sense that it functions through its knowledge which is determined by itself. Viśvanātha sums up the process in which *śakti* is an important causal factor, rather succinctly:

> *padajñānaṃ tu karaṇaṃ, dvāraṃ tatra padārthadhīḥ*
> *śābdabodhaḥ phalaṃ tatra śaktidhīḥ sahakāriṇī* [27].
>
> The awareness of the word is the instrument (of verbal comprehension), the awareness (through recollection) of the *meaning* of words is the operation *(dvāram:vyāpāram),* verbal understanding is the result, and the awareness of the signification function (*śakti*) of the word is the inter-mediary cause.

3.9 The *śakti* or 'power' gives the word its direct signification. It is not the mere perception of the word-form that gives us an awareness of what the word signifies, but the awareness of the *relation* between the word and its signification. It is through the *vṛtti* of *śakti* relation primarily (and *lakṣaṇā* relation secondarily) that word-meanings are understood. *Śakti* then is conceived as the essential meaning-*relation* that obtains between a word and that which it signifies. This capacity of word is analogous to the capacity of fire to burn, in virtue of its heat. To burn is the appropriate competency, *yogyatva*, of fire. It is the potency or inherent potentiality fire possesses even when it is not used for the purposes of burning. In cooking, for example, there is the realisation of its potentiality as an actuality. Similarly, the capacity of a word *to mean*, or *to signify* 'something' is its *yogyatva*. Another analogy is proffered which compares it to the function of the sense-organs, the *indriyas*: 'just as the *indriyas* as the organs of perception, have a natural capacity to perceive what comes into their purview, so also words have a natural capacity to convey sense.'[28]

Now this peculiar and ideal power or 'potentiality' is not an idea, but is a functional relation (*vṛtti*) that helps to bring about an operation by which the meaning of the word is actualised (*via* recollection) in awareness. When the meaning surfaces, as it were, there occurs an *actuality* of the meaning-relation. But in its *potential* state it exists, though non-ostensibly, as it does in the actual state. In actualisation it involves consciousness which apprehends the word. When we say the 'power' exists as a potentiality we mean the word has a "tendency" to operate in a certain way; this tendency is a *formal* condition for the operation. *Śakti*, in this respect, is the *formal* precondition for the operation of *artha* ('meaning') of words in speech-acts, or in any form of linguistic expression. Any power marks the formal structure of the situation in which it is operative, or in which it can operate. The powers or potentialities of a thing determine what that thing *can* do or can have done to it.[29]

To summarise the discussion so far, *śakti* is said to be the 'significatory power' a word has which determines its function in language, and by virtue of which the word signifies or has signification, designative and denotative functions of numerous sorts. This 'power' notion is comparable to the pragmatic concept linked to C. S. Peirce's idea of *power*. As Peirce puts it, the relation of a sign (word) and interpretant ('sense') must 'consist in a *power* of the representamen to determine *some* interpretant to being a representamen of the same object.'[30] And a power is a determinant because it has a tendency for forming a 'habit' of behaviour of some sort. But whilst Peirce's is a purely pragmatic consideration in arriving at such a notion of 'power', the Indian thinkers, in particular the Mīmāṃsakas, went a step further and postulated a much stronger nexus to account for the essentially permanent and immutable (*autpattika* = "originary") relation between word and meaning. We wish to explore in a little more detail this allegedly unique relation and its implications for the minimal theory of meaning necessary for an analysis of *śābdabodha*.

3.10 According to Mīmāṃsā, the relation between word and its meaning *qua śakti* is a natural or permanent one, because word is a naturally existing permanent power-entity (= *word-power*).[31] The *word*, as we saw in the previous chapter, according to Mīmāṃsā, is a subtle entity, subtler than sound-waves that carry it. As such it is an abiding substantive 'entity' (*dravya*) and its power to signify (i.e. its relation to the signified) is *intrinsic* (*sahaja*) to it in the sense that it is not instilled *ab extra: autpattikas tu śabdasyārthena sambandhaḥ.*[32]

Now although the significatory power is *intrinsic* to the substantive *varṇa* base, it is not identified with that. Nor is it just a *quality* of the substance. It is unlike any of the categories of reality, *padārthas*, and therefore has to be assumed to be a separate and distinct category of existent. Advaita joins Mīmāṃsā in this contention, arguing that *śakti* is the principal function (*mukhyavṛtti*) of a word with regard to its meaning which helps it to denote such and such an object or 'fact' directly (*viśiṣṭe vastu viśeṣe vṛttiḥ*). Dharmarāja claims that the significatory power is a distinct category, *padārthantaram*, because the power that produces the effect is a distinctly separate entity (from other causes)—for example, fire is the distinct cause of burning (the skin etc).[33] This *śakti* can be inferred, according to both Mīmāṃsā and Advaita, from the effect which manifests in the awareness of word-meaning generated by the awareness of word. From Patañjali's commentary on Pāṇini, we learn that in the Pāṇinian system also the relation between a word and its meaning was regarded as *established siddha*:[34] *siddhe śabdārtha saṃbandhe.*

To the Mīmāṃsā, because speech *qua letters* is eternal, it is impossible to conceive of a time when there was no speech. We might think that we learn the language we speak from our elders, but we forget that they in turn had learned that language from their own elders, and the latter from their elders, and so on *ad infinitum.*[35] But the main persuasion underlying the Mīmāṃsā view of the non-temporalness, i.e. the utter permanence (*autpattikatva*, and later '*nityatva*') of the relation between word and meaning is that ultimately the origin of the relation cannot be traced to a 'personal' source (*pauruṣeya*), the relation being *apauruṣeyatva* in its ultimate 'origin'—if we can speak in these terms. The relation cannot be traced to its establishment either by a deity or some humans, though admittedly preserved in their conventions. The relationship by which words denote meaning in human speech cannot be assumed to be created by human speech itself, for this relationship is itself a precondition for the possibility of speech. To presume that human speech itself establishes this significatory relation would involve the fallacy of *petitio principii* (*ātmāśraya*),[36] inasmuch as this relation is presupposed in any sentence uttered to make this statement. In objecting to the Mīmāṃsā position we may argue that without a force ('Creator', 'Maker') that establishes the relation in the first place, how could words function to indicate meaning? Is not the word-meaning relation established through use and passage of time? That is to say, it may be argued that if one *uses* a word with *reference* to a particular thing (*yatparaḥ*) the word would have the meaning (determined by that use); and likewise for its *relation.*

But Śabara, speaking for Mīmāṃsā, does not intend to make *meaning* a matter of 'choice' for the people speaking a language. They may choose or not choose to determine the meanings of the word—though they may vary the 'sense' in the appropriate context. The 'use' then is a possibility created by the pre-existing (functional) relation, and the use, and usages, reveals the relation. 'What men say is that this is how we *understand* the word, this is what we *take* the meaning to be, not that this *is* the meaning of the word'(*evam ayaṃ puruṣo veda iti bhavati pratyayaḥ, na tu evam ayam arthaḥ*).[37] The human in using and understanding the word presumes the word to have *potency*, the power or capacity to express what has been comprehended by the person addressed, and without *inferring* such a potency, we would not be able to explain how such understanding occurs in recurrent use of the word. It is in grasping the relation that their meaning is apprehended. Notwithstanding this empirical defence, Mīmāṃsā actually base their position on a metaphysical theory (which as such falls outside the scope of this enquiry), much as is its close analogue in the Bhartṛharian view of the eternal undivisiveness of speech. Both are in contrast to the more realist approach of the Nyāya, which has affinities to the 'use theory', on the one hand, and the pragmatic consideration of Peirce, mentioned earlier, on the other. We should look at the Nyāya view and its objections to the Mīmāṃsā position. This part of the discussion on relation of word and meaning will be concluded with a rejoinder from Mīmāṃsā in response to Nyāya.

3.11 Nyāya also holds that there is a relation between word and its meaning described earlier in terms of *vṛtti*, but Nyāya does not agree entirely with Mīmāṃsā. Nyāya, first of all, contends that, (*a.*) the significatory *power* is nothing more than a functional *relation* or the 'meaning-*relation*' that obtains between a word and what it signifies, usually its conventional meaning, but also the extended sense; and, (*b.*) that the 'power' is not *something* embedded in the word, nor is it due to some external source or determination *ab extra* which is not unaccountble in linguistic terms, or in terms of 'personal origin'. The Nyāya view is that the relation is a result of *convention*, which itself is established by the desire or *will* of Īśvara or God as understood by Nyāya, or at least of some supra-human agency (*puruṣaviśeṣa*). So the *śakti* of words consist in their being a collective determination by a *convention* willed by some transcendent being.

If, therefore, language can be taken to have its origin in some transcendent principle, then, according to Nyāya, it can only be understood as the revelation by the will of a Supreme Being that a word means such a thing.[38]

A thesis similar to this is to be found in Vyāsa's commentary on Patañjali's celebrated *Yoga-sūtras*: 'The usage as determined by Īśvara declares its existent meaning, as the relation of father, and so that is existent is expressed by the verbal statement 'this is his father', 'This is his son'.'[39*] In the sense that the relation is *established*, albeit by God, it makes it conventional. The 'convention' in this sense, however, does not necessarily mean 'human convention', which in fact is a distinct form of convention, that is also distinguished and accepted by later Nyāya. But the sense here has strictly to do with 'divine convention', for it is the desire or *will* of God that such and such be understood from such and such a word. Nyāya urges against the Mīmāṃsā theory of timeless relation between word and meaning, arguing that it is by *sāmayika* or conventional significance that the meaning of a word is understood when heard (or read). Thus, Gautama states: *na sāmayikatvāt śabdārthasampratyayasya.*[39]

The Nyāya and Vaiśeṣika [V.S.II.14-20] argue that if there were any *fixed* relationship between a word and its meaning, as between fire and burning, then the word should have already co-existed with the object denoted, but we do not observe any such relationship. A word does not co-exist with the object it denotes, for if it did, the word 'fire' should burn our mouth upon uttering it, and the word 'razor', for instance, should split our lips, and 'honey' sweeten our mouths, and so forth. But none of these 'objects' are experienced in uttering the word which is said to co-exist with what it signifies.[40] Obviously, Nyāya has displaced the Mīmāṃsā theory of immutability by interpreting it in more realist terms.

3.12 Another argument against the Mīmāṃsā thesis is that, if words had a natural relation with the objects denoted, the same word should mean the same thing everywhere; there should not be any variations in meaning – as the different 'senses' of the word. But there are variations and this is not sufficiently explained by postulating a *fixed* eternal relation. Nyāya reverts the 'use theory' proposition to suit its own position in arguing that in use we recognise the relation between word and meaning as a result of the wish and desire of personal beings. Hence, *śakti* is not eternal, it is a convention established by the will of God or of humans. Although, Mīmāṃsā would retort and explain that the variations in meaning that the Nyāya alludes to are not inconceivable within the permanency thesis it argues for.

The early Nyāya school, however, disallowed human intervention in language which would lead to the establishment of a purely human convention, as with the case of proper nouns and technical names, although it agreed that the convention established by God may undergo some variation at the hands of the human. And, further, the more varied the groups of humans, the more varied will be the meaning or 'sense'. But Vātsyāyana comments: 'The regulating capacity is not fixed in the cases of different groups of people (*jātiviśeṣa*), and they differ among the seers (*ṛṣis*), the noble ones (*āryas*) and the barbarians (*mlecchas*).'[41]

While the later Nyāya did allow for purely human convention to establish the relation between word and its meaning. When the conventional relation (*saṃketa*), is said to be established by the will of God, it is permanent and is called *abhidhā* or *śakti*; when it is established by the will of the human it is called *paribhāṣā*.[42] Jagadīśa attributing a similar view to Bhartṛhari quotes him as saying: '*Saṃketa* is of two kinds, *ājānika* or permanent, and *ādhunika* or modern; the former is the permanent primary relation, while the latter refers to the technical terms with their specialised and well-defined meanings, coined by writers of various scientific word.'[43] However, some in Nyāya school who came after Jagadīśa, though they accepted human conventionality, argued that ultimately such relations (*saṃketa*), were imbued with the *śakti* of God. Viśvanātha asserts that recent names also possess *śakti*, for (behind them) there is the divine will; and he gives an example accordingly: 'On the eleventh day, a father should name his child.' He continues, 'one school (the early Nyāya) holds that more recent (i.e. proper and technical) names possess no signification function (*śakti*).' The new school (Navya-nyāya), however, maintains that it is not the divine will that constitutes signification function, but any will. Hence even recent names possess *śakti*.[44] For example, *nadī* is a *vācaka* or articulated utterance, which with the help of the desire of God, denotes *river*. However, Pāṇini developed a system of grammatical terms in which *nadī* was used to signify something quite totally different from river. This use of *nadī* is said to be *pāribhāṣā-saṃketaḥ*. But Viśvanātha would argue that even then this could not have arisen without the *śakti* of God (as though looming somewhere in the background) that influenced or inspired Pāṇini to attribute such a *saṃketa* to *nadī*. Of course Pāṇinians would want to reserve their judgments on this matter.

The final objection of Nyāya against Mīmāṃsā is that *śakti* is not a separate category of existent (*padārtha*), it is rather subsumed under the accepted categories, and it is cumbersome to assume a *reality* for it over and above the accepted 'reals'. Dharmarāja retorts against the Nyāya objection to this point, by arguing that in any cause the power that produces the effect is a distinct entity (*padārtha*).[45] In other words, *padārtha* consists in the measure of a power (potential cause) instrumental in any causal process that produces an effect, such causal power or *śakti* is considered to be a distinct relation *vṛtti* (which Nyāya accepts) as well as a separate reality, *padārtha* (which Nyāya rejects).

3.13 Mīmāṃsā takes a rather defensive stance against the Nyāya objections and presents the following counterargument.[46] If the signification of a word is something created by some sort of a convention among humans, then there are only three ways on which this convention could function, (*a.*) a convention would be set up for the benefit of each person—each one being told that 'Such is the meaning of this word', or (*b.*) this convention would be set up each time the word is pronounced; or (*c.*) the convention would be set up by God for all time, at the time of creation. Now, under the first alternative (*a*) would the relationship established by such convention be one and the same for all persons, or would it be different with each individual? If it is one and the same for all, then it cannot be artificial; and the idea of its being diverse and different would be contrary to all experience. As for the second alternative (*b*) it is an impossibility, since a single utterance and the convention based thereupon can never fix *for all time* the convention between the word and its signification; nor could it account for the usage of the same for all time. As for the third alternative (*c*), in the first place, there is no such thing as the 'time' when there was a beginning of the world; and secondly, there is no God or 'creator' of the world (as Nyāya understands one), who could establish the convention. Kumārila goes on to argue that, even granting that there has been creation, the Vedas and the component words therein and their respective significations must have been in existence even before that, since the Vedas are '*śruti*,' 'in timeless hearing'; and the said relation between those words and their meanings could have had no beginning in time.

Having said this, Kumārila then presents his final view on the matter in dispute: In fact, in connection with all *verbal expression*, what happens is that when the inexperienced youth hears the use of certain words for the first time from people more experienced than him, he perceives the word-sound [coming] from the experienced persons, and the material objects handled by them in the course of their conversation. The fact that the person addressed has understood the meaning of the words used by other persons, is *inferred* by the speaker from the resultant activity of the person addressed. After which the speaker presumes the words to have *potency* or capacity to express what has been comprehended by the persons addressed, for without such potency the phenomenon noticed would be pretty well unaccounted for. Thus the presence of the relationship between the word and its signification is got at and comprehended through three means of cognition, viz. perception, inference and presupposition (*arthāpatti*).[47]

Mīmāṃsā would not allow for human conventionality even when it comes to accounting for the variations that emerge in human speech. According to Pārthasārathi, what variations there may be, could be attributed to the various aspects or functions related to the one signification capacity—such as *lakṣaṇā*, or the secondary function to imply a sense, *vyañjanā*, the suggestive function, and so forth. Pārthasārathi Miśra insists that 'the relation between the word and that which is signified is fixed and eternal and as such there is no possibility of human intervention therein.'[48] The relation is described as one between that which is signified and that which signifies: *pratyāyya* and *pratyāyaka*. Even without any other relations existing, the word by its very nature becomes expressive of the meaning (*pratyāyaka*) and the *meaning* is the signified (*pratyāyya*), and this itself constitutes the relation. Pārthasārathi explains, 'the word which expresses the meaning without depending on object-contact as do the senses, is called *abhidhāna* (which is another term for the significatory power of *śakti*), and relation is what is known as '*samjñā-samjñitva*—designation and the designated'. This relation (*prāpti-sambandha*) is considered to be a distinct category which is essential to the structure of language.'[49]

3.14 It may be argued, however, that there are cases where the relation between the word and meaning is one which is conventionally determined, or a conjunction (*saṃyoga*) as intended by the speaker in the particular context of its utterance. Every now and then a totally new word comes into vogue, which has a certain meaning associated with it, signifying something for which there may be no other word in the lexicon or in general parlance. For example, the term 'ball-point pen' came into being after the invention of a writing instrument making use of an inking ball-bearing in place of the time-honoured nib at the end of the inked scriber. And further, the significance of a word may vary in different ways when it appears in combination with other words, in expressions, that are contained in such phrases, clauses and sentences. For example "dog" in the sentence 'My dog is dark brown', and in the sentence 'A wolf is not a dog'. In the first expression "dog" has a definite *referent* corresponding to the individual dog of which I have a picture in my mind; while in the case of the second expression, "dog" does not have as its referent something as concrete and real in the world—viz. a biped—which corresponds to the cognitive content thus evoked. Most words, like "dog", "table", "book", have referents, but in certain contexts of their use, or usage, they do not perform an object-referring function. But this does not mean that such words in such contexts have no significance. What they do, or may, have in each such case, is one *aspect* of the signification which it is within the capacity of the word to have—namely, a "sense' or a mode of signification through the concept signified.

Ogden and Richards make a similar point when they distinguish a 'referent' from a 'reference' (our *referend*)—*signifié* of de Saussure—of a word: 'In stating that what they (words) direct and organise, record and communicate we have to distinguish as always between Thoughts and Things.'[50] The term "thought" corresponds to our use of *referend* or *concept-content*, which Ogden and Richards have called *reference*, and "thing" to our use of *referent*. They add that whilst there is a direct relation between symbols (word-forms) and *thought*, 'between the symbol and the *referent* there is no relevant relation other than the indirect one which consists in its being used to stand for a referent.'[51] Indeed, Mīmāṃsā also has a way of explaining the relation to referents by invoking the capacity of *lakṣaṇā* whereby individuals are designated indirectly through the direct signification, which for Mīmāṃsā is the genus or class, *qua referend*. But if there is some sense in making the distinction between signification as *referend* and 'signification' as (the) *referent* through the function of *use* or *reference* (or sense-relation(s)), then we can say that the relative fixity that there may be between word and its signification is in respect of its essential signification as the *referend qua concept* signified, not in respect of the *referent*, or 'object' it points to, or denotes, which may vary from one situation to another. It is also to be noted that by 'relative fixity' we do not mean an immutable relation which cannot in any way be varied by human intervention, as some Mīmāṃsā scholars (notably Pārthasārathi) would have it.

In reflecting on this discussion it may be of interest to pause a while to consider a somewhat similar remark from Ogdens and Richards, who write that: 'What is fixed is the reference [*referend*] which any member of (a) group will make in interpreting a symbol on any occasion within the relevant universe of discourse. It is no doubt very important that these meanings should not vary beyond narrow limits. But we may be legitimately anxious to maintain uniform standards of comparison without finding it necessary to presuppose them supernaturally established or in their own nature immutable.'[52]

3.15 It should not, though, be assumed that we are denying the inherent relation between word and its signification, in terms of its capacity to have *significance*. We defined 'signification' as the *power* or capacity a word has that enables it to obtain the same meaning in its recurrent uses; this is the capacity that enables the word *to convey the same meaning* through each use in language—that is to say, it enables the word to perform the same function, or aspect of the same function. This capacity, however, is not dependent on the *use* of the word, though the meaning or sense that a particular utterance has may not be obvious without observing how the word has been used in that context. But the *use* of the word need not be taken to be the sole determinant of the signification *qua śakti* of the word, nor also where meaning is invariably detected, though it is a place to look for one function of the basic signification. The point is subtle, and more needs to be said, as we shall do in a while.

The word has a 'formal function' in its primary capacity quite apart from its occurrence or use in an act of speech where its meaning is manifested. We are interested, all the same, in the function in respect of its meaning or 'signification', i.e. the many aspects of meaning a word may have. When we talk about one or other of the aspects of meaning we shall use the term 'significance', and shall describe the aspects as 'primary' or 'express', 'secondary' or extended, *significances*. We have earlier indicated that signification is more than just any one thing: essentially it is the *concept-content*, through which a word denotes, designates, indicates, points to, or refers to an object (the *referent*). Each of these are sometimes referred to as the different *significances* a word may have or manifest in different speech-acts. We shall now endeavour to examine the notion of *significance* as understood in the Advaita view.

3.16 The word, we said, has a power of effecting a certain attention, or communication when used in an act of speech. Now, the psychic act that follows the hearing or reading of a word on the part of another, can be any one or more of the following : thinking, imaging, feeling, judging. And the intentional or psychic contents corresponding to these acts can be described as idea, image, emotion, attitude and so forth. But none of them may be taken to constitute *meaning* in every instance of the act, for it may be that one uses a word to point to, or refer to a particular object, in which case the word would stand not for the idea or image, but for the 'object' referred to or designated by it.

But the referent may vary from one context of its use to another, and there must be some common intermediary through which *reference* is made to different things that are indirectly related to the word, or to its primary significance. And this intermediary is obviously the 'thought', 'idea',or 'image' that is evoked upon hearing the word, and through which the corresponding 'object' is referred to. The sameness of thought evoked would account for the sameness of the act of referring; but, as we pointed out earlier, only through being directly related to a thought, idea or image. Which is to say that a word has a corresponding psychic content to which it is related, and which accounts for the relation between the word and its significance, in different usages, where the significance may be *lakṣaṇā*, 'indicative sense' or 'implication', or perhaps 'suggestion', or even 'metaphor'. For otherwise, it may be argued, how could a word without a psychic-content evoked by it succeed in making reference to the same object or entity at different instances of its occurrence. It can be argued that it is through the psychic-content that reference is made, and that this is due to the identity of some such content in different uses and usages, with the consequence that there is the sameness of 'meaning' or signification.

The image, ideas, and attitudes evoked in each mind, however, are again capable of being as variant as the objects they refer to, for no two psyches mental states can be said to have an identical *viṣayatā* or noematic *Sinn* of anything. Therefore, we should postulate another 'element' associated with the words, which as 'entities' outside the minds of the speakers or audience, function to evoke the same images, ideas and so on in different psyches—or at least to convey the same significance. And this common factor is most needed in the use of words for the purposes of expressing and connoting 'attitudes' for which there are no corresponding objects as such outside in the world of everyday experience—though there may be some 'objects' in some other realm of existential possibility (*apūrva*). Whatever this 'locale of meaning' is, we shall regard it as the *concept-content* as distinct from the mental or psychic contents of images, ideas, feelings, attitudes. This *concept-content* is primarily the signification of the word, i.e. its *referend*, distinguished from the *referent* which is its reference or 'object' designated in an act of referring. The 'content' itself is more specifically a *concept* ('thought' in continental systems), and this is what the word *stands for, ipso facto*, independently of what image, idea, attitude or 'feeling', it evokes in the mind of the hearer. We have here made a distinction between *concepts*, as the essential *referend qua* the signification of the word, and the images, ideas, and so on, its use may evoke, as identifying correlates; and it is further distinguished from the 'object' or referent it may point to or indicate. In our discussion of meaning, the *concept-content* (the *referend*), and the *referential function* in use, which are the two most relevant dimensions of meaning-relation or *śakti*, significatory power, are given greater prominence over the subjective features of ideas, images, emotion and so on which are contingent upon the function of words in communication. The *concept-content* of the word is what we have already spoken of as the *referend*—the *vācaka* (i.e. the expressive) of the grammarians[53] which contains within it the modes of signification; and the *referent* aspect is identified with the *artha*, 'object' corresponding to the reference in the act of referring. *Significance* and the *referent*, may vary from one context to another. The *significance* is in the act of speaking (or writing) the word, and it links the *referend* with the *referent*.

The two meaning functions of *significance* and *referent* have parallels in Frege's own distinction between '*Sinn*' and '*Bedeutung*', the former of which is rendered as "sense", or as "meaning" by some; the latter is rendered as "indication" by Russell, and "reference" by Geach and Black.[54] However, since Frege's distinction does not concern itself with the *referend* so centrally in our tripartite analysis of meaning (except perhaps for his "*thought*"), we shall adopt the following convention. We shall continue to use *referend* for the "stuff" of signification identified with the *concept-content* (in an ideal hearer); and *significance* as the specific mode of signification, even more specifically as 'sense', and *referent* for the 'thing' (as the *individual* of Russell, and *fact*[55] of Wittgenstein) indicated, or pointed – if such is at all – as the 'object' ('ens', 'entity', or "event") of reference. Here *significance* or 'sense' stands for that which is signified or expressed, while its *referent*, identified with the 'thing' or 'object of reference', is what is indicated or denoted in an act of referring. And both the *vācyas* could be indirectly expressed or connoted in altered circumstances.

C. *The linguistic functions of meaning*

3.17 We are now in a position to represent the meaning-relation or *signification qua śakti* in terms of the triadic relations we have identified with the word in such functions, viz. the *referend* (*vācaka*), the *significance* ('sense') and the *referent* (*padārtha*). Though it is common in Indian linguistics to refer to all three as *artha* (particularly as Nyāya disregards the first), we have adopted a slightly different convention, and use *artha* for the significance-function identified as the *significance*, and *padārtha* ('object') for the *referent*, i.e. object of reference. The confusion that might arise through *padārtha* also continuing to stand for 'word-meaning' will be clarified by indicating the sense we intend in use of the term. We shall first present the classical representation in early Western linguistics[56] in order to show and stress the essential differences and departure of the Indian theories, at least on the Advaita presentation of it. Here we take issue with Kunjunni Raja's tendency to see overwhelming similarities.

Hence, for a word to have meaning, it would *ex hypothesi*, have a *referend*, i.e. a *concept-content* in an ideal speaker or hearer, which functions to manifest the *sense* or the significance in the act of referring. This may be contrasted with Husserl's ideality of meaning thesis. This *concept-content* is one, and the fundamental aspect of the word, to which is directly related the *significance*, and indirectly the corresponding *referent*, or 'object of

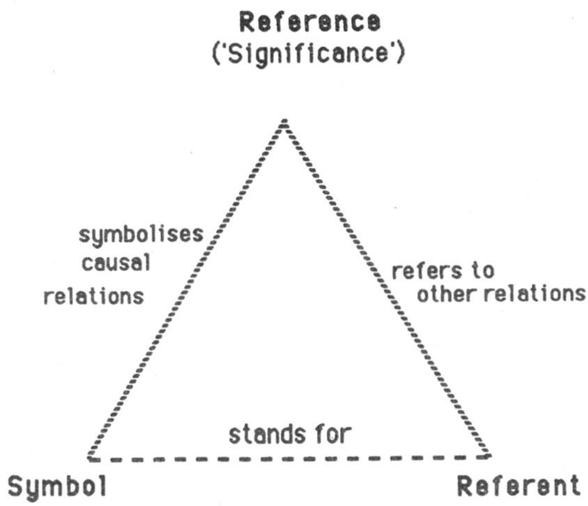

Fig I (Standard)

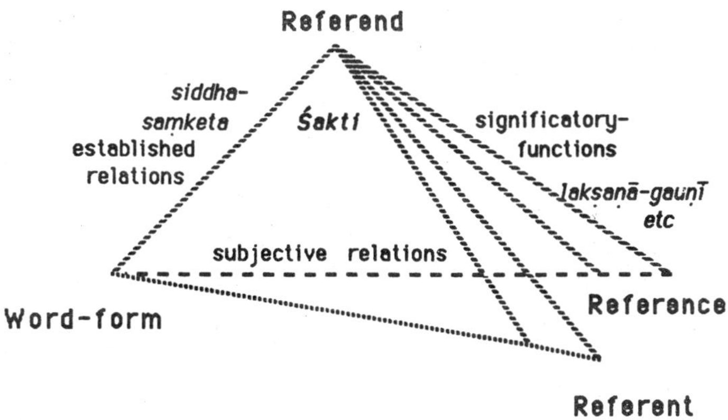

Fig.II (Advaita-Mīmāṃsā)

Diagramatic representation of meaning relations

reference'. But as we said, the *referend* need not have the same *significance* in different uses as this is a function of a subjective relation which necessarily changes from time to time and speaker to speaker; nor need there be the same significance-function in each use—or usages; nor need the *referent* be one and the same object in each use—for instance, "my dog", "your dog", "his dog". Indeed, it is not mandatory for it to have a *referent* in each use. Its *sense* may be such that it merely points to an idea or thought in someone else's mind who may be describing such an 'object', as for instance, when I relate the story about the 'wandering dog' I heard in childhood from my grandmother. On the other hand, the same object, for instance, 'that dog', may be the reference in different modes of signification using different words or expressions. We shall return to these points shortly.

What we are interested in doing now is explicating the different 'modes of signification' or the different *significances qua* different functional relations a word may evince. The Indian theories are unanimous in attributing at least two such functional relations, one primary and one secondary. *Śakti*, the significatory capacity we have been dealing with so far, is isolated as the primary function, *mukhyavṛtti*, while *lakṣaṇā* is identified as the secondary function. The significance got from the primary signification function is called *śakyārtha* or *abhidhārtha* or *vācyārtha* (*mukhyārtha*)—the primary sense or significance. And the significance called up by the secondary function is called *lakṣyārtha* or simply *lakṣya*. The word which possesses the 'power' to manifest the 'implied' significance is called *lakṣaṇā*. For its 'implied' significance it depends upon the primary signification function in such occurrences where the express significance fails to yield the 'sense' pertinent to the context of the word's utterance. There could be various 'degrees' of implications (*lakṣaṇā*) in different contexts, and it is to this analysis that we now turn.

3.18 Firstly we will make some general comments about the various dimensions of significance a word is said to have in virtue of its inherent *śakti* or significatory power. Most Indian grammarians accept the word to have three basic significance-functions, namely, *śakti*, or *abhidhā*, *lakṣaṇā* and *vyañjanā*, irrespective of whether the relation between the word and meaning is reckoned to be established by either divine or human convention. The most significant function of these however is *śakti*, which is the chief or 'primary' (*mukhya*) functional relation. The secondary significance is *lakṣaṇā*, which is the *indirect* capacity of the word. This depends functionally on *śakti*. Annaṃbhaṭṭa argues that *vyañjanā* or the 'suggestive power' of the word is not an indépendent relation (*vṛtti*). More will be said on this later. As for *lakṣaṇā*, the condition that calls for its use is said not to be 'syntax difficulty' (*anvayānupapatti*) but 'purport or intentionality discrepancy' (*tātparyānupapatti*).[57] The two functions are further divided into sub-functions of types, according to whether or not they are needed in speech. The four divisions of *śakti* are *yaugika, rūḍha, yoga-rūḍha, and yaugi-rūḍha.*[58] And *lakṣaṇā* is divided into three forms, viz. *jahal-lakṣaṇā, ajahal-lakṣaṇā, and jahad-ajahal-lakṣaṇā.* These are divisions of what is called simple and implicative functions, *kevala lakṣaṇā.* There is said to be another category of *lakṣaṇā* which is derived from this. This is called *lakṣit-lakṣaṇā or gauṇī*, which means 'indirect implication function'. It yields an indirect implication, as distinct from the more direct implication of simple *lakṣaṇā*. It will of course not be possible, nor necessary to go into any great detail about this, except for the two important functions, namely *abhidhā* (primary) and *lakṣaṇā* (secondary) in view of their significant role in the generation of *śābdabodha.*

The Advaita approach

3.19 Now *śakti* or *abhidhā* is the main function of the word with regard to its meaning. The function consists in the word being competent to signify such and such; for example, the word "pot" has the significance-function with regard to the *concept* of a particular thing by a broad-bottom hollow[59] – that is to say, the word "pot" has the function of denoting an object of such a description.

Now, what is most commonly and generally signified by a word is its *direct* significance (*śakyārtha*). That is to say, when the reference to that which a word signifies or denotes is direct the significatory power used here is *śakti*. This accounts, for example, when I point to a massive stream of flowing water within the confines of the two banks and say "river". But if I were to say "the goddess Gaṅgā [Ganges]", instead of "river", my reference to the river is *indirect* for I am implying a reference to the river through the goddess Gaṅgā – with whom, for some Hindus, the river is associated. The expression "goddess Gaṅgā" then helps me to make an indirect reference to the river; the signification function with regard to the river is *indirect*. It is unlike *śakti* whose reference to the river is *indirect*. However, in the context of illustrating the Hindu pantheon, if I were to use the same words "goddess Gaṅgā" to refer to the goddess who is said to flow out in the form of a stream of water from the head of the god Śiva, then I would be making a direct reference to the goddess and not to the river as such. Here I would be using the direct signification function of the words "goddess Gaṅgā".

But in the earlier use, the reference was to the river, and thus an indirect one. Again, this *indirect* significatory 'power' of a word, like the direct one, consists in its relation to that which is signified. But while in the case of 'śakti, a word signifies something directly, i.e., without the mediation of any other property or association of the word, in the case of *lakṣaṇā*, a word signifies something indirectly, i.e. through the mediation of that property which has been described as *śakti* or *abhidhā*. The signification relation that is known as *lakṣaṇā* is *indirect* in as much as it is the relation of a word to something that in its turn has a close relation to its object of reference in virtue of the primary capacity (*śakti*).[60] And it is through the awareness of the *śakti* of a word that its implicative function (*lakṣaṇā*) is known in any utterance in which such is utilised.

We may give an example using the case of Gaṅgā [Ganges] again in a slightly different context. Thiru A from south India goes with a friend B. to the river Gaṅgā in the north. They are told by their guide, 'This is Gaṅgā', whereupon B begins to recant with reverence how affectionate and comforting Gaṅgā is, as he bows and sprinkles water scooped from the river over himself. Now B, a visitor from abroad, appears to be a little puzzled by the ritualistic act and moving remarks of A, and so asks the latter whether he meant the river was being affectionate to him in some special way. Whereupon A. replies that he meant the *goddess* Gaṅgā is affectionate and comforting, and that it is to the goddess that his solemn act and remarks are directed. Here then is a clear case of someone using a particular word to indicate not what is signified or directly referred to, but to make reference to a 'sense' associated with the primary 'power' of the word and by virtue of which the word assumes an indirect signification function, which helps the visitor to make sense of the indirect reference—in this instance to the goddess Gaṅgā, which in the Hindu belief is associated with the river Ganges.

3.20 To reiterate a little more on *lakṣaṇā*, it is not unusual in speech to come across occurrences of words with meanings that may lead them to connote or signify more meanings or 'sense' than given in their express significations. For instance, a person turns around to another who is in a rage of anger, and calls him a "lion". Clearly, the angry person is not a *lion*, but the typical characteristics, such as ferocity, maybe violence, temper and so on, that he exudes in this state, are comparable to those associated normally with a lion. Thus, by virtue of an extension of the primary signification (*abhidhā*) of the word 'lion' characteristics of the lion are connoted in the use of the word in a context that are different from its usual occurrence. Here we say that the word is used in a way that may apply to a person who displays certain characteristics of behaviour comparable to those of a lion. This manner or mode of signifying a human is not primarily the signification function of the word 'lion', nor is the animal, *lion*, the direct reference of this utterance. This indirect mode of signification is regarded as a distinct linguistic function in respect of *lakṣaṇā*.

This category (*vṛtti*) marks the second significatory function or job-aspect of words in respect of their significance, i.e. the possibility of the word relating itself to another and other *significances* indirectly through its direct relation to its primary significance. The "new" function that the word assumes in such uses is not a new *padārtha* or existential category, but rather an extension of the chief (*mukhya*) signification function of the word and it comes to be related to this indirectly through the mediation of the *śakti* of the word.

The operation of this distinct but not separate function of *lakṣaṇā* may not be obvious in all cases, as it escaped the notice of the guide in the earlier example. But being a function that necessarily depends on the primary function, it is termed 'extended' or 'secondary' or 'indicated' or 'implied', and the *meaning* or actual significance yielded in such modes as *lakṣyārtha* or *indicative sense* (sometimes, 'implied sense') as distinct from the primary or express 'sense"—*śakyārtha*, i.e. *abhidhārtha* (or *vācyārtha or mukhyārtha*). This secondary signification function of words in certain circumstance of their occurrence, is particularly relevant to the analysis of *śābdabodha* since it explains how two or more words, or expressions, apparently denoting different "things" can be understood to be signifying or connoting an *identity relation* between the referents that appear to be disparate and yet related through their implied senses (*lakṣyārthas*). In so doing, we are given a *synthetic* judgment, which informs us of something we may not have known earlier. This mode of signification, then, as a linguistic device, could be said to give us an *understanding* that was hitherto unrealised by us, and which is therefore *novel*.

Thus, we see that *lakṣaṇā* fulfills an important epistemological function in sentence-meaning comprehension or *śābdabodha*, and it is precisely this that makes language such a good instrument of knowing.

3.21 It would appear from the Mīmāṃsā view of the immutable relation between word and meaning (as against the conventionalist views), coupled with the Jaiminian reservations about synonyms *(paryāyaśabda)*, that Mīmāṃsā would not accept the view that argues for a word to have more than one meaning or 'sense' for the reason that one word would be related more permanently to more than one meaning, and one meaning to more than one word. To check against the corruption of words, Jaimini ruled that 'it was not proper to assume many words (expressing the same meaning)': *anyāyaścānekaśabdatvam* (*MS* I.iii.26).

A corollary of this, given also the Jaiminian 'originary' or the *autpat-*

tika conditional, would be that it is not appropriate for a word to have many senses, as each word has its own potential with respect to its specific signification.

Of course, this does not mean, as Sabara points out, that synonyms are not accepted in the system, especially in normal speech if not in scriptural language,[61] nor that the 'implied sense' of words that is not sought after in interpreting Vedic texts. Śabara admits that humans understand words in different ways as a function of their speech: *evam ayaṃ puruṣo veda iti bhavati pratyayaḥ* (under *MS* 1.i.2). Though Mīmāṃsā would not agree that because the 'extended' sense is acceptable under certain circumstances that this is due to a distinct significatory power of the word other than its *śakti. Lakṣaṇā* as a dependent *vṛtti* is certainly admitted in Mīmāṃsā, and regarded (in Bhaṭṭa) to be important for two basic functions in speech – viz. (a) for indicating the individual of a word which primarily signifies a *class*; and (b) for 'revealing' the sentence-meaning based on *tātparyānupapatti* (intentional impropriety) which is resolved through *lakṣaṇā.*

Mīmāṃsā, while accepting the application or rather use of *lakṣaṇā*, calls for certain strictures in the use of synonyms and 'corrupt forms' (*apabhraṃśas*). Mīmāṃsā argues that if the meanings are so radically different then we have to assume that the words are not the same – that is, they are not different merely in respect of their signification, but are different words, though they may look alike. This can be taken to be valid in the case, say, of homophones, e.g. 'bear' [noun], 'bear' [verb], and homonyms, e.g. 'bare', 'bear'. These words, though they appear and sound alike, are different in respect of their meanings, as they are derived from different etymologies. Similarly, the English "ear" and "ear" are different words too as they signify different things – viz. a part of a body, and parts of cereal, such as wheat, barley, etc. respectively.[62] The same form 'ear' in both instances is derived from completely different roots that have completely different meanings as well – namely, *eare* for one, and *ear* for the other. The same could also be said of '*saindhava*', which means 'salt' as well as 'horse', but they are two different words since there is no connection between their respective meanings.

Mīmāṃsā would agree, though, that the strictures stipulated do not hold unequivocally for every pair of words, or "forms" of words that merely appear to be the same, for there are clear instances of the same word which functions to signify different, but related, meanings in certain usages. Mīmāṃsā would agree, for example, under its category of *sādṛśya*[63] that the use, or usage rather, of 'lion' in the earlier example is a case in point. But the same can be demonstrated with many other words also. For example, '*pravīṇa*' is a word which primarily signified 'good at playing on the *vīṇa*' (an ancient string instrument), and on account of the intensely demanding training and experience, and expertise acquired on the part of the musician, the word is commonly used in a metaphorical sense to mean simply 'having expertise', implying that the formidable and challenging task at hand is not beyond the individual in question. Thus, when the epithet *pravīṇa* is used to applaud the job done by a pilot, it does not mean that he has played the *vīṇa* superbly, but that he has shown remarkable *expertise* in his job in flying aeroplanes. Another word used in certain circumstances with the implication of *expertise* or proficiency is *kuśala*, but which primarily denotes 'one who is good at mowing grass or hay', since the word is formed from the root √*kuśa*, meaning *grass*. Now when the baker is commended for his excellent baking with the appellative *kuśala*, there is no intention to suggest that he is also good at mowing. But clearly, having an expertise in baking is not the primary or 'express' function of the word *kuśala*; likewise, being an adept at cutting grass is not the secondary or 'indicative' function of the same word used in a context different to its normal occurrence. All the same, what the word retains in both uses is the "core" sense associated with its the express function – viz. *proficiency*. It is this flexibility and indirectness of meaning which a word is capable of manifesting in different contexts of its occurrence that is attributed to the *lakṣaṇā* potential.

3.22 What, however, are the conditions that would ideally determine the shift or deviation from the express to the secondary sense? At least two conditions are discerned from empirical observation. One is in respect of the unsuitability or incompatibility of the express meaning to convey the 'purport' or intention of the speaker appropriate to the context.[64] The other is the indirect relation that a 'thing', event or situation may have with the primary meaning of the word, but which (express) meaning itself is not adequate in that context. To these we may add a fourth, namely, popular usage.[65] There may be some factors or elements too that may sanction a shift in the meaning of a word or expression in a particular context of its occurrence, such as simple conventions (e.g."Good morning", even on a decisively depressing beginning of the day), *via* poetical licence, and literary style in certain era.[66] But the most common condition among these is the first one. Nyāya also agrees that the inappropriateness of the primary meaning to the context of its occurrence naturally leads to the speculation whether an extension of the primary sense is more suitable to the circumstance, an adoption of which would yield the expected or intended understanding (*tātparyānupapattilakṣaṇābījam*). Thus, the association of 'lion' with Rāma's father in his state of ferocious anger leads the hearer to make the inverse inference (*arthāpatti*): 'One similar to a lion in anger, etc.'[67]

To take yet another example widely used in literature to illustrate this function, the expression *gaṅgāyāṃ ghoṣaḥ*, which translates as : 'The village (is) *in* the Gaṅgā (Ganges river)', is found to be worrying in that, if *gaṅgāyām* is taken in the literal or express sense, the village would be said to be "in the river (Gaṅgā)". But this is not compatible with the sense intended in this context, since the village is not located in the *pravahāḥ*, the rapid waters of the river, unlike say the house boats are in Lake Dal in Srinigar. The utterance 'the village in the Ganges' would not be intelligible *prima facie* at least to one hearing it. But as soon as he postulates another meaning, an indirect sense related to the primary meaning of *gaṅgāyām* through something that is known about any river—river itself being indirectly signified in *gaṅgā*—viz. its relation to the bank or banks is apprehended.

Thus, through this indirect association, *gaṅgāyām* is taken to mean "on the *bank* of the river (Ganges)". Hence, the *arthāpatti* derived is that the village is on the bank of the (river) Ganges. The expression then does not remain unintelligible any more than it did on hearing it. Since this indirect significance is only occasionally and not normally resorted to, the particular function is kept distinct from the more express and usual *śakyārtha* or primary meaning. It is important, however, to stress the essential *connectness* of the two meaning-functions or job-aspects of the same word.

The word '*saindhava*' provides a splendid contrast in way of illustration. Etymologically, it means 'that which is found in the land known as Sindhu' and in actual use it stands for both, a kind of 'salt' (i.e. rock-salt) and a kind of 'horse'. Now, these two things signified by the word *saindhava* are unconnected with each other and therefore the same distinction as made, say, between (the direct or expressive sense of) 'river' and (the indirect derivation of) 'bank' does not apply in this case. As Annaṃbhaṭṭa makes it clear, both the significances (of 'salt' and 'horse') are equally 'direct' or primary, and the word in question is often equivocally used to mean now one, now the other. For this reason such words are said to have *nānāśakti* or *multiple significatory power.*[68]

A problem, though, arises in the case of verbs and *verb*al bases: there is no agreement among Indian linguists as to whether *lakṣaṇā* is or is not to be admitted in such cases. Generally speaking, Mîmāṃsā accepts *lakṣaṇā* in the case of verbal forms, as the 'action' word is one among the many words embedded in a sentence whose whole-sense has to be derived through *lakṣaṇā*. In Nyāya, the function of *lakṣaṇā* with respect to verbal form would be restricted to specific cases where the context or the linguistic environment definitely requires this, otherwise the primary meaning should suffice; although Jagadīśa seems to be ambivalent on this point.[69]

It should be noted, however, that the secondary sense wherever it is required, is not comprehended directly from the word, but only indirectly through its function as signifying the primary and conventional meaning (*abhidhārtha*). Normally, the understanding that arises is in terms of the express sense, but where this is found to be non-intelligible or incompatible in the context, then one avails oneself of *lakṣaṇā* to obtain the connected implied sense. Also, it is emphasised by Dharmarāja that the 'incompatibility' or 'unsuitability' that one detects in such non-intelligible expressions is not in virtue of the *syntactical* relation among its component words, which may be quite intact, but in virtue of the *intentionality* of the utterance in the particular context of its occurrence [*VP* IV.30].

Two examples seem to support this qualification. Consider the expression: 'let the curd be protected from the crows.'[70] Here the primary meaning of the word *kāka* ('crow') is not inexplicable in the context, for the curd has to be kept away from crows; but crows as such are not the only threat to the curd, since other birds and animals, such as magpies, cats and dogs, are equally likely to spoil the curd, and thus, by implication, the cautionary advice includes protection from crows as well as threatening non-crows. The second example that is commonly mentioned is that about the village on the river, which we have already considered. Here too, the expression is syntactically immaculate, but the (semantical) problem arises in view of the incompatibility of the express meaning with the intended sense.

Lakṣit-lakṣaṇā

3.23 The third use of *lakṣaṇā*, as mentioned earlier, occurs in the popular or conventional usage of a word or expression in its implied or indicative sense. But one that is widely understood and has become popularly accepted. For example, the expression 'Adam's apple', primarily referred to a biblical legend, but gradually came to be used as a name for the vocal bone on the upper neck below the chin.

It may be remarked that sometimes the shift or transference from the primary to the secondary noun can, through popular usage, become so prominent and regular, that in time its original significance may be forgotten. This is more apparent with certain cryptic expressions than with individual words. 'Adam's apple' is a case in point. The *apple* that Adam supposedly ate in the Garden of Eden in time came to be associated with the natural bone that protudes from the neck of a large number of men, as though it was the same forbidden fruit that the first created man ate, or half ate, bringing thereby a wrath on all man thereafter. Thus, the protuded bone is assumed to be a symbol of that curse (of mortality).

However, this particular prophetic association is no longer evidenced in normal parlance, as, say, when the doctor examining a patient passes a comment about his Adam's apple. One might say that the expression makes a *primary* or direct reference to an object which is quite unrelated, in the mind of the speaker at least, to the alleged event through which it acquired currency in the first instance. And if the doctor wanted to make allusions, in passing, back to the biblical incident or the curse, he would have to invoke another *lakṣaṇā* if the patient is now to understand the non-clinical significance of the same expression uttered in a slightly altered context *qua* the intention of the speaker.

This form of *lakṣaṇā* is called *lakṣit-lakṣaṇā* or double-implication.[71] Likewise, when philosophers speak of exorcising Descartes' 'ghost' from the mind-body problem, they are making allusions, *via* double-implication, to the unrelenting influence of Descartes, particularly through his postulation of a categorically distinct entity of the 'mind' lodged as it were in the corporeal structure, as would a ghost in a possessed body (a description attributed by Gilbert Ryle).

Lakṣaṇā is therefore of considerable importance in linguistic comprehension. Indeed, it is one of the major devices utilised in scriptural expressions, particularly when a philosopher-seer is not able to give full expression within the available language to his insight or 'vision'. By manipulating words and expressions in particular ways, his narrative begins to communicate his perception and understanding of whatever problem he was concerned to address.

3.24 There are three or four major kinds of *lakṣaṇā* recognised, each one marking the extent to which the meaning shifts from the primary to the secondary. We have mentioned one of these in the example related to Adam's apple, namely, *lakṣit-lakṣaṇā*. The other two are : *jahal-lakṣaṇā* and *ajahal-lakṣaṇā*. The first one occurs where there is a total eclipsing of the primary meaning by the secondary sense, since the primary meaning would be unnecessarily obstrusive to a satisfactory understanding of the expression. The shift is adequate then to render utterance intelligible to the audience. The utterance of "Eat poison" on the part of a father reprimanding his son who announces that he will be taking his meal with the next door neighbours whom the father does not particularly like. Now what the father means to say is not that the son should go and take some verminous potion, but that he might as well be doing that if he goes without any scruples next door for his meal. But the father would not wish the death of the son as would be entailed if the latter were to carry out what the expression states in its primary sense. The primary sense would have to be completely submerged if the warning sounded by the father is to have any real effect. The son, thus, would need to heed to the father's reproach which he derives from the secondary or implied sense of the expression.

Likewise, when someone tells another "Go to hell!", one scarcely is supposed to make a descend to the nether-regions; but unless this literal sense is stripped, as it were, from the expression, and the sense intended in virtue of the *lakṣaṇā* used here is supposed, one is not likely to understand the expression, regardless of whether the audience will be satisfied with such a response to his request from the speaker.

3.25 *Ajahal-lakṣaṇā* on the other hand is not exclusive of the primary meaning when the secondary is invoked: in other words, it is inclusive of the former where the latter is primarily intended. Here the primary sense is not modified, it may be specified according to the context, or restricted by its syntactic relation to other words in the expression. To give an example, the expression 'The flagstaffs enter' is considered: *kuntāḥ praviśanti*. The word *kuntāḥ* here indicates by implication the flagstaffs, but also that the men who carry the poles are entering (the hall or whatever), since it would be difficult to visualise the flagstaffs making an entrance without some persons bearing them. Thus, the primary meaning of flagstaff is not abandoned but is implicated in the secondary sense, namely, of flagstaff-bearers.

Another illumining example is with the use of the expression, 'Norwood forest comes to Yorkshire.'[72] Of course, a whole forest cannot suddenly move from one place to another. The expression, however, can be seen to imply that the inhabitants of the forest are felling the trees and carrying them to Yorkshire for the purpose of building shelters. Though the implication is that the forest-dwellers are moving to Yorkshire, the primary sense of their taking the forest with them, in some way, is not excluded in the intentionality of the utterance. This particular *lakṣaṇā* is unique in that it enables a word to convey two sense, boosting, so to say, the scope of the expression from a simple to a rather more complicated understanding than is actually intended.

The third in this category is *jahad-ajahal-lakṣaṇā*, which, as the name indicates, combines the two above, and is known as the paradoxically 'exclusive-inclusive' implication. What it means is that the primary meaning is partly included while simultaneously it is also partly excluded. A simple example is with the expression '*grāmo dagdhaḥ*: the village is burnt down'. But the village comprises more than the huts that have actually burnt down; the people, the animals and pets and the well, for example, have escaped the devastating blaze of the wild fire. Thus only a part of the primary meaning is included, while another part is excluded in the secondary sense relevant in the context of its utterance.

A better example, more widely proffered, is that of the expression '*So'yaṃ devadattaḥ*' : 'This is that Devadatta'. Here the term *saḥ*, 'that', refers to Devadatta as seen at a past place and time, while the term *ayam*, 'this', points to the same Devadatta who is present here and now. But clearly, 'This' and 'that' in their primary senses cannot be compatibly identified, since they each refer to an 'object' situated in contingently different time and place; nor can we assume unequivocally that the person qualified by 'this' and the person qualified by 'that' are the *same person in every respect*, for then this would render superfluous the function of the disparate terms 'this' and 'that'. We thus have to assume that some differentiating sense is intended by the use of these terms, and yet their respective senses are not so distinct as to be irreconciliable to yield a more *unified* understanding in respect of the different things or persons referred to in such expressions. In this context, then, the two terms, despite the differences in the qualifications primarily expressed, are extended in their scope to cross their reference to the same substantive, namely, to Devadatta [=D]. Hence, Devadatta [D*a*] seen at one time ($t1$) is the same as Devadatta [D*b*] seen at another time ($t2$), but the prevailing conditions at $t1$ and $t2$ are relatively different, hence we cannot have the equation $t1 = t2$. Intuitively, however, we wish to affirm : $t1[a] = t2[b]$, since $Da = Db$ in respect of the pure substantive **[D]** (that abides in its self-identity), that both sides of the equation refer to, but which in itself is a tautology. The way to resolve this impasse is to give up some part of the primary senses of 'this' and 'that' while retaining some others. What is given up is the denotations that seem to wedge too sharp a distinction between Devadatta seen at $t1$ ('this') and Devadatta seen at $t2$ ('that') as though they were different persons. What is retained is the common substantive connoted equally in the usage of both 'this' and 'that', i.e. in this context Devadatta. The relation thus made compatible in this way renders the expression intelligible in respect of the conflicting, therefore doubtful, identity of the person seen at different times.

3.26 The various *lakṣaṇās* discussed here are widely utilised in scriptural hermeneutics for purposes of communicating more complex understanding that are not so straightforwardly obvious, such as with the classical use of the cryptic expression *tat tvam asi* : 'you are *that*'.

To say something very briefly on this example, the function of the two major terms in the expression, namely, *tvam* (you) and *tat* (that), is analogous to the equation of 'this' and 'that' in the earlier example about Devadatta. Both terms are used for qualifying a common substantive which is itself not obvious from their primary meanings alone, but only becomes apparent when their secondary senses are grasped or made clear. The identity established through the unitary sense conveyed is that of the individual self (signified by 'you') and the universal self (signified by *tat* or *'that'*, i.e. the other Self or *Spirit*). This non-difference relation – or non-dualness (*advaitatva*) – is supposedly established through *ajahad-jahal-lakṣaṇā*. This locates the common denominator, as it were, between the denoted and the connoted senses of two terms used qualificatively in respect of what appear to be two distinct entities or individuals related syntactically in the same expression. Since this significatory function is related to a 'part' only of the secondary sense, it is also called *bhāga-lakṣaṇā* by Sadānanda in his *Vedāntasāra* (#167).

The larger metaphysical claim, however, beyond the linguistic description of what is involved in such an utterance – i.e. that regarding the *true* or real, ontological, identity between the individual and whatever is denoted by *'that'* (which could well be an empty term in the proposition) – is clearly not part of the present analysis; that particular claim goes beyond the convenient illustration intended here.

Gauṇī and vyañjanā

3.27 Apart from *lakṣaṇā*, there are other significant linguistic devices that are also capable of extending meanings or relevant senses that are not normally part of the primary signification of the word. In poetical writings, for instance, such devices are used profusedly for suggesting a variety of senses that words are not normally used to mean. Sometimes, the sense of a word is extended to such a range as to leave only a vague or remote connection with its primary meaning. Even its figurative sense may suggest more than one *sense*, most or all of which may seem appropriate to the context, and convey the understanding the author intends to, or so it may appear. We shall consider two such devices: *gauṇī and vyañjanā.*

Gauṇī makes for a sort of 'signification of similarity'. An example of this is given in the use of the word *dvirepha*, which literally means 'a word having two '*r*'s'. The sound of the two 'r's, however, resembles the sound of the two 'r's in the word *bhramara*, which refers to bees, and by implication to the buzzing noise made by the wings of the bees. By analogy, therefore, *dvirepha* is used to signify 'bee' as well. Here the function of the word *dvirepha* comes to denote a referent different from that given in its conventional or primary signification, but in some ways connected with it, through a relation of similarity. And this type of secondary signification function of word is called *gauṇī*.

The other type of figurative sense is accomplished through 'suggestion' or *vyañjanā*, which includes emotive, aesthetic, and other associated meanings, such as are generally prevalent in poetry. *Vyañjanā* in the form of *dhvani* is defined by Ānandavardhana, a follower of Bhartṛhari, in the context of poetics, as; 'that kind of poetry wherein, either the (conventional) meaning or the (conventional) word renders itself or its meaning secondary (respectively) and suggests the implied meaning, is designated by the learned as *dhvani* or 'suggestive poetry'.'[73] *Dhvani* here refers to the suggestive function of *vyañjanā* of words or expressions in poetry and drama. We need not go into details here, save give some examples to illustrate the significatory function.

We may also mention here that Ānandavardhana included within the indicative category of the meaning of an expression its contextual factors, such as intonation, stress, gesture and even the pure sound used in making utterances that complement the literal meaning. And while the literal meaning is simply the thought, or idea signified, the suggested sense could be one of the three: an idea, a figure of speech, or an emotion or 'mood' (*rasa*). To this list of suggested aesthetic sense, which Kālidāsa exploited in his literary masterpieces, and around which, in another context, Abhinavagupta developed a theory of poetics. For example, with the use of the word '*gaṅgā*' in a poem, the *dhvani*, unlike its primary sense, is not river, but maybe 'coolness' or tranquility, suggested by the mood the river evokes in one watching it. One of the celebrated illustrations taken from Sanskrit literature is from Vālmīki's Rāmāyaṇa, in a narrative which captures the grief expressed by Vālmīki as he watched a female bird shriek with terror following the death of its male companion brought about by an arrow supposedly shot by a hunter. Vālmīki spontaneously broke into these moving words: 'Hunter, may you never get any peace. You have killed one of the pair of krauñcas in the state of being carried away with love.' This expression conveys the subtle sense of *grief* without mentioning the word grief or any word similar to that: yet the sense intended is conveyed indirectly by the composite sense created through the juxtapositioning of such words as 'peace', 'killed', 'love', 'krauñcas' and so forth, in a rhythmic structure. Analysing the poetic expression, K.C. Pandeya describes in equally colourful language the agony of the author:

> '[Vālmīki] speaks not as Vālmīki, but as the female Krauñca universalized. He views the situation as the latter. He, therefore, experiences the loss of what was the dearest and most precious. This has meant to him the irrecoverable loss of peace of mind. He looks upon the hunter as the author of his perpetual grief. He feels his helplessness against the enemy. And, therefore, in the characteristic manner of a widowed woman [whose husband has been senselessly murdered], he curses the hunter with a lot very much worse than his own.'[74]

One variation of *dhvani* is *rasa*, which is given prominence in drama and theatrical enactments. For instance, to get across a deeper impact of the suggestive idea of tranquility and coolness evoked by the river Ganges, it may be useful to introduce this to the audience in the course of a scene that makes reference to the river Ganges. This could be achieved by the actor first faking anger and remorse, then suddenly overcoming with peace and a calm resolve after hearing about the sacred attributes of the river. He gets up and in utter reverence makes a humble obesiance in the direction of the river (painted on the backdrop). The audience could not but help share the suggestive mood or *rasa* of calmness and pacificity evoked in this way.

Abhinavagupta was so intrigued by the suggestive quality of *rasa* that he extended its analysis for detecting the degree of suggestibility or dramatic quality of a play in proportion to its ability to evoke *rasa*. Abhinavagupta termed this 'mood' he considered so central in poetics and drama as *rasadhvani*, and through this he emphasised the 'complete identity of the aesthetic experience between the hero or character (*nāyaka*), poet *(kavi)* and the audience (*śrotṛ*)'.[75] He lay stress on the harmonious and 'sympathetic identification' or empathy between the emotions and feelings of the poet on the one hand and the audience on the other. Abhinavagupta's analysis could no doubt be of some use in grappling with some of the poetical verses in scriptures.

3.28 Of what use, it may be asked, could *vyañjanā* be to philosophy? Although it is admitted that vague suggestions do not solve any problems, *vyañjanā* has some use, such as a heuristic for suggesting plausible clues. First, it may help to dissolve some problems when it is recognised that these are pseudo-problems, being expressions more of linguistic confusions, or even concerns irrelevant to the problems of philosophy. Secondly, *vyañjanā* may help portend some cues by suggesting models and metaphorical structures for an understanding of the issues at hand. The descriptive and symbolic value of *vyañjanā* is evident, for example, in Descartes hitting upon the notion of the 'machine' in order to explain the workings of the human body, a 'model' he borrowed from physics and mechanics. Thomas Kuhn's popularisation of the idea of 'paradigm' in the context of the broad framework of theories and research projects governed by the prevailing consensus among the scientific community at any one period is another instance, particularly in view of the wide currency the term has gained in disciplines other than science, to whit, social sciences and even religion.

A third consideration that gives some weight to the function of *vyañjanā* in philosophical discussion is in situations where language fails to adequately represent reality, or some aspect of it, and attempt is made to express this by extending the figurative function of language. *Vyañjanā* is here seen to complement the functions of *lakṣaṇā* and *gauṇī* in as much as the latter two 'tip off', so to speak, the more salient or hidden and unexpressed (because unexpressible), *meaning* once the limit is reached with the usual *lakṣaṇās*.

Learning meaning.

3.29 One last issue in this chapter that remains for our consideration is that concerning the ways and means by which meaning is learned or assimilated. Observation of the use of words in particular contexts of their occurrence is the most commonly identified method. The younger of the two brothers hears the father utter this expression to the elder brother: 'Bring the cow'. The action that follows creates associations in the mind of the younger child. The process may involve assimilation (or agreement) of meaning, *anvayāvāpa*, or the elimination (or difference), *udvāpajñā*.[76] For instance, if the child later hears the uncle say to the elder brother 'Bring the horse', he notes that 'bring' is included here, but 'cow' is excluded, and he further observes the similarity and the difference in the action that follows upon the utterance of this expression. If he has any doubts, he might ask his father or someone senior to him what such an such a word meant. Children, and often those learning a new language, do this all the time. This method is called *āptavacana*. *Āptaḥ* refers to an authoritative person or source, and may include a teacher, mentor (spiritual), or an expert in lexical meaning (whose medium may be a glossary, dictionary, encyclopaedia or a catalogue or the thesaurus).

The grammarians insist upon some other ways by which meaning is learnt as well. They include the following: (i) *vyākaraṇa* or grammar, (ii) *kośa* or lexicon; (iii) *vākyaśeṣa* or contextual basis; (iv) *upamāna* or analogy (i.e. by the way of comparision); (v) *vivṛtti* or commentary; and (vi) *siddhapadasāṃnidhya* or syntax. The Mīmāṃsaka would add *prakaraṇa* or context and *liṅga* or indicative mark to these. We need not go into details on these since their function are all too obvious. Their relevance is more important in the context of sentence-meaning comprehension, a topic to which we shall be returning later.

Such then are the ways in which we come to the different meanings or senses words have in virtue of the different significatory functions they assume in linguistic communication, and through which our *understanding* is enhanced, and error and ignorance minimised if not removed. Admittedly, words used in isolation and unconnected to other words fail to convey anything very significant and coherent, since each utterance has to have a context in which the word, as it were, comes alive and manifests its primary, or secondary, or one of the other significatory functions. This context is given in a syntactic construction in the form usually of a sentence, and perhaps a phrase or a clause. In the next two chapters we turn to a detailed analysis of the *sentence* and the significantly dominant role it plays in the generation of *śābdabodha.*

Typology of meaning-functions

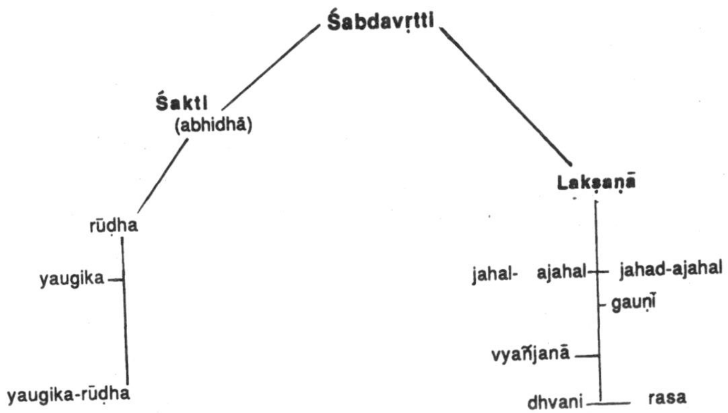

NOTES TO CHAPTER THREE

1. We have debated this issue in the previous chapter; one that will perhaps remain controversial.

2. As is remarked by Prof. Matilal, 'Sanskrit unfortunately has only one word '*artha*' which can ambiguously stand for 'meaning' or 'signification' or 'denotation' or 'connotation'. And also only one word *express* (*ucyate, vācaka*) is usually used to relate a word with its *artha*'. *ELG*, p43; also *NND*, p24ff for discussion.

3. Viśvanātha states: '. . .the comprehension of the meanings of *sections of a sentence* is followed by the comprehension of the meanings of the complete sentence. . .through the recollection of the meanings of the words.' *SM* on *BP*, under #82-83.

4. *Ibid* #81; see note 25 below.

5. Adaptation from Madhav Deshpande, in, 'Sentence-cognition. . .' p200.

6. This is in accordance with the Saussurean terminology, which gives the external facet of the symbol the term '*signifiant*' and the semantic facet '*signifié*'. This distinction loosely follows the duality between 'form' and 'meaning', or 'expression' and 'content' (*vācya-vācaka*), with which is to be contrasted our tripartite structure. See de Saussure's, *Cours*, pp100ff; S. Ullmann, *The Principles of Semantics*, 1963 p31ff. See also note 51 in previous chapter.

7. Or to put it in Russell's words, 'Words all have meaning in the simple sense that they are symbols that stand for something other than themselves.' *Principles of Mathematics*, 1903, p47.

8. See 'Uber Sinn and Bedeutung', p27; (Eng trs *RS* p119). Frege was clear that, even in the case of names, in grasping a sense, one is not assured of a reference (referent). *loc cit* and p28 (*RS* p120).

9. R.C. Pandeya, *The Problem of Meaning in Indian Philosophy*, p188.

10. *Śābarabhāṣya*, under I.iii.8 (GOI I, p109), I.IV.2 (1889, p127).

11. P. F. Strawson, 'On Referring' (reprint:) *Logico-Linguistic Papers*, Methuen 1977, p2 and pp4ff.

12. 'It is natural, now, to think of there being connected with a sign (name, combination of words, letter), besides that to which the sign refers, which may be called the reference of the sign, wherein the mode of presentation is contained. . .The reference of 'evening star' would be the same as that of 'morning star', but not the sense'. Frege *op cit.*, p27 (*RS* p119).

13. This is so, for Frege considers relations to be essentially not between objects, but between names or signs of objects – though only in analytic relations – no difference in the cognitive values of the relating signs need be assumed, as in $a = a$, in contrast to $a = b$. Statements of the latter form 'often contain very valuable extensions of our knowledge and cannot always be established *a priori* (*Ibid* p25); yet '*a*' and '*b*' may refer to the same object (of reference), while differing in their cognitive values or senses.

14. *Ibid* p26.

15. If $a = b$ is true as a factual statement, the reference is to an identical object, but the signs *a*' and '*b*' may be pointing to the reference through different cognitions, as such they have different cognitive values, in Frege's sense, which we here call the respective *viṣayatās* or 'intentional contents'. Taking *a* and *b* as the signs in Frege's equation, the cognitions expressed by each have different structures *qua viṣayatās* or their respective intentional contents. As for the 'objective' correlate, that comes closest to Frege's notion of 'thought', we have the *concept-content*, which too is capable of being the common property of several thinkers. The exception is in Nyāya, where the objective correlate is the *viṣaya*, the *real* object of reference.

16. *VKP*II.137: *ekasyāpi ca śabdasya nimittairavyavasthitaiḥ ekena bahubhiścārtho bahudhā parikalpyate.* (Limaye edition, p27.)

17. *Philosophical Investigations* II xi p220. *cf.* 'Language is an instrument. Its concepts are instruments' (569).'. . .our *meaning* that gives sense to the sentence. . .And 'meaning it' is something in the sphere of the mind.' (501, 358 resp.)

18. As J. N. Findlay remarks . . '.it is one of the extremely important discoveries of modern semantics that there are *some* expressions whose use, in certain contexts, is *not* to connote or denote anything, nor even to help to do either, but to do such things as give voice to feelings and wishes, evoke certain attitudes in others, or *perform* certain formal social acts, e.g. promises, which have certain definite social consequences, etc.' Ryle and Findlay, 'Use, Usage and Meaning', (reprint: *RS* p489).

19. *Cf.* E. Gellner, *Words and Things*, 1959.

20. Viśvanātha, *SM* under #80-81 (1920 p69).

21. *Tattvacintāmaṇi*, IV.ii. (*Śabdakaṇḍha*).

22. There are two senses in which Nyāya is realist, viz (a) in respect of its epistemological convinction that it is possible to have 'faithful and direct knowledge of the actual world', in which the *relations*, as distinct from the *relata*, are in some cases quite real (e.g. *samavāya*, inherence, and *saṃyoga*, conjunction); and (b) its belief in the reality of abstract entities like universals, or generic unities posited for general terms.

23. The Nyāya ontology requires that even in the case of the term 'sky-flower', each word has its own reference, viz. the objects *sky* and *flower.* Something similar is said about the compound *śaśaviṣāṇa* ('rabbit-horn') even though there is a false cognition of a relation between horns and rabbit (Jagadīśa *SSP* #6, p30). What this means is that the principle of *artha* is taken to its extreme in that the *viṣayatā* or intentional content of each cognitive episode is of necessity related to some *objective* correlate, *viṣaya*, regardless of whether the sign or linguistic representation is faithful to that particular or to some other actual object mistakenly identified—as when a post is taken foreman standing at a bus stop. Even the 'objects' in dream and hallucinations are actual in as much as they are connected, however remotely, to objects in the real world of normal experience. Dreaming, then, of the death of one's distant auntie is real at least in respect of the auntie and the phenomenon of death, despite their disjunction. Likewise, the legendary 'pegasus' is not unreal, since it has a resemblance in some actual animal or animals in the world. But to Quine this is one instance of where a word does not succeed in denoting a definite object, contrary to the Millian point of view.

24a. *Cf.* Pāṇini: *svaṃ rūpaṃ śabdasyāśabdasaṁjñā* (*PS* I.1.68, p275): 'A word (in a grammatical rule) which is not a technical term denotes its own form'.

24. Viśvanātha, *SM* #81: *vṛttiś ca śaktilakṣaṇānyataraḥ sambandhaḥ.*

25. Annaṃbhaṭṭa, *TS(D)* #59: *padalakṣaṇamāha-śaktaṃ iti. arthasmṛtyanukūlaḥ padapadārthasambandhaḥ śaktiḥ.* (BORI p50.)

26. *Ibid*, on #59. A restatement of this rather obscure phrasing would better read as: 'the *śakti* relation as the (primary) signification function of the word aids the understanding through recollection of what the word 'signifies' (denotes or designates). Its function is indirect in the sense that it operates through the 'meaning-content' (*artha*) potentially inhering in the word'. *Vide* Gopinath Bhattacharya's notes on *TS* p276ff.

27. *BP* #81, also in his *SM* on this: *padajanyapadārthasmaraṇaṃ vyāpāraḥ (śābdabodhe).* See also the discussion of Gaṅgeśa in our chapter one on *vyāpāra*. *cf. Mānameyodaya*, p93.

28. *VKP* III. iii. 29. See also I.50, 55.

29. *Ibid; Brahma-kāṇda*, I.i : *anādinidhanaṃ brahma śabdatattvaṃ yadakṣaram, vivartate'rthabhāvena prakriyā jagato yataḥ*—'The Brahman who is without beginning or

end, whose very essence is the Word, who is the cause of the manifest phonemes, who appears as the objects, from whom the creation of the world proceeds.' (Poona, 1965, Iyer tr. pl.) Thus Bhartṛhari identified speech (*vāc*) in its self-nature (*svarūpa*) with Brahman, the Absolute itself which manifests through its self-emanation in the form of syllables in four orders of subtle to the gross forms.

30. C. S. Peirce, 1.542, in Greenlee, *Peirce's Concept of Sign*, Mouton, The Hague, 1973.

31. Kumārila Bhaṭṭa, *Ślokavārttika, sambandhākṣepaparihāra*, #122-123: *siddhaḥ sambandhaḥ* (Varanasi edn. p478) (1898, ChSS, p498).

32. *Mīmāṃsā-sūtras* I.i.5; in *Śābara-bhāṣya*: '*Autpattika* ("inborn")—what we mean by this is 'constant'. It is *existence* (presence) that is figuratively spoken of as '*origin*'. What is meant is that the relation between word and its meaning is *inseparable*. It [thus] becomes the *means of knowing* (*jñāyate anena iti jñānam..*'). (Jha tr. GOI I p6).

33. *VP* IV 12-14, esp. 13 : *tatra śaktirnāma padināmartheṣu mukhyā vṛttiḥ*. See also Śaṅkara *bhāṣya* on *Brahma-sūtra* I.iii.28.

34. *Mahābhāṣya* (*Vārttika* quoted?), *Paspaśāhnika*, Kielhorn p6.

35. See note 32 above, 37 below.

36. Pārthasārathi Miśra in *Śāstradīpikā*, *tarkapāda*, under V.88, (Venkataramiah trans. p123).

37. *Śābarabhāṣya* on *MS* I.i.2. Of course, Śabara is setting up a fundamental distinction between 'ordinary language' terms and scriptural words related to action (*codanā*).

38. *Tarkasaṃgraha* of Annaṃbhaṭṭa, #59: *Āptavākyaṃ śabdaḥ. Āptaḥ tu yarthārthavaktā. Vākyaṃ padasamūhaḥ; yathā 'gām ānaya' iti. Śaktaṃ padam. 'Asmāt padāt ayam artho boddhavyaḥ' iti Īśvarasaṃketaḥ śaktiḥ* —'the statement of an authoritative person is *śabda* (as a *pramāṇa*); so sentence (*vākya*) that bears this statement is an instrument of knowledge'.

An authoritative person is one who utters what is in accordance with the real (*yathā*).A statement is a collection of significant words (*padas*), e.g. "Bring the cow"; a 'significant word' is that which has *śakti* or significatory power, and *śakti* is the will of God in some such manner: 'From such a word, such (and such) a thing be understood.' Also *cf. SM* on *BP* #81.

'God' indicates equivalence only, for *Īśvara*.

39*. *Vyāsa-bhāṣya* on *YS* I. 27 (Calcutta edn.).

39. *NS* II.i.55: 'convention'—*sāmayika*, (1920, p156).

40. Śabara also considers this objection, under I.i.5. See note 51 in previous chapter.

41. Vātsyāyana on *NS* II.i.56, on *jāti-viśeṣa* ('different groups of people' and their understandings), (1920, p156).

42. *Śabdaśaktiprakāśikā* #22-23, p117-122f. *Cf. SM* on *BP* #81 (*saṃpradāya* for human convention or regularity). Also, Vidyābhūṣaṇa, *op cit.* p449ff; S. C. Chatterjee, *op cit.* p325.

43. *Ibid*: *ājānikaś cādhunikaḥ saṃketo dvividho mataḥ nitya ājānikaś tatra yā śaktir iti gīyate. kādācitkas-tvādhunikaḥ śāstrakārādibhiḥ kṛtaḥ* (p124).

44. *SM* on *BP* #81.

45. *VP* IV.14.

46. Kumārila in *Ślokavārttika*, *loc cit* (see note 31 above).

47. *Ibid*; see also *Śāstradīpikā, tarkapāda, loc cit.*

48. *Ibid*; *cf. Mānameyodaya, dravya section*, p232.

49. *Śāstradīpikā (tarkapāda)* I.i.5-#89 (Banaras 1891 edn. p68ff).

50. Ogden and Richards, *The Meaning of Meaning*, p9-10.

51. *Ibid* (italics added). But 'thought' for Ogden and Richards is a rather subjective tendency, subject therefore to Frege's charge of 'psychologism'. The *thought* we speak of, much as in Frege, is more an objective content, characterised by its public shareability and recognisability. *Cf.* Husserl: 'An expression only refers to an objective correlate *because* it means something; it can be rightly said to signify or name the object *through* its meaning. An act of meaning is the determinate manner in which we refer to our object of the moment, though this mode of significant reference and the meaning itself can change, while the objective reference remains fixed.' In *Logical Investigations* Vol I and II (Findlay 1970). See also our discussion on Husserl's 'ideality of meaning' in the 'Introduction'.

52. *Ibid* p11.

53. See note 2 above, and discussion on *sphoṭa* of Patañjali in the previous chapter.

54. Russell, 'On Denoting' p45 (re: *RS*, p147), 'meaning' and 'denotation' is how Russell renders Frege's 'Sinn and Bedeutung'. Geach and Black in their trans. of Frege's '*Uber Sinn and Bedeutung*', (re: *RS* p117ff). Russell is not reliable on Frege.

55. As Max Charlesworth aptly points out: "Fact" for Wittgenstein here, means simply that which is asserted by a proposition such as "Socrates is wise"—that which is logically required in order that the proposition should 'propose'. In the same way Wittgenstein's notion of 'objects', the ultimate simples "Socrates", "wise", which are the constituents or elements of "facts", is not a metaphysical notion, as though Wittgenstein were trying to revive a metaphysical theory of atomism', in *Philosophy and Linguistics Analysis*, p84. Wittgenstenians may go even further and argue that 'facts' have nothing to do with internal features of mental states, rather that they are 'things', such as external events, explicable in the context of cultural practices and social norms. Obviously, the Nyāya notion of *viṣaya* is nothing like this; although the *vastu* and *artha* of Advaita-Mīmāṃsā may not preclude the Wittgensteinian 'facts'.

56. The traditional Ullmanian-Ogden-Richards signification triangle fits the diadic part of our triangle—viz. that of the relation between *significance* and *referent* of the word-form. The new linguistic element in our extended set of relations is obviously the *referend* or 'thought' (more Fregian than Ogdenian). Kunjunni Raja (*Indian Theories of Meaning, op cit*, p3-15) in drawing comparison between the Indian and Western views, stresses more the similarities than the differences, and although he goes beyond the Saussurean model, he does not see beyond the traditional model we are being critical of here. See also notes 50 and 51 above. And John Lyons, 'Semiotics', in his, *Semantics*, p95.

57. *Tarkasaṃgraha* #59, and *Dīpikā* on it. See *VP* IV.30 also.

58. *SM* on *BP* #88. *Yaugika* is 'etymological', *rūḍha* is 'conventional', *yoga-rūḍha* is 'etymological and conventional', *yaugika-rūḍha* is 'etymological or conventional'. These are useful for sorting out homophones from homonyms etc., as e.g. *hasta, kara, pāṇi* for 'hand', which are independent of each other and have their own fixed relations to the 'same' signification.But Śabara appears to want to regard homonyms as distinct words (*Bhāṣya* on *MS* III.ii.1).

59. *VP* IV 13: *yathā ghaṭapadasya pṛthubundhodarādyākṛtiviśiṣṭe* etc.

60. *Ibid*. Also see *Vedāntakalpatikā* #90 and *SB* pp4-7 (BORI 1962) for Madhusūdana Sarasvatī's interpretation.

61. Under *MS* II.i.4, *sūtra* 12, and III.i.5 (GOS I. p187), also under I.iv.2, where Śabara says something on *lakṣaṇā*, pointing to the general acceptance of a word in its *lakṣyārtha* form even when the express meaning has been forgotten (except by grammarians): *lakṣaṇā iti ced varaṃ lakṣaṇā kalpitā, na yāgābhidhānaṃ, laukikī hi lakṣaṇā haṭho'prasiddhakalpanā iti* (*Śābara-bhāṣya*, 1889, p87).

62. John Lyons, *Semantics*, (Vol II, p406).

63. One of the accepted marks for the use of figurative sense.

64. *VP* IV 30.

65. Since this leads to corruption and slang Mīmāṃsā would rather disqualify it or restrict its function.

66. Most of these come under *gauṇī, vyañjanā, dhvani* and *rasa* or poetics. (A good example is in the recent use of the symbols of *maṇḍala* and the 'chariot' in novels by Patrick White. Also to be noted is the profuse use of the symbol as in Carl Jung's psychology).

67a. *NS* II.ii.62: *sahacaraṇa-sthāna-tādarthya-vṛtta-mānadhāraṇa-sāmīpya-yoga-sādhan'ādhipatyebhyaḥ brahmaṇa-mañca-kaṭa-rāja-saktu-candana-gaṅgā-śāṭak'ānnapuruṣeṣu atadbhāve'pi tat-upacāraḥ.* (II.ii.61 in 1920, p220).

67. As in note 57 above.

68. *Ibid* under #59: *lakṣaṇā api śabdavṛtti. . .'*

69. *Śabdaśaktiprakāśikā* 16. See Matilal, 'Jagadīśa's classification of Grammatical Categories.' p227.

70. *VP* IV 31.

71. Dharmarāja, following Mīmāṃsā and Nyāya, is inclined to include *gauṇī* under *lakṣit-lakṣaṇā*, and not as a separate *vṛtti*, since this is part of its *yogyatā* or competency. Gajānanaśāstri in Hindi comm. on *VP*: *kārya utpann karaṇe ko yogyatā ko hi śakti samajña. . .sāmānya śakti (hei).* p209. *Cf* Gopinath Bhattacharya in *TS* p277; Kunjunni Raja, *op cit.* p240; Madhusūdana Sarasvatī calls *gauṇī* a 'qualificative' *lakṣaṇā*, since this concerns only the qualities indicated by the express sense of a word, *op cit.* p75.

72. Shakespeare, like his Indian counterpart Kālidāsa, knew this meaning-function too well, this being an adaptation from his own in *Macbeth*: '. . .till Bir'nam wood comes to Dunsinane'. Scene V.

73. Ānandavardhana in *Dhvanyāloka Uddyota*, also quoted in Harold Coward, ' Bhartṛhari's Dhvani: A Central Notion in Indian Aesthetics', in Coward and Sivaraman ed. *Revelation. . .* pp65-66.

74. *Ibid*, p66.

75. *Locana* p92; also in 'Abhinavagupta – The Literary Critic and Commentator (An Assessment)', by J. Tilakasiri, in ABORI XLVII, 1966 p9.

76. From various sources, notably *TS* (*śabda* section.), *Mānameyodaya* (*śabda* and *dravya* sections); *Siddhāntamuktāvalī* under #81; *VP* IV; Kuppuswami Sastri, *op cit*, notes p172.

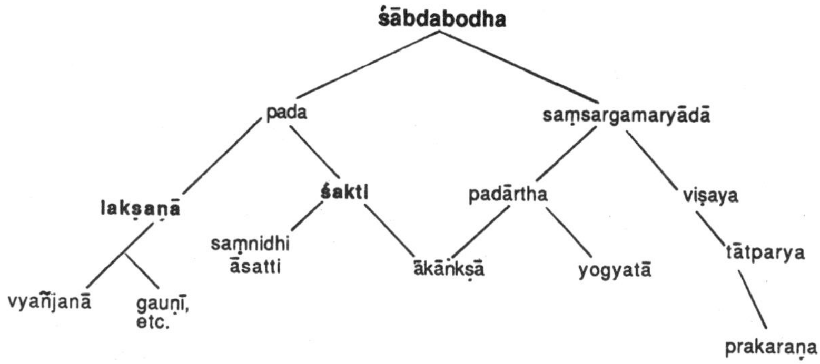

Generative tree for *śābdabodha*

vākyatvaṃ ca viśiṣṭārthaparaśabdatvam.

------ Gaṅgeśa on *śābdabodha*

4

ŚĀBDABODHA: PSYCHOLINGUISTICS OF SENTENCE UNDERSTANDING

A. *Śābdabodha*

4.0 While raising several issues about 'meaning' we looked at the relation of word and meaning, but we did not consider complex clusters of words, such as phrases and sentences. Something was said about the syntactic relation of words to the meaning of whole utterances. But does the utterance always take the form of a sentence, or are they two different things? And what relations do words have to the sentence: is a sentence analysable in terms of words, or word-meanings, or some other elements? We could go into great lengths on these issues, but we shall have to limit our concern to the role sentence plays in *śābdabodha* (linguistically derived understanding), and to that extent we would need a clear understanding of what a 'sentence' is or could plausibly be for our purposes at least.

More specifically, the aim of this and the next two chapters is to examine the role that a *sentence* plays in the structure of *śābdabodha* in terms of its component parts. To that end we concern ourselves with the structure of the sentence-whole in terms of its meaning-elements and the relations that obtain among them. We proceed with the analysis on the basis of the following propositions (under A, as outlined in chapters 1 and 2, and B, further issues that arise in this context).

A.

i. *Vākya* or 'sentence' is the basic unit of analysis of *śābdabodha*, whose utterance generates understanding of its meaning in the audience.

ii. An understanding of sentence-meaning involves first of all the 'perception' of the sentence and its component parts, which can be described in terms of the awareness of the surface structure of the linguistic expression.

B.

iii. The sentence itself is a composite structure that involves the syntactical connection of significant words *via* their 'meanings'; one part of the structure may be designated as the principal element (*mukhya viśeṣa*), the *qualified*, with the other parts as its *qualifier.*

iv. The meaning-content of the sentence (the 'sentence-meaning' or, better 'propositional sense') is greater and more 'holistic' than the meanings of the individual words or discrete meaning-elements of the sentence. Or in other words, what a sentence *qua* 'proposition' *means* is often more than what the constituent words taken individually and in isolation may mean; thus *vakyārtha* is not reducible merely to the sum of the *padārthas.*

v. The novel element in the sentence-meaning structure is the 'relation content', or simply the *relation* (*saṃsarga*) among the component parts of the expression, juxtaposed in certain (sometimes sequential) order, and syntactically connected in respect of their specific significations in the expression.

To begin with, we look at some views on what a 'sentence' is. There has been much debate on this question, and our sketch here is necessarily limited to our major concern with the structure of *śābdabodha* and no more.

The naïve view

4.1 According to the naïve view, known from very early times, as reported in Bṛhaddevatā,[1] a sentence is defined as *padasaṅghātajam (vākyam)* : a collection of words. The Nyāya discussion on this question often makes reference to a somewhat identical definition – viz. *vākyaṃ-padasamūhaḥ*:[2] a sentence is a collection of words (*padas*). But if either of these definitions were to be taken seriously then any cluster of words would qualify as a 'sentence' without, though, serving any particular linguistic function. The following expression is an example.

gaur aśvaḥ puruṣo hastī Ui (= utterance *i, etc.*)

(cow horse man elephant)

But is this a sentence? Some would say 'no'. Why? Is it because it fails to produce an intelligible sense in the audience? Or is it because it is not in the habit of humans to utter such expressions which appear to be lacking some grammatical element, such as a verb or perhaps an instrumental case-ending indicating some important feature, and so on and so forth? One may even argue that the words do not appear in their proper order. But will the alteration of the order of these words make any significant difference to the expression? would it make it any more intelligible? "Elephant cow horse man" seems to do no better, since the audience is likely to remain as perplexed as ever.

One verb (eka-tiṅ) view

4.2 Pāṇini had said that words can form a compound word only if they have the capacity to combine (*samarthaḥ padavidhiḥ*).[3] The 'capacity'—*sāmarthya*—was taken by some to signify a syntactic relationship which yields *ekārthībhāva*, a unification of meaning. This 'togetherness' or unity is achieved according to Kātyāyana, in his gloss (*vārttika*) on the Pāṇinian rule, by the presence of one finite verb: *ekatiṅ*.[4] Thus a sentence is an expression that possesses one finite verb and it seems, one and one only.

So if we were to add, for instance, a verb such as a copula ('is"), the expression would read a little differently, and we may get some sense out of it, thus:

gaur aśvaḥ puruṣo hastī asti Uii
(there **is** [a] cow, [a] horse, [a] man, [an] elephant.)

This expression looks more like a sentence in that it can be used as a whole expression in communicating some idea. The *verb*al form *(tiṅanta),* which this expression has, gives it the form of a sentence. A *verb*al expression (i.e. one that has a *verb*) should be as good as a sentence.

Does this however mean that each sentence has to be constructed from a cluster of words pulled together, as it were, by a verb? In other words, are there no cases of either single-word sentences, or sentences without verbs, or both?

One word sentence

4.3 There are cases of single-word utterances used by children when they are learning language, and by adults learning a new language, or who may prefer to utter single words. In both cases the audience tend to understand more than the single word taken in isolation would succeed in conveying. Take for instance these utterances:

pādapaḥ Uiii

deva Uiv

vṛkṣaḥ Uv

śrotiya Uvi

ghaṭam Uvii

pacati Uviii

Now one argument, which Vyāsa[5] in his *Yoga-sūtra-bhāṣya* seems to favour as well, is that each of the individual words above contains the force of a sentence *qua* sentence. That is to say, these singular expressions are shorter versions of what are complete sentences, and which would read as follow:

one that drinks through the legs Uiii *(a)*

one who shines Uiv *(a)*

this is a tree Uv *(a)*

one who is versed in the Vedas Uvi *(a)*

he makes a pot Uvii *(a)*

he is cooking rice Uviii *(a)*

Thus, when a word like *vṛkṣaḥ* (tree) is uttered we should consider associating '*asti*' ("there is") with it so as to complete the sentence, which takes the form in Uv(a). According to Vyāsa there is hardly any object in the world to which an existential predicate cannot be attached.[6] But we shall see in a while how this response is not acceptable to the Nyāya view, particularly with respect to Uvii and Uviii.

It is also to be noted that the single word in each case is an inflected word, which may involve a noun (*nāman*), a verb (*ākhyāta*), a preverb (*upasarga*) and a particle (*nipāta*). In this respect, some grammatical relationship already could be said to have taken place between or among the elements of the 'single word' expressions, such as between stem and suffix, or root and its radical ending. One can then say with some assurance that a sentence is at the least not a single *un*-inflected word. And as far as grammarians are concerned the 'single inflected word' definition can only be accepted provided it retains within itself the actions (*kriyā*) usually denoted by a *verb*al form (*ākhyāta*). This view will place strong stress on *action* (*vyāpāra*, to use another common term), whether a *nāman* or *ākhyāta* as indicative of action. Thus '*asti*' ("there is") performs the job of *ākhyāta* in Uv(a).

4.4Kātyāyana's definition then becomes a central part of the grammarians' conception and analysis of a sentence. The *verb* is the very heart of a sentence.[7] So there has to be an *ākhyātaśabda* is each sentence. *Varṣati* is as much a sentence as is *varṣati devo jalam*. A verb is efficient enough to constitute a sentence in combination with either an indeclinable, a *kāraka* (case or case-ending), an adjective, or an adverb. Thus, *uccaiḥ paṭhati*—'he reads aloud' (has a verb and indeclinable) and (Uviii) *odanaṃ pacati*—'he cooks rice'—has a verb and *kāraka*. By the same token, Uvii is read: *ghaṭaṃ karoti*—'he makes (a) pot'.

We can go on to give some examples from spoken English, such as when a one-word utterance like "---door!" is made in an angry tone by the master to the inattentive bell-boy. What the speaker means to say is "Shut the door", but he omits the finite verb in his utterance, which nonetheless is implied in the expression. Another example where the finite verb is not uttered but is implicit in the utterance, and which is comprehended as such by the word, is the sharp answer of "yes", and we may add "no". Thus, to the query :'Are you going to the market?', the listener replies "Yes"—meaning 'Yes, I am going to the market', or "No" as the case may be. For the purposes of speech, it may not be necessary to utter the finite verb but in a linguistic account, without assuming the function of a finite verb as the syntactic "cementing" element of the various words, such as nouns, adjectives and adverbs, the expression may not stand completed as a sentence. We may say that the verb plays a significant role in the sentence in which it occurs or is implied. The role of the finite verb could be extended to both the expressions in the earlier examples; although it does not appear that a finite verb occurs in every sentence—e.g. in "Wow!".

Whichever way one looks at a sentence, either as constituted of an inflected single word (*pada*) or a cluster of words, there should be at least one principal term around which the sentence is centered, and this *vibhāga* (unit) must be an action-word or have a *verb*al form. Sometimes, as Kātyāyana concedes, it may be accompanied by the particle, the normative, adjectives, and, he adds, even adverbs.[8] It is evident therefore that to the grammarians a finite verb is a central element, or 'nucleus' of a sentence. As P. S. Sastri aptly puts the case : 'The force of a sentence is said to be gathered in the verb and as a result a *verb*al form is enough to constitute a sentence. . .In every sentence, therefore, we face a verb and a verb refers to or implies a noun.'[9] The verb then is an centrally important element in a sentence, and thus the meaning of the sentence would to, a large extent, depend on the meaning of the verb too. It follows that the comprehension of the sentence-meaning also depends considerably on the comprehension of the meaning of the finite verb where one is present, or assumed where one is not present in the utterance itself.

4.5 On a related point, the grammarian's definition requires at least two words to constitute a sentence, one only of which is a verb Thus an expression like *'daṇḍa'* ("stick") is not a sentence, unless another word with a *verb*al ending is understood to be combined with it—such as *asti*, "this is". The important point, however, is that the centrality of the verb is emphasised, because it gives unity of structure to the sentence (*ekavākyatā*). But perhaps the grammarians failed to acknowledge that a verb is necessary for the removal of *ākāṅkṣā* or expectancy that arises in the syntactic structure of the expression when an important grammatical element becomes conspicuous by its absence in the structure, whether it be for a *verb*al or some other form. This is the sort of argument Mīmāṃsā and Nyāya also advance, as we will now go on to examine.

4.6 The Mīmāṃsā approached the problem of sentence from the point of view of their interest in interpreting rituals and sacrificial acts from the vast body of Vedic literature and evaluating their efficacy in terms of the 'efficiency' or 'potency' they could generate towards accomplishing a particular goal or purpose. The primary objectives that directed their analysis were the following.

One, the need to discern complete sentences from mere clusters of meaningless words; two, the need to discriminate between primary and secondary sentences; three, the need to detect and preserve the order of recitation of the *mantras* upon which the efficacy of the rituals were believed to be dependent; and, four, the need to be able to say which injunctions and optative efficiencies (as distinct from subsidiary qualifications) were being highlighted in any particular Vedic text. Obviously, for much the same reasons as the grammarians gave, Mīmāṃsā could not accept a mere cluster of words to be a sentence, since the expression serves no purpose (*arthaikatva*) or rather 'a single purpose'. And this is so because an utterance, such as Ui, rouses an expectation for further words to complete the sense of the expression, leaving one hopelessly to wonder: 'well, what about them?'. It is patently in need of *ākāṅkṣā*.

Ākāṅkṣā, then, is what a cluster of words is required to have if it is to be taken as a sentence. But although *ākāṅkṣā* is regarded to be one of the major contributions Mīmāṃsā made to Indian linguistics, Mīmāṃsā did not consider *ākāṅkṣā* itself to be either the central force of a sentence, or sufficient in the way Nyāya linguists, such as Jagadīśa, were to argue for later. For Mīmāṃsā *ākāṅkṣā* is an aid towards an expression obtaining a unity of purposive sense: *arthaikatvādekaṃ vākyaṃ sākāṅkṣaṃced vibhāge syāt.*[10] Jaimini wants to put some emphasis on *ākāṅkṣā* all the same:

> So long as a single purpose is served by a number of words, which on being separated, are found to be wanting ('incapable of effecting

the purpose'), they form "one sentence" (or one syntactical unit).[11]

In other words, if we have a cluster of words, and in taking them apart we find that they become *wanting* or deficient in their meaning while together they serve a single purpose or convey a particular 'import', then the cluster qualifies as a sentence. Śabara makes specific reference to Yajur Veda, indicating that this principle was formulated to ascertain the difficult passages of certain ancient texts (e.g. *Ṛg Veda*)—where it is sometimes difficult to ascertain how far a *mantra* reaches or extends in its import.[12] Its application to ordinary sentences was taken as matter of course by later Mīmāṃsakas. For as long as a group of words served a 'single purpose' (*arthaikatva*), they must have mutual expectancy as a unifying factor of their individual word-meanings. In Kumārila's judgement: It must be concluded that those words, on hearing which we are clearly cognisant of a *single* sense must be taken as forming a 'single sentence'; this definition is not found to be incompatible with the character of any sentence—either ordinary, or of the *Mantras* and *Brāhmaṇa*.'[13]

Prabhākara also stressed the unity of 'purpose' and 'meaning', but subordinates the latter under the former as he thought Jaimini and Śabara to have done.[14] And outside of itself a sentence as a complete whole of meaning does not require or expect words to complete its single sense. This is the principle of 'syntactical split' that marks off distinct sentences.[15] Again, the function of *ākāṅkṣā* is emphasised as the unifying factor for specific *śābdabodha*.

Bhāvanā: the actualising efficiency

4.8 It remained, however, that something else was to be considered more important than *ākāṅkṣā* in the structure of a sentence. To the Mīmāṃsā the purposefulness of the sentence is seen to converge on the 'action-word', in accordance with its commitment to interpreting Vedic sentences as prescriptive of optative counsel (*vidhi*)—or 'injunction' (which as such is an arguable rendering, with nowhere near the connotations attached to command, commandment, and imperative either in the strict categorical or the militaristic sense.)[16] Jaimini argued, as we reported a little earlier, that the unified meaning of a sentence depends upon the action-word, citing as evidence that upon hearing a (Vedic) sentence one becomes anxious to know what one should do (to accomplish a particular purpose or goal intimated therein).[17] No action is without purpose, and it could be in respect of some cognitive, affective or behavioural disposition. The action or performance enjoined is indicated by the essential optative *verb*al form in the sentence. In other words, action is denoted by the verb which presupposes an agent (*kartā*), action (*karma*) and the instrument (*karaṇa*), which together lead to the accomplishment of the purposive result (*phala*).

Thus, by definition a sentence has to have a verb (*ākhyāta*) that expresses *bhāvanā* or the 'efficient means for actualising (the purpose)', as its principal element (*viśeṣa*). This serves to indicate the specific process of activity required towards the accomplishment of the *apūrva*, the 'transcendental potency' that eventually brings about the desired fruit or result *qua bhāvanā.*[18] For instance, the following sentence expresses a typical conditional imperative: *svargakāmaḥ yageta*—'one who wishes for heaven ought to (make) sacrifice'. Here *jayeta* is the *ākhyāta* or *verb*al form, whose function it is to express an 'urge' or 'desire' (*kāmaḥ*), or the conditional 'act' towards a particular 'object' or end. This is very important to the Mīmāṃsā standpoint. For once the *verb*al root —*yaj(i)*— is isolated and through the suffix-ending—*ta*—the optative, *liṅ*, is determined one then sees what sort of a disposition it calls upon the person desiring some objective or goal, and what sort of an activity is required of him, as well as the degree of 'potency' or 'exigency' (*bhāvanā*) there is towards accomplishing that end-result.

The 'exigency' or efficiency implicated in any such expression is disclosed in two forms: through *śābdībhāvanā* and *arthībhāvanā*. The former is the *verb*al efficiency in respect of the action, while the latter is the objective efficiency in respect of the end-goal, indicated by the optative or the imperative form of the verbal element.[19] Once the act (of sacrifice, etc) is performed it deposits or establishes the efficiency for a transcendental 'fruit' to eventuate as a result : this is the working of the 'unseen (transcendental) potency' or *apūrva* that supposedly resides in the act or the agent, and is the link between the action and the result, or between earth and 'heaven'—i.e., between the moral force and the utopian 'kingdom of ends' (that the Mīmāṃsakas postulate).

This is at least how Kumārila interprets the situation, that is, he regards the force of the *verb*-al efficiency is a contigent one in that it is indicative of an hypothetical or conditional rather than a strict categorical imperative. For Prabhākara, however, the *apūrva* is not as such a potency but is indicative of an *ought*, a mandate (*niyoga*), much like the Kantian categorical imperative, and consequently the relation between the *bhāvanā* and the activity is more than a contingent one—it is of necessity. The injunction is not in respect of a goal, but in respect of the *act* as a moral imperative, fulfillment of which brings about the *phala* or the transcendental 'fruit'. The intervention of the *moral* injunctive here is not crucial to our analysis, but we may return to consider some of these issues when we look at the differences between statements of 'facts' and 'ought' statements. Nothing therefore can be more important to the Mīmāṃsā than 'action' (*kriyā*).

Kumārila categorically makes the assertion: 'Devoid of *kriyā* there can be no real mutual relation between the *kārakas* (words denoting *doer* of an act), and therefore words in a sentence are always connected with action.'[20a] Mīmāṃsā would then also agree with the grammarians that in a single word utterance such as *'ghaṭam'* the action-word *karoti* is to be assumed, in fact, that it already is assumed in the *kāraka* so that the sentence is in a complete form. And if there is more than one finite verb in a text or utterance, then it is a case of finding the one which is central to the single purpose proffered, as it were, to which any other verbs or verbal clauses are subordinated as qualifiers, or as modifiers, or perhaps even as interpretants of the *bhāvanā* (the *efficiency*), denoted by the principal *verb*al form. For the grammarians, such as Kātyāyana, this would be a difficult resolution to accept, since according to the *ekatiṅ* (one-verb view), one verb only per sentence is sufficient. Thus, in an expression like: *pūrvaṃ snāti pacati tato vrajati* (he first takes his bath, then cooks, then goes for a walk) one is not only left to discern the number of verbs it has—possibly three—but also to determine which one of them is the principal verb. Or could it be, as the grammarians might argue, that there are in fact *three* distinct sentences in the expression? But it would be too complicated a hypothesis to suppose that in every such utterance each verb makes for 'a distinct sentence' (*vākyamākhyātakāra*). The Nyāya critique comes in at this point and offers its own alternative view.

4.9 But before that, a word or two on *krama* or word order that was also considered by Mīmāṃsā to be of significant importance. They argue that every sentence has a special feature (*viśeṣa*), the special signification, which is to be comprehended. So a sentence is structured intransitively in a particular order in which words are uttered together in such a way as to express the intended, invariably purposive, sense. Usually it is the first inflected form that sets, as it were, the pattern of the ordered relation (*saṃghāta*) the words enter into. Consider the following sentence:

Devadatto grāmaṃ gacchati *Uix*
(Devadatta is going to the village.)

Uix has a *karmatva* that reveals the *vyāpāra* (activity) central to the sentence. It can be argued against the Mīmāṃsā that in spoken idiom at least, we do alter the order of words in a sentence without making the sentence any less comprehensible. Why can we not say that in the case of the above sentence, for instance:

'To the village goes Devadatta.'

But the Mīmāṃsā base their argument on the fixity and rigidity of order shown in Vedic language so as to prevent the *mantras* from being afflicted by linguistic distortions and corruption of form (as in *apabrahṃśa*). Reversion of order in the syntactical composition would be looked down upon in the context of Vedic language. Consequently, one could not change the order of words in the *mantra*: *agna ā yāhi*. . . ('O Agni, come. . .'; *Ṛgveda* VI.16.x), and utter '*ā yāhy agne*', as we may well do in ordinary speech. But if the suggestion in this argument is that the interference strikes at the level of the efficacy of the *mantra* in producing the particular result prescribed by the sacrifice undertaken, then this could not be a plausible reason to suppose that the interference occurs in the syntactical structure of the expression as well. But we may pass over this point for now.

The construction of a sentence then is not as contingent upon its order as Mīmāṃsā would have it. However, the order, or what we may call *sequence*, does have a relative role at the level of word-formation in a sentence, such that to alter, for instance, *bhavati* to *ti-bhava* by placing the ending in front of the root-base, would create problems in effecting the desired *śābdabodha*. We may grant Mīmāṃsā this point, though, for a better *argument* Nyāya deserves the credit.

4.10 Annaṃbhaṭṭa considers the naïve view (4.1) of *vākyaṃ padasamūhaḥ* but rejects it, not because the Nyāya regards sentences to be any more holistic (*ekavākyatātva*) than the Mīmāṃsā view does, but because the words lack *ākāṅkṣā* in order for them to yield a complete sense. When hearing an expression as Ui the audience may wonder whether the speaker is going to complete the sentence he seemed to have commenced. A fuller consideration of *ākāṅkṣā* led Nyāya philosophers to the belief that *ākāṅkṣā*, of all the linguistic features of an expression, is the most important one, and that in a strict sense it is sufficient for a sentence. Since we shall be looking at *ākāṅkṣā* in some detail in the next chapter we need not go into that here. But it may be noted that the reasoning behind such a view is to consolidate *the* form of expression towards a successful *śābdabodha*, to accomplish which certain syntactical requirements have to be met, the most important of which is said to be *ākāṅkṣā*. Nyāya then does not begin with an abstract linguistic problem as perhaps a grammarian would, even though what it comes up with is a mixture of grammatical and semantical considerations, sufficient to warrant the attention of modern-day linguists.

In appraising the Nyāya position we would do better to see, first of all which if any of the definitions we have so far considered the Nyāya accepts, or rejects, and their reasons behind the acceptance or rejection. Let us start with the single-word sentence argument (4.3). The question that the Nyāya asks is: what would be the minimum requirement to make the expression grammatically acceptable? Again it is *ākāṅkṣā* that constitutes the criterion of grammaticality for Nyāya. But one may ask, of course, how does Nyāya see *ākāṅkṣā* involved in a single-word utterance when expectancy would be seen to occur between two or more words? In what sense therefore do we say that *pacati* and *ghaṭam*, as instances of single-word utterances, have *ākāṅkṣā*? The Nyāya response is direct. *Pacati* is constituted of two words, basically, (stem) *pac-* and the suffix *-ti*, which here collaborate to denote an act or action on the part of the subject. *Pac-* is a root form which signifies the operation of cooking, and therefore *pac-a* is the implied *verb*al form. And this is possible in view of the fact that morphemes, roots, suffixes etc, as we showed in chapter two, have *śakti* or significatory power and therefore have the capacity to signify even if this is only feasible in collaboration with other significant elements in an expression, or with each other, as is the case here.[20]

One may doubt, however, whether the collaboration of the two 'words' succeeds in yielding a *completed* sense, as presumably *śābdabodha* is required to, since it is conceivable that on hearing this utterance the audience would expect a 'completion' of the expression. Perhaps a nominal base that qualifies the existing *verb*al base may be in order. But as it stands, the expression consists of a *verb*al base alone (apart from the suffix) and this is not adequate for the function. Either Nyāya is saying that *ākāṅkṣā* has been fulfilled in this expression, even though it is present only between the stem and the suffix, or that a finite verb can stand alone as a sentence. If it is saying the former then Nyāya has given us a criterion for the grammaticalness of an expression, but which nonetheless appears to be too strong for a sentence definition; but if it is saying the latter, then Nyāya could be taken to be in company with the grammarians and Mīmāṃsā, who together stress the *ākhyātatva* or *verb*-formality of an expression in their own definitions of sentence. Nyāya however would deny the latter interpretation of its position in this respect, and demonstrate its response with the use of a counterexample, namely the expression '*ghaṭam*' (Uvii).

4.11 Now in the case of *ghaṭam* Nyāya wants to argue that no *verb*al element is involved and it would not agree that the expression is grammatically acceptable merely on the ground of its lacking a finite verb. This expression is to Nyāya equally as much a sentence.[21] Would Nyāya then accept that a *verb*al item is understood implicitly in such an utterance? The Nyāya response is that *kriyā* (action) is understood from the context (*prakaraṇa*) and therefore as an action-word (*ākhyāta*), it does not have to be supposed or postulated. What does, however, add a special feature to this utterance, which the grammarians and Mīmāṃsā find in *ākhyāta* or *tiṅanta*, is *karmatvam* (being an 'object' [in the accusative] of an act, pertaining here to the pot (*ghaṭa*). The particle structure is as shown:[22]

ghaṭa-vṛtti-karmatvam (or *karmatvaṃ ghaṭīyam*)

In view of the fact that this and so many sentences would be ruled out of court, Jagadīśa therefore contends that it is quite illogical for the grammarian to assert that there cannot be any sentence without a verb ('action-word')[23]. Certainly, we may say there are expressions in spoken idiom, where no verb as such appears, for instance, when one asks *kuto bhavān*?: "Where you from?" And instances where the copula does not appear at all can be multiplied, not only in Sanskrit and English, but in other languages such as Russian, in the form of categorical sentences, which can be purely nominal expressions. For instance, the expressions *'daṇḍa'* ("err, stick"), *'ahaṃ bālaḥ'* (I [am] a boy), *'rāmo vaktā'* ('Rama [is] the speaker'), *'sa bhāravāhī'* ('he [is] a weight-carrier') and so forth. But while in English it may not be grammatically correct to write, or say, "the pot blue", when describing a pot, in Sanskrit, at least, it almost invariably takes this form. It may not be "aesthetically neat" either, but it is formally not incorrect, according to the Nyāya criterion for grammaticality at least, and it is no impediment to the generation of *śābdabodha*.[24]

We might as well say that such expressions, beside not being grammatically incorrect, are idiomatically correct so that its utterance succeeds in expressing and conveying an intelligible sense.

These instances support the Nyāya denial of the necessity of a verb in each and every sentence. Nyāya further argues that if the juxtapositioning of non-*verb*al words is sufficient to express a proposition and constitute a grammatical sentence, it would be wrong to insist on the presence of a finite verb which can be done without in a normal sentence.[25]

4.13 But is there a stronger consideration than that which has been suggested so far? It seems so. Consider for example the expression: *girir bhukto vahnimān Devadattaḥ*—'the hill has eaten has fire Devadatta'. This expression does not have just one finite verb, indeed it has two, and yet it is not half as intelligible as the expression we considered earlier, or as the expression *'surabhi candanam'* ("the sandal [is] fragrant"), which has no verb The Nyāya position can be better clarified by taking the sentence to have a propositional structure analysable basically in terms of the qualified-qualifier relation, where the principal element in the expression is qualified by the minor components or sections of the sentence. The propositional content of the expression or sentence can be analysed and related in the way contents of a qualificative cognition (*viśiṣṭajñāna*) are, as we saw earlier. This is represented in the following structure:

$Q(xy) - x$ qualified by y

That is, x is the qualified [*qualificand*] (*viśeṣya*) determined by the qualifier *y* (*viśeṣaṇa* or *prakāra*). Any two linguistic items that fit the terms of this relation can be said to constitute a sentence *qua* propositional structure. For example, the expression of the form *'ghaṭam'* can be analysed in terms formal structure in this manner:[26]

1. *ghaṭam*
2. *ghaṭa-* + *-am*
3. *ghaṭa* = (stem) *pot and '*-am*' = (to) the object*ness* [accusative].

The relation can be expressed as '(to) the object*ness* [accusative function] qualified by a *pot, which may generate a cognition of the form '*karmatvaṃ ghaṭīyam*' (the accusative function belongs to the pot)[27]. The single expression *ghaṭam*, then, equally fulfills the requirements of a sentence in terms of the relation stated above. Even a slightly more complex expression, such as *gām ānaya*, and *ghaṭo nīlaḥ*, can be analysed in terms of such relations. Thus *pacati*, the other single expression in question, can also be represented in the following terms:

> (He) is qualified by the effort of generating the activity of making contact (of, say, rice) with fire.

The single-word expressions in these examples qualify as sentences because, a) they may generate cognition of their meanings without the help of any further words or word-components; b) the unitary 'sense' derived, though not aesthetically complete, is logically or formally complete; and c) the propositional cognition can be construed in the qualified-qualifier relation, where the meaning of the principal component is qualified by the other component in the expression.[28] It would appear that in accord with such a formulation the *verb*al form need not after all be considered vital to a sentence.

4.14 The above formulation can be taken to be yet another statement of the necessity, for *ākāṅkṣā* among words in a sentence. If *x* is heard then an *akanksa* for *y* is registered as its qualifier, and vice versa.[29] If it is the case that an expression is used that signifies directly an action or some activity, as in *pacati*, then *ākāṅkṣā* between the two constitutive elements, one of which is primary (*mukhya*), is said to obtain. Generally speaking, the *mukhya-viśeṣa* is the agency (*kṛti*) not the *ākhyāta* (activity).[30]

Now having gone through these considerations the unequivocal definition of sentence may be stated, thus : a sentence is any number of significant words (*sārthaka*) that have *ākāṅkṣā* among them and that make for the syntactical whole, without which there is no *śābdabodha* of whatever is collectively signified by their utterance.[31]

If *ākāṅkṣā* (mutual syntactic expectancy) is to be considered so seriously, then the following expression should also be a sentence since it appears to satisfy this criterion – viz. *vahninā siñcati*: 'he sprinkles it with fire'. There is obviously nothing grammatically odd that one can point to in this expression, and the grammarians would also agree that the criterion of *ākāṅkṣā*, as stipulated by Nyāya, is satisfied here. Yet one would hesitate calling this a 'sentence', unlike when one is presented with an expression, such as, say, 'He sprinkles it with water'. We are inclined to say that this definition is rather wet and restricted, since it allows only partly-intelligible, though not nonsensical, expressions to pass as sentences.

On the other hand, however, if the concern is exclusively with explicating the marks of grammaticality, then this definition is a quite plausible one. Nevertheless, there remains one worry with this definition in that it pivots a very important feature of sentence on its 'grammaticalness' and does not take into account its *semantical* character. Should one not consider whether it is appropriate to allow semantically anomalous items to collaborate in an expression, which *may* have the form of a 'sentence', but which fail to generate an *intelligible* (as distinct from an 'incomplete') sense? Could not Nyāya qualify this definition in order to accomodate the issues which appear to be at stake here? Jagadīśa's response is that, in general terms, since the expression that has *ākāṅkṣā* satisfies a *formal* requirement, it should be accepted as a sentence – this is the argument of 'grammatical acceptability'.

However, in more specific and particularised terms, if the *śābdabodha* generated is not contradictory (*abādhita*) (unlike when one identifies some purposeful goal or end [perhaps sounding a cautionary note, in the above example, when superphosphate, or some weedkiller is being sprayed excessively]), then we have every reason to regard such expressions as valid sentences. Otherwise, of course, it is not to be regarded as such.[32] Jagadīśa is here qualifying sentence in terms of *śābdabodha* or the cognitive criteria pertinent to the comprehension of sentence-sense and not in terms of some abstracted grammatical consideration, or at least not purely in these terms. The *kāraṇas* or criteria of *yogyatā* and *āsatti* or *saṃnidhi* are added beside *ākāṅkṣā* in order to complete the analysis of sentence structure and its understanding.

4.15 *Yogyatā*, as we shall see in the next chapter, requires that the mutually associating words be compatible in their meaning-content : that is to say, they should be semantically competent. Thus, under normal circumstances, one would have no difficulty accepting the expression 'he sprinkles it with water' as a sentence that does not stand in need of another word to complete its utterance, nor does it conjure up the curious anxiety about what seems to be not-yet-said as the other expression we saw earlier would appear to. *Āsatti* requires that words in a sentence should appear in close proximity to each other in order for their *sāmarthya* to be effective.

In other words, *words* that are to be the constituents of sentence *A* should not be jumbled up with words of another expression *B*. *Āsatti* is also known as *saṃnidhi*.

We may note that the formal definition by Amarasiṃha ('the naïve view' 4.2) has undergone considerable modification and has developed in the background of the larger problem of *śābdabodha*. In this respect, the definition of a 'significant' sentence that Nyāya has come up with, could be regarded as quite plausible and suitable for our purposes, at least, and in so far as it assists with the analysis of *śābdabodha*, which afterall is our main concern here. Keśava Miśra sums up the modified definition for us:

> *vākyaṃ tvākāṅkṣā-yogyatā-saṃnidhimatāṃ padānāṃ samūhaḥ*[33] -

> A (significant) sentence consist of a collection of (inflected) words that has (in its interrelation) the properties of *ākāṅkṣā* (syntactic expectancy), *yogyatā* (semantic competence), and *saṃnidhi* or *āsatti* (contiguity or proximity of word-items).

But to be fairer to Keśava Miśra, we should give the fully-fledged definition he refurbishes from the above:

> *arthapratipādanadvārā śrotuḥ padāntaraviṣayāmarthāntaraviṣayāṃ vākāṅkṣāṃ janayatāṃ pratīyamānaparasparānvaya-yogyārthapratipādakānāṃ saṃnihitānāṃ padānāṃ samūho vākyam*[33a].

> A sentence is a collection of words. (These words) have the capacity to signify (or designate) 'objects', (and occur) in close proximity and are mutually (semantically) interrelated. Hearing (these words) generate, by virtue of their respective significations, an apprehension of expectancy either of words (to complement the other words), or of the signified 'objects' (to complement) those signified by the other words (in the utterance-whole).

B. *Saṃsargamaryādā*

4.16 Now if sentence is said to be the significant unit of speech then the *sentence* as such should have primacy over and above the constituent words of the sentence. But this raises a problem, in fact two problems—viz. (a) how are the constituent words related to the sentence? and (b) how does sentence-meaning *comprehension* arise from the words, or word-meanings?

Some responses to these questions have already been intimated in the earlier discussion on the definition of sentence. The implication is that, logically the *śābdabodha* that arises from apprehending a sentence is quite distinct from the meaning of each of the single words in the expression. This is so because the words have to be related to each other in accordance with the prerequisites for a significant sentence, such as *ākāṅkṣā*, *yogyatā* and so forth. But how exactly do the words contribute to the sentence 'whole'? and what becomes of the words once they collaborate to form a sentence? that is to say, do the words have any significant 'existence' outside of the sentence? There are even more problems in this context than we need concern ourselves with in the present discussion; but there are a few that we cannot ignore, such as those we have just stated, and which do require our attention.

It would appear that when one understands the 'meaning' of a sentence, one usually comprehends some 'whole' that is more than the meanings of the words taken in isolation. This is generally the case, though not invariably so. In other words, something different seems to occur when words, with respect to their distinct significations, are placed together in a composite expression, such as in a phrase or a sentence. For what they signify in isolation seem to undergo a transformation when a collective 'meaning' or sense arises from the sentence. While the constituent words, for example, "shut" and "door" could be uttered together in different contexts to convey quite a different sense—as, for instance, in "shut the door", or "shut-up and out the door!" What accounts for the difference is the nature of the interrelation that occurs between the constituent parts, and which may differ from one context to another. It is the interrelation between the constituent parts that, in the first instance, yields holistic meaning which is distinct from, and greater than, the 'sum' of the meanings of words in isolation. What is being stressed here is that the nature of the relation word-meanings enter into in a collective expression, as in a phrase or a sentence, is different from the sorts of relation, say, numbers in an arithmetical sum enter into, where the resultant number is not greater than the sum-total of the parts. For instance, 7 + 5 = 12. The number 12 does not embrace a numeral that is not already in the collection of 7 + 5. It is not as though the sum is totally new and distinct from its constituent parts, namely, 7 + 5. We could, moreover, break down the sum and rearrange it in terms of the different factors of '5 + 7', '6 + 6', '8 + 4', '4 + 8', '2 + 10', and so on, which would not make any difference to the total product. Thus the relation signified by the '+' sign is a constant one, in all the instances where the product is 12.

The same, however, cannot be said to be true in the case of the 'relation' of words and word-meanings in a sentence—much as we said of letters that go to make a word, or two (e.g. 'bear', 'bear'). Let us suppose the relation between the *word-meanings* is determined by the juxtaposition of words in a certain (syntactic) order. Now consider the expression '(The) dog drinks milk'. Can we rearrange the words with the hope of retaining a constancy in the relation among their meanings? For instance, can we say "milk drinks (the) dog", without altering the overall 'meaning' of the earlier sentence? Obviously we cannot. Hence, we are made to realise that a sentence-formation involves something more than a random collection of words in some undetermined order, and that the *relation* of their meaning is also a determined quantity which is not merely given as the 'sum' of their distinct meanings. This relation, however, is a novel element in the sentence, which is not present in the isolated words, but comes about when their respective meanings combine in a particular 'pattern' to yield a composite sense, which we call "meaning" of the sentence (*vākyārtha*). This *relation* is called *saṃsarga*; and as a unique linguistic property in *śābdabodha* or the understanding generated by a sentence, it is called *saṃsargamaryādā*[34] or 'relational coalescence'. Its importance is recognised in Navya-nyāya philosophy of language. Let us explore the implications of this unique factor for *śābdabodha*.

4.17 When someone understands the 'meaning' of a sentence, we most often assume that the person already knows the meaning of just about each of the words occurring in the sentence, i.e. an awareness of the meanings of the words occurring in a sentence is a necessary, although not a sufficient condition for knowing the meaning of the sentence as a whole. However, we cannot assume that knowing the meanings of words occurring in the sentence will *ipso facto* lead to the cognition of the meaning of the sentence – i.e. to an *understanding of the sentence-sense* (*śābdabodha*). This is so, for there are numerous cases in experience where one is acquainted with the words and their meanings occurring in a sentence, yet one either somehow misunderstands the sentence or fails to comprehend it. This presumably indicates that the awareness of the meanings of words in isolation from their inter-relation in an expression in a particular context of utterance is not sufficient to lead to a comprehension of the 'sense' of the sentence. And nor merely from a 'perception' of the sentence with respect to its constituent words. Evidently, something more has to be apprehended besides the constituent words and their meanings. But this implies that the comprehension of the meanings of words is different from the "comprehension" of the 'meaning' of the sentence.

On the other hand, one may never have heard that sentence before, but is yet able to understand it, or at least something from it. Children, for instance, show an incredible capacity to construct and understand new sentences, and this cannot be explained adequately in terms merely of the prior knowledge of meanings of constituent words, as we have just shown. For what accounts for the difference is the emergence from the sentence of the 'meaning' which is a product of the interrelation of the meanings of the individual words. However, when one utters a sentence, one does not think first of the words that would give rise to the 'meaning' of the sentence, but thinks usually of the proposition *qua* 'whole-sense' (*akhaṇḍārtha*), or subsentential parts such as clauses (*khaṇḍavākya*)[35] one wishes to convey, and then goes about, as best as one can, selecting from his vocabulary the words appropriate to express that. Which is to say that he finds words with those meanings whose interrelation would give rise to the overall desired sense on the form of the 'meaning' of the sentence he thus utters. Hence, the stress is not on the 'meaning of words', but on the meaning *qua* 'sense' of the sentence, prior to its division into constituent, 'meaningful' words. This is why Bhartṛhari and Prabhākara put much emphasis on *akhaṇḍārthatva*[36], the 'holistic' character of sentence prior to any consideration of the constituent bits, which in their view can never stand as meaningful units in isolation from the sentence. The division into word-meanings may be a necessary precondition for expressing the 'whole-sense' in meta-speech, but it is not necessary for its being what it basically is, namely the 'whole-sense' in understanding. Thus, what we see emerging here is the notion of relation among word-meanings which is determined by the prior requirement of conveying a *holistic sense, akhaṇḍārtha*, which is not always present singularly in any word or components constituting the sentence—allowing, though, for 'one-word' sentence.

This relation, or *saṃsarga*, then, is one precondition for sentence-formation and therefore of sentence-understanding or *śābdabodha*. Indian linguists, however, are not unanimous in regarding the relation to be among words, word-meanings, or word-powers (*padaśakti*)—i.e. it is not clear whether the *saṃsarga* is between *pada*, *padārtha* or *padaśakti*, or among some other 'parts' into which a sentence can be divided in accordance with the theory they each propose. We should now look at some of these issues and note how the responses bear on the analysis of *śābdabodha*.

4.18 Nyāya, as we saw earlier, describes the structure of a sentence in terms of a qualified-qualifier relation. The Nyāya theory is based on the logical commitment that an integrated whole, W (*avayavin*) is different from its parts, P (*avayava*).[37] Hence, the qualifying terms in an expression are integrated with respect to the meanings of each constituent word (*pada*). But the 'meaning-whole' that emerges is a separate whole (W_m) from its constituent parts (P_m).

Each word has the capacity to be related to its meaning, the functional relation termed *vṛtti*, as we saw earlier. Now in a sentence-utterance, this capacity is extended so that a novel sentence structure arises from the sequential interrelation of the relative significations of the component words with respect to the inflectional and syntactical rules. The *vṛtti* (or *padavidhi*, as it is also called) is capable of effecting a 'bridge' or a fusion among the mutually connected (*samartha*) words, and is, in a collective sense, responsible for generating a 'coalesced' understanding *qua saṃsargamaryādā* of the sentence, with which the audience may have had no prior acquaintance.[38] We need not, however, assume this capacity to be distinct to the *śakti* in virtue of which words can operate with either the *abhidhā*, primary signification, or *lakṣyā*, the secondary signification or 'implication'. This capacity enables two or more words to be related in respect of their individual 'meanings' in a certain sequence that yields an integrated whole of 'meaning'. It has also been called *tātparyaśakti* (which is quite distinct from the *kāraṇa* of *tātparya*, and with which it is not to be confused). Now formalising the structure of *śābdabodha*, we get the following:[38a]

'*x* qualified by *y*' or *Q(xy)*, where *x* is the qualified and *y* the qualifier. Let the following sentence be our example:

ghaṭam ānaya: 'Bring the pot.' (i)

The parts of this sentence that constitute its meaning-elements, in a non-syntactical structure could be represented as follows:

ghaṭaḥ karmatvam ānayanaṃ kṛtiḥ (ii)

'a pot, accusative relation (*karmatvam*) of bringing, an effort (mental disposition)'

The *śābdabodha* or the cognitive content, i.e. the propositional structure would have the following paraphrase:

ghaṭa-vṛtti-karmatānirupakānayanānukūla-kṛtimāṃ tvam (iii)

'you (*t*) are qualified by the effort (*k*) of generating the activity of of bringing (*a*) which has a pot (*g*) as its object' = *Q(tQ(kQ(ag)))*.

The analysis indicates that there is required some volitional effort that would cause the cow to be present in the intended place. Now even though an agency (*kartṛ*) is not expressed explicitly, (a convention in Sanskrit), Nyāya would regard this to be implicit in the *verb*al suffix '*hi*' signifying mental effort (*kṛti*) which is taken as being possessed by an agent.

The *kartṛ* is qualified by 'bringing', as it is causally related to the *kṛti*, and 'bringing' in turn is qualified by its predicate-entity, namely, 'cow' through the accusative relation (*karmatvam*) (which is why it takes the accusative *kāraka*,'*gām*', "the cow"). We should note that in the analysis neither the constituent 'cow' nor the activity of 'bringing' assumes the status of *mukhya-viśeṣa*, as they may in their counterpart in Mīmāṃsā or in the grammarian analyses. And further, because the second (analytical) expression does not have its components interrelated in conformity with the syntactic property of *ākāṅkṣā*, much less inflectional rules, it is not capable of generating *śābdabodha*, precisely because it is not a 'well-formed sentence'. But it does nevertheless succeed in showing how the constituents of the former utterance are connected and related, and how the prerequisite for a 'well-formed sentence', namely *ākāṅkṣā*, fails to do so. Nonetheless, in so far as the latter represents the *śābdabodha* generated by the former, its value lies in confirming that the 'coalesced meaning' arises not from discrete word-meanings but from interrelated word-meanings. Thus, what is novel here is the *saṃsargamaryādā*, the element of relational meaning fusion. It may be noted in this this connection that, here no recourse is taken to the meanings of the constituent words other than their primary significations or *abhidhā*. *Lakṣaṇā* (secondary signification) is not invoked for the sentence-sense, as Mīmāṃsā (Bhāṭṭa in particular) argues for.[39] The element of intentionality (*tātparya*) is taken into consideration in cases where something slightly different may have been meant, i.e. intended in the particular context of the utterance. In the case of the above example, the speaker may have intended the cow to be brought for inspection and not for the routine milking round.

4.19 What we are looking at here, I suppose, is whether the relation is between words alone or some other linguistic features in an utterance. A Nyāya response, just stated, is that the interrelation is between word-meanings, thus the capacity is with respect to their *mukhyavṛtti*—i.e. the capacity to express the primary meaning. But this could mean that the words together in a collection do not combine to yield a meaningful whole to the audience unless one also knows their meanings. For example, if the only two English words a newly arrived migrant to an English-speaking region has learned to recognise and pronounce were 'crossing' and 'train', and on his cross-country journey he catches a glimpse of these words apparently appearing together on a roadside sign-post, namely as "TRAIN CROSSING", could we not say with some assurance that the person would understand what he 'reads'? Nyāya would respond that the traveller would either have to know the 'meanings' of each term as the components of a linguistic expression, *or* that he would have to know them as some form of *signs* standing for or signalling some other thing or event, just as he would if two lengths of red boards, crossed to form an "**X**" sign, were posted by a railway level-crossing. While the former invokes a semantical criterion, the latter evidently involves a *signal* which can be operative independently of language.

Otherwise, all he would be able to say is that he 'knows' the words but he does not know what they mean, much less what they *express together.*[40] Even if he knew the meaning of one of the terms, let us say of 'TRAIN', he may be able to make some sense from the context – viz. through his concomitant awareness of the railway line, that a train could be making its way across the road at any time, probably without much warning. We catch ourselves often reading the work of another, or hearing them read, as we stumble upon some word in the expression which we recognise, even acknowledge acquaintance with it, but either do not recall its meaning, or find the meaning or 'sense' not to be too clear in the context. Thus, we constantly refer to lexicons for the 'meaning', or the different nuances the word is likely to have; yet these recursive meanings may be of little help when we are confronted with profound utterances that make use of the same words in ways that appear paradoxical, or equivocal, if not outright confusing.[41]

4.20 Bhāṭṭa Mīmāṃsā, agreeing basically with all that Nyāya has to say regarding the above, picks, however, on a more specific issue. It concerns the process of the assimilation of sentence-meaning to which Mīmāṃsā would like to add the function of *lakṣaṇā* to complement the function of *śakti.*[42] So Bhāṭṭas argue that since the primary or express meaning of the words in a sentence signifies only a universal, without indicating the particular (or individual), or space or time, there is need of another function to do the latter job. In the case of the expression "Bring the cow", the word 'cow' directly expresses the generic *cowness,* and only indirectly via the secondary signification function (*lakṣaṇā*), does it indicate or denote the *individual* cow as the particular object related to the *bhāvanā,* the actualisation by way of 'bringing', enjoined in the sentence. That is to say, the word "bring" directly expresses the *action of bringing* in general, but 'it indirectly indicates the particular act of *bringing* pertaining to the time.'[43] Thus, we cannot assume that *śakti* is sufficient for generating the 'meaning' of the sentence specific to the individual in the particular context in which the sentence is uttered. Hence, the meanings of words require first to be transformed from their more generic to the individual significations as ground for their application in the particular context of utterance.

Is there, however, any truth to the argument, that the express or primary (*abhidhā*) referend of a word is the 'concept' of the universal, and that the particular is indirectly indicated, whether in the 'same cognition' (*samān saṃvit*) or in a subsequent cognition where reference to the individual is apprehended? Now, not all the sentences are limited to expressing conceptual structures applicable in respect of the universal; many sentences are uttered to make direct reference to the individual or particular things and events in the course of daily experience. Though we hear sentences like "All swans are white" and "All elephants are huge", we also often hear sentences such as "A pair of swans is swimming in the Isis (river)", and "That elephant is called Rāja" and so forth.

Now, if in the case of the latter sentences we were to presume that the reference was to the universals of 'swan' and 'elephant' then this would not lead to a very intelligible sense: we can hardly imagine all the swans to be in the river Isis, or all elephants being called Rāja: nor, that in speaking of a pair of swans, we are making reference to the whole class of swans, or rather the whole class of water-birds called swans. We are, of course, making specific reference to some select members of the class-species, but this is hardly accomplished through the *abhidhā per se*. We have, then, to agree with Mīmāṃsā that *śakti* is not sufficient, however much necessary it is, for the delivery of the whole 'sense' of the sentence. Admittedly that this could be qualified in some way so as to take into account reference to the particular thing, i.e. the individual in the relevant context. Need we, however, agree that it is necessarily the function of *lakṣaṇā* to disclose the individual or specific meaning that is applicable in the context? If we consider that Advaita and Nyāya do not always require *lakṣaṇā* to disclose the individual or the particular thing or action, and considering that Advaita suggests other alternatives whereby such are also disclosed, (a thesis we shall consider later),[44] we can at least be assured that *lakṣaṇā* is not necessary in each such case of sentence-comprehension. We may agree that large numbers of sentences require this where the primary signification alone would lead to an incongruous 'sense', and where no other factors, like *tātparya*, or intention of the speaker, were present, as, for example, with the utterance 'The village on the Ganges'.

We may also reconsider the Nyāya view that the primary signification is invariably the individual, though qualified by the *jāti* or universal, though this latter is only so in specific uses of the words in sentences in particular instances, and since the accepted Advaita view is that the primary signification is the 'universal qualified by the individual', we find ourselves in half-agreement with the Bhāṭṭa Mīmāṃsā position in this regard. The more important point, however, that emerges from this analysis is that Advaita, Bhāṭṭa Mīmāṃsā and Nyāya all agree that in every sentence, each of the component words directly express its own meaning—be it universal or individual—and indirectly indicate that each word-meaning is *related* to the specific meaning of other words in the sentence. This view is characterised as *abhihitānvayavāda*—i.e. the *interrelation* of the given word-*meanings* is what is understood. Bhāṭṭa and Nyāya do insist, in explicating this view, that the capacity to interrelate is solely with the *meanings* of the words and does not rest with the component words themselves. 'This capacity, in other words, is invested in *artha* not in the *pada*.'[45] To Nyāya, this capacity rests solely with *śakti*, while for Bhāṭṭa it rests with *lakṣaṇā*. Advaita simply maintains that in some cases *lakṣaṇā* is resorted to, while in other cases, it is an extension of *śakti* in its instance-specific qualifications. This capacity has two aspects to it: (a) *smārikā śakti* or the capacity to recall and thus to present the meanings of words which are components of the sentence; and (b) *anubhāvikā śakti* or the capacity that enables the meanings of the components of the sentence to be related more holistically and in reference to the experience or activity in the given situation. In other words, according to the Advaita view, the express meanings or *mukhyārthas* of the words of the sentence have the relative capacity to be connected with each other (*vyapekṣā*). This 'power' rests with the meaning. The resultant 'sense' is the *vākyārtha*, which to the Bhāṭṭa is *lakṣyārtha* or derived through secondary meanings. But for this slight compromise to the Nyāya-Prābhākaran views, Dharmarāja follows Bhaṭṭa, as a rule.[46]

4.21 Now what is basically being suggested is that the meaning-whole is a product of word-meanings in interrelation, and since that which is *relative* cannot be known by itself, but through the knowledge of the relation of the component parts, the 'meaning' of a sentence can be known only if the component parts are known. This means, in Bhāṭṭa terms, that the awareness of *words* is to be supplemented with awareness of *word-meanings* as the other elements of the relational structure. And what is assumed, thus, is that in order to comprehend the *meaning* of the sentence, one has to know the meaning of each word occurring in that sentence. "Meaning", of course, is to be taken in the extended sense of specific signification applicable in the context, and which may be gathered from the context itself—such as from the intentionality involved in the particular utterance.

But does this mean that a sentence is not understood if some word occurring in it is not known, or if its specific sense fails to register in the mind of the audience? Or perhaps could we assume that the meaning of the sentence is first grasped, *after* which the meaning of the anomalous word is understood? One may, indeed, hear a sentence uttered in which words with unknown meanings occur, and yet, somehow, succeed in understanding the sentence. The Nyāya response is that, as with the case of elliptical sentences, one would tend to supply the 'meaning' by looking at the context and then understand the meaning of the sentence-whole. In other words, all the meanings of the relevant words and sections of the sentence are known either through recollection or through the context before *śābdabodha* arises. Nyāya denies the view that it is the *sentence* which is first understood as a meaningful unit, and that words come to acquire their relative meaning subsequently—from their use, or usage, in the particular context. But what Nyāya denies is exactly what the Prābhākara Mīmāṃsā maintains, namely that words are the constituent units (*padas*) of a sentence,[47] but disputes that the mutual relation is indicated by the word-meanings and not by the *words* themselves in consonance with the 'whole-sense' (*ekārtha*) one desires to communicate.

A corollary of Prabhākara's *anvitābhidhāna* theory of sentence-comprehension, as distinct from the Bhāṭṭa theory of *abhihitānvaya* ('meaning-constructionalism'), is that one first understands the sentence-meaning (*vākyārtha*) and then, if necessary, locates the meanings of the constituent word-units,[48] although their functional value would be considered to be negligible.

Prabhākara, however, was less insistent on the absolute indivisibility of sentences into word-components, as was the Bhartṛharian view, which stated that a 'sentence is indivisibly one and complete in all respects, wanting no help from any *outside* word, for a sentence is said to be *eko'navayavaḥ śabdaḥ*: a single undivided speech-unit.'[49] Prābhākara's seems to be a compromise to the Bhartṛharian position, in keeping with the *padavādins* ('word constructionalists'). Prabhākara, we must remember, took it for granted there were such linguistic items as words, and he assumed that it is possible to attribute to these words what we might call 'meaning'. He further accepted the divisibility of sentences into three basic parts which are linked by the requirement of mutual expectancy; the most important of these components being, as we saw earlier, the *verb*al element (*ākhyāta-śabda*), as we saw earlier. Yet to Prabhākara they each derive their relative significance from *within* the 'whole sense' of the sentence. In this respect, it could be said that Prabhākara's theory borders on the *akhaṇḍatva* ('holistic') view, but does not reach that far. In fact, Bhartṛhari is critical of the Prābhākaran compromise, since to Bhartṛhari, words are merely the artificial constructs of the grammarians, and therefore from this point of view, they are unreal (*asatya*). How can something 'unreal' give rise to the *real*?[50] But to Prabhākara, what were unreal were not so much the *words* as the *word-meanings* outside of the *context* of the sentence. If ever, therefore, we are to be concerned with 'word-meanings' we can do this only retrospectively by looking at the 'word-meanings' as *recursive* items in sentence utterance, which provide the context for the occurrence of words in virtue precisely of which there arises sentence-sense comprehension. This theory can thus be dubbed the 'context-meaning', as distinct from the Bhāṭṭa 'meaning-constructional' thesis.

4.22 Against the Prābhākara view we can say that however true this description may *appear* to be in everyday experience, that such instances of understanding the meanings of sentences first, and of the word-meanings later, occur only in cases where we have already known or memorised those sentences. And sometimes we do understand sentences with unknown words, but their omission does not alter drastically the overall sense of the sentence, as the Nyāya theory would seem to hold. Sometimes, superfluous adjectives and adverbs are used more for the sake of emphasis than for conveying the basic sense of the utterance.

The use, however, of unknown sentences with unknown or unfamiliar words that invariably generate sentence-meaning in the audience, are only few. While on the other hand, if a child, or a new language-learner, learns the meanings of words and the modes of their interconnection first, then he can understand the meanings of an unlimited number of sentences which he may never have heard before nor memorised.

This important and rather enigmatic point to be made about such instances is often overlooked, particularly in its implications for a theory which suggests that the apprehension of word-meaning precedes the awareness of word-meanings independent of each other. If it is suggested, as in some modern linguistic schools, that some basic organisational structures or 'patterning' of sentences—such as the Chomskian deep-structures—are innately or intuitively known prior to the encounter with specific sentences with those underlying structures, then there may be little dispute, for we will still have to admit that the surface-structure components are learnt beforehand, and this is the point Nyāya, Mīmāṃsā and Advaita also wish to make. To understand the sentence, then, we are still faced with saying that the 'surface' structure *qua meanings* of words and their interrelation occurring in the sentence are apprehended first, either by recollection from the perception of the words, or derived from the context with sufficient awareness of the meanings of most of the words in the sentence: *vākyārthajñāna or śābdabodha* is, therefore, *padārthasaṃsargajanyajñāna*. After which the *sense* of the sentence can be said to arise in a 'flash' of understanding (*pratibhājñāna*) in the audience.

4.23 To sum up the Mīmāṃsā position, before we apprehend the meaning-whole of the sentence, we must be pre-acquainted with the meanings of the words independently of each other. Their interrelation in a syntactical structure generates an independent meaning-whole we call *vākyārtha* or 'sentence-meaning' (may be 'sentence-sense' in some contexts), and the *understanding* of which is called *śābdabodha* : *athedānīṃ padārthā avagatāḥ santo vākyārthaṃ gamayanti.*[51] But the *padārthā*, like brick and mortar in a building construction, have to be structured and organised in a certain way, such that the arrangement can yield a relation which is distinct from the constituents themselves. The relation is really the way or 'form' in which the constituents have been arranged. What determines these relations, and what precise mechanism, so to speak, is involved in this stage of the process is something we shall raise in the next two chapters. But it is also important to emphasise that sentence-meaning does not consist merely in an apprehension of these relations but is supplemented by the awareness of word-meanings too. In short, a sentence does not merely indicate the relation of words, but the totality of word-meanings related together in a particular structure. For, as we set out to say, a mere collection of words, even when their individual word-meanings are known, is not sufficient, though it may be necessary, for generating an understanding of sentence-meaning. And unless one had a prior acquaintance with the sentence-meaning, without apprehending the 'relational coalescence' among the constituent word-meanings. In brief, without apprehension of the *relational content*, it would be difficult to derive an understanding of the sentence-meaning on the part of one who hears the construction for the first time.

We know from common experience that if the meanings of words are already known one may have less difficulty in understanding the meaning of the sentence, provided the relational construction does not present formidable difficulty, and other linguistic conditions are fulfilled. The same words, furthermore, would, in an altered structure, give rise to a different or slightly variant understanding, since the 'proposition' expressed by the sentence is also likely to be different. This still does not mean that a sentence-meaning as a *whole-sense* can be reduced simply to the constituent word-meanings, for even though the 'meaning' of a sentence is a relative product (*uktaram*), it can yet be conceived of as an 'entity' that is independent of the meanings of the constituent words and their interrelations.

We may agree with Prabhākara, and indeed with the *anvitābhidhāna* ('context-meaning') theory, that the division of a sentence into the constituent words *and* their distinct individual 'meanings' is artificial, in so far as we can also make the point that such a statement as we have just made, on the one hand, pertains to the 'whole-sense' that precedes the utterance of the sentence, and on the other hand, to what follows, namely, the *śābdabodha* that occurs. In other words, let us suppose we can distinguish the following two major stages. (a) The stage where the 'whole-sense' to be expressed - but is not yet expressed—first arises, and the later step in which the understanding (*bodha*) has arisen, from (b) the stage when the utterance is being made *expressing* this 'sense', and the hearing and processing-assimilative step that follows immediately (*vyāpārasagamyate*). If we succeed in this, then, the 'gestaltist' view of sentence represented by

Prabhākara's theory of 'context-meaning' can be retained without much damage to the 'meaning-construction' thesis, which, in our estimate, bases its analysis on the intermediate stage. Hence, the apparently conflicting theories can be integrated as *complementary* approaches to the problem of *śābdabodha* by shifting the locus more towards the audience.[52] And as we said earlier, some cases are explained by one view, while for others, especially where it concerns children and new language-learners, the latter is more adequate account of the process. It is then not a totally artificial operation when a sentence-meaning is analysed in terms of its constituent words and especially in terms of its word-meanings and their interrelations.

Some protagonists of either view go into much greater detail and debate over the differences represented in the two views, but we do not feel that our purpose here warrants a more detailed undertaking than that which we have already presented. That is to say, in as much as we have shown that *śābdabodha* can be accounted for and explained in terms of meaning-whole of a sentence, apprehended in a unified 'whole-sense' (*pratibhāk-haṇḍārtha*) that arises as one becomes aware of the meanings of the constituent words and their mutual relations, we have done enough. Śabara argues likewise, and presents his view on *śābdabodha* based on just this analysis, viz. that the novel element is not merely the awareness of the mutual relation (*sambandha*) of words and their meanings, but the *śab-davijñāna* or '(the propositional) understanding of things (*tasya*) signified by the words'; that is how the scripture gives us knowledge through an understanding of the sentential meaning (*śāstraṃ śabdavijnānād yadasan-nikṛṣṭārtha vijñānam*).[53] Since what is comprehended in this way is a distinct and novel *understanding*, Jagadīśa calls this *anvayabodha.*[54]

4.24 There are still a few issues outstanding in respect of the different views canvassed by their respective protagonists. A number of similar attempts have also been made to reconcile the two major theses. Professor Mohanty makes a useful observation in this regard: 'Both the theories have a concept of *padārtha* or word-meaning. They differ however as to what role such a concept could be allowed to play in semantic theory. Each word has its own meaning, hearing a word even reminds the auditor of its meaning *per se*. . .But this *reminding* is *not* signifying or denoting, and belongs not to the semantic theory but, let us say, to psychology.'[55] The *anvitābhidhāna* theorist would most likely agree with these characterisation of his position, but would presumably beg that their theory remain within the confines of linguistic analysis, as the denial of direct *meaning* comprehension does not entail the negation of syntactical and other grammatical criteria that are not parasitic upon any "psychological" explanation. Prabhākara would want to say that he is describing a linguistic disposition minus perhaps the semantic category at the *word* level.

In a similar spirit but from a different angle, J.F. Staal makes a suggestion that, perhaps we ought to look at the two theories in the context of their relative functions within the tradition. The Prābhākara, as we saw, was more concerned with *bhāvanā* or *kriyā* : 'what-ought-to-be-actualised or accomplished (*sādhya*)' through certain activities in order to succeed towards some end or goal. Now a sentence that embodies an injunction itself pertains to the whole without needing to go through the parts, or words and their meanings. The verbal case ending would be sufficient to show, (a) whether the sentence is a primary sentence or an *arthavāda* (elucidatory), and (b) the "efficient-force" (*bhāvanā*) could be called an extreme form of "syncategorematicism".[56] While the other theory, supported by Kumārila, is less concerned with 'what is to be accomplished' and is more interested presumably in what is already 'established' (actualised, *siddha*), for which knowledge is the key.[57] It thus makes it easier for Advaita to prefer this theory over the former.

4.25 The only crucial difference, for our purposes at least, that needs to be exposed between the Prābhākara and the Bhāṭṭa views in this regard is that with the former, words first give us a vague impression of the recollectable meanings and *then* the *significatory* capacity or *śakti* begins its operation of disclosing the 'meaning' as a related whole-sense. Hence, words in virtue of their *śakti*, yield related and not unrelated meanings in which conditioning factors of meaningful combinations are already implicated. Outside of the sentence, words have no real and substantive significance. But this is empirically weak, for we have lexical meanings of words, and we know meanings of several words in isolation, and not necessarily in their interrelational capacity in a sentence. However, Prabhākara's other strong point is taken when he stresses the unified structure of sentence-meaning, which cannot be easily reduced to isolated units, for each word is interrelated with the others. But, here, we need not concern ourselves further with the differences, for both Bhāṭṭa and Advaita also say that, first, unrelated meanings are recollected and then the related meaning or 'sense' arises. However, the inter-relating proceeds on the basis of the factors, such as the *kāraṇas*, that are often more overt than tacit as Prabhākara assumes them to be. The more familiar one is with a sentence, rather with the recursive structure, the closer one gets to the Prābhākaran criterion; and the more tacit the process is assumed to be, the closer to the Bhartṛharian view. But while in the process of learning a language (which involves a large degree of unfamiliar structures), our acquaintance with many of the words of these sentences may yet fail to yield their interrelated sense, and thus here the Bhāṭṭa criterion comes to the rescue, as it were, with the analysis of *śābdabodha* in respect of 'words' and 'meanings'. But here is another aspect of the extended *vyāpāra* on which both sides are agreed, and which Dharmarāja presents rather lucidly. This involves the causal factors (*kāraṇas*), (a) that determine the precise manner in which the mutual relations occur, and (b) that condition the *śābdabodha* in the audience. In the next two chapters we turn to examine these in some detail and this will take us towards the closing stages of the process that generates *śābdabodha*.

NOTES TO CHAPTER FOUR

1. Kunjunni Raja, *Indian Theories of Meaning*, p152. *Cf* P. S. Sastri, *op cit* p242.

2. Annambhaṭṭa attributes this view to Amarasiṃha, *TS* #59 (BORI, p50, also see notes p329). *Cf. Tarkabhāṣā* under *śabda: ata eva 'gauraścaḥ puruṣo hastī iti padāni na vākyam'* (p 13, 1959; p47, 1979).

3. *Pāṇini-sūtras* 2.1.1 (*PS*, Kielhorn 1892 = BORI 1962, p365 Vol I). N. B. The *Vyākaraṇa Mahābhāṣya (MBh)* of Patañjali includes Kātyāyana's *Vārttika*, hereafter *Vārttika.*

4. *Vārttika* on *PS* 2.1.1 (Kielhorn p367). *Cf 'ekatiṅ vākyasaṃjñaṃ bhavatīti vaktavyam, brūhi brūhi'*, Patañjali on *Vārttika* 10, *ibid.* Also *PS* 8.1.28: *tiṅṅ atiṅaḥ.* There is considerable dispute as to whether Pāṇini himself was of the view of 'one verb per sentence' as Kātyāyana took Pānini basically to be saying; Patañjali followed Kātyāyana, it would appear. Some have argued that Pānini, contrary to Kātyāyana's reading, may have allowed for more than one finite verb in a sentence in spite of the *tiṅṅ atiṅaḥ* rule. For review of this issue see S. D. Joshi *Patañjali's Vyākaraṇa-Mahābhāṣya, Samarthānika PS 2.1.1* (Poona p108ff), and B. K. Matilal, 'Indian Theorists on the Sentence.' (*op cit*) p377ff.

   Note also: *na ca samānavākye dve tiṅante staḥ (MBh* III p374,25). Other interesting features of the old grammarian definition to note are : *pṛthagarthānām-ekārthībhāvaḥ samarthavacanam ekārthībhāva* = 'singly integrated meaning', *Vārttika* no 1 (on *PS* 2.1.1). *samānavākye nighātayuṣmadasmadādeśāḥ (ditto*, no 11, p367). *parasparavyapekṣāṃ sāmarthyameke* (dependence rule), no 4.

5. *Vyāsabhāṣya* on *Yogasūtras*, III.17: *sarvapadeṣu cāsti vākyaśaktiḥ avṛkṣa ityukte astīti gamyate* (Calcutta edn. 1981).

6. *na hi sattaṃ padārtho vyabhicaratīti* (*Ibid.*).

7. The grammarians concentration on the utter importance of the verb in the sentence, either in the form of *ākhyāta*, expressing *kriyā* or *kartā*, or *bhāvanā* (dispositional) is rather aptly depicted in the accompanying 'spokes-on-wheel' chart:

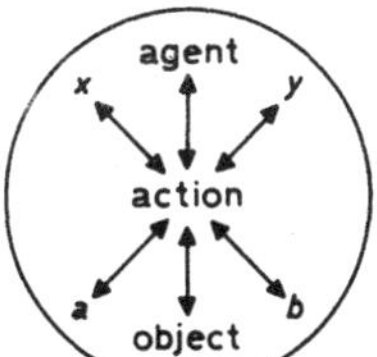

   (Diagram adopted from M. Deshpande, *op cit* p201.)

   Also, because the grammarian system is more action/act and less 'agency' oriented (*kriyā-bhāva vs kartṛbhāva*), certain seemingly unelegant sentences would appear to be acceptable – such as "the saw is cutting", "the ghost town sleeps", "the village went into frenzy", "the machine dictates letters", "the printer writes", "computers sake hands", "the syringe kills".

8. *Vārttika* 9 on *PS* 2.1.1: *ākhyātaṃ sāvyayakārakaviśeṣaṇaṃ vākyam*, (To Kātyāyana, '*atiṅ*' in *PS* VIII.1.28 is redundant). According to Dr Laddu a later commentator has revised this *vārttika* to read *ākhyātaṃ saviśeṣaṇam* (*op cit*, p227ff).

9. P. S. Sastri, 'The Ideal Content of a Sentence', *Calcutta Review*, (June 1957 pp239-56), p242. *Cf* Patañjali on *Vārttika* 9 above: *sāvyayaṃ sakārakaṃ sakārakaviśeṣaṇaṃ vākyasaṃjñaṃ bhavatīti vaktavyam . . . ākhyātaṃ saviśeṣaṇamityeva; sarvāṇi hyetāni kriyāviśeṣaṇāni.*

10. *MS* II.i.46 (text in *Mīmāṃsādarśana*, (I) p321; also discussed in *The Pūrva Mīmāṃsā Sūtra of Jaimini*, G. Jha, Vol I, p 213).

11. *Ibid.* (trans. from G.Jha in *Śābara-bhāṣya* GOS I p213); the translation given in the 1911 edn, though, is a slightly more Prābhākaran: 'So long as a single idea is expressed by number of words, which on being separated are found to be wanting in expressiveness, they should be taken as forming one sentence.' (p217). N. B. The occurrence of "idea" in place of "sense" or something more linguistic, or ontic. Note also Śabara's comment on this *sūtra* (text in 1889 p132; GOS I p214) : 'therefore it comes to this [,] a group of words serving a single purpose forms one sentence—but only if any one of the words, on being disjoined from the rest, becomes 'wanting' (defective).' (p213).

12. *Ibid.* Śabara is addressing the question: 'where the *mantras* are mixed, no clear indication of what is primary and what auxiliary to the sacrificial text -- how is it to be known that so far it is one *Yajuṣ mantra*?'

13. Kumārila in his *Tantravārttika* (gloss on *Śābara-bhāṣya*) Vol I p426 (Varanasi 1903; II.i.46): ***lokamantrabrāhmaṇeṣu avyabhicāri etadeva vākyalakṣaṇam sthitam. yattu na prāg vākyādarthatadekatvāvadhāraṇamastīti.*** See discussion in G. Jha, ***Pūrva Mīmāṃsā in its Sources,*** pp168–169.

14. G. Jha, *loc cit* (p169), quotes from Prabhākara's *Bṛhatī*: 'The comprehension of the *Mantra* is dependent upon its prescribed *use*. The meaning and purpose of the *Mantra* therefore can be ascertained from the metre. The present *Sūtra [MS* II.i.46] lays down the *extent* of the Mantra. The term '*Artha*' in the *Sūtra* stands for *Meaning* as well as *Purpose*; both being interrelated; but of the two, *purpose* is the predominant factor, that is why it has been emphasised by the author of the *Bhāṣya* [i.e. Śabara].'

15. *MS* II.1.47 : *sameṣu vākyabhedāḥ syāt* (trans by Jha GOS vol I p216; *Śābara-bhāṣya* in same, *loc cit*, text in 1889, p133):
yadyapi pratyakṣādinā pramāṇena nopalabhyate, śrutyā tu gamyate, iṣe tvā iti icchanatti, urje tvā iti anumārṣti. Śabara, in arguing for the independence of a sentence relative to each cluster of words, gives the above examples in which we find that the words '*Iṣe tvā' serve one purpose (being used in the 'chopping of the tree-branch') and the words 'urje tvā*', an entirely different purpose ('being used in the planning of the lopped branch' (Jha). Hence the two clusters of words ought to be treated as distinct sentences. See also Kumārila in *Tantravārttika* (1903, p431).

16. For a crypto-imperativist interpretation of Mīmāṃsā, despite the wide split within the school, see Shlomo Biderman, 'Religion and Imperative', *Religious Traditions* (1981, no. 4, pp59-70). Biderman's reading typifies a confusion of categories, particularly of the optativeness—i.e. the conditional—(*liṅtva*, as in the *codanā* or incentive-inducements, as in *svargakāmo yajeta*) on the one hand, with the strict "imperative" (*niyoga*), and *vidhi* or 'injunction', on the other hand, with 'command' (categorical and invoilable). The latter was perhaps more characteristic of the ancient, since extant, Old Testament-style, Bādari school, and Prābhākara to an extent, but not of Bhāṭṭa, which allowed for freedom within an autonomous morality. See next few notes.

17. *MS* I.1.25: *tadbhūtānāṃ kriyārthena sāmāmnāyaḥ arthasya tannimittatvāt* (1911, p18; Panini Office, Allahabad edition, 1923-5, p7): 'There (within sentence) occurs words with their own significations which merge with the word signifying action because the (unified) meaning (of the sentence) depends upon them.' In other words, all the constituent words in a sentence converge their purposefulness onto that of the 'action-word', because the unified meaning depends upon the interrelation of these words. See also I.1.2: *codanālakṣaṇo'rtha dharmaḥ* : Dharma is indicated by the incentive-inducing texts (of the Vedas, since they are conducive to the *summum bonum*).

18. *MS* II.1.1 : *bhāvārthāḥ karmaśabdaḥ tebhyaḥ kriyā pratīyeta, eṣa hi arthaḥ vidhīyate* (GOI 1)—'Words that express *bhāvārthāḥ* (the way it is to be or to be brought about [the way of 'be-ing' or 'be-coming'] are words that signify activity (*karmaśabda*), (and) from them is known the *kriyā* (action) that leads to the objective-result enjoined.' *MS* II.2.1 describes the different classes of 'action-words' or *verbs* in respect of their function

wholly and totally within a sentence-structure, but not outside of it.

Śabara's *bhāṣyas* on these *sūtras* are illuminating. Śabara aligns *bhāvanā* to the 'urge' or the 'incomparable desire or want' (*bhāvārtha*) that connects one with objects or some objective state of affairs that await to be brought about (*bhāvayet*). In pursuit of these humans are led to performing various kinds of acts, with the use of varying instruments that are conducive to short to long term goals. And it is only through *karmaśabda* that one comes to learn which is the appropriate means and how exactly the goal or purpose is to be achieved. Thus the *bhāvārtha karmaśabda* is a verb. *Yajeta* in *svargakāmo yageta* is a good example of this, since from this verb is known the *kriyā* (action) that has to be perfomed, and this in turn answers the expected question: what sort of objective accomplishment or *real*-isation (*artha*) does this word point to? The answer, obviously, is *Svarga* or 'heaven'. The *bhāvārtha,* or the incentive induced, then, could be analysed in terms of two significant dispositions or 'exigencies'—viz. *arthībhāvanā* (realisation of the significance of some objective goal or purpose) and *śābdībhāvanā* (the 'efficient force') impressed upon by the word (i.e. the 'action-word' or verb), as indicative of the wherewithal for the actualisation of the *artha,* which may be *apūrva* or quite novel and 'unseen' (*adṛṣṭa*). All verbs, in Mīmāṃsā view, invariably express *bhāvanā.* The more lofty the goal, the more complex the nature of the *bhāvanā* expressed. *Cf MS* II.1.5 (*codanā punarāmbhaḥ*). See also *Śābara-bhāṣya* on I.1.8 (32), where he shows how the *karmaśabda* functions to raise and respond to three expectations: 'what should be performed?', 'with what', and 'to what end?' Perhaps also 'How?'.

19. *bhāvanā nāma bhavitur-bhavanānukūlo bhāvayituḥ vyāpāraviśeṣaḥ sā dvīdheḥ śābdībhāvanā arthībhāvanā ceti*, in *Arthasaṃgraha* of Laugākṣi Bhāskara (1915, Varanasi, p18; 1977, p31ff). To elaborate: the injunctions in the Vedas are taken to be expressing *bhāvanā* or 'efficiency' ["exigency"], which is not a 'commandment', like 'Do this, or else. . .', but rather conditionals, like 'Should you wish *x*, you ought to do *y*'. This is more so with Kumārila who admitted that even a fool would not do something without a purpose or end in mind : *prayojanaṃ anuddiśya na mando'pi pravartate, ŚV, Sambandhākṣepaparihāraḥ* #55, p463 (1978 Varanasi edition).

As indicated in the previous note, the two terms of the conditional correspond to two sorts of 'efficiencies', namely, *arthībhāvanā* (the end-goal efficiency) and *śābdībhāvanā* (the verbal instrumental efficiency). The former is expressed by the *verb*al form, the latter by the optativeness (*liṅtva*). Thus, to make an appraisal of the sorts of actions, performances and 'instruments' required for the actualisation, one looks at the relevant texts and the sorts of things said about the undertaking, including those mentioned in the explicative or eulogistic passages (*arthavāda*). Even *mantras* are considered useful for such intellectual appraisal *qua śābdībhāvanā.* (*vide, Mīmāmsā Paribhāṣā,* p73). Criteria are given for discerning the *śruti,* the relevant scriptural texts from the irrelevant and subsidiary sentences (*ibid* p23); and for assessing the *śruti* itself. Among the six criteria proposed, 'reasoning' (*upapatti*) is deemed particularly important. See D'Sa, *Śabdaprāmānyam in Śabara and Kumārila,* p44f, n15. But for a contrast, see Prabhākara, Introduction to his *Bṛhatī*; and Kunhan Raja, 'In Defence of Mīmāṃsā'. Also, Chapter 7 (*infra*).

20a. *kārakāṇāṃ kriyāparihāreṇānyonyasaṃbandhābhāvāt; tena vākyamapi kriyáyaiva saṃbandhnīyāt, eka ca sa,* in *Tantravārttika* on *MS* I.2.31 (1903, p53).See note 18 above.

20. Jagadīśa, *Śabdaśaktiprakāśikā*: *vākyabhāvamavāptasya sārthakasyāvabodhataḥ, sampadyate śābdabodho na tanmātrasya bodhaḥ* (1934, p63, no 12); and *śabdāntaramapekṣyaiva sārthakaḥ svārthabodhakṛt* (no 6). Such words he specifies to be radicals (*prakṛti*), suffixes (*pratyaya*) and particles (*nipāta*). *Cf.* Śabara on *MS* I.1.25: 'what happens is that each of the words (composing the sentence) ceases from activity after having expressed its meaning, and the meaning of the word thus comprehended bring about the meaning of the sentence (as a whole).' (G. Jha tr.)

21. *śabdāntaraṃ sahakṛtya janayanti, vākyāni punarasahakṛtyāpi* (Jagadīśa *Śabdaśak-*

tiprakāśikā, p30).

22. *Dīpikā* on *TS* #61; see also n38a below. More will be said on this shortly, but see discussion in Jagadīśa *op cit* under 4, p12-13, regarding the role of *ākāṅkṣā* here. The example given in the text may, however, pose some difficulty in English where the equivalent of the accusative (*-am*) is non-different in form from the nominative (viz. 'pot'), and both are not distinguishable in their stem forms either (viz. *pot).

23. *Suptiṅantacayo naivamitivyāptyādidoṣataḥ* (#13, i). *yattu 'suptiṅantacayo vākyami' tyamarasiṃhairuktam, tanna yuktam, subantādeḥ pratyekasamudāyavikalpenātivyāptyavyāptyoḥ prasaṅgāt* (*Śabdaśaktiprakāśikā* p66).

24. Jagadīśa gives counterfactual cases wherein the presence of *verb*al ending does no better to turn certain 'ungrammatical' *qua nirākāṅkṣatva* expressions into sentences, such as *ghatam patam* and *pacati gacchati : na hi ghatam patamityākārah pacati gacchatītyanupūrvīko vā śabdasamūho vākyaṃ, na vā ghaṭa pacatītyetayoḥ pratyekanna vākyam (Ibid*, #13.ii).

25 Bimal K. Matilal in 'Indian Theorists on the Sentence.', p380.

26. In effect, this representation is that of the *śābdabodha* generated, which itself is also called *śābdabodha* in the sense of 'proposition'. *Cf.* Gadādhara. *Śaktivāda*, p87ff (Varanasi, 1976); *vide*, Matilal, *NND* Chs 2. (p15ff) and 15 (p146-7).

27. *Śabdaśaktiprakāśikā*, under no 5, p24.

28. *Cf.* Gaṅgeśa's definition : *vākyatvaṃ ca viśiṣṭārthapara-śabdatvam*. It could, however, be argued against the restrictiveness of the qualified-qualifier structure, since (a) not all grammatically acceptable sentences consist of qualificative relations between two (clusters of) terms; and (b) some languages do not involve a subject-predicate type structure of sentence. Under (a) come the 'identity' statements, single term assertions, and exclamations, etc, such as "blue (is) blue", "Stop" (sign), "Wow!". Attempts however can be made to reduce these to the *Q(xy)* type.

To be sure, where the relation is significant is in determing what is qualified by what. In the Nyāya view it is the *agent* (which is an existent) that is qualified (e.g. the 'cook' in our example), and the act of cooking is the qualifier. While in Mīmāṃsā, the *act* of cooking that is qualified, which is not an existent as such. Rather, for Mīmāṃsā the act results in the producing a potency (*apūrva*) for a result which may be an existent; the potency could be transcendental in the case of ritual acts, whose sacramental result might be a perceived, or an 'unseen' existent. In this sense, the verb-form, indicating the action in respect of what is to be accomplished (*sādhana*) or what is thereby accomplished (*sādhya*) is central to the sentence-structure.

29. V. N. Jha, 'The Structure of Śābda-bodha' (typescript, Poona, CASS, p3).

30. *Ibid.* See also note 20 above.

31. *Śabdaśaktiprakāśikā* no 12; and no 3: *sākāṅkṣaśabdairyo bodhastadarthānvayagocaraḥ*.

32. *śābdamaterāhāryatvopagame 'nirvahnirvahnimān' 'pacanna pacati' tyādikamapi vākyameva, no cedapārthameva, yādṛśabodhatvāvacchedenāhāryyatvaṃ tādṛśabuddhyarthaṃ prayuktapadānāmeva tathāvidhārthabodhaṃ pratyapārthakatvāt*, Jagadīśa, *SSP*, under no. 13, pp65-66.

33. *Tarkabhāṣā* (p17, 1953; p47 1979); *cf.* Annaṃbhaṭṭa *TS* #60-61 (BORI)

33a. *Ibid.*

34. For Jagadīśa, see note 53 below; see also Gadādhara *Śaktivāda* (1929, p43). Gopikamohan Bhattacharya gives the following definition of *saṃsargamaryādā* from Gadādhara : *śābdabodhe caikapadārthe aparapadārthasya saṃsargaḥ saṃsargamaryādayā bhāsate*: 'In the comprehension of sentence-meaning the relation between one word-meaning with the other (word-meaning) is known through *the relational seam*' [italics added]. As Bhattacharya rightly points out, *saṃsargamaryādā* is not be confused

with other linguistic capacities, such as *tātparya* (intentionality), and *tātparyaśakti* (a syntactic function). We also consider *saṃsargamaryādā* to be more than a mere 'sequential arrangement' of the word-meanings so that it is extended to the more complex forms of interconnectedness between word-meanings—thus, a collaboration, or better, *coalescing* of word-items in syntactic and grammatical relations. Deshpande's rendering conveys this sense a little better: 'The word *saṃsarga* stands for 'relation, connection, contact', and *maryadāyā* means 'boundary'. Thus, *saṃsargamaryādā* refers to the point of contact or a relational seam between two words. It is something like a feeling of interrelatedness created by the juxtaposition of words.' (*op cit,* p214 n30). See also Kuppuswami Sastri, *Primer to Indian Logic*, p258ff; and *cf.* Jayanta: *abhidhātrī matā śaktiḥ padānāṃ svārthniṣṭatā teṣāṃ tātparyaśaktistu saṃsargāvagamāvadhiḥ*, *Nyāyamañjarī* I (1936, p372). Gadādhara, *Vyutpattivāda*, pl (cited in Gopikamohan Bhattacharya, 'On Saṃsargamaryādā' (1980), p81). Also see Gopikamohan Bhattacharya (*ibid*).

35. *khaṇḍavākya*, 'section of sentence' is introduced, it seems, by Viśvanātha (*SM* under *BP* 82-83). We also have not considered when sentences can be parts of a larger sentence, and what it would take to form a 'minimal' sentence. For example, could a single stem like 'g' [Sanskrit] be regarded a sentence, if say someone who was listening understood its reference to be Bossie the dog? See Karl Potter, 'Some Thoughts on the Nyāya Conception of Meaning', in examining some claims by P. C. Chakravarti *The Linguistic Speculations of the Hindus* (Calcutta, 1933—among the earliest pioneering works in this area, sadly out of print).

36. Or '*akhaṇḍatva*', 'indivisibility of sentence'. Bhartṛhari gives the analogy of the multi-coloured picture which in spite of its analysis into its constituent colours is seen as a unitary image. *VKP* II 8-9. Likewise, he states that a man-lion (*narasiṃha*) is also a single entity and is quite different from either a man or a lion placed side by side. (II 90-91). See also II.71-7, 235-240, and *cf.* S. D. Joshi, 'Bhartṛhari's Concept of *Pratibhā*', p71.

37. Just as two halves cannot carry the same quantity of water as a single pot made from the two parts, thus the 'whole' is greater than the sum of the parts.

38. With Jagadīśa, we should stress that there must be an ordered interrelation among the meaning-contents of the parts of the expression in accordance with syntactical and inflexional rules, which interrelation is called *ākāṅkṣā*, 'expectancy', by Jagadīśa, and contrasted with the *kāraṇa* of *ākāṅkṣā* (for later). *Cf* Madhusūdana Sarasvatī: *padajanyasmaraṇasya nirvikalpakavākyārthanukūlasya nirvikalpakatvaṃ anubhavavādevaviruddham. savikalpakavākyārthabodhe ca savikalpaka-padārthopasthitiraṅgam* (*Siddhāntabindu, 'kāṅkṣā'* ch. 1928, p64ff)

38a. As we said, something that has relational *content* is a qualificative cognition. Representations are from Gaṅgeśa, *TC*, IV. pp241-2ff, and Raghunātha Śiromaṇi. The grammarians would represent (ii), giving centrality to the *verb*al form, thus: *kartṛkaḥ vyāpār'anayaḥ ghaṭānukūlaḥ*, an activity conducive to the activity of bringing. *Cf.* Gaṅgeśa on another : *agniḥ karaṇatvaṃ odanaḥ karmatā pākaḥ kṛtiḥ* ; *TC*, IV.1, p233.

39. Nārāyaṇa Bhaṭṭa reports this in *Mānameyodaya* (p96): '. . .we say that the sense of the words conveys the meaning of the sentence only by secondary implications (*lakṣaṇā*)': *vayaṃ tu padārthā lakṣaṇayai, vākyārthaṃ bodhayantīti brumaḥ*. See also *Śabdasaktiprakāśikā*, pp66-89, 104ff

40. J. N. Mohanty presents the problems succinctly: 'One is pushed back to the question, how one learns the meanings of new words. But the theory of *anvitābhidhāna* does have *some room for the pure word meaning per se*, only he does not want to assign a place to it within his *semantic* theory. This accommodation is done in the following way : as a word is heard, it *reminds* the auditor of its pure meaning, *but it does not signify* that pure meaning. . .(and so) the pure word meaning is of no relevance for it.' From, 'Frege's Context Principle and Indian Semantics.' (—presentation, International Philosophy Conference, Jadavpur, Jan 1983.)

41. Sibajiban Bhattacharyya points to this problem with some illustrations: '. . .although I know the meaning of

(si) All the world's a stage

by knowing how to work out this meaning from the words occurring in it, still I do not have any idea of the meaning of

(s2) The world is all that is the case.'

From, 'Meaning of Words and Sentences', (paper, *ditto* conference, Jadavpur). See also his 'Some Indian Theories of Meaning' (*op cit*).

Quine made a point here which is relevant, namely that, words are limited in number while sentences are limitless, therefore as the unit of meaningful communication sentence is the primary unit, as it is in sentences that meaning comes alive. But he confesses that in learning sentences we use lexiography, recursive definitions, and starting with a finite array of words, we bring in words as devices to illustrate meaning of sentences. In this way, Quine seeks a reconciliation of the 'context' (*anvitābhidhāna*) and the 'constructional' (*abhihitānvaya*) theories. (Jadavpur, *ditto*, response).

42. See note 39 above. Also, Pārthasārathi Miśra, *Śāstradīpikā* I.1.7: *tasmātpadābhihitaiḥ padārthair lakṣaṇayā vākyārthaḥ pratipādyate*: hence, meaning of words is obtained via primary signification, the sentence sense via the secondary. (1891 Banaras edn. p129.)

43. *Cf.* G. Jha, *The Prābhakāra School of Pūrva Mīmāṃsā*, p63.

44. See Madhusūdana Sarasvatī on the relative merits of these views, in *Vedāntakalpalatikā* p65ff; also Gaurinatha Sastri, *The Philosophy of Word and Meaning*, 'Import of Proposition' section, esp. p234ff

45. Some Nyāya thinkers regard this functional capacity to be a distinct *śakti* or 'power' of linguistic elements apart from those considered earlier. But there is no need to regard this as a distinct 'power' since it is reducible to pure *śakti* or *lakṣaṇā*, and to the capacities for interrelation, such as *saṃsargamaryādā*. *Cf.* *Ślokavārttika* : *na vimuñcanti sāmarthyaṃ vākyārtheṣu-padāninaḥ; tanmātrā'vasiteṣveṣu padārthebhyaḥ sa gamyate* (*Vākyādhikaraṇa*, no 229, 1889, p909): 'the words (composing) a sentence do not lose their significance (potentiality), and it is only because the direct function of the words endings in the signification of their own individual denotations, that we hold the meaning of a sentence to be deduced from meaning of the words (not otherwise).'

It may also be noted that the term *abhihitānvaya* is short for *abhihitānāṃ padārthānāmānvayaḥ* : 'the separate meanings of the words are first conveyed by the separate words, and then the words and their meanings are grasped as entering into syntactical relation.'

46. Though Dharmarāja admits that *lakṣaṇā* belongs not only to single words but also to 'a group of words' as in a sentence; the example he gives of the sentence is the same as that about the village in the deep water, which clearly is not an ordinary sentence. However, it could be said that Dharmarāja did allow the possibility of a Bhāṭṭa-type (i.e. constructionalist) analysis of sentence—i.e. *abhihitānvayavāda*— *VP* IV.31. Again, he illustrates how *lakṣaṇā* is used in understanding certain subsidiary sentences in Vedic texts, as if they were 'words' used metaphorically or suggestively in a sentence. And for this he invoked Kumārila Bhaṭṭa.

47. G. Jha, *The Prābhākara School of Pūrva Mīmāṃsā*, p62ff. Prabhākara argued that the *abhidhā* or primary signification with the intentionality is sufficient to generate sentence-meaning. But this *abhidhā* is itself dependent on the 'whole-sense' of the utterance, in Prabhākara's view. He seems to have got his clues from Jaimini's *MS* I.1.25. But how he got this is puzzling : compare text in n17 above. Śabara in his *bhāṣya* makes it clearer: '(In a sentence) there is only a predication (or mention) of words with definite denotations along with a word denoting an action; as the meaning (of a sentence) is based upon that (i.e. the meaning of the word).' (G.Jha tr. p44 GOS I).

48. This is the Quinean type view.

49. *Vākyapadīya*, II.1, 2, 9, 13-14, 92; II.28-29ff.

50. J. Brough, commenting on this, argues that Bhartṛhari, in so far as he is talking not about the procedure of grammatical analysis, or a retrospective look at a sentence uttered, is telling us something valid about 'language operation', as distinct from language-material considered and described by a grammarian. 'Indian Theories of Meaning', J. Brough, in *RSG.*, Staal, edited, p416-417.

51. Again, from Śabara's commentary on *MS* I.1.25, this lends support to Kumārila Bhaṭṭa's view (text in 1889, p34); see also n17 above. Prabhākara is of the view that the text supports his position.

Prof. Karl Potter contends that the Nyāya view could be seen as a hybrid of the 'context' and the 'constructional' views, and explains: 'the former pattern used in accounting for our understanding "minimal sentences" (those sentences expressed in *varṇas*), the latter pattern used in accounting for our understanding of complexes of minimal sentences.' In 'Some Thoughts on. . .Meaning', p212. But *cf.* fn 41 above for argument to the contrary.

52. Kunjunni Raja sums up the Prābhākaran position aptly, as follows: 'The Prābhākaras do not deny the existence of individual words and their isolated meanings; they only assert that it is impossible to comprehend the isolated meanings of a word apart from its relation in a sentence. Words certainly recall their senses [meanings] separately; but they do not stop with that. Even though the listener knows the general meaning of the words, his experience tells him that the words are meaningful, only when they are connected in a sentence and not when isolated. The words themselves convey their meanings only as related to one another on the strength of three well-known factors, *ākāṅkṣā, yogyatā and saṃnidhi [āsatti]*. The words convey not only their individual meanings, but also their syntactic relation. Thus, the sentence meaning is directly conveyed by the words themselves', *Indian Theories of Meaning*, p198

53. *Śābarabhāṣya* on *MS* I.1.5 (*autpattikastu śabdasyārthena saṃbandhaḥ*). The difference is that while for for Mīmāṃsā the composite sense is comprehended through *lakṣaṇā* (secondary signification), for Nyāya this occurs through the *śakti* or primary signification in the first instance. Also, for Naiyāyikas like Jagadīśa and his commentator Kṛṣṇakānta, *śābdabodha* is obtained only from sentences (and not, say, from perception), and where (a grammatically correct) sentence alone is *pramākaraṇa* and *śābdabodha* its valid end-product (i.e. *pramā*).

54. *Śabdasaktiprakāśikā* : *asti tāvad gaurasti-gāmānayetyādi-sākāṅkṣaśabdebhyaḥ svasvavṛttiyā padārthānāmupasthityuttaraṃ gavādāvastitvāderanvayāvagāhī* (no 3, p7). *Cf.* Viśvanātha in *BP*: *dvāraṃ tatra padārthadhīḥ, śābdabodhaḥ phalam, śaktidhī sahakāriṇī.* (See ch. 1.)

55. J. N. Mohanty, see note 40 above.

56. *samūhya-padārtha-vācī* versus *svayaṃ-padārtha-vācī* ('categorematic'). J. F. Staal, 'Sanskrit Philosophy of Language', pp511.

57. *Ibid*, p512. See also pp182ff in next chapter (*infra*). For earlier example of *agna ā yāhi*, see also J. F. Staal, *Word Order in Sanskrit and Universal Grammar*, p 25.

5

THE KĀRAṆAS

A. *Ākāṅkṣā* - syntactic expectancy
B. *Āsatti*—word-element contiguity

Kāraṇa

5.0 One part of the argument we looked at in the previous chapter stated that if *śābdabodha* is to arise words and their meanings must be interrelated in certain ways, and that this would bring the process of *sābdabodha* to a completion. But this also means that there are a number of causal conditions (*kāraṇas*) without which the process of sentential comprehension would not be complete. Four such determinant factors are recommended as being central to the *saṃsargamaryādā* or relational coalescing of the sentence components, with the addition of other auxiliary conditions (*sahakārikāraṇas*) where the sense is more complex than in ordinary utterances.

The four significant *kāraṇas* are: *ākāṅkṣā* or syntactic expectancy, *āsatti* or contiguity (proximity) of word-elements, *yogyatā* or semantic competency (compatibility) and *tātparyajñāna* or intentinality. (*VP* IV ii) The first two of these pertain to the formal properties, while the last two to the semantic properties. The other factors that influence a specific sentence and its understanding are the context, the different nuances a word can be used with, the tone of the speech-act, the manner or character of the speaker and of the audience, the relative disposition of both, the time, place and occasion of the utterance, and the idiom and propriety of the utterance, amongst others. Compared to the first two these are minor. In the present chapter we will concern ourselves with the first two *kāraṇas*, namely *ākāṅkṣā* and *āsatti*; in the next chapter with the other pair.

5.1 Of the *kāraṇas* that contribute to *śābdabodha*, *ākāṅkṣā* is regarded to be one of the most important and comprehensive 'cementing' factors. *Ākāṅkṣā* is perhaps one of the more significant contributions to linguistics made by non-grammarians in India. We have already covered much ground on this in the previous chapter in our search for a workable definition of a sentence and its implications for *śābdabodha*. We noticed that much hinged on the syntactic property that *ākāṅkṣā* lends to a cluster of words which then collectively obtain a sense of logicality about them, which they seem to be in dire need of before their utterance achieves the semblance of a sentence. One wonders not whether what one hears in this way is a sentence or not, but whether the speaker has completed what he had begun to say. And this concern or anxiety is roused precisely in the emergence of *śābdabodha* such that, we could say, the function takes on a subjective, or better, cognitive role. But what sort of a *function* does *ākāṅkṣā via* the sentence-structure have in *śābdabodha*, and why is this so very important?

We emphasised in the context of sentence construction how *ākāṅkṣā* added the *syntactic* property to a cluster of words. But what role does *ākāṅkṣā* play in the actual hearing of the sentence? Does it continue its function. The short answer is, yes. Some may argue, however, that in that case the function should not be called as such 'syntactical' since the process of generating a sentence is not quite the same as generating *śābdabodha*, despite the latter's dependence upon the former. We may recall, as Jagadīśa remarked, that Indian linguistic speculation did not take place outside of the concern with knowledge or *understanding* and purpose, conveyed through language-behaviour, which therefore made the definition of a sentence itself parasitic on the fulfillment of the requirements for a successful 'verbal' understanding (*śābdabodha*). In other words, if one has a sentence then it is possible to have *śābdabodha*; but if one does not achieve the intended *śābdabodha*, then there can be some doubt as to whether the utterance heard was a sentence in the first instance. The concern with *śābdabodha* precedes the attempt to define a sentence. Nevertheless, we can say that the attempt to define in some *a priori* manner the parameters of what is 'meaningfully utterable' in terms of what is 'comprehensible' is not totally misguided as some useful insights are contained therein. If our concern were purely with linguistics and the process of generating linguistics expressions then it would be a different matter; but since our concern is more specifically with cognitive *understanding* generated through such expressions, we cannot but take seriously the claim made here. The definition of the sentence couched in terms of the definition of *śābdabodha* facilitates this concern. It would be an interesting challenge, though, to generate definitions of the sentence that were significantly better than those considered earlier.[1]

5.2 Secondly, and perhaps more importantly, if the end-product is causally related to the process preceding it, then one cannot be considered without the other. Thus, if syntactical relation plays an important part in the sentence structure it must also effect the process that follows when this structure is made use of in its proper context. The end-product here, namely, *śābdabodha* cannot therefore be immune from the impact such a property might be said to have (or *not* have, in its absence). In other words, if the absence of this property does not have any significant consequence on the character of the end-product then we could forget about the matter and be rest assured that such problems are of no consequence to the argument. But if its absence can be shown to have some significant consequences then these are necessarily consequences for the argument as well. We are, it seems, here talking about some preconditions for the possibility of successful linguistic communication, in wanting to ensure that the elements of communication are not devoid of such properties as would render them unintelligible. And this requirement, we shall argue, gives what we may call 'logicality', or a formal property, to the sentence utterance. By 'logicality'[2] we mean a degree of plausibility and intelligibility, that is not necessarily conteminous with analyticity, consistency, semanticity and intentionality. These latter fall more or less under the *kāraṇas* of *yogyatā* and *tātparya*. Thus, for example, if it is deemed that in a structure **S**, *x* and *y* go together, then in the absence of, say, *x*, the structure remains incomplete and the anomaly that arises is attributed to the non-presence of *x*, as *x* and *y* are said to have 'mutual syntactic expectancy' (*ākāṅkṣā*). And in the nonfulfillment of *ākāṅkṣā*, or pervasion of *nirākāṅkṣā*, the *śābdabodha*, if it were to arise, would most probably lack intelligibility, hence logicality. Attempt will now be made to describe logicality in terms of grammatical or syntactical plausibility by examining *ākāṅkṣā* more closely (bearing in mind the ground already covered in the previous chapter).

5.3 It appears that the grammarians were the first to make use of the concept of *ākāṅkṣā*, although the same term was not consistently used. Patañjali was one who discussed this issue under the concept of *vyapekṣā* or 'meaning inter-dependence',[3] while Pāṇini himself spoke of *sāmarthya* or the 'capacity' for words via syntax to be mutually interconnected.[4] Even Kātyāyana's insistence on one verb per sentence (*ekatiṅ; ekārthībhāva*) could be looked upon as a statement in this respect, for without a verb the limits of sentence utterance would be too narrow, and with more than one verb, would be too wide.[5] With Kumārila Bhaṭṭa, the Mīmāṃsā view began to take a more syntactic character, taking after Jaimini, as he was concerned to distinguish between sentences that involved injuctives (*liṅ*-), optatives, and 'exigencies' (*bhāvanā*), from those that were mere expositions or glosses on these (i.e. *arthavāda*). For Mīmāṃsā, simply put, *ākāṅkṣā* is seen as the need of a word to be complemented in its meaning by other words in the linguistic structure in order to bring about a completed sense, a unity of idea or of purpose.[6] *Ākāṅkṣā* is the chief basis for the cognition of the syntactic unity of a sentence. If *ākāṅkṣā* is lacking, then, it is argued, one of the major conditions for understanding the 'meaning' or sense of a sentence is said also to be lacking. Mīmāṃsā, however, did not distinguish sufficiently the grammatical or syntactic criterion from semantic and psychological expectancy, as is evidenced by the wide-ranging debate over the exact intention of '*artha*' occurring in Jaimini's *sūtra* and on the primacy of word *or* of meaning implicated in the maxim: *sākāṅkṣaṃ ced vibhāge*. And further, the Mīmāṃsā scholars could not explain how, i.e. in virtue of what 'power' or 'capacity' of word (or words together), this property comes into operation. For such problems, theorists like Dharmarāja had to turn to the wealth of reflections of the Nyāya thinkers, especially those of the Navya-nyāya school. We shall present a rough sketch of their view now.

5.4 *Ākāṅkṣā* is derived from the root *kāṅkṣ*, which means "to expect", "to desire (for something to follow)", "to thirst after". *Ākāṅkṣā* can accordingly be rendered as: expectation to learn more – the anxiety, in other words, that is roused in one through what is already known but not known sufficiently or adequately, or through what has just come to the attention of the audience, but not in any coherent form. One gets the dreadful feeling that something is amiss, that something is lacking and unspoken, and so his understanding is thwarted and therefore frustrated. In one sense, then, it could well mean "the expectation or 'desire' (*icchā*) on the part of the audience roused by the incompleteness of an utterance".[7] This definition arguably gives *ākāṅkṣā* a psychological coordinate as it speaks of 'expectation', 'desire', 'want(ing)' and so forth on the part of the individual who comes to hear or read some words. Surely, one may say, when I hear a speaker ramble on rapidly through his topic of discourse I want to know what he meant by such and such, what more he may have meant, and what follows from his statements; one might even say, this is an 'intellectual expectation'.

Nonetheless, could one really speak of a linguistic property of expectation, or expectancy, in this context? Suppose now, I was complaining about the way the speaker ran one sentence into another in quick succession and moved to the next sentence before finishing off the previous one, and so on and so forth, would I not be making a comment on his linguistic behaviour? Would I not be saying that some bits of his utterance did not 'hang together' or tally with each other. I am, it seems, saying something about his use of words, or about the way the words in his utterance relate or do not relate. Still, one could argue that my expectation need not be called 'linguistic' since it appears to be more of a subjective or psychological nature, and besides, the problem expressed could well be resolved by *āsatti* or contiguity of utterance-bits.

Some early thinkers, particularly Mīmāṃsakas like Śālikanātha, would have been happy to accept this criticism[8], but not so Dharmarāja, who took a somewhat different approach. Dharmarāja would not deny that the expectation, desire or whatever, is roused on the part of the audience to know the 'other' words to which the ones he has heard are related, but he makes a distinction between actual (*utthit*) and potential (*utthāpy*)[9] expectation, and attributes this function to a special *capacity*—viz. *yogyatva* [not to be confused with *yogyatā* as a *kāraṇa*]. It is in virtue of this *yogyatva* of words that the actual *jijñāsā* or 'anxiety' to "hear" more is made manifest in certain contexts of utterance. Its function nonetheless is concomitant and intact even if the actual expectation in the psychological sense does not arise. By emphasising this capacity or *yogyatva* for *ākāṅkṣā qua jijñāsā*, Dharmarāja attempts to remove *ākāṅkṣā* from the psychological-subjective to the linguistic-expressive (*vācaka-śabda*). Of course, from a phenomenological point of view this step may appear to be reductive and hence unnecessary. But the consoling part is that the reduction is not intended to be total, and is not devoid of references to the cognitive *qua śābdabodha* anyway. Thus, the chief element in Dharmarāja's definition of *ākāṅkṣā* is *yogyatva*, which refers to the *potential* for *jijñāsā* or '*icchā*'—'the desire to know the other word (linguistic component)'—when a word is heard.

In keeping with the above line of thought, the following definition is given: *padārthānāṃ paraspara-jijñāsā-viṣayatva-yogyatvaṃ ākāṅkṣām*[10]—

> *Akanksa* is the capacity (*yogyatva*) of word-meanings to become the content of enquiry or (the desire for) understanding in mutual relation to each other.

That is to say, *ākāṅkṣā* is the capacity to rouse the expectation of one word in mutual interrelation with the other word, or word-meaning. It is the precondition for the possibility of understanding one word as related to the other *qua* their meaning-content. To explicate this definition a little further, suppose we hear two words, and impute or recollect the meaning of one of them. As soon as we recognise the meaning of one term of the relation there arises potential for the expectancy of the content of the other word to which the content expressed by the different components of this expression are related. Thus the mutual interrelation or *paraspara* of the components *qua* word-meanings is stressed. Which is to say that the relation must be reciprocal.

5.5 Consider in this light Annaṃbhaṭṭa's statement on *ākāṅkṣā*:

> If a linguistic item *x* cannot generate an integrated meaning-cognition due to the absence of a linguistic item *y*, then *x* is said to have mutual expectancy with respect to *y*.[11]

The shift towards grammaticalness of the utterance is evident here. For *ākāṅkṣā* is more than the function of rousing interest in the meaning of related words in an utterance. It is a condition that requires a mutual connection of words for a *syntactic* completeness of the utterance. If a word, in the absence of some other word or words, cannot effect the completion of the syntactic relation in an utterance then that word is said to have *ākāṅkṣā* for the other word or words. In whatever linguistic convention, it could be said, certain words require certain other words to complete the sense. For example, in the expression "the boy eats an apple", if the word 'eats' is left out, the resulting expression is syntactically and grammatically incomplete, and therefore unintelligible. In other words, the resulting expression [2] "the boy an apple" is syntactically incomplete. One may argue, however, that since the copula ("is") is not considered to be necessary, in Sanskrit at least, and its implicit presence could be assumed, should we not understand the expression to read "the boy is an apple", which on the face of it is a grammatically legitimate *sentence*, as much as Nyāya would want to say that expression *'ghaṭo nīlaḥ'* ('the pot blue') is legitimate. We would have to agree with this argument up to a point, provided we recognise that, even though grammaticality of the expression no longer appears to be in question, there is a glaring semantical problem with the expression, and one cannot but be aware of this. Nyāya would say that in that case the problem is passed over to the next *kāraṇa*, namely, *yogyatā* which detects semantical incompatibility between the terms of an expression. But the matter does not rest there. *Yogyatā* may very well decree that the copula only goes so far as to indicate the tense of the *ākhyātatva* (verb-form), but is not the verb-form itself (verb-form being the responsibility of *ākāṅkṣā*), for without *yogyatā* the syntactic expectancy could not be fulfilled. Thus the problem remains basically one for *ākāṅkṣā* in the example above, the verb-form, "eating", is still wanting in the expression [2]. According to Gadādhara, at least, the anomaly ought to be resolved within the function of *ākāṅkṣā* itself, with the rider that it should be possible to extend the functional capacity of *ākāṅkṣā* to overlap, so to speak, that of *yogyatā (yogyatājñāna)* or the awareness of semantical compatibility.[12]

If the above argument is to have any force then we would definitely have to accept the expression *'vahninā siñcati'* ("he sprinkles with fire") as a sentence whose utterance should lead to a particular (qualificative) *śāb-*

dabodha. In *'vahninā siñcati'*, for instance, one notices that the mutual syntactic expectancy leads to a particular (qualificative) *śābdabodha*. In this expression the mutual syntactic expectancy has been fulfilled in as much as the expectancy is not apparently illogical. However, one might ask: upon hearing the expression is one not likely to become a little apprehensive about the seeming incongruity in speaking of fire as though it could be sprinkled like water, or as though it were water? One can accept the fact that there is nothing terribly illogical about this, and concede that syntactically the expression is sound, but that somehow semantically it raises a curious doubt whether the hearer is going to be able to make 'full sense' of this. And that even if he did make sense of it for himself, how is he going to be able to represent the *vācaka* (the expressed) to another? To take another example, while describing rabbits, suppose someone makes the utterance, 'Ah, rabbits have horns'. In the normal circumstance of speech, and for one who is reasonably acquainted with the language of the speaker, there is not likely to be any *mis-understanding* of what has been said, for the sentence at least is intelligible. Alternatively, however, he could begin to visualise Alice in her Wonderland murmuring something to that effect when she notices a rabbit humbling itself in her presence. But at the same time, the instinctive response would be to turn around and beg of the speaker: 'You don't say that, do you?' To which, one may get the reply: 'I say what I mean.' Now in both instances, do the difficulties expressed by the audience have anything to do with the function of *ākāṅkṣā* in the way we have been exploring it? It would appear not: for the only way in which this could be so, would be if we were to *presuppose* a semantic structure in the syntactical criterion, i.e. in the conception of 'grammaticalness' that one takes to be adequate for generating well-formed sentences that lead to *meaningfully complete śābdabodha*. That the Navyanaiyāyikas attempted this is undeniable; even though they did not cease to place equal weight on *yogyatā* as well, but perhaps for reasons different than usually thought so.[13]

Even the grammatically sensitive Jagadīśa, who wanted, in an ideal sense, to make *ākāṅkṣā* the sufficient condition for a sentence, nevertheless, appears to be ambivalent on this issue, at least, when counterfactuals of the above sort are raised. He, accordingly, proceeds to qualify *ākāṅkṣā* with the aid of further logical rules, such as the absence of self-contradiction and falsification, and so on, which are, he concedes, properly the concerns of *yogyatā*.[14] And if he also says, as he appears to, that *ākāṅkṣā*, as a syntactic property, "belongs to component-words and not to the concepts or entities expressed by those words",[15] then the above-mentioned qualifications cannot form part of the syntactic structure as these necessarily deal with 'concepts and entities' designated by the word-meanings and their relations. Unless therefore some further explication can be offered for a satisfactory marriage of *yogyatā* to *ākāṅkṣā*, it would be better to keep their functions categorically distinct, as we have attempted to.

5.6 The strength however of the Nyāya contribution to *ākāṅkṣā* lies particularly in their analysis of the grammaticality of an expression, insofor as *ākāṅkṣā* has been used as a formal criterion to explain certain grammatical rules, concerning order, the sequence of minimal word-constituents, combinations in compound words, subsentential elements or word-complexes, and for subject-predicate relations (NP + VP). The fulfillment of these rules makes the cluster of words communicable in the composite sense they express or signify. But how *ākāṅkṣā* exactly operates in generating satisfactory *śābdabodha* and what specific sorts of problems arise when *ākāṅkṣā* is not fulfilled, are better articulated in Dharmarāja's analysis. However, before returning to Dharmarāja, let us complete the Nyāya account of *ākāṅkṣā* with some more examples.

As we said, *ākāṅkṣā* requires that the words of a sentence be syntactically connected to yield a unified sense or purpose. And in the Nyāya theory, by 'syntactically connected' is meant the mutual coalescing or interrelational compounding of the words which enable them to generate a collective and unified *meaning*.[15a] To illustrate this, let us consider, for example, the expression: *gām ānaya* : "bring (the) cow". In the previous chapter we saw how this expression could be analysed in terms of the qualificand-qualifier relation. We need not repeat that here. We can say here that the significant content of the accusative, namely, '*gām*' ('cow'), that of the verb '*ānaya*' ('bring'), and the *kartṛ* or the agent, understood in the vocative as '*tvam*' ('you') (which or who generates the 'act of bringing') are interrelated in a particular manner in accordance with certain syntactic and inflexional rules. And this 'order' of the interrelation of significant items (*sārthaka śābda*) is *ākāṅkṣā*, without which there would be hindrance to the generation of *śābdabodha*. It is also said that there is *ākāṅkṣā* within the verbal unit '*gām*', between the word-base '*go*' and the accusative inflexion '*-am*'. In the absence of this ending inflected to the word-base, the *expectancy* would not have been fulfilled and this would have rendered the whole expression ungrammatical. Thus, coming back to a previous example, the following analysis is said to lack expectancy regardless of the order of its component parts:

> *gaur karmatvam ānayanaṃ kṛtiḥ*: 'the cow, in accusative relation, act of bringing, an effort'.

Though the same items are used here as in the former expression for the previous chapter, the grammatical connections are the same, as the discrete elements lack adequate *syntactic* relation with each other. The question does arise of course, whether the expression could still be meaningful even though it appears to be lacking any proper grammatical connections. One response to this question is that 'if we rule that ungrammatical combinations are, in general, not meaningful'[16] then such an expression would be declared meaningless, and therefore a comprehension of the 'connected' meaning of the whole is not possible. And, from the Nyāya point of view, it follows that it will be improper to say that the sort of example (rather counter-example) we have just considered lacks the syntactic property of *ākāṅkṣā*, and hence does not generate any cognitive meaning as such.[17] But it is obvious that, apart from providing something of the 'raw stuff' for a proper understanding to arise, this string of 'unconnected' words does *not*, under normal circumstances, fail to generate *any* comprehension in an audience. One will construct out of it some meaning and no doubt will want to know more (or more clearly, what is only *vaguely* comprehended). The *ākāṅkṣā* remains unfulfilled, unless, of course, the one hearing the expression modifies it to the proper structure, perhaps as indicated in the earlier example. At any rate, the expression is less than plausible for the purposes of generating a 'good' *bodha.*[18]

To sum up the Nyāya view, we may say (and here we follow Gaṅgeśa) that the *ākāṅkṣā* is 'the accompaniment of one string *x* with another string *y* in such a way that *x* would not generate a cognition of the meaning (*śābdabodha* or *anvayabodha*), unless accompanied by *y*.[19] Now Dharmarāja, while not opposed to the Nyāya view, wants to define *ākāṅkṣā* more in terms of the *modus operandi* of the capacity to rouse the expectation where *expectancy* is unfulfilled, rather than merely in terms of the *lack* of syntactic relatedness among the sentence components. And he further qualifies the sorts of situations or contexts where *ākāṅkṣā* is likely to be actually unfulfilled. The significance of these qualifications or 'delimitors' of *ākāṅkṣā* is that they give us some understanding of the ways in which *ākāṅkṣā* contributes to the emergence of successful and satisfactory *śābdabodha.*

5.7 Dharmarāja points out three specific situations which particularly call up the requirement for *ākāṅkṣā*. He states that when we hear about an *action* (*kriyā*), expectation is roused for the *kāraka*, the accomplisher or doer of the action. That is to say, there is desire to enquire after the agency that accomplishes the action, or causes it or is related to it.

Secondly, when we hear of a *kāraka* or agent ('the doer'), then this rouses the expectation to know something about the action (*kriyā*) that is to be accomplished; and thirdly, when one hears of a *karaṇa*, a particular cause for an action, one enquires after the *modus operandi* or the know-how, *kartā*, by which the action is to be effected.[20]

To illustrate with an example, when a number of boys hear the expression 'fetch firewood', each one may wonder whether it is he alone or someone else, or all of them that are being summoned to gather firewood. On the other hand, if one of them or all of them hear 'You there. . .', there may be roused an expectation as to *how* exactly this is to be accomplished. And when told that firewood can be got by chopping wood, they may want to know how exactly, or by what *instrumentation* this is to be effected, whether with the use of a knife, or an axe, or a chain-saw. On the other hand though, an utterance like "cow, horse, man, elephant", is merely a string of words, none of which possesses the property of *ākāṅkṣā*, because there is no *kriyā, kāraka*, nor *kartā* between or among them. That is to say, there is no indication of what it is to be accomplished, who accomplishes it, and how it is to be accomplished. Even a *copula*, such as "is" would have given the utterance relatively more significance than it presently could be said to have. For then, there would have been some suggestion as to how one is related to another, how they are interrelated to each other in the expression, and so on.[21]

It appears, however, that Dharmarāja's definition of *ākāṅkṣā* is restrictive. To say that the string of words "cow, horse, man, elephant" is grammatically incomplete is one thing, and is acceptable; but to say that this is so because it does not tell us anything further about the *action* to be accomplished from hearing these words, is really to stretch the notion of 'syntactical unity' a bit far. Surely, someone hearing these words may expect to be told something further that relates their contents into some cohesive and completed whole. Someone, for instance, may ask, "Well, what about them?". In responding to this query one need not say anything about what they are doing, nor what is being or is to be done , or by whom, or through what. One may as easily say, supposing the utterance took place at a zoo, "They are colourful creatures!"

But a question arises here : in making a descriptive statement about something or somethings, one is not necessarily *fulfilling* any of the three 'delimitors' for *ākāṅkṣā* that Dharmarāja has suggested. Certainly, one would like to know what the speaker is getting at in reeling off the string of words which seem remotely connected to form a complete sentence, but one does not expect that the information forthcoming will be in terms of the three cases—of *kāraka, kriyā*, and *kartā*—as Dharmarāja has stipulated. One could, for example, quite meaningfully utter the expression "Blue is blue", or 'Good is plain good", "A spade is a spade", without necessarily conveying anything, or rousing the expectation for a *kriyā, kāraka. . .kartā* trio. Even if one were to stop short at "Blue is. . .", it is not necessary that another person hearing it will want to know what is to be accomplished, whom by, or through what instrumentation. This is so, particularly in the case of poetical and aesthetic musings.

5.8 It is, then, not necessary to restrict the application of *akāṅkṣā* to the narrow cases to which Dharmarāja would have us do. The utterance mentioning the word "blue" is just as capable of rousing some expectation on the part of the audience as is the expression "bring" in the earlier example.[22] In other words, the expression possesses *ākāṅkṣā* for the reason that it has the capacity, with respect to the constituent words, of calling up, as it were, other words required for completion of its 'whole meaning' or sense. The word or words required for completing the sense need not necessarily fall into the category of *kriyā, kāraka or kartā.*

The question then arises, whether in these instances of *śābdabodha* the actual *desire* to know or inquire further is roused through this capacity for *ākāṅkṣā* when one encounters such sentences.[23] We might think of a sentence such as 'Bring the cow' being uttered, but with gaps or pauses between each word. And we can ask in this case whether, after the first word "bring" is heard, an expectancy for another word before "(the) cow" is heard? We may accept that when the cryptic and forceful utterance "--door!" is made, there might just arise the expectation on the part of the audience for another word or cluster of words to complete the sense of the utterance. One might expect to be told to 'shut' or to 'open' the door. This expectancy is the "desire", as we said earlier, to know what further follows from the sense of this incomplete utterance. We may even say that subjective response is elicited where the "sense of the utterance" is wanting in the absence of other terms required to complete the utterance.

But, for argument sake, the question we are raising is, whether it is necessary that in each case of sentence-comprehension, the *ākāṅkṣā* as a *subjective* response on the part of the audience actually arises? The logical case which Nyāya makes ought also to be acceptable, for otherwise we could be undermining the integrity of the relation between the components of the sentence which, as the definition earlier indicated, is secured by the syntactic property of *ākāṅkṣā.*

The query that we are raising here is whether the grammatical or syntactical property has to be *psychologically* manifest as one hears and understands a sentence utterance? We are raising this issue again since we wish to clarify the precise link Dharmarāja makes between the logical and the psychological processes.

5.9 Dharmarāja's view is that so long as the capacity (*yogyatva*) for the mutual interrelatedness of meaning-content is there, the requirement for *ākāṅkṣā* is said to be fulfilled. This is why he argues for the introduction of the term '*yogyatva*' in the definition of *ākāṅkṣā*. He goes on to say, "so that even to one who has no desire to inquire comprehends the sentence".[24] In other words, someone hearing a cluster of words, even though he does not intend to understand what is being said, may often find himself quite able to comprehend the interrelated sense though he may not be consciously aware of the expectancy that each component has for the other. What Dharmarāja is suggesting is that the words have the potentiality or '*capacity*' to be mutually expectant of each other, and so long as this capacity is there in the sentence-structure, it could be said that the requirement for the syntactic relation has been fulfilled, regardless of whether the *actual* desire or expectation on the part of the audience is roused for (an)other word(s) upon hearing the partial utterance.

Still, one may wonder whether a *śābdabodha* would arise without the actual expectation or desire, and if it did, then what would be the need for *ākāṅkṣā*? Again, Dharmarāja makes the point that he is not talking about the absence as such of *ākāṅkṣā*, rather that he is laying stress on the *yogyatva* or *capacity* for *ākāṅkṣā* to be there. He wants to disavow the notion that there has to be an actual manifestation of this *ākāṅkṣā* on the part of the audience. In other words, *ākāṅkṣā* is the potentiality that words *qua* word-meanings have in order to be in mutual interrelation with each other (*padārtha-sambandha*). And so long as this 'capacity' is there, the actual desire (*icchā*) need not manifest upon hearing the utterance. Since the potential or *yogyatva* for *ākāṅkṣā* is there, its function is assumed to be licit and the actual expectation need arise in all but a few instances. Mostly though, the understanding occurs unimpeded, and here the manifest function of *ākāṅkṣā* is deemed to have been exhausted. In effect, Dharmarāja is talking about a quasi-linguistic property, and not a psychological disposition. Rather, he means a *mentalistic* construct attributable to a sentence or any utterance that fulfills the requirement of syntactical expectancy. Thus, for instance, of the two examples we considered earlier, namely, "bring" and "bring the cow", the former, unlike the latter, is likely to rouse expectation on the part of the listener for the fulfillment of the syntactic relation of the components to each other, while the latter expression has the *capacity* for *ākāṅkṣā* which is fulfilled without necessarily rousing the expectation. This fulfillment makes the expression grammatically acceptable and logically plausible such that its utterance should be capable of generating a satisfactory comprehension.

5.10 Dharmarāja would want to say, with Nyāya, that in the example of the utterance "cow, horse, man, elephant", there is no *ākāṅkṣā* as there is no syntactical connection between the words.[25] As such the expression uttered is grammatically incomplete, and it would thus not generate *śābdabodha*. Logically this verdict is acceptable, but one wonders whether this is true in each case of the utterance of such an expression. We have looked at this issue earlier, but there may be another approach that remains to be considered.

Supposing, as we said earlier, the utterance took place in a zoo in response to the question, by a mother to her child: "What do you see in the zoo?" Now the response to this as a collective expression (i.e. 'cow, horse, . . .etc') has the capacity of rousing the expectation in another to the effect: "Well, what about them?" But to the mother, the understanding derived from this expression would be clear : she would understand that little Tom means that he sees a cow, a horse, a man and an elephant in the zoo grounds. Could we then not say that *ākāṅkṣā*, as qualified by Dharmarāja, is present in the words in the above utterance? It may not be syntactically complete for another reason, namely, for not having a verb in it, but that should not detract from its being capable of generating *śābdabodha*. Why, then, would one want to deny *śābdabodha* to such utterances on the ground that they lack *ākāṅkṣā*? We get a further response from Dharmarāja in which he qualifies the condition of what we might call 'the automatic fulfillment of *ākāṅkṣā*'. That is to say, the capacity-for-expectancy (*yogyatvākāṅkṣā*)[26] is delimited to two specific cases viz. *kriyātva and kārakatva*—i.e. to *actionness* and *action-promoter* in utterances.

What Dharmarāja is saying is that, the *yogyatva* for *ākāṅkṣā* as a quasi-linguistic property that does not require a psychological manifestation is delimited to words that express some involvement with an *act* or *action*, or refers to the *actor*, or to one *doing* an act. The *yogyatva* for *ākāṅkṣā* is then invariably with respect to some act being done, or some action, or alternatively with respect to the 'doer' (*kāraka*) of the action. The capacity in such cases would be the potential expectancy that may well rouse the desire to know such things as 'what act?', 'which action do you mean?', 'who did it?', 'how did he?' 'whom was it done to?' 'is that so. . .but why?', and so on.

Most gossips and hearsay reports, we might add, centre largely around these sorts of "expectations" for they are either about some event or about some person or persons, about which some people generally are interested. Even at a casual gathering, when someone catches the tail-end of a conversation to the effect, ". . .died", he is likely to turn around and ask "Who died?"; and when told the name of the departed, he may express shock at the news and proceed to ask how did such a tragic death occur, and whether it was due to an accident, some sort of viral infection, a collapse of the internal system of the person, or what? He may further enquire about the person's most recent movements, physical and mental dispositions family situation, work environment and so forth. Depending on how closely one knew and was associated with the person whose death is being reported, one may come up with strings of other questions and for many days may brood on just how such a tragedy could have befalled an otherwise healthy and energetic person.

To take another example, when someone reports that Jack went to the gaol, another is likely to turn around and inquire about the particular act (*kriyā*) that led him to be gaoled. But if the utterances were complete in both cases, then the desire to enquire would presumably not arise in the audiences' minds; they would understand what they do when their respective queries have been responded to. This indicates that the complete utterances possessed *yogyatva* for *ākāṅkṣā*, which would have been wanting, as they clearly are in the above two examples, had the *kāraka and kriyā* in each utterance been omitted, or not heard. In the case of the earlier example about the cow, horse, man and elephant, there is an absence of *kriyātva*—i.e. the action-determinant, pertaining to the contents of the utterance, and hence the utterance lacks *yogyatva* for *ākāṅkṣā*. And thus the question that arises in this regard cannot be resolved within the utterance in terms of the mutual relations among the word-meanings. If the *yogyatva* is present then there would be no need for the 'expectancy' to go beyond, as it were, the expression for its fulfillment. For a sentence to retain its syntactical unity, *ākāṅkṣā* must be met with from within the sentence, for otherwise it would not qualify for generating *śābdabodha*. Thus, it is not necessary that an actual *desire* to inquire after the *kriyātva* in an utterance should arise, so long as the potential for the 'syntactic expectancy' required with respect to these two delimited conditions (*avecchedaka*) is present in the words of the utterance. And, as *kriyātva* is absent as a *yogyatva* in the utterance "cow, horse, man, elephant", Dharmarāja deems it to be unqualified for *śābdabodha* without the further requirement for a *kriyā*-term, which could require a separate utterance. If the *śābdabodha* is to be complete, the *ākāṅkṣā qua yogyatva*, should be fulfilled in the same utterance. Hence, the requirement for *ākāṅkṣā* in view of the qualifications introduced through, (a) the linguistic criterion (*yogyatva*) of *ākāṅkṣā*, and (b) through the two delimitors of *kriyātva* and *kārakatva*, cannot be said to be too wide, nor too narrow. And this is an important contribution for a theory of *śābdabodha*.

5.11 Dharmarāja goes on to clarify the situation by specifying that when there are two words in an expression with the same case-ending, and an *expectancy*, or potentiality for the *ākāṅkṣā* with respect to one, then there is assumed to be *yogyatva* for the other as well.[27] That is to say, the syntactical relation is complete for both the terms with the same case-ending if there is *yogyatvākāṅkṣā* for one at least. For example, the author uses the Upaniṣadic utterance *tat tvam asi* ("That you are"), to illustrate this. Here *'tat'* and *'tvam'* have the same case-ending, and in this respect they are non-different to each other (*abhedānvaya*), and hence the capacity inhering in '*tat*' is also conferred to '*tvam*' in fulfillment of the requirement for *ākāṅkṣā*. But could we not say that the same is true of "cow", "horse", "elephant" in the utterance mentioned earlier – are they also not of the same case-ending? Here, it seems, Dharmarāja would want to invoke the delimitors of *kriyātva* and *kārakatva*, and have us realise that *kriyātva* is lacking in this utterance, and therefore the expectation does not apply to the utterance in question. If, for instance, in the case of the utterance, '*tat tvam asi*' someone were to ask "Well, what about '*tat*'?" – the response would be, "It is said *to be tvam* itself; in other words, the requirement of *ākāṅkṣā* in respect of the *kriyātva* is deemed complete in this expression."

In contrast to this, in the case of the "cow. . .elephant" utterance, the *ākāṅkṣā* does not obtain completion within the expression, and, as we said a little earlier, one may have to await another utterance for it to be completed. This is clearly not the case with '*tat tvam asi*' where the *copula* serves the function of the *kriyātva* required for *yogyatvākāṅkṣā*. In a sense the '*copula*' is tantamount to the *kriyātva*', for, in Sanskrit especially, the verb 'to be' is as much an action-verb indicating the state of an 'event' as much an adjunctive action-verb indicating 'doing': if he is 'being' someone or somebody, then he is either *doing* the act of *being* that, or somehow this is being *done* to him. Thus, this also clarifies our earlier reference to the *copula* as a differentiating factor between the utterance "cow, man, horse, elephant" and the response "There is (a) cow, (a) man, (a) horse, (and an) elephant (in the zoo)" – unless we took the former to be an elliptical utterance in place of the latter or as intending the latter expression.

However, as Jaimini points out, elliptical utterances also have to be completed before they are understood.[28] Or, as Dharmarāja might add, the elliptical utterances must have *yogyatva* for the omitted words, otherwise they would be different to the utterance in question, for the reason that they become the 'objective correlate' of the potential desire of some *kriyā*-term, such as 'see' or 'bring', which would, were the query to arise, answer the questions, "What about them?", "What do I do with them?", and so forth; after which the expression is no longer a jumble of words, but a sentence, with a unified sense.

5.12 Now the final issue that we wish to consider here concerns the question of the specific nature of the 'contents' to which *ākāṅkṣā* is applicable. This is to ask, whether *ākāṅkṣā* is between words themselves, or between word-meanings or between objects (*viṣaya*) or "entities" referred to by an expression? Now if we take the view that *ākāṅkṣā* is a causal relation between word-meanings, then there can be a case made against this contention. Consider, for instance, a hypothetical scene of crime at which a parrot caged nearby reels off a string of what appear to be unconnected words. Now, one hearing this string of words is not likely to make much sense of them, since parrots are not expected to construct intelligible sentences. Suppose a detective strolls in at that moment and hears the parrot spout off the same string, he is most likely going to be interested in making a mental note at least of the words he hears from the caged bird, because they could well be the very last words of the gasping victim as he fell to the assailant's weapon. If the detective hears two words in this way, say, "you. . .", "cruel. . .", he is likely to want to know more to add to the cues he picks up from the scene surrounding the crime. However, the expectation which the detective comes to have is not based merely on his recognition of the "words" of the victim, but on his understanding of the *meaning* of each word in the context and circumstance in which he takes them to have been uttered in the first instance, by the victim. We could say then that the expectancy, though ostensibly for another word or words, is implicitly for word-meanings whose interrelation would yield a unified sentence-sense.

Suppose now, soon after the parrot shrieks in a resounding tone: "You!. . .my uncle!. . .", this would, to a large extent, go towards satisfying the expectation roused on the part of the detective. He would then proceed to look for some concrete evidence that would corroborate his suspicion that the uncle of the victim was the likely assailant. To an innocent bystander the words uttered by the parrot may appear to be no more than some nonsensical babble; but to the detective they are, as the saying goes, food for the forder, which have the potential for *ākāṅkṣā*, through which a meaningful understanding is, as it were, in the making.

We would then have to agree that it is possible for *ākāṅkṣā* to hold between word-meanings, as we realise that cognitive expectancy arises usually after the meanings of the individual words of an utterance have been recollected or gathered. If one does not understand the meaning of a word, one is more interested in knowing or finding out what the word means *before* he could be expected to enquire for the other words of which this word is mutually expectant. But Nāgeśa reports the Nyāya reply that, in such cases expectancy is "superimposed" on to the meanings. That is to say, through superimposition *ākāṅkṣā* may also be said to be related to the meaning.[29] But the persuasion here, on the part of Nyāya at least, is that *ākāṅkṣā* is essentially a *syntactical* property among words. And hence it could not belong to the *concepts* or 'contents' as such expressed by the words in a sentence, except by superimposition. The effectiveness of *ākāṅkṣā* manifests itself in the particular word-order or sequential arrangement of the sub-sentential elements in the expression.[30] Thus we could say that the Nyāya consideration is basically a *structural one in respect of ākāṅkṣā*, and that Dharmarāja obviously derives part of the strength for his argument from the position that pertains to the 'logical coherency' of the utterance.

5.13 There is one rather minor problem that arises here, namely, that of how we determine which word has expectancy for which other word if *ākāṅkṣā* is with respect to the word-order in a sentence. Is this given by the word-order itself? That is to say, does the structure of the sentential word-group make manifest the *ākāṅkṣā* or mutual expectancy between the relevant components? Consider the expression:

Caesar crossed,	on horse-back,	the rubicon.
(1)	(2)	(3)

If the response to the above query is in the affirmative, then we would expect in a sentence with this structure, that word-components (1) and (2) have *ākāṅkṣā* for each other. But clearly, there is no mutual expectancy between (1) and (2), because (1) is connected with (3) alone; the *ākāṅksā* would be determined (effected) either by looking at the semantic link that (1) has with the rest of the terms of the sentence, or by considering the intention (*tātparya*) of the speaker. However, in either case, merely looking at the grammatical elements and the structure of the sentence for mutual expectancy between the components will not suffice: one has to look at the *meaning* of the words as well. One could then argue that the *akāṅkṣā* is a relation of expectancy foremost between *meanings*, and only secondarily between words that express or manifest these meanings. The harmonious interrelation of the respective significations is therefore more important than the order of the words. The *ākāṅkṣā* operates, albeit licitly, towards the fulfillment of this interrelation and its success in generating a completed *śābdabodha*.

Part B:: *ĀSATTI – linguistic contiguity*

5.14 The other condition (*kāraṇa*) for understanding sentence-meaning considered to be of importance is *āsatti*.[31]

Āsatti, which is also called *saṃnidhi*, is more of a formal property, than *ākāṅkṣā*. It is normally rendered as 'proximity'; however, we prefer 'contiguity' to 'proximity' as the former connotes a sense of *continuity* which the latter does not necessarily convey. Still, both terms will be used interchangeably in different contexts.

Now, in early Nyāya understanding *āsatti* or *saṃnidhi* referred to the absence of any unnecessary intervention or interval between the string of words in the utterance (*uccāraṇa*) of a sentence.[32] The argument is that if there is to be a meaningful understanding of a sentence utterance, then its constituent words must be continuous with one another in *temporal* (when the string is spoken) and *spatial* sequence (when the string is written). Commonsense confirms this view, for if long intervals separate the words uttered then a unified sentence cannot emerge, especially as other activities and "noise" tend to distract one's attention.

Likewise, if the first few words of a sentence are spread over three pages, and the rest appear elsewhere in the book, then again a sentence as such cannot be said to have been presented to the reader—unless, of course, he were to search through the book for the words, as in a 'mystery word-game'. Thus, it cannot be consistently asserted that words uttered (or appearing) at long intervals can generate the understanding of any interrelation among them, even if other syntactical conditions are fulfilled.

To give an illustration, suppose someone utters the word "bring" today, and another word, say, "cow", the next day. The auditors may not be able to recollect and associate the words the following day as they would have heard a number of words in the meantime from other persons, and also perhaps on radio and television. Even if they succeed in recalling the words the next day, they could have difficulty connecting the words in such a way as to yield the composite sense of the utterance. To give yet another example, let us take the utterance "the hill has eaten fire Devadatta" (*girir bhukto vahnimān Devadattaḥ*).[33] But the 'sense' of the utterance is thwarted if we take this as a single sentence. The Sanskrit equivalent sounds rather meaningless, even though there is no strict rule for word-order in Sanskrit (language).[34] *Ākāṅkṣā* alone cannot resolve the anomaly altogether, for if we ask, "What did Devadatta do?" one could well be led to believe that Devadatta 'has eaten fire' - much as stage-magicians and fire-eaters make a show of. But if we were to look for those words in the utterance that are most likely to be continuous with one another, as words in a sentence, then we would find the following break-down of the string of words into two separate sentences—viz. "The hill has fire", and "Devadatta has eaten". Hence, it cannot be denied that 'proximity' of words is an important factor in understanding a sentence.

From the consideration just outlined, it may appear that the condition of *āsatti* pertains to the ordered juxtaposition of words in an utterance only if the string of words are the constituents of a single sentence. But if this is all there is to *āsatti* or *saṃnidhi*—i.e. that there should not be any unnecessary interval or interruption between words uttered to form sentence — then, as J. Brough also points out, this is not a linguistic condition as such, and itself betrays a sort of *naïvity* on the part of Indian linguists.[35] What we see in the above discussion, however, is merely one view of the condition under consideration, and perhaps an early and undeveloped one at that. (It was perhaps current among the earlier logicians.) The condition is really a little more complex and sophisticated, and for this more defined analysis we will now turn to the early grammarians, and especially to the Mīmāṃsā and Advaita.

Word-order vis-à-vis contiguity

5.15 It may appear strange that while the linguistic tradition denied any specific word-order in a sentence, the linguistically-inclined philosophers insisted on a notion of the contiguity of words in a sentence. How is this so? And what is then the difference, if any, between word-order and contiguity? Let us consider first what the early grammarians and, later, Bhartṛhari had to say regarding *word-order.* After this we will turn to Mīmāṃsā.

Pāṇini gives rules for ordering the *parts* of words (e.g. stems, suffixes, etc),[36] but in general in Pāṇini's grammar the order of words, as such, is relatively free. In the same vein, Patañjali, commenting on Pāṇini, makes the following observation : 'words are generated in accordance with grammatical rules, but their order (*abhisaṃbandha*) is free, as in *āhara pātram* and *pātram āhara* ("fetch the bowl").'[37] And Bhartṛhari, in a rather dramatic manner, says the following:

> Though sound is produced in a fixed order
> Speech itself has no earlier or later
> Itself without order, it is produced
> As if divided by the appearance of order.[38]

It is to be noted then that the grammarians worth their name actually denied there to be any rigid fixity in word-order in sentences, other than what appears to be so in manifest "sound". One might argue, however, that the view represented here applies to Sanskrit and perhaps to a few other languages, and that there are some languages in which word-order is of prime importance. For instance, using the translation of Patañjali's own example, while "fetch the bowl" is what is intended by either of the 'orders' Patañjali gives, in English at least, to reverse the order would be to destroy the fabric of the intended sense — viz., "bowl the fetch", or "the fetch bowl", since this leads to an incongruous sense. But if the article stays linked to bowl one gets "the bowl fetch" and "fetch the bowl".

Hence, we may need to make some reservations about the maxim regarding word-order. This, however, is not what *āsatti* was all about to Mīmāṃsā and others concerned with language in the context of *śābdabodha* generation. This same sort of objection (as we raised in relation to the English syntax), was directed against the Mīmāṃsā, who were taken to be denying a rigid fixity of words in Vedic sentences (*mantras*). Jaimini reports this objection in dealing with the issue of sentences, in these words: 'Because the order of the word (in *mantras*) is irrevocably fixed.'[39]

Śabara, in examining this objection, makes a useful distinction between 'order in utterance' and 'order in sentence', and states that if the speaker intends that (order) ought to be apprehended as such, this is what is important, not necessarily what is presented in the sentence which is but a token for what is uttered.[40] And, we may add on behalf of Śabara, a 'token' does not always correspond to the 'type'. It may also be remarked here that J. Brough is not wrong in his observation that *āsatti* is not a linguistic property, but is more a cognitive requirement for the operation of understanding (i.e. *śābdabodhavyāpāra*). And the distinction that Śabara has made here sets the tone for the formulation of a theory of *āsatti*.

Kumārila Bhaṭṭa does honour this task, though not before Śabara had settled the matter with the opponent in consonance with Jaimini's own noncommittal reply—which was that 'the opponent's view (of fixed word-order) is not inconsistent (i.e. with our own view that *mantras* are meaningful).[41] Śabara reasons thus: 'Perhaps the fixed order (rule) is pointless; at any rate what is observed (i.e. that the words *do* convey meaning in whatever order they occur) cannot be rejected.'[42] With regard, however, to ordinary language, as distinct to the Vedic *mantras*, word-order was regarded to be relatively free.

5.16 Kumārila, not unlike Patañjali, said that 'the meaning of *agnir-mūrdhā* is the same as *mūrdhā-agniḥ*; hence, fixing the order (of words) is pointless.'[43] But Kumārila does not deny the order of stems, affixes and compounds, as for example in '*Indrāgnī*' (Indra and Agni), *rājapuruṣa* (king's man—and man's king). Thus, Kumārila observes : 'here it is reasonable (to maintain word-order), since if the order is reversed, an incorrect form (*apaśabda*), a different meaning (*arthānyatva*) or no meaning at all (*ānarthakya*) would result.'[44] Kumārila then makes further distinction in Śabara's (above) account. Kumārila distinguishes *saṃnidhi* or *āsatti* from 'the mere immediate sequence of utterance (*anantara-śruti*).'[45] Thus *āsatti* is not merely the 'order of utterance' as was alluded to in Śabara's distinction. Kumārila's explanation of *saṃnidhi* or *āsatti* is that it is 'the continuous moving about of the words or their meanings in the mind (*buddhau viparivṛttiḥ*).'[46] But one wonders whose 'mind' it is that Kumārila is referring to here : is it the mind of the speaker or of the auditor? If the former, then this would be little different to what Śabara had already proclaimed. But if the latter, then this would constitute a shift to another level of the problem. The Bhāṭṭa does seem to stress this requirement in terms of the *utterance* (or at least the occurrence) of words, and consequently of their meanings, without undue delay and interruptions.

5.17 Nārāyaṇa Bhaṭṭa makes the Bhāṭṭa view a little clearer. He states first that, 'to be signified by words in contiguity is indeed (to be speaking about) the contiguity of the *meanings* of words.'[47] In other words, it is the notion of the contiguity of the meanings of words rather than the mere immediacy of words that is being emphasised here.

The second negative point that Nārāyaṇa makes, is that *saṃnidhi* is absent (a) where the utterances are not contiguous – i.e. the string of words are not uttered together, and (b) where something (apprehended) is not signified or expressed by the words.[48] With regard to (a), if we take Nārāyaṇa's opening statement about the contiguity of *meaning* then we must take him to be suggesting that the speaker must intend the 'contiguity of meaning' in uttering the particular sentence. And the speaker presumably intends the auditor to understand the sentence components in this order – viz. 'the order of meaning-content'.

Nārāyaṇa, however, qualifies his statement lest it be understood that the contiguity implied is between any pairs or 'bits' of understanding irrespective of whether they arise from words or not. Thus the requirement is about the contiguity of word-meaning, and this is why the counterfactual (b) is stated above. Suppose, an example is given[49]; someone utters the sentence 'tie up the cow', someone hearing this may take this to mean that the horse he sees in front of him needs to be tied up before it runs off. Now this is clearly an incorrect understanding. But even if it were true, this is not a case of *śābdabodha*, as this understanding is lacking in *āsatti* or *saṃnidhi*. Why is this so? Because, replies Nārāyaṇa, the required contiguity between word-meanings is lacking here, because no word remotely connected to a horse had been uttered here. If the word 'horse' in place of 'cow' had been uttered then there could have been no dispute : the *āsatti* between 'tie' and 'horse' would then have been accepted. Since, however, the understanding of the 'horse' is derived from perception, its contiguity with 'tie' cannot be said to serve the purpose of generating *śābdabodha* proper.

We may note that Mīmāṃsā is not necessarily denying the possibility of an understanding arising. Rather, they deny that there is any syntactical connection between its parts, for the vital condition of *āsatti* or *saṃnidhi* has already been fulfilled. According to Nārāyaṇa, Prabhākara, the other rival Mīmāṃsā Guru, did not understand this requirement, as he considered *saṃnidhi* to involve a mere 'contiguity of understanding (*buddhisaṃnidhi*)'. Whilst the Bhāṭṭa view is that *saṃnidhi* should be interpreted as the condition referring to sounds, or better, words (*śabdasaṃnidhi*) comprehended. Prabhākara would have the horse no sooner tied up if someone happened to utter "tie up the cow" in the proximity of a horse. But Nārāyaṇa admits that Prabhākara was not so narrow and that he realised that syntactical relation occurs among words.[50]

The Bhāṭṭa view in this regard had an influence in time among the Indian philosophers and linguists. But some schools did not change their views so easily. The Jaina school, for instance, accepted contiguity of sense or meaning, but did not require the contiguity to be necessarily of words actually uttered. For example, in elliptical utterances, such as that of "door!", all that the Jaina view requires is that one understand the sense of *shut* without the actual provision or providing of the word "shut".

On the other hand, the Bhāṭṭa school insists that the missing word 'shut' must be supplied by the auditor if there is to be syntactical relation between the terms of the sentence intended to be understood if not so uttered. Thus, though Bhāṭṭa does not deny that contiguity is between what is *expressed* (actual or intended), the 'expressed' must be what arises from *śabda* (or *pada*), and not something inferred or gathered from some other means. Advaita supports Bhāṭṭa on this, as we shall go on to see.

Meaning contiguity

5.18 In passing, we may note that even Annaṃbhaṭṭa in his *Dīpikā* on his earlier *Tarkasaṃgraha* treatise, moves towards the more complex view of the Bhāṭṭa's we have just presented. His earlier view, as we have already seen, was that there should be no delay or interval in the utterance of the several words that constitute a sentence. In his *Dīpikā* he clarifies that *saṃnidhi* is to be understood not merely as the *utterance of words* without undue delays between the words, but rather as the *presentation*, also without delay, to the mind of *what is signified by the words* of a sentence.[51] And, more interestingly, Viśvanātha in his own commentary on *Bhāṣā-Parichedda*, makes the modified Nyāya view on *āsatti* even more succinct. He states that contiguity is the apprehension, without any intervals, of the *meanings* of two or more words, one of which must be connected to the other (in order for the syntactical relation to be complete).[52] Thus Viśvanātha is basically referring to the apprehension of word-meanings and their connections in some order that yields a composite sense to the utterance.

One of the examples considered here is the following : "Blue, jar, substance, cloth".[53] Now this makes little sense as it stands. The auditor might attempt at rearranging the words to get some sort of sequence himself. Let us suppose he comes up with the following: 'A blue jar', and 'A substance as cloth'. There is apparent contiguity among the apprehended words and their meaning. But is this what the speaker intended him to understand? No, not quite : the speaker intended the following : 'A blue cloth' and 'A jar is a substance'. Accordingly, the *āsatti* or contiguity the hearer guessed in terms of what was presented to him was mistaken; however, according to Viśvanātha, even then "there is no harm".[54] Viśvanātha also argues that in the case of elliptical utterances, the supplying of words, such as "shut" is necessary when only "door" has been uttered; it is not sufficient that there be a mere apprehension of the meaning of "shutting"—'for the apprehension of particular meanings of words, which is generated by those words, is the cause of a particular verbal comprehension.'[55]

5.19 But, looking at it from another angle, what if it were the case that the words that constitute a sentence are uttered without any intervals, and that the auditor also hears them without any intervals or interruptions, and yet fails to grasp the connection between the words? What explanation can we give of this situation? Why has the auditor failed to grasp the meaning of the sentence even after hearing the words?

Viśvanātha considers an opponent's view that such a situation can arise when one forgets the impressions of the first few words while awaiting for the final impressions to register. To this, Viśvanātha replies that the apprehension of the last impressions actually revives the collective impression of the whole, hence keeping contiguity fairly intact. On the other hand, what the auditor fails to do in such a situation is to apprehend the *meaning* collectively in their mutual syntactical connection. Viśvanātha does not actually say this, but this is what one could expect him to say, given the definition of *saṃnidhi* that he advances.

A more clear response, though, can be gotten from considering the statements of Dharmarāja in this regard. Dharmarāja is forthright in his view of *āsatti*, that 'contiguity' consists in the proximity of word-meanings in the actual understanding, as distinct from the utterance, without any unnecessary interruption, and that this contiguous apprehension must arise from *words*. That is to say, the arising of word-meanings—solely from words and nothing else—must be contiguous in the understanding, without undue delays and interruptions. Thus, when we apply this definition, let us say, to the problem raised here, we should understand Dharmarāja's response to be that the auditor has failed to derive a contiguous understanding of the word-meanings from the words he has heard.[56a]

That is to say, the contention of Dharmarāja is that, though the words are uttered and heard without an interval, the *meanings* of each of the words have not been comprehended without interruption in a continuous sequence. In other words, despite hearing the words, in the order presented, the auditor fails to recollect or associate in *that order* the exact sense of one or more of the words uttered by the speaker as part of the sentence. Sometimes it happens that several sentences are heard before the auditor manages to recollect the meanings of each of the words in the very first sentence. And while he is concentrating on another sentence that marks off a distance from the first sentence, he suddenly recollects the meanings of the word with which he had difficulty much earlier. But in the meantime, he has recollected meanings of many other words; and so many other meanings and connections have occurred. Consequently, many other expectencies and contiguities would have been created and thus would alter the meaning of the initial and temporally recalled words. This unfortunate interval in his recollection of the meaning of the inter-related words, and not the interval as such between the occurrences of the two (or more) words—as there has been no significant interval between the hearing of the two words—is what has impeded the emergence of mutually connected word-meanings, and thus of a unified sentence-sense in the mind of the auditor.

5.20 The qualification that Dharmarāja has introduced in regard to the condition of *āsatti* is quite a significant one. For if mere proximity of words were the condition then it could be quite legitimate to object that this feature is of no avail at all since the 'slow-witted' will have no difficulty in connecting the words of the same sentence though they may occur at different intervals. But the same cannot be maintained if word-meanings were the issue, as then the slow-witted will be faced with considerable difficulty if he does not recollect the meanings of words as they are heard.

There is yet another reason why the qualification aforementioned is significant. For often we hear the first few words of a sentence, and grasp the sense of the sentence even before the speaker completes his utterance of it : e.g. 'a friend in need. . .' There are also instances of the elliptical sentence where the speaker breaks off in the middle of a sentence or utters only a very small portion of it. In such cases the syntactic affinity of the words that actually constitute the sentence has certainly been interfered with and the omitted words many never be heard—as in the case of man dying in the middle of uttering a sentence, but all we hear is something like, "Yes, I do believe in. . ." Yet the particular auditor in the dialogue often has no difficulty filling in the missing bit or in completing the sentence-sense for us since he or she is more than aware of the subject matter of the query to which the dying person was making a final response, even though the exact words may not have been uttered. Sometimes, in a less defined context, only a 'general sense' of the utterance is possible, but that too is more than what the hereto words would directly signify. The auditor then is not deprived of the relation among the meanings of the different 'bits' of the sentence, where the meanings of some 'bits' have been anticipated or interpolated. Here too, therefore, we notice the importance of *āsatti* as the condition that contributes towards an understanding of the sentence-sense, or *śābdabodha*.

Word contiguity revisited

5.21 Some philosophers, such as Kumārila as already noted, would object to the above analysis, and argue instead that the omitted word ought actually to be supplied before the syntactic connection with the rest of the parts can be made. Kumārila would be of the view that if a man died in the middle of uttering a sentence, then it is up to the auditor to provide the omitted words if the latter is to comprehend the intentionality of the utterance. But the difficulty with this contention is that one cannot be expected in such cases to suppose, off-hand, which words would have been uttered had the sentence been completed—unless such a sentence in its complete form had been heard before. If, however, the auditor has some intimation or idea of the purport of the utterance, then, on that basis, one may be able to postulate the words that would best complete the utterance. But we notice that the comprehension of the sense of the whole utterance, however vague it be, precedes the provision of the omitted word.

As an example of what is being said against Kumārila's view, let us consider the following Vedic text:[56]

Iṣe tvā : Thee, O Iṣa (grass)

In interpreting this text, one would need to supply the words "I cut" *(chinadmi)*[57] to complete the sense of the sentence. Dharmarāja insists that the understanding must arise from the words. But these words are supposed from the 'general thrust' of the text, or what the text attempts to convey. This process of 'supposition' resembles the *pramāṇa* of *arthāpatti* ('postulation'), albeit from a *verbal* rather a *perceptual* context.

Thus it is called *śrutārthāpatti*, which here plays a significant role in aiding the postulation of the omitted meaning of the word or words in order to complete the syntactic structure in the case particularly of elliptical or broken-off sentences.[58] Hence, it is important that words and word-meanings be postulated to complete the verbal comprehension of certain sentences, some of whose words are either unheard before, or not heard at all.

In supposing the sense or meaning of the omitted 'bit', the auditor may not immediately be able to recall the word appropriate to that sense, but may yet have no difficulty in conveying the sense of the speaker's utterance to a third party who cannot even make out the sense of the omitted 'bit'. To illustrate this, suppose a person *A* asking for an airline ticket is asked whether he wants a first class ticket, begins to answer "Ah, the . . .", and breaks off as he attempts to recall the term for the exact class of ticket he wants. He is asked again :"Which do you want?" Blushing, he looks around, as though for some assistance with his failing memory. The passenger behind him, anxious to have his turn, tries to help out, but he too is not able to work out which one the other passenger is after; at least, though, he is able to tell the clerk at the desk that maybe passenger *A* wants the next cheaper one after first class but not the economy class. To which the clerk immediately responds: "Oh, *clipper* class! Is that what you want, Sir?"

5.22 Disregarding elliptical sentences, the function of *āsatti* in normal conversation where principal sentences are used, cannot be overemphasised. For it is often, though not always the case, that when one is listening to three people speaking at once, even though the sequence in which one hears the words of the three speakers would be jumbled, one needs to mentally isolate the words of one sentence from those of the others, and also to recollect the meanings of each word in the order in which *each sentence* is uttered by each speaker and not in the order in which the words are heard, since this makes for an interruption between the words of the respective sentences. The auditor may find himself asking one of the speakers what he said such and such to be, and of another speaker, what word he uttered following the word at which his attention was distracted by one of the other speakers, and so on.

Speaking generally, it would be difficult if not impossible for an audience to follow the conversation of each speaker for any length of time if they all continued to speak at once. Some people, however, and in particular teachers and interpreters, develop a capacity to extend the application of *āsatti* in such situations as well, and recollect the meaning of the words only after the order of words which constitute each sentence have been mentally isolated. It may be finally remarked, that without the aid of *āsatti* the meaning of the different parts of the respective sentences may not be isolable, and therefore, the audience's understanding of the utterance would be severely impaired, if not made impossible. Let us take an example of a series of jumbled words that one might hear in a crowded bus: "Cow is Latin gives John dead went milk languages to London."

Now *Āsatti* is seen to have the function of separating the distinct sentences that are involved. The person listening should be in a position to understand that one speaker is saying, "Cows give milk"; another, "Latin is a dead language"; and a third, "John went to London". Thus, we can recognise the importance of *āsatti*, or contiguity of word-senses, in comprehending sentence as a whole utterance : that is to say, for a successful *śābdabodha*.[59] Its implications for other areas of learning and inquiry should be obvious, given that language is an important instrument in such processes.

NOTES TO CHAPTER FIVE

0. Much was gained from comments at a seminar on *ākāṅkṣā* I presented at the Oriental Institute, Oxford University. A version of this chapter was published in two articles in *JIP* (see bibiliography in Appendix).

1. But see Strawson on sentence understanding, in discussion in ch. 7, esp. notes 57 and 96a (*infra*).

2. As emphasised in another context by R. M. Hare in his, *Moral Thinking, (passim).*

3. *parasparavyapekṣāṃ sāmarthyameka icchanti. kā punaḥ śabdayoḥ vyapekṣā. na brūmaḥ śabdayoḥ iti kiṃ tarhi arthayoḥ.* :
Some prefer (to take that) semantic connection as mutual requirement. But what (do you mean by) requirement between two words?*
We do not say: 'between two words.'
What then?
Between two meanings.
* = interdependence. Trans. S. D. Joshi, *Patañjali's Vyākaraṇa-Mahābhāṣya Samarthānika (P 2.1.1)*, Poona, 1968, p87. *Mahābhāṣya # 98* on *PS* 2.1.1 (Kielhorn, p365)

4. *Pāṇini's sūtra* 2.1.1 is itself interesting: *samarthaḥ padavidhiḥ*—a rule which relates to complete words (is to be understood to apply only to those words the sense of) which are mutually connected. (S. C. Vasu, tr. p192 Vol 1.) Consider parallels : *ekārthībhāva* of Kātyāyana; *vyapekṣā* of Patañjali, and *arthaikatva* of Jaimini; also *sākāṅkṣā* of Nyāya.

5. *ekatiṅ* in *Vārttika* 10 (Kielhorn p367), and *ekārthībhāva* in *Vārttika* 1, both in Pāṇini 2.1.1 (*loc cit*): 'singly integrated meaning'.

6. Jaimini-sūtras, II.1.46 (see notes 10, 11 in previous chapter).

7. B. K. Matilal, in 'Indian Theorists on the Nature of the Sentence.', p383.

8. In his representation of Prabhākara's position which he supported; see Kunjunni Raja *Indian Theories of Meaning*, p158.

9. These are terms used by Kunjunni Raja (*loc cit*), and they also appear in commentaries.

10. *VP* IV 3.

11. *padasya padāntaravyatirekaprayuktānvayānanubhāvakatvamākāṅkṣāṃ. Tarkasaṃgraha* #60 (BORI). Rendering adopted from Deshpande, 'Sentence-cognition in Nyāya Epistemology', p198.

12. Prof. Matilal in the seminar, mentioned in note 0 above; *cf. TS* #60 : *ākāṅkṣā-yogyatā-saṃnidhiśca vākyārtha-jñānahetuḥ.*

13. Although Udayana seems to say that *āsatti* and *yogyatā* together cannot lead to *śābdabodha*, without *ākāṅkṣā*. *Cf.* Haridās Bhattācārya: '*nanu yogyatāsahitā āsattiveva heturastu'tatrāha yogyastirabandhanā iti vyāpti-śūnyā, ayameti putro rājaḥ puruṣo' pasāryatāmityatra nirākāṅkṣayorājapadapuruṣapadayorvyabhicārāt.*'(on III.13 *Nyayakusumāñjali*, edited by Cowell, 1864). Gadādhara also seems to have taken such a view. But more work needs to be done here as yet. *Cf.* also Nāgeśa Bhatta: *ayamartho'rthāntaramākāṅkṣatīti vyavahārāt ... padaṃ sākāṅkṣamiti tu sākāṅkṣārthabodhakamityrthakam. ata eva ghaṭaḥ karmatvam ānayanaṃ kṛtirityato ghaṭamānayetivannānvayabodhaḥ ākāṅkṣājñāvirahāt. ghaṭamānyeti vibhaktyantākhyatāntāyoreva sākāṅkṣājñāt vācca.* In *Paramalaghumañjūṣā* (ed. Pt Sadasiva Sarma Sastri, Banaras, 1946, pp34–35) See also note 29 *infra.*

14. *Śabdasaktiprakāśikā : vahninā sekha ityādyapi vākyameva, parantu bādhatārthakatvādayogyam, śābdamaterāhāryatvopagame 'nirvahnirvahnimān' 'pacanna pacatī' tyādikamapi vākyameva, no cedapārthameva, yādṛśabodhatvāvacchedenāhāryyatvaṃ tādṛśabuddhyarthaṃ prayuktapādānameva tathāvidhārthabodhaṃ pratyapārthakatvāt* (under no 13, pp64-66.) See next note. N. B. Although self-contradiction is not men-

tioned as a separate category and though Indian logicians did not make the analytic-synthetic distinction as sharply as made in recent Western philosophy, it might be a little presumptuous on our part to assume this. There is, however, considerable evidence in the literature to suggest that they were equipped with the tools of critical thinking based on the logical principles of non-contradiction and consistency, and other normative principles of thought. While in an expression like "fire wets" there is the realist intuition of 'empirical inconceivability', elsewhere we come across logical categories such as the following : *bādha* ('contradiction', 'falsity'), *prati-* ('opposed to'), *pratibandhaka* ('counterfactual'), *viruddha* ('contrary'), *vākchalam* ('equivocation'), *anekārthatā* ('ambiguity'), *viśaleṣaṇā/vaiśaleṣika* ('analytic'), *vyāghātā* ('contradictory'), *pratijñāntar* ('against evidence'), *pratijñāsaṃnāsya* ('reproof'), *hetvābhāsa* ('without reason'), *viruddhāvyabhicārī* ('contrary'), *anaikāntika* ('discrepant'), *āśrayāsiddhi* ('unreal combination'), and the more well known ones like *asiddhi* ('non-established'), *vyabhicāraḥ* ('incongruent'), and *satpratipaksa* ('questionable'). See *Nyāyakośa*.

Cf. Gaṅgeśa: *vahninā siñcati—ayogyatajñānam* (p235); *pratibandakaṃ dāhe* (p236). *Tattvacintāmaṇi* IV. See note 15 in next chapter.

15. See notes 20, 24ff, and discussion under 4.11 chapter 4, and note 2 in chapter 6.

15a. *Sabdaśaktiprakāśikā*, no 6: *śabdāntaramapekṣyaivasārthakaḥ svārthabodhakṛt; (cf) anvayabodhānukūlānupūrvi paryavasitā tv-ākaṅkṣā*, p12 under no 4. See also *NND*, p19, n42. And as shown in the previous chapter, '*ghaṭaḥ karmatvam*' ('a pot accusative') does not have *ākāṅkṣā* (*na ākāṅkṣodāharaṇaṃ, ghaṭaḥ karmatvaṃ iti*) *Dīpikā* on *TS* 61.

16. Matilal, *NND*, p19-20, and 'Indian Theorists on the Nature of the Sentence.', p383ff, and seminar comments. J. Brough, likewise, considers *ākāṅkṣā* to be of linguistic importance; 'Some Indian Theories of Meaning', p415.

17. Matilal, *ibid.*

18. The use of 'good' here (and 'bad' elsewhere) is merely a normative characterisation of 'knowledge' in terms of the epistemological capability of some structure of experience and is not in any way a value-judgement, much less a moral evaluation.

19. **_Tattvacintāmaṇi_, under _śabdakhaṇḍa_ (i): _yasya yena vinā svārthānvayānanubhāvakatvaṃ tasya tadaparyavasānam, nāmavibhaktidhātvākhyāta-kriyā-kāraka-padānāṃ parasparaṃ vinā na parasparasya svārthānvayānubhavajanakatvaṃ_. p208ff (Kashi edition).**

20. *VP* IV 3(b): *kriyāśravaṇe kārakasya tasya śravaṇe kriyāyāḥ, karaṇa-śravaṇe itikartavyatāyaśca jijñāsāviṣayatvāt. Cf. Mīmāṃsā Paribhāṣā*, delineating *ākāṅkṣā* between *arthībhāvanā* and *śābdībhāvanā* : *sā cārthabhāvanā kiṃ, kena, kathamiti aṃśatrayaviśiṣṭā* : the objective urge consists of three parts - 'what, through what, and how?' (Mādhavānanda, ed. 1948, p46). And *cf. Tarkabhāṣā* in rather more realist strain (under *ākāṅkṣā*): mutual dependency of the referential designation makes for dependency of meaning-content of significative utterances; thus words, expressive of them also become interdependent. *arthastāvat svapadaśrotaryanyonyaviṣayākāṅkṣājanakatvena sākāṅkṣā ityucyate* (p17, 1953; p48, 1979).

21. This is different from the use of the copula in the expression "the boy is (an) apple"; for, as we indicated in chapter four, 'copula', in Sanskrit particularly, is taken to be a *kriyā*-form, that is to say, an implication of a continuous activity, or simply 'of being there somehow' (*bhāvanā*, again). As such the process of *be-ing*, is involved. Compare, the vernacular English : "Be yourself!" *cf. Astimat*: possessing property; *bhāva* and *bhāvanā* could also be taken to signify this in certain contexts, or simply to connote "being somehow", or just "being" (v).

22. It may well be that in taking *kriyā* so seriously the author has been persuaded by the grammarians' insistence, in contrast to the Nyāya's, on the utter necessity of at least one finite verb for a completed syntactic structure, as we saw in the previous chapter. The reinforcement for this comes from the Mīmāṃsā preoccupation with *bhāvanā*—

the 'efficient force' bringing about a result – which in a syntactic structure is represented by an *ākhyāta*-suffix. Patañjali spoke of *kriyā* in a manner somewhat similar to the Mīmāṃsakas.

23. The use of mentalistic and quasi-psychological terms in Indian epistemology, does not indicate, as Prof. Mohanty has pointed out, a resort to psychologism of the form that, say, Frege and Popper, repudiated. Rather it attempts to expose epistemic constituents and theoretical structures underlying the processes of knowing, meaning and expressing. And although the terms are not as incorrigible as Ryle would wish them to be, one could be assured that, for instance, no Cartēsian ghost lurks behind the *manas* ("mind") in epistemological analysis, whatever its status might be in the more ontological preoccupations of Sāṃkhya and the like.

24. *VP* IV 4: *ajijñāsorpi vākyārthabodhād yogyatvamupāttam.*

25. The same is said by Nārāyaṇa Bhaṭṭa in *Mānameyodaya*, no 10:*gauraśvaḥ puruṣo hastītyākānkṣārahiteṣviha. anvayādarśanāt tāvadākāṅkṣā parigṛahyate.*

26. *VP* IV 4 : *tadvacchedakaṃ ca kriyātva-kārakatvādikamiti nātivyāptiḥ gauraśvaḥ [puruṣo hastī]' ityādau.*

27. *Ibid* IV 4c: *adbhedānvaye ca samānvibhaktikapadapratipādayatvaṃ tadavacchedakam iti tatvamasyādivākyeṣu nāvyāptiḥ.*

28. See previous chapter. *Cf. Mīmāṃsā-sūtras* II.1.48 : *anuṣaṅgo vākyasamāptiḥ sarveṣu tulyayogitvāt.* (p174 G. Jha ed. 1911 *(SBH*).

29. *sā ca ekapadārthajñāne tadarthānvayayogyārthasya yajjñānaṃ tadviṣayecchā 'asyānvayyarthaḥ kaḥ' ityevam rūpā puruṣaniṣṭhaiva, tathāpi tasyāḥ svaviṣaye'rthe āropaḥ*. Nageśa Bhaṭṭa, *Paramalaghumañjūṣā (op cit)* pp33–34.

30. See note 15a above, which construed in a wider sense could be said to extend to the order of sentence-components or sub-sentential elements, although Jagadīśa may have not meant that.

31. Again, much was gained from the seminar mentioned in note 0.

32. *Tarkasamgraha: padānāmavilambenoccāranam samnidhih* 60.4 (BORI) p52.

33. *SM-BP* under #82 (p166.) Also quoted-discussed in the item in the next note.

34. Matilal, 'Indian Theorists on the Sentence.' p384.

35. J. Brough in 'Some Indian Theories of Meaning', p145.

36. See 5.13 in text, and chapter four discussion *PS* 2.1.I – notes 3 and 4 above.

37. J. F. Staal, *Word Order In Sanskrit and Universal Grammar*, p25-6.

38. *Vākyapadīya* I.48: *nādasya kramajanmatvān na pūrvo na paraś ca saḥ akramaḥ kramarūpeṇa bhedavān iva jāyate* (trans. in Staal, *loc cit*, see note above).

39. Jaimini in *Mīmāṃsā Sūtra* I.2.32 (p45): *vākyaniyamāt*. See discussion on *'agnimūrdhā' 'mūrdhāgniḥ'*, by G. Jha in accompanying English commentary ('and so the order of the sentence is irrevocably fixed').

40. *Śābara-bhāṣya* on above *sūtra*. Vol I p76 (GOI 1889, p56) *agniḥ-mūrdhā-divaḥ. . .(divaḥ-agniḥ-mūrdhā)*

41. Jaimini in *Mīmāṃsā-sūtras*, I.2.44: *aviruddhaṃparam* p50 (1911).

42. *Śābara-bhāṣya* on *sūtra* above; trans. from Staal (*op cit* p45ff). *Cf.* Staal discusses Śabara's review of the example concerning the *mantra*: *agnir mūrdha diva:* An opponent argues that, if *mantras* had meaning, reversing the order would mean the reversal of the meaning of the expression as well. A distinction therefore is suggested between 'utterance' and 'sentence', the former having more to do with *performance* than with (linguistic) *competence*, and it would appear that word order is fixed in utterances, even if it be not fixed in sentences. Śabara more or less accepts this view. For Kumārila the

word order is pointless in expressions such as *mūrdhā agniḥ*, which means the same when reversed; although word order becomes meaningful 'in the case of stems, affixes and compounds'. But both Mīmāṃsakas also indicate the significance of word order for establishing unseen result (*apūrva*). Staal does not stress this point sufficiently and seems to rest his conclusions on the view that because *mantras* are meaningless they do not share the same characteristics with sentences in ordinary speech (such as free word order), and are therefore not relevant for linguistic investigation. (*Loc cit.*)

43. Kumārila Bhaṭṭa in *Tantravārttika*, G. Jha. Eng trans. Vol I pp83-85, and quoted in Staal (*loc cit*, p46). Also note 39 above.

44. *Ibid.*

45. *saṃbandhakāraṇatvena kḷptaṃ nānantaraśrutiḥ*, Kumārila Bhaṭṭa, *Tantravārttika* (in Kunjunni Raja, *op cit*, p166 n3).

46. Kunjunni Raja (*loc cit*, n4).

47. *śabdaḥ saṃnihitatvena bodhatitvam hi padārthānāṃ saṃnidhirityucyate, Mānameyodaya*, Āgama section (VII, p101).

48. *ataḥ saṃnihitatvābhāvāt śabdabodhitatvābhāvācca dvedhā saṃnidhyabhāvo bhavati. tatra bhinnakāloccāritayoh gāṃ ānaya iti padatoḥ saṃnihitatvābhāvādanvayaḥ—(ibid).*

49. *gāṃ bādhana ityatra bandhanāpekṣasya dṛśyamānasya aśvasya śabdabodhitatvābhāvādevānanvayaḥ ataḥ śabdapratipannānāmevānvayaḥ iti niyamaḥ siddhaḥ—(ibid, and continuing).*

50. *Ibid.*

51. *Dīpikā* on *Tarkasaṃgraha* #61 [BORI] : *ghaṭaḥ karmatvamityanākāṅkṣodāharaṇaṃ 'dravyaṣṭam'* (Mehendale edn., variant reading: *dṛṣṭavyam*).

52. *SM-BP*, under #82-83 (1883 edn. p75ff).

53. *Ibid.*

54. *Ibid.* He continues: 'Moreover, since words denoting actions and their objects are necessary to make sense in their particular forms, how can there be verbal comprehension without words denoting actions? Similarly, since in words like 'for flowers' the use of the dative case-ending is inexplicable without supplying some such word as 'craves', the supply of *words* is a necessity.'(p169.)

55. *Ibid.*

56a. *VP* IV 10: *āsattiścāvyavadhānena padajanyapadārthopasthitiḥ, mānāntareṇa upasthāpitapadārthasyānvaya-bodhābhāvāt padajanyeti.*

56. *Ibid*, IV 11: *ata eva aśrutapadārthasthale tattatpadādhyāhāraḥ, - dvāram—ityādau—pidhehi—iti. Ata eva—Iṣe tvā—ityādau chinadmi—iti padādhyāhāraḥ; ata eva vikṛtiṣu—sūryaya juṣṭaṃ nirvapāmi—iti padaprayogaḥ.*

57. *Ibid.*

58. This is gone into in some detail in the Hindi commentary on the same text, by Gajānana Śāstri. pp204ff.

59. Remarking on a similar view in Western linguistics, albeit on a more psychological note, it is said that 'Sapir has proved that in all languages, juxtaposition is the simplest, most economical method of binding words together and of bringing them into some relation to each other. The very process of juxtaposing. . .forces some kind of relational feeling, if nothing else, upon us. Words and elements when they are listed in a certain order, tend not only to establish some kind of relation among themselves, but are attracted to each other in greater or in less degree', O.Hobart Mowrer in 'The Psychologist Looks at Language' (*Readings in the Psychology of Language*, ed. by L. A. Jakabovits and Miron, Prentice-Hall, N. J., 1967, p13 fn 17; in Deshpande, *op cit*, p203).

6

THE PHENOMENOLOGICAL KĀRAṆAS

Phenomenological *kāraṇas*[0]

A. ***YOGYATĀ – semantic competency***

B. ***TĀTPARYA – intentionality***

A: *Yogyatā*

6.0 In this chapter we wish to continue the analysis of the *kāraṇas*, two of which remain, namely, *yogyatā* and *tātparya*, which, in varying degrees are said to determine the structure of *śābdabodha – yogyatā* is said to be more important than *āsatti*, and *ākāṅkṣā* perhaps the most important of them all. We shall deal with *yogyatā* in part A and with *tātparya* in part B.

The factors that generate *śābdabodha*, propositional understanding, often exceed the syntactic and grammatical factors involved in *vākyārthajñāna*, i.e. the comprehension of the 'meaning' of the sentence uttered. Such factors could be semantical, logical and contextual determinants. *Yogyatā* is considered to be one such, and is basically a *semantical kāraṇa*. It has been rendered variously as '*semantical* compatibility, competency, acceptability, consistency. congruity and so forth.'[1] In a general way, *yogyatā* can be defined as the mutual congruity or fitness of one word-meaning or 'significant-content' with another word-meaning or 'significant-content' in accordance with the syntactical-grammatical connections of the respective words expressing those meanings.

6.1 To put matter more precisely, *yogyatā* is the absence of absurdity or incompatibility among the relations of the word-meanings or 'significant-contents' intended by the speaker : *yogyatā ca tātparyaviṣayasaṃsargābādhaḥ*.[2] In other words, the 'significant-contents' or what is signified by the constituent words of a sentence must be in harmonious and consistent relation, and this in turn depends on the absence of contradiction or incongruity among the 'contents' signified. Thus, the *relation* (*saṃsarga*) that is being considered here is not the purely grammatical and syntactical relations among the word-elements, but one that goes a little beyond word-meanings and their respective referents. Of course, words are not always used to refer to particular objects or 'referents',[3] they are also used abstractly, often to designate some concept or universal, and thus the *saṃsargaḥ* or relation would extend to these as well. Hence, the relational principle is to be construed more in a *logical* sense as the relations that obtain between epistemic items in an episodic act (*jñāna*), towards which the absence of self-contradiction,[4] contradiction by another *jñāna* (i.e. falsification), and contingencies that would militate against their consistent relation, would be significant determinants.

We pointed out that *yogyatā* is to be distinguished from *yogyatva* (as involved in *ākāṅkṣā*), which also implies 'fitness' or the capacity of two or more word-meanings to be mutually related. Unlike *ākāṅkṣā*, which is focused on mutual expectancy, *yogyatā* is a criterion all to itself, and is not subordinated to another relation: it is a causal relation itself. But *yogyatva* also has application in *yogyatā* in the same way that it does in *ākāṅkṣā*. For example, the *kriyātva-kārakatva* delimitors in respect of *ākāṅkṣā* are also the delimiting conditions for 'competency' of the relation determined by *yogyatā*. But with one important qualification, namely that, while *jñāna* or awareness is not required in the case of *ākāṅkṣā*, its function here being as it were automatic, with *yogyatā* its occurrence is concomitant. In some ways this is an added advantage for *yogyatā* since it is able then to deal with anomalies not within the scope of *ākāṅkṣā*. We shall look at this a little later.

6.2 To return to the above example, in the utterance "Bring the pot", there is no inconsistency or incompatibility between the terms of the expression in respect of the *kriyātva-kārakatva* relation. Thus *śābdabodha* should arise unimpeded. Some utterances, however, are made that do not accord with this delimiting condition, and so are devoid of *yogyatā*. Let us consider some examples of expressions we considered earlier:

(i) *vahninā siñcati* : '(he) sprinkles (the field) with fire.'
(ii) *jalena siñcati* : '(he) sprinkles (the field) with water.'

Now (i), as distinct from (ii), is said not to possess *yogyatā*, for though both are grammatically and syntactically appropriate and acceptable, (i) is not semantically appropriate – i.e., it is lacking in semantical *yogyatva*, while (ii) is semantically appropriate as well. But why is (i) semantically inappropriate or 'incompatible'? Allowing now for the category 'semantical' to have a wider nuance than it ordinarily has in view of the definition of *yogyatā* given here, we can look for a response by analysing the distinct parts or elements of the sentences, and by considering the mutual interrelation among the 'senses' intended in the utterance; we will then be in a position to question their compatibility or otherwise. Now in (i), we observe that someone is said to sprinkle the field with fire, in the way that water is used for making the soil in the field moist. But the word used for the *verbal* element is *'siñcati'*, which has the *abhidhā* or express sense of "sprinkles" and which *connotes* the act of "wetting" or "flooding", or even "watering". Thus, that to which this act of watering is done would become *wet* or *watery*, as the garden is after being hosed with water. But this also indicates that the object that is most appropriate or *fitting* for the purpose of sprinkling or "wetting" is the fluid we know as water, whether it is in the form of water pumped out of a well, or irrigated off a river or a sea, or as rain. Thus, while it is appropriate to relate sprinkling with 'water', as it is in sentence (ii), which is consistent with the *kriyātva-kārakatva* delimitor, such that *yogyatā qua* its fitness capacity (*yogyatva*) is not frustrated in this sentence (ii), this is not the case with sentence (i), where, on the other hand, *fire* is being presented as the 'object' for the purposes of sprinkling or "wetting".

Fire, however, cannot be said to be the *fit* or proper object with which to sprinkle or moisten things with. On the contrary, for the purposes of analysis at least, fire, even in the form of strong sunlight, is opposed to wetness, and its use therefore would be antithetical to the purpose desired. Presuming that this is not a metaphor, fire is therefore incompatible with the activity of irrigating the field. But this is what the speaker or the utterance seems to intend : the grammatical construction, which is perfectly acceptable, and the use of the instrumental indicates that the activity of sprinkling is to be related to fire. But, as we said, the relation between these two is semantically inappropriate in the sense that the *kriyātva-kārakatva* relation is frustrated here so long as we take the intent (of the speaker) to mean that sprinkling is to be related to fire. It is evidently the case that fire is impossible as a means of wetting or sprinkling, just as it is impossible to *burn* with water. There is little reason, then, to believe that a syntactical connection between the two terms of the relation can occur without giving rise to an inconsistent sense in sentence (i).

6.3 The response to the above query is that syntactical connection is not being denied here. What is being said is that the connection or the intended relation between the two elements or 'contents' in the sentence (*tātparyaviṣayasaṃsarga*) does not give rise to a consistent sense, and this is possibly due to the incompatibility or inappropriateness between the senses or 'contents' (*viṣayasaṃsargabādha*). It is not that the sentence (i) does not make *any* sense, but that it does not make 'good sense', or generate an unimpeded *śābdabodha*. Nyāya would deny that in such instances as utterance (i), any *śābdabodha* arises at all. Of course, the example used for illustrating this point is perhaps a weak one, for one can easily say that expression (i) is used in a metaphorical sense, as might occur in poetry and creative forms of writing.

There can be two sorts of response to the question just raised. One, is to say yes, a metaphorical sense is being used here, and the other to say that the specific use is made of for a particular purpose, as Jagadīśa says.[5] In either case, one could say that the absence of *yogyatā* or the presence of *ayogyatā*, is exploited in order to shift, as it were, the level of meaning to the implicative or *lakṣya* function. It is assuredly not the case that the affirmative proposition 'this is a metaphorical sense' is given with expression (i) since its syntactical structure, at least, is identical to expression (ii) which is not a metaphor. That it is a metaphorical use of the term in (i) has to be cognised *ab extra*, through the awareness first of the discrepancy involved in the conventional relation of the terms of the sentence. Admittedly, in a language-community where metaphors and other non-literal senses, along perhaps with humour, are not tolerated, an expression such as (i) would probably be discarded on the grounds that it is lacking in *yogyatā*. Unless, of course, even in such communities expressions like (i) were made use of under extra-ordinary circumstances to alert one to the dangerous consequences of one's act or to warn another of the futility of his act. This would occur (following Austin here) in illocutionary, and maybe perlocutionary, speech-acts. For example, when one screams "Oh good Lord! They are sprinkling (with) fire!"—he is expressing horror at the sight of a field being sprayed with a film of some inflamatory chemical used in warfare, or simply with an unwarranted quantity of a potent fertilising agent. It would be a cold euphemism to suggest that the enraged citizen was resorting to a metaphor here, as though he were some sort of a romantic.

6.4 Anticipating some uneasiness with the above response, Jagadīśa proceeds to give another example where the absence of *yogyatā* is perhaps more obvious, namely, the expression 'fire is in this place (where) it is not'.[6] Obviously, there is a self-contradiction involved here; how can fire be in a place where it is denied to be at the same time? Either the fire is there where it is said to be, or it is not. Just as we cannot say the dead man is alive if we mean that the man is dead and pronounced dead. If we say 'Caitra is cooking' (*caitraḥ pacati*), we cannot turn around and say 'Caitra is not cooking' (*caitraḥ na pacati*). Can one affirm and deny something in the same breath without being involved in a contradiction? Would they not annihilate themselves? Now here a rather more logical consideration is invoked for discerning *ayogyatā* or semantic incompatibility among the terms of an expression. 'Semantic' here is taken broadly to include, as we said earlier, both logical and empirical discrepancies given through experience. *Yogyatā* can then be taken to mean that there should be harmony and consistency or mutual congruity among the referents or 'objects' (*artha*) designated by the terms of an expression. To say, therefore, that a spade is a shovel (as in some vernacular idiom) is acceptable, but to say that a spade is a donkey, is not acceptable for the reason that this relation goes against, or at least is not given in, empirical experience.[7a]

6.5 It would be illustrative to consider an example of an expression that is totally lacking in *yogyatā*[7] – viz. 'There goes the barren woman's son with a chaplet of sky-flowers on his head; he has bathed himself in the waters of a mirage and is holding a bow (made out of) rabbit's horn.' This is lacking in *yogyatā* because one cannot ostensibly make sense of an utterance which implies that a barren woman has had an offspring – an unlikely biological feat (notwithstanding *in vitro* fertilisation and such new reproductive technologies) – who is running around with flowers snatched from the sky. There is further suggestion that he has bathed in the illusory water created by a mirage-effect and is displaying a bow that is said have been made from something that rabbit's are not known to have, even if they did, the horn would be too small for a bow.

Udayana proposes other sorts of characteristics that could frustrate *yogyatā*, namely,[8] gesturing, punning, equivocating, withdrawing parts of coherent statements, as well as those considered above. If language is considered to be a mirror of the world (of 'real objects', *yathārthas*) then it should not, without good reason, reflect more than there is. And this is where *yogyatā* has its legitimate function: it asks, roughly, whether a word or an expression is being used in its valid (normative) occurrence, and if it is not then why and exactly how it isn't; otherwise the expression in which these occur would be less than capable of generating satisfactory *śābdabodha.*

6.6 It would appear that requirement of *yogyatā* arose from the need to formulate some sort of a rule to interpret the apparent incongruity of one sentence following another, taking into account the overall purpose of the passage or verse. Dharmarāja gives an example to illustrate how *yogyatā* resolves an apparent inconsistency between two Vedic sentences, one of which refers to the nature of a particular sacrifice to be performed, while the other states: 'Prajāpati even tore his own skin (*vapā*).'[9] The apparent inconsistency is between the sacrifice and Prajāpati tearing his own skin which in effect has nothing to do with the sacrifice. Hence, one would be led to believe that there is an incongruity between the two statements. This, however, is *not* the intended purport of the text; if it were, there would evidently be *ayogyatā* (inconsistency) between the two. By contrast, the second sentence is used here merely as an eulogy (*arthavāda*) to elucidate the principal sentence concerning the sacrifice to be performed. Its purpose and intent is not to explain the procedure or detail of the sacrifice as one might expect, but merely to lend support to the sacrifice in praising it in a high-faluted way, by implicating an illusory infliction on the part of the god who incurs this in accepting the offerings from the sacrifice. Hence, if anyone's skin is torn it is that of the animal to be sacrificed, which in this case the god receiving the sacrifice reciprocates, in a manner of speaking. It would be like saying "I will give my life to show that there is life after death." It is not at all obvious, regardless of whether there is life after death or not, that by giving up one's life here one will provide any evidence to another of life anywhere, much less hereafter. Likewise, to say that the killer killed himself, presumably not killing anyone else then or before, would be to commit, in Udayana's term, a *pratisaṃdhānam* in view of the fact that the two terms in this expression tend to annihilate each other. Suppose, however, with the earlier example, that the intended purport was that Prajāpati also tore his skin *open* in the process of officiating the sacrifice. This, then, would properly lead one to ask, "But why?" "What has this to do with the sacrifice proper?" and so forth, indicating that there is something inappropriate in this sentence. Hence, in that case there would be *tātparya-viṣaya-saṃsarga-bādha*: contradiction in the relation among the intended 'objects'. Which is to say that there is absence of *yogyatā*, and without *yogyatā* the intended *śābdabodha* from the scriptural statements would be frustrated. Later the Mīmāṃsā and the linguistic thinkers adopted this 'criterion' for adjudicating the appropriateness or otherwise of the mutual relation of distinct elements within the same utterance, i.e. within the same sentence. And this gave them a yardstick, so to speak, by which to measure whether a sentence was qualified for *śābdabodha*, at least in respect of one of the *kāraṇas*. Only after that questions of truth or falsity of the propositions expressed in respect of the congruent qualifier-qualified relation would be appropriately raised.

6.7 The grammarians, though, entertain a slightly different notion of *yogyatā* and do not extend its function quite so far. As the grammarians are concerned, *yogyatā* is a purely formal property of a sentence, and it does not extend to considerations of logical and empirical compatibility as has been argued for in the earlier analysis. To the grammarian, sentence (i) would be as acceptable as sentence (ii), for the linguistic structure is the same in both, though they differ in their respective 'meanings'. But it is not upon the grammarians to make the judgements about the truth or falsity of the 'propositional sense' of the utterance. Whether the referents of 'fire' and 'water' serve the same purpose or not outside of the sentence could be of little or no concern to the linguistic structure proper of the sentence : its concern is to convey the sentence-meaning, whatever it be, in as best a way as possible.

Thus, someone like Nāgeśa would reject the view represented earlier, that an utterance such as *'vahninā siñcati'*, 'he sprinkles with fire', does not succeed in conveying any meaning whatsoever.[10] It is undeniable that someone hearing this expression, which afterall is a grammatically and syntactically sound sentence, will understand something from it in order to be able to say that it makes no sense to utter such a thing.

The audience might argue that such a state of affairs in the world is not possible. But this itself indicates *prima facie* that the audience has understood the sentence-meaning (*vakyārtha* as distinct from *śābdabodha*). This is what the sentence conveys to him, so much so that he is able to challenge the authenticity of what appears to be intended by the speaker, and in expressing his doubt he is also calling for clarification. Stating the grammarians' case, Deshpande remarks : 'We must distinguish the stage of apprehending the sentence-meaning from the stage of evaluating its logical or empirical validity. A sentence-meaning may be logically or empirically invalid, and yet there is nothing to stop that sentence from conveying its meaning.'[11] It is further observed that even though there may not be the exact correspondence in the external reality to whatever is being expressed by a word or a cluster of words, as in a sentence, this does not mean, therefore, that this word-expression is not capable of generating legitimate meaning-apprehension.

The Sanskrit grammarians (who are committed exclusively to the consideration of the formal features of a sentence) looked at this issue in another way. For them, the 'soundness of a sentence' is really about the lexical and structural appropriateness of the sentence and they do not in this regard consider extra-linguistic issues, such as its correspondence, truth-value, and so forth. The grammarians' conception of what is acceptable and what is not is therefore based, by and large, on the formal properties of a sentence. So much so that, to them, expressions like '(He is) a barren woman's son' [regardless of the *in vitro* surrogate 'motherhood' technique of late], and the Chomskian example, 'Colourless green ideas sleep furiously', are perfectly 'meaningful' sentences, for they are in harmony with grammatical and syntactical requirements, and there would be little difficulty for an audience to comprehend their respective meanings. Though the grammarians might perhaps admit that the occurrences of such sentences in actual speech are actually rare, and are likely to provoke confusion or strong reactions on the part of the audience. This is particularly so since expressions like 'all bachelors are not unmarried men' and 'nuclear warfare can renew life on earth', and 'dump this file, PIP to drive B, stripp off controls and trail it down Modem', tend to become common idioms in certain areas of ordinary discourse and work-a-day life.

6.8 At any rate, because the grammarians do not regard *yogyatā* to be a necessary condition for *śābdabodha*, *yogyatā* has been regarded as an *ab extra* logical and an empirical requirement that involves a judgement of either the truth or falsity of the statement expressed through this sentence, or of the sense or nonsense of the utterance. In other words, it is claimed that the requirement, is totally extra-linguistic and is in way incumbent upon the internal structure of *śābdabodha*.

Now it is true that those schools, such as Advaita, Mīmāṃsā and Nyāya, that maintain *śabda* or 'word' to be a means of knowledge (*pramāṇa*), would want to define a sentence in such a way that only those expressions that lead to *valid* knowledge would be regarded as 'valid sentences'. And such a definition of a sentence would perforce involve considerations of a logical and empirical sort in terms of the nature and relation of its factual contents. By 'factual' we mean here the actual 'things', 'objects', or some state of affairs – i.e. referents – that the words in the sentence denote or designate, individually or collectively. Consequently, the truth-value of the proposition expressed in the sentence would be dependent on the real 'correspondence' of the external (i.e. extra-linguistic) state of affairs that the sentence refers to. Hence, *yogyatā* can be interpreted as a requirement that helps make judgements about the 'contents' (material or conceptual) that are related in this way and the appropriateness or otherwise of the relation therein.

However, while this would not be denied by those of a non-grammarian persuasion, it should be pointed out that such a consideration would become applicable only *after* the sentence has been uttered and understood. The alternative viewpoint, to be sure, stresses that *if* the sentence is intended to generate valid knowledge, *śābdabodha*, then such considerations must occur *prior* to its utterance. That is to say, if someone uttering the sentence intends that a true understanding be conveyed, he would presumably make sure that *his* understanding is not self-contradictory or logically inconsistent, nor amiss in its reference to a state of affairs in the world. And because he has this expectation, and because he knows something about the world and so forth, his understanding would, to a large extent, depend upon the absence of internal inconsistency within the sentence. Otherwise it would betray a misunderstanding of some real state of affairs. Once the audience is led to suspect that there is some incongruity within the sentence (particularly in regard to the constituents in the expression and their interrelation) then this would impede the emergence of a clear understanding of the sentence sense.

The audience might be led to wonder, for example, how the speaker intends two disparate contents to be related when they are incompatible or inconsistent with known facts. Thus, the relation would appear to be incongruous to him, and, therefore, whatever he comprehends from the sentence (*vākyārthajñāna*) would be unacceptable. In this sense, it would be said, the requirement of *yogyatā* has not been fulfilled, and a *śābdabodha*, at least a successful and unhindered one, could not be said to have been generated. It is not that the sentence would be *totally* unintelligible to him, although it may be in some cases, but rather that his understanding would be as though *petrified.*[12]

6.9 Now surely, if this were the case, then the substantive and logical aspects cannot be said to lie entirely outside the scope of the sentence, for they are at least one part of its structure, viz. its 'semantical relation'. It is not being said that what one understands from a sentence has to be *ipso facto* true. Rather we are suggesting that one can reasonably expect that every caution is taken on the part of the speaker to see to it that his understanding is not erroneous before he makes the utterance in question. This, of course, includes the assumption that he does not attempt to convey what might be ostensibly meaningless, empty, incoherent or factually incongruous. For one would trust the speaker to be reliable in the normal world of commerce and discourse, and would expect that his utterance is not a lie, or a misrepresentation or a travesty of some real 'fact' or state of affairs in the world or known universe at large. And if one expects this from the speaker of a sentence then one also expects this from the sentence encountered where perhaps the speaker is not immediately present (as in written text).

Putting it another way, one expects the sentence to be grammatically and syntactically acceptable. But perhaps this is too much to presume on the part of the audience before what is expressed can be put to test for its truth or falsity (with respect to, say, the criterion of verification or of falsification). At least, one like Ayer might argue that the statement expressed ought to be verifiable (or falsifiable) for it to be meaningful. Otherwise one might be led to make utterances whose contents are rather more abstract and not directly presented in nor relatable to experience.

On the other hand, one could argue that if we could think of or imagine the *conceivable limits* within which even the most abstract sort of understanding can be expressed—and which are at the same time not merely ideas given in flights of fantasy or in some vague fancy—then we could make sense of the expression. Where this is not possible, only then we concede to the meaninglessness of the expression. Thus, again, a sentence like 'Quadraplicity drinks triangle' has a sound grammatical structure, but the semantic interpretations we put on, or can put on it, would undoubtedly get us into trouble, for however far we stretch our imagination within conceivable limits, it still makes very little sense to speak of 'quadraplicity'.

The problem, to be sure, is a conceptual one, not a straightforwardly empirical one, although in the last analysis one might have to turn to empirical instances to, as it were, sort out the conceptual incongruity. Indeed, for any sentence, we first grasp it at its conceptual level and then relate it to its respective designations in the specific context of its utterance. The utterance that rabbits have horns, as we stated earlier, is an instance of such a troublesome expression. Admittedly, then, there is something of an empirical ring around the criterion of meaningfulness proposed here.

It is, nevertheless, at this conceptual level also that judgements are made about the *viability* of the sentence-sense in respect of the verifiability (or falsifiability) of the 'contents' of the utterance. A *prima facie* judgement sometimes proves to be wrong, as the sense intended can often be more subtle than at first appears.

Consider, for example, following two utterances : "Consciousness begins at the third month of the foetus' life."(a Hindu belief); "To become big, you have to become small" (a moral saying of the New Zealand Maori). The first reaction usually to such utterances (particularly on the part of those outside the community of the respective speakers) would be one of uneasiness. For, in the case of the first expression, one may have no familiarity with such a discourse, apparently as it relates to pre-natal consciousness, and in the case of the second, there is an unobvious paradox involved.

To consider yet another example, suppose the question 'Where are you sleeping tonight?', provokes the response: "On the river."An innocent by-stander may make an immediate response with the query: "But you will drown there!" We could say that the audience has misunderstood the speaker's intention – until the latter decides to clarify himself, by adding perhaps: "The house-boat is quite safe." It is only then that the perplexed audience becomes aware that the speaker did not intend to be understood that he was going to actually rest his head on the waters of the river, rather that he would sleep in the house-boat which happens to be in the river and not in the village grounds. Had the speaker intended the audience to understand what the by-stander earlier took him to be saying, then that 'petrified' reaction could not have been avoided. Why? Because he would have apprehended that the sentence just uttered is lacking in *yogyatā* : which is to say that there is inconsistency between the elements related in the sentence, namely, "sleeping" (elliptically understood) and "on the river".

Thus, within a reasonably conceivable limit the audience would have to question the integrity of the speaker's utterance (if not of the speaker himself), if he is to accept what he initially understood from the utterance. It then seems reasonable to suggest that, if one is to take a sentence-sense understood to be a 'true cognition' then the *contents* presented by the sentence-components and their interrelation, would need to be consistent and compatible. In fact, the Nyāya thinkers go a little further by arguing that one cannot even *understand* a sentence if the meaning-contents are incompatible or inconsistent. In effect they may deny that such utterances are sentences *at all*. But this requirement is built into the definition of sentence – viz. that, given the optimal conditions, the sentence ought to be capable of leading to a 'true cognition' (i.e. valid *śābdabodha*). By the grammarian's standard this definition is too rigid, as we saw earlier.

The Advaita definition is a little more open-ended than the Nyāya one, in that while it emphasises the *power* and the potentiality of a sentence leading to 'true cognition', it does not preclude sentences that do not generate valid *śābdabodha*, or which inadvertently lead to *mis*-understanding or error or doubt, since each of these is an instance of *jñāna* even though none may qualify as *pramā*.

6.10 We have asked this question before, but perhaps for the sake of clarity we should ask it again: is the incompatibility merely with respect to the actual factual contents that prevent the comprehension, or is it in respect of the inconceivability of the mutual connection of the 'meaning-contents'?[13] We can approach this question by considering another example, namely that of the following: "the circular square". Now the description that fits the two terms, namely, 'circular' and 'square', appear to be incongruous when one is taken as qualifying the other. In other words, even as universals (*jātis*), they are distinct, just as the universal of cow, *cowness*, is distinct from the universal horse, *horseness*. Likewise, the figure (*ākṛti*) or geometric shape symbolised by a circle cannot be the same shape as that symbolised by a square.

Putting the matter more simply, a *square* cannot be a *circle*. In other words, it is inconceivable that the geometric figure of a square would at once have the shape of a circle as well (in Euclidean geometry at least). Thus their combination in respect of the meaning-contents in the above expression has to be discarded because there is incongruity in the combination. This is the real issue, for what appears to be the case in the context or a particular situation would depend upon the relation and identification possible at the descriptive, conceptual level first, since particulars, in most Indian systems, are more like shadows of the universal and the possibilities therein. There are, however, exceptions, as when the same terms are used either metaphorically, or as signifying different universals to those that they are directly related, or perhaps as *names* denoting particulars devoid of universals as their significations.

Suppose, therefore, the use of "square" in the particular context of its occurrence is not intended to be taken in the usual sense of the geometric shape it signifies, but as a name, as in "city square", which distinguishes an open area in the middle of the city where common citizens congregate for recreation and civic functions. The term "square" in this sense is then not to be identified with the geometric shape with four equal sides to it. A 'city-square', on the other hand, need have no shape or ostensible "sides" at all. But a particular city-square in a particular town we are describing, say, happens to be a circular enclosure, marked off by paths and roads that curve around the general area set aside for civic mingling. Now, in such a case, it is not inconceivable that a 'square' can have a circular shape, for there is no conceptual problem regarding the identification of a 'square' (*qua* city-square) with a circle, unlike in geometry. There is, therefore, no incongruity in saying that a *square*, for all intents and purposes, has a circular form if what we mean by a 'square' is the civic assembly area in the city. But this sort of an identification cannot be made in the case of contents that are purely conceptual (e.g. geometrical), as distinct from any factual contents.

The meaning-contents (i.e. the 'senses') are such that there can be no adequate relation between them; and when this is lacking it is said that words signifying these contents are semantically incompetent to combine to yield a properly meaningful sentence. Again, this is so because one of the conditions governing the comprehension of sentence-sense is that there be compatibility among the different word-meanings that combine to constitute sentence-sense. And if the meanings of words that occur together do not combine adequately to present a composite sense, then their being together cannot be said to serve any significant purpose. Their occurrence, therefore, does not amount to constituting a sentence in any significant *sense*. But in so far as the grammatical structure is concerned, the concatenation of words, as say in "Quadraplicity drinks triangles", cannot be denied to constitute a sentence, and because this sentence is drastically in want of *yogyatā* its relative scope for *śābdabodha* is significantly restricted. And that is the basic point that Advaita wants to make in its lengthy discussion on *yogyatā*.

6.11 Now it remains to be asked whether the audience has to be actually aware of the presence of *yogyatā* in the sentence, or whether it is sufficient that the incompatibility between the intended relation be simply of its constitutive elements. In other words, in comprehending a sentence does one have to be consciously aware of the compatibility of the relation between, or among, the 'contents' signified? If there is such a distinct awareness, is it concomitant with the awareness of the sentence-sense?

Viśvanātha states clearly that where there is lack of awareness of *yogyatā* 'there is no comprehension from sentences like, "They are sprinkling (with) fire".'[14] Annaṃbhaṭṭa is also of the same opinion.[15] That is, a decisive awareness of *yogyatā* is a prerequisite for a linguistic comprehension or *śābdabodha*.

Dharmarāja also argues that the audience has to be aware of the presence of *yogyatā*, on the basis that, in metaphorical and allegorical sentences, if one were not aware of the mutual compatibility of the elements of the sentence in their non-literal or some other intended sense, then one might well fail to understand the sentence. An example is given, of the Upaniṣadic sage making the utterance, "That you are" (*'tat tvam asi'*). One would respond that such a relation is impossible because the individual *qua* his body and mind cannot be identified with a conception of some absolute. However, if he were to become aware that the identification intended is between the 'contents' signified through the secondary implication (*lakṣyārtha*) of each of the major terms of the expression, then he should be in better position to comprehend the intended sense.[16] Otherwise he would find himself conceptually in the same predicament as the person who hears the sentence "Kṛṣṇa is his brother Balarāma", and so forth, unless certain ontological assumptions are made through *lakṣaṇā* or some other relevant significatory function.

6.12 Viśvanātha and some others mention that there are some, even among the Nyāya thinkers, who maintain that 'the apprehension of consistency (*yogyatā*) is not a cause of verbal comprehension (*śābdabodha*).'[17] Rather, they claim both that it is the awareness of the absence of inconsistency or incompatibility that leads one to a clear comprehension; and the corollary, that the awareness of the presence of incompatibility between the elements would impede a successful *śābdabodha*. Thus, according to this 'revised' interpretation, one does not have to be consciously aware of *yogyatā* (i.e. *yogyatā-niścaya*) for *śābdabodha* to arise. The moment one becomes aware of this or has doubts or suspicion about the incompatibility of the relation between or among some elements in the sentence, not only does the expression lose its status of being a sentence (*vākya*), but it becomes an obstacle to an unimpeded arising of *śābdabodha*.

The argument alluded to here is reported by Viśvanātha as follows : 'an apprehension of this consistency is not possible anywhere before verbal comprehension (has arisen); for the meaning of a sentence is not something that is already known.'[18] Viśvanātha gives a short and pointed reply to this: '(That is) not so; for when particular meanings of words are recollected, it is possible to have an apprehension of consistency (*yogyatā*), sometimes in the form of doubt and sometimes in that of certainty.'[19] This is a plausible response for, in the examples we have already discussed, some expressions clearly do not lead to any understanding since it becomes difficult at the very outset to mutually relate some of the terms and their contents in order for them to yield a cogent sense. We often cut short a speaker the moment he utters, say, the first two words of a would-be sentence, such as 'Colourless green. . .'. But on the other hand, it is only after hearing the whole sentence and grasping or apprehending some general 'sense' of the utterance, that we make judgement to the effect that this is nonsense, since the speaker has confused different issues, categories, ideas or simply 'contents'. Thus the relation he intends between these is incompatible (*ayogyatā* = *tātparyaviṣayasaṃsargabādha*). Were the counter-instance to be absent, the comprehension would be successful, and the question of *ayogyatā* would not arise in the audience's mind in all but a few instances—where, for example, there is distrust towards everything the speaker says. The differences, however, appear to us to be matter of emphasis. Kunjunni Raja sums up the situation succinctly in the following words : 'According to the former view it is a positive condition, whereas according to the latter it is only the absence of an impediment in verbal cognition.'[20]

6.13 Finally, it needs to be emphasised, despite the reservations of the grammarians, that *yogyatā* is a very important *kāraṇa*, not merely for its linguistic importance but also for its logical and empirical contributions towards the generation of *śābdabodha*.

It is not sufficient that the grammatical and syntactical requirements be attended to, for then we would be hearing a lot of sentences which no one significantly understands. There are a few other factors which are preconditions for the possibility of adequate linguistic communication; for example, the intentional element in the utterance, the proximity of the verbal constituents and so forth. This in turn would mean that the sentence should be constructed in such a way that its 'meaning-contents' are (a) truly *meaningful*, and (b) are mutually and *compatibly* interrelated, at least in consonance with the overall intention of the speaker or author (or 'source') in uttering that. If, after that, the audience still fails to gain a 'meaningful' sense from the sentence, then the fault would not be with the speaker for misunderstanding the situation spoken of, nor for failing to adequately articulate what he wishes to convey, and nor would it be with the audience's unfamiliarity with the subject matter and the terms used for the expression. But before dismissing the sentence to be nonsense, one often resorts to the speaker's intention in uttering the same. The intentional element, or what we might call the 'intentionality' of the utterance, becomes of prime importance. And this takes us to the second of the 'phenomenological' *kāraṇas*, namely *tātparya*.

B: *TĀTPARYA*

6.14 We shall call the *kāraṇa* of *tātparya*[21] 'intentionality', i.e. the *intentional* factor in the utterance and comprehension of a sentence. Intentionality is not fully realised in the semantical structure of the sentence, basically for the reasons that follow. (We should point out that we are here drawing from the Strawson-Austinian classifications with their parallels in Bhartṛhari):[22]

i) A sentence can be used in different contexts of utterance by the same speaker to express different things.

ii) The *same* sentence can be uttered by different persons to express the *same* thing; and conversely, the same sentence can be used by these speakers to express *different* things.

iii) Apart from the differences in the locutionary act, indicated above, the same sentence may be used in different contexts of utterance for quite different illocutionary, *and* perlocutionary acts.

An example of i) would be, a speaker X saying 'Good morning' to his spouse as they wake up, but using the same expression with his children to draw their attention towards him or her, or to get them ready for school. To give an illustration: Suppose X and Y both say "Rādhikā is beautiful". They have both uttered the same sentence. Now if one of them is talking about his wife, while the other is talking about his favourite cow, then they have used the same sentence to occasion a *śābdabodha* or propositional understanding, but they intended different *śābdabodhas*. On the other hand, if each is talking about the same individual, they have made two different utterances of the same sentence to occasion the same *śābdabodha* (in terms of the common signification); that is, they have each made the same use of the sentence.

As for iii), the shepherd who climbed on top of the tree and shouted 'There is a fox', may actually have been describing the advent of a fox on the field, or he may have been delighting himself after a boring day by simply shouting (- thus an illocutionary act); or alternatively, he may have shouted with a view to alerting the villagers of the help he needs to chase the fox off the field, in his employment as a shepherd (- thus a genuine perlocutionary act).

Now, in the Nyāya view, *tātparya* pertains to the speaker's actual *intention* in uttering the word-complex (*vākya*) that he does, and therefore a complete comprehension of a sentence (i.e. *śābdabodha*) entails a concomitant apprehension of the speaker's intention (*vactur-icchā-tātparya*).[23] And *tātparyavṛtti* or *tātparyaśakti*, in Jayanta's opinion, is a special function in sentential comprehension, namely the power of conveying the speaker's intention or general purport of the utterance.[24]

There is a distinction, however, which is sometimes not made very clear between the different viewpoints. For, Advaita, while it insists on the necessity of *tātparyajñāna* (awareness of intention) for *śābdabodha*, interprets *tātparya* as the meaning, or better, the 'sense' *intended to be conveyed by a sentence or expression*. In other words, *tātparya* is the 'intentionality' of the sentence required to be understood. There is no direct reference here necessarily to the speaker's wish or intention in uttering the sentence. This debate has been hitherto neglected in recent Indian linguistics,[25] particularly as regards its implications for *śabdapramāṇa*.

Indian linguistics, generally speaking, would tend to explain these differences in terms of the different *tātparyas* involved in each distinct utterance of the same sentence or sentences, given their respective contexts. *Tātparya*, in a very broad sense, has to do with the 'intention' required in order that a sentence be understood. It is the 'intentional' factor embedded in the utterance, but not necessarily discernible in the grammatical and syntactical construction of the expression or sentence uttered. But this could mean that *tātparya* can range in function from what is in the mind of the speaker when he utters a sentence, to what he intends the audience to understand from his utterance, to even what the audience actually understands. There is no unanimity in the Indian tradition as to what *tātparya* does or ought to stand for.

The closest analogue to *tātparya* in the Western context is the '*intentio*' of the Scholastics, and the more recent 'intentionality' (*meinen*) in the phenomenology of Brentano and others.[26] For Brentano intentionality consists in its being consciousness always "about" or "of" something. Although, generally speaking, in phenomenology there is some dispute as to whether *intentionality* is a property or characteristic of consciousness whereby it refers to or intends an "object" (i.e. the feature of having 'intentional content'), or whether it is merely the abstracted function of referring to or pointing to something "other", regardless of the specific 'mental life' with which it is descriptively identifiable. Further, when it is said that an utterance made by someone refers to or *intends* an object, the 'object' of the intentional content need not necessarily have real properties or be an existent, but, in phenomenological terms, could be just that of which it is a mental phenomenon. (It could, for example, be another mental state.) It is *of* or *about* 'something' that is not straight-forwardly given in the semantical structure of the sentence. This aspect of meaning construction is therefore made possible, it is said, by a quasi-linguistic causal operator or *kāraṇa*, which is related to the 'mental life', so to speak, of the speaker (or author, or an *apauruṣeya* 'source' - i.e one devoid of 'personal' constitution) – that is, to the 'intentionality' of the utterance *qua text*. And this, therefore, gives the scope for a phenomenological analysis.

A sentence that has such an 'intentional' character is said to have *tātparyavṛtti*, without which a *śābdabodha* would not be complete, and the 'central thrust' or *purport (tātparya)* of the sentence utterance may remain elusive to the audience. But, again, there is no unanimity on how exactly *tātparya* is thought to function.

6.15 An approach to this problem is to look at *śābdabodha* from two different angles, as the Indian approach overall suggests.[27] One is to look on it, on the one hand, as the linguistic event that leads to the utterance of a sentence, and the other, on the other hand (and quite differently), as the episodic event that issues upon the utterance of the sentence. In other words, we can look at the problem from the viewpoint either of the speaker *or* that of the audience. The speaker has a particular attitude when he utters a sentence, and he chooses a particular set of words and construction that best reflect his attitude, and usually a pattern is discernible in the words, etc., used to express the same or similar 'intention' in this sense.

It is also true that the speaker's intention may introduce a contingent element in the association of the relatively fixed word-meanings, for the overall sense formed by the word-complex could then depend on how the speaker intends it to be construed over and above the sum of the syntactically related meanings, however meaningful that expression may be independently. People often do make utterances with the intention of conveying something specific or to induce a particular belief. Consider in this respect the point H. P. Grice makes about what it is to say that a speaker A meant something by uttering X: 'A uttered X with the intention of inducing a belief by means of the recognition of this intention.'[28] Grice emphasises here the importance of the recognition of what is intended, and, we may add, to the extent that he feels the same sentence may be uttered with the intention to induce yet another belief in a different context. This is also true, in Frege's illustration, of expressions such as '(The planet) Venus', which in the morning is intended to refer to the 'morning star' and in the evening to the so-called 'evening star'.

While what has been said in the preceding paragraph is true, it is also the case that contingent elements enter the cognition arising from listening to the sentence, as the audience is as much a participant in the process, and that his *understanding* is determined by certain conditions, which understanding may not coincide with what the speaker wants to convey. Hence the conditions that generate *śābdabodha* ought to be looked at from, as it were, the audience's or the hearer's side.[29] For it is ultimately what the hearer understands that counts as *śābdabodha*; the speaker may have a particular intention but whether he succeeds in *conveying* it can only be known from the audience's understanding or what he recognises as being intended by the utterance. There may be a number of other factors that condition the process from the audience's side, and therefore these too ought to be considered in the causal nexus that leads to *śābdabodha*. From the standpoint of *śabdapramāṇa*, it is *śābdabodha*, the resultant understanding in the context of certain appropriate conditions, that is more important in any linguistically successful communication than a mere understanding of the expression.[30] The early Nyāya philosophers centred their approach on the *speaker*, concentrating on issues such as his intention, his own understanding and reliability (*āptatva*).

Dharmarāja, on the other hand, while not denying the significance of these factors, concentrates more on the audience's understanding, their relative ability and disposition; and more importantly he emphasises the capability of *language* to convey, *qua tātparyavṛtti*, the intended understanding to the audience.[31] In this he follows Jayanta. But this thesis of *tātparyavṛtti* is also in consonance with the Mīmāṃsā view that denies a 'revealer' or a 'creator' of the words of *śruti* (the "revealed scriptures"), which nonetheless have been understood by those who have "heard" these words.[32] The problem of *tātparya* has thus been tackled from this perspective.

6.16 A typical analysis of what is involved in this stage of the operative process (*vyāpāra*), where *tātparya* becomes relevant, can be sketched in the following terms:[33]

(i) that which is in the mind of the speaker when he utters the sentence (*vactur-icchā*);

(ii) that which the speaker wants to convey to the audience through the utterance;

(iii) that which the utterance actually means – i.e. the 'meaning' of the sentence;

(iv) that which the audience understands to be the 'meaning' of the sentence;

(v) that which the audience thinks the speaker has in his mind in uttering this – i.e. that which he thinks is intended to be conveyed by the utterance.

The foregoing breakdown is very important indeed, for the distinctions made here are useful when looking at more complex utterances, such as, successful lies, deliberate mis-representation, equivocal and ambiguous expressions, and so forth. We shall consider the case of successfully lying later, with an illustration. Dharmarāja, however, would not agree that the foregoing represents the complete process in so far as his understanding of *tātparya* is concerned, and while Advaita would want to reverse the order of priority stated here, it would also urge the addition of two further factors. These are :

(a) the fitness or capacity (*yogyatva*) of the words of a sentence to generate a particular intended meaning *(tatpratīti-jananayogyatvam)*; and

(b) the *non*-utterance with the 'intention' or desire to generate another apparently equally applicable meaning or 'sense'.

6.17 Before we proceed to examine the Advaita critique, it would be helpful to consider the early Nyāya view a little more.

Nyāya first responds to the objection that *tātparya* is not an independent and necessary condition for *śābdabodha*, by saying that it is already implicated in the other conditions (*kāraṇas*), especially in *ākāṅkṣā* or mutual expectancy.

Ākāṅkṣā, as we saw in the previous chapter, is defined as the relational requirement that one word depends on another in order to complete the syntactic relation, so yielding the coalesced meaning expressed. Where *āsatti* and *yogyatā* have become deficient, *tātparya* is appealed to in order to resolve the 'petrified' judgement. The 'sense' of elliptical utterances are also completed with the awareness of the intention of the speaker in making the particular utterance. Again, when the collective sense from the *abhidhā* or express meaning of constituents words of an expression – such as, e.g. "The village (is) on the river" – is frustrated, it is *tātparya* that tells us whether *lakṣaṇā* or 'secondary implication', will help us to understand the sentence. Annaṃbhaṭṭa further argues, that what leads to *lakṣaṇā* is not *anvayānupapatti*, or 'syntax-difficulty', but *tātparyānupapatti*[34] or 'purport difficulty'. But Mīmāṃsā, in opposition to the Nyāya claim, would argue that *tātparya* is subordinated to other more important causes (*hetu*-s) of syntactical relation that generate *śābdabodha*. Annaṃbhaṭṭa himself did not mention *tātparya* as a condition separated from the other *kāraṇas*; but in his *Dīpikā* he is emphatic of its necessity for deriving the 'intentional' sense of the utterance in question. He follows Viśvanātha, who explains *tātparya* as the 'intention, *qua desire (or wish* of the speaker) in wishing to convey a particular sense.'[35] It is argued that unless *tātparya* as characterised here is taken into account, one may fail to understand the *particular sense* intended by the speaker in uttering that sentence, since it would be possible for him to mean something different by uttering the same sentence in a different context or, say, in a different speech-act. And unless one apprehends the intention of the speaker, how would he know which is the 'real sense' to be had from the utterance in that context. How, one might ask, does the audience apprehend the 'intention' of the speaker? Annaṃbhaṭṭa's reply is that the *context* (*prakaraṇa*) helps to ascertain this. Thus, the Nyāya writers argue that *tātparya* has a broader function than being merely an accessory to the other *kāraṇas* for *śābdabodha*.

6.18 Invariably, the example of the ambiguous sentence "Bring (the) *saindhava*" is invoked to illustrate the point, since *saindhava* can mean both 'rock-salt' and 'horse', and without an awareness of the speaker's intention, it can be argued, it would be difficult to know which of the two senses is intended. And Viśvanātha argues that it would be too simplistic to assume that the *context* will make clear the proper sense without any reference to the speaker's wish or desire. His reasoning is that 'context and the like cannot be grouped under the common denomination'[36] of *tātparya* since these are merely accessories for apprehending the *tātparya* itself.

To illustrate the above example in a concrete situation, let us imagine Devadatta is taking his food and calls out to his new attendant: 'Bring the *saindhava*.' Firstly, it can be dismissed that *ākāṅkṣā* is lacking here. For if there is expectancy it would be in respect of either 'bring' or '*saindhava*', but the expectant elements of both these words are mutually given in the utterance, and thus there would be no query in this regard. It cannot, then, be said that there is a need for fulfilling the requirement of *ākāṅkṣā* here for the syntactical completeness of the sentence. However, this does not mean that the audience has completely understood the sense of the sentence uttered in exactly the same sense that the speaker intends him to. For, again, the attendant knows that '*saindhava*' is a term that commonly designates both 'salt' and 'horse', and he may not be sure which of the two is meant here unless he queries the intention of the speaker, which in one sense is the speaker's 'expectation', although this is not the same as *ākāṅkṣā* or syntactical expectancy.

That is to say, the question that arises in the case of this expression is not with respect to what other words and word-meanings are required for completing the construction of the sentence, but with respect to the specific *meaning* a particular word has in association with other words in the structure, that would yield the 'proper sense' intended by the utterance. And it is only by making recourse to the speaker's wish or desire that the ambiguity or query could be resolved. Indeed, it would be correct to say that the condition of *ākāṅkṣā*, as much as those of *yogyatā* and *āsatti*, have been fulfilled in the sentence, while what is lacking is the provision of the actual *sense* intended on the part of the speaker.

Since, according to the Nyāya thesis, it is the speaker's *intention qua his wish or desire* that would fulfil this condition, the attendant can come to this in one of two ways. He could simply ask Devadatta, using other terms, whether it was the four-legged animal *or* some sort of salt that Devadatta had called for. Devadatta may respond to this by uttering another expression, or by making the appropriate gesture (as though moving the salt-shaker over his food), thereby indicating to the attendant his particular wish to have salt for his food. Alternatively, the attendant may recall previous instances of the same utterance in a similar context – viz. at the dinner table. Thus, he would gather from the context of the utterance that Devadatta requires a little more salt for his meal, just as he did the previous evening while taking his food. What the attendant has done, in Nyāya terms, is to make a judgement about the speaker's particular need, thus providing him with the particular sense intended in the utterance of that expression. Hence, the pending condition of *tātparya* has been fulfilled, and an apprehension of the 'proper sense' of the sentence is thus acquired – i.e. a successful *śābdabodha* has been generated.

Suppose, however, the same sentence, "Bring the *saindhava*", was uttered outside in the fields as Devadatta emerges from the house in a jockey's outfit. The attendant should in all probabality apprehend that Devadatta has called for his horse. It would be unlikely that Devadatta was wishing for salt to be brought in that context when on similar occasions in the past the same utterance had led to the horse to be brought to him. Such judgement would not be beyond the attendant.

But to change the scenario slightly, suppose now the same expression was uttered in quite a different context to those considered here, say, for example, in a lecture-hall. What difference would that make? Would it not make it difficult for the attendant, or for anyone listening, to comprehend the exact significance of the sentence, since the appearance of '*saindhava*' does not seem to be appropriate to the present context? He may ponder: "Does Devadatta want a horse or some salt. . .but what would he do with either in the classroom?" Perhaps, the attendant might resolve, Devadatta wishes to give a demonstration of some property of salt to his students. But it could equally be the case that Devadatta wants to demonstrate some skills he has taught his *horse* (as Hans Christian Anderson once attempted to in a class-room setting). This then could be quite confusing for the attendant, as the 'context' here gives very little clue as to what particular sense is intended through the expression. It is all the more necessary in such a context that the speaker's intention is sought and understood if the proper *śābdabodha* is to result.

Some Nyāya thinkers have also argued in deference to the sort of situation we have exemplified here, that it is only in such cases of ambiguity and equivocation that awareness of the speaker's wish or desire becomes necessary, otherwise it is not imperative.[37] At any rate, in such instances of obscurity where understanding is thwarted, the Nyāya thinkers are agreed, one has to quiz the speaker of his intention in using such an ambiguous expression, so that the audience could pursue the course of action most appropriate to the speaker's request. But first a clarification of the speaker's intention has to be sought. And this, according to Nyāya, is the *tātparya* required for completion of the *śābdabodha* proper. So the criterion evolved for *tātparya* in the *early* Nyāya school is a subjective one, since it is in reference to the speaker's intention *qua his wish or desire* in making that particular utterance. This particular approach differentiates it from the quasi-linguistic and objectivised understanding that Advaita proposes, and which some later Nyāya writers, like Jayanta, have been moved to entertain seriously.[38]

6.19 The view of Nyāya as regards the nature of *tātparya* raises some interesting issues, however common-sensically self-evident the notion might appear to be. For one, it may be asked, where does the power to effect *tātparya* lie, with the words or with the speaker? If it is with the speaker, as Nyāya tends to argue, then how does this extra-linguistic aspect enter, so to speak, the sentence-structure? Or would it be correct to say that *tātparya* is not part of the sentence construction and hence not to be considered an important linguistic aspect of verbal communication. It could be thought that it somehow drags along with the sentence, depending largely on the effort that the speaker makes in choosing the words and grammatical structure appropriate to the context.

The early Nyāya view, for example, denied that *tātparya* was anything like a *vṛtti* (established relation) between word and meaning in the same way as *śakti* is said to be a relation between word and meaning. And when the *abhidhārtha* (express sense) is incompatible in a context, it is *tātparya* that helps to identify whether *lakṣaṇā*, and which type of *lakṣaṇā*—such as analogy, metaphor, or suggestion—is the appropriate signification in the context of the utterance.

Mīmāṃsā also agree with this, for it denies that *tātparya qua* 'intention of the speaker' is needed in all but the instances of ambiguity and doubt. Here too, *tātparya* is made subordinate to *lakṣaṇā*, and in the case of ordinary expressions, is identified on the basis of contextual factors, and with the use of a set of interpretation-criteria in the case of *śruti* or Vedic statements.[39]

Jagadīśa, speaking for Nyāya, is not persuaded by the considerations advanced for taking *tātparya* so seriously. Unlike Gaṅgeśa and Viśvanātha, he appears to be rather sceptical about the role of *tātparya* as a separate *kāraṇa* in *śābdabodha*. Jagadīśa is aware of the standard Nyāya argument that as contexts (*prakaraṇa*) vary considerably it is only proper to consult the intentions of the speaker in order to determine the precise *śābdabodha*. In responding thus, he asks, whether, with the passage of time, especially the intentional agency for each utterance (even of the same sentence) would vary given also their differential contexts, and also whether we are to determine the *śābdabodha* in light of the intentionality attributed to, say, sentence X at *t*(1), or at *t*(2)?

It may be found helpful to return to the *prakaraṇa* or context that specifically determined the particular instance of the utterance of that sentence. Referring to our earlier example, it follows according to Jagadisa that it is precisely the awareness of the *context* specific to the utterance (*prakaraṇajñāna*) that leads to the *śābdabodha* proper – namely, the context of eating (*bhojana-prakaraṇa*).[40] If, however, the sentence were uttered in the field, the context would obviously alter, thereby effecting a different *śābdabodha*. Here, therefore, there is a need to refer to the intentional agency as such.

6.20 There is one other concern that Jagadīśa expresses in this regard. If we say that *tātparyajñāna* or awareness of the intention with which an utterance of a sentence is made in a given context, is a necessary condition for *śābdabodha*, are we not also committed to saying that there are two sorts of awareness here, namely, awareness of the sentence sense (*vākyārthajñāna*) *and* an awareness of the *intention* relative to the utterance? Suppose, for instance, *S* utters '*x* is a pot (*y*)', its *śābdabodha (sb*1) would have the following structure:

Q(xy) (where *x* = 'a thing', *y* = 'pot', and *Q* = the function of qualifying *x* by *y*).

Now if we were required to take cognisance of the *tātparya* in addition to the *śābdabodha* (*sb*1) that has arisen, then we would need a further awareness to qualify the above – namely, *Q(TQ(xy))* (where *T* = *tatparya* or intention).[41] But this is obviously cumbersome; for we do not in the normal circumstances understand the *intention-content* apart from the sentence-sense. That is to say, using the above example, the attendant does not first understand that his master wants salt and then qualify this by an awareness of the master's intention to this effect. Rather, Jagadīśa wants to say that the intentionality is already part of the semantic structure of the sentence, inasmuch as the relevant intentionality determines the *saṃ*-

sargamaryādā or the relational structure a sentence assumes in a specific context of its utterance. He thus argues that it is not something over and above the sentence-whole. If this view were to be taken seriously then we could not say it would be possible to extract the 'literal meaning' devoid of the intentionality,[42] precisely because the form of the *śābdabodha* (that Jagadīśa could be said to agree to as well), would be thus : *Q (Txy)*. That is to say, *T* becomes a determinant in the relation between *x* and *y*; or in the case of the sentence "Bring the *saindhava*", *T* would already be regarded to have qualified *saindhava* relative to the context of the utterance. Thus the structure of the *śābdabodha* would be:

'(you) the act of bringing, qualified by *T.saindhavam*

Jagadīśa has made a very pertinent observation regarding the linguistic 'power' to absorb, as it were, the context-specific intentionality, in terms of the desire to utter something, into the sentence-structure. Dharmarāja takes this analysis a few steps further in support of his own argument.

6.21 The Advaita approach records some reservations with the characterisation of *tātparya* as merely an extra-linguistic factor identified as the 'intention' or 'intentional agency' *qua* the 'personal wish or desire (*icchā*)' implicated on the speaker's side as he makes the particular utterance. Dharmarāja sums up the Advaita critique in these words:

> *Tātparya* cannot be defined as the *'utterance with the desire* to effect the cognition of (what is intended to be conveyed by the speaker).'

Let us look at some of the arguments advanced in support of this view. (i) *Arthajñāna śūnyena.*[43] On account of the absence on the part of the speaker 'uttering' the expression of any knowledge of *what* he utters, it is argued, how could we say that the 'speaker' has any 'intention' in uttering what he does to convey a particular sense? Two cases are given as examples, namely the "utterances" of a priest and a parrot respectively. To these we may add the babbling, mostly in the form of imitation, of a child.

Consider the predicament of the priest entrusted with the task of reciting 'sacred' hymns but who does not necessarily understand what the hymns actually mean, nor has any intention of conveying anything particularly significant to his audience. But for his skill at reading the text (as distinct from the narrative), and intonating the hymns with the correct accent and pitch, he may not have any definite idea as to what the text is really saying. He, as anyone hearing, would gather from stray occurrences of names of deities, such as Indra, Agni, Sūrya and so on, that the particular text has something to do with invoking and supplicating the gods. Now, if the apprehension of the 'proper sense' or *purport* of the hymns were dependent on the concomitant awareness of the speaker's intention in uttering these, the audience would be no further in understanding the *meaning* of the text than the 'speaker' or priest himself would be. The audience might feel that there is some significance in the complicated ritual, given the sanctimonious performance of the priest, but that need have nothing to do with the *meaning* of the expressions or compositions being uttered.

We are next asked to consider the case of the trained parrot that reels off a number of words, indeed a well-constructed sentence or two, as one enters its master's home. We may feel we are being greeted and that the master has been made aware of our presence in the house. But, could we say in this case also that 'the speaker utters with an intention to convey a particular sense'?

No less typical are the cases of the child learning to articulate words and phrases after hearing them from another more elderly person; and that of the demented patient who also imitates or utters words of which he has no understanding. Often politicians and spokespersons for certain professions blurt out jargons and clichés which they may scantly understand or have any much sympathy with, but hope that these may help to impress, or confuse, their clientele. Thus, in such cases, one does not get far by looking at the speaker's intention to get to the proper understanding of the linguistic expressions, as highlighted in the examples with the parrot and the priest. And yet one who hears these expressions is able to comprehend something from them quite apart from whatever may be in the speaker's mind at that moment. We say 'comprehend', for the hearer may have grasped no more than what the linguistic structure conveys, and could still complain that he has not fully understood what was intended of him. (A subtle distinction is being made between what the speaker might intend and what is intended of the hearer : any given linguistic expression may not succeed in accomplishing both of these simultaneously.)

6.22 (ii) Dharmarāja offers another example in giving his second argument, which we shall reconstruct more slightly. There is the case of the teacher who sets out to expound a particular theory or text and in all sincerity believes that his understanding and exposition of the theory is correct. Thus we might say that he is uttering a number of sentences with the desire to convey a particular view. But a sharp student picks up some discrepancy in what the teacher says and what he understands from his own reading of the text. Now the teacher has actually got the text wrong, and yet the student has been able to get to the correct purport of the text, though it appears to be at variance with the 'speaker uttering with the desire to convey the intended sense.'[44] Therefore, it may be argued, the *purport* apprehended by the student is something independent of and does not always correlate with the speaker's intention in respect of the 'proper sense' or purport of the text. But for Advaita it is just this 'purport' which is the *tātparya* of the sentence in the text.

Now this argument has some plausibility, as here we see that if one were to depend on the speaker's intention in uttering a particular expression, one will comprehend perhaps the speaker's intention but not necessarily 'intentionality' *qua purport* of the sentence utterance. This is to say that expression has, in a manner of speaking, an intentional feature quite apart from the wish or desire of the speaker, but which may be implicated in it. To the objection that the teacher may have 'borrowed' the expression of another speaker, whose intentions he has misunderstood or misrepresented, Dharmarāja may have no response, but he would argue that the case in question at least of "utterance with the desire to convey such and such. . ." is certainly a more complex aspect of sentential comprehension, and it is to this that Dharmarāja is pointing in his critique. He goes on to a third reason.

6.23 (iii) One cannot say, as the early Nyāya view appears to, that ultimately it is the *icchā* or 'willing wish' of God (as *Īśvara*) that such and such be understood from such and such sentences, especially those of the Vedas. Dharmarāja argues that, even those who do not believe in the existence or interference of God in this regard, are still able to understand such sentences without having to resort to the 'will' of God while he uttered them.[45] This objection is in consonance with the view that the 'source' of the Vedas as *Śruti* or 'what has been heard', is devoid of personal origin, being beginningless and endless in their nature—thus *apauruṣeya*. The task of 'God is merely to preserve the Vedas during the time of *pralaya* or cosmic dissolution, and to hand them down again to the beneficiaries of the next world-emergence (*sṛṣṭi-prapañca*).'[46] It is then, not the 'will of God' that could be called the intentionality of the Vedic sentences, and therefore there is no need to make reference to the intention of God in attempting to understand the abstruse Veda-statements, taken as a body of texts complete in its own meaning for which it is not dependent as it were on an external meaning-giver but is dependent on "other utterances of the same order".[47] In other words, intentionality, so understood, lies in the interconnectedness of the parts of the texts rather than in any subjective feature, such as the 'will' or intention of the speaker or author necessarily extraneous to the text.

The seers *(ṛṣis)* of old, apparently, had little difficulty comprehending these texts in both their performative and speculative contents, without having to suppose the 'intentions' of their authors, since these were regarded to have had no authors. What, in our postmodern era, has come to be known as the 'authorless text' thesis was evidently not without its parallel in the orthodox Indian schools, such as with the Mīmāṃsā notion of *apauruṣeya*.[48]

It needs, however, to be said that even if we hypothetically assume that there are texts which comprise of a series of well-formed sentences, but which in themselves, either for historical or literary reasons, cannot be attributed to any known or particular author or authors, we still need not presume that because we do not have access to the 'intentions of those who uttered these sentences', we therefore have no way of fully comprehending their respective meanings or senses whatever their context of utterance. If we were to presume this, it may render language deficient in its instrumental efficiency of being able to communicate what is relatively independent of the intentions of its speakers. We do not always have to assume that the intentions of the speakers are very much part of what is uttered and therefore to be understood. Our attention is being drawn here to an important point so often overlooked -viz. the instrumental capacity or 'power' (*śakti*) of the word. It is in terms of this 'power' that Dharmarāja explains the 'capacity' (*yogyatva*) words *qua* sentences have, (a) to involve the *purport* as a linguistic property in the sentence, and (b) to enable the *tātparya* to be conveyed to the audience—given other factors, such as the disposition, preparedness and attentiveness on the part of the audience, and non-interference in the communication environment. In terms of this particular linguistic consideration Dharmarāja frames his definition of *tātparya* according to the criterion that follows.

6.24(iv) *Tatpratītijananayogyatva*:[49] 'the fitness or capacity (of the text) to generate a particular sense'. What this means is that it is possible for the purport to be comprehended by virtue of the capacity of words to generate the cognition *intended* in the sentence. Thus, the *kāraṇa* or causal condition of *tātparya* lies within the *śakti* of the words themselves. *Tātparya*, then, is understood as the capacity to generate comprehension of just that *understanding* which is the sentence-*sense* (*tātparya śābdajñāna-janakatva-svarūpa*). To elaborate further, *tātparya* is one of the generative causal conditions of sentence-comprehension that arises from the 'perception' of the ostensive sentence-structure. And the *yogyatva* in the definition indicates the capacity of words to generate apprehension of the relation of word-meanings that yield the *sense* appropriate to the context. Dharmarāja goes on to illustrate with the following example. The expression "Pot (is) in the house" is fit to indicate the relation of the house to the pot, but not to the cloth or whatever else may also be in the house.[50] It is important to emphasise the capacity of words in this respect that can be considered apart from the intentions of the speaker, the subject or being, in uttering a sentence. It is clear that in this case the relation of the house to the pot is conveyed regardless of whether the speaker intends this or the pot specifically. To this extent, at least, we can speak of the expression as having an 'intention' (*tātparya*) of indicating the relation of house to pot. If this *tātparya* is at variance with what the speaker *meant* to express (perhaps he meant the relation of house to cloth), this is a separate issue that pertains not so much to the inefficiency of the medium as to the failure of the speaker to construct the appropriate sentence. Thus, in Advaita view, *tātparya* is better characterised as the *fitness of words* themselves to give a particular meaning quite apart from the intentional agency involved in the utterance. Hence this argument aims to refute the view that *tātparya* has basically to do with the utterance of a sentence with a specific desire or intention to convey what the speaker wishes to convey. Advaita's own alternative is that *tātparya* is the fitness or capacity (*yogyatva*) of the text *qua text* to generate just that sense made possible by the *saṃsargamaryādā* relational structure of the text. It is this that is called the 'intentionality' of the sentence and is not, as such, isomorphic to the subjective intentionality of the agent, subject or being, involved in the act of uttering (or making the speech-act). And, of course, this renders the task of deconstruction, particularly of scriptural sentences, less problematic than if one were to be involved in speculating about what the respective authors might or might not have meant in uttering these sentences. One looks to the movement within the narrative itself, assuming a logical—as distinct from a psychical—priority of its semantic content, as it were, in the interiority of syntagm, for whatever sense the text might have or might have been intended to convey.

However, even if this were true, an objection can be made to this argument. Consider again the expression "Bring (the) *saindhava*", where we might accept the 'sense intended' to be a request for salt to be brought. But is it not the case, given the afore-stated argument, that the expression has the natural capacity (*svarūpa-yogyatva*) to generate an apprehension of the association of "bring" with *horse* in view of the contingency present within the word '*saindhava*' to indicate this association as well? In other words, because '*saindhava*' has the inherent potentiality of signifying both salt and horse, is it not possible that it signifies *horse* while also signifying *salt*?[51] Within the limits of the criterion presented herein, this possibility cannot be denied. Dharmarāja is acutely aware of such an objection and therefore qualifies the criterion in the following terms.

6.25(v) *Tadanyapratītīcchayānuccaritatvam*:[52] the (above) criterion for *tātparya* is qualified with the delimitor : *non-utterance* with the desire to convey a sense *different* from what is intended.

What Dharmarāja seems to be suggesting is that, in so far as the sentence is not uttered with the intention to convey any other or a sense different from that which is understood from the sentence, then the contingency, which may not be denied to be present, fails to have any effect. Indeed, Advaita would argue that the objection really brings out the subtle point being made in the criterion – viz. that words have the fitness to convey particular significance relevant in that context, and as the word '*saindhava*' has the capacity to convey both salt and horse, either could be applicable in the sentence utterance.

The qualification, however, also checks which one of those two senses is applicable in that context. And this is accomplished by the negative consideration that, if the sentence has not been uttered with the desire (*icchā*) of conveying anything other than what it significantly conveys, then there is no reason to take the 'other' as the appropriate *tātparya* here. Thus, with example at hand, if the sentence is not uttered with the desire to convey anything other than salt, while Devadatta is taking his meals, then there is no reason for taking *horse* as the *tātparya*. If, however, the association with the aid of the context (*prakaraṇa*) of the occurrence of the sentence disclosed is that with *salt*, why should one take the *saṃsarga* nexus to be with horse, even if the possibility of this association is there?

6.26 In presenting the second criterion Dharmarāja has not said that we ought to look at the actual *desire* (*icchā*) of the person making the utterance to determine the *tātparya*; rather, he is saying that one looks to see what has been *excluded* even if that sense would have been a strong contender, as it were, in this construction. He is not denying that the 'other' sense would be totally ineffectual in such a sentence, but if this has been excluded (as no utterance has been made to this effect, and the content does not point to it), then it would be inconsistent to take this as the *tātparya-proper*, when clearly it is not. An important point is being made here, that the fitness of words to convey a particular sense is not undermined when one of the senses is excluded from a sentence. It just so happens that the particular sentence or its occurrence in the particular context, appropriates one and not the other of the possible *yogyatvas* for *tātparya*. Now the particular desire or intention of the speaker has not as such been invoked to establish the *tātparya*, rather it is utilised where doubt may arise as to which of the possible senses has been excluded. And apart from such ambiguous and equivocal causes, one may not need to make such a circumspect reference to the speaker's intention in understanding the sentence.

It may be argued, on the other hand, that we do not always judge in such negative terms, as we often tend to ask the speaker (such as one might in the example under consideration), 'Well, what exactly do you mean?' Thus, it could be said, that Dharmarāja has side-stepped the issue in throwing the intentional agency, as it were, out with the speaker. But has the issue been side-stepped with the introduction of the second criterion? Surely, the question of what is to be included and what is to be excluded arises in cases where the expression betrays an ambiguity or unclarity as to which of the possible senses has been intended. In such cases it may be necessary to refer to the speaker's intention. But by so doing are we necessarily identifying the *tātparya* of the expression with the intention of the speaker, or are we looking for an indication as to which of the contending *tātparyas* we are to understand from the expression?

Now in the instance narrated in the foregoing, the intention of the speaker would be of help; but there are cases where the *context* of the occurrence of the expression would be sufficient to help us establish this too, and there are a number of other factors that could be of aid as well in this regard. What in effect we are doing in such cases is making a judgement about, (a) what the speaker has *not* uttered, and, more importantly, (b) what has therefore been excluded from the expression. Admittedly, we do not go to this extent in comprehending such sentence we hear, but nor do we, by the same token, refer separately to the intention of the speaker to establish the *purport* of all the expressions we hear and come into contact with. Thus Dharmarāja has not exaggerated the cause nor deviated from the real issue. For, again, if the desire or intention to convey any other sense is absent, then that intention is absent, and there is no question of avoiding reference to this intention. And this is also reflected in the typical response often made when the audience attempts to paraphrase what he takes to be the purport of the expression uttered by another : "No, I did *not* say that!. I meant just what I *said*", and he would thereupon repeat the expression or sentence uttered or written earlier.

One other objection against the qualification is that it is too narrow, and thus it restricts the possibility of *both* the senses being intended, as, for example, in the case of the sentence "Bring (the) *saindhava*", with a view to have both the salt and horse being brought. But if one were to look for the sense excluded, one might mistakenly exclude what is not intended by the speaker to be excluded. Dharmarāja replies that since the sentence is not uttered with the wish or desire to convey either one *or* the other of the senses—i.e. other than what is intended - then both are to be taken as the *tātparya* of the sentence. In other words, as the desire to convey any other sense or senses intended is absent, this again proves the point that the sentence has not been uttered with the wish to convey anything other than both the senses sanctioned by the *yogyatva* present in the sentence. But this also on the other hand may be too wide, as then the imitative utterance of the same expression by the parrot may be taken to have the *tātparya* in respect of both senses.[53]

Dharmarāja makes a swift response to the objection just raised : that the parrot has not made the utterance with the wish to convey either one or the other – that is to say, neither is there the wish for *salt* nor for horse, nor for that matter for anything else – in the "utterance" of the parrot. Hence, even in the case of the parrot's utterance, or rather non-utterance with the wish to convey anything other, the second criterion holds true.[54]

With this objection answered, Dharmarāja gives his definitive account of *tātparya* – namely : a sentence which has the capacity to generate a particular comprehension and at the same time is not uttered with the intention or wish (*icchā*) of generating awareness of anything else or different. That sentence is said, therefore, to bear association (*saṃsarga*) to the 'intentionality' (*tātparya*) of *that* (which the sentence expresses through its *sense*).[55]

6.27 It may be well to note that the definition of *tātparya* in these terms also brings out the crucial differences in the conception of word-meaning and their relation between the Advaita and the Nyāya schools. Advaita, following Mīmāṃsā, regards (a) the primary signification (*śakyārtha*) to be a power that resides, as it were, in the words, and (b) the relation between them to be *autpattika* or 'relatively fixed'. While Nyāya considers the relation to be imported into the words in virtue of the intention or '*icchā*' of the person using it, who in turn owes it to the 'convention' of the language community he is part of, and which in turn owes it to the determination of God (*Īśvara saṃketa*).

Thus, while Advaita confines *tātparya* within the bounds of language, as it were, and characterises it as a quasi-linguistic property on the assumption that the 'capacity of words to convey a particular sense' is an independent function of words in virtue of the inherent *śakti* or words in interrelation with one another, Nyāya specifices *tātparya* as a somewhat psychological property implicated in making a particular utterance. Thus it follows, according to the Advaita view, that *tātparya*, as a determinant of *śābdabodha*, is constituted by the inherent fitness of words collectively to convey a particular sense independently of the conscious-intentional agency. Furthermore, given the theory of meaning that underpins this view, a word is not a mere sign or symbol that acquires 'meaning', inasmuch as it is 'consciously designed to stand for something other than itself'.[56]

6.28 Dharmarāja explains further that it is this delimiting factor (*yogyatva'vecchedaka*) of language in its capacity of containing the intentionality within its own structure that is the novel 'power' that becomes transparent when words combine to yield a collective sense. This 'collective power' one may call *vākyaśakti*, the special strength of the sentence. The *tātparya* as such is not given through perception or inference. In the case of ordinary sentences one may be aided by the speaker's disposition and the context of his utterance, but in the case of the Vedic texts, since one may have no access to such supposed speakers and their supposed intentions or wishes, their intentionality cannot be at all confined within these limits.

6.29 A question arises as to how the *tātparya* is determined in the case of *śruti*? In response to this question the Mīmāṃsā evolved a system of rules, collectively called *tātparyaliṅgam*. They were designed to assist with interpretation of the text. Interpretation, in the sense relevant to hermeneutics, aims to bring to light an underlying coherence or sense, and clears away puzzles, obscurities, confusions, and seeming contradictions in texts. But the prime motive of Mīmāṃsā is to throw light on the specific liturgical/ritual process enjoined as well as to enlighten the adherent of the 'transcendentally signified' (*apūrva*) in the relevant texts. Since these rules are elaborate and complex we can only descriptively list them here.[57]

(i) *upakramopasaṃhārau* - consistency in what is introduced with what is concluded

(ii) *abhyāsa* - repeating of the main subject-matter

(iii) *apūrvatā*— the novelty of the subject-matter

(iv) *phala* - the end-result (i.e harmony with that intended)

(v) *arthavāda*—corroboration of the principal intent through the eulogical or subsidiary sentences

(vii) *upapatti* - argumentation for the actual intent.

6.30 Let us now see how context or *prakaraṇa* is supposed to disclose the *tātparya* in ordinary sentences. We will consider the sentence "The sun has risen". Now with respect to criterion (i), we looked at earlier, this expression is competent to convey the relation of the sun to the act of rising, as distinct from the act of setting, for which sense another term would be appropriate. This, we may say, is the 'general purport' or intentionality of the sentence. But in the more specific *context* of the time, the reference is to day-break and the advent of a new day. This is the purport in this particular context. But let us consider two different contexts : one in which the utterance is made in a warehouse by a watchman on night duty, and another in which the same sentence is uttered in a bedroom where a mother is attempting to awaken her children. While the first context conveys the meaning of 'knocking-off from duty', the second conveys that it is time for the children to get up and prepare for school. Thus, we notice that the same sentence can be used to convey differently intended senses. If we regard the *vākyajñāna* or awareness of sentence-structure as the first-order signification of the sentence in virtue of the association of word-meanings that creates a particular relation (*saṃsarga*), which in turn yields the specific sense, then the second-order, third-order and so forth senses, would be the respective *tātparyas* in the relative contexts of their occurrences. And a grasp of *tātparya* accordingly is indispensible for a fuller understanding of the sentence. But the intention of the speaker need not be kept completely at bay as its interrelation with the context could be a significant *grāhaka* or 'provider' of the appropriate sense. Yet, a mere appeal to either the grammatical and syntactical structure of the sentence, or to the intention of the speaker in uttering the same, cannot guarantee the successful grasp of the *purport* of the *sentence*.

Given the argument just stated, Advaita would suggest that rather than talk about the *desired* overall sense, we could talk of the *intended* association of word-meanings that have the capacity to convey the overall sense through the particular relation that results from the construction, which in turn yields the specific sense intended. And this is distinct, as we remarked already, from the analysis which concentrates on the desire or wish (or 'will') of the speaker, without showing adequately how such subjective elements become part of the linguistic construction. Advaita, it seems to us, has addressed this problem constructively : the speaker's desire may enter the sentence-meaning, but if all one comprehends is the sentence-meaning (i.e. the semantical and syntactical construction), then how does the speaker's 'intention' come across to the audience, particularly when the speaker is not there to provide this directly or confirm this in some non-linguistic way?

Now, if it is said that the 'intention' is 'superimposed' on to the meaning-structure of the expression, then again, it needs to be explained how this is made possible. But if, on the other hand, we look at the structure as a complete relation of 'significant contents', which the audience assimilates as determined by the context, then it is the apprehension of these specific relations, aided perhaps by an awareness of the intention of the speaker to exclude others, and perhaps by the audience's own disposition and appraisal of the situation, that the *tātparya* of the sentence as applicable in the particular context is said to be apprehended. In the case of *śruti*, given the Mīmāṃsā-Advaita view of its *apauruṣeyatva* or non-personal authority, we would seem to be deprived of even the little help we could have expected in respect of the 'intention of the *speaker* and his/her reliability'.[58]

6.31 Finally, we should look at the case of successful lying or deceptive utterances in order to identify the *tātparya* in such cases where it appears that the sentence sense is perfectly compatible in that context for one member of the audience, but not for another. For instance, two persons, A and B are seated on a bench. A third, C, arrives , looks at A and says : "Your father is calling for you". A gets up and leaves for his home. But A, remaining seated, carefully observes the situation and intuits from C's triumphant response that his utterance was merely worked up to get A off the seat, which C then promptly occupies. A, of course, took the utterance to mean that a message had come from his father; while B took it as a ploy to get A off the bench. Now what is the true *tātparya* of C's sentence? Is it sense as comprehended by A, or is that comprehended by B,or is what C intended A to comprehend (but not B since he wanted his company)? Then again, C could have intended something quite different to what either A or B comprehended. But for now, we may neglect the last possibility and pay attention to the differently apprehended senses of the same sentence uttered once. Or should we say that A comprehends the 'meaning' of the sentence, but not its *sense* proper, since he is not aware of the intentions of the speaker; while B comprehends both. But can we say that the 'meaning' of a sentence is graspable without awareness of what is intended in the context of its utterance? In other words, is the 'intentionality' cognised separately from the (express) meaning of the sentence (*vākyavācaka*)? But the present instance is confounded by the fact that the speaker is deliberately lying and hence does not want his real intentions exposed. To that end he does not let his intentions enter, as it were, the sentence or his utterance of the sentence : if this is to be known it has to be cognised *ab extra*—as B does—and it forms no part of the intentional structure of the actual sentence uttered.

On the other hand, if A were not lying, and the father of C had actually called for him, then the *śābdabodhas* that was had by A and B respectively would coincide, and there would be no concern with the speaker's "real" intentions in uttering the sentence so as to grasp its *tātparya*. But because the speaker is *lying* in this context, the *tātparya* would have to be that sense which the hearer is intended to comprehend *as determined* by the speaker in that context.

The significance of *tātparya* as a *vṛtti* cannot be overstated in the above example. The speaker has determined, somewhat deviously, that a particular member of his audience does not become aware of the actual intention with which he utters a sentence since it is at variance with the intentionality of the sentence his audience hears. The contingency of this deceit mars the hearer's proper understanding of the sentence sense in that context. The by-stander who perceives the element of deceit in the speaker's utterance appreciates the contingency and therefore brackets the intentionality of the sentence he hears, and on which he would normally base his belief. But this class of utterance along with ambiguity, doubt and equivocations are more exceptions and rather extreme instances where the speaker's intention, because it overrides the intentionality of the sentence he utters (or writes), has to be apprehended and ascertained *ab extra.* In such cases, awareness of the speaker's personal or idiosyncratic desires, wishes or intent to deceive helps remove the difficulty and impediments posed in the way of fully understanding the sentence uttered by complementing and qualifying intentionality embedded in the speech-act or an utterance. This awareness then renders the *śābdabodha* distinct, unambiguous, and intelligible, but it does not make the function of *tātparya* any less significant.[59]

NOTES TO CHAPTER SIX

0. An earlier version of Part A of this chapter appeared as, '*Āsatti* and *Yogyatā* in Sentential Comprehension : *Vedānta Paribhāṣā*', *JIP* Vol 8 No 4 1980 pp393-399; and Part B as, '*Tātparya*: Intentionality in Sentential Comprehension—in Advaita linguistics', in *Annali (Sezione Orientale)*, dell'istituto Universitario Orientale, Napoli, Italy, Dec. 1985 (45/4, pp 599-627).

Yogyatā. section **A.**

1. These and more nuances are found in different translations and expositions of texts dealing with the issue—such as in the translation of *Tarkasaṃgraha* 61, *Dīpikā* on it, *Tarkabhāṣā*, and *Mānameyodaya*. But the differences perhaps also reflect the difference in the understandings on the part of respective authors.

2. *VP* IV (= *Āgama* chapter) #8

3. See notes 13, 14, 15 and discussions in previous chapter. B.K. Matilal represents the Nyāya delimitation of the definition of *yogyatā* in respect of 'objective consistency' in these terms: 'the compatibility of one object (or, rather the absence of absurdity or incompatibility in one *object*) with another *object* in accordance with the syntactical (grammatical) connection of the respective words denoting the *objects*' (italics added), in his 'Indian Theorists on the Nature of Sentence. . .' (p377ff). But could such a definition deal adequately with logical relations between 'possible world objects' and abstract and nominalistic entities etc., as within these realms also, it could be argued, 'incompatible' associations may arise which are not necessarily, in the straightforward Nyāya terms, self-annihilating (*pratijñāvirodhatva*)?

   Surely, 'Hare's Horn' and 'wetting with fire' are good counterintuitive instances from an empirical point of view, but would that preclude us from talking meaningfully about, say, a 'bad God', 'the stationary raindrop', 'killing the already dead' (in the "Divine Eyes", *cf. Bhagavadgītā* chp XI, theophany), "the dead living; the living dead".

   We may also mention Gödel's theorem along with the issue of congruency among 'non-existent objects'.

4. We remarked in note 13 and 14, ch. 6 (*supra*), that a purely analytical concept of contradiction appears not to have been prevalent in the Indian systems; though, this does not mean they ignored other and recognisable forms of self-contradiction (*svataḥ-bādha*), as in the examples—'*ahaṃ maunī*' : 'I am (presently) mute'; 'the headless Rāhu' (Rāhu being a mythical being with head alone); 'fireless fire'.

5. That is to say, that if it were made in fulfillment of a purpose then its use, metaphorical or otherwise, would be justified. For instance, one may say (extrapolating from Jagadīśa's example): 'the fire-walker's feet are not burnt by the red-hot coal'; *cf.*: *Śabdaśaktiprakāśikā : vahninā sekha ityādyapi vākyameva, parantu bādhatārthakatvādayogyam, śābdamaterāharyatvopagame 'nirvahnirvahnimān' 'pacan na pacatī' tyādikamapi vākyameva, no cedapārthameva, yādṛśabodhatvāvacchedenāhāryatvaṃ tādṛśabuddhyarthaṃ prayuktapadānāmeva tathāvidhārthabodham pratyapārthakatvāt*.

6. *Ibid. SSP*, under no. 13, pp65-66.

7a. *Cf.* Gaṅgeśa in *Tattvacintāmaṇi : tatsaṃśaye'pi śabdādanvayabodhaśca śabdaprāmāṇye tu yogyatāyāḥ saṃśaya niścayasādhāraṇaṃ jñānamātraṃ prayojakamiti śabdaḥ pramāṇamiti*.p79 *Śabdakhaṇḍa* IV. Haridāsa Bhaṭṭācārya on Udayana points out that the absence of manifest contradiction is *yogyatā* (under III.15) *bādhakapramāvirahārūpayogyatājñānavilambādevāyogyaye'nvyadhīvilambhavāt*. (Cowell ed 1864 Calcutta p35; *cf. SM* on *BP* #80-81 : *pratibandhakatva*).

7. J. F. Staal cites B. Bhattacharya's (1962) use of this not uncommon example, in 'Sanskrit Philosophy of Language', 1969, p525.

8. *Pariśuddhi*. Quoted by Matilal in 'Indian Theorists on . .Sentence. . .', p380.

9. *VP* IV 9: *'Sa prajāpatirātmano vapāmudakhidat' ityādāvapi tātparyaviṣayībhūtapaśuvapāyāgaprāśastyābādhād yogyatā.*

10. See note 15 below. *Cf.* Jagadīśa: *yogyātāḥ saṃśayasthale'py anvayabuddher ānubhavikatvāt*, under no 4, *Śabdaśaktiprakāśikā*, p12. *Vide* Deshpande, *op cit*, p201.

11. Jagadīśa *op cit* under 4, p12-13.

12. A description used by Kuppuswami Sastri, *A Primer. . .*, p250.

13. Viśvanātha raises this issue as well, see *SM-BP*, under #82-83 (p 169).

14. *Ibid; cf* Gaṅgeśa *vahninā siñcati. . .ayogyatājñānam* (*TC* IV, p235).

15. *Tarka-saṃgraha* #61: *agninā sincediti na pramāṇaṃ yogyatāvirahāt. Tarkabhāṣā* : *agninā siñcediti navākyaṃ yogyatāvirahāt.na hyagnisekhayoḥ parasparānvya-yogyatā asti.* (1979, p47). *Cf* Nāgeśa Bhaṭṭa: *ata eva vahninā siñcatīti vākya prayokturadravena vahninā katham sekam braviṣītyupahāṣaḥ saṃgacchate. abodhe hi etadarthakadrāviḍabhāṣāśravaṇottaraṃ pāścāttyasyeva mūkataiva syāt* ? *Paramalaghumañjūṣū* (p36ff) and comm: on Jagannātha's *Ṛg.rūpakālaṅkāra*.

16. *VP* IV 9: *'tat tvamasi'ādivākyeṣvapi vācyābhedabādhe'pi lakṣyasvarupābhede bādhābhāvāda yogyatā.*

17. *SM-BP (loc cit. p169).*

18. *Ibid* p166ff.

19. *Ibid.*

20. Kunjunni Raja, *Indian Theories of Meaning, p165.*

Tātparya section **B.**

21. The etymological root is obscure, but it could have meant 'what is aimed at (*tāt-para*)' (Monier-Williams, *Sanskrit-English Dictionary*, reprint, Motilal Banarsidass, Delhi, 1981, p442 col. 1), or 'a character being for that'. Monier-Williams also indicates that it could be a 'purpose, meaning, purport (esp. of speech or work)' and also that *tātparyārtha* is the 'meaning of a sentence'. It appears that the 'speaker' and his '*icchā*' are not central features of the term as described here. There is, however, no unanimity on this issue. We use 'intentionality' and 'purport' relatively interchangeably though not identically.

22. The model is adapted from L. Goddard and R. Routley *The Logic of Significance and Context* 1973 p24-25. See note 3 Ch. 1 *(supra)* (Strawson on referring).

23. *Siddhānta-muktāvalī (SM)* of Viśvanātha on *BP no* 84.

24. Athough Jayanta's conception of *tātparyaśakti* hinges on the notion of *saṃsargamaryādā*, which we have discussed in 4.6ff. n34, ch. 2 (*supra*). It is the 'power' of words that continues to operate until the intended meaning-whole of the utterance is presented to the mind. See Kunjunni Raja, *Indian Theories of Meaning*, pp222-223.

25. For example, J. Brough in his 'Some Indian Theories of Meaning' does not even mention *tātparya* as one of the *kāraṇas* for *śābdabodha*. B. K. Matilal makes passing reference to *tātparya* resolving that they are 'particularly needed in order to disambiguate an otherwise ambiguous expression', in 'The Nature of the Sentence.', p283; although in *NND* a little is more said (under 2.11). M. Deshpande is equally silent on this. Gaurinatha Sastri devotes a little more to the discussion of this *kāraṇa* under 'Import of Proposition', in *The Philosophy of Word and Meaning*, p243. It is only with Kunjunni Raja that we get a more extensive discussion and I am grateful to Raja's mapping of this discourse (see also note 33 below). But an analysis that utilises the cognitive and phenomenological framework has hitherto not been developed, which is my aim here. *Cf.* Husserl : 'while speaking we perform an inner act of meaning which mingles itself with the words and at the same time animates them', *Edmund Husserl's Theory of Meaning*, J. N. Mohanty, 1964 p63; and E. Husserl *The Idea of Phenomenology*, 1964.

26. Strictly speaking, the 'intentionality' referred to here is to be distinguished from Brentano's *intentionality*, which, unlike our use of it, is a property of 'the mental life capable of relating itself to objectivity'. ('Objectivity' here need not imply real or existent objects. This property of consciousness of relating itself to objectivity while at once being a fundamental property of inner experience is, of course, taken up and developed further by Husserl.) *Tātparya*, one might say, is the objectivised 'mental life' of the linguistic expression that becomes transparent in *śābdabodha*; the latter being an awareness "about" or "of" something other than itself. One can easily see the disjunction between Brentano's *intentio* (and the intentionality in Husserl's phenomenology) and *tātparya*. For this reason, some might find the rendering of *tātparya* as 'intentionality' rather awkward.

27. Some modern Indian writers have began now to concentrate on the 'hearer's side', i.e. the audience's involvement in the process of linguistic communication as a vitally important factor in the analysis. Kalidas Bhattacharyya is a good example (in lecture in Jadavpur (1983) and personal communication).

28. Even though this is from a perlocutionary standpoint – H. P. Grice in his "Meaning", reprinted in *RS* (pp501-512) p508.

29. As in John Searle's words, the 'hearer's side'; *vide*, *Speech Acts: An Essay in the Philosophy of Language*, p 37; see also ch 1 n3 (*supra*).

30. Consider J. N. Mohanty's statement: 'Neither the Mīmāṃsā nor the Nyāya is concerned, in *the strict sense*, with what one can call "understanding the meaning of an expression". One is rather *concerned* with how hearing a sentence under appropriate conditions (e.g. when the speaker is honest and reliable) serves as a means of acquiring valid knowledge, i.e. as a *pramāṇa*', in 'Frege's Context Principle and Indian Semantics', Jadavpur International Conference in Philosophy (1983, paper, p8).

31. Questions arise as to whether *intention* can be conveyed without, or rather outside of, the bounds of linguistic communication. For example, by getting another to see something in a particular way, through the medium of art for instance, or music , or some other system of signs and motifs.

32. See note 48 below for reference to work-in-progress.

33. Adapted with modifications from Kunjunni Raja, 'The role of *Tātparya* in Sentence-Meaning' (ed. Joshi, Winter Institute, Poona), p94; see also note 25 above.

34. *TS-Dīpikā*: *tātparyānupapattilakṣaṇābījam*: *lakṣaṇā* is resorted to when the express or primary sense is unsuitable, not where the relation between the words, but where the intention is concerned (under v 59-61). In Mīmāṃsā view even the sentence-sense is based on *tātparyānupapattiḥ*.

35. See note 23 above. A better rendering is perhaps 'an utterance with the intention of (generating in the mind of the hearer) comprehension (*pratīti*) of *that* (i.e. that particular thing)' : *tatpratītīcchayoccaritatvam*). See also Nāgeśa Bhaṭṭa *Paramalaghumuñjūṣā*(1946) p39 on *prakaraṇa*.

36. *SM-BP, ibid; cf* Kuppuswami Sastri in his edition and notes to *TS* (*Primer*) p257 (1961).

37. We would consider this to be the case with the earlier Nyāya.

38. Jayanta in his *Nyāyamañjarī*; see note 24 above. Although, as we said, Jayanta argues that *tātparya* is a linguistic function and gives an indication of the 'form' of relation between word and meaning, which is fairly fixed. And the capacity to indicate or determine this relation affords the category *tātparyaśakti* to this function. This capacity is then identified with that of syntactical relational nexus, i.e. *saṃsargamaryādā*. See also Gaurinatha Sastri (*op cit* p243). Viśvanātha and Gaṅgeśa at least were quite clear about the role of *tātparya* in its essential and indispensible *kāraṇa* function in the generation of successful *śābdabodha*. See section on *tātparya* in *TC* IV (i) pp319-323.

39. It is indeed intriguing that Mīmāṃsā, in view of its *autpattika* ('originary') theory of word-meaning relation, did not take the Advaita line seriously. It could not accept *tātparya*

as a linguistic function of *lakṣaṇā* and *abhidhā*. But it would have to agree that if either possibility is open, then something like *tātparya* would be needed for deciding which of the two is applicable in the context. And that the Mīmāṃsakas evolved the *tātparyaliṅgā* criteria for *śruti* indicates that the 'purport' for Mīmāṃsā was not to be found in any '*auctor*' or 'speaker', but rather in the inherent capacity of the words or expressions, for to them the Vedas as such did not have any 'Creator'.

40. *ata eva saindhavamānaya ityādāvapi lavaṇaparatvadhīrna lavaṇādyanvayabuddhau hetuḥ; kintu tadarjakatvenābhimataṃ bhojanādiprakaraṇasya pratisandhānamiti nyāyasiddhāntaḥ.Śabdaśaktiprakāśikā* p27; (also see Nāgeśa, *op cit.*, p38-39).

41. *nanu mābhudāptoktavasya niścayānurodhena siddasādhanaṃ tātparyasya tu syāt, tanniścayasyasyā'nvayadhīhetutvāt, anyathā ghaṭa-karmatvādiparatvābhāvasya ghaṭakarmatvādhyanyamātraparatvasya vā niścaye'pi ghaṭamityādivākyāt karmatvaṃ ghaṭīyamityādyanyabodhāpatteriti cet. na, karmatādharmikaghaṭādyanyadhīparatvābhāvāniścayadasāyāṃ prameyatvādiprakāreṇa ghaṭakarmatvādiparatvasya niścaye'pi, ghaṭīyaṃ karmatvamityanvayamateranutpattyā karmatādharmikaghaṭānvayabodhaparatvaprakārakaniścayatvenaiva tātparyyadhiyastasyāṃ kāraṇatvamna vākyārthasya tatrāniveśāt.* (Jagadīśa, *ibid*, pp 24-25.)

It may also be said that we do not always recognise that an expression has ambiguity, rather, we understand it in one or other of its ambiguous senses. Strawson explains the "less tidy referential apparatus of English language" (*pace* Quine) with the help of some examples, one of which is worth mentioning here : 'Most of the girls love one boy', could be taken to mean, 'one particular boy is loved by each girl', or, 'majority of the girls love one boy'. The sentence on its face-value does not tell us the definite relation between the numbers on each side (Oxford, Hilary lectures, 1983, writer's notes).

42. On the contrary, as Donald Davidson points out, even to get to the literal meaning of a sentence we might need to seek out the intentions, and even then we may be no closer to the literal meaning : 'there are intentions embedded in all linguistic utterances such that if we could detect them we would know what the words uttered literally meant' (Davidson, 'Communication and Convention', Calcutta University Philosophy Conference, Jan 1983, paper p10-12). Consider again, in this light, Jagadīśa's understanding of what occurs when the master utters to the servant "Bring the *saindhava*". Is there a 'literal' meaning other then the intentionality-embedded meaning?

43. *VP.* IV 38a.

44. *VP* IV 38b: '*ayamadhyāpako'vyutpannaḥ*' *iti viśeṣadarśanena tātparyabhramasyāpyabhāvāt.*

45. *na caīśvaratātparyajñānāt tatra śābdabodha iti vācyam īśvarānaṅgīkarturapi tadvākyārthapratipattidarśanāt* (*Ibid*).

46. *Ibid*

47. *VP* IV 55: *tathā ca sargādyakāle parmeśvaraḥ pūrvasargasiddhavedānupūrvīsamānānupūrvīkaṃ vedaṃ viracitavān na tu tadvijātīyaṃ vedam.*

48. For discussion of *apauruṣeya*, see Kumārila Bhaṭṭa, *Ślokavārttika*,I. 27-32; Āpadeva's *Mīmāṃsā-Nyāya-Prakāśa*, '*vedāpauruṣeya* sect. (with discussion on role of *ākāṅkṣā*, *yogyatā*, etc.) (Vasudeva Shastri Abhyankar ed. BORI, Poona, 1971, p7ff). Hitherto there is no significant modern work on this fascinating notion; for some attempts, see ch. 7 n125 (*infra*).

49. *VP* IV 39. This is said to be the final view.

50. *gehe ghaṭaḥ iti vākyaṃ gehe ghaṭasaṃsargapratītijananayogyaṃ na tu paṭasaṃsargapratītijananayogyam. iti tad vākyaṃ ghaṭasaṃsargaparaṃ na tu paṭa-saṃsargaparamiti vyapadiśyate. (Ibid.)*

51. *VP* IV 40: '*saindhavamānaya*' *ityādivākyaṃ yadā lavaṇānayanapratītīcchayā.*

52. *VP* IV 41.

53. *na cobhayapratītīcchayoccarite'vyāptiḥ; tadanyamātrapratītīcchayānuccaritatvasya vivaksitatvāt (ibid).*

54. *Ibid.*

55. This has been extrapolated from IV. 40 and 42 (*loc cit*).

56. *ibid* (#42).

57. Mādhava in his *Sarvadarśanasaṃgraha* [chapter on: 'Pūrṇaprajñadarśana', an earlier system of absolutist Mīmāṃsā] cites these, ascribing them to *Bṛhat Saṃhitā* in the Vedas:
upakramopasaṃhārāvabhyāso'pūrvatā phalam,
arthavādopapattiś ca liṅgaṃ tātparyanirṇaye. (Ānandāśrama edn. p60)

For further discussion of the six critical criteria for determination of textual intentionality (*sadliṅga*) in conjunction with the Mīmāṃsā rules for establishing meaning (*samanvaya*) of (injunctive) texts - to whit, (in descending order of strength): *śruti* (direct statement), *liṅga* (implied derivation from coventional usage), *vākya* (syntactic relation), *prakaraṇa* (contextual circumstance), *sthāna* (place or position), and *samākhyā* (etymological) - see Jaimini *MS* I.iii; Laugākṣi Bhāskara, *Arthsaṃgraha*, (Varanasi, 1983, pp59-100); Kṛṣṇa Yajva, *Mīmāṃsā-Paribhāṣā* (ch 1); Vedānta appropriates Mīmāṃsā hermeneutical techniques, though with a somewhat different outcome. Sadānanda, for instance, quotes the aforementioned text cited in Mādhava's *SDS* (*vide Vedāntasāra*, V. #183-4), and Śaṅkara variously utilises the Mīmāṃsā principles in his interpretation of *Brahma-sūtras* and a number of Upaniṣadic texts (such as *Chāndogya Up.* VI.ii.1). For discussion of the latter, see S. G. Moghe, *Studies in the Pūrva Mīmāṃsā* ('Śaṅkarācāraya and Pūrva Mīmāṃsā', ch 1, pp 1-13; Ajanta Publications, Delhi, 1984). See also *Mīmāṃsā-Nyāya-Prakāśa* with comm. of Vasudeva Shastri Abhyankar (see n48 above), p27 #20-24; Edgerton trans. p9 and paragraphs 68–181.

58. But to the Mīmāṃsakas, not having to rely upon the word of a person or 'personal authorship' is a way of avoiding talk about subjectivity and the subjective dimension in the knowledge process altogether, along with its possible defects, biases, errors, etc. Yet they do not deny the capacity of the Vedic expression to convey 'intentional' sense : '*tātparyamapi sujñānam svato jñānānumāṃ vinā, yathā vede yathā cānyeṣvanālocitakartṛṣu*', in *Mānameyodaya*, section on *Āgama*, (*loc cit*, V-15, p107).

59. *Cf.* Donald Davidson's remark : 'Lying is a case where meaning is essential; the liar has an ulterior purpose that is served only if his words are understood as having the meaning he *intends*.' (*op cit* p12; italics added).

7
ŚABDAPRĀMĀṆYA
PROBLEM OF TRUTH AND AUTHORITY OF THE WORD

(T)he theory of *śabda* as a *pramāṇa*, indeed as the one mode of knowing which can override all others, needs to be looked at afresh. It is here that tradition and modernity come headlong into conflict. Even if it is true that the life-world does not fully determine the philosophical problems, it nevertheless appears that for a people whose faith in the infallibility of the scriptures is considerably weakened . . . *śabdapramāṇa* cannot any longer provide the theoretical basis for a satisfactory philosophy. But that is *not* to reject *śabda* altogether as a *pramāṇa*. What is necessary is to re-examine the priorities and relative strengths and weaknesses . . .. But one also needs to recall the distinction between understanding a sentence *p* and knowing *p*, the *different ways* in which language is central to cognitive enterprise and to moral and religious life, and the problems connected with the notions of a text and its interpretations. The methodological insights would, I believe, rehabilitate the tradition's self-understanding, without returning to the naive use of *śabdapramāṇa* to which a return is just impossible.

-- *J. N. Mohanty*[0]

PART A:—Truth and falsity of *śābdabodha*
PART B: - 'Authority and praxis' – *āptabhāva*

A: *Truth and falsity of śābdabodha*

7.0 In concluding this study we intend to examine some crucial epistemological issues that concern the analyses of *śābdabodha* (linguistically derived understanding) in the preceding chapters, against the background of the kind of challenge that has been generally posed, and articulated in the excerpt from J. N. Mohanty (above). The principal issues that we will be concerned with are—a) the problem of the truth or falsity of *śābdabodha*, in the broader context of the problem of understanding, knowledge and truth, and b) the issue of the the 'authority' of the *śābdabodha*, bearing in mind the context of the discourse that we have been engaged in. Under b) we will also look at the issue of the independence or otherwise of *śābdapramāṇa* from other means of knowing. Although, without preempting the discussion, it might be added that this last problem is not considered to be as important as it has been made out to be in traditional scholarship.

The aspect of the overall thesis we shall be arguing for here is the following:

The *tātparya-viṣayībhūtatva* or the intentional *contentness* in the understanding or judgement derived (*śābdabodha*), which is a qualificative awareness (*viśiṣṭajñāna*), is more than the comprehended linguistic 'meaning' (*śabdārthajñāna*), for the reason that the intentional content involves a significant epistemic relation with the 'given' in the episodic act.

We had occasion earlier in the discussions of *jñāna* and *pramā* [especially in the 'Introduction', and under *śābdabodha* (1.19) and *prāmāṇya* (1.20)][1], to make a number of points regarding the relation of the intentional content (*viṣayatā*) in an awareness to the 'objective' content it represents or signifies, and the claim to the truth of the cognition in terms of one or more conceptions of truth (*prāmāṇya*) proposed by Indian theorists. *Prāmāṇya* is what defines a *true* awareness and differentiates it from a *false* awareness (*apramā*, or *mithyājñāna*, *bhrama* or *viparyaya* or 'error') and doubt. Since *śābdabodha*, derived from understanding the meaning of a sentence heard, is a kind of awareness, albeit an occurrent judgement (which presumably carries conviction), its analysis would be in line with the analysis of all awarenesses. Thus, the question of whether and to what extent truth (*prāmāṇya*) can be predicated of *śābdabodha* must naturally arise. We wish to take this discussion further here by recapitulating and extending the analysis of the problem of *prāmāṇya*.

Nyāya theory of *jñāna*

7.1 In the Nyāya view, an awareness is neither an activity of the 'mind' (*manas*) nor a *vṛtti* or 'modification' of the inner sense (*antaḥkaraṇa*, the unifying psychic apparatus), but a property (*guṇa*) of the self that results from the interaction of a collocation of causal conditions (*bodhābodhas-vabhāva sāmagrī*). It is better understood as an episodic occurrent that has no parts and assumes no form (i.e. the shape of the object).[2a] Rather, an awareness is, in manner of speaking, something of a *conscious-link* between the subject and the object that is being experienced. It is not, however, an 'event' in consciousness, but is identified with 'consciousness' itself, as an act, which has no lasting duration (since it arises as a property of the self with each apprehension), although it may leave behind (psychic) impressions (*saṃskāras*) and 'dispositions'. What is most significant in this view of awareness as 'modal' consciousness is that awareness transcends itself to achieve a complete reference to the object without requiring any other intermediary process or mental state.[2]

Now, what distinguishes *jñāna* or awareness generated through one of the recognised *prāmaṇas* from other awarenesses is not the fact merely of its being a novel piece of awareness (as the Mīmāṃsakas would have it), but in having *contentness* (*viṣayatā*) or in its being an 'intentional presentation' (to borrow Brentano's terminology). While we may also compare *viṣayatā* to the 'intentional inexistence' of medieval scholastics, we must note that the object the awareness is directed to has more than an 'immanent objectivity'; rather, the object is substantively real. If the awareness is of black swans, it cannot be that the *viṣayatā* is about a class of swans that does *not* exist anywhere (or exists merely in imagination).

In other words, *jñāna* is any awareness, cognition or judgement (henceforth used interchangeably) that is characterised by intentionality or the the property of being directed towards an objective state of affairs or an 'other' (*saviṣayatā*), where the '*viṣaya*' is a reference to a *real* object or entity.

Thus the *relata* in a determined (*savikalpa*) awareness always answer to *real* relational characters of objects or entities *as they are*. (A *jñāna* without *viṣayatā* would be like 'experience' devoid of *content* to Kant.) Also, the antecedent in the awareness and its features are not borrowed from or juxtaposed on the 'contents' of some other experience, or mental state (or, some other property of the self or Being), but are substantively related to the object that is causally efficacious in giving rise to the awareness.[3a] (Although we might note that the truth of the 'awareness' need not necessarily be defined in terms of the *causal* determinants of the awareness.) In perceptual awareness, for instance, the percept bears a direct relation to the object, and no extra 'psychical entity' or ideation need intercede between the knowing 'self' and the known.

Now the *viṣayatā*, in terms of the *relata* of a judgement, comprises three components, namely its own *viśeṣyatā*, *prakāratā* (*viśeṣaṇatā*),and *saṃsargatā* as their relations. Using a 'subject-predicate' model, we may say that the *viśesya* is the subject term (say, *x*), or the *qualificand*, the *prakāra* or *viśeṣaṇa* is the predicate term (say, *y*), or the *qualifier*, and the *saṃsarga* is the 'R' that links the two in terms of the particular relation obtaining in, and therefore delimited by, the object being cognised. Although this does not give us a *proposition* as in a (dispositional) belief or 'an impersonal' judgement *qua* 'eternal sentence' (of, say, logic and mathematics), this property, however, renders the cognition in question a qualificative apprehension (*viśiṣṭajñāna*).

A *viśiṣṭajñāna*, as we explained in our 'Introduction', is an awareness which has a 'propositional' structure, as could be said of an occurrent belief state, or of a 'propositional attitude' towards what it is that one is actually *believing* or judging at some moment. The *viśiṣṭa*- (*Q*) is described as the minimal relational structure *qua viśeṣya-viśeṣaṇa sambandha* obtaining in the 'objective' content in the awareness. In other words, the (epistemically) significant *jñāna* (=*j*) is an episodic occurrent that has *contentness* with a qualificative or relational structure, which, like any conception, is potentially expressible in linguistic form and analysable in terms of logical principles, i.e. in notational representations such as $j = Q(xy)$ and $j = Q((xy)(z))$. It is this 'propositional' character that helps to distinguish 'determined' (*savikalpa*) awareness from awareness-states that are said to be 'primitive' or indetermined (*nirvikalpa*). In more precise epistemological terms, a determined awareness ought to be described as a 'judgement' and a 'true judgement' as 'knowledge'. (But this convention has been avoided by modern writers and translators.)

The relational structure referred to in such an awareness is determined by the specific features that constitute the chief distinguishing property of the entity or object of presentation in the awareness, such that if, say, an object appears or 'floats' into my awareness, the *visayatā* in terms of its qualificand, *x* ('this' *contentness*), is presented as qualified by a distinguishing property *y*, or as being an awareness of a relatedness of *y* to that which possesses *y*. Thus, $j = Q(xy)$. But, if instead of *y*, the qualifier in the *viṣayatā* in question happens to be *w*, which, however, is a qualifying feature of another entity (real or psychical)—thus $Q(xw)$—then it follows that the truth-value (*prāmāṇya*) of the cognition is false. For, a *true* cognition is one in which there is an accurate apprehension of the feature just as it is in the object (of which it is an awareness, and not of any other (*arthāvyabhicāritā*)).[3]

As well as being *avyabhicārin*, non-erroneous or 'non-deviating' from the object, Gautama adds that the (true) awareness should also be *vyavasātyātmaka*, that is, of 'definitive' character (*NS* 1.1.4; *adhyavasāya* in Śrīdhara, *arthajanyatva* in Jayanta or *arthaniścaya* in Gaṅgeśa). Vātsyāyana comments that this further restriction (in Gautama's definition) is added so as to exclude doubtful awareness, which may not have deviated substantially from the object but is not definite whether the awareness is actually of that or some other object (as, say, in the awareness: Is this smoke or fog?).[4a]

Annambhaṭṭa formulates the structure of such an awareness in the following terms: *tadvati tatprakārako'nubhavo yathārthaḥ* (which maybe paraphrased as *tadvadiviśeṣyakatve sati tatprakāratvam*):[4] a true awareness is an apprehension of the object with its distinguishing property *such as* it is in reality (*yathābhūto'rtha yasmin saḥ*). ('Distinguishing property' is mentioned so as to exclude *saṃyak* or general features, which several objects may share, such as the floor-space occupied by a pot and cloth.) In Gaṅgeśa's terms this reads as: *tadvati tatprakāraka(jñāna)tvam*,[5] which is equivalent to *tadvadviśeṣyakatvāvacchinnatatprakāraka.*[6] Stated more explicitly, an authentic presentation is an awareness that is constituted by the equiformity or agreement (*yāthārthya*) with the features of the selfsame object (*ekasmin dharmiṇi)* of which it is an awareness. That is, the subject term of the cognitive content (*viśeṣya*) must be characterised by just those features (*prakāraka*) in the awareness as are present in the correlative objective situation (*tadvati*). The judgement only then discloses the entity just as it is in itself, or in just the manner *as* the thing presented to consciousness is. This is the directive that a judgement must follow if it is to be 'true'. Although *yāthārthya* may, in the definition of the earlier Naiyāyikas, be taken to imply a pictorial resemblance between the awareness and the object, in Gaṅgeśa it is clearly restricted by *tadvattva* to mean the immediacy or directness of the presentation of the object (*tadvati*) as and where it is: *yatra yad asti tatra tasyānubhavaḥ.*[7a]

Herein lies the 'essence' of truth. This theory of truth has often been compared to the 'correspondence to the *facts*' theory.

7.2. Consider, for example, the cognition 'This is a pot'. Now the awareness is that there is *something* (*tadvati*) that is experienced as pot, i.e. qualified as *potness* (or possessing *tat* [in *tadvati*]). Now if it is the case that *potness* is the distinguishing property of the object cognised, i.e. the pot, and it (*tat* in *tatprakāraka*) conforms to the *viśeṣaṇa*, i.e. *potness* in the awareness, then the cognition is true or a *pramā.*

Note that *tat* is the variable, which is filled in by 'potness', now as the qualifier of the qualificand (*viśeṣya qua tadvati*) (i.e. the ontological predication), and then as the epistemic qualifier (*viśeṣaṇa, prakāra*) of the object in awareness. Its selfsame conformity in respect of the *prakāra* (in the awareness) and the object designated by *tadvati* is what constitutes *prāmāṇya*, according to this definition. Gaṅgeśa consolidated the definition and made it more precise by including reference to the third factor in the cognitive process, namely the relation or *saṃsarga*, as :

> *tadvati tatprakārakajñānatvaṃ tadvati tadvaiśiṣṭyajñānatvaṃ vā prāmāṇyam* -

'*Prāmāṇya* is either (a) an awareness whose chief qualifier, *x*, is in what possesses *x*, or (b) an awareness of a relatedness of *x* to what possesses *x*.'[7] A *false* cognition, it follows, would be one where such features as ascribed to the qualificand of the content presented (*upasthita*) in awareness are not really in the object of awareness (*tadabhāvavati tatprakārakaḥ*,[8] or where the awareness deviates from its object (*ayathārthas tu arthavyabhicāri)*[9], or where two *viṣayatā*s are wrongly juxtaposed in an experience (as in the alleged awareness: 'hare's horn'). Doubt or doubtful awareness, such as 'Is this a man or a tree?', is also excluded since two or more contrary or diverse features or *viśeṣaṇas (viruddhanānādharmās)* are 'juxtafused' in a way that does not give the awareness any certainty (*niścaya*).[10] *Prāmāṇya*, then, is an essential property of an awareness which obtains the relational structure in agreement with the objective situation towards which it is directed and whose 'opposedness' (*pratibandhaka*) it has overcome. Such a *jñāna* is known as *pramā*, 'true' awareness, cognition or judgement. And a 'false' *jñāna* is *a-pramā*, since it is opposed to *pramā*.

In more general philosophical terms, *pramā* is the objective fruit (*phalajñāna*) of the quest for *tattvajñāna* or knowledge of the real nature of things ('Things' being covered by the general term *'artha'*). *Tattvajñāna*, it is believed, comprises not only knowledge of objects (*viṣayas, padārthas*), but also knowledge of 'purpose' (*prayojana*), 'the highest good' (*niḥśreyasa*), and the de-ontological ends (*puruṣārthas*), that may be conducive to proper and successful activity (*saphalakriyākāritvam*) on the part of human beings. (Thus, Vātsyāyana's cryptic introductory comments on the *Nyāya-sūtras*: *pramāṇataḥ arthapratipattau pravṛttisāmarthyāt arthavat pramāṇam*; and Gaṅgeśa's defence: *niṣkampapravṛttyaṅgasya prāmāṇyaniścayadhīnatvāt*).[11a]

Utpatti (genesis) of *prāmāṇya*

Now this is as far as the definition (*pramālakṣaṇa*) of the nature of truth goes. But it is not to be assumed that the very conditions that give rise to *jñāna* are also the conditions that determines its truth or *prāmāṇya*. The truth condition is not the same as *jñānajanya* (awareness-genesis) conditions. That is to say, truth is not identified with the genesis of the awareness, but is analysed as a species of *jñāṇa*, which becomes present in it by virtue of some special condition, called *guṇa* that is causally related to the object or objective state of affairs of which this is an awareness.

We are now being asked to conceive of 'truth' in a causal sense, which may sound peculiar indeed, since truth is usually regarded to be an uncaused universal. Nor is this a nominalist conception, for the Nyāya is committed to a realist ontology wherein particulars are the *reals*, and hence more significant than the universal (*jāti*) which is said merely to 'inhere' in the particular. Perhaps it is here that we should look for the sense of this extended conception of truth. We should note, therefore, that the truth condition is closely aligned to the ontological component in the awareness-complex. And since the ontic status of the known is a particular, each judgement must relate itself to that particular at the moment of its emergence.

Truth, then, is a measure of the condition that *guarantees* or assures this specific relation, and cannot be said to be given among the more general causal conditions of *jñāna* (as the *svataḥ* or intrinsically valid or self-evidence thesis of Advaita-Mīmāṃsā would claim). And this later distinction is crucial in Nyāya view, for otherwise, it is argued, false or erroneous cognitions, and even doubt, that arise from the selfsame conditions as a *pramā* would also pass as having *prāmāṇya*, and it would then not be possible to discern the false cognition as being *false* immediately as it arises. Further, doubt is also ruled out if the doubtful cognition is not apprehended for what it is immediately as it arises (since doubt vacillates between two or more noetic 'givens'). Besides, it is not obvious that the truth of a cognition is self-presented or intrinsic, for if it were it ought to be directly evident with the illumination of the cognition.

For example, when an awareness of the pot on the floor emerges, the awareness does not necessarily carry the *certainty* that the object cognised is a pot and its locus is the floor. And even if the awareness did emerge with *certainty*, it does not follow that an objective situation obtains exactly as the awareness points to. There has to be something 'extra' ('from other sources': *parataḥ*) that is appended to the awareness, which would make its truth-value *evident*, without necessarily manifesting it directly. The 'extra' condition (*asādhāraṇakaraṇam*) that accounts for the genesis of truth is called *guṇa: 'excellence'*; and the adverse condition that is involved in false cognition is called *doṣa: defect.*[11b] The presence of *guṇa* deems the awareness as possessing *pramātva* (truth), while the presence of *doṣa* determines a negative truth-value, *apramātva* or falsity.

One might object that there is no uniform *guṇa* for all true cognitions, unless we also admit a generic property that defines the different *guṇas*; nor does it appear that there is some one basic *guṇa* for each *pramāṇa.*[11] This does not seem to concern the Naiyāyika, for he admits a different *guṇa* for each *pramāṇa*. For example, in perception the *guṇa* pertains to the veridicity of the awareness in terms of the specific relation of the intentional content (*via* sense-organ contact) with the substantive and the parts thereof (*viśeṣaṇadviśeṣyasannikarṣaḥ*), so that the object in the awareness is 'such-as' as it is in reality.[12] In inference the *guṇa* would pertain to the correct relation of the concomitance (*vyāpti*) in the subject of inference (*pakṣa*). And in *śabda*, the *guṇa* may be said to pertain specifically to the correct apprehension of *yogyatā* (compatibility) with regard to what is spoken about a particular state of affairs—but this may also include considerations of *tātparyajñāna* (intentionality) and *āptajñāna* (reliability of the speaker).

In any case, the talk about *guṇa* is a way of saying that an ideal cognition must exude the characteristic of being adequately aligned (*yathārtha, avyabhicārita*) to the specific *species* of reality of which it is an awareness. This is hardly satisfactory in terms of a consistent account of the essential property of truth. Put rather crudely, the *guṇatva* is construed as the compatibility of the awareness in relation to the 'facts' (in broad terms of the Nyāya theory of reality). A surreptitious commonality is thus assumed in the various *guṇas*, and it must be so if the analysis is to be consistent across the accredited *pramāṇas*.

It is also admitted that although the conditions that determine a *jñāna* and those that determine its 'truth-value' are different, they may nevertheless arise together. Thus *jñāna* either arises as a *pramā* or it does not. And it is the difference in these conditions that differentiate true from false or erroneous cognitions. The *apprehension* (*jñapti*) of the truth-value, however, may not arise with the awareness, but that is not at all the same issue. For an awareness may be true (in respect of the *guṇatva* possessed) and yet its truth may not be apprehended then, or even moments later. For example, John sees a tree at a distance; there is actually a tree there and he has perceived it correctly; the awareness is therefore true, but it is not immediately self-evident to him that his cognition is true, for the truth of the awareness has not presented itself simultaneously with the awareness. Another mental or psychical act may be required for the disclosure or perhaps even the *discovery* of the truth *qua* its having *guṇa*.

7.3 Taking into consideration all that we we have said so far, it should be clear that the optimum condition under which a *jñāna* would be said to possess *guṇatva* or 'evidence of excellence', is when it is *yathārthānubhava* : an authentic experience of the object as it is in reality, and one that is identifiable as such by some mark or characteristic other than the awareness itself (free from any possible *doṣa* or defect, nor given merely through impressions left from a previous experience, as it is in the case of objects of memory: *saṃskāramatrājanyaṃ jñānaṃ smṛtiḥ*, *TS* #34). Thus the presence of of *yāthārthya* ('such-as it actually is') in the awareness is the presence of *guṇatva* or special mark of 'excellence', which makes the awareness a *true niścayajñāna*. The *guṇa*, then, may be described as *yathārthayogyatva*: the *objective competence* of the awareness, in terms of enabling its intentional content to achieve satisfactory correspondence with its objective correlate—i.e. in successfully yielding its object of awareness.

Again, there is no suggestion here that the *guṇa* would 'show-up' immediately. According to this thesis, that the awareness is possessed of *guṇatva* is not given in the awareness itself. That is to say, the apprehension of the truth-value (*jñapti*) is not intrinsic to the conditions that account for its 'truth-making' (*utpatti*), but may be affirmed or ascertained *ab extra* (i.e. consciousness of it arises extrinsically). Overall, some instances of awarenesses succeed in this characterisation, while some do not.

Memory (*smṛti*), for instance, is ruled out since the connection between the qualifier in the recollected content and the objective correlate is so tenuous as to render it difficult to establish that the qualifier (*tat*) is selfsame and bears the same relation in the *viṣayatā* as it does in the non-present object. Or as Locke said, the object corresponding to the idea in the recollection is sought after and found with difficulty and effort.[13] Thus we could not speak of 'authentic presentation' (*tadvattva*)—i.e. that the awareness is 'true' to its object, notwithstanding the resemblance (*sārūpya*), without further qualification or an additional judgement as to its authenticity or otherwise. To be sure, it is not that memory, which may be true to its object as experienced previously, does not have *yāthārthya*, but memory is excluded from the class of *anubhava*, apprehension, whose object must be actually present, *sattā*. Memory would be said to lack the characteristic of *arthajanyatva* (object-generated), and may be hindered by doubt about its *avyabhicāritā* ('non-deviation'). To Jayanta's thinking the object of memory is as good as non-existent.[14a]

Likewise, *pramā* is not extended to guesses, hunches and dreams, which are even more susceptible to error than, say, recognition would be, because of the possible confusion of their *viṣayatās*, their inability to achieve a direct reference to an object, possibly also the non-existence of the objective reference, and the involvement, particularly in dreams, of non-cognitive—i.e. affective, conative, and subconscious - factors.[14]

7.4 A corollary to the foregoing analysis of truth conditions, we have noted, is that error is a contingent element in the awareness brought about by the presence of defects (*doṣas*) which are due to conditions other than those that determine the awareness itself. The error *qua* defect is said also to be ascertained *ab extra*, that is by an extrinsic process, just as it is for the ascertainment of the 'evidence of excellence' in a true *niścayajñāna*. The extrinsic process in both instances could involve an introspection (*anuvyavasāya*) or an inference.

Although, it would be more to the point to say that while an awareness *per se* is disclosed in a subsequent introspective awareness (*anuvyavasāya*), its truth-value (*prāmāṇya*) is disclosed in a follow-up inference.[15] It may be argued, however, that the *anuvyavasāya* must disclose the *guṇa* or the *doṣa* (as the case may be, in terms of the relation of the qualifier and the qualified, *tadvati* etc.), in the same species-moment as it discloses the awareness, and that therefore the truth-value of the *jñāna* should become self-evident. That may be so, but this will not do for at least two reasons: a) no one will claim that an introspective awareness is necessarily related to the the ontological component (i.e. it merely marks out the epistemic features of the preceding awareness, however representative these may be), and b) the actual judgement of truth or falsity of the awareness would still be required so as to obviate doubt and to achieve conviction about the truth or falsity of the initial awareness. And for this to be possible, there has to follow a kind of inference (known as *vyatireki*, that deduces from mutual *co-absence*) on the basis of a corrobarative instance, or the successful activity the awareness leads to, or some familiar knowledge or convention (*tajjātīya*), or yet another cognitive awareness of the same object that could be taken to be decisive. Or perhaps this may be established on the basis of evidence of a different, but related, kind (such as its consequences, satisfaction-relation, after-effects, pay-offs, etc).

Whatever the means, it is clear in the Nyāya view that the conditions that disclose the awareness are *not* the very set of conditions (*yāvatsāmagrī*) that discloses its truth-value. Thus, the conditions that generate an awareness and the conditions that determine its truth-value, as also the conditions that 'reveal' both, are not commensurate (i.e. they are different and extrinsic to each other). This thesis, in respect both of the genesis and apprehension of truth, is known as *parataḥprāmāṇya.*

Again, why the Nyāya view seems to be insistent on this extrinsically established characteristic; is because of the belief that, a) an erroneous cognition could well have the same qualifier as a true cognition (but not qualifying the same qualificand) thus allowing room for confusion of one with the other, and b) a doubtful cognition may appear to have the same content as a cognition of which there is no doubt. Consider, for example, the sentence 'This is a tree: is this a tree?'[16] What would distinguish the qualifier of '*this*' in one part of the awareness from the qualifier in the other part without leading to mutual contradiction? Ideally, nothing would. Yet there might be *yāthārthya* in one part ('this is a tree) but not in the other. Such an awareness cannot be said to have *yathārthayogyatva*, for there can be no certainty or conviction about the object of this awareness (*arthaniścaya). Being aware with certainty (niścaya*), of course, is no guarantee of *prāmāṇya*, for the truth with regard to the first part would be frustrated by the second part; and besides, there could be mistaken certainty in false cognitions as well. (Hence the inclusion of *arthavat.*)

But, by the same token, if doubt about the truth of a cognition is said to arise extrinsically, Nyāya should admit the same in the case of a false or erroneous cognition, so that there might be no inkling of the possibility of falsity until a while later perhaps. This charge, if conceded to, would diminish the Nyāya objection against the impossibility of doubt implied in the *svataḥ* or intrinsic (truth) thesis, for the latter thesis also agrees that doubt is apprehended *ab extra* just as falsity is. That is to say, even if the doubt does not arise at the moment of the awareness in question, if there is a cause for it, by virtue of the presence of some defect, *doṣa*, or 'juxtafusion', the awareness would *not* arise with certainty (*niścaya*), and the doubt would manifest itself in a subsequent awareness.

Thus, even though truth might be given intrinsically with the awareness, it is not beyond doubt in some other species-moment. But this is a not a very damaging rebuttal, for the real danger in the *svataḥ* thesis, as we shall see shortly, is in saying that *jñāna* is *presented* as true (even if it is not directly evident) when it might not be so. Doubt may or may not arise (as when a cognition is accidentally true), and it sometimes arises even where a cognition happens to be true.

7.5 In sum, the Nyāya thesis may be formulated in the following representation.

For an awareness *j*, that something, *x*, is *y*, only where the *niścaya* ('conviction that *x* is *y*)' is backed unequivocally by *yāthārthya* [*Q(xy)*, leaving out fortuitous correspondence] can truth be said to have been predicated, and only then is *j* a true *niścayajñāna* or *pramā*. In more general terms, we might then say that there is truth in the certainty of the awareness that has some relevant affirmable 'evidence of excellence' attached to it in terms of yielding its object, which is analogous, though not identical, to a 'justified' true belief account of knowledge (for reasons we shall remark on a little later).[17]

It follows that if an awareness is to be true, in addition to carrying conviction (*niścaya*), it must be characterised by *guṇatva*, explicated in terms of *yāthārthya*, specific to that mode of knowing. And this in turn implies that the awareness is not a memory and is brought about by a recognised or 'accredited' means of knowing (*pramāṇa*). Extending this principle to *śābdabodha* (*sb*), the structure of the cognition would be something like this: *g(sb)*—i.e. a linguistic awareness qualified by *g* (= the *guṇatva*). Here *g* is the 'competency for *objectness*' (*yogyatāyāthārthya*), or the 'purposive objective',[18] designated by the sentence structure and correlated to the intentional content of the *śābdabodha*. But since the relevant 'objective' state of affairs may not be co-present, as it would in the case of perception, apprehension of the correct *yogyatā*, perhaps also the reliability of the authority (i.e. 'testimonial evidence', *t*) may have to be invoked to confirm the presence of the *guṇatva* valid for that *pramāṇa*. At any rate, the structure of this analysis could be formalised as follows:

$g(sb) \rightarrow (aF)$ [where *a* is *visayatā* or *artha*,[19], *F* is the *viśeṣaṇa*]

That this *śābdabodha* has *guṇatva* may not be directly evident, but may be disclosed in an *anuvyavasāya* or reflective judgement of the form:

$$sb = ((aF))(t).$$

In Gaṅgeśa's terms (i.e. his general thesis of *prāmāṇya*), we may say that the qualificand of the *śābdabodha* possesses a certain property as its chief qualifier, and that that feature really belongs to the *artha* designated by the sentence structure apprehended. To put it another way, a correct *śābdabodha* ascribes to its content the feature(s) in accordance with the 'objective' state of affairs represented in the sentence structure which gave rise to that awareness.

In summing up the rather simplified account of the Nyāya thesis, we note that the conditions that determine truth of an awareness are distinguished from the conditions that give rise to the awareness itself. The truth-character consists in its being a cognitive occurrence in which the qualifying features of the qualificand and their relatedness conform to the relevant qualifier in the objective correlate. Such a cognition is said to possess *guṇatva* or 'evidence of excellence', whose awareness, though, does not arise simultaneously with the cognition itself, since the disclosure of the presence of *guṇa*, as also of defects (*doṣa*) in the case of erroneous cognitions, requires a separate cognitive act, possibly an inference, an introspection, or simply another confirmatory awareness (such as the quenching of thirst upon drinking water), or some related circumstantial evidence.

Advaita and Mīmāṃsā views on truth

7.6 The Advaita and (Bhāṭṭa) Mīmāṃsā theories of truth are, by and large, not totally consistent with Nyāya theory, particularly in respect of their respective descriptions of true cognition (*pramā*), although there is considerable convergence in respect of false cognition or error (*apramā*). That is to say, they may be mutually in agreement about the conditions of falsity as being *parataḥ*, both in respect of its genesis and its apprehension, but they are in disagreement about the conditions that generate truth.

The Advaita-Mīmāṃsā view is that the conditions of truth (*utpatti*) are *svataḥ* or intrinsic to the set of conditions that generate the cognition of the unknown object.[20a] In other words, the truth of an awareness is not dependent upon some other conditions, such as those identified by the *guṇas* in the Nyāya theory, and inferred from a confirmatory evidence, or practical success, and so forth. (Although, as we noted earlier, the Nyāya view does not entail that truth is an additional confirmation that occurs *after* the awareness has arisen; rather that, though generated together, they do not arise in the same species-moment, i.e. *jñāna* arises indifferently to its truth or falsity.)

Further, it is claimed by the *svataḥ* thesis that the conditions that disclose the *jñāna* are the conditions that also disclose or illumine the truth of the awareness (*jñapti*). So, for instance, according to Bhāṭṭa Mīmāṃsā, what is disclosed is not really *jñāna* or the awareness (which in itself is an unintuitable act of consciousness) but the *jñātatā* or 'knownness' (or "cognisedness", which is a property acquired by the hitherto unknown object). And this is disclosed in a sort of unfailing spontaneous inference as soon as the awareness occurs. However, it is in this selfsame disclosure of *jñātatā* that the truth of the awareness is also made manifest. For the Advaita, the *jñāna* is a 'modification' of the inner psychic apparatus that itself is inert. Nonetheless, the *jñāna* is illumined by virtue of its proximity to the ever-luminous witness-consciousness (*sākṣin*), and the same consciousness illumines (or gives witness to) the *truth* of the awareness. In short, then, the conditions that generate the awareness are commensurate with the conditions that generate its truth; likewise with the respective conditions that disclose the awareness and its truth. (We shall not here concern ourselves with variations in details on the *svataḥ* thesis.)[20]

There is, however, controversy as to whether the *svataḥ* thesis does not analytically entail the denial of error or false *jñāna*, for if *jñāna* is intrinsically true but is discovered to be false afterwards, then it could not have been a *jñāna* at all! And one wonders whether the *svataḥ* theorists could be too concerned with giving a description of *apramā* or false cognition (so that *apramā* is excluded from the genus of *jñāna*, or that there is no *apramā* at all, as in the Prābhākara version).

But to say this is to attach too strong a sense of 'knowledge' to *jñāna* and to deny that truth could be predicated of it. Certainly, we might agree that error is not *jñāna*, but nor is it *ajñāna*—'ignorance *par excellence*'—(the opposite of *jñāna*). *Apramā* is not *ajñāna*, but is best construed as a false awareness-state lacking in *prāmāṇya* by virtue of the non-fulfillment in the awareness of the characteristics of *anadhigatatva* (novelty), *abādhitatva* (unfalsifiedness), *niścayatva* (certainty), *avyabhicāritatva* (unerringness), and *saṃvāda* (coherence with other knowledge).

Further, the qualification of *yathārthānubhava* (i.e. *arthatathātva* or *viṣayatathātva* in Mīmāṃsā)[21] or 'as the thing truly is' is generally insisted upon in most standard accounts of *prāmāṇya*. Dharmarāja expresses this in terms of the *tadvati tatprakārakajñānatvam* definition (*VP* VII.1), very much as it is in the standard Nyāya definition (stated earlier). This definition is applicable to both cognition and recollection, but is not normal in the instance of error—at least this is the firm view of Dharmarāja, although Madhusūdana Sarasvatī and other commentators seemed to be of a somewhat different opinion, as Mohanty reports.[22] (We shall come back to this issue a little while.) Also, it is *because* a cognition possesses *prāmāṇya* that it is conducive to successful activity or capable of satisfying the condition of yielding a productive outcome (*saṃvādipravṛtty'nukūlam; ibid*).

That is to say, *pravṛtti* is possible just if the condition of awareness 'fits' the object of awareness. According to this thesis, however, the fulfillment of those determining characteristics, enumerated in the preceding paragraph, is assured only if a recognised *pramāṇa* (in terms of the relevant causal conditions and restrictions) is nondefectively deployed. A *pramāṇa*-generated awareness succeeds in revealing the thing that has been hitherto unrevealed, or has remained veiled, and is other than the prior non-existence of that awareness (i.e. it is not a repetition, notwithstanding the case of recollection).

This definition, by and large, is consistent with the realist epistemology that undergirds both the *parataḥ* and the *svataḥ* theses in almost all Indian schools, with the possible exception of Prābhākara and most Buddhist schools. For the latter, truth was generally a matter of *arthakriyākāritva*: what leads to successful activity or workablility, which in turn determines the 'object' or *artha* of awareness as being *avisaṃvāditā* or congruent with the awareness.[23] That is to say, *pravṛtti* is possible just if the object 'fits' the condition of its awareness. The awareness picks out the object in terms of the characteristics that are most satisfying to the awareness itself (i.e. in terms of some goal, purpose or end to be achieved).

7.7 In essence, *prāmāṇya* in the Advaita approach is consistent with the requirement that the awareness in question must apprehend the qualificand (*viśeṣya*) as qualified by the chief qualifier (*viśeṣaṇa, prakāra*) in accordance with the correlative 'object' that informs it. In the terminology of *Vedāntaparibhāṣā*, again, this is stated as *tadvati tatprakārakajñānatvaṃ prāmāṇyam*. This does look curiously similar to Annaṃbhaṭṭa's definition if not identical with Gangesa's formulation. Annaṃbhaṭṭa uses the term *anubhava* in his definition to refer to 'experience', while Dharmarāja uses the term *jñānatva* specifically to avoid confusion with conative and affective (*icchā*-) states, which may also have *viśeṣaṇas* (intentional qualifiers) identical to the *viśeṣaṇa* in a cognitive act.[24]

Dharmarāja is aware of the importance of grounding his definition of *prāmāṇya* in an ontological situation: thus he does not dispense with *tadvati*. His analysis would run along the following lines. When one has the awareness of the form : 'this is a pot', the *pot* in the awareness is the *viśeṣya*, characterised by the *dharma* of *potness* (the *viśeṣaṇa* of the awareness). But unless *potness* is the very feature that qualifies some object out there (*tadvati*), the awareness will fail to have *prāmāṇya*.

A Naiyāyika, like Gaṅgeśa, may still want to argue that it is not sufficient that an awareness has a qualifier and that there be a qualificand that possesses that qualifier. An awareness, in addition, should give assurance that the qualifier qualifies the right qualificand and has encompassed the precise relation that obtains among the components of the object. Dharmarāja's response to this would be that he intends these additional requirements to be covered by the *tadvati* component, and that the correct deployment of the causal conditions that generate a *jñāna* would need to be assured. If there is any doubt this should become obvious when the awareness fails to yield some determined outcome, or when there is another (confirmed) awareness that contradicts it (*bādhita*). He is not suggesting that the awareness might not be mistaken, and that there are no limitations in this definition of truth, but he does not believe that his definition is too wide off the mark. One serious limitation, we feel, in his definition is the inclusion of recollection (*smṛti*), which he had explicitly excluded from his earlier definition of *pramā*, while requiring *anadhigatatva* or novelty as one of the marks of *prāmāṇya*, along with non-contradiction (*abādhita*) (*VP* Intro. #4).

Dharmarāja obviously sees no difficulty in extending this definition to recollection, suggesting that the *viśeṣya-viśeṣaṇa* (*(Qxy)*) relation holds true even though the *viṣaya* or the objective state of affairs is not immediately present (as is also the case in inferential knowing). It might be suggested that novelty is only required in the case of *śabda* or verbally-generated awareness, for one does not want to know from another source what one can or has already come to know through one's own resources, while it might so be fruitful to use all the knowledge and experience one has had in the past in order, say, to solve a difficult problem or to even recognise its familiar features. Certainly, *smṛti* in the form of *pratyabhijñā* or 'recognition' is accepted by Jayanta even though he (along with the rest of the Naiyāyikas) rejects *anadighatatva* or novelty as a characteristic of *prāmāṇya*.[25a] Perhaps Dharmarāja had this in mind, but he does not make it clear. Or perhaps, he was making room for the derived authenticity and, therefore, acceptance of the class of scriptures that fall under the category of *smṛti*, literally, 'the recollected', such as the *Purāṇas*, epics, and the *dharmaśāstras*.

Neveretheless, and this is an important point, Dharmarāja does *not* extend this definition to the case of *erroneous* awareness (*bhrama*). Indeed, there is reason to believe that he excludes the application of this definition to *bhrama*, so as to pick out true *niścaya*-awareness from erroneous awareness. At least one of the traditional commentators confirms this, as he suggests: *bhrame tannirāsāya—tadvatiti*: 'that (*tadvati*) is excluded in (the case of) erroneous cognition.'[25] Now here Dharmarāja clearly departs from Madhusūdana Sarasvatī. But this is contrary to what Anantakrishṇa Śāstrī suggests. Śāstrī is of the view that Dharmarāja's definition extends to *bhrama* as well.

This point is worth dwelling on, for Anantakrishṇa Śāstrī, whom

Mohanty quotes, is simply wrong.[26] Śāstrī's qualification of *sādhāraṇam* (common to), which he attributes to Dharmarāja, is completely misplaced; he thereby misconstrues Dharmarāja's text (or rather forces it to fit Madhusūdana's alleged view). Śāstrī does not mention in his gloss two most important categories, namely, *anubhava* and *smṛti*, which *sādhāraṇam* is meant to qualify. Instead, Śāstrī mentions *bhrama* (error), which he takes *sādhārana* to be qualifying. But this is false, since *bhrama* does not fall within the *tadvati* definition, while *anubhava* certainly does (*pace* Annambhaṭṭa), even though *smṛti* might not (except perhaps in the form of *pratyabhijñā; cf.* Jayanta). This is an exceedingly serious oversight on the part of Anantakrishṇa, for Dharmarāja is quite clear in his statement on those categories of experience to which the *tadvati* description applies. He names them as we just stated: *smṛtyanubhavasādhāraṇam*. If it extended to *bhrama*, it would be under the most extra-ordinary circumstances (*asādhāraṇam*), and even then that would be at the cost of the ontological component in the definition.

Now even if most (other) Advaita writers took the contrary view (i.e. that the definition covers error, *bramasādhāraṇam*) there is no compelling reason to attribute this view to Dharmarāja in his *Vedāntaparibhāṣā* (emerged as it did in the post-Gaṅgeśa spirit). Thus, the *prakāra* in the definition in question is taken as having a generic character, but it also answers to real features of particular objects (*viṣaya*): hence 'silverness' cannot be said to work in the oft-cited example (of the experience of a silver-like shinning shell), for 'silverness' is not a property of an existent in that species-moment of awareness.

To digress a little here, it might be well to see whether Madhusūdana was indifferent to the ontological demands that a rigorous *prāmāṇya* thesis would make. In his earlier work, viz. *Vedāntakalpalatikā*, Madhusūdana admits, time and again, that true awareness has an ontological correlate even though it is not evident in the awareness. His description of the *viṣayatā* (intentional content) is that its character is general - thus 'jarness', 'mother-of-pearlness' – and it is aligned to an *individual*, though not to the particular object, such as a *jar*, etc. But he insists that there has to be an *object*, otherwise the situation would be anarchic, and the affairs of the everyday world would break down. And further that, without the presence of an object the subject-object dichotomy, common to all empirical experience, would not arise (although there is no compelling reason why a mistaken object or illusion cannot give rise to this differentiation).[27]

It is true that Madhusūdana is suggesting that at the moment of awareness the intentional content (as the epistemological component) is all that is directly evident. But he does not think that this is sufficient for true awareness to arise since the connection to the object is not directly given: which is why the *viśeṣaṇa* could be 'silverness' or another ('clothness') recollected from memory. Though he would also want to say that, in the case of memory-recollection, the *viśeṣaṇas* are there only by virtue of the respective substantives of which these are 'images', such as 'mother-of-pearl', 'jar', etc. At one time, that is in a previous experience, they each answered to the description of *tadvati* or a real object and were qualified by just those features (*prakāra*) that now re-appear (as *viśeṣaṇa*) in the memory-given 'objects'. But of course, if these persist as though they were possessed of real substance, then doubt would arise and an introspection might make clear their real scope. In view of this doubt, one might look to *pravṛttisāmarthya* – their conduciveness towards activity – as well as their authenticity in terms of the presence of something novel or original. And these are looked at not for their own ends, but as tests and means for detecting falsity or error. Still, however, one could argue that despite these strictures, Madhusūdana does not intend to exclude the possibility of an erroneous awareness possessing the same property-qualifications that an otherwise true awareness would possess. Nevertheless, for Madhusūdana this is merely one moment in a process that is rather more complicated, and thus it should not unnecessarily blur the distinctions that ensue in the subsequent moments in the same awareness. It is precisely to aid the clarification of these internal distinctions that Dharmarāja brings in the condition of *tadvati* in his revised definition.

One hopes that the discussion so far would bring to relief one of the quandaries that led Mohanty to remark, in his celebrated work on Gaṅgeśa's *prāmāṇyavāda*, that the *svataḥ* and *parataḥ* theories are irreconciliable as to their epistemological description – a conundrum that Karl Potter takes up in arguing for a radically different approach to the problem of *prāmāṇya*.[28]

7.8 The real difficulty with the standard Advaita position is not that it is *not* ontologically sensitive, or that the whole thrust of its epistemology (as Potter seems to suggest for all Indian theories of truth), one way or another, hangs on 'workability', but that at some point the Advaitin wants to be able to say that the *viṣaya* of all empirically-derived knowledge is ultimately not the 'real thing' (*paramārtha*). The *viṣaya* of the empirical - *vyāvahārika* – realm is contingent, from the level of the *pāramārthika* , and for that reason empirical knowledge is not good enough for removing the root substratum of *ajñāna* or *avidyā* (the 'indescribable', *anirvācya*, in the given world). From the *pāramārthika* level, which alone is the realm of true reality, the *vyāvahārika* is no more real than the snake is in the snake-rope illusion (which, as such, is said to belong to a lower, *prātib-*

hāsika, level).

The shift in levels of the discourse on reality and the 'sublation' or overriding of each lower level occurs by virtue of the *ambiguity* of all levels of reality other than the limitless *real*. But it would *not* be fair to conclude that objects in the *vyāvahārika* level are of illusory nature in the way that 'objects' of dreams are, for then there would be nothing to distinguish empirical experience from dream or hallucinatory experiences. The objects of dreams, etc., do not have substantive reality, but this is something we know only from our common-sense experience. At best, their epistemological status could be said to be *anirvacanīya* or 'inexplicable', which implies an experience of something that is neither straightforwardly real nor unreal. But the material cause of the 'inexplicable' is attributed to *avidyā* or *ajñāna*, which enters, as it were, the 'space' between the object (the known) and the subject (the knower) and becomes inextricably associated with the awareness. And this leads to an alogical identification (in terms of a superimposition, *adhyāsa*), of the false intentional content with the objective 'state of affairs'. The snake-rope illusion, which also has its cause, albeit at a more degenerate level, in *avidyā*, provides a good analogy here.

On this view, the alogical identification of *ajñāna* with truly real is a phenomenon which afflicts our whole life-world, and indeed all our knowledge. What confounds our knowledge is that the subject-object relation itself is constitutive of the alogical identification, that is to say, the subjective and the objective are not free from the ambiguity of their reality status (from the the point of view of the *pāramārthika* level). True *jñāna* or *pramā* (knowledge), as we showed earlier, only arises in the context of a subject-object relation. This dichotomy of the subject and object is, therefore, indispensible for all empirical knowledge (with perhaps the single exception of the direct intuition of self-subjectivity). Then what happens to *ajñāna*?

The Advaita view is that *ajñāna* is not sufficiently opposed by *pramā* or knowledge, because the latter deals only with particulars and generals, whereas *ajñāna* is more pervasive than, say, the false snake in the instance of the snake-rope illusion. Empirical knowledge of any form thus is tinged with *ajñāna*, which imposes a limit on the knowledge, even if it does not render it false. Empirical knowledge is therefore categorically incomplete, the full truth of which could be known only if *ajñāna* is overridden in some way. Only in the transcendence of all class of objects of common experience, indeed only in the transcendence of all modes of ordinary knowing, is insight into the Real, the 'unlimited', possible. That Real is designated in Advaita by the word 'Brahman'. Still, transcendental knowledge or *Brahmavidyā* cannot be knowledge unless it too conforms to the 'object' or *thing* (in the broadest possible sense) of which it is the knowledge. This 'object', unlike the objects of ordinary knowledge, would be bereft of *adhyāsa* or the superimposition of the alogical conditional that afflicts the mundane state of affairs and their respective modes of knowing.[29]

7.9 The thrust, then, at least in Madhusūdana's thinking, at a deeper level, is a metaphysical one: Brahman does not fit into the *viṣayatva-ghaṭatvaprakārakajñātvam* configuration because Brahman is not a particular object qualified by attributes and distinctions (such as the subject-object differentiability), and is thus not revealed by the modes of the mind or by *vicāra* (thought), or, for that matter, by any of the recognised instruments of knowing. But the *analogy* with respect to the removal of false knowledge (of, e.g. 'silverness') by true knowledge (of 'mother-of-pearl') holds true here for the very reason that knowledge, in addition to having a substance for its reference, has the capacity, (a) to negate its own opposition (*qua apramā*), and (b) to oppose the prior unknownness of the object, (which error is not capable of doing, for which there is no unknown object, or if there is, it is not the correct one).

The concern, it may be noted, is every bit realist orientated, even though there is a shift in the discourse of the limits of 'knowledge' as ordinarily understood. Even Śaṅkara was consistent in this matter. His arguments evince a set of basic philosophical concerns that do underscore realist considerations. He argued that a judgement depends for its truth on the *thing* itself and not on some fanciful human idea conjured in a dream-like experience (*vikalpa, saṃpat*). Correspondence to the object accounts for true awareness, so that an awareness, such as, 'Is this a pole or a man' cannot be true, while the awareness, such as, 'This certainly is a pole' (where there is a pole) is true. Thus the truth of a judgement of real object or thing is determined by the *object* itself. Such a knowledge alone is *tattvajñāna* and it has the characteristics of being precise, definitive and unambiguous as to its real object (*vastutantra*). Such being the case, knowledge of Brahman can be no less determined by the *thing-itself*, if Brahman is also (as he believes it to be) a real existent.[30a]

Again, Śaṅkara continues, (when) knowledge is *pramāṇa*-generated, which discloses the object as it obtains in reality, only then is there *yathārtha*; and this truth has nothing to do with whether an action is to be performed, not to be performed, or performed otherwise; nor is it dependent on the subject or any moral command. Whatever the consciousness discloses, says Śaṅkara, must be related to the object, and nothing should be added to it, nor should any discrepancy vitiate it. And as the nature of objects vary so do the *pramāṇas* for arriving at their respective knowledge. Therein lies the justification of the *jñāna.*[30]

Thus a kind of realism, albeit a 'transcendentalised' realism (in the Kantian sense of *transcendental*), runs through Advaita epistemology. There is at once a genuine concern with knowing the world as it is, or as it is presented to human experience. While coming to know the world in all its particularities, one also wants to discover the condition of the possibility of all such knowledge, and, of course, ultimately the *ground* of the possibility of the being of such things as our knowledge discloses.

Beneath its search for knowledge is undoubtedly a metaphysical quest, but it would be false to suggest that a pre-determined metaphysics fundamentally dictates or determines the terms of its epistemological inquiry. The metaphysical *angst*, if one could put it this way, is 'bracketed' or set aside, while the inquiry into the means of knowledge (*pramāṇa*) and the conditions of its validity (i.e. truth and falsehood) is pursued with vigilance in a framework that is, as best as humanly possible, neutral as to some ulterior motive or to the 'ultimate' concerns, although the latter might form the 'background' for its subsequent critique. This point has not been brought out sufficiently in recent disputes on the status of *prāmāṇya* in Indian thought. Of course, this cannot be the last word on the controversy we are alluding to, which has recently surfaced in a significant and powerful way.[31] We shall be referring to this issue a number of times again.

This discussion has ramifications for a number of issues we are dealing with in this chapter, and it is an ongoing debate, which is not likely to be resolved before the present work reaches print. (I do hope to throw more light on the issues raised by looking closely also at the (Pūrva) Mīmāṃsā responses in due course of time.) We might mention in passing that what has contributed, in no small measure, to the controversy is the diverse and often confusing senses of the term '*artha*' (as in *yāthārthya*) that appear in different constructions and in various different contexts.[32]

In one context it might refer to *viṣaya* (*bhūtavastuviṣaya* as being *vastutantra*, the 'real' of the *pramāṇas*), or 'thing', 'object' (as in *pramānato'rtha, arthasārūpya, arthatathātva*), or a 'transcendent' object; in another to 'meaning', 'signification' (as in *sabdārtha, padārtha, arthavāda*), in yet another to 'purpose' or 'goal', 'satisfaction-giving', 'fulfillment' (as in *codanālakṣaṇo'rtho dharmaḥ* [*MS* I.i.2];[33] *arthībhāvanā* and *śabdībhāvanā*, or *bhavārtha*) and last but not least, the play of two senses of *artha* in *arthapratipattau pravṛttisāmarthyāt arthavat pramāṇam* (the controversial opening line of Vātsyāyana, which we referred to under 7.2 *supra*).[34]

As Mohanty points out, either way we cannot rely merely on the etymology of the term,[35] nor, for that matter, in its popular occurrences in non-philosophic contexts. For a strict critique of *prāmāṇya* we have to confine the meaning of *artha* to its occurrence in logical and epistemological discourses. (Just as we might say of the term 'mass' when talking about the sale of a quantity of gold, but at another time referring to the 'weight' of a planet in Newtonian physics, and yet at another time to the minute quantifications in the wave-particle theory or in the formula: $E = mc^2$.)

7.10 To return from this lengthy digression to the question of the conditions that give rise to truth of a cognition, Dharmarāja states, as we noted earlier, that *prāmāṇya* is generated by the sum total of the antecedent conditions that gives rise to the awareness itself (*jñānasāmānyasāmagrīprayojyam*), thus requiring no extra 'excellence' (*adhikaguṇam*) since there seems to be no constant condition for this.[36] And since no 'extra' condition is required (which it would if the genesis of the truth was dependent on some positive extrinsic condition), it follows that *prāmāṇya* is intrinsic to the awareness (in respect of its origin)—i.e. it is *svataḥ*.

Again, a further claim is made that the *prāmāṇya* of the awareness in question is apprehended intrinsically—i.e. by the very aggregate of conditions that illumines the awareness in its locus (*vṛttijñānagrāhakasāmagrī*), which is attributed to the so-called 'witness-consciousness' (*sākṣin*). The overall contention is that however little of an object we see, we experience it without fault at first encounter; and if we are mistaken, however much we see of it we remain mistaken about it, even after repeated attention is directed to it. Thus, all our awareness emerges with a truth-value attached to it. If the *tadvati tatprakārakatva* structure is intrinsic to awareness, and if it is apprehended *ab initio*, then it is consistent to claim that truth is apprehended intrinsically—i.e. the truth of a cognition is self-presented and self-evident.

The problem, as we anticipated earlier, raised by this contention is : how would doubt, error and other such awarenesses be distinguished if each *jñāna* arises as self-evidently true? Indeed, how could one even doubt such knowledge, for if truth is self-evident and the *niścayajñāna* presents itself as 'indefectible' (to use a term from Cardinal Newman)? Yet, there might be some legitimate grounds to doubt its truth and therefore suspend our conviction about it. And further, could such a knowledge ever turn out to be false if its truth is given from the beginning? Common sense would tells us that we do entertain doubt well after our conviction about some knowledge has worn off. At least in the case of doubt, it cannot be said that the awareness in question is free from all defects, for this incongruency is part of the structure of a doubtful awareness: thus it would not arise as a *pramā*.

Dharmarāja admits that both doubt and *pramā* are equally competent of being intrinsically illumined, but he suggests that doubt is actually not so apprehended (being defective),[37] This qualification, like the earlier implied qualification in regard to *bhrama*, is intended to distinguishe doubt from a true *jñāna*. But, as we argued earlier, this is not attested to in real life experience. Doubt does arise as self-evidently as any judgement, and it does not stand in need of recurrent conditions to illumine it.

The real challenge, however, as we have just stated, rests with the question of the intrinsic origin of *truth*, which would *a fortiori* make it impossible for such a *jñāna* to ever turn out to be false, not merely known to be false. To argue, as Dharmarāja does, that 'absence of defect' is one of the prior conditions for the genesis of a true *jñāna* is not sufficient for, again, as with doubt, we do discover later that we were mistaken in our certainty of some knowledge, and that it had pretensions of being *knowledge* when it was not. We are then analytically forced to say that our knowledge was not *knowledge* (*qua* true *niścayajñāna*), at best it was pseudo-knowledge.

7.11 These are questions that are not satisfactorily answered in the *svataḥ* thesis, as in any self-evidence theory of truth. But one significant advance that the thesis under consideration makes over traditional accounts is in not suggesting that the apprehension of *prāmāṇya* is 'indefectible' and permanent—thus admitting fallibility and possibility of falsification. Its disadvantage is in suggesting that the criteria it can propose are only good for disclosing error and falsity, but not for truth-making. What is true cannot be made more true; but what is not true, or only partly true, can be shown to be so.[38a] Madhusūdana wants to reject *saphalapravṛttisāmarthya* as he reasons that even in dreams there appears to be efficacy in respect of what is desired.[38] Pārthasārathi Miśra brings a similar argument against practical success as an evidence of truth, although he does admit that an awareness, whose truth appears to be self-evident now, could actually be in error. But then Pārthasārathi seems more committed to the *svataḥ* in respect of the apprehension of truth than to its origin.[39a]

Alternatively, the Advaitin might acquiesce in the suggestion that in real life no *jñāna* ever completely succeeds in disclosing its truth-value. The best that we can do is to discount those that continue to be doubted, and discard those that are subsequently falsified, or which have been found to have defects. At least, the thesis under consideration compromises on the issue of the apprehension of truth, by admitting that, while no *jñāna* arises bare without an attached truth-value, the truth-value apprehended might be incorrect and therefore the *claim* (in respect of the apprehension of its truth) would stand to be affirmed or denied. In other words, there might occur a mistaken apprehension of falsity or error for the truth of an awareness. The *apprehension* of an erroneous judgement, manifesting as a true judgement, is in this sense *intrinsic* to the awareness (while its truth is not), which is why there is certainty in the awareness of the snake mistaken for the rope (or of silver mistaken for mother-of-pearl). Doubt about the truth and apprehension of falsity occurs only in another species-moment (i.e. extrinsically).

In that case, it may be asked, why insist on truth at its origination? why not settle for truth as a claim merely asserted with the apprehension of the *jñāna*, which nevertheless still requires 'justification'? But that is not what is being conceded to, for there is no suggestion that error *qua error* (or falsity) is intrinsic to the conditions that generate the awareness, and therefore a distinction between an awareness that is true and one that is in error is *not* absent in the awareness itself, although the awareness might fail to indicate which it is. And all we need do now is to establish whether it is in error. And if the awareness is not erroneous or false, then it is true, and known to be true. That is to say, if all doubt is dispelled and the awareness is shown not to be false, this does not make its truth an extrinsic property. Need truth be added to what already has truth?

The charge that this assertion might involve a circularity can be dealt with easily: it is not that 'truth' is being defined in terms of the *what is not false* or inerrant, and 'falsity' as *what is not true*; rather, the negative description pertains only to the *apprehension* aspect, so that what is not apprehended as false and is known not to be in error is known to be true. That it is either true or false is for reasons that have nothing to do with how its truth or falsity is apprehended or made transparent.

Further, if truth can be ascertained by showing the absence of error or falsity, what need would there be of 'justification' in a *svataḥ* theory? How more *true* can it be if it is already true? Besides, *justification* is too strong a category here for it undermines the 'right to be sure', especially if the *jñāna* has been brought about through a recognised *pramāṇa*, which implies, all things being equal, *yathārthānubhava* or experience of things as they are, and the possibility of error has been excluded. That the *jñāna* is *pramāṇa*-generated is its *justification.*[39] But, we may agree that, in terms of a weaker sense of justification, if the truth of the *jñāna* is to be *asserted* it must be done so on adequate grounds in terms of the correct apprehension of its truth-value. One such ground, it might be suggested, would be the absence of *bādha* or falsification in the awareness. But does this suggestion not involve us in a circularity, for can the characteristic that is said to define truth as an intrinsic property, be invoked again as a criterion of its evidence.

The precise point of this exercise surely must be to take recourse to some ground, in addition to the supposedly self-presented characteristic (*dharma*) that would confirm or deny the characteristic. So if one of the characteristics is *abādhaditatva*, there must be some independent way of showing that this obtains in reality, not the mere presence of nonfalsifiedness in the awareness. One may need to propose potential falsifiers and make attempts to confirm these. Although, it would be fair to remark here, that there are problems with this test as well.

Briefly, a false judgement may escape falsification; another unsuspected false judgement might falsify a true judgement; a false cognition may falsify another false cognition, and the former might acquire a positive value. Thus, can these tests ever be decisive? Presumably, Advaita would press for a more 'open-ended' approach with respect to this test — a point to which we shall return shortly.

7.12 To state what is being said in another way, according to the Advaita-Mīmāṃsā thesis, since falsity is a species of *jñāna* (even if truth might not be since, in a strict sense, truth coincides with *jñāna*), there might be a way of ascertaining the falsity of a cognition. The thesis makes this possible by admitting that some extrinsic circumstances, such as vitiating defects, are responsible for error, and therefore falsity is to be ascertained extrinsically. Thus even though a direct test of confirmation of the truth is not proposed, it does provide a set of marks or criteria for the detection of possible defects (*doṣa*s), thereby exposing the source of falsity or error, as the case may be. In this way the awareness whose truth is at fault could be picked out from those that are not in error or known to be not so. Doubt is acknowledged as the prime instigator of such a process of clarification and definitiveness.

This is analogous to the preference given to the falsificationist methodology as providing the decisive test-situation for reasons of obvious difficulties with the verificationist approach.[40] Since the defects are necessarily extrinsic to the conditions that generate a *jñāna*, it should be possible to propose tests for determining the presence or the absence of falsity in this way. And thus, if it could be shown that falsity is absent, then one could say that falsification has not occurred and, by implication, the 'truth' of the cognition can be regarded to have been established beyond doubt. In fact, Advaitins, notwithstanding the commitment *in principle* to the self-evident character of truth, for practical reasons would insist that the knowledge be thoroughly scrutinised in order to be assured that it is free from any possible flaw, misconception, and deception.

Furthermore, the thesis allows for *corroboration* of the *prāmāṇya* of the *jñāna* in question in terms of the some of the marks that the rival thesis proposes for its confirmation. In particular, are mentioned the marks of *anadhigatatva*, an original or novel presence (so as to rule out re-assertion of things already known, as in memory); the satisfaction in terms of successful fulfillment of activity or some anticipated result (*saphalapravṛttisāmarthya*), and *saṃvāda* or congruence or coherence with other relevant judgement of the same kind, or with generic knowledge and evidence of a different or related kind. Another mark useful in the case of a *śabda* (word-generated) judgement would be the reliability of the author or authority (*āptabhāva, āptopadeśa*) of the utterance. And further, if inference is used to adduce a generalisation or to conclude a test, the rules and arguments invoked must be rigorous in form, and not vitiated by fallacies.

7.13 It is more than likely that the traditional Nyāya logician will express reservations about the alternative suggested, for to him what the Advaita-Mīmāṃsā thesis might succeed in doing in this way is in showing that the *jñāna* is *not known to be false, that it is in all probability true.* But since the *guṇa* ('evidence of excellence')—the only valid test of objectivity—as such has not, in principle, been demonstratively established, in principle at least, there would still be room for doubt, and as such it is not certain that such a *jñāna* is ever true (not merely taken to be true) i.e. a *pramā*. At best this is a negative approach to the problematic and thus has less of an appeal against a more positivistic account.[41]

At this point, the traditional Advaitin, like Madhusūdana, might fall back on the *svataḥ* conviction, and refrain from all argumentation.[42] This fundamental difference seems irreconciliable between the two schools, and although Dharmarāja is much persuaded by the logic of the Nyāya rejoinder, he too may appear hesitant to compromise any further. But then there is much in the Advaita view that commends itself to the Nyāya position, since historically, particularly with the increasing interaction between the Navya-nyāya ('New Logic') scholars and Advaita thinkers, the two schools were moving closer to each other, at least in their epistemological ruminations. One evidence of this, as we have already noted, is in the shared commitment to realism, another is in the almost identical terminology Dharmarāja uses to re-state the Advaita definition of *prāmāṇya*, in terms of the *tadvati tatprakārakatva* formulation. Yet another evidence is in the emphasis he places on the pragmatic, perhaps psychological, value of *prāmāṇya* as being conducive to successful consequence or satisfaction (*saṃvādipravṛtty'nūkula*), and a test for inferring false judgement, which are of immense importance to the *parataḥ* thesis as well, although with a somewhat different emphasis (as we shall consider shortly).

7.14 While on the issue of the apparent 'incommensurability' of the Advaita-Mīmāṃsā versus the Nyāya theses, it may be mentioned that some modern writers, notably, Mohanty, do suggest that a 'reconciliation' can be broached in the following terms, without putting too fine a line to this analysis. If *jñāna* is construed in the *svataḥ* thesis as ' 'knowledge' in a strong sense according to which to know is to know the truth', then *prāmāṇya* is understood as a 'predicate of knowledge'; while in the *parataḥ* thesis *jñāna* is construed in the weak sense of generic knowledge or, better, *belief*, so that *prāmāṇya* here is a 'predicate of belief'.[43] Thus, while 'true' and 'false' can be predicated to the latter as significant opposites, it makes it trivial to predicate 'true' of knowledge, which by definition must be true, and 'false' knowledge is a contradiction in terms.

But as Potter has pointed out, and Mohanty has agreed, the sharply drawn distinction between 'knowing' and 'believing' in ordinary (English) language usage does not quite work in the Indian epistemological context, although they are more compatible in the 'justified true belief' account of truth.[44]

If we forget about the qualification of 'justification' in this account—for reasons indicated earlier—and concentrate on 'true belief' as 'true *yathārthajñāna*', *qua* its structural correspondence together with the characteristics of *niścaya* (certainty), *abādhitatva* (unfalsifiedness), *anadhigatatva* (novelty), *saṃvāda* (coherence), *avyabhicārya* (unerringness), and *saphalapravṛttisāmarthya* (pragmatic/successful), (taken collectively as a vindication of the presence of *guṇatva*), we may then be coming close to a theory of truth that is as fair to the *svataḥ* as it is to the *parataḥ*. For, while the latter will propose empirical tests for truth-claim of all *jñāna*, the former will concede to the testing of any truth-claim about which doubt has been raised, or which appears to be falsified by subsequent judgement or knowledge elsewhere.

In other words, it should be possible to state the conditions under which a judgement would be true, and conditions under which it would be false. It would be vanity on our part to suppose that the Advaita philosopher would be so dogmatic as to refuse challenges to their truth-claims, even if their theory, in a strict reading, does not seem to entail that.

In a phenomenological vein, it should be possible to suspend certainty about truth of a judgement, or understanding (if derived from *śabda*), and proceed to test it for its likely falsity by looking for the conditions that would falsify it and by seeking confirmatory evidence for the potential falsifiers. Further steps may be taken to corroborate the evidence at hand. If a decisive falsification is not forthcoming, and all efforts to this end have been exhausted, and its characteristics have withstood the tests and, by implication, achieved corroboration, then one could be said to be reasonably justified in holding tenaciously to the truth of the judgement. This seems also to fit in well with Ayer's stipulation of the three necessary and sufficient conditions for knowing something to be the case -viz. 'first that what one is said to know be true, secondly that one be sure of it, and thirdly that one should have the right to be sure'.[45]

7.15 At the risk of repeating ourselves, what is important to recognise is that Dharmarāja begins by recounting the theses presented by both the schools (i.e. Mīmāṃsā and Nyāya), and appears at first to side with the Mīmāṃsā (for example in his introductory chapter, #4), and finishes his treatise on *pramāṇas* characteristically with a position that has a strong leaning towards the Nyāya. (In saying this we might bear in mind that Udayana and Jayanta compromised to accept self-evident confirmation at some point in the test-situation,[46] and that Gaṅgeśa was amenable to the falsificationist criterion.) What Dharmarāja ends up with could be called a 'combined' or *'syncretic'* theory of truth,[47] while insisting that the characteristics of truth he proposes are given not by any one but by the totality of the antecedent conditions efficacious in producing the particular cognition (*tacca jñānasāmānyasāmagrīprayojyam*). Being by nature so complex and 'holistic', no one condition can be isolated to account for the origin of the truth. Taken in one cluster, we might say, these constitute the *guṇatva* Nyāya is insistent upon (without admitting that extrinsic conditions are necessary to validate its presence). But obviously, the tests of falsity are indirectly checks on the strength or weakness of the *guṇa*.

Two considerations are to be borne in mind before we move any further by way of qualifying the tentative resolution alluded to with regard to Dharmarāja's position. First, as we just noted, the Nyāya logicians were sensitive to the problem of coming up with decisive confirmation of a true cognition through recursive tests. If the truth of a cognition is not confirmed *ab initio* then one obviously has to look to other, extrinsic, means of arriving at the confirmation. But could another cognition suffice? What would be the valid grounds for assuming, or accepting, the truth of the latter? And what guarantee is there that that cognition is not in error itself?

Any knowledge-claim (*p*) that is not self-evident, or axiomatic, would require for its validation another (*q*) and yet another bit of knowledge (*s*), or circumstantial evidence supporting this (*e*), and a rule (*r*) that will relate *e* to *s* to *q* to *p*. But *e* and *s* may in turn need further corroboration if doubts continue to arise and persist as to their own grounds or their relevance in the particular context, and so on *ad infinitum*. However, there is no reason to assume that each successive confirmation requires either to be self-evident or to be as strong as the preceding one, given that their function is to *confirm* and not to replace the core judgement. Also, a cognitive occurrence elsewhere may logically constitute a confirmation even if we are not immediately aware of its truth – i.e. if a confirmatory cognition is true it is no less successful in its task even if its truth is not directly evident. Or, the confirmation may be found in a performative outcome. To illustrate with an example, suppose I walk into an electronic hardware 'expo' and find myself fascinated by an equipment displayed there. I am not sure whether this sophisticated equipment is a typewriter or a cashregister (since the *viśeṣaṇa*, keyboard*ness*, appears as though it might belong to either *viṣayas*). I want to know which it is. Now I could right away depress a few of the familiar keys on the keyboard and keenly watch what happens. If the equipment responds by printing the letters indicated on the keys that I depress, then it is most likely a typewriter. Or maybe not. To be secure in my judgement, however, I could depress the keys with numeral markings, as I would on a cashregister. I could then look to see what kind of print is displayed, and what kind of noise is made when I manipulate other keys and buttons on the far side, as well as wonder whether a money tray might open out. I now suspect that the equipment might be a cashregister. So I would look carefully at what happens when I continue to depress keys that have arithmetical signs, such as '+', '-', '=', '$', and emulate all the familiar operations on a storekeeper's till. The numbers seem to add up, and the print-out indicates the results of the quick calculations, whereupon a tray also springs open! My impression that the equipment is a cashregister has therefore been confirmed. If I still have any doubts I could ask the sales attendant, and pick up a brochure.

Alternatively, in more general cases, there might be some other confirmatory cognitions, in terms of giving evidence to the presence of the *guṇatva* of the core judgement, which are directly evident—i.e. in someways are intrinsically true—such as could be said of certain sorts of performatory consequences. Quenching of thirst from the water one sees and reaches out for could well be a case in point. Either the thirst is quenched or it is not quenched: what further confirmation could one look for in such an instance?

Jayanta argues that people could not be fooled about trusting their day-to-day judgements. Given the common-sense appeal, it is reasonable to argue that 'second-order' judgements are capable of confirming 'first-order' judgements which may not have obtained confirmation. The confirmation may be obtained from the apprehension of some successful practical result that follows on from the 'first-order' judgement, on the grounds that what is not true does not yield successful result. It may be noted that the reasoning here is based on agreement in the mutual *absence* of the major and middle terms (i.e. *prāmāṇya* or truth and *saphalapravṛttijanakatva* or the achievement of practical success). This category of negative inference is known as *vyatireki*.

Now a confirmed 'first-order' judgement is said to become a 'familiar' instance (*tajjñāna*) that helps to confirm a similar judgement that might arise later, or corroborate the later judgement when doubt arises about its truth. In other words, if judgement *j* has achieved confirmation (through the *parataḥ* process), then when a similar cognitive situation is encountered in the future, the newly arisen judgement may receive confirmation by virtue of its *familiarity* with the earlier confirmed judgement (as, e.g. could be said to occur in recognition).

This 'extraordinary', almost intuitive, process by which verification is achieved for a later judgement is termed *tajjātīya*[48a] *('via familiarity': tajjñānaviṣayakajanyajñāna).* The previous knowledge, as it were, presents itself in the introspective apprehension (*anuvyavasāya*) of the later judgement, generated by the same set of conditions, in such as way as to 'transfer' its truth to the truth-value of the latter. The truth of the previously confirmed judgement, say, *A*, becomes the mark (*liṅga*, middle term) through which the truth of the current judgement (*sādhya*, the major premise), say, *B* is inferred.

The *vyatireki* syllogism, which, as we said, was previously used to (negatively) infer the truth, *T*, of the earlier judgement on the grounds of the non-absence of successful activity (or the successful case, *abhyāsadaśāpanna*), *C*, in respect of the particular judgement, is combined with an inference based on the agreement in presence (*anvaya*) of the two terms, and is applied to this instance, on the grounds that there is a 'familiarity' factor involved here. Intuitively, the inference might proceed in this way: What does not have *T* does not yield *C*, but *A* has yielded *C*, and *A* and *B* converge in their conditions, so *B* should also yield *C*, therefore *B* has *T*. This form of inference is known as *anvayavyatireki*. (From *tajjātīya* to *'samarthapravṛttijanakajñānajātīyatvāt'* as its *hetu*.) In other words, the inductive inference is based on the observation of agreement both in absence and presence of the middle and major terms. The reasoning may be unpacked and formulated into the following syllogism [where *P* is the major term, *M* the middle term, and *S* the minor term in the equivalent formal schema]:

What does not have *T* does not yield *C*	[no non.*P* is *M*]
but *A* has yielded *C*	[*all S* is *M*]
therefore *A* is *T*	[therefore, *all S* is *P*];
now *A* and *B* converge in their conditions	[substitute $M^{(1)}$ for *M*],
so *B* will yield *C*	[*all* $S^{(1)}$ is $M^{(1)}$]
what yields *C* has *T*	[all $M^{(1)}$ is *P*]
therefore *B* has *T*	[therefore *all* $S^{(1)}$ is *P*].

What is interesting here is the implicit suggestion that the truth of *B* is very nearly self-evident.

What is worrying here, however, is whether the indication of 'familiarity' is sufficient to account for the convergence of the conditions that generate the same truth-value in two temporally distinct judgements. As in the case of recognition, one could easily err in the intuition of the 'familiar' case, for there may be other variables that considerably differentiate one judgement from the other. On the formal aspect, there is a logical shortcoming in the *vyatireki* class of inference that seems not to have overly concerned the Indian logicians (with the exception maybe of Gaṅgeśa and some later Advaitins). It is that, if the major premise in a syllogism has a negative sign then the conclusion must also have a negative sign, so that what one may obtain, referring to the above formulation, by observing that no non.*T* yields *C* [i.e. no non.*P* is *M*], is that '*A* has not non.*T*' [i.e. no *S* is non.*P*]. But one cannot be said to observe from this that what yields *C* necessarily has *T* [i.e. *M* is *P*], which really has not been established but assumed as the major premise in the second half of the syllogism. The validity of this affirmative universal is wanting in the above syllogism, while the validity of the negative universal remains intact. Thus, by the convergence of *A* and *B*, which becomes the middle premise, all that we can obtain is that '*B* has not non.*T*' [i.e. no $S^{(1)}$ has non.*P*]. What it shows is that the later judgement is *not false*, or rather not known to be *false*, but its truth has yet to be confirmed. And pending this confirmation we can only say that *B* is not known to be false.

What we are questioning here is the claim that *anvayavyatireki*, as an affirmative inference on the grounds of the familiarity of a latter judgement with an earlier confirmed judgement, is what is involved in the *tajjātīya* case. This claim does not really hold weight for the reason that the truth-value of the previous judgement is itself dependent upon a *vyatireki* inference, which gives a conclusion with a negative sign. Unless the *vyatireka* is resolved in such a way as to yield a more positive conclusion in respect of the truth-value of the earlier judgement, the *anvayavyatireki* cannot be said to succeed where its key premise relies upon the truth-value of the earlier judgement. For the sake of logical precision, what the *vyatireki* delivers is that if *A* yields *C* it is not non.*T*, and therefore the *anvayavyatireki* cannot go any further than to allow one to say (in respect of *B*) that *B* is *not* non.I; the latter, for all practical purposes, cannot be simply construed as having *T*.

Although the following analogy might be a bit stretched here, we could say that the procedure described above is a little like the use of inductively established premise in a deductive reasoning where the truth-value of the premise strengthens, or weakens, the conclusion. However, just as there are problems with accepting reliance upon an inductively established premise in a deductive inference, even if we grant some virtue to the *vyatireki* argument, there might still be questions about the exact relation between the extrinsically established truth of the earlier judgement and the inferred truth of the later judgement in the *tajjātīya* model. These difficulties apart, however, the *vyatireki* inference does have one significant advantage, as already hinted at in the foregoing discussion, which will be brought out in the discussion of the pragmatist interpretation of *prāmāṇya*. But the Mīmāṃsā counter-thesis that we must therefore accept the truth of the earlier judgement to be intrinsically revealed in the *jñātatā*-apprehension of the judgement does not help resolve the issue in any more convincing way.

7.17 To take a more conciliatory approach, one implication of the above analysis would be that one could begin by assuming the core judgement to be *false*, and then proceed to show that it is *not* false. It might be sufficient in some instances to be convinced that a judgement is not false, perhaps only that it is not known to be false even if it cannot be shown to be true. A false judgement, as we noted earlier, is defined as *ayathārtha tu arthavyabhicārī apramāṇajaḥ*[48]—that which does not conform to the property of the object or thing it is an awareness of. A 'proof' can then be set up comprising a number of supporting and auxiliary hypotheses derived from the judgement. These hypotheses are then tested. This may be formalised in the following way:

If $a \rightarrow b$,
for a judgement j = aF because G is b.
Assume it is false = $-aF$ because G is $-b$.
$-b$ iff $-(q + t)$
q has s but not f, etc.

Suppose the tests fails to show f, but shows s, and its locus is q. There is independent evidence that q, together with t, does occur. But this is opposed to $-(q + t)$, which in turn denies $-b$.

Thus a confirmation of $-b$ has not arisen; and if b is not negated, then a is also not negated (from $a \rightarrow b$): it follows that the j has not been shown to be false. And this much is enough for the judgement to lead to some appropriate activity, if one looks to knowledge as a guide to one's activities.

Gaṅgeśa uses just such an argument against the Mīmāṃsaka who tries to persuade his opponent to the view that the there has to be incontrovertible certainty about such a judgement, and that given the *anavasthā*, *regressus ad infinitum*, charge, the self-evidence theory of truth would have to be accepted.[49a] But the charges have been answered satisfactorily, and Gaṅgeśa's final position reinforces the 'syncretic' theory of truth, which involves a complicated process of ascertaining the *yāthārthya* of a judgement *via* a transparent secondary cognition (*anuvyavasāya*) (as distinct from a first-order apprehension of its truth). In terms of this theory, then, a judgement which is not known to be false, and has been corroborated against doubt, could be taken to be true (*avisaṃvādy'nubhavaḥ pramā*).[49] Such a move, it appears, was foreshadowed by Rāmādvaya,[50] which compares favourably with that of the later Nyāya view and is undoubtedly characteristic of Dharmarāja's own approach.

One of the tests referred to in the preceding formalised example could, in large part, involve *saphalapravṛttisāmarthya*—i.e. satisfactory or the successful fulfillment of activity. (*Pravṛtti* implies activity or practice, and *sāmarthya* its capacity to be realised.)

But there is some dispute about the precise interpretation of what this enterprise entails. If suppose the *jñāna* is shown to lead to satisfaction or successful activity, should it be inferred that the *jñāna* led to successful result *because* it is true, or whether that it *is* true because it led to successful practice? Would it fail to be true if there was no successful activity? Or more radically, is its truth wholly in its satisfaction principle? But it is no part of the definition that every true *jñāna* must of necessity lead to successful practice, only that it might be conducive to *pravṛtti* (pragmatic move), and perhaps also that only a true *jñāna* can succeed in leading to satisfactory working.[51] So that if there is successful practice, this can only have a confirmatory or corroborative value, but it cannot be taken to constitute the truth of the cognition; to concede the latter would be to compromise the theory of which this mark (*dharma*) is a contingent consequence. At best, 'workability' or *pravṛttisāmarthya* is the *ratio cognoscendi* but not the *ratio essendi* of truth. Thus what is regarded as *a* test of truth or the potential outcome of a true judgement (in terms of its 'workability'), cannot at the same time, be the *definition* of truth. And there are further reasons for this consideration.

For one, the successful result or satisfaction can only occur at some future moment and is therefore not a *given* in the awareness; secondly, some *jñāna*, by nature, may lead to no productive outcome, since their 'object' might be non-empirical, or no action might follow. One may want to contemplate a truth for its own sake and not expect any extrinsic satisfaction or activity from it.[52] Potentially, most true *jñānas* may be *conducive* (*anukūla*) to unwavering activity (*niṣkampa pravṛtti*) or satisfaction; but if they do not lead to this, or are frustrated in the attempt, it would not automatically constitute a decisive falsification of these *jñānas*. And if there is satisfactory consequence we might conclude no more than that the cognition is now known *not* to be false, in as much as it was able to 'pick out' the object to which it is cognitively related. That is all that is required in the 'syncretic' theory of truth and is consistent with Gaṅgeśa's alternative proposal.

7.18 Keśava Miśra argues that for practical purposes one may draw up an inference based on negative generalisation (*vyatireki*). When a man looking for water has the cognition of water, he reasons in the following way (in setting up a working hypothesis): Either that it is *samartha*, 'fit' or 'capable of leading to satisfactory result', or that it is not *samartha*.[53] If there is *samartha* then the cognition is true (on the premise that 'that which is not true does not yield *samartha*'); if (there is) no *samartha* the cognition is false.[54] (We should note also that 'satisfaction' is understood not necessarily in terms of meeting or satiating some psychological need or drive, but rather the practical accomplishment of some real 'state of affairs'. Thus, it involves an ostensible pragmatic rather than a subjective consideration.)

Now if experience confirms that the liquid quenches thirst, i.e. it is *sāmarthya* or is empirically productive in satisfying thirst, then the first inference is rendered valid; at least, he could be confident that his judgement is not false. But if no satisfactory result is observed to follow, he has good grounds to assume that the cognition is not known to be true, until some other evidence can show otherwise. Keśava Miśra goes on to suggest that when confronted again with a similar cognition, before seeking a practical confirmation of the (newly generated) cognition, the man may reason, *on the strength of the analogy* with the previous cognition, that this cognition will be as effective as the previous one, as it bears similarity in all respects with the previous cognition, and dissimilarity with others.[55] This alone is enough to drive him towards the object of his cognition.

To take the example further in order to illustrate the workings of the 'syncretic' theory in the case of a *śabda*-generated judgement, consider the plight of the the thirsty person wandering through the desert. He cannot trust his perception any more, for each time he moved towards a spot further on where he 'saw' water, it turned out to be a mirage. Then he comes across another traveler who, pointing to a spot nearby, tells him 'that is water'. His judgement bears the structure *aF* (where *a* is *that something* liquid, *F* is water*ness*). The thirsty person might be said to reflect in the following way.

He would like to disbelieve the judgement he has been led to in the present circumstance, for all he knows, the spot may turn out to be yet another mirage. But, by the same token, he may have something to loose if the judgement turned out to be true. On balance, the traveler seems quite reliable and, from his other utterances, appears to have good knowledge of this region. But the thirsty person still has some doubts. Well, at least he could assume that his judgement has not yet been shown to be false, although it might well be false; but he does not know that, so he should give benefit to the conviction or doubt to the contrary. He could argue with himself that if that is water, it should have the *guṇatva (G)* of *waterness* (*b*). And if it has *b* it should quench his thirst (*q*), as well as take the dryness away from his mouth (*t*); furthermore, it should not be like, say, fire (*f*), which burns the mouth, but perhaps like milk, which has a rather soothing effect (*s*).

Alternatively, he could assume that whatever he finds is not going to be like milk, it will not quench his thirst nor take the dryness away from his mouth. He then decides to move towards the spot the traveller has pointed to. On reaching the spot he initiates the activity with his hands stretched out and his palms together, as he would when reaching out to scoop water running from a tap. What follows next is either of two events: he feels the sensation of liquid sipping down his throat that at once quenches his thirst; or, he feels no sensation of any liquid passing his tongue and his thirst is not quenched. If it is the latter of the two, then in that case he could conclude that there is no evidence of *s*, there is no satisfactory result to the effect either *q* and *t*, which implies that there is no *b* either; thus there is no good reason for him to give up his initial doubt. However, if it is the former, the situation would be something different. The conditions have been fulfilled, although he cannot immediately conclude that he knows the judgement to be true. But if there is evidence of *s*, and a satisfactory result to the effect *q* and *t*, then, at least, he could infer that there is good grounds to believe that there is *b*, and it would follow that he has good reason to discard his doubt and say with some *assuredness* (*niścaya*) that he knows the judgement not to be false.

He could go a step further. He might look to other 'tests' and corroborative support. For instance, he might try to light it with a match, or take some of the liquid back with him and run positive and negative electrodes through it. If one of the gases collected from one of the electrodes ignites with a match, then he could claim to have found a decisive confirmation of the truth of his judgement. And he has a 'right to be sure' about this.

7.19 Others may want to argue that in the case of the *śabda*-generated cognition, we could say that, the thirsty person makes a similar move in light of his previous experience of water. Thus, it may be said that, he proceeds towards the spot not because he wants to have his cognition confirmed by finding *samartha*, but that he proceeds *because* he is convinced that his cognition will bear out the *samartha* he has deduced on the basis of previous experience. That is to say, because he is sure that his activity or behavioural disposition is 'justified', and that, given the reliablity of the testimonial evidence, he has a right to be sure about this. We may as well say that he knows his judgement to be true.[56] It follows, incidentally, that the systematic determination of the sentence-meaning by the meanings of its constituent parts and construction is not enough : we are also to be concerned with how the meanings so determined are *understood*, and as a meaning-whole how it is understood to be *true*. The criteria for its probable truth-character is to be kept in mind when such evaluations are made.[57]

Naiyāyikas, as we have seen, will have little difficulty in accepting the rider that each time one understands a sentence one should be in a position to say what would be the characteristics of this understanding if it is to be true, and what if it is to be false. Advaita would go along with this principle, urging at the same time that ideally the utterance understood need not be unnecessarily restricted to the empirical realm, for there may be 'states of affairs' or "facts" (in the broad Wittgensteinian sense) that transcend empirical experience and go beyond the purview of perceptual experience and inference, and it may yet be successful in presenting the non-empirical. Utterances about moral values, it could be argued, in some instances belong to this class, and though they might not make reference to 'real objects', they could be pointing to some state of affairs in the world, such as the attitude, disposition or behaviour of the individual.

Some extra-empirical considerations

7.20 There are other instances too, some of which may pertain to so-called 'deep experiences'. Insights and intuitions from sources other than reason and empirical experiences about matters too subtle to be passed over are clear instances of these. And they may derived be from expressions, literal and metaphorical, some of which might be in the *śāstras* or scriptures (the well-known *koan*-like *mahāvākyas* or exponibles of the Upaniṣads are good examples that come to mind here). The hermeneutical tradition developed by Mīmāṃsā, and adopted with some modifications by Advaita, for interpreting such sentences are usually invoked to facilitate understanding *qua meaningfulness* of such non-conventional and non-conversational sentence-types.[58] Likewise, when Sabara takes up the enquiry into *dharma*.

What we should be able to say now is that with regard to the property of any recognised or accredited *pramāṇa*, the emergence of particular instances of false awareness through such a *pramāṇa* need not to be taken to constitute a falsification of the entire *modus operandi* of the *pramāṇa*, just as one irrational consequence does not render the whole system of belief from which it is derived irrational.[59] There is obviously room for doubt but not a hasty rejection of the system in its entirety. Paradigms in science are not discarded with the appearance of failed predictions and a large number of anomalies; there is always the possibility of internal adjustments and attempts to bring about greater coherency and cogency within the different parts of the system. No methodological program is so simple as to be rejected off-hand merely because it does not seem "to fits the facts". *Ad hoc* devices are at times used so as to remedy certain methodological defects and to enable the program to complete its operation. If after that it continues to fail, and an intolerably large degree of anomalies and defects continue to vitiate the operation, then there would be reason to assume that the program is degenerating and there would be grounds to dismantled it, possibly for a complete overhaul. Then again, with the emergence of a strong and successful alternative program the current one may be considered fit for discarding. Some antecedents of the program may, of course, remain as 'die-hards' and continue to be used in the alternative program. This analogy with the scientific process is not exaggerated, we believe, for no epistemological discourse is to be seen in a narrow context of the few instances that do not appear to tie in with the system as a whole in virtue of the principles enunciated therein.

7.21 We might also exercise some caution before we surmise that the Indian theorists were any less aware of the practical difficulties in fulfilling the varied conditions for the successful achievement of a *pramāṇa*-derived knowledge. There is awareness, for instance, of the variables and adventitious factors that could vitiate the efficient operation of a particular *pramāṇa*, and of the necessary steps to be taken to guard against any methodological deficiencies. And there might be consideration to limit the extent of such knowledge or understanding within a specific context, so that its scope does not reach out to areas where it does not have competence, and its falsification or its confirmation would then be sought in terms of the more accessible methodological tools at disposal. Doubt obviously will often drive one to this; but such doubt is to be regarded as a rather healthy disposition, otherwise, as Jayanta pointed out, error may flounder unabashed.[60]

In this regard, Śaṅkara, for example, was adamant that no amount of scriptural assertion would justify that fire is not hot, or is wet or whatever.[61a] Thus it is possible, and perhaps imperative, to reject scriptural claims that are in flagrant contradiction to what is known to be true in common experience or what reason could establish for us. If Śaṅkara downplays the role of reason. sometimes rather cagely—as has been pointed out by a number of writers[61]—it is not because he wants to oppose reason against the verdict of scripture, but because he believed that reason (*tarka*) does not have the scope to extend to areas of enquiry (such as self consciousness) for which we have to look to other possible sources. He thought scriptures embodied insights from such other sources. That he might have overestimated the worth of these insights does not diminish the force of his transcendental strategy (no more than Kant's preparedness to believe in the existence of angels diminished the force of his transcendental dialectic, by which he attempted to map the 'bounds of reason').[62]

These and similar considerations have led us to the argument that it would be methodologically more convenient to look for likely falsification and where possible confirmation, and where there is conviction of certainty (given the modified *svataḥprāmāṇya* thesis), a further corroboration of the *śābdabodha* generated. If there is still doubt then one could inquire further to see why the *pramāṇa* failed and what sorts of defects (*doṣa*), faults and flaws have impeded its success. Which also means, of course, that one should be prepared to make adjustments in proportion to the degree of failure and difficulties encountered with respect to the particular awareness derived. Likewise, where success and fulfillment of the purposive or goal-directed awareness is in sight, humility and acceptance become prudential dispositions. It is clear that intellectual integrity is very much a prerequisite for there to be any progress in such an approach to understanding.

7.22 In bringing the discussion on truth to a conclusion, let us move to consider how the major characteristics of truth in terms of the definition of *pramanya* enunciated (here and in earlier parts) are seen to apply to judgements derived from hearing utterances.

First, the truth condition, which, as we explained is given, the following proposition: *tatprakārakatvam* (or more precisely: *tadvati tatprakārakānubhavo yathārthaḥ*). In a narrow and restricted sense this lays down that a judgement is true on condition that the state of affairs as understood does occur. In other words, we must be able to say that the judgement 'corresponds with the facts' and that these *facts qua* state of affairs actually obtains. (We need not go over the qualifications on the notion of 'correspondence' that were added in earlier discussion.)[63] In a broader sense this condition is to be interpreted as one that requires conformity of the features of the judgement with the qualifying features of the 'object' or reality being made aware of. For instance, if one has an awareness of a typewriter, the object of that awareness (*viṣaya*) should have all the features of the typewriter, and not, say, of a calculating machine sitting nearby.

Is it, however, self-evident that the said state of affairs actually obtains in reality? We have seen that the *svataḥprāmāṇya* thesis has no hesitation in giving a positive response to this question, with the proviso that the *modus operandi* is a recognised *pramāṇa*. But even if something x is evident, does it necessarily follow that it might not turn out to be false? It might appear *evident* from hearing John say that it has been raining (because the weather report the day before said it would rain, the ground and the window look wet, and, besides, it has been cloudy all day). On further investigation, however, it is discovered that the sprinkler had been turned on accidentally by someone and that had caused the ground and the window to be wet. Thus what is evident is not always true; and this objection becomes even more relevant when we consider that the state of affairs referred to, suggested, or asserted, by *śabda* may not be such as to be evident in the ordinary sense in which we understand some state of affairs to be evident – i.e. that *facts* are not present in that moment for there to be direct evidence of correspondence (or *tadvati*, conformity). Either the *śābdabodha* has then to be rejected, or some other characteristics would have to be looked at that would vindicate the judgement.

Given this difficulty, in qualifying and tempering the *svataḥprāmāṇya* thesis with the *parataḥ* thesis, we suggested that the characteristics of truth shared between Advaita-Mīmāṃsā and Nyāya could be utilised as 'criteria' of evidence in terms of the conditions under which an utterance is understood and understood to be true. This procedure is adopted not so much to adjudicate the truth or falsity of a judgement as to measure the degree of positive and negative support it is able to muster through the various tests proposed. This might be compared with Strawson's remarks: 'To know a sentence *p* is to be aware of the conditions under which *p* is understood and the conditions under which the proposition it expresses would be true.' We shall consider the application of the following major criteria.

7.23

a. *Abādhitatva* (*jñānaprāmāṇyaṃ nāma abādhitārtha viṣayakatvam*).[64] We can call this the falsificationist criterion. This criterion requires that the judgement ought not to have been contradicted or falsified by knowledge pertaining to the same state of affairs. One implication of this test is that it helps to prevent a premature rejection of judgement whose direct confirmation has not been forthcoming (in terms of the evidence of *guṇatva*, etc.)

Thus, rather than rejecting the *śābdabodha* about which some doubt may have arisen one has to see if there is some judgement based on evidence either from another, or maybe from the same, *pramāṇa*, which falsifies the *śābdabodha* and therefore validates the doubt. It is sometimes easier to find evidence that refutes a cognition than one that confirms it. It is not surprising, therefore, that this particular methodological principle has given rise to much debate and has been recommended widely in current philosophy of science.[65] Its many difficulties have also been acknowledged, particularly in respect of practical application of the test. Various such questions are raised such as: when has a falsification been constituted, by what means has it occurred, how is it decided, and what are its ramifications for the larger body of knowledge within which such a theory is placed?[66]

Śrīharṣa and Citsukha raised similar problems with this criterion. We had occasion to look at some of these earlier on in the discussion. By far, the strongest point made in their critique was that we can never be sure that a judgement taken to be true now will not be falsified at a later time. But that the judgement might be falsified is a sufficient acknowledgement of the viability of the falsificationist criterion.[67] (This surprising admission might go to show that not all Advaitins adhered rigidly to the *svataḥ* thesis: there are sceptics within even the apparently more orthodox and self-assured schools of Indian thought!)

Similarly, there are problems associated with interpreting the sentence-generated judgement for its application in one context and its non-extension in another. There are questions raised as to how evidence from, say, perception can be commensurable with a *śābdabodha*, which may make reference to a state of affairs that is not categorically about what is perceptible but maybe about matters that are said to go beyond common-sense experience. Such problems arise especially in regard to scriptural sentences, which purport often to be about unknowables, about which, however, there might be some insight possible through some sort of 'uncommon experience' or 'intuition'; or they may be expressive of certain values and 'significances' or 'authenticities' that are evidently not given in ordinary human discourse.

b. Anadhigatatva : tatra loke vede. . .apūrvatayā prāmāṇyam[68] – This criterion states that 'both, in the case of ordinary or common and scriptural (Vedic) sentences there is said to be the character of novelty (of the what is understood from these sentences)'. That is to say, the *śābdabodha* should illumine some state of affairs or some aspect or other of enquiry about which there is no awareness or previous knowledge. This is an important requirement, for otherwise a method such as *śabda* could be merely engaged in repeating what is already known or what can be known through other *pramāṇas*, and that would render *śabda* fortuitous. But then, sometimes there are things we might come to know through other available sources, but as yet have not managed to; here too, 'testimony', if it does not given us that precise knowledge, may inspire, as it has in some instances, a different attitude and approach to the problem.

It is the excessive repetition of what we do 'see' or are already reflecting on that renders *śabda* a rather trivial source. It is because of the repetitive feature of recollection through memory (*smṛti*) that recollected judgement is not regarded as a *pramāṇa*. (Paradoxically, we might be reminded, memory, but not verbal testimony, is accepted as an accredited source of knowledge in traditional western philosophy).[69] Though in a sense, especially in the case of common or *laukika*, as distinct from scriptural sentences, there is bound to be repetition, as Dharmarāja acknowledges, for in such a case a listener *A* comes to know something that *B* is already acquainted with, through understandingly hearing a sentence utterance from *B*. But the repetition is not in respect of *A*'s understanding, but rather betrays a sense of complete novelty to *A* who might otherwise have remained totally ignorant of the matter in question.

The character of 'novelty', like that of novel predictability in science, remains an essential feature of what is to be 'new' knowledge. Sometimes, however, something quite new is discovered when one pays concerted attention to what is heard, and it yet need not be a repetition of what another person has known as, for example, in the case of utterances which are conjectures. According to a much-acclaimed account of the scientific methodology, scientists are said to present 'conjectures' to the scientific community which are then developed into well-constructed research programmes, experimentally tested so that there might be some justifiable grounds for their acceptance.[70]

For our purposes, this would mean that the validity of the *śābdabodha* generated by the conjecture would have to be established if it is to be acceptable as 'new' knowledge which was hitherto not part of the community knowledge. The 'conjectures' of the scientists in that regard do not necessarily lead to a repetition of what is already known, and less so when they were confirmed experimentally : they are thought to disclose something *new*, and apart from making and confirming novel predictions, may even spark off a revision of a whole cluster of hitherto received knowledge. They are even said to bring about 'revolutions' which result in a 'switch' from one paradigm to another.[71] The implication of this for *śabdapramāṇa* is that, suppose a *śābdabodha* is generated by some conjectured utterance, then it would have to be established that at least a 'novel' knowledge is in the making, which was hitherto not part of the community knowledge. And in a similar vein, for *methodological* purposes, scriptural sentences could be regarded to be making 'conjectures' whose fuller implications await to be worked out. (We are making these generalisations in respect merely of sentence-types; how it is worked out in respect of sentence-tokens would need to be considered carefully in the appropriate *context* of the utterance and in concert with the other criteria that have been stipulated.)

Admittedly, as in any system of philosophy there are always a number of trivially conceived conjectures—the products oftentimes of 'hunches' and 'guesses'—but that does not preclude there being some worthy 'conjectures' that may arise from deep reflection on philosophical and religious problems of some magnitude and value. Thus the school-theorist pleads that before *śruti* sentences are rejected, or for that matter accepted hastily they deserve to be considered in terms of what they might be attempting to convey, and what they might mean, how their truth or falsity is to be established, and, indeed, what new light they might throw on what is presently not known. Even if this might be achieved dialectically or *via negativa*.

c. *Asaṃdigdhatatva*[72] (or *niścaya*) : tenacity of conviction or certainty of the judgement arrived at. According to this criterion, there should be no doubt (*saṃśaya*) about what has come to be known, which is to say that there should be conviction (*niścaya*) that the state of affairs given with the understanding or awareness obtains. As Professor Potter puts it succinctly: 'Now a *pramā* must be a believing, a *niścaya jñāna*. . . That is, it must be an awareness involving conviction or felt certainty, though it should be emphasized that this believing which is a *niścayajñāna* is an episodic state and not a disposition to assent or something along those lines (as belief is frequently analysed in Western thought [*sic*]).'[73] Thus if doubt arises, one would have to retrace the steps of the process to locate the source of the suspected error or defect. Holding on to a judgement with tenacity in the face of contradiction and opposition from what is already known and well-established would, of course, be an irrational move.

Nevertheless, it is not being suggested, as we argued earlier, that certainty is all that is necessary for the judgement to succeed in its claim. *Niścaya* is one mark, albeit a very important one, and in some instances clinches an issue when there is no good reason to slip into the dubious process of *deinfinitum*. But the *tenacity* has to be shown and rationally defended rather than being merely felt as a psychological disposition. Otherwise, one could not claim the 'right to be sure' about anything that one thinks one knows or has a belief about.

d. *Saṃvāda*[74] : congruency or coherency with other body of knowledge or evidence of the same kind. This is another important consideration, for what is the point of any judgement that does not seem to be related to anything else that we know, or does not cohere with the body of knowledge on aspects of the matter already enquired into.

If suppose, a scriptural utterance tells us something about the self, but this understanding bears little or no relation to the awareness of the self through our subjective processes, and, in fact, depends on an uneconomical postulation of properties and extensions that do not seem to answer to any description, actual or possible. In such instances there would be good reason to doubt that the judgement has *saṃvādaka*. Again, that there might be *saṃvāda* would not be enough to settle the dispute, for there can be any number of internally cogent and coherent system of judgements that are however not about any particular state of affairs (as, say, in mathematics). It is, therefore, important to keep in the forefront the overall perspective of the truth condition of which *saṃvāda* constitutes one obvious criterial mark.

Since a symmetry between 'correspondence' and 'coherence' is not assumed, it is quite legitimate to include coherence as a condition of truth within the broader parameters of a basically correspondence *qua tadvati tatprakārakatva* test. If Gaṅgeśa rejected *saṃvāda* he might have done this on the assumption that coherence was being proposed as a self-sufficient condition of truth. And he probably rejected the other conditions we are examining here on a similar questionable assumption.

Now we come to what is perhaps the most controversial of the criterion that can be proposed for the problem in hand. It is not because this particular criterion is considered to be weak in its scope, but rather because that is supposed to be so strong that it has tended to usurp the truth condition approach and proposed itself, in a manner of speaking, as a theory of truth in its own right, or so it has been understood by some writers. Since we have already gone over this ground we need not dwell at length on this here, though some recapitulation is unavoidable.

e. Pravṛtti-sāmarthya[75] : being productive of successful result or leading to satisfaction. That is to say, *śābdabodha* should lead to some fruitful or satisfactory fulfillment of some practical need in the appropriate context. We often use such pragmatic tests in daily life where we hope to achieve adequate results and find fulfillment in whatever we undertake : more so if we are taking another's word for it. Similarly, *śabdapramāṇa*, interpreted in this way, fulfills a function when it can lead to successful achievement or satisfaction in respect of the 'object' or state of affairs about which knowledge is being sought.

'Does it work?' is a query often raised in our day-to-day living, and from the moment an infant learns to hold a toy-object to the moment one is on the death-bed wondering if the penultimate medication will keep one alive. In the later case, the success or failure of treatment determines its worth or otherwise.

7.24 William James and other pragmatists developed a theory of truth based on a consideration similar to this, for whom truth consisted in a kind of satisfaction, and falsity in a kind of dissatisfaction. But James also insisted that truth entailed that there is 'correspondence with the facts'.[76] In other words, our judgement would lead to satisfaction only if there is correspondence with the state of affairs about which it is a judgement. But, as Chisholm points out, along the lines we have remarked earlier: 'The satisfactions or dissatisfactions to which the man's belief may lead. . .will be a function, in part, of his *other* beliefs. And these other beliefs may combine with a true belief to produce dissatisfaction, or with a false belief, to produce satisfaction. Thus the belief that there are tigers in India [which James uses as an example], even if it is true, need not lead to satisfaction (the man may encounter tigers in India, but mistakenly think that they are lions or that he is not in India) and it may even lead to dissatisfaction (he goes to Syria, finds no tigers, and mistakenly believes that he is in India).'[77]

Thus, it is not the case that there is fulfillment or satisfaction of a state of affairs if and only if the state of affairs occurs, and non-satisfaction if such a state of affairs does not occur.[78a]

If the foregoing proposition is true then satisfaction or 'workability' is not an adequate measure of truth in terms of the 'correspondence' condition. But this particular problem with most versions of pragmatism is too often overlooked (except perhaps in Peirce, who is a much more rigorous realist than James, Dewey or Pepper [78]). A weaker version of pragmatism may stipulate that if there is no satisfaction then one could be reasonably secure in inferring that there is no correspondence (on the generalisation [i] that if *p* is not true *p* does not work), and that if there is satisfaction then one might be reasonably secure in inferring that there is correspondence (on the generalisation [ii] that *p* works if and only if *p* is true). And it might be added that neither inference would be sufficient unless it is corroborated by other relevant considerations and evidential support.

Professor Karl Potter, as we said a while earlier, wants to argue that the 'workability' principle (as against, say, the truth conditional theory), has been the major thrust in the Indian quest for truth, in however many different forms it might have appeared. Like James, Potter does not want to deny the importance of the 'correspondence' notion in the Indian theory of truth, but he argues that the 'real' (*artha*) to which there is to be correspondence or 'equiformity' (with regard to the *tadvati tatprakārakatvam* description of the judgement), pursued in Indian thought, 'is an ontologically-neutral hierarchy of values'[79]. And this hierarchy of values, he suggests, fundamentally 'stems from a graded acquiescence of drives, and thus satisfaction led to by purposive activity relative to each drive in the appropriate context.'[80] And from this he reflects that, whether the relation of the content of an awareness to satisfaction of a drive only occurs when the content corresponds to a real object, or whether it does not is not pertinent to the *meaning* of the term *prāmāṇya*. In itself, this is a valid question, but however it may be answered, 'it does not affect the appropriateness of using the term *prāmāṇya* when the satisfaction-relation is believed to obtain.'[81]

Surely, one might say, such an approach basically has to do with adjudicating the satisfaction-relation between those purposive activities (*pravṛtti*) undertaken in such a context that are productive 'of acquiescence of drives and thus satisfaction' and those that are not. [*ibid*, p11] In Potter's terms, it is a rationalisation of a 'workability' consideration with a weighted concern for a 'means-to-end' fulfillment than for a considered theoretical analyses of truth and falsity (i.e. in terms of the conditions under which our thoughts correspond to reality or not).[82]

Professor Potter, however, is aware of the pertinent questions that arise in this regard—viz.: Is a judgement, *p*, *true* because it works? Or does the judgement, *p*, *work* because it is true? And he admits that it cannot be had, as it were, both ways. But in his understanding, the Indian wisdom is decidedly in favour of an affirmative response to the latter question—i.e. *p* works because *p* is true (generalisation ii. above).[83] Well, if Potter is sure about this ground, then there is no real issue, for he is not now suggesting, as he seemed to be earlier, that a judgement is adjudicated to be true merely on the grounds of its workability or satisfaction-fulfillment *qua* satisfaction. If, on the other hand, he was asserting that the tradition vouchsafed a positive response to the former question, then the same sorts of objections as raised against James' theory would apply here. In addition to these there are some difficulties we intimated earlier, such as: how good an estimate is a measure of 'drive-satisfaction' to the testing of *yāthārthya* or 'equiformity to the state of affairs in reality'? (Or, as Pārthasārathi Miśra quipped: what is the difference, even in dream state one has the satisfaction of drinking water [when there is no real water], or the satisfaction of meeting a lover!)

But evidently, Professor Potter is careful to retain the basic structure of the Indian theory of truth in terms of the *tadvati* definition. The difference he sees is that the 'real' (*artha*) in the definition is itself a notion that is to be defined and interpreted within the parameters of a notion of 'workability' or 'acquiescence of drives and thus satisfaction'.[84] Simply put, if the reason for some judgement working or satisfying is because it is true, but it is true because it conforms to an *artha* ('object-value'),[85] then its workability is in virtue of the *artha*, and we cannot have an *artha* that does not lead to satisfaction,[86] or that has nothing to do with satisfaction in terms of a set of values and goal-directions.[87] Thus the key question is whether the satisfaction-relation obtains or not in the judgement, and if it obtains (setting aside Chisholm's strong reservations for now) then, in all probability, there is *arthatathātva*[88] or the relevant state of affairs is said to have occurred.

Still, there is a problem here. What this reading seems to have done is to have reduced *artha* to an unequivocal rendering of all the various uses and occurrences of *artha* (in its etymological root-sense)[89] to some one meaning of what satisfies or frustrates a 'purpose', 'goal object', or 'drive'. While, as we pointed out earlier, *artha* has other meanings, the most specific one (in the epistemological context) being *viṣaya.*[90] These pertain to two different levels of discourse, and though there might be some overlap, they are not identical (just as the term 'mass' means different things in Newtonian mechanics and in wave-particle physics).

Secondly, as Professor Mohanty has rightly argued, it is not clear that *artha* is ontologically-neutral, and therefore that truth is free of the concept of any ontological commitment (i.e. so as to render it neutral as between realism and idealism).[91] This may be so in most Buddhist approaches to truth, and to some extent in (Pūrva) Mīmāṃsā (in which perhaps even *svarga* ['heaven'], the ultimate *lakṣaṇo'rtha* of all injunctions, is the *summum bonum* of all earthly values). But one would have to show that the *padārthas* of Nyāya-Vaiśeṣika and the *prakṛti*-extensions of Sāṃkhya (both of which influenced Vedānta cosmology), are in any sense empty terms that upon analyses do not answer to any ontological descriptions and can be replaced by absolute value terms. Likewise, for *ātman* and Brahman, in most versions of Vedānta.[92]

Thirdly, there is tendency in Potter's strategy of reducing the *definiendum* (*prāmāṇya*) to the *definiens* (the elements *w, x. . .z,* in terms of which *T* is defined or explicated), and it is here (in the *definiens*) that 'workability' makes a significant occurrence as one of the more important discriminatory marks of the *definiendum*. So that:

if T = Df. w, x. . .z; then one cannot say $w \rightarrow T$.

Finally, on this point, the satisfaction-relation is not always the worthiest consideration when deciding on a judgement (or on a belief). Like utilitarianism, pragmatism has the weakness of supposing that there can be definitive measures of satisfaction-dissatisfaction, pleasure and pain, gains and losses, and that incontrovertible decisions could be based on such judgements.[93] This sort of a rigid measure, especially if it turns into being prescriptive, could be a hindrance to moral imperatives and more rationally intuitive grounds for accepting or rejecting a judgement; and this is no less pertinent in the realm of values, once the necessity of 'object' has been dispensed with in the notion of *objectivity.*

Thus, an objective intuition in regard to a state of affairs may not conform to any pragmatic consideration, however persuasive that might be. Surely, it might pay to have each and every melancholic and manic-depressive client take substances that induce in them a state of semi-euphoria or a tranquilising effect. But since this treatment does not get to the root of the anguish, and does not prevent the recurrence of the condition for which each is being treated (in asmuch as it only works towards suppressing the symptoms) this treatment would not be fair on the clients concerned. It may serve a functional end, in respect, say, of remedying a socially embarrassing situation. In a worsened stage of such a condition, coupled with advancing senility, it might appear more rational on utilitarian grounds for the client to opt for voluntary euthanasia. Although, it is arguable whether this is a more *rational* ground, or whether this is a rationalisation based on the inability to cast a different perspective on the situation encouraged by an urgency to find short term, practically accessible, solutions.

Even so, it could be urged from another perspective that, the current condition of anguish or dissatisfaction might be a pointer to a deeper existential disposition of dissatisfaction (*duḥkha*). Further that, the antithesis of the dissatisfaction is not necessarily satisfaction, but perhaps a cessation of *both* the conditions of satisfaction and dissatisfaction, in terms of dealing with some overarching (or undergirding) condition that is responsible for the more ostensible conditions. The value-orientation that would be required here would be quite different from a pragmatist ('means-end') approach, and the schema for 'liberation' from such a disposition could not be mapped out simply on some 'workable' principle, without heeding to an insightful and searching *understanding* of the problem in hand. 'Truth' then would lie in the complete and adequate understanding or appraisal of the problem-situation in all its ramifications, rather than in what might just work to resolve the problem.

To indulgence in a rhetoric: wisdom proper (i.e. 'truth' as distinct from 'received wisdom', as in "received science") cannot be substituted by mere workability. The *paramārtha* or ultimate 'object' of truth-questing (*satya-jijñāsā*) could, perhaps, be interpreted in this light.

None of the qualifications emphasised in the above argument, however, should in any way be seen to diminish the *function* of the 'workability' principle in the *modus operandi* of the different *pramāṇa*s, and particularly in *śabdapramāṇa*. In other words, through *workability* it may be possible, and indeed necessary, to establish a *prima facie* case for the truth or falsity of the judgement. Alternatively, if an action is to follow from a judgement that is true, it may be prudent to have an intimation of the sort of action that will follow and whether or not it might satisfy the conditions. For if there is to be movement (*pravṛtti*) towards an object or state of affairs (*nivṛtti*), which may not be immediately given or accessible, then some assurance that it would led to satisfactory result (*sāmarthya*) would tend to lend credibility to the judgement, and may therefore inspire one to undertake appropriate steps to test the truth of the judgement. Dissatisfaction need not mean that the judgement is necessarily false, but may raise doubts about how its truth is known, and perhaps even about the extent or limits of the judgement in the particular context in terms of its correspondence and the other conditionals of coherence, novelty, and so forth.

As we illustrated earlier, Keśava Miśra's experiment requires the setting up of an hypothesis, which involves 'workability' in asmuch as it enables one to make a tentative inference that if *j* does not work then *j* could not be true (based on the generalisation that what is not true does not work).[94] This, at least, motivates the subject to proceed with the tests he may decide upon. If he does not score 'satisfaction' (in terms of the projected successful productive activity), he has immediate grounds to seriously doubt the truth of the judgement. We shall now move to examine the next criterion.

f. Āptabhāva[95] : trustworthiness or reliability of the speaker or 'source' from or through which the particular judgement is derived. What this means is that if the 'source' can be trusted and has been shown to be reliable in matters of concern to one and all, then there is immediate confidence in the authoritative character of the *śābdabodha*. The *āptabhāva* of the 'source' is here looked upon as lending authority to the understanding derived through hearing the words of the speaker or from some remote source. For example, doubts may persist in the hearer about what he reads or what he has heard from the another, and he may therefore choose to exercise some restraint before he goes any further with the matter in hand.

The speaker, however, might say to him, 'But you have it on my word!',[96a] and if the hearer considers the speaker to be sufficiently reliable, at least in the matters he speaks on, and given that he has a choice, he is likely to take his understanding seriously. He may then decide to set about establishing for himself the 'truth' of what has been said. The speaker's word proves to be of assistance in fulfilling this quest on the part of the hearer. And until he gains a first-hand acquaintance (*aparokṣānubhūti*) of this matter under discussion, he may, given there are no extenuating circumstances, decide to accept the understanding to have *provisional* truth, since he has obtained it from a reliable source. Had it not been for the speaker he might have not come know about this anyway. He would reflect that, it pays to move confidently but cautiously through such a procedure. (Of course, some classical thinkers would reject the qualification of 'provisionality' we have attached to the truth discovered through this process, since they would want to argue that the *jñāna* derived through the *śabda* of a reliable source is either *true* or *not*-true, there being no question of its being merely provisionally true.[96] But we have modified this commitment in accordance with our overall revision of the *prāmāṇya* thesis.)[97]

Admittedly, it is often difficult to have access to the 'object', 'event', 'situation' or 'state of affairs' about which one comes to have some understanding, since these are not given widely in the course of common and everyday experience. For example, when a novice is told by his master that certain practices and mental disciplines lead to the pacifying of the mind, the present state of the novice's mind may fail to disclose a conformity between the master's utterance and his own state of mind. He might, though, be able to perceive a harmony in the master's own state, which perhaps manifests certain attributes that are consistent with his statement. And the hearer might attempt the course of action he is instructed in. If there is truth in the master's word then it should work. The pragmatic overtones in this criterion, however, makes it more fitting for consideration under *pravṛttisāmarthya.*

7.25 One implication of the latter qualification is that the function of *yogyatā* (semantical competence) as Nyāya conceived it, may need to be modified somewhat. That is to say, the pertinent consideration would be seen to alter – in terms of the *prāmāṇya* (objective) category – from 'measure of logical and empirical congruency or compatibility', to a measure of 'pragmatic viability (*samartha*)' in accordance with the other criterial marks of *pramātva* that we have considered above. This may even require the hearer to temporarily suspend or 'bracket', in the spirit of *epoché*, any judgement of truth or falsity of the *understanding* derived from the master's word, until he is convinced otherwise. (And, of course, the question of *ultimate* or absolute truth would have to be completely 'bracketed'. The empiricist strain in Indian epistemology is quite amenable to this phenomenological move.) He would presumably proceed to reflect on the conditions under which such a *jñāna* would be true, and under which false. It would be easier still for him to continue to doubt the judgement. It is something of a truism that it is less problematic to justify *doubt* concerning a particular awareness than it is to affirm its truth.[98] But he might persevere until the fruits of his understanding are borne out (*phalaṃ tvasya vākyārthajñānam*).[99] And if the speaker is reliable and trustworthy, then he could take the heard word to be 'true', and subject his understanding thus derived to the rigours of the *prāmāṇya* considerations already enunciated. The *pramāṇa* of *śabda* should then be taken as seriously as any other *pramāṇa*. Reliability might be one valid *ground* that justifies the acceptance of *S* which one understands (i.e. has *bodha* of) from another person's utterance, though this would not be the only defence against continual doubt. (*Cf.* Keśava Miśra: *vākyamāptapuruṣeṇa prayuktaṃ śacchabdanāmakaṃ pramāṇam*).[100]

Of course not every speaker is reliable, and there would be no good reason to assume this given the human tendency to err. Thus not all sentences prove to be instruments (*karaṇa*) of true understanding. It would then not be too gratuitous, nor unphilosophical in attitude, for one to accept as true the understanding derived from sentences whose source of utterance is a reliable authority. It goes without saying that one need not take the 'authority' to be in any sense absolute, nor need one be undisposed to further questioning and possible delimiting of the scope of the understanding gained in this way. But to stop with the linguistic analysis of *śabda* without due acknowledgment of its epistemic worth would be deemed to be an unnecessarily restrictive stricture.

7.26 At one extreme, one may be more insistent about the worth of this criterion and recommend *āptokta* as efficacious in generating 'truth' since the reliable person confers, as it were, the 'truth' of his understanding to another. The word of the *āpta* is then not only a source or 'instrument' (*karaṇa*) for *śābdabodha*, but is also a source for its truth. The *āptavacana* or 'word of the reliable source', it is said, is *pramāṇa par excellence* as it leads to *(śābdī-)pramā* without the need of any other conditions to vindicate its validity.[101]

There is understandable resistance to taking this extreme position without some qualification, for what I have from another is an *understanding* and not *knowledge* as such, and this distinction is to be kept in mind when appraising such views. But it should be clear that the foregoing analysis in no way seeks to collapse this distinction; indeed, the additional requirement of such understanding and on the grounds on which it could be justifiably accepted as knowledge would need to be shown also. If no judgement (or belief in the Justified True Belief account) arises as knowledge, but is an awareness (or belief) that is accepted only if there are grounds beyond reasonable doubt that justify its acceptance, then there is no reason to expect that *śābdabodha* should also arise as knowledge, and that if it does not, but is at best an *understanding*, then there could be no possible grounds for its acceptance as *knowledge* (*qua* 'true *niścaya* awareness', in analogy with *justified true belief*). We have argued what some of these *grounds* might be and how they might be operative in *śabdapramāṇa*. Reliability, though not the strongest, is one such consideration towards establishing grounds for accepting or rejecting a verbally-derived understanding.

Problems, of course, arise in deciding *who* is reliable and *when* reliability obtains, and also in deciding whether or not to accept the authority in the particular context of the utterance. Advaita could be seen to go along with this view inasmuch as it emphasises that the 'source' ought not to be unreliable. While Mīmāṃsakas, like Kumārila Bhaṭṭa, accept *āptabhāva* only in the context of scriptural sentences and not with regard to sentences that arise in the course of the more mundane and day-to-day affairs of living, since the utterances of persons do not have the same goal-potential as statements of scriptural sources are supposed to, and nor are people infallible. The best that one can do is guard against unreliability and fallibility on the one hand, and excessive credulity and dogmatism on the other.[102]

7.27 When all is said and done, the Indian theorist's point is that each of the truth characteristics discussed above should help towards effectively determining the epistemic character of the awareness that emerges through understandingly hearing the words of another. And, therefore, in so far as care is taken to ensure the effective fulfillment of the considerations that these criteria require, possible interference from extraneous defects, limitations of one sort or another (e.g. contextual errors), as well as subjective attritions that would distort clear apprehension (e.g. jaundice in vision), there should be grounds not to doubt the emergence of a valid *śābdabodha*. One could still suspend judgement and become critical; and others may seek direct confirmation and corroboration where doubt arises. But if the conditions have been fulfilled in respect of both the linguistic processes and the validation criteria, then one could be assured that a 'true' *śābdabodha* should emerge. In due course, should the need arise, the hearer could proceed to inquire further, and reflectively arrive at the 'intuitive' or whatever form of knowledge his informant seems to be in possession of and from which he speaks. This could be particularly relevant in the context of *śruti*, where uncommon 'intuitions' concerning problems of existence, and in morality and ethics, are sought to be communicated through the reflexive use of language.

In considering the scope of the preceding argument, however, one may wonder if the initiated is predisposed to accepting what is taught in this way, and that even if one is to approach scriptural utterances equipped, as it were, with the considerations pertaining to *prāmāṇya* (as we have discussed), there is still the chance that the hearer might accept rather naively all that is said and implied or metaphorically suggested. Admittedly, one cannot sufficiently stress the need for a critical acumen and the methodological refinements with respect to the sorts of phenomenological and epistemological principles we have attempted to highlight in this work.

At least, Śaṅkara raises the question of the *pramāṇa* for understanding the assertion that Brahman is the ultimate source of the universe. (*BSB*

I i 3). In so far as he has raised this question, he has implicitly made a distinction between understanding and the grounds for accepting the understanding. He first considers that reason might provide us with the necessary grounds; but he rejects this in favour of the authority of the scripture. The arguments he produces for his preference may be inadequate and indeed faulty, but the procedure he has adopted in terms of which he commences his enquiry is not without its merits. It would seem, from his later comments, that he might consider yet another *pramāṇa* - viz. that of *aparokṣānubhūti* or 'direct (intuitive) experience'. What is important, from an epistemological point of view, is not his conclusion on the matter, but the way in which he seeks to address the problem and different possibilities open to him in terms of finding the answer.

7.28 A hypothetical example of a sentence from *laukika* or ordinary experience is often used to illustrate the efficacy of the hearing (*śravaṇa*) of *śabda* (word) in generating 'immediate undisputable awareness' that could be seen to meet the requirements of *prāmāṇya*. This story-form is known as *daśamastvam asi*[103] : 'You are the *tenth* (person)'. Ten persons cross the river, and one of them decides to make sure that all of them have got across safely. But his count revealed that only nine had got across. Then each member of the group decides to count, but none of them counted himself. Puzzled by the commotion, a wayfarer, who happens to be passing through, comes to their rescue. His intuition tells him that there has been some mistake.

The wayfarer begins to count, and as he reaches the ninth person, he sees that there is one more in the group who in numerical terms would be the 'missing' member. Thereupon he moves his finger and exclaims: 'You are the tenth!' The words themselves were sufficient to convey the information. Now self-conscious, this person comes immediately to the realisation that *he* is the alleged missing person. Perhaps like John Wisdom's hunter he could not have been expected to hunt himself. To drive home this new-found awareness, the wayfarer repeats the procedure, until each individual has come to this self-understanding. Each of the ten persons would presumably respond with a self-conscious reflection 'Well, I suppose *I* am the tenth person!' : the self-consciousness that characterises this particular awareness is evident in the self subjectivity expressed as '*I am*'.[104]

The foregoing story, then, is a good example that shows the viability of *śabdapramāṇa* in one of its numerous applications. Awarenesses of certain sorts of ideal 'possibilities', optatives, imperatives and injunctions that lead one in the direction of some object or towards the realisation of some *value* or purpose, and perhaps also to some rewarding activity, have a direct efficacious force in the words of another who is perhaps far better and more sensitively informed than another might be.

7.29 Before we conclude this part of the discussion, there remains one other pressing question we need to look at, but only briefly—viz. can one say that *śabdapramāṇa* is an independent means of knowing, or dependent on another, *or* is it one which in the last analysis could be reduced to the other recognised or accredited *pramāṇas*, namely *pratyakṣa*, *anumāna*, and so forth?

In other words, the question is: does this particular means of knowing depend for its success solely on the success of perception and inference, or is its success independent of these other *pramāṇas*? This question was raised in a discussion in an earlier chapter (2) where it was asked to what degree perception could be said to be involved in the *vyāpāra* or process of the generation of *śābdabodha*, particularly in view of the obvious fact that words or expressions have to be assimilated through hearing, reading or the use of the Braille and other 'reading' devices. It was pointed out that it is not *perception* as such of the sentence in its outer structure that accounts for the principal instrument (*karaṇa*) in the complex process, but that the perception contributes towards the assimilation of the sentence structure, and for that reason perception is *sādhāraṇa* or 'ordinary' determinant, which does not explain the larger causal process effective in this *pramāṇa*.

The overall process, as made clear in the preceding analyses, is a lot more complex, and it involves among other things, perception, recollection and maybe inference, none of which are singularly sufficient, in the sense that they are invariably necessary and indispensible for *śābdabodha*. We need not repeat here what has already been argued, but may mention that the use of perception is acknowledged in obtaining *śabdajñāna* as the initial source, although this in itself is not *śābdabodha*. Thus, the complex *vyāpāra* or the operative process, which involves no doubt the mediating function of the 'perceived words' that leads to the presentation of the different word-meanings (*padajanyapadārthopasthitiḥ vyāpāraḥ*), becomes differentiated from perception as it generates the new 'whole-meaning' (*viśiṣṭaḥ ekārthaḥ*) identified as *śābdabodha*. And this is the distinct linguistically generated cognition.[105] For its truth-character also, as shown earlier, there is no direct dependence on evidence provided by perception, for the reason that in some instances this would not be available, and in other instances of no avail (due to the difference in the level of discourse). The categorically distinct character of *Śrutijanyabodha* or the *śruti*-given awareness may not lend itself to either a confirmation or a refutation from the sorts of evidence that perception and inference, or both together, could provide.[106a] That does not preclude some other ways of explaining the phenomenon (or phenomena) that, say, *śruti* aims to enlighten upon. But unless this alternative mode of understanding, be it perceptual, inferential or other, can explain all that *śabda* or *śruti* is considered as being capable of, and over and above that, can provide useful novel information and directive, even if by way of implication, then there would be no good grounds for rejecting the argument for the methodological independence of *śabda* relative to other *pramāṇas*. A maxim that comes to mind here is the following :

T(i) can be reduced to T(ii) only if the latter explains (and not merely describes) all that the former does, and in addition is capable of explaining, by way of prediction or implication, more than what T(i) has been capable of.

7.30 By the same token the reduction to memory-recollection is not feasible. For, as we also pointed out earlier, while word-meanings are recollected from previous awareness of their connection, in the context of the sentence, new connections also emerge, and the 'significations' are somewhat modified to suit the emergence of a 'whole-sense' which is different from the sum of the meanings of the constituent words. The relations (*saṃsarga*) that arise between words and word-meanings in a sentence, are not given in recollection but are a linguistic property given in the sentential structure itself, and these determine the nature of the combined sentence sense that emerges in apprehension as the *śābdabodha*. Thus, the *śābdabodha* is not itself recollected, except in cases where that same sentence had been heard before in the same or a similar context. But even the 'same sentence' can be used with different intentions to convey quite different senses to what was understood in previous utterances of the same. If such new relations between and among word-meanings were not possible, and if different uses were also not possible of the same sentence, then very little of a 'new understanding' could be said to arise through linguistic communication, which is something even common sense would not deny.[106]

7.31 What about inference then, can *śabdapramāṇa* be reduced to the inferential mode of knowing? There are two ways in which this question can be broached, one of which admits of a partial dependence upon inference, the other denying any significant dependence and therefore the attempted reduction. In more recent times, D. M. Datta has advocated the former approach as a plausible resolution,[107] while others, such as Kunhan Raja,[108] following Mīmāṃsā and Sāṃkhya, defend the latter approach.

The first approach accepts *śabda* as being significantly dependent upon inference, and this arose as a concession to the objections of the Vaiśeṣikas, who reduced it to inference.[109] Accordingly, the response to the objection is that, even if *śābdabodha* were to depend upon inference for its truth, this does not entail that as a basic *understanding qua śabdajñāna* (i.e. *padajanyapadārthasaṃsargabodha*) it has to depend upon inference. That is to say, for the source of its *content* (*viṣayī-bhūta), śābdabodha* is not as such dependent upon inference, as it is on the cluster of processes that give rise to the rather complex awareness. Although it may be true that for its validity, inference (in the form of inferring the reliability of the 'source', or of inferring its truth from a previous awareness of the same and so forth), may be involved. Thus, as Datta, in attempting to defend this compromised position, has stated: Often there is confusion between a method as 'a *source* for the attainment of knowledge of fact' and the means by which the truth of that knowledge is determined and those by which this truth is 'known or ascertained'.[110]

Śabda, like any other *pramāṇa*, is a source of information about 'facts' and therefore should be regarded as a method of knowledge irrespective of the conditions upon which it depends for its truth and for the awareness of its truth (notwithstanding the theory that makes no distinction between the conditions that give rise to knowledge and those that determine its truth and the awareness of this). Datta goes on to point out that there are cases where even perception, when it is doubted, depends upon inference for the confirmation of its truth; but we do not say that therefore perception ought also to be brought under inference (*ibid*).

Sometimes, it may be argued, perception and inference themselves would depend on (other) inferences for their confirmation, particularly when there is considerable doubt about their truth. Conventions and normative evaluation of evidence, for example, emerge in this way. Likewise, when the understanding derived from hearing an utterance is in doubt, inference is called upon to evaluate the conditions under which such an understanding would be true and under which false. *Śabda* in some ways is left open as the only option in instances of speech-acts that stand in need of understanding and reciprocation on the part of the hearer—viz. questions, commands and expression of requests, wishes, feelings and ideas of other persons. Thus *śabda* can be regarded as an independent means of knowing as could be said of perception and inference. On balance we are more inclined, in principle, to favour Jayanta's view, that the process here is a rather complex one of collective interdependence (*bodhābodhasvabhāva sāmānyasāmagrī*) and that the question we have laboured on here is largely irrelevant. Of course, Dharmarāja will not agree with us on this.

We can therefore conclude at this point that even if *śabda* is not an independent *pramāṇa* it nevertheless has distinctive features which it does not share with other recognised sources of knowledge. That is to say, *śabdapramāṇa* is distinct in respect of the 'content' even though it is not different in respect of the 'truth' of the *jñāna* it yields.[111] There will inevitably be instances of doubt about the authenticity of understanding so derived and there will be even greater scepticism about the truth of such *jñāna*. But then, which means of knowing is immune from such challenges? Doubts are continually raised, for example, about the whole edifice of knowledge built upon the scientific enterprise as perhaps the only authentic source of knowledge the modern world has been disposed to accepting.[112] Still, one can accede to doubts and find it methodologically expedient in such instances to resort to other forms and means of knowledge to make further enquiries, and seek either corroboration or disconfirmation of the truth of the judgement in question. Again, reason should become a useful guide, such as when we ask how reliable and truthworthy is the speaker or source of the utterance through which the *jñāna* is had, and how else we might go about determining the truth or falsity of the judgement drived. We may err sometimes in our evaluation, and we may not be able to derive a normative rule according to which all such future judgements are to be evaluated, but we may be able to come up with working guidelines and some principles. We do this continually in our day-to-day living, although as philosophers we may find it difficult to accept the common-sense practice and the ordinary use of language as a very satisfactory arrangement. But we must begin by stating what is or appears to be the obvious.

There is a third view that argues for a total dependence on a relatively weak form of 'reasoning' (or rather unreason) and seeks to explain away *śabda* or 'testimony' as being tantamount to what Bertrand Russell, a Western proponent of this critique, calls 'animal inference' since the 'probable trustworthiness of testimony' is a premise yet to be established.[113]

We are more than credulous, says Russell, in common-sense practice, and tend generally to accept testimony unless some positive reason prevents us from doing so in the particular case. Russell tries to explain that the 'cause', though not justification, of this practice, is the animal inference from a word or sentence to what it signifies.[114] He goes on to give an example of the exclamation "Tiger!" and what it does to one's body when one is engaged in a tiger hunt : the body gets into a state of frenzy similar to that which would occur if one actually encountered the tiger in real form. The hearing of the exclamation merely triggers certain impulses, and evokes an emotional response that one would evince towards a tiger. Russell argues that such a state characterises the belief that a tiger is in the neighbourhood. Even in a different context when one is told about huge tigers found in the forests of India and South East Asia, though the impulse will not be overtly manifest, they may yet 'cause during the following night a nightmare from which you wake in a cold sweat, showing that the impulses appropriate to the word "tiger" that survived subconsciously.'[115]

Russell, however, is showing here some naïvity in choosing to argue from such a flimsy and extraordinary example neglecting what he admits to be 'the niceties of grammar and syntax', while trivialising the issue by creating a rather sensational context in illustrating the workings of 'animal inference' as though all speech operated in this way. If all linguistic communication occurred in the manner Russell describes then he would not have been one of the most learned and informed thinkers of his time, nor would there be any need to distinguish individual words from sentences, and the meanings of individual words from more complex meaning-wholes—even ones which may have never been heard before. One need not disagree with Russell that in the humdrum of day-to-day living and common-sense practices, such a form of testimony does feature, sometimes rather prominently. But to suggest that all forms of testimony is to be reduced to this is simply gratuitous.

Evidently, Russell does not ignore the testimony in law that has the potential of leading a convict to the gallows where the only evidence on the judgement passed down may be that of the witness or witnesses who are summoned to the court to provide testimony of their knowledge or involvement in the case in hearing. Many important decisions in life and in the world of business and professional enterprise are made on the basis of testimony, solicited or volunteered. Russell also acknowledges the testimonies of the 'soap-sellers' and the politicians, but these (too) he concludes are based on 'primitive credulity' which are not in the interest of philosophers. But he does go on to raise what he considers to be the important question from the point of view of the philosopher, namely, *not* whether the testimony one hears is intended to be truthful, but whether it has any intentions of conveying any significant information.[116]

It is baffling, however, why the philosopher should be any less interested in the question of its truth than in the significance of the information it conveys, for it would appear that the former presents a more formidable challenge to the philosopher, while the linguist may be contend to concern himself with the latter. It is, afterall, one major responsibility of the philosopher to adjudicate over problems of truth and falsity in any discourse that claims to make a positive contribution to human knowledge. Perhaps Russell was not persuaded that 'testimony' belonged to this class of discourse, and hence he looked upon testimony as a rather uninteresting means of conveying equally uninteresting information, whether it concerns alerting another of the presence of a tiger in the vicinity (which one could also by making a loud coded bang on the gong), or, as in the case of the soprano, giving 'pleasure in contemplation of an imaginary sorrow', or as in the case of people dreaming, uttering whatever they are preoccupied with in their subconscious mind. By contrast, Śaṅkara somewhere mentions that even if one gets terrified by imagining a tiger (supposing that tigers, like all things are illusions), the episodic process reveals one significant truth—

viz. the existential fact of being terrified and it uncovers the being who is, as it were, possessed by an inauthentic dread. What gets demonstrated (using a Heideggerean twist), is the 'disclosedness of Being-in and of the Self'.[117]

The analysis in the preceding chapter showed that not only does 'testimony' *qua śabda* succeed in conveying information, by no means meagre or uninteresting or merely repetitive, but that it succeeds in many instances of conveying that which is true or truly the case. Truth, then, is not the exclusive prerogative of perception and rational inference, but is a possibility within *śabda* as well. If there is inference involved it is certainly not, except perhaps in the trivial cases of the sort Russell chooses to highlight, some kind of 'animal inference' [not withstanding the unfairness such an attitude may reflect on the animal species]; nor does the involvement of inference necessarily impair the efficiency of *śabda* as a legitimate *pramāṇa* for knowing, nor does that make it any less significant in what awareness it gives rise to. Language *qua* word does more than clarify propositions, and a little more than convey useful and interesting information. It also portends meaning, refers to objects, reveals what is not known (hitherto or to another), and in its negative function 'speaks' of the 'unspeakable' by negating appearance, false ascriptions and descriptions, thus unconcealing the *ground* that remains hidden (and this *ground* need not be an object).

The Upaniṣadic usage of *neti neti* or 'not *this*, *not* this' is a classic example of such an approach, for it begins by negating appearances, the instrument used is language, and the appeal is to experience. If one goes further and assumes for the purpose of the exercise that one's experience of oneself as the body-subjectivity complex (in waking as also in sleep state) is a result of some alogical identification, then a systematic negation of this experience should disclose something rather interesting. The experience can be analysed in terms of the several stages through which the identification arises, and each stage would then be described in verbal terms. The negation would proceed with a conceptual reduction of each term of the description such that its affirmation would lead to a contradiction (eg. 'consciousness is this body'), until the residual conception is also negated. What remains might require a deeper intuitive awareness, although it might well defy further description, except in some sort of exponible expression. The *word*, it could be said, leads one into realms of experience that is not commonly pursued.

Thus, there is something distinctive about *śabda* which it does not share with other means or ways of knowledge. Long discarded as a distinct source of knowledge in western philosophy (largely in order to reject the authoritative reign of centuries of unquestioned theological dogmas and doctrines that were accepted *ex cathedra*), 'verbal testimony', as it has been crudely termed, is not accepted as a legitimate means of knowledge in modern western philosophy.[118] Perhaps there might be occasion, if the critical Eastern wisdom has anything significant to contribute to this silenced debate, to re-instate the 'word' as a legitimate source of knowledge. Our analyses and arguments might be seen to be an attempt at reviewing the impasse that has also affected mutual dialogue between philosophy and religion. The dialogue may possibly make way for speculative yet critical metaphysics in some restraint manner.

PART B

AUTHORITY AND 'PRAXIS'

Āptabhāva : authoritativeness (*qua* the reliability criterion.)

8.0 The preceding remarks take us to the final section in which we wish to briefly, and more informally, discuss the notion of 'authority', or what Ninian Smart has elsewhere rendered as 'Doctrine', specifically as it relates to *śabdapramāṇa.*[119] Rather than offer a 'final' view, if such is at all possible, in this section I merely present a broad overview of the discourse on 'authority' in the Indian philosophical tradition. It is thus more experimental in nature and is not likely to engage one who might be led to expect a continuity of the analyses and arguments as have been attempted in the preceding section and chapters. (For this reason also a separate chapter did not seem warranted; or to do justice to this discourse would require a whole separate work.)

To begin with a comment on the standard criticism of *authority* in the form of testimony of another, it is not altogether wrong to suggest that humans are only too prone and credulous in accepting testimony and relying uncritically on this source of knowledge in common-sense matters.[120] We can make two responses to this. (a) The problem is not so much with the tendency of humans to rely too strongly on words uttered or written by another authority, as it is with the unguarded and indeed uncritical tendency with which the words of another are accepted. (b) It is not only in common-sense matters but also in many spheres of human activity and intellectual endeavour that there is reliance upon 'authority', albeit, in less uncritical ways. It follows that if authoritative testimony is acceptable in whatever degree in the latter case, then there might arguably be good reasons for its acceptance in common-sense practice as well.

What should not be acceptable in common-sense practice is the naïve and often credulous reliance on the words of another or others. Perhaps this is an area where philosophers have not been able to provide adequate guidelines and the wherewithal for a more critical pursuit that the common person could relate to and make the most use of. The world of common-sense is not usually troubled by the same sorts of problems that concern say a philosopher or a scientist. The Indian tradition attempted at various stages to develop something along these lines, although perhaps in not as consistent a manner as may be desirable. However, there are snippets of wisdom here that it would not be proper for us moderners to dismiss quite as swiftly as we do anything that vaguely smacks of *tradition*. To say this, is not to share either the romanticism of the apologetic for 'the tradition', or the eagerness of the fundamentalist dogmas and details of the past.

Āptopadeśaḥ

8.1 The issue first addressed pertains to *attitude* with which the words of another is accepted, if it is to be accepted. It should not be a vain belief or 'faith' in another's word, bereft of intellectual honesty and awareness of the possibility of error and relativity of the source. Authority is certainly accepted with some passion and respect in tradition, but it urges at the same time that maximum intellectual freedom be exercised in regard to the content of what is learned through this process and that queries be made regarding the *reliability* of the source or speaker. If these queries are not satisfactorily answered then the judgement derived stands in need of review and the authority should be bracketed. Certain characteristics of the person whose authority is in question are stated : these include good and honest character, non-intention to deceive, being unsullied in motivation, not being self-contradictory, taking precaution in arriving at and articulating the understanding to be conveyed, reliability and trustworthiness, among others.

8.2 Gautama from the Nyāya school states categorically that '*śabda* is the *upadeśa* (testimony or instruction) of an *āptaḥ* (or reliable person).'[121] Vātsyāyana, commenting on Gautama remarks, says that an *āptaḥ* is a person who has distinct knowledge of *dharma* or the ethico-ecological laws on which the universe rests and which determine the results of human action.[122] The *āptaḥ* is the "scientist" [from *scire*] in that special sense as he is one who knows or claims to know the 'categories' (*padārthas*) of reality and the relations that obtain among them. If such a one can communicate this knowledge in terms of the relevance it has for humans living in as many aspects as life's concerns demand upon the *homo sapiens*, then he is truly said to be an *āptaḥ*. He or she ought though, as Jayanta insists, have every intention of imparting nothing but the truth (*cikhyāpayisa*) and, of course, he should be well-informed himself (*upadeṣṭā*).[123]

Any partiality or partisanship would only detract from the authoritative character of whatever is being conveyed, as would any self-interest or ambivalence in the motive with which this is done. Adequate awareness about the matter in hand as well as an openness to question and further enquiry are the hallmark of one given to the qualities of authority. A real *vidvān* or learned person is deserving of such authority. *'Science'* (by which we do not necessarily mean what goes by the name of 'science' in our times), is a mark of authority when it is not abused or over-extended.[124]

8.3 A good deal of reservation, however, is encountered in the Mīmāṃsā school on the question of authoritativeness of any *personal* source (*pauruṣeya*), i.e. the authority that pivots itself on the experience and verdict of a person *qua* human as distinct from the authority of the Vedic scriptures (*śruti*). There seems to be an irrevocable suspicion in this school of the irremediable deficiencies (or the 'bad') in human constitution despite the earnest pursuit of the 'good', and the *summum bonum* that is *dharma. Śruti*, as Vedas on the other hand, according to this school, is not subjected to these deficiencies for *śruti* is not the 'word' of any human or personal source since the words of the Vedas are regarded by the Mīmāṃsakas to be without origin (*apauruṣeya*).[125] An argument is given to justify the suspicion of human-based authority where reliability has been the chief consideration. Nārāyaṇa Bhaṭṭa comments that if 'reliability' is to be considered as the absence of delusion (misunderstanding) and so forth, then it is 'not possible to establish this in the case of (each) person in virtue of the dictum, Delusions have been suspected even among the sages; what, then Sir, about the delusion in this person'.[126] Nārāyaṇa is expressing what in effect is the Mīmāṃsā rejection of 'secular' authority of any sort in deference to the authority of the 'sacred' word of *śruti* ('what has been heard'), which to Mīmāṃsā is the ultimate pinnacle of knowledge, being *apauruṣeya* or transpersonally given, so to speak.

8.4 Śaṅkara, in a similar vein, throws doubt on the whole-hearted acceptance of the words of the most respected sages in the tradition. He states that the reasoning of someone who has wide fame and acceptance is relied upon in the belief that his (reasoning) must be conclusive; but surely, he says, this must remain inconclusive in asmuch as persons whose greatness accords recognition and who are founders of philosophical schools (and as instances he mentions Kapila and Kaṇāda and others), are seen to hold divergent views.[127] Perhaps Śaṅkara would not regard himself to be above these either, though he takes the seers of the Upaniṣads and Bādarāyaṇa (the author of *Brahma-sūtras*) to be supremely reliable and conclusive in their metaphysical speculations, at least as he understands them.

We have remarked earlier that Śaṅkara was perhaps unnecessarily suspicious of the role of reason in enquiry into just the sorts of problems he was concerned with. Paradoxically, he shows himself to be something of a doyen of the rationalist in using reasoning to demonstrate the intent of the scriptures and, more particularly, in combating all variant interpretations and any denial of the sort of metaphysics and soteriology he sets to construct, or rather re-construct. He supports his speculations with reasoned arguments and appeal to analogical examples, while asserting that 'this is what is presented in the scriptures' (when other philosophers, like Rāmānuja and Madhva, might read the same text in an entirely different way). Śaṅkara's methodology is double-edged: he uses reason to support the word, and uses the word to support what is got from rational reflection. In other words, while setting the limits of reason, he does not consider rational reflection to be in any way antithetical to the 'revealed words' of the scriptures; rather he saw them to be compatible. Like some medieval Western thinkers, he believed that scriptures give scope to reason, in terms of clarifying and elucidating 'authentic' propositions, whatever their source.

It is clear that Śaṅkara places an enormous pedagogic and dialectical value on reasoning. The former follows from the need to reflectively understand the meaning after *śravaṇa* (hearing) and *adhyayana* (learning) the text from the teacher have occurred. The latter arises when there is difficulty encountered in comprehending various paradoxes and apparent discontinuities in the relevant discourse. Suppose it is claimed that the only possibility of knowing anything real is to be identified with it, for without this identity there would be an incommensurate distance between the subjective knowing process (*pramātṛ*) and the objective (to be known, *viṣaya*). But once this has occurred, there can't be a reflective assertion of this awareness without creating a rupture in the identity-awareness, which, of course, would bring back the dichotomy. Any account, thought or linguistic expression, of this experience would tend to negate or falsify the experienced reality. Any linguistic assertion would be an assertion of reflective appearance of the reality, and as such it would be a falsification of the reality.

Now it is here that dialectics can be of help. It involves a systematic process of negating all descriptions and assertions of what is effectively appearances or empty attributions. The argument is that by negating and falsifying the false, the way is made clear for the *ground of falsity* to manifest itself. Language and reasoning are utilised to their fullest in the dialectical process of describing, expressing, asserting and for negating or falsifying the appearances, until that of which it is appearance presents itself. Ultimately, according to Śaṅkara, the confirmation is to be realised in experience (*svānubhava*), albeit in 'depth intuition'.[128] (*sākṣādaparokṣajñānam* or *prajñā* of what is *svarūpajñāna*).

Gauḍapāda, the precursor and in some ways father of the Advaita system, mentions a number of 'personal' sources whose views he suggests may be accepted with approval; some of them are *'buddha'* or 'enlightened ones'. Other characteristics and marks of the person also go towards qualifying him as a reliable 'authority'. It would appear, however, that to Gauḍapāda, as to the Advaita traditionalists, such an 'authority' was one who is qualified to interpret the *śruti* texts for their subtle meaning, not unlike in the manner we have exemplified in the preceding discussion.[129] Certain rules and guidelines for such hermeneutics is provided by Mīmāṃsā, which tend to be rather useful given the obscurity prevalent in much of the scriptural text. Among those that Gauḍapāda saw suitable for representing authority are *munis* or sages, *manīṣins* or the wise, *vicakṣaṇas* or the 'deep' seers, *tattvavids* or the knowers of truth, *veda-pāragas* or the interpreters of Veda, *vidvāns* or the learned, *mahādhīs* or the great intellects, and *mahājñānas* or the great knowers. While those that are categorically disqualified from representing any authority are the *abuddhas* or of unruly intellect, *bāliśas* or of childish disposition, *avipaścids* or the unwise and the knave.[130] But it would be a matter of course that those qualified to interpret the *śruti*, and those not qualified to do so, would accord similar respect and disrespect in giving their 'word' on secular matters as well.

Thus, despite the reservations expressed by Śaṅkara, the Advaita tradition does not reject human (or personal) authority (*pauruṣeya*) as radically as Mīmāṃsā does. Advaita does insist on certain requirements before there is acceptance of such an authority. Mastery of the subject of discourse, a deep understanding of the issues in hand, reliability, trustworthiness, the ability to reason and make critical assessment of every situation, would be some of the characteristics looked for here. It could be said that traditional schools florished on account of such an acceptance of authority, especially where the authority or 'doctrine' was ultimately seen to be grounded on *śruti*. Indeed, the culture of the so-called *guru-śiṣya* or teacher-pupil relationship, before it got widely maligned, was based precisely on such understanding and stringency of prerequisites on which the authority of the guru was to be accepted, coupled with mutual respect.

8.5 In Madhva's view, valid testimony consists of 'defectless words'. The defects of words, Jayatīrtha argues[131], are of the following class : (i) the non-intelligible (*abodhakatva*), which arise from two causes, (a) by the use of non-sensical words (*nirabhidheyatvam*) and (b) by the use of words which have no syntactical relation (*anvayābhāva*); as well as those (ii) that give rise to erroneous cognition (*viparītabodhakatvam*); (iii) that explain the already known (*jñātajñāpaktvam*); (iv) that teach the useless (*aprayojanatvam*); (v) that have a non-intended use (*anabhimataprayojanatvam*); (vi) that state the unaccomplishable (*aśakyasād-*

hanapratipādanam); and (vii) that teach a difficult method where a more parsimonious one is available (*laghūpaye sati gurupāyopadeśaḥ*). Thus, words other than these can be relied upon for their defectlessness, and therefore for their epistemic worth. These stipulations may be reminiscent of the Nyāya requirement for *yogyatā* in *śābdajanyabodha* (understanding derived from words).

8.6 The second point concerns some of the reasons and considerations advanced for a more accommodating attitude towards 'authority'. There is a general acceptance and realisation of the limitations of the individual. But there is more expected of the individual's potentiality. There is sensitivity, however, to the lack of appropriate power and ability for a more direct acquaintance with what may be thought of as going beyond the range of common experience, which, in large part, is determined by the prevailing normative and scientific commitments of the community. It is undeniable that authority in some form or other begins to take effect very early in the individual's life with the more mundane aspects of living, such as toilet training, physical welfare, parental love and so forth. Then the process of education and the mental and intellectual training the individual goes through are based on the tacit (sometimes explicit) acceptance of the efficiency of *āptopadeśa* (authoritative instruction). But the individual is no less reliant, perhaps over-reliant sometimes, on the authority of those 'experts' who are supposedly trained to provide advice and care on other aspects of life, some relatively more important than others, such as may concern the individual's medical, economic, social and political well-being. When existential problems, hightened sense of anxiety and depression arise in the individual then help is sought from those who have the appropriate expertise. (In our culture these may be involved in the practice of psychiatry, or psychoanalysis, or maybe psychology.) The anguish may lead some individuals to seek for a more fulfilling intellectual life; some may quest after a spiritual understanding and a harmonious orientation to life within a broader or more universal perspective. The uncertainties in many of the leading disciplines, such in modern physics and biology, have led some thinkers towards just such a quest. (But some of them then begin to dabble in what is at worst bad metaphysics.)

We see, then, that there is no branch of living that does not involve in some way or other the 'word' of authority adequately qualified, one hopes, for guidance and direction. Often it becomes incumbent upon some members of the community (it used to be with the philosophers or philosopher-kings) to see to the continuity of at least the principles and ideals and values enshrined in the social institutions. It is their responsibility to maintain, as also to take measures to improve and modify these as circumstances and contexts necessitate that. Some individuals may be required to critically review even the ideals and values from time to time as the understanding of the community broadens and deepens and to convey their views to the community. Some may be entrusted with the task of taking the quest for an even deeper understanding and awareness of the intricacies and 'mysteries' of life and reality at large. Words of course are one of the means for effectively passing on the cumulative wisdom : they may be complemented by such media as mythical signs, icons, symbols, images, and musical compositions. Of course, these media are not exclusively used for communicating effectively the insight whose truth is beyond doubt, no more than language is invariably used for this purpose (soft-selling advertisements and media reporting come to mind here). Indeed, nor are words used only for communication : they are used non-communicatively as well, as in the poet's musing to himself, or in one uttering 'Good morning' out of sheer habit or without meaning it at all. Communication is possible only when there is a mutual agreement to exchange understanding and when the speaker can put, so to speak, him/herself in the hearer's 'self' and assume that what he/she is about to utter will be as effective as it would if he/she were the one to hear that. Monologues proceed on just such a supposition.

In dialogue the identification on the part of the audience with the 'self' of the speaker is not *advaita* (non-dual, though it might even be that in certain instances, as for instance between two lovers, a devotee and the worshipped, the poet's 'alter ego'). All this makes for a greater efficiency (*jñānakaraṇa)* on the part of language as a means of communicating understanding. When there is a breakdown in communication and mutual trust is lost between the parties concerned, or if this trust is abused, then there is danger of misunderstanding, even chaos when this occurs in a larger scale among the citizens of a society : the result is typified in Hobbes' 'natural state' and in the so-called 'Tower of Babel' scenario in the biblical legend. Misunderstanding and 'power' can easily replace *trust* in an authentic authority.

What we have pointed out is often true in the context of religion, science and politics, as also in bureaucracy and institutional structures : if the basic trust in an authority becomes, from one extreme of vain susceptibility or what Russell rightly calls 'primitive credulity' on the part of the votaries of the structure in question, to the other extreme of coercion and authoritarian reign on the part of the torch-bearers, then a situation ripe enough for some form of despotism could be said to have been created. Thus, while there is virtue associated with the principle of 'trust' or trust-worthiness, there is also room for its abuse and dangers when one who claims authority turns as a predator upon those who entrust the authority.

If criticism, legitimate censure and self-criticism are looked upon as threats rather than checks against possible divergence and failings of the *āptaḥ*, then *āptabhāva* cannot work. As the structure gets larger, and convictions and doctrines become institutionalised into dogmas and creeds, the checks and appraisals become more and more difficult. Challenges to authority are then judged as heretical and subversive attempts at uprooting the established order. The Indian tradition has been no less guilty of this unfortunate tendency and unself-reflective censure; it is for this reason that modern thinkers, such as Professor Mohanty, believe that a naïve return to *śabdapramāṇa* is just impossible. Who could deny this resolve in the latter part of this century?

jijñāsāsādhana-saṃpatti: "praxis" or *'disciplinary matrix' in enquiry.*

We would like to add some remarks to the discussion, we entered into a little earlier (7.21), on Śaṅkara's two-tiered use of scripture and reason for enquiry into matters of philosophic concern. For one who is keen on embarking on such a pursuit, but is beset with doubts and lack of guidance, certain disciplines and practices are recommended in order to provide support to the process of enquiry. These may be put under a common heading of *sādhana* or 'praxis' or *saṃpatti.*

Sādhana does not entail another mode of knowledge but is a disciplinary matrix, comprising a number of practical steps, in order to facilitate the process of achieving deeper philosophic understanding. Thus it must have something to do with the disposition of the adept in terms of his or her mental capacity to assimilate the complexities of the various views about the subject matter under investigation. *Sādhana* may variously comprise prescribed actions (*karma*), *yoga* and *upāsanā*; the latter is a kind of meditative reflection performed on scriptural texts with the view to deriving a clear and distinct understanding of the substantive thrust of the teaching involved.

For brevity's sake, *sādhana* will be considered under the triune disciplines of *śravaṇa*, *manana* and *nididhyāsana*. We shall not concern ourselves with the significance of *karma* and *yoga*, since their function is more of a preparatory 'purificatory' nature for one keen on commencing enquiry, and they result in steadfastness of conduct, self-control and tranquility, but not necessarily in deeper understanding or knowledge.[132] And without knowledge of true reality *(tattvajñāna)*, there is no 'enlightened freedom' (*mokṣa*). In other words, we are particularly concerned with what is usually called *jñānamārga* in Śaṅkara's thought – i.e. the 'path' of knowledge and the facilitative processes therein. *Śabdapramāṇa*, from this perspective, is the basic element, and the disciplines mentioned are the manifold 'signposts' and, as it were, the driving force. Now we shall not enter into discussion on the issue whether Śaṅkara thought these disciplines to be at all necessary for knowledge of true reality, or whether for him the knowledge arose on the instance of merely hearing the *śruti.* (The later Advaitins concerned themselves excessively with this issue:[133] I would refer here to Śaṅkara's *Upadeśasāhasrī*, and to S. Mayeda's[134] and J. Taber's[135] balanced discussions of this rather entangled issue.)

Śravaṇa: 'hearing'.

Śravaṇa or attentively hearing, is the first of these disciplines. 'Hearing' of course is inevitable in human discourse and is widely recognised to be so, since hearing is perhaps the most common means of assimilating information. But the *śravaṇa* that the traditional texts speak of is intended to be a deeper and rather more significant way of 'hearing' concomitant with an intense focussing of one's attention and powers of concentration on what is heard. One is, as it were, to holistically 'hear' not just the words, but the cluster of meaning in its proper hermeneutics. Without *śravaṇa*, it is said, the true *tātparya* or 'intentionality' of a text or utterance is not assimilable. This phenomenological-hermeneutical perspective on 'hearing' is explored in great detail in some Upaniṣadic and commentarial literature (particularly in Vedānta and Mīmāṃsā).[136a]

When *śravaṇa* is accompanied with *manana*, a meaningfully reflective attitude towards what is heard, with every effort by the intellect to probe further behind what is outwardly presented to its deeper 'intentionality', then one is said to minimise the risk of error and enhance understanding. One may need to mentally go over and over the words heard. Here 'epoché' plays a significant role in asmuch as the hearer's initial task of understanding is served better if questions of truth and falsity of the statement in question are 'bracketed' or momentarily suspended, so that the 'essence' of the text presents itself in immediate acquaintance to the intellect. Doubt, in this initial stage of reflective 'openness', is also not allowed to interfere until an understanding in its completeness has occurred. Too often doubt and perplexity tend to mince what might be a matter of some complexity or even abstrusenes to common-sense disposition. What is involved is not only a reflection on what is heard and being processed to result in understanding, but also a 'depth' reflection (*reditio completa*) on the very process of understanding—i.e. a turning back on the operation of the intellect to inspect precisely the steps and moves by which it derived the understanding. That is to say, it tries to intuit the 'logic' of the understanding.

The phenomenological ramifications of *manana* are indeed significant here. Presumably, such a 'praxis' orientation in gaining insightful awareness would call for long moments of undistracted attention and pacificity, qualities or dispositions of the mind that are not normally given nor cultivated for their own sake. But *manana* presupposes such a non-contentual disposition as an *a priori* condition of the possibility of 'depth' understanding. The *Yoga* tradition, from which the notion of this intellectual discipline is most likely derived, mapped out a series of mental exercises that are supposed to aid one in achieving what it considers to be a pristine disposition of the mind, unencumbered by the hurly-burly preoccupations of ordinary existence. These exercises are elaborated under the *yogic* categories of *dhāraṇā*, *dhyāna* and *samādhi*, which together, in more contemporary parlance, would be called 'meditation'.

Śaṅkara on sādhana

Śaṅkara, it might be noted, was not averse to these *yogic* exercises, as we remarked earlier, even if only for their mediate transformative utility and as ancillary props in facilitating the larger and more demanding intellectual task at hand. (This point is too often glossed over by those who either, on the one hand, attempt to align Śaṅkara strongly with the traditional *Yoga* school, even claim him to be its lapsed member,[136] or who decry any attribution of even a moderated concern with *yoga* on the part of Śaṅkara [137]). Useful and necessary as it is thought to be, however, one is not to remain locked in this mode of repetitive reflexion. There is yet another stage in the intellectual process, but one that continues the reflection in a more detached and perhaps less passionate frame of mind than is assumed under *manana*. This next stage is called *nididhyāsana*, and it involves a sustained contemplation on the *significance* of the utterance, in its broader context of what else is known about the matter being enquired.[138] The dimension of the understanding is taken to its more profound levels. This is what Descartes and the phenomenologists might call *meditationes* (hence the titles of some of their works bearing the term: 'Meditation'—in sharp contrast to the yogic exercises also rendered 'meditation', as we mentioned above—and perhaps compares more favourably with *ādhyāna*, or intense reflection, aided by *manana* and *nididhyāsana*, —as we go on to discuss (and return also to Śaṅkara shortly).

Nididhyāsana

Nididhyāsana calls upon the enquiring mind to consider all the possible ramifications the understanding derived has for the problem under investigation. The contemplation does not proceed *in vacuo*, nor is it supposed to involve an empty recanting or repetition of the syllabic form of the text heard in the hope that that itself might ensue in some profound insight. (Thus contemplations that involve *mantra* recitation and prayers are categorically part of another process altogether, with a similar functional relation as was said of yogic exercises.) Rather, it involves a disciplined dialectical process wherein the judgement is evaluated from all possible points of view, and each inadequate perspective is discarded in the graduated progression to one whose negation involves improbable consequences (such as when one denies one's own being in the locus in which this assertion is made), or which easily lead to *reductio ad absurdum.*

The kind of intensely inward-probing contemplation(or *ādhyāna)* that is spoken of here has as much to do with the eidetic and logical relations that obtain among the concepts refined through *manana*, as it has to do with their relation to experience in its noematic frame of reference. The parameters of understanding are extended to include considerations of the possibility of contradiction (*bādhita*) in what the intellect has delivered, or its incoherency with what else is known on the same problem (*asaṃvadita*), or its nonconsonance with conscience or some more intuitive understanding, such as in reason, or what might be self-evident and *a priori.* These considerations stem from the criteria for *prāmāṇya* we looked earlier. The basic point is that only what remains noncontradicted, and withstands any number of attempts at contradiction or falsification, is ultimately worthy of the characterisation of truth. And *truth* is the fundamental quest here, that is the penultimate goal of *brahmajijñāsā* or this particular form of enquiry.[139]

Altogether, then, *śravaṇa*, *manana* and *nididhyāsana* constitute an intense form of what some have insisted on calling *listening* (distinguished here from merely verbally attending), since 'listening' is a form of hearing that involves 'intending' (in a phenomenological sense) and 'constructing' (in a Kantian transcendental sense). The reflective awareness that this process generates is said to be distinct from ordinary awareness or judgement, since its orbit is a concern with the ultimately valuable and with freedom (or transcendental 'epoché').

As Kalidas Bhattacharyya acutely observes: 'This attitude of *commitment* [is] more an insistence on listening than on speaking, i.e. insistence on cooperation by traditional Indian mind for learning from authority (*śabdapramāṇa*). This is of course not merely in the transcendental field. . . but too often in our mundane life also.'[140] Bhattacharyya concludes :'*Śabdapramāṇa* is just that which generates knowledge in the mind of the listener.'

Āptaḥ revisited: a reliable teacher

The practical disciplines described, and especially 'hearing', are supposed to take place under the guidance of an *āptaḥ*, a reliable authority or teacher in this context. In recommending the help of an *āptaḥ*, traditional wisdom does insist that the candidate does not acquiesce merely in the words of the 'expert guide', but that searching questions be raised that pertain to the 'authority' of the *āptaḥ* itself. The following would seem to be some of the pertinent concerns: (a) has the *āptaḥ* expressed himself sufficiently adequately for the communication to take place, (b) has the communication been freed from vitiating defects, (c) is the *āptaḥ* claiming the authority actually in possession of the knowledge in question and that too derived or acquired on firm grounds, (d) can the *āptaḥ* be trusted to be reliable, particularly in the context of the understanding being sought, (e) are there other avenues through which the same knowledge could be had, or confirmed, or falsified, (f) could the understanding be corroborated in the seeker's own experience, (g) does it hold coherently with the general body of knowledge in that area? There are other questions which become more specific in the actual context of the problem in hand to which reasoned responses are sought.

For instance, to use an example Śaṅkara fondly invoked, if the scripture tells that fire is cold against all empirical evidence then there would be reason to doubt the authority of the scripture particularly on that issue. The discipline of *guru-śiṣya sambandha* incorporates such considerations while remaining uncompromising in its reliance upon the authoritative word of another. At the same time, intellectual freedom and its unhampered growth is to be given full encouragement. Free-will and discretionary use of reason in choosing one option of action against another is left entirely on the individual's judgement.

Thus we have Kṛṣṇa, towards the end of his lengthy and hair-raising sermon to Arjuna in the *Bhagavadgītā*, stepping down from the pedestal and saying to the despondent warrior : 'Reflect upon this knowledge I have propounded to you, this mystery of mysteries, in its entirety, and then do as you are pleased to do'.[141] Further, to give the benefit of the doubt that the human ears may have yet not understood the 'mystery' imparted, Kṛṣṇa's final words are in the form of a question (and not, say, a warning of damnation): 'Have you listened to this with concentrated attention? . . . is your ignorant delusion gone?'[142]

Authenticity and intellectual honesty are thus valued in the place of blind assent; a state of healthy anarchy may even be preferable if the latter were the only option, as clearly this is not if *āptabhāva* is to be true to its intentions. Tradition vouchsafes this noble sentiment and accordingly elevates *āptabhāva* to the status of a doctrine, (or the 'Doctrine' where *āptabhāva* is identified with *śruti*)—which C. Kunhan Raja expresses succinctly and eloquently in these words:

> In this doctrine of "Authority" developed in the Indian philosophy we see the supreme example of honesty of intellect, the bold confes-

> sions of the limitations of man's normal capacities to know, and the assertion of the maximum abilities of man's life. There is a recognition of the possibilities of man in his intellectual pursuits with an admission of the bare facts of man's life that man, though perfect, is not exhibited always as a perfect being, the possibility being that man in his true nature is free from all limitation in his powers of knowing and that there is nothing in the universe that is really and eternally concealed from man's knowing powers. The "Authority" in Indian philosophy is the most misunderstood and most misrepresented doctrine in the entire range of Indian philosophy.[143]

However, in seeking to limit the force of Kunhan Raja's austere remarks, I would tend to agree with the plausible criticism that no amount of talk about *trust* takes us towards a resolution of some of the basic logical issues with respect to the *truth* of what is to be taken on the trust of authority. There then has to be caution in any discussion on authority, which cannot stand on its own without the tested theoretical foundations that a thesis such as *śabdapramāṇa* attempts to examine and seeks to vindicate. But as we also remarked, the scope of this *pramāṇa* has not been examined far beyond its application to the world of empirical experience.

In fact, Madhusūdana Sarasvatī argues that in the last resort *śabdapramāṇa* fails as an adequate means of transcendental knowledge. His reasoning is that while *śabdapramāṇa*, like any *pramāṇa*, deals with the configuration of several elements in some ordered relation, transcendental knowledge answers to no such configuration or structuring, since the subject matter of the latter is one unitary whole and as such is one truly knowable in the most direct, immediate and intuitive experience of identity with that. And to achieve this realisation, he commends an inward openness to the revelation of scriptures (*śruti*).[144]

Thus the limitations of *śabdapramāṇa* are the limitations of ordinary experience, language, reasoning and the world as it is presented through these venues of human knowing. Either the world is what it is, or it is not what it is. *Śabdapramāṇa* according to Madhusūdana reinforces the former, but cannot demonstrate the truth of the latter, while other Advaitins might want to argue that *śabda* in any form is capable of the latter.

Śaṅkara, for instance, was aware (as should be apparent from our earlier citations) that most knowledge involves configuration (*saṃpat*) of disparate elements (*nāmarūpopādhyanurodhī*),[145] and that most sentences give knowledge of this form. But the authority of the sentence has nothing to do with this, nor with the action it enjoins, or does not enjoin, or whatever other option there might be, but in its being certain and satisfying knowledge with regard to the object of enquiry (*vastutantra*). Brahman is such as 'object', and Śaṅkara is of the firm view that the *pramāṇa* of *śabda* is efficacious in giving rise to the knowledge of Brahman (as being one with the self). His appeal to *śruti* is an appeal to the incorrigibility of this *pramāṇa*: it is not that *śruti* alone is the way to this knowledge (for what attests to the *wisdom* about a means is not necessarily the *means* itself).

The word, however, being other than the reality to which it leads necessarily has a limited purpose, and is virtually useless after the goal of knowledge has been reached, in the same way as the mother-of-pearl looses its charm once the fact of the illusion of 'silver' has been recognised, or when the student has learned all he or she could from the teacher.[146] It follows that once this is accomplished, it would be recognised that language *qua śabda* and scriptures *qua śruti* have exhausted their use, and should therefore be thrown away (like the ladder after it has been climbed!).[147]

We may remind ourselves again of the reflections of Kalidas Bhattacharyya on the significance of *śabdapramāṇa*:

> *Śabda-pramāṇa* is critically relevant for all transcendental Indian philosophy, and also. . . for much of Indian ethics (life of action). That is why all forms of Vedānta, Sāṃkhya, Yoga, Jainism and Mīmāṃsā speak so much, and in such finest details, on *śabda-pramāṇa*, taking the scriptures (of various sorts) as (probably) the only anchorage ground for all that is transcendental and ethical. (The first four schools mainly for transcendental knowledge and Mīmāṃsā for all injunctions and prohibitions in (Hindu) social life).[148]

It follows that the scope of one's inquiry is extended when one grants due acknowledgment to the limitations of one's own intellectual capacities and recognises the merits of a methodology that would enable him or her to expand the limited span of awareness. This requires a philosophical attitude and openness to the words of another, but at the same time it does not dispense with the critical faculties. Faced with such limitations it would be foolish if one were not to take the word of another seriously, though not conclusively. There should be nothing to prevent a proliferation of awareness and 'evidence' from as many other legitimate sources as possible at least as a means to challenging the accepted wisdom from a paradigm that is commonly recognised. There need be no 'unconditional acceptance of the inviolability of statements of the scripture' or of any authority. One meets with frequent warnings that no scriptural testimony can make a thing what it is not, at least as and in the manner given in perception and judged through reasoning. Again, Śaṅkara's point that no amount of scriptural testimony can falsify common-sense experience is relevant here.[149]

To say a little more on the last statement, attention may be drawn to the formalised rules for conceptual clarification and distinctiveness, and an intelligible approach to *śruti* utterances evolved in the Indian tradition, particularly by Mīmāṃsā in accordance with its hermeneutical pursuit, which we discussed under *tātparya*. Explaining that scriptures themselves might not have formulated these rules, Kalidas Bhattacharyya argues that 'they could be formulated only by those for whom scriptures were an integral part of their being, whose living and thinking were verily in the line of scripture – in older language, those to whom the ultimate truths regarding [the hu]man and the world came more or less to be revealed, or, if one admits an omniscient God, to whom God spoke more or less directly – in short, in our present-day language, those who are original thinkers on ultimate truths and values.'[150]

To the methodological subtleties these hermeneutical rules give evidence to, we may add the following considerations towards a more formalised procedure for an authentication of the 'depth' *understanding*' (or 'deep experience'[151]) derived from scriptural utterances, bearing in mind the consequence this has particularly towards a paradigm for *śrutiprāmāṇya*:

(a) the reliability of the instructor or preceptor guiding one through *śruti* (in terms of both the character of the teacher and the interpretation of the substantive content of the teachings);

(b) the reasonableness of the knowledge (of fact or action) derived in terms of its tenacity to withstand reasoned scrutiny, analysis and normative evaluation;

(c) the noncontradiction or unfalsifiedness of the *śrutijanyabodha* by truths already accepted, and its coherency (*saṃvāditā*) with the same in the relevant context;

(d) the pragmatic consequence or successful 'satisfaction-relation' of the *jñāna* in terms of its incentive towards activity conducive to the purpose or result portended;

(e) the repeatability of the outcome, in terms of achieving some degree of subjective corroboration and predictable novelty of the outcome, however intangible (*apūrvatva*), relative to the general body of accepted knowledge; and

(f) its consonance with ethical principles and and the moral implications of the potential course of action (i.e in terms of whether it helps decide towards the intrinsically *good* and valuable that enrich human life and potentials, such as preventing its destruction – self or other propelled – and averting adversities that tend to manifest much after the cause, and so forth).

8.11 In bringing this study to a close, it would be well to formulate in way of a summary, the gist of the argument for the thesis investigated herein. In point form we have argued the following:

a. *Śabdapramāṇa* is a valid means of knowing (i.e. it is that which generates knowledge in the mind of the 'hearer').

i It begins with 'hearing' words or utterances of another and results in *śābdabodha.*

ii. *Śābdabodha* is a particular form of cognitive awareness derived from understanding the meaning of the utterance. It is a distinct *karaṇa* for verbal knowledge.

iii. *Śābdabodha* has a propositional structure (of qualificand-qualifier relation), that itself involves *śabdajñāna* or *vakyarthajñāna*—i.e. the comprehension of the 'meanings' of the constitutive parts of the sentence utterance; but the factors that generate *śābdabodha* often exceed the linguistic and grammatical factors involved in *vākyārthajñāna*; thus circumstantial context (*prakaraṇa*) and intentionality (*tātparya*) and logical-referential compatibility (*yogyatā*) are also significant.

v. The significant 'meaning-content' of the sentence (i.e. the propositional sense *qua* the embedded 'intentional content') is greater and more 'holistic' than the meanings of the individual words or component parts of the sentence taken in isolation, for what a sentence *qua* its propositional sense 'means' is often more than what the constituent words taken individually mean (signify, indicate, denote stand for or refer to) : *vākyārtha* is then not reducible to the sum of the component *padārthas.*

vi. The novel element in the construction of sentence-meaning is the *saṃsargamaryādā* or collective coalescing of the relations (*saṃsarga*) among the component parts of the expression, with an added dimension of intentionality relevant to the particular speech-act or utterance. In part, this is due to the particular juxtapositions of the constituent words, sometimes in sequential order, and in large part to the syntactical connection of the meanings of the individual words in virtue of their specific signification function in the expression.

The semantic and syntactic connections are comprehended in accordance with *kāraṇas* that are structurally responsible for generating a non-empty *śābdabodha*: the are the formal and phenomenological operants of sentential comprehension. These operants are *ākāṅkṣā* (semantical expectancy), *yogyatā* (syntactical competency), *āsatti* (contiguity of verbal items), *tātparya* (intentionality of the utterance). But if, as Bhartṛhari and some grammarians argue, the apprehension of the sentence-meaning occurs in a 'flash of conceptual unity' (*sphoṭa-pratibhā*), then this last premise may need to be modified.

vii. The *viṣayībhūta* or the qualificative content (i.e. the *contentness*) in the understanding derived is intentional i.e. the content of the qualificative cognition involves an epistemic relation with the properties of the object (*viṣaya*) or the relevant objective state of affairs about which this is an understanding. If the *śābdabodha* is to be significant (in the epistemological sense) it must have a noëmatic relational structure, and it must be illumined in consciousness. It is then said to be a *jñāna* or judgement.

According to the theory of truth, a *śābdabodha* is true, if the features in its content correspond to the relevant features of *viṣaya* or the object, etc. of the judgement. The *śābdabodha* is a *pramā* if the state of affairs obtains, and it is false if the relevant state of affairs does not obtain. There is debate as to whether the truth of the judgement is self-evident, or whether it is determined extrinsically in virtue of its possessing *guṇatva* or 'evidence of excellence'. Either way, there are certain truth-characteristics any 'true' judgements would have. Its being *pramāṇa*-generated would be one such; in a weak sense this is its *justification*.

viii. For the validation of these characteristics or 'marks' of truth, the following set of criteria is proposed: non-contradictedness or unfalsifiedness (*abādhita*); novelty (*anadhigatatva*); certainty or conviction (*niścaya*); coherency with relevant knowledge (*saṃvādakatva*); pragmatic capacity to lead to successful activity (*pravṛtty'nukūla*); last not least, reliability (*āptabhāva*) of the source ('authority') of the utterance or information. The result, in all probablity, should be *yathābhūtavastuviṣayam*, which, in Śaṅkara's words, is *niścitaphalavadvijñānam* or 'certain and satisying understanding of the real'.[152]

Further corroboration may be sought by appeal to various tests and counter-tests, a program of intuitive and empirical investigation engendered by the understanding, and perhaps further systematic enquiry with the aid of phenomenological reflection, 'praxis' involving deeper understanding, contemplation, and 'deep experience' under carefully evaluated conditions and guidance. A critical, discerning and self-reflective disposition is the bedrock for such a pursuit to yield even a modicum of truth, especially where the source of the testimony or evidence is remote, or non-personal (*apauruṣeya*) as is said of a class of scriptural source by some.

The foregoing considerations, it can be seen, are as applicable for determining the authenticity of 'ought-sentences' (that might be based on some *a priori* principle) as they would be for so-called 'fact-sentences' (i.e. empirical statements). *Śabdapramāṇa* is relevant for both, though it begins to show signs of weakness in areas such as the quest for transcendental knowledge; unless, of course, *śabda* is identified with *śruti*—an identification and subsummation we have avoided in this work.

There is not scópe enough now and here to develop the implications, philosophical, ethical and religious, of these remarks further (though that may be done elsewhere). However, as an attempt at making sense of the thesis, and in so far as providing a *theoretical* framework, in terms of the epistemological underpinning and correlate ontological assumptions of the so-called 'doctrine of the word' or *śabdapramāṇa*, not altogether unique to Indian thought, we hope the present work can claim a modest contribution.

NOTES TO CHAPTER SEVEN

0. J. N. Mohanty, 'Indian Philosophy Between Tradition and Modernity' in S. S. Rama Rao Pappu and R. Puligandla (eds.), *Indian Philosophy: Past and Present* (Delhi, 1982, pp233-252), p237 & p250. (See also n2 Intro. *supra*.)

1. A reference that will occur often in this chapter is the writer's paper on '*Jñāna* and *Pramā* : The Logic of Knowing – A Critical Appraisal', *Journal of Indian Philosophy*, 13 (1985), pp73-102.

2a. For discussion see J. N. Mohanty, *GTT* [see note 7 below for details], p25-26; and 'Introduction' (*supra*), Ch. 1, and '*Jñāna* and *Pramā*', pp79-82.
Cf. Udayana, *Nyāyakusumāñjali* IV i-iv: *avyāpteradhikavyāpteralakṣaṇamapūrvadṛk, yathārthānubhavo, mānamanapekṣatayeṣyate. . . arthenaiva viśeṣo hi nirākāratayā dhiyām*. Most simply stated as: *yathārthānubhavaḥ pramā*.

2. *Ibid.*

3a. See Karl H. Potter, 'Towards a Conceptual Scheme for Indian Epistemologies', in *Self, Knowledge and Freedom, Essays for Kalidas Bhattacharyya*, Mohanty and Banerjee (eds.), 1978, pp17-30.

3. Although the definition is of perceptual knowledge, Gautama describes the *jñāna* as being *avyabhicāri vyavasāyātmakam, NS* I 1 4. Udayana is more explicit: *Iyam eva ca arthāvyabhicāritā pramāṇasya yat . . . avisaṃvādaḥ arthasvarūpaprakārayoḥ, Pariśuddhi* (in *Nyāyadarśana*, Mithila, 1967, p24; also cited in K Chakrabarti, 'Indian Theories of Truth', n15 [see note 28 below for details]); *cf* Jayanta: *avyabhicāriṇīmasandigdhām-arthopalibdhaṃ vidadhatī*, in *Nyāyamañjarī* (CSS 1971, vol I, p. 12).

4a. *Nyāyabhāṣya* I.1.4 (Uddyotakara's variant reading need not detain us here).

4. *Tarka-saṃgraha* (=TS) #35 (BORI edn. 1974 p23); author's *Dīpikā and Govardhana's Nyāya-bodhinī* (*ibid*). *Bhāṣā-Pariccheda* (=BP): *tatprakāraṃ yajjñānaṃ tadvad-viśeṣyakam* (#135, see also *Siddhānta-muktāvalī* on same).

5. Gaṅgeśopadhyaya, *Tattvacintāmani* (=*TC*) vol.I (*pratyakṣakhaṇḍa*, N. S. Rāmānuja Tātāchārya (ed.), Tirupati, 1973):*pramāṇajñaptivāda* pp177; for convenience (and because recent discussions have focused on this, and since it also has a translation of the *prāmāṇyajñaptivāda* [=*prāmāṇyavāda* section] with notes), we shall also refer to Jitendranath Mohanty, *Gaṅgeśa's Theory of Truth* (1966), hereafter *GTT* – thus, no. 15, p111, and discussion on p42-44.

6. *GTT* p46; and Commentaries on *TC* (*prāmāṇyajñaptivāda*) pp128-129, 177.

7a. *TC, loc cit.*

7. *TC, Ibid* (p177) (*GTT* p111; Potter's translation is preferred ('Indian epistemology', p312, see note 28 below).

8. *Ibid*, p181; *GTT*, p119; and *Tarkasaṃgraha* #35 (*loc cit): tadabhāvavati tat-prakārako'nubhavo'yathārthaḥ*.

9. See Jayanta, *Nyāyamañjarī, pratyakṣa* in (discussion on *avyabhicārī* (p82), and *Tarka-bhāṣā* (p2. p37. Poona edn. 1953).

10. *TS #64 (op cit): ekasmin dharmiṇi viruddhanānādharmavaiśiṣṭyāvagāhi jñānaṃ saṃśayaḥ; yathā sthāṇurvā puruṣo veti*. Likewise in *BP* #129, and *Nyāya-sūtra (NS)* I i 23, and *bhāṣya* thereon; putting together *samānadharma* and *anekadharma*: same and diverse characteristics.

11a. *Nyāyabhāṣya, op cit*, Introduction. We may attempt the following reading : successful activity in respect of an object is obtained through a (valid) means of knowledge (*pramāṇa*); hence *pramāṇa* is invariably connected with an object (*arthavat*). Could Diṅnāga, the Buddhist logician, have meant something similar when he suggested that *prameya* (object of knowledge) depends upon the nature of the *pramāṇa*? (See note 23 below.) Gaṅgeśa in *TC, prāmāṇyavāda* #5, p123. See Jayanta on *tattvajñāna* and *niḥśreyas* (arguing against the Mīmāṃsakas that the *summum bonum* has to do merely with results of sacrifice) in *NM* (p6 ff.)

11b. *pramāyā guṇaganyatvamutpattau paratastvam, pramā'sādhāraṇakāraṇam guṇaḥ; apramā'sādhāraṇakāraṇam doṣaḥ – Tarkasamgraha-Dīpikā,* under #63 (BORI p56). Jayanta's view is that *guṇa* is in addition to the entire collocation of causal conditions for the purpose (*op cit* p150).

11. *Vedāntaparibhāṣā (VP)* VII 1: *na tu adhikaguṇamapekṣate pramāmātre anugataguṇābhāvāt.*

12. *TS-D* #63 (BORI), and continues: *anumittau vyāpakavati vyāpyajñānam. . . śābdajñāneyathārthayogyatājñānam. Cf.* Dharmarāja's further objections, VII 2-3 (*qv.* preceding note), suggesting that there is no contact between the sense-organ and the parts, particularly in the case of colour and self-awareness.

13. John Locke, *Essay on Human Understanding*, Book II, ch.19. *Vide: Nyāya-Bodhinī* on *TS* #34 and #65 (BORI p22, p65).

14a. *na smṛterapramāṇatvam gṛhitagrāhitākṛtam. api tvanartha-janyatvam tadaprāmāṇyakāraṇam. (nanu kathamanarthajā smṛtiḥ tadāruḍasya vastunaḥ tadānīmsattvāt.) Nyāyamañjarī (loc cit,* p21).

14. See Vātsyāyana and Uddyotakara on *NS* IV 2 33-37. And the notion of *anāhārya* (unconscious) in *mānasaviparyaya* ('mental illusion'), under which come dreams, *TS-D* #64 on *apramā*) And Jayanta's notion of *bodhābodhasvabhāva* is interesting, but he is using this against the Buddhist who argue that consciousness is sufficient for *pramāṇa*, by adding non-conscious factors.

15. For a discussion of differences between *svataḥprāmāṇya* and *parataḥprāmāṇya*, and the role of *anuvyavasāya* (introspection) and *anumāna* (inference), *Tarkabhāṣā prāmāṇyavāda* section (pp136-142); *Tarka-samgraha-Dīpikā* under #63 (BORI p55f; Udayana in *Nyāyakusumāñjali* (Kashi Sans. 1957, p. 220ff.); Jayanta *NM* (pp. 146-166); and for a discursive analysis, *GTT,* Introduction and pp. 111ff.

16. *Tarkabhāṣā* (1953) p39: *kimayam sthāṇurvā puruṣo vā*? Also see note 10 above.

17. In both its traditional and revised forms (post 'Gettier problem' and Lehrer qualifications) – see R. M. Chisholm *Theory of Knowledge*, Ch. 6, p103; and his *Perceiving: A Philosophical Study,* (Cornell University Press) Ithaca, 1957, p. 16ff, where a distinction between 'know' and 'belief' is made.

18. In deference to Potter's objection that *yogyatāyāthārthya* need not just mean 'things' or 'objects', but could indicate competency in yielding some purpose, goal or satisfaction. (In personal comment on earlier work). This, as he also points out, is the problem with the ambiguity implied in the term *artha*. (See note 28 below). This apparent ambiguity arises because the object of knowledge as also the satisfaction achieved through the action it leads to are both called *artha*. That is, both the antecedent and the consequence are identified by the same term, but possibly not with the same intent or epistemological significance. Vātsyāyana's opening statement of his *Nyāyabhāṣya* on *NS*, as we remarked earlier, only helps to confound the issue. See note 11a above; and more to follow.

19. Although in perceptual knowing at least the *viṣayatā* would be directly linked with the object or thing of which it is an awareness – i.e. it is an awareness not in the representational connection but in the directly illuminative presentation. Thus it is not the awareness that is known but the object *itself* (e.g. 'This is a cat'), this stage of the cognitive process is called *vyavasāya*. (We noted this in note 30, 'Introduction'.)

The reflective or introspective awareness, which is called *anuvyavasāya*, on the other hand, makes the former awareness known, in the form, say, 'I am aware that this is a cat', or more precisely as Gaṅgeśa would have it: 'I have a knowledge of *this* (*viśeṣya*) as having 'thisness' and 'catness' (*prakāra*) as its qualifiers', but no *relation* is apprehended, which is in the actual awareness, and without apprehension of the relation (of *samavāya* or 'inherence' between *viśeṣya* and *prakāra*) the *prāmāṇya* or truth-value is not made evident. For this reason, an inference is necessary to apprehend the relation and its rightness in the context. The fact of *anuvyavasāya* in respect of the apprehension of the cognition, and the inference in respect of the apprehension of the truth-value means that both are 'known' from 'other sources' (*parataḥ*). See *TS-D* under #63; also *GTT* pp154-157; *TB, prāmāṇyavāda* section (BORI, 1979, pp50-56),; for other places, refer to note 15 above. 'Introduction'.

20a. *prāmāṇyaṃ svata evotpadyate jñāyate ca. . .tacca jñānasāmāṇyasāmagrīprayojyam*; *VP* VII 1; stated another way, by Kumārila: *tasmāt bodhātmakatvena prāptā buddheḥ pramāṇatā, arthānyathātvahetūtthadoṣajñānādapodyate, Ślokavārttika* (*codanāsūtra* #53, 1978, p46) See also Pārthasārathi Miśra's comments on this in *Nyāyaratnākara*, and *Śāstradīpikā* (*codanāsūtra, Tarka-pāda* #14-18, 1940; txt in *SD* ed. Rāma Miśra Śāstri, Banaras, 1891, pp13-14).

20. *jñāna-prāmāṇyaṃ tadaprāmāṇyāgrāhakayāvajjñānagrāhakasāmagrīgrāhyatvam* (stated in *TS-D* #63). We have presented a rather simplified view of the *svataḥ*;there are different versions within it: according to Prabhākara, in each awareness, the content of the experience, the subject, and the object experienced are self-revealed, and with the exception of memory every awareness is true. Murāri Miśra accepts that an awareness or rather the *jñātatā* (the *knownness* or *apprehendedness* of the object) is revealed in an *anuvyavasāya* (reflective or introspective awareness), but he wants to argue, unlike the Naiyāyikas, that *prāmānya* (truth) of the *jñāna* is *also* revealed in this second-order reflection because here the relation of the awareness to the object is brought to light. Falsity, on the hand, though is not revealed in *anuvyavasāya*, but in a distinct inference as a result of doubt brought about by some defect (*doṣabādha*) in the situation. While Kumārila rejects *anuvyavasāya*, he maintains that the same process that self-presents the *jñātatā*, curiously in a kind of intuitional inference (*jñātatāliṅgakānumitti*), also reveals its truth, and that falsity is apprehended *ab extra* at the recognition of some defect in the means of knowing (e.g. jaundice in the eyes), or when the awareness is found to be contradicted by another awareness or rather knowledge.
Keśava Miśra objects that both these views should then admit that the falsity of an inerrant awareness is also self-presented (*svataḥ*) in the same way. *Tarkabhāṣā*, (*op cit*, 1979, p55), where the Mīmāṃsā· views are canvassed then refuted.) Pārthasārathi Miśra defends Kumārila in *Śāstradīpikā* (*loc cit*).

Echoing the Advaita view, Dharmarāja states that truth is intrinsically apprehended in the awareness, while falsity is inferred from the the failure to lead to successful activity, or *via* the evidence of contradiction or falsification (*VP*, VII.10, Intro.#4, and VI 1). It is curious that Dharmarāja does not mention *abādhitatva* as such and novelty in his short treatment of *prāmāṇyavāda*, but it is clear that this is a conciliatory move, for he brings in both memory and *pravṛttisāmarthya* (successful activity), that would please most Naiyāyikas. It may also be noted, however, that *pravṛttisāmarthya* to Dharmarāja, as to other Advaitins, is a test of *abādhitatva* or unfalsifiedness, and not *vice versa*. See also note 64 below.

To mention one or two Buddhist views, In Yogācāra psychology, consciousness alone is *pramāṇa*, there being no other 'instruments' of knowledge *nor* any awareness apart from modes of consciousness; awareness being consciousness in self-nature it is self-revealed. Diṅnāga also accepted that awareness as *pramāṇa* is self-apprehended (*sva-saṃvitti*) (in *Pramāṇasammucaya*, *qv.* M. Hattori, note 23 below). On the question of truth, the standard account would seem to be that every awareness at its origin is 'invalid' (*aprāmāṇya*), and remains so until it leads to some actual practical outcome (*arthakriyākāritā*). The awareness is then said to be *avisaṃvādaka*, in conformity with the object, *because* or as a consequence of its pragmatic character, and not that it achieves its pragmatic success because it is true to reality. For a contrast, *cf. TB: yathārtho avisaṃvādi* (BORI, 1979, p78).

21. The 'real' (*viṣaya*) in Mīmāṃsā is tied to the notion of *jñātatā*, the *knowness* of what is unknown object; it could be argued that this is more of an epistemological concept that does not show a *direct* connecting link with the ontological correlate. But Nārāyaṇa Bhaṭṭa makes a lot of *jñātatattvārtha* as the *viṣaya* or *yathārtha*, arguing against the Prābhākarans for whom the word 'real' has no significance and there is no false cognition, and so there is no need for them to distinguish delusion, doubt, etc, from true apprehension. Nārāyaṇa Bhaṭṭa states that since there are awarenesses like delusion, error, etc., in which a thing is apprehended otherwise than what it is, the word 'real' (*tattva*) is meant to exclude these: *anyathāgrahaṇapabhramādijñānasadbhāvāt tannirāsārthaṃ tattvapadam, Mānameyodaya*, I.10 (*pramānāṇi*) also 2, 8, and 15: *jñātatattvārthajñānsādhanameva naḥ.pramāṇamiti nirṇītaṃ tadviśeṣaṇātha bruve*. Thus *yathārtha* is restricted in its application to true awareness in terms of the categories we have been discussing.

Pārthasārathi has no difficulty using *yāthārthya* in this sense, as being synonymous with *viṣayathātva* (and not in the sense intended by the Prābhākarans), and therefore this cannot be the character of each and every awareness, even if it might appear to be so in the apprehension of the *jñātatā*. (*Śāstradīpikā, op cit*, p15 and pp28-29). Curiously, this would mean that in the case of some awareness falsity is intrinsically mistaken for *viṣayathātva*!
But this a problem created by Kumārila's insistence that every awareness is true by its very nature (i.e. as a product of the appropriate functions) so long as there is no apprehension of defect (*Ślokavārttika, codanāsūtra*#47: *svataḥ sarvapramānāṇāṃ prāmāṇyamiti gamyatām, na hi svato'stī śaktiḥ kartumanyena śakyate*, and #80: *tasmād dṛḍhaṃ yadutpannaṃ napi saṃvādamṛcchati, jñānāntareṇa vijñānaṃ tatpramāṇaṃ pratīyatām;* and Pārthasārathi's comments on same (*ibid* p45). Kumārila obviously thinks that 'non-apprehension of defects' is tantamount to 'non-presence of defects'. This confusion is not there in the Advaita and later Mīmāṃsā views.

22. Certainly this would be true of *tatprakārakatva*, but not if *tadvati* is added, which is meant to relate the cognitive configuration to the objective correlate. So it is a curious thing for an Advaitin to suggest. Mohanty puzzles over this admission on the part of Madhusūdana Sarasvatī, in *GTT* p15 (and refers to *Advaitaratnarakṣaṇam*, in *Advaitasiddhi*; note 36). Still, Madhūsudana must tell us then how a true *jñāna* would be distinguished from a false *jñāna* or *bhrama*. Perhaps to him the criterion is in the latter's failure to lead to unwaveriung activity and in not revealing something unknown. See also note 25, 26 that follow for another view.

23. See end of note 20 above. Although Diṅnāga seems to have made *artha* as *prameya* every bit depended upon *pramāṇa*, as a means of knowledge rather than just a means to fruitful activity. See M. Hattori, *Diṅnāga, On Perception*, 1968 (p76 and *passim*).

24. *Arthadīpikā* on *VP* by Śivadatta, (Chow. Sans., 1968, p121).

25a. Jayanta, in *Nyayamañjarī*, I, p96-98.

25. *Arthadīpikā* (*op cit*), p121. Also in Gajānanaśāstri Musalagaoṅkar's *Prakāśa* (in Hindi), (Varanasi, 1963) p316.

26. in *GTT* p15, note 36: *yadvapi vedāntināṃ mate tadvati tatprakārakatvarūpaṃ prāmāṇyaṃ bhramasādhāraṇameva*; which is meant to be a comment on the passage in *VP* VII 1: *smṛtyanubhava-sādhāraṇam (saṃvādi-pravṛttyanukūlam) tadvati tatprakārajñānatvaṃ prāmāṇyam. Cf* Pt Pañcānana Bhaṭṭācārya Śāstrī, Sans. comm. p220. Now, although memory is regarded as a *pramā* (*VP* Intro. 4), it is not considered to be false awareness in any sense; in fact, memory is valid if it has for its content a non-contradicted *viṣaya* (*ibid*). To have this it must have *tadvati tatprakāraka*, that is why the *tadvati* definition is common (*sādhāraṇa*) to both true *jñāna* (judgement) and *smṛti*

or memory (VII 1), and must, therefore, *a fortiori* exclude *bhrama*.

27. *Vedāntakalpalatikā* (ed/tr, R.D. Karmarkar, BORI, 1962). pp100-103, p106-108.

28. *GTT* Introduction, pp1-2, *passim*.

Professor Karl Potter takes up these remarks in the context of the ambiguities evident in the different uses of *artha* (note 18 above), along with the Madhusūdana's inclusion of *bhrama* in the *tadvati tatprakārakatvam* defn. (*cf.* n22), and the pragmatic concern (*arthakriyākāritva*) of the Buddhists (such as Dharmottara), as well as William James' and Stephen Pepper's subordination of correspondence under a pragmatist (or instrumentalist) theory. Potter concludes that ' "prāmāṇya" does not translate as "truth" (i.e., correspondence with reality), despite standard translation practice, but rather connotes a more pragmatic criterion of being capable of producing or helping to produce satisfaction in action'. The moral, therefore, is that 'the correspondence assumption should not be imposed on the *pramāṇa*-terminology'. And unlike the justified true belief account, which is a descriptive theory of truth, Potter strongly suggests, the Indian concern does not make the absolute fact-value distinction, and is not devoid of ethical and aesthetically normative concerns; concerns that have to do with values, human aspirations, goals, purposes, in short, *satisfaction*. Karl H. Potter, 'Does Indian Epistemology Concern Justified True Belief?', *Journal of Indian Philosophy*, Vol 12, no 4 Dec. 1984, pp. 307-328. (Hereafter Potter, 'Indian Epistemology'). An earlier statement of this, based on an hierachical value-satisfaction model, was presented in his '*Prāmāṇya* as Meaning Divorced from Truth-Conditions', International Conference in Philosophy, Jadavpur University (Calcutta), Jan. 1983 (unpublished). Hereafter Potter, '*Prāmāṇya*' (Jadavpur).

Two papers in response were presented in a subsequent symposium (where Professor Potter's 'Indian Epistemology' was read), namely by Professor J. N. Mohanty and Dr Kisor Chakrabarti. These have been published in the same issue of *JIP* (vol. 12, no 4, Dec. 1984) - viz. J. N. Mohanty: 'Prāmāṇya and Workability—A Response to Potter', pp329-338. (Hereafter Mohanty, 'Prāmāṇya and Workability'), and Kisor Kumar Chakrabarti: 'Some Remarks on Indian Theories of Truth', pp. 339-356.
Since the present writer participated in the Jadavpur debate on *prāmāṇya*, following up discussions with first two of the writers, and subsequently published '*Jñāna* and *Pramā*' (n1 above), this contribution is, in its own way, part of the on-going disquisition on *prāmāṇya*.

29. *Vedāntakalpalatikā (op cit)*, pp106-110 (see also n27 above).

30a. *Brahma-sūtra-bhāṣya (BSB)* I.i.2: *na vastu-yāthātmyajñānaṃ puruṣabudddhyapekṣam, kiṃ tarhi vastutantram eva tat. na hi sthāṇāvekasmin sthāṇurvā puruṣo'nyo veti tattvajñānaṃ bhavati tatra puruṣo'nyo veti mithyājñānam. sthāṇuretveti tattvajnānam, vastutantratvāt. evaṃ bhūtavastuviṣayānāṃ prāmānyaṃ vastutantram. tatraivaṃ sati brahmajnānamapi vastutantrameva, bhūtavastuviṣayatvāt.Brahmasūtraśaṅkarabhāṣyam. Catussūtrī* section (ed. Viśveśvar Siddhānta Śiromaṇi, Vidyābhawan Sanskrit Granthamālā no 137, Varanasi, 1966; pp66-67).

30. *BSB* I.i.4: *jñānaṃ tu pramāṇajanyam, pramāṇaṃ ca yathābhūtavastuviṣayam, ato jñānaṃ kartumakartumanyathā vā kartumaśakyaṃ kevalaṃ vastutantrameva tat, na codanātantram, nāpi puruṣatantram, tasmānmānasatve'pi jñānasya mahadvailakṣaṇyam.* (*Ibid,* p133).

31. As mentioned in note 28 above, Professor Karl Potter raised this issue at a conference in Jadavpur, in 1983, and discussions have continued in subsequent symposia and published papers.

32. We have already referred to the apparent ambiguities, notes 18, 21, 23, 30a.

33. For detailed explanation of *artha* in *arthībhāvanā* and *śābdībhāvanā*, see Kumārila Bhaṭṭa, *Ślokavārttika*, and *Arthasaṃgraha* (*qv, supra* ch 4, p135ff, p148, p159).

34. See note 18 above, and 'Introduction' (*supra*), under *pramāṇa*, on discussion of *tattvajñāna*.

35. 'Prāmāṇya and Workability', p333, and p335 respetively.

36. *VP* VII,2-4. See also *Arthadīpikā* p121-2. Also notes 20 and 20a above, respectively *Cf.* Jayanta: *bodhābodhasvabhāva sāmagrī prāmāṇyam (op cit.* p12).

37. *Ibid* VII 7.

38a. J. N. Mohanty, *GTT*, p24.

38. *Ibid*, and *passim*.

39a. Pārthasārathi Miśra uses the term *arthakriyājñānam*; he further argues that it cannot be *avyabhicārī*, for: *svapnāvasthāyāmasatyapyudakāharaṇe'rthakriyāvijñānadarśanāt*. . . *priyāsaṅgamavijñānena svapnāvasthāyāṃ sukhadarśanāt. (Śāstradīpikā, tarkapāda, op cit.* p15); Pārthasārathi then suggests that although awareness is self-evidently true it loses this when there is evidence of defect or it's incongruency with another experience (*ibid*). See also discussion in J. N. Mohanty, *GTT*, p22.

39. Mohanty, 'Prāmāṇya and Workability', p333.

40a. *VP* Intro. 4; Pārthasārathi Miśra in *Śāstradīpikā* under *autpattikasūtra*: *kāraṇa doṣabādhakajñānarahitamagṛhītagrāhijñānam* (*op cit*, p28), elsewhere: *jñānaprāmāṇyaṃ nāmābādhitārtha viṣayaktvam* (cognition is said to be true whose content is not falsified).

40. The problem with verification is both a logical and a practical one. Logically, the problem is with its inductivist assumptions; and also if *p* entails *q*, and *q* is demonstrated, it does not necessarily follow that *p* also obtains. On the practical side, apart from the *infinite regress* problem, there is also the problem of determining which evidence is confirmatory and which not, and whether any of them is final. The alternative to this is the *falsificationist* approach. Logically this seems quite more plausible, for if *p* entails *q*, and -*q* is shown then (by *modus tollens*) it follows that *p* does not obtain. One then makes predictions and looks for their potential falsifiers. If the predictions are not falsified, and instead are corroborated, then the theory is said to have withstood refutation. This theory becomes operative, until a rival theory falsifies it or undermines its explanatory power. There are, however, practical problems of translating this logical convinction into actual and decisive test-situations, but at least the shortcomings of the *infinite regress* and the inductivist problems are not there. These are its merits. And I believe this is the sort of paradigmatic matrix Indian epistemology should be moving towards, as I attempt to argue for in this chapter.

As a one-time ardent pupil of Popperian thought (under Professor Alan Musgrave, Otago), I can't resist quoting Sir Karl Popper in this very connection: 'the criterion of the scientific status of a theory is its *falsifiability*, or *refutability*, or *testability*', and 'there is no more rational procedure than the method of trial and error – of conjecture and refutation', in *Conjectures and Refutations: The Growth of Scientific Knowledge*, 1965, p37, 51.

One question that Indian epistemology will have to face if it takes the sort of falsificationism suggested here, is whether it would be happy to accept the reduction of evidence into *formal* logical contradictions (as derived, say, from *modus tollens*). The other question has to do with the provisionality in the Indian thesis of what is accepted as true until falsified; it could be said that the Indian commitment to truth is of a *kind* rather than of a *degree*. But by the same token, the problem (evidently serious one in the Popperian scheme), of determining the legitimate basic observation statement as the decisive falsifier in a theoretical system (as distinct from a formal logical equation) does not threaten to give way to indeterminancy or (epistemological) anarchy in the Indian system where the test situation is intended to be a more direct one between experiences (*anubhava, jñāna*). The latter too, of course, has its own problems.

41. Gaṅgeśa, for instance, might object that a falsifying judgement would have to be shown to be true, and therefore its own unfalsifiedness would have to be established, for from the fact that *p* is falsified by *q* it does not follow that *p* is false and *q* true. Mohanty, *GTT*, p41.

42. At least a Mīmāṃsaka, like Pārthasārathi Miśra, would argues that if one judgement were to depend on another judgement for its corroboration and confirmation of the successful utility, then it might take thousand lifetimes before we can said to know an object truly! (*loc cit*).

43. 'Prāmāṇya and Workability', pp331-333.

44. Potter, 'Indian Epistemology', pp318-320; Mohanty, 'Prāmāṇya and Workability', p334. See also R. Chisholm, *Theory of Knowledge*, p18, p103ff.

45. A. J. Ayer, *The Problem of Knowledge*, (1964),p35.

46. On Udayana's attempt to reconcile *svataḥ* with *parataḥ*, see *GTT*, p49, & n.41, (even though this applies to inference only), on a 'weak' sense of intrinsic truth in Nyāya. Admittedly, this attempt at a hybridisation has to be investigated further, and its parallel in other similar and radically different attempts have to be looked into. (*Vide*, Jayanta in *Nyāyamañjarī* pp55-60, *passim*). Gaṅgeśa, while not admitting intrinsic truth even in the case of awareness of an (introspective) awareness of an earlier awareness, retorts that it is enough that the judgement should not be known to be false – *GTT*, p65.

Pārthasārathi Miśra admits that, due to defects in the human channel of information-gathering, there do occur mistaken ascriptions of truth to what is later contradicted and therefore shown to be false (*op cit*, p15, *qv.* n40a above). To be definitive on this he would have to give us conditions under which contradictions would occur and falsity would be detected.

47. Admittedly this attempt at breaking the hiatus between the *svataḥ* and *parataḥ* has to be developed further, in light of the debate mentioned earlier (in note 28 and comments in note 40, above). See also discussion in Mohanty, 'Indian Theories of Truth' (1980) pp. 447ff, especially on the question that if *svataḥ* is applicable to 'ought-sentences' and the *parataḥ* theory does well for factual statements, then how would the 'combined' theory fare unequivocally with both sentences?

48a. *Tarkabhāṣā*: *anena tu kevalavyatirekyanumānenābhyāsadaśāpannasya [jñānasya] pramāṇye'vabodhite taddṛṣṭāntena [jala]pravṛtteḥ pūrvamapi tajjātīyatvena liṅgenānvyayatirekyanumānenānya-jñānasyānabhyāsadaśāpannasya prāmāṇyam-anumīyate [iti]*. (BORI, 1979, p56: also see Cinnambhaṭṭa, in *Prakāśikā*, *ibid*, p195-6) Annambhaṭṭa, *TS-D* on #63: *prathamaṃ jalajñānānantaraṃ pravṛttau satyaṃ jalalabhe sati pūrvotpannaṃ jalajñānaṃ pramā samarthapravṛttijanakatvāt yannaivaṃ tannaivam yathāpramā iti vyatirekiṇā pramātvaṃ niściyate. dvitīyādijñāneṣu pūrvajñānadṛṣṭāntena tatsajātīyatvaliṅgenānvyavatirekiṇāpi gṛhyate*. See also Jayanta *NM* (I pp149-150.), and Gaṅgeśa's more moderate version in *GTT* in p64 and pp206ff. At least Gaṅgeśa realised that *not false* is all that one can say from a *vyatireki* inference, but as for the implied *anvaya* he may not agree with our reservations.

48. *TB*, (*ibid*) p78.

49a. See note above, and 48a and comments therein.

49. For discussion, *vide* Phyllis Granoff, *Philosophy and Argument in Late Argument* p35. *Cf.* The Buddhists do not understand the same thing by the term *avisaṃvāditva*, eg. in Dharmakīrti (*Pramāṇavārttika* II.1). See also note 20 and 23 above.

50. *Vedānta Kaumudī*, cited in P. K. Sundaram, *Advaita Epistemology*, (p7 n18a).

51. K. Chakrabarti, *op cit*, p340.

52. As A. N. Whitehead noted, apart from action, contemplation of truth has an interest of its own. *Adventure of Ideas*, (1942) p281. Dewey and other pragmatists admitted

this at least in regard to logical and mathematical truths. Dewey, *How we Think* (London, 1909), p182-3; *Logic: The Theory of Inquiry* (Boston, D. C. Heath, 1933). See also notes 76-79 below.

53. *Tarka-bhāṣā: tatra sapahalavatī yā pravṛttiḥ sa samarthā tayā [taj]jñānasya [yāthar-thyam] prāmāṇyamanumīyate. prayogaśca. vivādādhyāsitaṃ jalajñānaṃ pramānaṃ samarthapravṛttijanakatvāt yattu na pramāṇaṃ na tat samarthāṃ pravṛttiṃ janayati yathā pramāṇabhāsa iti kevalavyatirekī. atra ca saphalapravṛttijanakaṃ yajjalajñānaṃ tat pakṣaḥ. tasya prāmāṇyaṃ sādhyam. yathārthatvamityarthaḥ.* (*op cit*, 1979, p56). See also note 48a above.

54. *Ibid.*

55. *Ibid, qv.* note 48a above.

56. See note 45 above.

57. Compare Strawson: 'To understand a sentence is to know what thought it expresses or is capable, in given contextual circumstances, of expressing; and to know this is to know what we would be believing if we took that thought to be *true*' – 'Knowledge and Truth', (IPQ, Poona, April 1976 No 2, pp273-282, p274).

58. *VP* IV 25. The chief amongst these hermeneutical principles are: 1) consistency of substantive and concluding passages; 2) repeatability; 3) novelness of the descriptive content; 4) degree of satisfaction yielding; 4) commendation and disconfirmation in other passages – i.e. coherency of whole text; and its rational persuasiveness. We mentioned these in the previous ch. as well, and say just a little more towards the very end of this ch. But a more thorough and critical work on Mīmāṃsā hermeneutics of textual interpretation is far from complete. An attempt towards commencing this (based on Kumārila and Pārthasārathi Miśra) has been made in the writer's working monograph '*Apauruṣeya* in Mīmāṃsā – a possibility of trans-personal word, towards a paradigm for *śruti*', presented as part of a symposium on '*Apauruṣeya*' in the Congress of the International Association for the History of Religions, Sydney, August 1985. See also note 124 on a complementary project.

59. There is a similar criticism against the revolutionary conception of scientific progress of Thomas Kuhn made by the piece-meal protagonists, particularly Karl Popper. But we have also in mind the Quine-Duhem thesis that aims to protect a theory of some magnitude from too earnest a rejection. See *Criticism & Growth of Knowledge*, Lakatos & Musgrave (eds). Popper himself later shows conservatism towards a hastily rejection; and Lakatos makes a case for degenerating programmes to survive yet longer. See issues in Paul Feyerabend's *Against Method*, 1975.

60. *NM*, (*op cit*, p84-85, & *passim*). *Cf. Nyāyakalikā*, p4. See also J. N. Mohanty, 'Nyāya Theory of Doubt' (*qv.* note 98 below).

61a. *na hi śrutiśatamapi sītaḥ agniḥ aprakāśo veti bhruvatprāmāṇyaṃ upaiti. yadi brūyāt sītaḥ agniḥ aprakāśo veti tathāpi arthāntaraṃ śruteḥ vivakṣitaṃ kalpyaṃ prāmāṇyānyathānupapatteḥ* : a hundred *śrutis* may declare that fire is cold or that it is dark; still they possess no authority in this matter. If *śruti* should at all declare that fire is cold or that it is dark, we would still suppose that its purport is something else quite other than the apparent one. Śaṅkara on *Bhagavadgītā* XVIII.66-67 (Gokhale edn. Poona 1950; also in *Complete Works of Śaṅkara*, Madras, 1981, vol. VI.) Likewise, in *BSB* II i 13, Śaṅkara states that if *śruti* contradicts reason the *śruti* must be interpreted in another way. . .it follows that it would be unreasonable for *śruti* to contravene what has been established through other sources of knowledge.

61. See Śaṅkara in *BSB* I iii 28. K. Satchidananda Murty in his *Reason and Revelation in Advaita Vedānta*, has been most unfair to Śaṅkara; for a more balanced critique, see Wilhelm Halbfass, *Studies in Kumārila and Śaṅkara* (Ch. II on 'Human Reason

and Vedic Revelation in the Philosophy of Śaṅkara', *Studien Zur Indologie Und Iranistik*, Monographie 9, Reinbek, 1983 [courtesy of author].
Compare Paul Hacker, his numerous papers and references to Śaṅkara, especially, 'Śaṅkara der Yogin und Śaṅkara der Advaitin einige beobachtungen', *Weiner Zeitschrift für die Kunde Süd-und Ostasiens*, vol XII-XII (1968-69) pp119-148), and 'Śaṅkara's Conception of Man'—both reprinted in Paul Hacker, *Kleine Schriften*, edited by L. Schmithausen, Franz Steiner, Wiesbaden, 1978 (pp213-242 and pp243-251 resp/ly); see notes 127 and, especially, 136 below. Also see J. Taber, (*qv.* notes 135 below, and elsewhere).

62. On matters such as 'freedom of human will, the hope of a future life, and the existence of God', and so forth, the transcendental critique has 'convinced completely me that, as reason is incompetent to arrive at affirmative assertions in this field, it is equally unable, indeed even less able, to establish any negative conclusion in regard to these questions'—Immanuel Kant, *Critique of Pure Reason* (Kemp Smith tr., 1970, p602), also his openness to certain other questions, on purposive unity, etc. (pp565ff).

63. For Pārthasārathi Miśra's attempt to deal with the issue of 'correspondence' (*yathārthajñāna*) see *Śāstradīpikā*, on *autpattika-sūtra* (op cit p29, p31-35, p51)

64. *VP* Intro.#4: *abādhitārtha-viṣayakajñāntvam*; more significantly, in the context of *śabda* generated judgement, his opening statement in the *śabdapramāṇa* ch. IV 1: *mānāntareṇa na bādhyate.* And Pārthasārathi Miśra, preceding note and note 40a.
Vacaspati in his *Bhāmatī* on *BSB-catussūtrī*) states three criteria for *prāmāṇya*, one of which is *abādhitatva*, (trns. S. S. Suryanarayan Sastri and Kunhan Raja, Adyar, pp 159-160).

65. Compare Imre Lakatos on Research Programmes, in the context of remarks in note 59 above; in Lakatos & Musgrave (eds), *Criticism and the Growth of Knowledge.*

66. *Ibid*, and various contributions in the same volume, such as Feyeraband's.

67. '*Jñāna* and *Pramā*', pp95-96, and note 37; Phyllis Granoff, (*op cit*, p37, & *passim*). See also note 41 above for Gaṅgeśa's objection.

68. *VP*, IV 45-46. Dharmarāja suggests there is repetition in the case of secular sentences, though not in scriptural sentences, but he is prepared to accept both as expressing something novel, at least from the point of view of the hearer. Madhusūdana supports this criterion extensively *(ajñātārtha-niścayatmakameva..)*; see his *Advaitasiddhi* on *mithyātvanirūpaṇe*, esp. third definition (Varanasi edn. pp123ff). It is also interesting to see how the notion of 'novelty' of a theory or its predictive ability has played a strong role in philosophy of science as a measure of verisimilitude between rival theories.

69. Chisholm, *Theory of Knowledge*. p122.

70. Popper, *The Logic of Scientific Discovery* (London, 1968), and *Conjectures and Refutations* (RKP, 1965; 1969). See also W. V. O. Quine, *Word and Object* (Camb. MIT Press, 1960), *passim*, and his reservations on the absoluteness of 'objectivity' in science, from an epistemological footing: *From a logical point of view: Logico-Philosophical Essays*' (Harper Torch, N.Y. 1963; Camb. Mass, 1964, p44ff).

71. Thomas Kuhn, *The Structure of Scientific Revolution.*

72. *Asaṃdigdhata* is discussed extensively in *Śāstradīpikā*; see notes 38, 40, 42 above.

73. Potter, '*Prāmāṇya* as Meaning', p5, (and see note 28 above).

74. Naiyāyika's generally understand *saṃvāda* in the context of some previous judgement that had proved to be successful (*arthakriyājñānasaṃvāda*). For a critical discussion, see Jayanta *NM (op cit* p149), and for Gaṅgeśa's objection to *saṃvāda*, see *GTT*, p41. See also note 20 above.

75. *Ibid*: *pravṛtty'nukūla*, or *saphalapravṛttijanakatva*. See *Śāstradīpikā* (*loc cit*).

76. William James, *Pragmatism* (New York, 1907), VI., and *The Meaning of Truth: a sequel*

to pragmatism (New York, 1909; Harvard University Press, in *The Works of William James*), Ch.2. See also note 52 above.

77. Chisholm, *op cit*, 97-98.

78a. Compare text related to note 51 above.

78 See A. J. Ayer, *The Origin of Pragmatism: studies in the philosophy of Charles Sanders Pierce and William James*, London, MacMillan, 1968. To be fair to Potter, he rejects William James' pragmatism as being too 'foundationalist' ('Indian Epistemology', p321; for discussion of Pepper, see *Prāmāṇya* as Meaning, ppl-3).

79. Potter, '*Prāmāṇya* as Meaning', p7, pp10-11ff, and build-up of argument in preceding pages.

80. *Ibid*, p9, pp11-12, see pl-4; and as expressed in discussing the paper in Jadavpur.

81. *Ibid* p5; see also 'Indian Epistemology', discussion on 'workability'.

82. Using Pepper's model, *ibid*, p2, p7-8, p14. This, indeed, is the thrust of Potter's argument in the two papers cited in these discussions, and he blames in part the language of Western philosophy (apparently imbued with the correspondence notion) and within whose ambience much of recent articulation and defence of Indian epistemology, and Indian thought in general, has been carried out. However, we might be reminded that modern Indian writers have been as alive to Continental thought (such as phenomenology, with less of a commitment to the correspondence principle) as to the analytical tradition, though they perhaps payed less attention to the American pragmatic development.

83. Potter, '*Prāmāṇya* as Meaning', p7; and see 'Indian Epistemology', *passim*. But, of course, this is a tricky spot, for as Potter argues 'truth' is not a condition of correspondence, for that would beg the realist assumption, but that its meaning is determined in terms of the satisfaction-relation that a cognitive activity obtains. Yet he does not deny that the 'Indian philosophers are concerned about what reality is, what exists, what is true. That is precisely what they are concerned with' (*Prāmāṇya*, p9, p11), and that concern apparently off-sets the standard objections to western pragmatism when extended to the type of pragmatism prevalent in Indian philosophy.

84. *Ibid*. See also 'Indian Epistemology' : 'There is little or no disagreement among Jains, Buddhists and the various Hindu philosophical *darśanas* about values', after questioning Western scepticism—shared by rationalism, empiricism, modalism and absolutism—about any hierarchy of values in deference to the realist hypothesis of a single reality (p323).

85. Thus Potter rejects the 'fact-value' distinction as being too rigid, but which apparently suits the JTB account. Instead, Potter invokes Nelson Goodman's 'relativity to purpose' utility account of truth; but later reneges the implicit relativism in this account as well. *Ibid* pp322-323.

86. On Potter's reading of *artha*, see pp313-315.

87. Here Potter would argue that the Buddhist and Mīmāṃsā would understand *artha* to be a *purpose* object, which commends itself to pragmatic verification (*ibid*). The ontic status of *artha* is questioned. It would seem, however, that to the Nyāya, even if the *artha* of perceptual object is not the substance, it is clearly the qualities or properties of the *object of cognition (prakāra* in *tad*, thus *tatprakārakatvam*).

88. *Ibid*. Actually, Potter usues the term '*viṣyatathātva* in referring to the Bhāṭṭa view on the relation (R) of the content to the objective of successful activity; but he intends Nyāya's (Udayana's) use of *arthatathātva* in a similar vein. He says the R 'nicely satisfies Gaṅgeśa's analysis of *prāmāṇya*'. (*Ibid*.) *Cf*. Chakrabarti, (*op cit*, p347).

89. *Ibid, passim*; and '*Prāmāṇya* as Meaning', p 10.

90. See notes 32-33 above. To which Mohanty adds: *yāchñā, dhanam, kāraṇam, śabdapratipādya, nivṛtti, prayojanam*, 'Prāmāṇya and Workability', p335.

91. *Ibid*, p337.

92. Dharmarāja likens the efficacy of *śruti* in yielding knowledge of Brahman to the instrumentality of ordinary *śabda* in giving knowledge of (existent) objects (*siddhārtha* or *siddhavastu*), as, e.g., when someone says, 'You have given birth to a son', etc. *VP* IV. 46. See references to *BSB* I i 2; I i 4 earlier, and discussion later. See also Pārthasārathi Miśra on two types of valid locutions: factual and performative, *Śāstradīpikā*, (*autpattika-sūtra*. I v 63).

By contrast, Potter must imply that Brahman is also an ontologically-neutral *value* term, since it is another term for the 'Word' that designates the ultimate purpose of all activity in terms of the penultimate value of liberation. This would be the 'highest reality' as what is 'true' ultimately (*satyasya-satyam*). He sees no difficulty thinking this through for *dharma* as the supreme value that, say, generated the Pūrva Mīmāṃsā ontology. For, Potter reminds us again, 'the ultimate criterion which grounds any ontology is satisfaction'. 'See *Prāmāṇya* as Meaning' on *paramārthasat*, p10-11.

93. See Bernand Williams and Amartya Sen *Utilitarianism and Beyond*, (Camb. Univ. Press, 1982), and recent criticisms of.

94. K. Chakrabarti (*loc cit*).

95. Pārthasārathi Miśra accepts two sorts of reliable authority, that of the *āptaḥ* and that of the Veda (*śruti*); but while the former is liable to defects, and since people are not always trustworthy, its authority is not absolute. *Śāstradīpikā* (I ii 23 [1891 p16]; *& cf* I ii 21 p15:) *pauruṣeyavacanāni tu purusabuddhiprabhavatvādāntyā vipralipsayā vā prayukttāni mūladoṣeṇa dṛṣṭatvādayathārthāni bhavantīti vaiṣamyam*. He also begins to develop Kumārila's *apauruṣeya* argument hereon.

Nyāya writers give strong defence to the *āptaḥ* criterion, even though inference (on the grounds of the reliability of the speaker) is not ruled out in the process, and invalidity is not merely attributed to defect or deceit in the the speaker (as distinct from defects in the utterances and their failure to correspond to reality). This is something that the Bhāṭṭa Mīmāṃsā writers would want to deny. Udayana for the Nyāya and Kumārila and Pārthasārathi for the Mīmāṃsā are the best sources for this debate, in their respective works cited elsewhere. See also 96 below.

96a. Or, to follow Strawson's line: 'one who expresses a supposition expresses a true supposition if and only if things are as, in expressing that supposition, he expressly supposes them to be'; 'Meaning and Truth', *Logico-Linguistic Papers* (1975) p180.

96. Udayana *Nyāyakusumāñjali* III.xvi (for he denies this to the untrustworthy person), and Gautama in *Nyāya Sūtras* 1 i 7; I vii 1: *āptopadeśaḥ śabdaḥ*, puts stress on the reliability of the instructor or speaker. Annaṃbhaṭṭa, likewise : *āptavākyaṃ śabdaḥ; āptastu yathārthavaktā* (*TS*, BORI #59): 'sentence uttered by an authoritative person (is *pramāṇa*); an authoritative person is one whose words are true-to-the-facts'. Also *Tarkabhāṣā* (pp 49-50, 1979; p18, 1953); and Jayanta : *āptopadeṣaḥ śabdaḥ*, *Nyayamañjarī* (pt 1, p137ff); and *Caraka Saṃhitā*, where also the tradition of *āptopadeśaḥ* seems to have originated in the form Nyāya has taken and developed further, although in the former the demiurge Brahmā would perhaps be the first real *āptaḥ* since he holds the Vedas in his hands.

97. N. S. Junankar, *Gautama The Nyāya Philosophy*, (Delhi, 1981), traces the 'besetting sin' of *śabdapramāṇa* to the orthodox espousal of *āptabhāva* ('authority'). He does not regard this part of *śabdapramāṇa* to be 'logically connected with the Nyāya theory of *pramāṇa*', since it underscores an attempt at maintaining ties with the 'holy strings'. pp 493-495, p505. (See the present writer's review of Junankar, elsewhere). We disagree with Junankar that *śabdapramāṇa* deals exclusively with 'belief in' in contradistinction to 'belief that' (p618). For, the analysis of the structure of sentential understanding in the context of the *prāmāṇya* requirements should make it clear that *śabda* relates to

'knowledge *that*' (the distinction between 'knowledge' and 'belief' being spurious to Indian epistemology).

See also Arindam Chakrabarti's response in his incisive review of Junankar in *JIP*, vol. 8, no. 4, 1980, pp401-407, esp. p406.

98. For instance, *A* may readily doubt proposition *x* of *B*, so that *A* does not have to look at its potential refutation of proposition *y*, and whatever performative value it might have for *A*. *Vide*, Mohanty, 'The Nyaya Theory of Doubt', reprinted in his *Phenomenology and Ontology*, (The Hague, 1970).

99. *Tarkabhāṣā*, *śabdanirūpaṇam* section II, (*loc cit*).

100. *Ibid.*

101. See note 96 above. And Vātsyāyana, Uddyotakara and Vācaspati on *NS* 1.1.7. And Jayanta *NM*, I. p138.

102. Cf. Quine, 'From a Logical Point of View', see n 70 above; Feyeraband, *Against Method*.

103. *VP* I.30: *daśamastvam asi ityadau*. . . *śabdādapyaparokṣajñānābhyupagamāt*.

104. Śaṅkara, who also mentions this illustrative story in his *bhāṣya* on *Bṛh. Up* I.iv.7, also on *Tait. Up.* II.i.1, backs it up with another *cogitatio* example : how one can deny the immediate awareness of the intimate subjectivity of oneself? Compare Descartes: *ego cogito, ego sum*. (*Meditations*). Obviously, though, for Śaṅkara, there is no need of *cogito* in pure self-awareness (*sākṣātkārāparokṣātmajñā*), for reasons of the limitations of *cogito* as an adequate indictor of the 'I', no more than could be said of 'I am dreaming' (which to Śaṅkara would succeed in maintaining the delusion where Descartes' evil-intending spirit eventually fails). See *BSB* II.i.14 on dreaming and dying in dreaming.

105. Once *śābdabodha* is distinguished from *śabdajñāna* (or better, from *padajñāna* as *śabdārthajanyajñāna*, as we have repeatedly done in earlier chapters)then the propositional cognition that is generated from the prior cognition of the verbal elements and their mutual juxtaposition, stands to be differentiated. It is for this reason that Vedānta commentators emphasise the 'objective contentness' of 'word'-derived understanding (*śabdajanyabodha*).

106a. Jagadīśa argues that the objects of knowledge in an inferential process are not as well determined and identified as they are in *śabdapramāṇa qua śābdabodha*, which is more directly related to the objects concerned and presented through *śabda*. And in turn is related to the experience of the speaker, making it all the more empirical. See his *Śabdaśaktiprakāśikā*, p7ff: *so'yaṃ niyantritārthatvānna pratyakṣam na cānumā*.

According to the Mīmāṃsā view, every word is capable of generating knowledge – even with regard to the inaccessible (*atyantisatya*). And *śabda* is a different species of *pramāṇa* with regard to the past; the scriptural sentence (*codanā*) is a species of *śabda* and for this reason it is able to connect with the past. But *laukikavacanam* (secular sentences) are not as corrigible as *śruti* is, particularly in respect of *dharma*.

See, Pārthasārathi Miśra, *Śāstradīpikā* : on the redunancy of inference in *śābdabodha*: *avaśyaṃ hi buddhiviśeṣamanumitsatā prathamaṃ padārthasteṣāṃ cānvayayogyatā alokolacayatvyā te calocyamānā drāgeva vākyārthaṃ bodhayantīti nānumānaṃ pratījñanta* (*op cit* p16).

106. See D. M. Datta, *Six Ways of Knowing*, ch. on *sabda*, pp. 338ff.

107. *Ibid.*

108. Kunhan Raja, *Some Fundamental Problems in Indian Philosophy*, p97ff.

109. Jayanta, Jagadīśa, and Gaṅgeśa direct their arguments largely against such charges brought against the Nyāya position; see *Śabdaśaktiprakāśikā*, pp9-29. But are not the Buddha's 'wisdom words' *śabda*, and do not the instructions in the graded steps to enlightenment make recourse to *śabda*, and do not the *mantras* in Mahāyāna-tantric practices

have both intellectual and spiritual efficacy? No Buddhist thinker would deny these, of course, but may continue to stand by the traditional rejection of *śabda* in the form of *āgamapramāṇa*, since this was viewed by Buddhists as a surreptitious means of vindicating the unquestioned authority of the Vedas (and it is the ritualistic *contents* of the Vedas, for most part, that the early Indian Buddhists had difficulties with). However, normative and soteriological concerns and differences should not lead to an unreasonable denial of an epistemological thesis merely because it might have been used or misused for other purposes. Those Buddhists who are inclined to accept *śabda* tend generally to reduce its workings to inference, and thus do not admit the uniqueness of *śabda*. But their linguistic analyses would suffer for this, and there would be many questions on language and knowledge that would remain unanswered. Although, perhaps, one can't say the latter with the same force about Nāgārjuna.

110. Datta, *Six Ways of Knowing*, (*loc cit)*.

111. A point that Datta has made ably (*ibid*).

112. Again, see Quine (note 102 above), and it is interesting to note Kuhn's reflections on the role of 'convention' and '*community*' structure of scientific decision-making, which Masterman explores for their sociological implications. Kuhn, *Scientific Revolution*; and Masterman in *Criticism and Growth of Knowledge*, Lakatos and Musgrave (eds. See notes 71 and 65 above).

113. Bertrand Russell, 'Common-sense Inference', in *Science and Perception in Human Knowledge, its scope and limits*, Clarion Books (N.Y. 1948).

114. *Ibid*, p90.

115. *Ibid* p57 It is interesting in this regard also to note Montagues's views on 'testimony'. Montague is more modest than Russell in dismissing 'testimony' out of court; in fact Montague goes a long way towards accepting the independence of its source, but not of its validity, which is subordinated under inference. This is not an unsound move, and such a position is not without its parallel in the Indian system, particularly in Vaiśeṣika (See *Śarvadarśanasaṃgraha*, ch. X under 'The Vaiśeṣika or Aulukya Darśana'- trs. Cowell & Gough, pp144ff. *Cf. Sāṃkhya Kārikā* #4 & #5, on the proof of reason for the accomplishment of valid knowledge: *prameya-siddhiḥ pramaṇād dhi*).

Montague's discussion is all the same quite intriguing - esp. chapter on 'Methods of Authoritarianism', *The Ways of Knowing* (Allen & Unwin, 1952).

116. *Ibid.*

117a. *Cf.* Śaṅkara, *BSB*, II i 14, of dreams and snake-bites.

117. I get this sense from Richard Campbell's discussion of Heidegger's 'Being-uncovering' in his 'Heidegger: Truth as Aletheia', *Dialectic*, vol. 23, 1984, pp. 1-13.

118. Compare Chisholm's classification of the accredited sources of knowledge, *Theory of Knowledge*, p122.

119. *Doctrine and Argument in Indian Philosophy.*

120. *Cf.* Santayana, *Scepticism and animal faith* (New York, 1955.) Vācaspati Misra, *Bhāmatī-catussūtrī, (op cit* p51).

121. *Nyāya-sūtras* I i 7, and note 101 above.

122. **Vātsyāyana's commentary on above; he sees the *āptabhāva* extending to mlecchas ('aliens'), āryas ('noble ones'), and *ṛsis* or 'seers'. Though the ultimate or supreme court of *āptabhāva* to Nyāya is *Iśvara,* the Hindu concept of a supreme being.**

123. Jayanta in his *Nyāyamañjarī* I (*op cit*, p138), and: *cikhyāpayiṣaya prayukta upadeṣṭā ceti (ibid*).

124. *Cf.* Udayana's statement: 'An omniscient (and) immutable (*Īśvara*) can be established from effect, combination, from support etc., from human usages, from authoritative-

ness, from the sacred scriptures, from sentences and from special number'. *kāryāyojanadhṛtyādeśaḥ padāt pratyayataḥ śruteḥ, vākyāt saṃkhyāviśeṣāc ca sādhyo viśvavid avyayaḥ, Nyayakusumāñjali* V.1 (Kurukshetra, 1974, p69); translation from G. Chemparathy in his *An Indian Rational Theology*, Introduction to Udayana's *Nyāyakusumāñjali*, (Vienna 1972, p85)—a worthy treatise itself.
Incidentally, it is the profoundly authoritative character of the scriptures that leads Udayana to argue for the existence of a supreme deity (*Īśvara*) as their only possible source.
It must be noted, however, that *Īśvara* as 'God' in Nyaya is comparable but not identical to the living and willing God of Judaeo-Christianity. Nor is *Īśvara* comparable to the All-Knowing *Buddha* of some Buddhists doctrines.

125. Kumārila Bhaṭṭa is by far the most rigorous exponent of this view, esp. in his *Ślokavārttika* (*tarkapāda*, the last two chs. *vākyādhikaraṇa* #365-69; *vedāpauruṣeyatva*) which deal with the question of the authorlessness (*apauruṣeyatva*) of the Veda-sentences; Pārthasārathi Miśra's commentary on this, *Nyāyaratnākara*, and his independent works, *Śāstradīpikā* and *Nyāyatnamālā* expand on the thesis. Some issues in this context were first explored in a symposium on *Śabda and Śruti*, in the International Research Conference in Asian and Comparative Philosophy, Honolulu, August, 1984 (presentations by Frits Staal, Ninian Smart, and the writer; a further symposium was held a year later in Sydney (IAHR), with presentations from Ninian Smart, K. Sivaraman, G. Chemparathy, Harold Coward, and the writer (see note 58 above). Publications resulting from these, as well as the writer's projected work on *Apauruṣeya*, in the near future, may throw more light on this neglected doctrine.

On some historical reflections on *śruti* and *apauruṣeya*, see Smart (*op cit*); J. N. Mohanty, 'Philosophy as Reflection on Experience', in *Indian Philosophy Today*, N. K. Devaraja (ed.), (Delhi, 1975, pp 169-171). On the attempt to de-mythologise this doctrine, see Francis X. D'Sa, S.J.,*Śabdaprāmāṇyam in Śabara and Kumārila : Towards a study of Mīmāṃsā Experience of Language*. On the possible absurdity of this doctrine, see K. Satchidananda Murty (*loc cit*) p330. Other useful and related (even if only for their methodological relevance) works worth noting are: Raimundo Panikkar, *Mantramañjarī The Vedic Experience* (esp. the Introductory chapter); D.M. Datta, *Six Ways of Knowing* (chapter on 'Verbal testimony'); Swami Satprakasananda, *Methods of Knowledge* (ch on *Āgama*); Ramachandra Gandhi, *Availability of Religious Ideas*, and *Presuppositions of Human Communication*; Coward & Sivaram (eds.), *Revelation in Indian Thought*; J.G.Arapura, 'Language and Phenomena', *Canadian Journal of Theology*; Kalidas Bhattacharyya, *Logic, Language and Truth*; Paul Ricoeur, *The Rule of Metaphor*; Karl Barth, *The Doctrine of the Word of God* (1936 Edinburgh); Ian Ramsey, *Religious Language* (SCM, London 1967); A. J. MacDonald, *Authority and Reason in the Early Middle Ages* (OUP, 1933); last but not least, Ian Kesarcodi-Watson, 'Hindu Metaphysics and Its Philosophies—*Śruti* and *Darśana*', *IPQ* (Fordham), (Vol XVIII no. 4, December, 1978, pp. 413-432).

126. Nārāyana Bhaṭṭa, *Mānameyodaya*, p108. This is really showing the Mīmāṃsā distrust ultimately for all secular as distinct from Vedic statements, because the former is potentially vitiated by human error and defect while the latter is free from such. But Pārthasārathi Miśra is a little light on this, he accepts *āptaḥ* in mundane matters as well. *Śāstradīpikā* (*autpattikasūtra*, 63; see note 92, 95, 105 above).

127. Śaṅkara's commentary on *Brahma-sūtras*, II i xi-xii, I iii 28, II i 6, II iii 40, III 3 50. See also notes 61-62 *supra*.

128. *Ibid* II i 14: *brahmaṇa ātmaikatvadarśanaṃ mokṣasādhanameva. pramāṇābhāvāt kūṭasthabrahmātmatvavijñānādeva hi phalaṃ darśyati* (after the liberating oneness-experience of self and Brahman, that *pramāṇa*-awareness has no other residual content but the self).

129. See Gauḍapāda in his *kārikā* on *Māṇḍūkya Upaniṣad*.See also writer's *'Guru-śiṣya,*

Teacher-Pupil Relationship, *Journal of Dharma* (Bangalore). *Cf.* Søren Kierkegaard, 'The essential author is essentially a teacher; and, if he is not and essentially could not be the real author, he is essentially a learner', *On Authority and Revelation*, Walter Lowrie (tr. & ed.) Harper, 1955, p9.

130. In his *kārikās* (various) on *Māṇḍūkya Upaniṣad* (esp. II & IV). See also discussion on *tātparyaliṅga* in Mādhava's *Śarvadarśanasaṃgraha* (ch. on *pūrṇaprajñadarśana*), (ch.6 6.29, n57, and ch 4(B) *supra*).

131. *Pramāṇacandrikā* in *Madhva Logic* (text & trans.) by S. K. Maitra (Calcutta, p156); and *Pramāṇapaddhati* in P. Nagaraja Rao, 'Problems Relating to Verbal Testimony with Special Reference to Dvaita Vedānta', *Poona Orientalist*, (vol 2. No 4, 1937-8, pp. 212-226) p212.

132. *Cf. Bṛh. Up. Bhāṣya* IV.iii.1-7; IV.iv.1-3/22; *Tait. Up. Bhāṣya* I.ix.11ff.

133. Mostly of the Vivaraṇa persuasion in contradistinction to the Bhāmatī school, that follows the ex-Mīmāṃsaka, Maṇḍana Miśra (esp.Govindānanda's *Ratnaprabhā* and Vācaspati's *Bhāmatī* respectively). Bratindra Kumar Sen Gupta, *A Critique of the Vivaraṇa School, studies in some fundamental Advaitist theories* (Calcutta, 1959) is a good discussion of the Vivaraṇa position, which argues that mere 'hearing', *śravaṇa*, of the *śruti* is sufficient for immediate Brahman-realisation (implying that no understanding or contemplation is necessary at all, or that if they are brought in, they have a contingent role of facilitating awareness). The word, then, is what really yields the final awareness. The *Bhāmatī*, first book of which is translated by S. S. Suryanarayan Sastri and Kunhan Raja (Adyar, 1933), presents the rival thesis according to which Brahman realisation is (indirectly) mediated through the disciplinary practices in question, and that all of them are equally important. But the word does not yield the final awareness. There is a third position that regards *manana* as primary, and the other two as secondary (*Kalpataru* of Amalānanda on *Bhāmatī* seems to come close to this view).

134. Śaṅkara's *Upadeśasāhasrī* has received a commendable treatment in Sengaku Mayeda's *A Thousand Teachings The Upadeśasāhasrī of Śaṅkara*, (tran. with Introduction and Notes), University of Tokyo Press, Tokyo, 1979. Śaṅkara certainly says here that 'hearing' *śruti* is all that is necessary, and for one established in this firm understanding, after assimilating the meaning of the sentence through recollecting the meanings of its constituent words, no action of any kind is incumbent (I, 18, 188-226). Obviously, he is referring to ritualistic and prescriptive actions as enjoined in the scriptures, and which the Mīmāṃsakas followed to the hilt to derive gains of one (earthly) sort or another (heavenly). Paradoxically, the last chapter is on *parisaṃkhyāna* or 'concluding meditative reflection', although he seemed to have discarded a similar type of practice, under *prasaṃkhyāna*, earlier (I, 18, 9-21; and in *BSB*). Then there are the *sādhana-catuṣṭayā* that border on yogic disciplines that Śaṅkara also recommends. (These are enunciated in his commentaries on the various Upaniṣads, particularly *Bṛh.Up*).The purpose of all these practices and disciplines is undoubtedly to achieve *citta-śuddhi* in the first instance, but also to enhance understanding at deeper levels of consciousness – thus, like *epoché*, they are as much of *phenomenological* significance, as they would seem to be spiritual in orientation.

135. Remarks similar to the above are developed into cogent arguments in John Taber, *Transformative Philosophy A Study of Śaṅkara, Fichte and Heidegger*, (University of Hawaii Press, Honolulu, 1983).

136a. For example, in *Upadeśasāhasrī*, part II (*op cit*), and parts of *BSB*, II i 14ff.

136. *Vide* Paul Hacker, '*Śaṅkara der Yogin und Śaṅkara der Advaitin*, (*q.v* 61a above). Although admitting that Śaṅkara was familiar with the yoga tradition generally, and probably authored *Patañjaliyogasūtrabhāṣyavivaraṇa* (trans. by Trevor Leggett, Boston, RKP, 1980), a number of scholars have raised doubts about the alleged transition of Śaṅkara from Yoga to Advaita. S. Mayeda, for instance, does not consider this a fully acceptable suggestion, and thinks that this 'opinion' should be re-examined, *A Thousand*

Teachings (pp4, 8, n.15); *cf.* H. Nakamura, 'Notes to Śaṅkara's *Yogasūtrabhāṣyavivaraṇa* [I]', *Journal of Indian and Buddhist Studies*, vol XXV, no. 1, 1976, p77). (Even stronger reservations were expressed by both scholars in conversations.)

137. For example, T. P. Ramachandran, *The Concept of Vyāvahārika in Advaita Vedānta* (Madras, 1969); C. Markandeya Sastri, *Sureśvara's Contribution to Advaita*, (Vemur, A. P., 1973?).

138. Bādarāyaṇa describes this as *ādhyāna* ; and see Śaṅkara on *BSB* III iii 14)

139. Peter Geach :'All true propositions point towards the True, all false ones away from it', and 'if True is not God, there is no God' (Peter Geach 'Truth and God' *Aristotelian Society* 1982 vol LV1, pp83-98, p97) ; see also Stewart Sutherland's response, *ditto*, pp99-116, p116). Cf. M.K.Gandhi '[I]t is more true to say that Truth is God, than to say God is Truth.' (M.K.Gandhi on 'M. K. Gandhi', in *Contemporary Indian Philosophy*, S.Radhakrishnan (ed.), London, 1966, p21).

140. Kalidas Bhattacharyya, 'Traditional Indian Philosophy as a Modern Thinker Views It', (pp. 171-224), p216.

141. *The Bhagavadgītā in the Mahābhārata*, J.A.B. van Buitenen, (tr. and ed.), (Chicago, 1983), XVIII. 63: *iti te jñānam ākhyātaṃ guhyād guhyataraṃ mayā, vimṛśyaitad aśeṣeṇa yathecchasi tathā kuru*. (Translations, for this and next verse, *ibid*, p143-4.)

142. *Ibid* 72: *kaccid etac chrutaṃ Pārtha tvayaikāgreṇa cetasā, kaccid ajñānasaṃmohaḥ pranaṣṭas te Dhanaṃjaya*.

143. Kunhan Raja (*op cit*) p94.

144. Madhusūdana Sarasvatī in *Vedāntakalpalatikā*: words themselves are only capable of producing indirect knowledge, which might be followed by direct realisation, but only *śruti*, he says, is capable of the ultimate self unconcealing, there is no need for contemplation and so forth either.(This suggests yet another alternative to the two approaches considered in note 133 above—namely, *śabda-parokṣa prasthāna*).23, pp. 58-60, and p146.

145. *Vide BSB* II iii 40, III iii 5O. *Īśvara* is also part of the 'name' and 'form' manifestation in the limited reality: *evamvidyākṛtanāmarūpopādhyanurodhīśvaro bhavati*, *BSB* II i 14.

146. *Ibid*. Śaṅkara considers the objection that if words, like all else in the world, is unreal, how could it lead to the knowledge of the real. He responds that until the final realisation occurs, everything is *real* and all the relations are logical and transactable: the world is as it is, until it is contradicted by a 'higher' level experience. He invokes the anology from dream experience: though the snake-bite in a dream is unreal to one who has woken up, still, it is taken to be real while one is dreaming; and after one has woken up, the *awareness* that such and such occurred in the dream is not false, even though the awareness within the dream is false. Here an unreal item gives awareness about a 'state of affairs' *qua* dream that itself is not false. Presumably, then, the unreal words give an awareness of the reality of the world, which turns out to be false. That awareness of the falsity of this awareness, is already quite an accomplishment for *śabda*, Śaṅkara would say. (Coversely, if the dream event were absolutely real, and it affected, apart from the actor in the dream, the actual dreamer, then death in a dream would prove to be rather fatal!) Thus, if the word or its reference in the world were taken in some sense to be absolute, then the overall impact could be devastating, and there would be no possibility of transcendence. Śaṅkara is, therefore, persuaded that once something is falsified or its efficacy is exhausted it should be discarded in the same way as illusions are once a more sober vision returns. This is one way of 'worldmaking' that does not set unalterable limits to what our knowledge and language could plausibly yield.

147. Ludwig Wittgenstein, *Tractatus*, 6:54. (Although the Śāṅkaran strain of 'mysticism' seems to be conspicuous by its absence in the rest of the *Tractatus*.)

148. 'Traditional Indian Philosophy' (*op cit*, p217).

149. See note 61, 61a, and note 127 above.

150. Kalidas Bhattacharyya (*loc cit*). It would be true to say, though, that Krishnachandra Bhattacharyya, writing in the 1920s, was the first to bring the doctrine of *śabdapramāṇa* into a more systematic philosophical light. K. C. Bhattacharyya devoted a chapter to 'Vedānta Logic', basing his discussion on *Vedānta-paribhāṣā*, and informed by Kant's 'paralogisms of Pure Reason'. (*Studies in Philosophy*, ch III, vol 1; ed. Gopinath Bhattacharyya, Progressive Publishers, Calcutta, 1956 (re: MB, Delhi, 1983), pp 69-90)). K.C. sees the value of *śabda* in its *suggestive* and 'provisional' function, which intimates knowledge of the noumenal by phenomenal signs (although not positive proofs). Thus he writes: 'Some provisional belief (*Śraddhā*) is required to start the enquiry. A mere thought, even though necessary, can never induce belief, can never be mistaken for knowledge ; for in knowledge there is an unmistakable intuitive or 'given' character. This provisional belief can only be induced by authoritative statement (*śabda* or *āgama*) which may, for aught we know, be disproved afterwards. But the statement gains in reliability if on acting on it or after contemplation of it we attain a progressive *satisfaction or realisation*. That is the only justification which we may expect to have of the truth of what is claimed to be revelation, from below, i.e., before we have finally realised its truth.' (p 69) K.C. then goes on to argue that a word *qua* sentence refers '*directly* to the thing, expresses the thing, *touches* it (*Bṛh. Upaniṣad* I. V, 3) in a sense.' (p 83) And the sentence at once refers to an objective relation, through which it obtains objective reference. Although this gives us provisional belief, it is *continuous* with knowledge in the absence of conflict with other evidence: 'we do not require a positive confirmation by other evidence'. (*ibid*) Among the *kāraṇas* necessary for *understanding* the *thought* or belief expressed by the sentence and transforming it into knowledge, the writer locates *tātparya* ('objective intention') as the most significant. As he says: '*Tātparya,* is the capacity of a sentence to produce objective knowledge. It is not the subjective intention of the person uttering the sentence, though in cases of ambiguity the subjective intention has to be taken into account. It is the objective intention which, in cases of ambiguity or the like, is not contradicted by the subjective intention. So a true sentence, even when uttered by one not understanding or misunderstanding it, has an intrinsic *tātparya*.' (p 87) As to 'revelation', K.C. has this to say: 'Whether metaphysical enquiry necessarily presupposes a revelation is an issue which need not be confused with the other issue whether the *Veda* itself is revealed or not. If it be granted that the spirit can only teach spirit and that truth can only be *recognised* and not created by mental activity, it must also be granted that revelation is necessary, and that the Word is God, and that accordingly there should be an eternal succession of omniscient teachers.' (pp 69-70).

Cf again, Mohanty's objections: 'But neither the understanding of the meaning of a sentence nor that belief in its truth amounts to knowing that the facts are as stated. Knowing requires that mere understanding is supplemented by verificatory evidence, the grasping of the meaning-intention be fulfilled, and the belief be supported by adequate evidence. Failure to distinguish between 'understanding', 'believing', and 'knowing' is at the root of the epistemological status accorded to *śabda*.' ('Philosophy as Reflection on experience,' *loc cit*, p175ff). Well, we hope this objection has been taken care of in this work, and the spirit of K. C. Bhattacharyya has been returned to the discussion of *śabda*.

151. *Vide*, Richard L. Franklin: 'A Science of Pure Consciousness?' (*Religious Studies*, Vol 19, No 2, June 1983, pp185-204).

152. *BSB* I i 4 (*loc cit*) and *Bṛh Up. Bhāṣya* I iv 7. See also discussion under 'Revelation', in *A Source Book of Advaita Vedānta*, (Eliot Deutsch and J A B van Buitenen, eds. University Press of Hawaii, Honolulu, 1971, pp 5-32).

APPENDIX A

The following is a transliterated text of *Āgama* (or *Śabdapramāṇa*) chapter (IV) and *svataḥ-prāmāṇyam* (VII) (with a few related bits from the Introduction) from the *(Advaita) Vedāntaparibhāṣā*. Various editions have been consulted (i.e. palm-leaf and published mss; see Bibliography A under Dharmarājādhvarīndra), in particular the manuscript in Chandra Shum Shere collection (d. 560 [5]) held in the Oriental stack of the Bodleian Library, Oxford. Although the S. S. Suryanarayan Sastri (Adyar) edition* (1942) is not the most reliable, it provides a convenient numeral break-down of the text, issue-wise. The numeral ordering of the text of *Vedāntaparibhāṣā* has been adopted from this edition (and used throughout in the preceding chapters). Also, where appropriate, for compound resolution and break-up of complex constructions we have followed this and other editions. Some variant reading and interpolations by other editors have been noted within square brackets [ ]).

(*It would appear, from a reference in Sastri's note in his Introduction, that he has used the Tanjavur Library MSS, catalogue XI. He may have also used other editions he mentions on page xiv, note 2.)

ĀGAMA

1. athāgamo nirupyate/ yasya vākyasya tātparyaviṣayībhūtasaṃsargo mānāntarena na bādhyate tadvākyaṃ pramāṇam//
2. vākyajanye ca jñāne ākāṅkṣāyogyatā'sattayastātparyajñānaṃ ceti catvāri kāraṇāni//
3. [tatra] padārthānāṃ paraspara-jijñāsā-viṣayatva-yogyatvam ākāṅkṣā/ kriyāśravaṇe kārakasya kāraka tasya śravaṇe kriyāyāḥ karaṇaśravaṇe itikartavyatāyāśca jijñāsāviṣayatvāt//
4. ajijñāsorapi vākyārthabodhād yogyatvamupāttam/ tadavacchedakaṃ ca kriyātva-kārakatvādikam iti nātivyāptiḥ gauraśva [puruṣo hasti] ityādo/ abhedānvaye ca samānavibhaktika-padapratipādyatvaṃ tadavacchedakam iti tattvamasyādivākyeṣu nāvyāptiḥ//
5. etādṛśākāṅkṣābhiprāyeṇaiva balābalādhikaraṇe sā vaiśvadevyāmikṣā vājibhyo vājinam ityatra/ vaiśvadeva-yāgaśyamikṣā'nvitatvena na vājinākāṅkṣetyādivyahāraḥ//
6. nanu tatrāpi vājinasya jijñāsāviṣayatve'pi tadyogyatvamastyeva/

pradeyadravyatvasya yāganirūpita-jijñāsāviṣayatā-[yogyatā]vacchedakatvāt//

7. iti cet na/ svasamānajātīya-padārthānvayabo*dha*[**dhāsaha*]-virahasahakṛtapradeya-dravyatvasyaiva tadavacchedakatvena vājinadravyasya svasamānajātīyāmikṣādravyānvayabodhasahakṛtatvena tādṛśāvacchedakatvābhāvat/ āmikṣāyāṃ tu naivam vajinā'nvayasya tadānupasthitatvāt/ udāharaṇāntareṣvapi durbalatvaprayojakākāṅkṣaviraha eva dṛṣṭavyaḥ//

8. yogyatā ca tātparyaviṣay[ībhūt]asaṃsargābādhaḥ//

9 vahninā siñcati [siñcedityā°, siñcyati°], ityādau tādṛśasaṃsargabadhanna [ativyaptih] yogyata/ sa prajapatiratmano vapāmudakhidat ityādāvapi tu tātparyaviṣayībhūta-paśu[vapāyāga]prāśastyābādhād yogyatā/ tattvamasi ādivākyeṣvapi vācyābhedabādhe'pi lakṣyasvarūpābhede bādhābhāvād yogyatā//

10. āsattiścāvyavadhānena padajanyapadārthopasthitiḥ/ mānāntareṇopasthā'pitapadarthasyānvaya-bodhābhāvāt-padajanyeti//

11. ata eva aśrutapadārthasthale tattatpadādhyāhāraḥ dvāram ityādau pidhehi iti/ ata eva iṣe tvā ityādau [mantre] chinadmi iti padādhyāhāraḥ/ ata eva vikṛtiṣu sūryāya juṣṭaṃ nirvapāmi iti padaprayogaḥ//

12. padārthaśca dvividhaḥ śakyo lakṣyaśceti//

13. tatra śaktirnāma padānāmartheṣu mukhyāvṛttih yathā ghaṭapadasya pṛthubudhnodarādyākṛtiviśiṣṭe vastuviśeṣe vṛttiḥ//

14. sā ca śaktiḥ padārthāntaram/ siddhānte kāraṇeṣu kāryānukūla-śaktimātrasya padārthāntaratvāt//

15. sā ca tattatpadajanya-padārthajñānarūpakāryānumeyā//

16. tādṛśaśaktiviṣayatvaṃ śakyatvam/ tacca jātereva na vyakteḥ/ vyaktīnāmānantyena gurutvāt//

17. kathaṃ tarhi gavādipadād vyaktibhānam iti cet/ jātervyaktisamānasaṃvitsaṃvedyatvāditi brūmaḥ//

18. yadvā gavādipadānāṃ vyaktau śaktiḥ svarūpasatī na tu jñātā [hetu]/ jātau tu sā jñātā hetuḥ/ na [tu] vyaktyaṃśe śaktijñānamapi kāraṇaṃ gauravāt/ jātiśaktimattvajñāne sati vyaktiśaktijñānaṃ vinā vyaktidhī-vilambābhāvācca/ ata eva nyāyamate'pyanvaye śaktiḥ [svarupasatīti siddhāntaḥ]/ [=jñāyamānaśaktiviṣayatvameva] vācyatvamiti jātireva vācyā//

19. athavā vyakterlakṣaṇayā'vagamaḥ/ yathā nīlo ghaṭaḥ ityatra

nīlaśabdasya nīlaguṇaviśiṣṭe lakṣaṇā/ tathā jātivācakasya tadviśiṣṭe lakṣaṇā/ taduktam ananyalabhyaḥ [hi] śabdārthaḥ iti/ evaṃ śaky[ārth]o nirūpitaḥ//

20. atha lakṣyapadārtho nirūpyate/ tatra lakṣaṇāviṣayo lakṣyaḥ lakṣaṇā [ca] dvividhā/ kevalalakṣaṇā lakṣitalakṣaṇā ceti//

21. tatra śakyasākṣātsambandhaḥ kevalalakṣaṇā/ yathā gangāyāṃ ghoṣaḥ ityatra pravahāsākṣātsambandhini tīre gaṅgāpadasya kevalalakṣaṇā//

22. yatra śakyaparamparā-sambandhenā'rthāntarapratītistatra lakṣita-lakṣaṇā/ yathā dvirephapadasya rephadvaya-śaktasya bhramarapada-ghaṭita-paramparā-sambandhena madhukare vṛttiḥ/ gauṇyapi lakṣita-lakṣaṇaiva/ yathā siṃho māṇavakaḥ ityatra siṃhaśabdavācyasambandhi-krauryādisambandhena mānavakasya pratītiḥ//

23. prakārāntareṇa lakṣaṇā trividhā/ jahallakṣaṇā ajahallakṣaṇā/ jahadajahallakṣaṇā ceti//

24. [tatra] śaky[ārtha]manantarbhāvya yatrārthāntara[sy]pratītiḥ tatra jahallakṣaṇā/ yathā viṣaṃ bhuṅkṣva iti/ atra svārthaṃ vihāya śatrugṛahe bhojananivṛttirlakṣyate [=lakṣitā]//

25. yatra śakyārthamantarbhāvyaivā arthāntarapratītiḥ tatra ajahallakṣaṇā/ yathā śuklo ghaṭaḥ iti/ atra hi śuklaśabdaḥ svārthaṃ śuklaguṇamantarbhāvyaiva tadvati dravye lakṣaṇayā vartate//

26. yatra hi viśiṣṭavācakaśabdaḥ svārthaikadeśaṃ vihāya ekadeśe vartate, tatra jahadajahallakṣanā/yathā so'yaṃ devadattaḥ iti/ atra hi padadvyavācyayorviśiṣṭayoraikyānupapattyā padadvyasya viśeṣyamātraparatvam/ yathāvā tattvamasī ityādau tatpadavācyasya sarvajñatvādiviśiṣṭasya tvaṃpadavācyenāntaḥkaraṇaviśiṣṭenaikyāyogāt-ekyasiddhyarthaṃ svarūpe lakṣaṇeti sāmprādayikaḥ//

27. vayaṃ tu brūmaḥ so'yaṃ devadattaḥ tattvamasi ityādau viśiṣṭavācakānāṃ padānāmekadeśaparatve'pi na lakṣaṇā/ śaktyupasthitayorviśiṣṭayorabhedānvayānupapattau viśeṣyayoḥ śaktyupasthitayorevānvayā[bodhā]virodhāt/ yathā ghaṭo'nityaḥ ityatra ghaṭapadavācyaikadeśaghaṭatvasyāyogyatve'pi/ yogyaghaṭavyaktyā sahānityatvānvayaḥ/ yatra padārthaikadeśasya viśeṣaṇataya upasthitiḥ/ tatraiva svātantryeṇopasthitaye lakṣaṇā 'bhyupagamaḥ/ yathā nityo ghaṭa ityatra ghaṭapadād ghaṭatvasya śaktyā svātantryeṇānupasthityā tādṛśopasthityarthaṃ ghaṭapadasya ghaṭatve lakṣaṇā/ evameva tattvamasi ityādivākye'pi na lakṣaṇā/ śaktyā svātantryenopasthitayoḥ tattvampadārthayorabhedānvaye

bādhakābhāvāt/ anyathā gehe ghaṭaḥ ghaṭe rūpaṃ ghaṭamānaya ityādau ghaṭatvagehatvāderabhimatānvayabodhāyogyatyā tatrāpi ghaṭādipadānāṃ viśeṣyamātraparatvaṃ lakṣaṇayaiva syāt//

28. tasmāt tattvamasi iti vākye ācāryānāṃ lakṣaṇoktirab-hyupagamavādena bodhyā//

29. jahadajahallaksanodāharaṇaṃ tu kakebhyo dadhi raksyatām ityādikameva/ tatra śakyakākaparityāgena aśakyadadhy-upaghātakatvapuraskāreṇa kāke'kāke'pi kākaśabdasya pravṛtteḥ//

30. lakṣaṇābījaṃ tu tātparyānupapattireva/ na [tu] anvayānupapattiḥ kākebhyo dadhi rakṣyatam ityatrānvayānupapattyabhāvāt/ gaṅgāyaṃ ghoṣaḥ ityādau tātparyānupapatterapi saṃbhavāt//

31. lakṣaṇā ca na padamātravṛttiḥ/ kiṃtu vākyavṛttirapi/ yathā gambhīrāyāṃ nadyāṃ ghoṣaḥ ityatra gambhīrāyām nadyām iti padadvayasamudāyasya tīre lakṣaṇā//

32. nanu vākyasyā'śaktatayā kathaṃ śakyasambandharūpā lakṣaṇā//

33. ucyate śaktyā yatpadasambandhena jñāpyate tatsambandho lakṣaṇā/ śaktijñāpyaśca yathā padārthaḥ [tatha] vākyārtha'pi itina kācid anupapattiḥ//

34. evamarthavādavākyānāṃ praśaṃsārūpānāṃ prāśastye lakṣaṇā/ so'rodidītyādinindārthavākyānāṃ ninditatve lakṣaṇā/ arthavādagatapadānāṃ prāśastyādi lakṣaṇā'bhyupagame ekena padena lakṣaṇayā tadupasthitisambhave padāntaravaiyarthyaṃ syāt//

35. evaṃ ca vidhyapekṣitaprāśastyarūpapadārtha-pratyāyakatayā arthavādapadasamudāyasya padasthānīyatayā [vidhi] [padasaṃnid-hanena] padenaikavākyatvaṃ bhavati/ iti arthavāda-vākyānāṃ padaikavākyatā//

36. kka tarthi vākyaikavākyatā/ yatra pratyekaṃ bhinnabhinnasaṃsarga-pratipādakayoḥ vākyayoḥ ākāṅkṣāvaśena mahāvākyārthabodhakatvam [tatra vākyaikavākyatā]/ yathā dar-śapūrṇamāsābhyāṃ svargakamo yajeta ityādivākyānāṃ samidho yajatītyādivākyānāṃ ca parasparā-pekṣitāṅgāṅgibhāva-bodhakatavaikavākyatvam/ taduktaṃ bhaṭṭapādauḥ:-

> svārthabodhe samāptānāmaṅgāṅgitvādyapekṣayā
> vākyānāmekavākyatvaṃ pūnaḥ saṃhatya jāyate// iti/

evaṃ dvividho'pi padārtho nirūpitaḥ//

37. tadupasthitiśca āsattiḥ/ sā ca śābdabodhe hetuḥ tathaivānvayavyatirekadarśanāt/ evaṃ mahāvākyārthabodhe avāntaravākyārthabodha hetuḥ/ tathaivānvayādyavadhāraṇāt//

38. kramaprāptaṃ tātparyaṃ nirūpyate/ tatra tatpratīticchayoccaritatvaṃ na tātparyam/ arthajñānaśūnyena puruṣenoccaritād vedādarthā[pratyaya]bhāva[nā]prasaṅgāt/ ayamadhyāpko'vyutpannah iti viśeṣadarśanena [tatra] tātparyabhramasyāpyabhāvāt/ na caiśvariyatātparyajñānāt tatra śābdabodha iti vācyam/ īśvarānaṅgīkarturapi tadvākyārthapratipattidarśanāt//

39. ucyate tatpratītijananayogyatvaṃ tātparyam/ gehe ghatah iti vākyaṃ gehe ghatasaṃsargapratītijananayogyam, na tu paṭasaṃsarga-pratītijananayogyam iti tad vākyaṃ ghaṭasaṃsargaparam/ na tu paṭasaṃsargaparam iti vyapadiśyate//

40. nanu saindhavamānaya ityādivākyaṃ yadā lavaṇānayanapratīticchayā prayuktam; tadāpyaśvasaṃsarga-pratītijanane svarūpayogyatāsattvāt lavaṇaparatva[jñāna]daśāyāmapyaśvādi-saṃsargajñānāpattiḥ//

41. iti cet na/ tadītarapratītīcchayā'nuccaritatvasyāpi tātparyaṃ prati viśeṣaṇatvāt/ tathā ca yadvākyaṃ yatpratītijananayogyatve sati yadanyapratītīcchayānuccaritaṃ tadvākyaṃ tatsaṃsargaparamityucyate/ śukādivākye'vyutpannoccaritavedavākyādau ca tatpratīticchāyā evābhāvena tadanyapratīticchayoccaritatvābhāvena lakṣaṇasattvāt nāvyāptiḥ/ na cobhayapratītīcchayoccarite'vyāptiḥ/ tadanyamātrapratītīcchayā'nuccaritatvasya vivakṣitatvāt//

42. uktapratītimātrajanana-yogyatāyāścāvacchedikā śaktiḥ/ asmākaṃ [tu] mate sarvatra kāraṇatāyāḥ śakterevāvacchedakatvāt/ iti na ko'pi doṣaḥ//

43. evaṃ tātparyasya tatpratītijanakatvarūpasya śābdajñānajanakatve siddhe/ caturthavarṇake tātparyasya śābdajñānahetutvanirākaraṇavākyaṃ tatpratītīcchayoccaritatvarūpatātparyanirākaraṇaparam/ anyathā tātparyaniścayaphalaka-vedāntavicāravaiyarthyaprasaṅgāt//

44. kecitu śābdajñānatvāvachedena na tātparyajñānaṃ heturityevaṃparaṃ caturthavarṇakavākyam/ tātparyasaṃśayaviparyayottaraśābda-jñānaviśeṣe ca tātparyajñānaṃ hetureva/ idaṃ vākyametatparam/ utānyaparam iti saṃśaye tadviparyaye ca taduttaravākyārthaniścayasya tātparyaniścayaṃ vinā'nupapatteḥ ityāhuḥ//

45. tacca tātparyaṃ vede mīmāṃsā-pariśodhita-nyāyadevāvadhāryate/ loke tu prakaraṇādinā/ tatra laukikavākyānāṃ mānāntarāvagatārthatayā anuvādakatvam/ vede tu vākyārthasyāpūrvatayā nānuvādakatvam//

46. tatra loke vede ca kāryaparāṇāmiva siddhārthānāmapyapūrvatayā

prāmāṇanyam putraste jātaḥ kanyā te gambhirṇī ityādiṣu siddhārtheṣuvapi padānāṃ sāmarthyāvadhāraṇāt/ ata eva vedāntavākyānāṃ brahmaṇi prāmāṇanyam/ yathā caitattathā viṣayaparicchede vakṣyate//

47. tatra vedānāṃ nityasarvajña-parameśvara-praṇītatvena prāmāṇyam iti naiyāyikaḥ//

48. vedānāṃ nityatvena nirasta-samastapuṃdūṣaṇataya prāmāṇyam ityadhvara mīmāṃsakāḥ//

49. asmākaṃ tu mate vedo na nityaḥ utpattimattvāt/ utpattimattvaṃ ca asya mahato bhūtasya niḥśvasitametadyadṛgvedo yajurvedaḥ sāmavedo'tharvāṅgirasya ityādi-śruteḥ. [(*Bṛh. Up.* 2 iv 10)]

50. nāpi vedānāṃ trikṣaṇāvasthāyitvam/ ya evavedo devadattenādhītaḥ sa eva vedo mayā'pi ityādipratyabhijñāvirodhāt/ ata eva gakārādivarṇā-nāmapi na kṣaṇikatvam so'yaṃ gakāraḥ iti pratyabhijñā-virodhāt / tathā ca varṇapadavākyasamudāyasya vedasya viyadādivat sṛṣṭi-kālīnotpattikatvaṃ pralayakālīnadhvaṃsa-pratiyogitvaṃ ca/ na tu [madhye] varṇānāmutpattivināśau anantagakārakalpanāyāṃ gauravāt//

51. anuccāraṇadaśāyāṃ varṇānāmanabhivyaktiḥ taduccāraṇarūpa-vyañjakābhāvāt na virudhyate/ andhakārastha-ghaṭānupalambhavat//

52. utupanno gakāraḥ ityādipratyakṣaṃ tu so'yaṃ gakāraḥ iti pratyabhijñā-virodhādapramāṇam/ varṇābhivyañjaka-dhvanigatotpatti-nirūpita-paramparā sambandha-viṣayatvena pramāṇaṃ vā/ tasmāt na vedānāṃ kṣaṇikatvam//

53. nanu kṣaṇikatvābhāve'pi viyadādiprapañcavadutpattimattvena parameśvarakartṛkatayā pauruṣeyatvasiddhau apauruṣeyatvaṃ vedānāmiti tavāpi siddhānto bhajyeta//

54. iti cet na/ na hi tāvat puruṣeṇa uccāryamānatvaṃ pauruṣeyatvam/ gurumate'pi adhyāpakaparamparayā pauruṣeyatvāpatteḥ/ nāpi puruṣādhīnotpattikatvam [pauruṣeyatvam]/ naiyāyikabhimatapauruṣeyatvānumāne asmādadinā siddhasādhantvāpatteḥ/ kiṃtu sajātīyoccāraṇānapekṣoccāraṇaviṣayatvaṃ pauruṣeyatvam//

55. tathā ca sargādyakāle parameśvaraḥ pūrvasargasiddhavedānupūrvīsamānānupūrvīkaṃ vedaṃ viracitavān/ na tu tadvijātīyaṃ vedam/ iti na /sajātīyoccāraṇānapekṣoccāraṇaviṣayatvaṃ pauruṣeyatvaṃ [vedānāṃ]/ [mahā]bhāratādīnāṃ tu sajātīyoccāraṇamanapekṣyaivoccāraṇamiti teṣāṃ pauruṣeyatvam/ evaṃ

pauruṣeyāpauruṣeya-bhedena āgamo dvividho nirūpitaḥ//

iti vedāntaparibhāṣāyām āgamaparicchedaḥ

Other relevant texts:

Definition of 'true' knowledge (*pramā*)-

pramākaraṇaṃ pramāṇam (#3) *tatra smṛtivyāvṛttaṃ pramātvaṃ anadhigatābādhitārtha-viṣayakajñānatvam/ smṛtisādhāraṇaṃ tu abhādhitārtha-viṣayakajñānatvam* (#4)

On 'worldly' falsification-

brahmasākṣātkārānantaraṃ hi ghaṭādīnāṃ bādhaḥ. . .na tu saṃsāradaśāyāṃ bādhaḥ—yatra hi dvaitamiva bhavati taditara itaraṃ paśyati—iti śruteḥ/ tathā ca abādhitapadena saṃsāradaśāyāmabādhitvaṃ vivakṣitamiti na ghaṭādipramāyāmavyāptiḥ. . ./. . . laukikaṃ tadvadevedaṃ pramāṇam tvā'tmaniścayāt// (#8-9)

Svataḥprāmāṇyavāda (VII): theory of self-validation-

1. *evamuktānāṃ pramāṇānāṃ prāmāṇyaṃ svataḥ evotpadyate jñāyate ca/ tathā hi smṛtyanubhava-sādhāraṇaṃ saṃvādipravṛttyanukūlaṃ tadvati tatprakārakajñānatvaṃ prāmāṇyam/ tacca jñānasāmānyasāmagrīprayojyam, na tu adhikaṃguṇamapekṣate pramāmātre'nugataguṇābhāvāt//*
2. *nāpi pratyakṣaprāmāṇyaṃ bhūyo'vayavendriyasaṃnikarṣaḥ/ rūpadipratyakṣe ātmapratyakṣe ca tadabhāvāt satyapi tasmin pītaḥ śaṅkha iti pratyakṣasya bhramatvāt//*
3. *ata eva salliṅga-parāmarśādikamapi anumityādiprāmāṇyaṃ na guṇaḥ/ asalliṅga-parāmarśādisthale'pi viṣayābādhenā anumityādeḥ pramātvāt//*
4. *na caivampramāpi pramā syāt/ jñānasāmānya-sāmagrayā aviśeṣāditi vācyam/ doṣābhāvasyāpi hetutvāṅgikārāt/ na caivaṃ paratastvam/ āgantuka-bhāvakāraṇāpekṣāyāmeva paratastvāt//*
5. *jñāyate ca prāmāṇyam svataḥ/ svatogrāhyatvaṃ ca doṣābhāve sati yāvatsvāśrayagrāhaka–sāmagrīgrāhyatvam/ svāśrayo vṛttijñānaṃ tadgrāhakaṃ sākṣijñānaṃ tenāpi vṛttijñāne gṛhyamāne tadgatprāmāṇyamapi gṛhyate//*
6. *na caivam prāmāṇyasaṃśayānupapattiḥ/ tatra saṃśayānurodhena doṣasyāpi sattvena doṣābhāva-ghaṭitasvāśrayagrāhakābhāvena tatra prāmāṇyasvaivāgrahāt//*

7. *yadvā yāvatsvaśrayagrāhakagrāhyatvayogyatvaṃ svatastvam/ saṁśayasthale prāmāṇyasya uktayogyatāsattve'pi doṣavaśeṇāgrahāt na saṃśayānupapattiḥ//*

8. *aprāmāṇyaṃ tu na jñānasāmānya-sāmagrīprayojyam/ pramāyāmapi aprāmāṇyāpatteḥ/ kintu doṣaprayojyam//*

9. *nāpyaprāmāṇyaṃ yāvatvasvāśrayagrāhakagrāhyam/ aprāmāṇyaghaṭaka-tadabhāvavattvādervṛttijñānā'nanupanītatvena śākṣinā grahītumaśakyatvāt//*

10. *Kintu visaṃvādipravṛttyādiliṅgakānumityādiviṣaya iti parataḥ eva aprāmāṇyamutpadyate jñāyate ceti/*

iti svataḥprāmāṇyavādaparicchedaḥ

Dharmarāja's *vitae*:

śrīmadveṅkaṭanāthāravyān velāṅguḍinivāsinaḥ
yena cintāmaṇau [*TC* of Gaṅgeśa] ṭīkā daśaṭīkāvi[pra]bhañjinī
tarkacūḍāmaṇirnāma kṛtā vidvanmanoramā
ṭīkā śaśadharasyāpi bālavyutpattidāyinī
padayojanayā pañcapādikā vyākṛtā tathā
tena bodhāya mandānāṃ vedāntārthāvalambinī
dharmarājādhvarīndreṇa paribhāṣā vitanyate.

(End of *Vedāntaparibhāṣā* texts)

* * * *

śāntipāṭha

ādyante jyotistasya vācaḥ . . .
kastarhi śabdaḥ?
mahān devaḥ śabdaḥ.

* * *

kleśaḥ phalena hi punarnavatāṃ vidhate. (Kālidāsa).

iti śrīmadpuruṣottamapadmākṣabilimoriaviracitaḥ
śabdapramāṇavādaḥ prayojanaparicchedaḥ samāptaḥ

* *amā śāntiḥ* *

APPENDIX B
BIBLIOGRAPHY

The Bibliography is in two parts. Part A comprises mostly primary material in Sanskrit. Although not intended to be comprehensive, a number of different editions (with commentaries, translations in English or Hindi, notes, annotations, etc.) have been noted. This has partly been necessitated by the span and nature of this work (specific references in the notes to each chapter indicate which particular edition, etc., has been used or consulted for each such reference). Besides, it is hoped that the bibliography will prove to be a useful reference-source for other purposes. Part B provides a list of useful and interesting secondary and some related material, drawn widely from sources East and West.

ABBREVIATIONS (of series, publishers, institutes and journals):

ABORI	–	*Annals of the Bhandarkar Oriental Institute,* (Poona).
A&U	–	(George,) Allen and Unwin (London)
AJP	–	*Australasian Journal of Philosophy* (Victoria).
ALRC	–	Adyar Library and Research Centre (Adyar, Madras).
ASS	–	Ānandāśrama Saṅskritgranthāvali Series (Poona).
BHU	–	Banaras Hindu University (Varanasi).
BORI	–	Bhandarkar Oriental Research Institute, (Poona).
BSOAS	–	*Bulletin of the School of Oriental and African Studies*, University of London.
CASS	–	Centre for Advanced Study of Sanskrit (Univ. of Poona).
ChSS	–	Chowkhamba Sanskrit Series (Office: Varanasi). (or Chowk. Sans.)
CUP	–	Cambridge University Press (Camb).
DCPG	–	Deccan College Postgraduate Research Institute (Poona).
EIP	–	*Encyclopedia of Indian Philosophies*, General Editor, Karl Potter (see under title).
GOS	–	Gaekwad's Oriental Series, Baroda Oriental Institute (Baroda).
IIO	–	Indian Institute Library, Bodleian (Oxford).
IOL	–	Indian Office Library (London).
IPQ (Fordham)-		*International Philosophical Quarterly* (Fordham, N.Y.).
IPQ (Poona)-		*Indian Philosophical Quarterly* (Poona and Amalner).
JAAR	–	*Journal of the American Academy of Religion.*
JAOS	–	*Journal of the American Oriental Society* (U.S.A.).
JIP	–	*Journal of Indian Philosophy* (Dordrecht).
KSS	–	Kashi Sanskrit Series (some re: Chowkhamba) (Banaras).
MGOS	–	Madras Government Oriental Series (Madras).
MB	–	Motilal Banarsidass (Delhi).
MUSS	–	Madras University Sanskrit Series (Madras).
NSP	–	Nirnaya Sagar Press (Bombay).
OUP	–	Oxford University Press (Oxford).
SCM	–	Student Christian Movement Press (London).
PEW	–	*Philosophy East and West* (Honolulu).
RKM	–	Ramakrishna Mission Math, (Mylapore, Madras).
RKP	–	Routledge, Kegan and Paul (London).
SBES	–	Sacred Books of the East Series (ed. Max Muller).
SBH	–	Sacred Books of the Hindus (Allahbad).
VSS	–	Vizianagram Sanskrit Series (Banaras).
VVS	–	Vāṇī Vilās Sanskrit Series (Srirangam).

comm. = commentary; ed./eds = edited by or editor/s; edn. = edition; txt = text; tr./trs. = translated by or translator/s; trans. = translation; re: = re-issued or reprinted; * = see under title or name.

PART A (*Primary Sources*)

ABHINAVAGUPTA, *Dhvanyālokalocana* (or *Locana*) in K. Krishnamoorthy II.*
AMALĀNANDA, *Vedāntakalpataru* on Vācaspati Miśra's *Bhāmatī*, with Appayya Dīkṣita's *Parimala*, VSS L, 1914–1915.
ĀNANDAGIRI, *Nyāyanirṇaya*, (with *Brahmasūtrabhāṣya, Ratnaprabhā* and *Bhāmatī*) ed. J. L. Shastri, MB, Delhi, 1980.
ĀNANDAPŪRṆAMUNĪNDRA, *Nyāyacandrikā* (on Advaita epistemology), with comm. *Nyāya-prakāśikā* of Svarūpānandamunīndra, ed. N. S. Anantakṛṣṇa Śāstrī and Rāmamūrti Śāstrī, with Intro. MGOS, CLIV, 1959.
———, *Nyāyakalpatikā* (comm. on *Bṛh.bhāṣya-vārttika*), ed. V. Subramanya Śāstri, Kendriya Sanskrit Vidyapitha, Tirupathi, 1976.
ANANTĀNANDAGIRI, *Śaṅkaravijaya* , ed. N. Veezhinathan, Univ. of Madras, Madras, 1971.
ANNAṂBHAṬṬA, *Tarkasaṃgraha* (*TS*) with *Dīpikā* (D) and comm. of Govardhana: *Nyāya-bodhinī*, ed. tr. notes, Y. S. Athalye, Bombay Sanskrit Series No. LV (1918); re: BORI, Poona, 1974.
-*Tarkasaṃgraha-dīpikā* (*TSD.*) *on Tarkasaṃgraha*, tr. notes, Gopinath Bhattacharya, Progressive Publishers, Calcutta, 1976
-*Tarkasaṃgraha*, txt. tr. Kuppuswami Sastri: *A Primer of Indian Logic*, The Kuppaswami Sastri Research Institute, Madras, 1961.
-*The Tarka-saṃgraha* . . . with critical notes, by K. C. Mehendale; Radhabai Atmaram Sagoon, Bombay 1908.
-*Tarkasaṃgraha* (*Dīpikā*), ed. A. Jha, Uttar Pradesh Hindi Grantha Academy, Lucknow, 1976.
ĀNANDAVARDHANA, *Dhvanyāloka*, ed. K. Krishnamoorthy, Karnataka University, Dharwar, 1974; tr. K. Krishnamoorthy, Poona Oriental Book Agency, Poona, 1955.
ĀPADEVA, *Mīmāṃsā-nyāya-prakāśa* - ed. with comm. V. S. Abhyankar, BORI, (Govn. Oriental Series A3), 1937; re: Sri Satguru Pub., Delhi 1986.
-ed. tr. Franklin Edgerton, New Haven, Yale, 1929.
APPAYYA DĪKṢITA, *Siddhāntaleśasaṅgraha* ed. S. R. Krishnamurti and N. Veezhinathan, with comm. of Acyutakṛṣṇānanda Tīrtha, Secunderabad, 1973.
-tr. S. S. Suryanarayana Sastri, University of Madras Philosophy Series 4, vol 1, Madras, 1935.
———, *Parimala*, in Vācaspati Miśra's *Bhāmatī*, and Amalānanda's *Kalpataru*.
BĀDARĀYAṆA, *Brahmasūtras*: *Brahmasūtrapāṭha* (BS) (with Word-Index), S.K. Belvalkar, The Bilvakunja Publishing House, Poona, 1938.
-*Brahma-sūtra of Bādarāyaṇa* (with comm. of Śaṅkaracarya), text, tr. and notes by S. K. Belvalkar, I-1, Poona, 1923; II – 1 & II, Bilvakunja Publishing House, Poona, 1938; II – 2, The Oriental Book Supplying Agency, Poona, 1924.
-Also see *Brahmasūtra*, Śaṅkara, Rāmānuja, and Vācaspati Miśra.
BHARTṚHARI, *Vākyapadīya* (*VKP*) *of Śrī Bhartṛhari* (complete txt. eds. K.V. Abhyankar and V. P. Limaye, Sanskrit and Prakrit Series. Vol. II. University of Poona, Poona, 1965 (cited as Limaye edn.).
-*The Vākyapadīya of Bhartṛhari with the Vṛtti*, tr. K. A. Subramaniya Iyer, Deccan College Postgraduate Research Institute, (Poona), Kāṇḍa (ch) I (1966), Kāṇḍa III pt 1, (1963), Kāṇḍa III pt 2 (1973) – re: MB (Delhi), 1974, Kāṇḍa II, MB, 1977. Various txt. some with Helārāja's comm. Deccan College Monograph Series, 1963.

-*Vākyapadīya* (txt and tr. cantos I, II) K. Raghavan Pillai MB Delhi, 1971.
-*The Kālasamuddeśa of Bhartṛhari's Vākyapadīya* (III-9) with Helārāja's comm., Peri Sarveswara Sharma, MB, 1972.
BHAGAVADGĪTĀ (*BG*) (from *Bhīṣmaparvan*) ed. by S. K. Belvalkar, BORI, Poona, 1968. (From BORI Critical Edition of the *Mahābhārata*).
-J.A.B. van Buitenen, (Bi-lingual edn) tr. with notes, University of Chicago Press, Chicago, 1983.
-F. Edgerton (translation and interpretation) Part I. Harvard Oriental series No. 38. Harvard University Press, (Camb) Mass., 1946.
-with the *Sanatsujātīya* and the *Anugītā*, tr. by K. T. Telang; SBES, vol. 8 (1882); MB, Delhi, 1975.
-for *Bhāṣyas* (comm) see under Śaṅkara, Rāmānuja, Madhusūdana,
-W. D. Hill (OUP, 1928); S. Radhakrishnan (Blackie, India 1979);
-*A New Translation*, Kees Bolle, University of California, Berkeley, 1983.
BHĀSARVAJÑA ĀCĀRYA, *Nyāyasāra* (with *Nyāyasārapadapañchikā* of Vāsudeva of Kashmir) ed. V. S. Abhyankar and C. R. Devadhar, R. S. Gondhalekar's Book-Depot, Poona, 1922.
BRAHMASŪTRA-PRAMUKHABHĀṢYA-PAÑCAKA-SAMĪKṢAṆAM (main *bhāṣyas* on the *Brahmasūtras*, by Śaṅkara, Rāmānuja, Madhva, Nimbārka, and Vallabha), txt. ed. R. S. Tripathi, KSS 213, Chowkhamba, Varanasi, 1972.
CARAKA SAṂHITĀ, txt and Eng. tr. Ram Karan Sharma and Vaidya Bhagawan Dash, ChS Studies XCIV, Varanasi, 1976.
CĀRVĀKA, in *Śarvadarśanasaṃgraha* of Mādhava*.
CITSUKHA, *Tattvapradīpikā* or *Citsukhī*, ed. with auto-comm. Yogīnanda, Banaras, 1956; also NSP, Bombay 1931. (See also Padmapāda, Maṇḍana Miśra.)
DEVASŪRI (VĀDI), *Pramāṇanayatattvālokālaṃkāra*, tr. with auto-comm. Hari Satya Bhattacharya, Jain Sahitya Vikas Mandal, Bombay, 1967.
DHARMAKĪRTI, *Pramāṇavārttikam*, ed. Swāmī Dwārikādās Śāstrī, Bauddha Bharati Series 3, Varanasi, 1968.
-*The Pramāṇavārttikam of Dharmakīrti*, Kārikās I-LI. (tr. with intro. comm.) S. Mookerjee and H. Nagasaki; Nava Nalanda Mahāvihāra, Nalanda, Patna, 1964.
-*Nyāyabindu*, with *ṭīkā* of Dharmottara (Hindi and Sanskrit), Śrīnivās Śāstrī, Sahitya Bhandara, Menatha, 1975.
DHARMARĀJĀDHVARĪNDRA Dīkṣita, (*Advaita*) *Vedānta Paribhāṣā* (*VP*), (c. 1682—1700 A.D.); palm-leaf mss, Adyar Mss Collection (ARLC): 1174, 20H. 32 & 1184. 33. B 11; printed in Calcutta, 1847 (Bengali, 1855)(Burnell: 'A classified index to Sanskrit mss in Palace of Tanjore'; Trübner, London 1880, p90); Mss. Chandra Shum Shere d560(5), Oriental Collection, Bodleian Library, Oxford. Another early edition consulted belonged to J. R. Ballantyne (signed, Banaras, 1850) (IOL, London, E2338/3067).
-txt. Trivandrum Sanskrit Series XCIII, 1928. (with comm. of Pedda Dīkṣita*).
-ed. N. S. Anantakṛṣṇa Śāstrī with his comm: *Prakāśikā*, Calcutta, 1930.
-ed. tr. notes, S. Suryanarayan Sastri, ALRC, Madras, 1942; re: 1974.
-ed. with Śivadatta's *Arthadīpikā*, Pt. Tryambak Rāma Śāstrī, Chowkamba Sanskrit Series 6, 1968. (with Pedda Dīkṣita's comm.).
-ed. with Hindi comm. *Prakāśa*, Gajānanaśāstri Musalagaoṅkar (*Prakāśa*), Chowkhamba Sanskrit Series, Varanasi, 1963.
-tr. Swami Mādhvānanda, RKM, Howrah, Calcutta, 1942.

———, *Tarkacūḍāmaṇi*, on Rucidatta's *Dīdhiti* on *Tattvacintāmaṇi* (*śabdakhaṇḍa*) of Gaṅgeśa, (incomplete mss ALRC 985E 71728); Sarasvati Mahal Library, Tanjore Mss; see also Rāmakṛṣṇādhvarīndra.

DIṄNĀGA, *Pramāṇasamuccaya* ed H. R. Rangaswamy Iyengar, University of Mysore, Mysore, 1930.
-See also Hattori.

GADĀDHARA, *Śaktivāda*, ed. Goswāmi Dāmodar Śāstrī, KSS 77, Banaras, 1929, Varanasi 1976.

———, *Vidhisvarūpavicāraḥ*, ed. with comm. *Vidhibodhinī*, Pt Yādavendra Nāth Roy, Bibliotheca Indica, Asiatic Society, Calcutta, 1973.

GAṄGEŚA (UPĀDHYĀYA), *Tattvacintāmaṇi* (*TC*) *of Gaṅgeśopādhyāya*: Vol I; II-IV1; IV2
-ed. Pt. Kāmākhyā Nāth Tarkavāgīśa; Bibliotheca Indica 98, The Asiatic Society of Bengal, Calcutta, 1888–1901.
-*ditto* Vol I (*pratyakṣakhaṇḍa*) with S. C. Vidyābhūṣaṇa's Intro., Calcutta, 1897, re: MB, Delhi 1974.
-Vol I (*pratyakṣakhaṇḍa*) with *Prakāśa* of Rucidattamiśra and *Nyāyasikhāmaṇi* of Rāmakṛṣṇādhvarin, ed. N. S. Rāmānuja Tātāchārya, Kendriya Sanskrit Vidyapeetha Series no 20 (Foreword by V. Raghavan), Tirupati, 1973.
-*Prāmānya(jñapti)vāda* section, txt. tr. in Jitendranath Mohanty, *Gaṅgeśa's Theory of Truth* (*GTT*), Viśva-Bharati, Santiniketan, West Bengal, 1966
-with Pakṣadhara's *Āloka* (in parts), ed. Umesha Misra, Mithila Vidya-pitha Granthamala, 1957.

GAUḌAPĀDA, *Bhāṣya on Sāṃkhyakārikā of Īśvarakṛṣṇa*, txt. tr. and notes T.G. Mainkar, Oriental Book Agency, Poona, 1972.

———, *Gauḍapāda-kārikā* on the *Māṇḍūkya Upaniṣad* (with Śaṅkara's comm); tr. Swami Nikhilananda, Sri Ramakrishna Ashram, Mysore, 1974.
-*Gauḍapāda-kārikā*, ed. and tr. by Karmarkas, R. D. Bhandarkar Oriental Research Institute, Poona, 1953.
-*Gauḍapāda: A Study in Early Vedānta*, by T. M. P. Mahadevan,*

GAUTAMA, (AKṢAPĀDA), *Nyāyasūtras* (*NS*): *Nyāyadarśana*, txt. with Vātsyāyana's *Bhāṣya* and gloss of Viśvanātha, ed. Lakshmana Sastry Dravida *et al.* ChSS, Banaras, 1920.
-*Nyāyadarśana*, ed. Pt. Jayanarayana Tarkapanchanana, Bibliotheca Indica 1865, Calcutta.
-*Nyāyadarśana*: *The Nyāyasūtras with Vātsyāyana Bhāṣya* and extracts from *Nyāyavārttika* and *Tātparyaṭīkā*, ed. Gaṅgādhara Śāstrī Tailaṅga, ed Banaras 1896, re: Satguru Publication, Delhi 1984.
-ed. with *Nyāyabhāṣya*, Anandasrama Sanskrit Series, Poona, 1922.
-*Nyāyadarśana* with *Bhāṣya* of Vātsyāyana, *Vārttika* of Uddyotkara, *Tātparyaṭīkā* of Vācaspati & *Pariśuddhi* of Udayana. Vol I, ed. Anantalal Thakur. Mithila Institute Series no 20, Mithila, 1967.
-*Nyāyasūtras of Gautama*: *A System of Indian Logic with Vātsyāyana's Nyāyabhāṣya* ed. Ganganatha Jha (with two independent comms: G. Jha and Dhundiraja Shastri), ChSS, 1925; re: Poona Oriental Series, 58 (ed.), 59 (tr.), Poona, 1939 (txt only in no. 62).
-*Die Nyāyasūtras* (txt), W. Ruben, Übersetzung Erläuterung und Glossar, Leipzig, 1928; re: Nendeln, Mraus Reprints, 1966.
-*Nyāya Philosophy*, tr with Vātsyāyana's *bhāṣya* (4 parts), D. Chattopadhyaya and M. Gangopadhyaya, Indian Studies, Past and Present, Calcutta, 1975.
-*Nyāyadarśana*, ed. Tārānātha Nyāya Tarkatīrtha *et al*, Metropolitan Printing

and Publishing, Calcutta, 1936–44; re: Rinsen Sanskrit Text Series I-1 (2 vols), Rinsen Book Co., Kyoto, 1982.

HARIRĀMA, TARKAVĀGĪŚA, *Prāmāṇyavādaḥ*, ed. Viśvabandhu Bhaṭṭāchārya Sanskrit College, (Research Series Text, No. 17) Calcutta, 1964.

HELĀRĀJA, comm. on Bhartṛhari's* *VKP*, various, in Iyer edn. Deccan, 1963.

HEMACANDRA, *Pramāṇa-Mīmāṃsā*, ed. txt, tr. Satkari Mookerjee, Tara Publications, Varanasi, 1970.

ĪŚVARAKṚṢṆA, *Sāmkhya-kārikā*, txt. tr. Kunhan Raja, with *Gauḍapādabhāṣya*.

-*Sāṁkhya-kārikā*, with *Gauḍapādabhāṣya*, ed. Bhāvārtha Bodhikā comm (Hindi), Vimla Karnataka, Gokuldas Sanskrit Series 13, Chow. Orientalia, Varanasi, 1976

JAGADĪŚA, (TARKĀLANKĀRA) *Śabdaśaktiprakāśikā* (*SSP*), (with two commentaries *Kṛṣṇakāntī* of Kṛṣṇakānta Vidyāvagīśa and *Prabodhinī* of Rāmabhadra Vāgīśa), ed. Pt. Dhundhiraja Sastri, KSS 109; ChSS Office, Varanasi 1934, 1971.

JAIMINI, *Mīmāṃsasūtras* (*MS*): *Mīmāṃsādarśana*, with *Śābarabhāṣya* of Śabara Svāmī, ed. Pt Maheschandra Nyāyaratna, Bibliotheca Indica; Vol I-II, Asiatic Society of Bengal, Calcutta, edited 1863-1867, printed 1873–1889 (first published as 'The Aphorisms of The Mīmāṃsā'); re: Biblio Verlag, Osna-bruck (2 vols) 1983.

-*Mīmāṃsādarśana*, Vol I, II. IV with *Śābarabhāṣya*, and *Tantravārttika* of Kumārila Bhaṭṭa, ed. V. G. Apte, Ānandāśrama-saṃskṛta-granthavāliḥ, Poona, No. 97, 6 vols, 1930–33ff (re: 1970–76).

-*The Pūrva Mīmāṃsā Sūtra of Jaimini* tr. of I-III adhyāyas (chs), (with original Eng. comm.) Mh. Ganganatha Jha, SBH Series X, Panini Office, Allahabad. 1911–12 (1916); re: Ames, N.Y. 1974.

-*Mīmāṃsā-sūtras of Jaimini*, txt., complete tr. Mohan Lal Sandal, SBH, Vol XXVII, XXVIII, Panini Office, Allahabad, 1923–25; re: AMS, NY, 1974; MB. 1980 (2 vols).

JAYANTA BHAṬṬA, *Nyāyamañjarī*, ed. Pt Surya Narayan Śukla, KSS 106, Chowkhamba Sanskrit Office, Banaras, 1936 (part I); tr. Janakivallabha Bhattacharya, *Calcutta Review*, serially Oct. 1952- Nov. 1955 (re: MB, Delhi, 1978).

JAYATĪRTHA, *Pramāṇacandrikā*, txt. tr. in *Madhva Logic*, by S. K. Maitra, University of Calcutta, Calcutta, 1936.

KAṆĀDA, *The Vaiśeṣika sūtras* (*VS*) *of Kaṇāda* (with various comms.), tr. Nandalal Sinha; SBH. Vol.16 Allahabad, Panini office; 1911 (AMS Press, N.Y. 1974).

-*Vaiśeṣika-sūtra*, in Ui. H: *The Vaiśeṣika Philosophy* (According to the Daśapadārtha-Śāstra). Chinese text, Eng. tr. Oriental Trans. Series XXIV; Royal Asiatic Society, London, 1917.

-with comm of Candrānanda, ed. Muni Sri Jambuvijayaj, GOS (Baroda) vol 136, 1961

KĀTYĀYANA, *Vārttika* on *Pāṇinisūtras*, in (*Vyākaraṇa-)Mahābhāṣya*, ed by F. Kielhorn. 1st edn. 1880; re: 1892; revised, BORI, Poona 1962, 1965.

KAUṆḌA BHAṬṬA, *Sphoṭanirṇaya*, ed. tr. S. D. Joshi*, CASS, Poona, 1967

KEŚAVA MIŚRA, *Tarkabhāsā* (*TB*), with Cinnaṃbhaṭṭa's *Tarkabhāsāprakāśikā*, ed. D. R. Bhandarkar and Pt Kedarnatha, Bombay Sanskrit and Prakrit Series No. LXXXIV re: BORI. Poona, 1937, 1979.

-*Tarkabhāṣā*, ed. N. N. Kulkarni, 1920; re: Poona Oriental Series no. 16, Poona, 1953; tr. G. Jha, same series 17: 1940s, 1967.

-*Tarkabhāṣā* with *Tarkabhāṣādīpikā* (Hindi comm.), ed. Viśveśvara Siddhānta

Śiromaṇi, KSS 155, Chowkhamba Sanskrit Sanstha, Varanasi, 1982
-*Tarkabhāṣā*,ed. txt, tr. S. R. Iyer, with Foreward by Gaurinatha Sastri, Ch. Orientalia, Varanasi, 1979.
-*An Indian Primer of Philosophy, or, The Tarkabhāṣā of Keçavamiçra,* tr. P. Tuxen, A. F. Hoef, Copenhagane, 1974.
———, *Gautamīyasūtraprakāśaḥ*, ed. Kisoranatha Jha, Ganganatha Jha Kendriya Sanskrit Vidyapitham, Allahabad, 1978.

KṚṢṆA YAJVA, *Mīmāṃsā-paribhāṣā*, txt. tr. Swami Mādhavānanda, Belur Math, Ramakrishna Mission Sarada Pitha, Howrah, 1948.
-ed. Nārāyaṇa Rāma Ācārya, NSP, Bombay, 1950.

KUMĀRILA BHAṬṬA, (*Mīmāṃsā*)*Ślokavārttika* (*SV*), *with Pārthasārathi's Nyāyaratnākara*, ed. Rāma Śāstrī Telaṅg, Chowkhamba Sanskrit Series 3, Varanasi, 1898-99.
-*Ślokavārttika* (with comm. by Pārthasārathi Miśra, *Nyāyaratnākara)* ed. Swami Dvārikādāsa Śāstrī, Prāchyabhāratī, Series 10; Tara Publications, Varanasi, 1978.
-*Ślokavārttika*, (*tarkapāda*) tr. with extracts from Sucaritamiśra's *Kāśikā*, Ganganatha Jha, Bibliotheca Indica 146, Asiatic Society of Bengal, Calcutta, re: Sri Satguru Publications, Delhi, 1983.
-in *Ślokavārttikaṭīkā* (called *Sarkārikā*) of Bhaṭṭaputra Jayamiśra, MUSS no 17, ed by Kunhan Raja, Univ of Madras 1946.
-*Ślokavārttika* with comm. of Sucaritamiśra, ed. Sāmbaśiva Śāstrī, Trivandrum Sanskrit Series 90, 1926–43.
———,*Tantravārttika*, ed. Gangādhara Śāstrī, Benaras Sanskrit Series 3, 1882–1903 (also referred as 1890 edn), Chowk. Book Depot, Varanasi.
-ed. V. G. Apte, with *Śābarabhāṣya* (Jaimini*), ASS, Poona, 1930–33ff.
-tr. Ganganatha Jha, Bibliotheca Indica 161, Asiatic Society of Bengal, Calcutta, 1903–1924 (1927); re: (2 vols) Sri Satguru Publications, Delhi, 1983.

LAUGĀKṢI BHĀSKARA, *Arthasaṃgraha*, (with Sanskrit and Hindi commentaries)
ed. by Pt. Ram Chandra Jha, ChSS, 228, Varanasi, 1915, 1979.
-ed. with Hindi comm. by Vācaspati Upādhyāya, foreword by B. K. Matilal, Chaukhamba Orientalia, Varanasi, 1977.

MĀDHAVA (Chalāriśeṣācārya, ?son of Sāyaṇa), *Śarvadarśanasaṃgraha* (*SDS*),ed. Pt. Iswarachandra Vidyasagara, Bibliotheca Indica, Asiatic Society Bengal 62–142, Calcutta 1958;
-ed. V. S. Abhyankar, Govn. Oriental Series, Poona, 1924; re: BORI, 1978;
-trs. Cowell & Gough, Trubner, London, 1882; re: ChSS 1979.
-ed. with comm. *Prasthānabheda* of Madhusūdana Sarasvatī*.

MADHVĀCĀRYA, also known as Ānandatīrtha, see *Brahmasūtra-pramukha-bhāṣyas*; and Jayatīrtha.
———, *Brahmasiddhi*, ed. Raghavendra, with intro. notes T. Burrow, Mysore University Press, Mysore, 1965.

MADHUSŪDANA SARASATĪ, *Advaitasiddhi* (*AS*),ed. Sitansuśekhar Bagchi (with comm. *Bālabodhinī*, by Yogendranāth Bagchi) 2 vol. Tara Publications, Varanasi, 1971.
-*Advaitasiddhi*—with *Advaitaratnarakṣaṇa* ed. N. S. Anantakṛṣṇa Śāstrī, NSP, Bombay, 1937.
-part tr. Ganganatha Jha, *Indian Thought*, vol 6. 1914-vol 10, 1910.
———, *Siddhāntabindu* (*SB*) (on Śaṅkara's *Daśaślokī*),ed. by V. S. Abhyankar (1928) BORI Poona, 1962; ed. Tryambakarām Śāstrī KSS, 1928.

-*Siddhāntabindu* with Puruṣottama's *Saṃdīpa*, ed. tr. P.C. Devanji, GOS, Baroda, No. 44, 1933.

———, *Vedāntakalpalatikā*, ed. and tr. R.D. Karmarkar, BORI, Poona, 1952.

———, *Gudhārthadīpikā* on the *Bhagavadgītā*,ed. V.S.R. Kashinatha Śāstrī Agase, ASS 45, Poona, 1901. (Parts ed. by N.L.H. Sarma Bombay, 1916); see also Gupta. S.

———, *Prasthānabheda*, comm. on Madhva's *SDS*, ed. pandits of Ānandāśrama, ASS 51, Poona, 1906, 1928, 1977.

THE MAHĀBHĀRATA Text as constituted in the Critical Edition, ed. V.S. Sukthankar, S.K. Belvalkar, P.L. Vaidya, *et al.* 3 vols. 1971-1974.

———, tr. and ed. by J.A.B. van Buitenen, The Univ. of Chicago, Chicago and London, 1973 (Books I-IV) .

———, tr. Pratap Chandra Ray (re): Munshiram Manoharlal, New Delhi. 1972 (vol. I-XI, various).

MAHEŚA CHANDRA NYĀYARATNA, *Navyanyāyabhāṣāpradīpaḥ*, ed (with Bengali tr.) Kalipada Tarkacharya, Calcutta SCR Series No. LXXIX, Sanskrit College Calcutta, 1973.

MAṆḌANA MIŚRA, *Sphoṭasiddhi—La Demonstration du Sphoṭa*, Madeleine Biardeau; Institut Francais, No. 13, Pondichery, 1958.

-ed. with comm. *Gopālikā* of Parameśvara, MUS 6, 1931

-*Sphoṭasiddhi of Maṇḍana Miśra*, tr. Subramania Iyer, Deccan College, 1966.

———,*Brahmasiddhi*, with Abhiprāyaprakāśikā of Citsukha, ed. A.N. Anantakṛṣṇa Śāstrī, MGOS 161, 1963.

-with comm. of Śaṅkhapāṇi, ed. S. Kuppuswami Sastri, re: Delhi, 1984.

———, *Vidhiviveka*, ed. in *Paṇḍit* XXV-XXVII 1903-6.

MANUSMṚTI, (Ch. 1-2) ed. S.B. Yogi: with tr. G. Buhler. MB, Delhi, 1975.

MĪMĀṂSĀKOŚAḤ, ed. Kevalānanda Saraswati and V. G. Joshi, Prajña Pathasala Maṇḍal, WA I, 1952-56.

NĀGEŚA BHAṬṬA, *Paramalaghumañjūṣā*, ed Pt Sri Nityananda Panta Parvatiya, Banaras, Haridas Sanskrit Series, 93, 1946.

-ed. Kapila Deva Shastri, Kurukshetra Visvavidyalaya Prakasha, 1975.

———, *Sphoṭavāda*, with com. *Subhodinī*, ed. V. Krishamacharya, ALRC, Madras, 1946.

NĀRĀYAṆA BHAṬṬA, *Mānameyodaya* (An elementary treatise on Mīmāṃsā), ed. tr. C. Kunhan Raja and S. S. Suryanarayan Sastri, ALRC, No. 105; Madras, 1975.

NIMBĀRKA, see *Brahmasūtra-pramukha-bhāṣya*.

NṚSIMHĀŚRAMA, *Advaitadīpikā*, with *Vivaraṇa* of Nārāyaṇāśrama, Banaras, 1919?.

NYĀYAKOŚA, ed. Bhīmācārya Jhalakikar, revised V. S. Abhyankar, Poona, 1928.

PADMAPĀDA, *Pañcapādikā* (*PP*) with *Prabodhapariśodhinī* of Ātmasvarūpa, *Tātparyārthadyotinī* of Vijñānātman , *Tātparyadīpikā* of Citsukha, *Bhāvaprakāśikā* of Nṛsimhāśrama and Prakāśātman's *Pañcapādikā-vivaraṇa*, ed. S. Srirama Sastri and S. R. Krishnamurti Sastri, MGOS 155, 1958.

-tr. D. Venkataramiah, GOS. no. 107, Baroda, 1948.

PĀṆINI, *Aṣṭādhyāyī* (*Ashṭādhyāyī*),ed. tr. with notes S. C. Vasu, Panini Office, Allahabad, 1891; re: (2 vols), MB, Delhi, 1962, 1977. 1980.

-*Pāṇinisūtras* (*PS*) in *Vyākaraṇa-Mahābhāṣya*, ed. F. Kielhorn, 1st edn. 1880; re: 1892; revised BORI, Poona, 1962, 1965; see also S. D. Joshi.

PĀRTHASĀRATHI MISRA, *Śāstradīpikā* (*SD*) with comm. *Yuktisneha*, *Prapūrāṇi* of Pt Rāmakṛṣṇa Miśra, ed. Laksman Shastri Dravida, (ChSS 188,

190, 220–226), Banaras, 1916 (1919).
-ed. Rāma Miśra Śāstri, Banaras, 1891 (*saṃvat* 1949).
-ed. P. P. Subrahmanya Sastri, Madras Govn. Oriental Series 9, *c.* 1945.
-*Tarkapāda* section, tr. D. Venkataramiah, GOS. No. LXXXIX Baroda, 1940.

———, *Nyāyaratnākara* (on Kumārila's* *SV*).

———, *Nyāyaratnamālā*. ed with Intro. notes, Pt. Subrahmanya Sastri, Sanskrit Mahavidyalaya, BHU, 1972.
-GOS vol 75, 1937.

PATAÑJALI, (*Vyākaraṇa-*)*Mahābhāṣya*, ed. F. Kielhorn; 3rd edn. K. V. Abhyankar, 3 vols, BORI, Poona, 1962, 1965.
-*Mahābhāṣya-pradīpa-vyākhyānāṇi*, comms. of Patañjali and Pradīpa of Kaiyaṭa, ed N. S. Narasimhacharya, Adhyāya 1–8, Institut francais d'indologie, Pondicherry, 1973–83.

PATAÑJALI, *Yogasūtras* (*YS*) – (no relation): *Pātañjaliyogasūtrāṇi*, with comm. of Vyāsa and *ṭīkā* of Vācaspati Miśra, ed. pandits, ASS 47, 1899, 1978.
-ed. txt with *Vyāsabhāṣya: Yoga Philosophy of Patañjali* ed. Swami Hariharānanda Āraṇya (tr P. N. Mukerji) Univ. of Calcutta, 1981
-*The Yoga-Systems of Patañjali* – J. H. Wood, Harvard Oriental Series, (1914) No. 17. re: MB, Delhi, 1966.; see also Śaṅkara and Legget.

PRABHĀKARA MIŚRA, *Bṛhatī* (*Śābarabhāṣyavyākhyā*) with comm. Ṛjuvimala of Śālikanātha Miśra, ed. A. Chinnaswami Sastri, ChSS 391, Banaras, 1929.
-(*Tarkapāda*) (*on Śābarabhāṣya*) ed. by S. K. Ramanatha Sastri, Uni of Madras, 1934, MUSS no. 3.

PRAKĀŚĀNANDA, *Vedānta-Siddhāntamuktāvalī*, tr. notes by Arthur Venis, (Gokuldas Sanskrit Series 4) Chaukhambha Orientalie, Varanas: 1975.

PRAŚASTAPĀDA, *Padārthadharmasaṅgraha*, ed. with Śrīdhara's *Nyāyakandalī*, tr in Hindi, Durgadhara Jha Sharma, Ganganatha Jha Granthamala, Varanasi, 1963 (Eng. tr. G. Jha, *Pandit* NS 1903–1915).

PRAKĀŚĀTMAN (YATI), *Pañcapādikāvivaraṇa* – on *Pañcapādikā*, see Padmapāda.

PEDDA DĪKṢITA, *Prakāśikā*, ed. Sāmba Śiva Śāstrī, with Advaita *Vedāntaparibhāṣā*), Trivandum Sanskrit Series, No XCIII, Book House, 1928.

PUṆYARĀJA, comm. on Bhartṛhari's* *VKP*.

RAGHUNĀTHA ŚIROMAṆI, *The Padārthatattvanirūpaṇam*, ed. tr. Karl H. Potter, Camb. Mass. 1957.

RĀMĀDVAYA, *Vedāntakaumadī*, ed. Radhesyama Caturvedi (Hindi and Sanskrit), Kashi Hindu Visvavidyalaya Samskrtagranthamala, Varanasi, 1973
-ed. S. Subramanya Sastri, MUSS, Madras, 1955.

RAMAKṚṢṆĀDHVARĪNDRA, (*Vedānta*)*Sikhāmaṇi* (on *Vedāntaparibhāṣā*), with Amardāsa's *Maṇiprabhā*, ed. Govinda Simha, Bombay, 1901.

———, *Nyāyasikhāmaṇi* on *Prakāśa* of Ruccidatta on *TC* of Gaṅgeśa *(pratyakṣa khaṇḍa)*, Tirupati edn of *TC* (see Gaṅgeśa).

RĀMĀYAṆA (Vālmīki), tr. R. T. H. Giffith: *Rāmāyaṇa of Vālmīki*, ChSS, (XXXIX) Varanasi, 1977.

RĀMĀNUJA, *Gītābhāṣya*, comm. on the *Bhagavadgītā*: *Rāmānuja on the Bhagavadgītā* (with notes and Intr.) rendered by J.A.B. van Buitenen, MB. Delhi, 1974.

———, *Śrī Bhāṣya* (comm. on Bādarāyaṇa's *Brahmasūtras*), ed. with Śrīnavāsa's *Yatīndramatadīpikā*, ed. Ratna Gopal Bhatta, Benaras Sanskrit Series 133, Varanasi, 1907.
-see *Brahmasūtra-pramukha-bhāṣya*.

-ed. V. S. Abhyankar, Bombay and Prakrit Series 68, Bombay, 1914–1916
-*The Vedānta-sūtra with Rāmānuja's Śrībhāṣya*, tr. G. Thibaut, SBES (1904), Vol. 48, MB, Delhi, 1976.
-*Śrībhāṣya* with intro. notes R. D. Karmarkar, Univ. of Poona, Poona, 1959–64.
_______, *Vedāntadīpa*, ed. Acharya Bhattanathaswamy, Benaras Sanskrit Series, 70, (3 parts) 1902–1904.
_______, *Vedārthasaṃgraha*, ed. with Intro. & tr. J.A.B. van Buitenen, DCPR, Poona, 1956.

RATNAKĪRTI, *Apohasiddhi*, in Six Buddhist Nyāya Tracts, Bibliotheca Indica, 185, Calcutta, 1910; tr. Dhirendra Sharma.*
_______, *Ratnakīrtinibandhāvalīḥ*, ed. Anantalal Thakur, (2nd rev. ed; Tibetan Sanskrit Works Series 3) Kasi Prasad Jayaswal Research Institute, Patna, 1975.

ṚGVEGA, (See *Veda*).

ŚABARASVĀMĪ (ŚABARA), *Śābarabhāṣya*, in *Mīmāṃsādarśana*, ed. V. G. Apte (see Jaimini); first published with 'The Aphorisms of the Mīmāṃsā' *Mīmāṃsādarśana*, Bibliotheca Indica, Asiatic Society, Calcutta, 1873–1889 (see Jaimini);
-tr. G. Jha, 3 vol. Gaekwad's Oriental Series, nos. 60, 70, 73; Boroda, 1933; re: 1973.

SADĀNANDA, *Vedāntasāra*, ed. with Kaumudī (Hindi comm.) R. S. Tripathi, Gokuldas Sanskri Series 34, Chow. Orientalia, Varanasi, 1983.
-*Vedāntasāra (Essence of Vedanta)*,txt. tr. M. Hiriyana, University of Mysore, Mysore.
-ed. Sudarśan Ācārya Śāstrī, CHSS 251, 1954.
-txt. tr. with notes, G. A. Jacob, (1904) in *The Philosophy of the Vedānta and the Vedāntasāra*, by P. Deussen and G. A. Jacob, Susil Gupta Ltd, Calcutta, 1957.

ŚĀLIKANĀTHA SVĀMĪ, (See Prabhakāra)

ŚAṄKARA (or SAṄKARĀCĀRYA BHAGAVATAPĀDA), *Śrīśaṅkaragranthāvali*: *The Works of Śrī Śaṅkarāchārya*,(ed. txt) Vāṇī Vilās Press, Srirangam, 1910–14 (Vols. I-VIII); reissued as: *The Complete Works of Śrī Saṅkarāchārya*, Samata Books, Madras, 1981 (10 vols):
_______, *Bhāṣya on Brahmasūtras* (*BSB*) (Madras, 1981) Vol VII.
-See also *Brahmasūtra-Pramukha-bhāṣyas*;
-*Brahmasūtra-Śaṅkara-bhāṣya*, with five commentaries, ed. with Eng. trs. intro. Anantakṛṣṇa Śāstrī, Metropolitan Printing & Publishing Co, Calcutta, 1941.
-*Brahmasūtra-bhāṣya*, with Govindānanda's *Ratnaprabhā*, ed. Rama Narayana Vidyaratna, Bibliotheca Indica 22, Calcutta, 1854–1863 ; re: Osna-bruck, Biblio Verlag, 1980.
-*Brahmasūtra-bhāṣya* (with other works), ed. Mahādeva Śāstri Bākre, revised W. S. Śāstri Paṅsikar, NSP, Bombay 1934.
-*Śāṅkarabhāṣya* (*Catussūtrī*), with comm. *Brahmatattvaprakāśikā*, (Hindi) by Viśveśvara Siddhānta Śiromaṇi, Vidyanatha Sanskrit Granthamala 137, Vidyabhavan, Varanasi, 1966.
-*The Brahmasūtrabhāṣya*, ed. txt, note, Nārāyaṇa Rām Āchārya, NSP, Bombay, 1948.
-with *Dīpikā* of Mahādevānanda Saraswatī, ed. Rāma Śāstrī Tailaṅga, BSS, Banaras, 1904-.
-ed. G. G. Gokhale, ASS 75, Poona, 1915.
-ed. J. L. Shastri, with *Ratnaprabhā*, *Bhāmatī* and *Nyāyanirṇaya* , MB, Delhi, 1980.

-tr V. M. Apte 1882; re: Popular Book Depot, Bombay, 1960.
- *Vedānta Sūtra with Śaṅkarāchārya's comm.* (2 vols) tr. G. Thibaut, SBES, 34, 38; re: Delhi, 1979. (text in:-)

_______, *Bhāṣyas on Upaniṣads*, in *Complete Works* (Vol II, XI, VII-VIII). *The Bṛhadāraṇyaka Upaniṣad*, with comm. of Śaṅkarācārya, tr. Swami Mādhavānanda, Advaita Ashram, Calcutta, 1975.
-*Eight Upaniṣads with the comms. of Śaṅkarācārya*, tr. Swami Gambhīrānanda, 2 vols. (Īśa, Kena, Kaṭha, Taittirīya; Aitareya, Muṇḍaka, Māṇḍūkya, Praśna), Advaita Ashram, Calcutta, 1972.
-*Chāndogya Up. bhāṣya*, tr. G. Jha, with intro Umesha Misra, POS, 78, Poona, 1942.

_______, *Vivekacūḍāmaṇi*, with comm. of Jagatguru Chandraśekhara Bhāratī Vidyātīrtha, tr. T. Sankaranarayana, intro Subramanya Iyer, Bharatiya Vidya Bhavan, Bombay, 1973.

_______, *Upadeśasāhasrī*, in: S. Mayeda, *A Thousand Teachings The Upadeśasāharsī* of *Śaṅkara* (with tr, intro, notes), University of Tokyo Press, Tokyo, 1979.
-Ch. 18 in '*That Thou Art*', tr by J. A. Alston, Shanti Sadan, London, 1967.

_______, *Bhāṣya* on *Bhagavadgītā*: VOL VII (*Works*, Madras, 1981)
-tr. Mahadeva Sastri, *The Bhagavad-Gītā*, with Commentary of Śrī Śaṅkarāchārya, Samata Books, Madras, 1892, 1947, 1971
-ed. D. V. Gokhale. POS I, 1931, 1950.

_______, *Yogasūtravyāsabhāṣyavivaraṇa* (See Leggett, Nakamura).

ŚĀNTARAKṢITA, *Tattvasangraha* (with comm. of Kamalaśīla), tr. Ganganatha Jha, GOS 80, 1937.

SARVAJÑĀTMAN MUNI, *Pramāṇalakṣaṇa*, ed. with Eng. intro, notes, Easwara Nampoorthiry, Univ. of Kerala, Trivandrum, 1973.

_______, *Saṃkṣepaśārīraka*, ed. with Puruṣottama Miśra's *Subodhinī* V.R. Sastri, ASS, no. 83, Poona, 1918.
-ed. tr. N. Veezhinathan, Univ. of Madras, Philosophy Series 18, Madras, 1972.

SĀYAṆA, *Sāyaṇa's Preface to the Ṛg-Vedabhāṣya*, tr. Peter Peterson, BORI, Poona, 1974. (See Devasthali, Garge).

ŚRĪDHARA, (see Praśastapāda).

ŚRĪHARṢA, *Khaṇḍanakhaṇḍakhādya*, ed. with comm. and extracts of Ānandapūrṇa, Citsukha, Śaṃkara Miśra and Raghunāth Śiromaṇi, ed. by L. S. Dravida; ChSS XXI, 1914 Varanasi
-tr. Ganganatha Jha, Indian Thought Series 4, 1915; re: Sri Satguru Publications, Delhi, 1985 (2 vols).
-with *Śāṅkarī*, comm. of Śaṅkara Miśra, and *Tattvabodhinī* (Hindi comm.) of Svāmī Hanumāndās Satsāstrī;Navikanta Jha, KSS 197, Chowkhamba, Varanasi, 1970; see also Phillis Granoff*.

ŚRĪNIVĀSADĀSA, *Yatīndramatadīpikā*, tr. notes by Swami Adidevānanda, Sri Ramakrishna Math, Madras, 1967. (See Rāmānuja).

SUREŚVARA, *Naiṣkarmyasiddhi*, txt. tr. by S. S. Raghavachar, Univ of Mysore, Mysore, 1965.

_______, *The Naiṣkarmya Siddhi of Śrī Sureśvara*, tr. A. J. Alston, Shanti Sadan, London, 1959.

_______, *The Saṃbandhavārtika of Sureśvārācarya*, ed. text tr. notes, by J. A. Alston, Shanti Sadan, London, 1971, 1976.

-*Bṛhadāraṇyakopaniṣadbhāṣyavārtika* (*BUBV*) (see Hino*)

______,-*The Taittirīyopaniṣad Bhāṣya-Vārtika* (*TUBV*) of Sureśvara, ed. tr. by R. Balasubramanian, Univ. of Madras, Madras, 1974.

-*TUBV*. tr. ed. notes by J.M. van Boetzelaer, J. Brill, Leiden, 1971.

______, *Mānasollāsa*, comm. on Sankara's Daksinamurtistotra, Bhavnagar, 1911.

TOṬAKĀCĀRYA, *Śrutisārasamuddhāraṇam*, ed. Kevalānanda Swami, ASS 103, Poona, 1936.

UDAYANA, *Nyāyakusumāñjali*, Ganganatha Jha Granthmala (vol 6), ed. with Hindi trs. Pt Durgadhara Jha, Varanasi, 1973.

-ed with comm. of Haridāsa Bhattācārya tr E. B. Cowell, asst. by Pt Maheśa Chandra Nyāyaratna, as: *The Kusumāñjali or Hindu Proof of the Existence of A Supreme Being by Udayana Acharya*, Calcutta, 1864 re: Bharat Bharati, Varanasi, 1980.

-txt in *Kusumāñjali-kārikā-vyākhyā*, of Nārāyaṇa Tīrtha, ed. Srinivasa Shastri, Kurukshetra University, Kurushetra, 1974.

-trs. and elucidation in George Chemparathy*

______, *Kiraṇāvalī*, with comm. of Vardhamān, ed. M.M. Shiva Chandra Sarvabhauma, Calcutta, 1911; re: Bibliotheca Indica, Calcutta, 1956.

-Gaewkad's Oriental Series, Baroda, 1964 (two parts).

-see also Tachikawa.

______, *Pariśuddhi*, see Gautama: *Nyāyadarśana*.

UDDYOTKARA, *Nyāyavārttika*, ed. Pt. Vindhyeśvari Prasad Dube, ChSS, 21, 1919.

-see Gautama: *Nyāyadarśana*.

UPANIṢADS, *Eighteen Principal Upaniṣads*, Vol. I txt, ed. V. A. Limaye and R. D. Vadekar; Vaidika Saṃsodhana Maṇḍala, Poona, 1958.

-*108 Upaniṣads*. txt, NSP, Bombay, 1930

-*The Bṛhadāraṇyaka Upaniṣad*, see R. D. Ranade and Belvalkar.

-*The Kenopaniṣad*—with Śaṅkara's Comm. txt, tr. by M. Hiriyanna, Karyalaya Publishers, Mysore (1912), 1974.

-*The Principal Upaniṣads*, ed. text, tr. by S. Radhakrishnan; George Allen and Unwin, Humanities Press, 1974.

-*The Upaniṣads*; tr. by Max Müller, 2 vols. Dover Publications, N. Y., 1962; Sacred Books of the East Series Vol. I, XV.

VĀCASPATI MIŚRA, *Bhāmatī*, with *Kalpataru* of Amalānanda and *Parimala* of Appayya Dīkṣita*, KSS 116, 1935.

-*The Bhāmatī (Catussūtrī)*, comm. on Śaṅkara's

-*Brahmasūtrabhāṣya*, I-IV), ed. tr. S. S. Suryanarayana Sastri and C. Kunhan Raja, The Theosophical Publishing House, Madras, 1933.

______, *Tattvabindu* (*śābdabodhakaraṇa*), ed. Kasinatha Sarma, E. J. Lazarus & Co., 1917.

-*La Tattvabindu*, edition/critique, traduction et introduction, M. Biardeau, Institut francais d'indologie, Pondicherry, 1979.

VAIDYANĀTH BHAṬṬA, *Nyāyabindu* (a treatise on the study of Pūrva Mīmāṃsā) with comm. of Madan Pathak, ed. Mahādev Gaṅgadhar Bākre, The Gujarati Printing Press, Bombay, 1915.

VĀTSYĀYANA, *Bhāṣya* on *Nyāyasūtras* of Gautama*, ed. G. S. Tailaṅga, Banaras, 1896.

VIDYĀRAṆYA (Bhāratītīrtha), *Pañcadaśī*, ed. with comm. of Rāmakṛṣṇa, V.S. Paniskar, NSP, Bombay, 1949.

Pañcadaśī, txt. tr. Swami Swahananda, Ramakrishna Math, Madras, 1968.

———, *Jīvanmuktiviveka*, ed. V. S. Pansikar, ASS 20, 1978.

———, *Vivaraṇa-prameya-saṅgraha*, ed. Rāma Śastrī Telaṅg, VSS n 7, Banaras, 1893. (See Mahadevan).

VIJÑĀNABHIKṢU, *Vijñānāmṛtabhāṣya* (on *BSB*), ed. Kedarnatha Tripathi, BHU, 1979.

VIMUKTĀTMAN, *Īṣṭasiddhi*, Gaekwad Oriental Series, vol 65, Baroda, 1963.

-txt, with preface by P. K. Sundarama, Swadharma Swaarajya Sangha, Madras, 1980.

-ed. with extracts from Jñānottama's *Vivaraṇa*, M. Hiriyana, Kevalya Publications, Mysore.

VIŚVANĀTHA. *Bhāṣā-pariccheda* (*BP*)(*Kārikāvalī*), with *Siddhānta-muktāvalī*, (*SM*), ed. Jivānnanda Vidyāsāgara Bhaṭṭāchārya, Bibliotheca Indica, Calcutta 1883.

-ed. NārāyaṇaRāmaĀchārya, NSP, 1952.

-*Kārikāvalī*, with Dinakara's *Prakāśa* (*Dinakarī*), ed. Harirāma Śuklaḥ Nyāyācārya, KSS 6, Varanasi, 1972.

———, *Nyāyasiddhāntamuktāvalī*, (ditto), with comm. *Kiraṇāvalī* by Pt. Kṛṣṇavallabhācārya; ed. Nārāyaṇa Caraṇa Śāstrī and Svetavaikuṇṭha Śāstrī, KSS 212, Chaukhambha, Varanasi, 1940, re: 1983.

-tr. Swami Mādhavānanda, Advaita Ashram, Calcutta, 1954.

VEDAS Ṛg Veda, *Sāyaṇabhāṣyabhūmikā*, with Hindi comm. V. K. Varma, Chowk. Orientalia, Varanasi.

-*Ṛg Veda Saṃhitā* (txt) with comm. Sāyaṇa, Vaidika Saṃsodhana Maṇḍala, Tilak Maharastra Vidyapitha, 1946, 1972. (Vol I-IV), Poona.

-*Ṛg-Veda, padapāṭha, bhāṣyas:* Skandaswāmī, Mādhava, Sāyaṇa *et. al*; ed. Vishva Bandu; Parts I-VII, Vishveshvarananda Vedic Research Institute, Hoshiapur, 1965. (esp. Part VII-*maṇḍala* X. 46–191).

-*Atharva Veda Saṅhitā*, ed. R. Roth/W. D. Whitney, Ferd-Dummlers, Bonn, 1966.

-*Artharva Veda*, tr. Whitney, Harvard Oriental 7–8, 2 vols; M. B. Delhi, 1971.

-*Text of the White Yajur Veda*, TR R. T. H. Griffiths; Lazarus, Ben. 1925.

-*Taittirīya Saṃhitā*, with comm. Bhāskara Miśra, Sāyaṇa; ed. Sontakke and Dharmadhikari, Vaidika Saṃsodhana Maṇḍala, Vol I-II, Poona, 1970.

YAMUNA, *Āgamaprāmāṇya*, as *Yamuna's Āgama Prāmāṇyam*, txt, tr. J.A.B. van Buitenen, Rāmānuja Research Society, Madras, 1971.

VYĀSA, Comm. on *Yogasūtras*, see Patañjali, Leggett.

PART B (Useful secondary and related sources, and others of interest.)

ABHYANKAR, K. V., *A Dictionary of Sanskrit Grammar,* 2nd edn. Oriental Institute, Baroda, 1961 (re: 1977)

AQUINAS, ST THOMAS, *Summa Theologiae*, Latin txt. Eng. trans. intro. notes, etc. (Gen. Editor: Thomas Gilby), Blackfriars, Eyre and Spottiswoode, London, 1964-8. (See also Pegis.)

_______ DE VERITATE, Qu 21. (Robert W. Schmidt, tr.) *Truth* (vol III), Henry Regnery and Co, 1954.

ARAPURA, J. G., 'Language and Phenomena', *Canadian Journal of Theology*, Vol. XVI, 1 + 2 (1970), pp. 41-53.

_______, 'Māyā and the Discourse about Brahman', in Sprung, M. (ed.) *Two Concepts of Truth* (1973) pp 109-121.

_______, 'Some Perspectives on Indian Philosophy of Language', in *Revelation in Indian Thought*, Coward* and Sivaraman (eds), pp. 15-44.

ARISTOTLE, '*De Anima*', in *The Basic Works of Aristotle*, Random House, New York, 1941.

_______, *Metaphysics*, (W. D. Ross, tr.) The Clarendon, Oxford, 1924.

ATREYA, B. L., *The Philosophy of Yoga-vāśiṣtha: a comparative, critical and synthetic survey,* Darshana International, Moradabad, 1981.

AUROBINDO, Sri, *The Secret of the Veda*, Sri Aurobindo Ashram Trust, Pondicherry, 1972.

_______, *Collected Works*, Aurobindo Ashram Trust, Pondicherry, 1979.

AUSTIN, J. L., *How to Do Things with Words*, OUP, NY, 1965.

AUUNG, SHWE ZAN and RHYS DAVIDS, C.A.F., *Compendium of Philosophy, Being a translation of the Abhidhama-matta-saṅgaha*,. Pali Text Society translation series, Vol II, OUP, London, 1910.

AYER, A. J., *Language, Truth and Logic*, Gollanzce, London, 1536.

_______, *The Problem of Knowledge*, Penguin, Middlesex, 1964, 1971.

_______, *The Origin of Pragmaticism: studies in the Philosophy of Charles Sanders Peirce and William James*, Macmillan, London, 1968.

BAGCHI, S., *Inductive Reasoning, A Study in Tarka and Its Role in Indian Logic* Calcutta, 1955.

BALASUBRAMANIAN, R., *Advaita Vedānta (based on Brahma-siddhi)*, Madras University, 1976. (See also Sureśvara.)

BARLINGAY, S. S., *A Modern Introduction to Indian Logic*, National Publishing House, Delhi, 1965.

_______, *Beliefs, Reasons and Reflections*, Indian Philosophical Quarterly (Publications), Poona, 1984.

_______, 'Indian Epistemology and Logic', in *Indian Thought, An Introduction*, Donald H. Bishop (ed.), Wiley Eastern, Powaite, New Delhi, 1975, pp. 148-163.

BANERJEE, A. C., *Sarvāstivāda Literature*, Oriental Press, Calcutta, 1957.

BANERJEE, N. K., *The Concept of Philosophy*, K. C. Memorial Lectures, University of Calcutta, 1968.

_______, *Language, Meaning and Persons*, A&U, London, 1963.

BANERJEE, S. P., and MOHANTY, J. N., (eds) *Self, Knowledge and Freedom, Essays for Kalidas Bhattacharyya*, The World Press, Calcutta, 1978.

BARTH, KARL, *The Doctrine of the Word of God*, (tr. G. T. Thomas), Clark, Edinburgh, 1936.

de BARY, THEODORE, (ed.) *Sources of Indian Tradition*, Basham, Dandekar Raghavan, Weiler, *et. al.*, 2 vols. Columbia Univ. Press, N.Y. 1970.

BASHAM, A.L., (ed.) *A Cultural Heritage of India*, Oxford Univ. Press, Oxford, 1975.

———, *History and Doctrine of the Ājīvakas*, MB, Delhi, 1981.

———, 'Hinduism', in R. C. Zaehner (ed.) *The Concise Encyclopedia of Living Faiths*, Beacon Press, Boston, 1967, pp. 225–260.

BELVALKAR, S.K. and RANADE, R. D., *History of Indian Philosophy—Creative Period*, (1927), Oriental Books Reprint, New Delhi, 1974.
- see *Brahmasūtra*

BERKELEY, BISHOP, *The Principles of Human Knowledge*, (ed. G. J. Warnock) Fontana/Collins, London, 1962.

BHADURI, S., *Studies in Nyāya-Vaiśeṣika Metaphysics*, (1947), BORI, Poona, 1975.

BHARATI, AGEHANANDA, 'Radhakrishnan and the other Vedānta', in P. A. Schilpp (ed.) *The Philosophy of Sarvepalli Radhakrishnan*, N.Y. 1952, pp459–480.

BHATTA, GOVARDHANA P., *Epistemology of the Bhāṭṭa School of Pūrva Mīmāṃsā* ChSS Studies, vol xvii, Varanasi, 1962.

BHATTACHARYA, H., (ed.) *The Cultural Heritage of India*, IV vols, Ramakrishna Mission, Calcutta, 1969.

BHATTACHARYA, GOPIKAMOHAN, 'On Saṃsargamaryādā in Navyanyāya', in S. D. Joshi* (ed.) *Winter Proceedings on Sentence-Meaning*, 1980, Poona, pp. 79–84.

———, 'Śābdabodha as a separate type of pramāṇa', *JIP*, vol. 5, 1977, pp. 73–84.

———, *Navya-Nyāya—Some Logical Problems in Historical Perspective*, Bharatiya Vidya Prakashan, Delhi/Varanasi, 1978.

BHATTACHARYYA, GOPINATH, 'A Study in the Dialectics of Sphoṭa', *Journal of Department of Letters*, 29, 1937, University of Calcutta.
-see Annaṃbhaṭṭa, *Tarkasaṃgraha* .

BHATTACHARYYA, KRISHNA CHANDRA, *Studies in Vedāntism*, Calcutta University Press 1970.

———, *Search for the Absolute in Neo-Vedānta; Studies in Vedāntism*, G. B. Burch, ed.), Univ. Press of Hawaii, Honolulu, 1976.

———, *Studies in Philosophy*, (Gopinath Bhattacharyya, ed.), 2 Parts (esp. 'Knowledge & Truth', and 'Vedānta Logic'), Progressive Publishers, Calcutta, 1958; re: MB, Delhi, 1983.

BHATTACHARYYA, J. V., *Jayanta Bhaṭṭa's Nyāyamañjarī* (trans. etc.), vol 1, MB, Delhi, 1978.

BHATTACHARYYA, KALIDAS, *Object Content and Relation*, Das Gupta, Calcutta, n.d.

———, *Philosophy Logic and Language*, Allied Publishers, Bombay, 1965.

———, 'The Absolute as Pure Consciousness', in *A Modern Understanding of Advaita Vedānta*, L. D. Series 45, L. D. Institute of Indology, Ahmedabad, 1975.

———, 'The Fundamentals of K. C. Bhattacharyya's Philosophy: The Definite and the Indefinite-I', *Bulletin of the Ramakrishna Mission Institute of Calcutta*, Vol.XXIV, Oct. 1973, No.10, pp. 345–350.

———, *On the Concept of Relations and Negation in Indian Philosophy*, Sanskrit College, Calcutta, 1977.

———, 'Traditional Indian Philosophy as a Modern Thinker Views It', in

Pappu* & Puligandla (eds) *Indian Philosophy Past and Present*, 1982, pp 171-224.

_______, 'Indian Concepts of Knowledge and Self', *Our Heritage*, Bulletin of the Dept. of P/G Training, Sanskrit College, Calcutta, vol 2, 1954, pp 221-248 (and seriatum, later numbers).

_______, (ed.) *Recent Indian Philosophy*, Progressive Publishers, Calcutta, 1963.

_______, 'Hearer's Meaning', inaugural paper, Darshan Bhavan, Philosophy Dept, Jadavpur Uni, Calcutta, Jan. 1983 (recorded)

BHATTACHARYA SIBAJIVAN, 'Some Indian Theories of Meaning', *The Journal of The Indian Academy of Philosophy*, Calcutta, vol. XXIII no 2, 1984, pp 25-41.'Meanings of Words and Sentences',paper delivered in International Philosophy Conf. Jadavpur. Jan 1983.

_______, 'Knowing That', in *Contemporary Indian Philosophy*, Margaret Chatterjee (ed.), Allen & Unwin, London/NY 1974, pp. 254-272.

BHIDE, V. V., 'The Concept of the Sentence and the Sentence-Meaning according to the *Pūrva-Mīmāṃsā*', in S. D. Joshi (ed.) *Winter Proceedings on Sentence-Meaning*, 1980, pp. 137-142.

BIARDEAU, MADELEINE, *Théorie de la connaissance et philosophie de la parole dans le brahmanisme classique*, Mouton, Paris, 1964; see also under Mandana Misra, Vacaspati Misra.

BIDERMAN, SHLOMO, 'Imperatives and Religion in India', *Religious Traditions*, vol 4, no 2, Oct-Nov. 1981, pp 59-70.

BIJALWAN, C.D., *Indian Theory of Knowledge, based on Jayanta's Nyāyamañjarī*, Heritage Publishers, Delhi, 1977.

BILIMORIA, PURUṢOTTAMA, '*Ākāṅkṣā*: 'Expectancy' in Sentential Comprehension. An Advaita Critique', *JIP*, Vol.9, No.1, 1981, pp. 85-98.

_______, '*Āsatti* and *Yogyatā* in Sentential Comprehension: *Vedānta Paribhāṣā*', *JIP*, Vol.8, No.4, December 18, 1980, pp. 393-399.

_______, '*Perception (pratyakṣa)* in Advaita Vedānta', *PEW*, *30*, no. 1, Jan. 1980, pp. 35-44.

_______, '*Tātparya*: Intentionality in Sentential Comprehension in Advaita linguistics', Sezione Orientale dell'intituto, Universitario Orientale, Napoli, Dec 1985, 45/4, pp 599-627.

_______, '*Jñāna* and *Pramā*: Logic of Knowing – a critical appraisal', *JIP*, vol. 13, no 1, March 1985, pp 73- 102.

_______, '*Pramāṇavāda* – towards an Indian Theory of Knowledge – outline for a programme', *Darshana International*, Moradabad, April, 1980, pp 72-78.

_______, 'Renaissance Reaction to Śruti', ABORI, (Poona) 1984 vol LXV, pt I-IV, pp 43-58.

_______, '*Śruti & Apauruṣeya* – an approach to scripture and revelation' *Journal of Dharma*, Bangalore, July-Sept. 1982 Vol II no 3, pp 275-291.

_______, '*Apauruṣeya*: Possibility of Trans-personal Word', IAHR paper, Sydney, 1985 (under revision).

BOTHRA, PUSHPA, *The Jain Theory of Perception*, MB, Delhi, 1976.

BOWES, PRATIMA, *Hindu Intellectual Tradition*, Allied Publishers, Delhi, 1977.

BLOOMFIELD, LEONARD, *Language* (1935), MB, Delhi (reprint) 1964.

BRENTANO, FRANZ, *Psychologie vom empirischen Stanpunkt*, (D. B. Terrell and Linda McAister, trs), RKP, London, 1973.

_______, *The Theory of Categories*, (R. M. Chisholm and Norbert Guterman, trs), Martinus Nijhoff, The Hague, 1980.

BRADLEY, F. H., *Essays on Truth and Reality*, Clarendon Press, Oxford, 1914.

BROUGH, JOHN, 'Some Indian Theories of Meaning', Transactions of the Philological Society, 1953, pp 161–76, reprinted in J. F. Staal (ed.) *A Reader on the Sanskrit Grammarians*, M. I. T. Mass, 1972, pp. 414–423.

———, *Theories of General Linguistics in the Sanskrit Grammarians*, Philological Society of London, Transactions, 1951, pp. 27–46.

BUBER, MARTIN, *I and Thou*, (Ronald Gregory, tr.) T. Clark, Edinburgh, 1966.

BUITENEN, J.A.B. van, *Rāmānuja on the Bhagavad Gītā*, MB, Dehli.

———, and DEUTSCH, E., (eds) see Deutsch; and *Bhagavadgītā*

CASSIRER, EARNEST, *Language and Myth*, Dover, N. Y., 1946.

———, *Philosophy of Symbolic Forms*, (R. Manheim, tr.) Yale Univ. Press, New Haven, 1953–57.

CENKAR, WILLIAM, *A Tradition of Teachers: Śaṅkara and the Jagadgurus Today*, MB, Delhi, 1983.

CHAKRAVARTI, P. K., *The Linguistic Speculations of the Hindus,* Univ. of Calcutta, 1933.

CHAKRABARTI, KISHOR KUMAR, *The Logic of Gotama*, Monograph of the Society for Asian and Comparative Philosophy, No.5, The University Press of Hawaii, Honolulu, 1977.

———, 'Some Remarks on Indian Theories of Truth', *JIP*, Vol 12, No 4, Dec. 1984, pp 339–356.

———, 'The Nyāyavaiśeṣika Theory of Universals', *JIP,* 3 (1975) pp. 363–382.

CHARI, C.T.K., (ed.) *Essays in Philosophy, Presented to Dr. T. M. P. Mahadevan,* Ganesh & Co., Madras, 1962.

CHARLESWORTH, MAX. J., *Philosophy and Linguistics Analysis*, Duquesne Univ., Pittsburg, 1959.

———, 'The Problem of Religious Language', *Religione*, Ateismo, Filosophia 1.3, Roma. pp 47–51.

CHATTERJEE, A. K., 'Predicates', *IPQ* (Poona), vol V no 4, 1978, pp 549–576.

CHATTERJEE, JAGADISH, *The Hindu Realism*, Indian Press, Allahabad, 1912.

CHATTERJEE, S. C., *The Nyāya Theory of Knowledge*, Univ. of Calcutta, 1978.

CHATTERJEE, K.N. *Word and Its Meaning: A new perspective in light of Jagadīśa's Śabdaśaktiprakāśikā*, Chawkhamba Oriental, Varanasi, 1980.

CHATTERJEE, MARGARET (ed.) *Contemporary Indian Philosophy*, Allen & Unwin, London/NY, 1974.

———, *The Language of Philosophy*, Allied Publications, Delhi, 1981.

CHATTERJI, S. K.,RAGHAVAN, DANDEKAR, *et al* (eds) *Some Aspects of Indo-Iranian Literary and Cultural Traditions*, Commemoration volume to Dr. V. G. Paranjpe, Ajanta Publications, Delhi, 1977.

CHATTOPADHYAYA, DEBIPRASAD, (ed.) *Studies in the History of Indian Philosophy*, 2 vols. K. P. Bagchi & Co., Calcutta, 1977.

CHATTOPADHYAYA, S. K., 'The Concept of Adhyāsa and the Vedānta of Śaṅkara', *IPQ* (Poona) Vol VI no 1 Oct. 1978, pp 81–100, part 2 in July, Vol VI no 4, 1979, pp. 683–696.

GHEMPARATHY, GEORGE, *An Indian Rational Theology, Introduction to Udayana's Nyayakusumāñjali*, Indologisches Institut der Universitat Wien, Vienna, 1972.

———, 'Three cardinal thesis of the Nyāya-Vaiśeṣikas concerning the validity of the Vedas', IAHR paper, Sydney, 1985.

———, 'The Veda as Revelation', *Journal of Dharma*, July-Sept 1982 vol VII no 3, pp. 253–274.

_______, 'Nyāya-Vaiśeṣikas as interpreters of Śruti', *Journal of Dharma*, July-Sept, 1978, vol III no 3, pp 274–294.

CHISHOLM, R. M., *Theory of Knowledge*, Prentice-Hall, Englewood Cliff, 1966.

_______, *Perceiving: A Philosophical Study*, Cornell University Press, Ithaca, 1957.

_______, *Realism and the Background of Phenomenology*, Free Press, Glencoe, 1961

CHOMSKY, Noam, *Syntactic Structures*, The Hague, Mouton, 1957.

_______, *Language and Mind*, Harcout, Brace and World, New York, 1968.

CHRISTIE, E., *Indian Philosophers on Poetic Imagination (Pratibha)*, *JIP*, vol. 7, NO.2, pp. 153–207.

COBURN, THOMAS B., 'Scripture in India: towards a typology of the World in Hindu Life', *AAR*, LII/3, 1984 pp 432–458.

COHEN, M., and NAGEL, E., *An Introduction to Logic*, RKP, London, 1963.

COOMARASWAMY, ANANDA KENTISH, 'Angel and Titan: An Essay in Vedic Ontology', Journal of American Oriental Society', (New York), Volume 55, Dec, 1935, pp. 373–419.

_______, *Hinduism and Buddhism*, Greenwood Press, Westport, Conn, 1971.

_______, *Spiritual Authority and Temporal Power in the Indian Theory of Government*, Munshiram Manoharlal, New Delhi, 1978.

COPLESTON, FREDERICK, C., *A History of Philosophy*, (in 2 volumes), Image Books, New York, 1960.

_______, *Philosophies & Cultures*, OUP, 1980.

_______, *Religion and the One: Philosophies East and West* (Gifford Lectures), Crossroads, New York, 1980.

COWARD, HAROLD G., *Bhartṛhari*, Twayne Publishers, Boston, 1976.

_______, 'Bhartṛhari's Dhvani: A Central Notion in Indian Aesthetics', in *Revelation in Indian Thought*, Coward* and Sivaraman (eds), pp. 65–86.

_______, *The Sphota Theory of Language*, A Philosophical Analysis, MB. Delhi, 1980.

_______, and SIVARAMAN, K., (eds.) *Revelation in Indian Thought*, A Festschrift in honour of T. R. V. Murti, Dharma Publishing, California, 1977.

_______, (ed.) *Studies in Indian Thought*, (collected papers of T. R. V. Murti) MB, Delhi, 1983.

_______, (ed.) *Language in Indian Philosophy and Religion*, with Intro., Canadian Society for Studies in Religion, Supplement 5, Quebec, 1976.

DANDEKAR, R. N., *et.al.* (eds) *Sanskrit and Indological Studies, Dr. V. Raghavan Felicitation Volume*, MB, Delhi, 1975.

_______, R. N., *Some Aspects of the History of Hinduism*, Univ. of Poona, Poona, 1967.

_______, *Insights into Hinduism*, (select writings II), Ajanta Publjications, Delhi, 1979.

DAVIDSON, DONALD, *Semantics of Natural Language* (edited with Gilbert Harman), D. Reidel & Co., Dordrecht, 1972.

_______, 'Communication and Convention', paper delivered in International Philosophy Conf. Calcutta, 1983, printed in, *Journal of Indian Council of Philosophical Research*, Delhi, I, 1, 1983.

DASGUPTA, S. N., *A History of Indian Philosophy*, Vol.III, Delhi, MB. 1975, (CUP, 1947).

DATTA, D. M., 'Indian Epistemology', *The Cultural Heritage of India*, Vol. III, The Ramakrishna Mission of India, Calcutta, 1953.

———, *Six Ways of Knowing*, Calcutta Univ. Calcutta, 1972.
———, 'Testimony as a Method of Knowledge', *Mind*, Camb. 1927.
———, 'Verbal Testimony as a Source of Valid Cognition', in Kalidas Bhattacharyya* (ed.) *Recent Indian Philosophy*.
DAYA KRISHNA, 'Adhyāsa – A Non-Advaitic Beginning in Śaṅkara Vedānta', *PEW*, XV, no 3, 1965, pp 243–249.
DERRIDA, JACQUES, *Position* (Allan Bass, tr.) The Athetone Press, London, 1972.
DESCARTES, RENÉ, *Meditations on First Philosophy*, (L. J. Lafleur tr.) The Library of Liberal Arts Series, Bobbs-Merrill, N. Y., 1960.
DESHPANDE, MADHAV, 'Sentence-cognition in Nyāya Epistemology' in *Indo-Iranian Journal* (Dordrecht), vol. 20 (1978) pp. 195–216.
DUESSEN, P., *The System of the Vedānta,* Dover, N. Y., 1975.
DEUTSCH, ELIOT, *Advaita Vedānta: A Philosophical Reconstruction*, The University Press of Hawaii, Honolulu, 1973.
———, 'On Meaning', in Banerjee* and Mohanty (eds) *Self, Knowledge and Freedom, Essays for Kalidas Bhattacharyya*, pp. 1–16.
———, and J.A.B. van BUITENAN, (eds) *A Sourcebook of Advaita Vedānta*, The University Press of Hawaii, Honolulu, 1971.
DEVARAJA, N. K., *An Introduction to Śaṅkara's Theory of Knowledge*, MB, Delhi, 1972.
———, and HIREMATHA, (eds) *A Source Book of Śaṅkara*, BHU, Varanasi, 1971.
———, 'Contemporary Relevance of Advaita Vedānta', in *Indian Philosophical Congress Proceedings*, 1967, BHU, pp. 1–11.
DEVASTHALI, G. V., *Mīmāṃsā: The Vākyaśāstra of Ancient India*, Bookseller's Publishing Co. Bombay, 1959.
———, *Religion and Mythology of the Brāhmaṇas*, University of Poona, Poona, 1965.
———, 'Pāṇini and Ṛg Vedic Exegisis', in *ABORI* (Golden Jubilee) Vol. XLVIII, XLIX, 1968, pp. 75–81.
———, '*Vākya* According to the Munitraya of Sanskrit Grammar', Charudeva Shastri Felicitation Volume, Delhi, 1974.
———, 'Śabara and Nyāya-Vaiśeṣika darśanas', *Journal of Oriental Research*, 18, 1948, Madras, pp 16–24.
DEWEY, JOHN, *How we Think*, (London, 1909), D. C. Heath & Co., Boston and NY, 1933.
———, *Logic: The Theory and Inquiry*, D. C. Heath, Boston, 1933.
DRAVID, R. R., 'Pramāṇavāda', *IPQ*, IV, 2. Jan, 1977, pp. 135–146.
———, 'Language, Thought and Reality', in R. C. Pandey and S. R. Bhatt (eds), *Knowledge, Culture and Value*, Delhi, 1976, pp 447–453.
D'SA, FRANCIS, S. J., *Śabdapramāṇam in Śabara and Kumārila: Towards A Study of a Mīmāṃsā Experience of Language*, de Nobili Library Research series, Vienna, 1980.
———, 'Revelation without a God: Kumārila's theory of śabdapramāṇam', in D. S. Amalorpavadass (ed.) *Research Seminar on Non-Biblical Scriptures*, Bangalore, 1974, pp 469–487.
DE, S. K., *Studies in History of Sanskrit Poetics*, 2nd rev. edn., Calcutta, 1960.
DUMMET, M.A.E., 'What is a Theory of Meaning', in *Mind and Language* (see Guttenplan (ed.), OUP, 1975.

_______, *Frege, The Philosophy of Language*, Duckworth, UK. 1973.

EDGERTON. F., 'Some linguistic notes the Mimansa system', *Language*, 4, pp 171–177.

ELIADE, MIRCEA, *Yoga, Immortality and Freedom*, (N. R. Trask, tr.) Princeton (1954) Princeton Uni. Press, 1958.

_______, *The Two and the One*, The University of Chicago Press, Chicago, 1962.

ENCYCLOPEDIA OF INDIAN PHILOSOPHIES (General Editor, Karl H. Potter): Vol I - Bibliography (1970, 1974, 1980, revised 1982, MB, Delhi); Vol II. Nyāya-Vaiśeṣika: Indian Metaphysics and Epistemology, The Tradition of Nyāya-Vaiśeṣika up to Gaṅgeśa (part 1), (1st edn. Princeton Univ. Press, Princeton, 1977; MB, Delhi 1977), Vol III. Advaita Vedānta up to Śaṅkara and His Pupils (part 1), (Princeton, 1978; re: MB, Delhi, 1981).

EVANS, J. L., 'On Meaning and Verification', *Mind* LXII, p. 327.

FINDLAY, J. N., and RYLE, G., 'Use, Usage and Meaning', in *Proceedings of the Aristotelian Society*, Supp. Vol. 35 (1961); reprinted in *Readings in Semantics**, Zabeeh *et al.* (eds) pp. 477–497.

FLEW, A., and MACINTYRE, A., (eds) *New Essays in Philosophical Theology*, SCM, Press, London, 1963 (1966) (includes symposium on 'Theology and Falsification', discussions by Flew, R. M. Hare, Basil Mitchell, I. M. Crombie).

FEYERABEND, PAUL, 'Wittgenstein's Philosophical Investigations', review in *The Philosophical Review*, LXIV (1955) pp. 449–83; reprinted in *Readings in Semantics**, Zabeeh *et al* (eds) pp. 381–417.

_______, *Against Method: An Outline of An Anarchistic Theory of Knowledge*, New Left Book, London, 1975.

FODOR, J.A. and KATZ, J. J., (eds) *The Structure of Language: Readings in the Philosophy of Language*, Prentice Hall, Englewood Cliffs, N. J., 1964.

FRANKLIN, R. L., 'A Science of Pure Consciousness?', *Religious Studies*, Vol 19, No 2, June 1983, pp185–204.

FRAUWALLNER, E., *History of Indian Philosophy*, 2 vols. MB, Delhi, 1974.

_______, *Materialien zur ältesten Erkenntnislehre der Karmamīmāṃsā* (included trans. of *Śābarabhāṣya* I.i.1-I.i.5, H. Bohlaus, Wien, 1968.

FREGE, GOTTLOB, *Begriffsschrift* (Halle, 1879) (trans.) in *Philosophical Writings of Gottlob Frege*, P. T. Geach and Max Black (eds), Blackwell, Oxford, 1960 (pp. 117–135).

_______, 'Uber Sinn und Bedeutung' (trans. as): 'On Sense and Reference', in Geach and Black (1960) (above) pp. 56–78; reprinted in *Readings in Semantics**, pp. 118–140).
(see also under Dummet; Mohanty)

FOUCAULT, MICHEL, *The Archaeology of Knowledge*, Pantheon Books, 1972.

GADAMER, HANS-GEORG, *Philosophical Hermeneutics*, University of California, Berkeley, 1976.

GANDHI, MOHANDAS KARAMCHAND, 'M. K. Gandhi', in *Contemporary Indian Philosophy*, Radhakrishnan* and Muirhead (eds), London, 1966, 1st entry.

_______, *Hindu Dharma*, Navajivan Publishing House, Ahmehabad, 1950.

GANDHI, RAMCHANDRA, *The Availability of Religious Ideas*, Macmillan and Co. New Delhi, 1979.

_______, *Presuppositions of Human Communication*, OUP, 1974.

_______, 'What we Do and Say in Saying and Doing Something', International Philosophy Conf. Jadavpur, 1983 (paper); printed in *IPQ* (Poona), XI. 2. April 1984, pp145–160.

GANGULI, H. K., *Philosophy of Logical Construction*, Sanskrit Pustak Bhandar, Calcutta, 1963.
GÄCHTER, OTHMAR, *Hermeneutics and Language in Pūrva Mīmāṃsā: A Study in Śābara Bhāṣya*, MB, Delhi 1983.
GARBE, R., 'Mīmāṃsā', in *Encyclopedia of Religious Ethics*, Vol VIII, pp648ff.
GARGE, D. V., *The Contribution of the Śābarabhāṣya to Ṛg Veda Exegesis*, Bulletin DCPG, Poona III.4., pp 531–546.
———, *Citations in Śābarabhāṣya*, DCPG, Poona, 1952.
GARDINER, A. H., *The Theory of Speech and Language*, Clarendon Press, Oxford, 1951.
GEACH, PETER, *Truth, love, immortality, an intro. to McTaggart's philosophy*, Hutchinson, London, 1979.
———, 'Truth and God', *Proceedings of the Aristotlean Society*, 1982, Vol I vi, pp 83–98.
GELLNER, ERNEST, *Words and Things: a critical account of linguistic philosophy*, Gollancz, London, 1959.
GHATE, V. S., *The Vedānta*, A study of the Brahma-sūtras with the bhāṣyas of Śaṁkara, Rāmānja, Nimbārka, Madhva and Vallabha, Poona, 1960.
GODDARD, LEONARD and ROUTLEY, RICHARD, *The Logic of Significance and Context*, Scottish Academy Press Edin/London 1973.
GOKAK, V. K., *The Poetic Approach to Language*, O.U.P., London, 1952, (Darby, Pa. 1969)
———, *Four studies in the Language of the Veda,* Mouton, Gravenhage, New Haven, 1959.
GONDA, JAN, 'The Historical Background of the Name Satya assigned to the Highest Being', in *ABORI* (Golden Jubilee Vol.) XLVIII and XLIX, 1968, pp. 83–93).
———, 'Pāṇini and Modern Linguistics', in *Studies in South Asian Culture*, Vol. XII, E. J. Brill, Leiden, 1978 (Senarat Paranavitama Comm. Vol.)
———, *Vedic Literature*, Vol. I of *A History of Indian Literature*, Otto Harrassowitz, Wiesbaden, 1975.
GOODMAN, NELSON, *The Structure of Appearance*, Camb. Mass, 1951.
GRANOFF, PHYLLIS E., *Philosophy and Argument in Late Vedānta : Śrī Harṣa's Khaṇḍanakhaṇḍakhādya*, Classical Studies of India, vol I, D. Reidel & Co, Dordrecht, Holland, 1978.
GREEN, T. H., *Prolegomena to ethics*, (A. C. Bradley, ed.), Clarendon Press, Oxford, 1906.
GRICE, H. P., 'Meaning', re: *RS*, pp 501–512.
GUHA, D. C., *Navya Nyāya Systems of Logic*, MB, Delhi, 1979.
GUPTA, RITA, 'Some Significant Contributions of Buddhist Logicians in the Development of Indian Philosophy', *IPQ* (Poona), XI 2, 1984, pp 161–170.
GÜTTENPLAN, SAMUEL, (ed.) *Mind and Language*, Wolfson College Lectures, 1974, Clarendon Press, Oxford, 1977 (contributions by D. Davidson, Føllesdal, Anscombe, Quine, Dummet, Geach).
HABERMAS, JURGEN, *Communications and the evolution of society* (tr. Thomas McCarthy), Beacon Press, Boston, 1979.
———, *Knowledge and Human Interest*, (tr. J. Shapiro) Beacon Press, Boston, 1971.
HACKER, PAUL, 'Śaṅkara's Conception of Man', reprinted in *Kleine Schriften*, L. Schmithausen (ed.), Franz Steiner, Weisbasden, 1978, pp 243–251.

_______, 'Saṅkara der Yogin und Śaṅkara der Advaitin: Einige Beobachtungen', in Oberhammer (ed.) Festschrift für Erich Frauwallner, Weiner Zeitschrift für die Kunde Süd- und Ostasiens 12–13 (1968–69); reprinted in *Kleine Schriften*, L. Schmithausen (ed.), Franz Steiner, Wiesbaden, 1978, pp 213–242.

HALBFASS, W., 'India and the Comparative Method', *PEW*, vol 35, no 1, 1985, pp 3–15.

_______, *Studies in Kumārila and Śaṅkara*, Verlag für Orientalistische Fachpublikationem, Studien zur Indologie und Iranlistik, Reinbeck, 1983 (esp. 'Human Reason and Vedic Revelation in the Philosophy of Śaṅkara', see review by Taber).

HARRISON, B., 'Meaning and Mental Images', in *Proceedings of the Aristotelian Society*, (1962–3) pp. 237 ff.

HINO SHOUN, *Sureśvara's Vārtika on Yājñavalkya Maitreyī Dialogue*, MB, Delhi, 1982.

HARE, R. M., *Moral Thinking*, Clarendon Press, Oxford, 1981

HAJURKAR, S.S, *Vācaspati Miśra on Advaita Vedānta*, Mithila Institute series 3, Durbangh, 1958.

HATTORI, MASAAKI, *Dignāga, On Perception* (trans. with annotation), Harvard University Press, Camb. Mass, 1968.

_______, '*Pratyakṣabhāṣā*—Dignāga's View and Dharmakīrti's Interpretation', *Miscellanea Indologica*, Kyoto, Vol. 6–7, 1965, pp. 122–128.

_______, *Dignāga's Theory of Direct Knowledge* (tr. of *Pramāṇasamuccaya*, Chp. I) in Furitsu Daigaku, Bakai, Jimbun Shakai, Bulletin Series C. Vol. 7, 1959 pp. 1–20.

HEAL, JANE, 'On the Phrase';'Theory of Meaning' (re:) *The Philosopher's Annual*, Boyer, Grim, Sanders (eds), Basil Blackwell, Oxford, 1970/2 pp. 111–127.

HEIDEGGER, MARTIN, *An Introduction to Metaphysics*, (Ralph Manheim, tr.), Doubleday and Co., N.Y. 1961.

_______, *Poetry, Language and Thought*, (with Intro. Albert Hofstader, tr.), N.Y. 1952.

HICK, J., *Faith and Knowledge*, Oxford Univ. Press, London, 1957.

_______, *Philosophy of Religion*, 2nd edn. Prentice-Hall, N. J., 1973.

HIRIYANNA, MYSORE, *Essentials of Indian Philosophy*, George Allen and Unwin, London, 1974.

_______, *Indian Philosophical Studies*, 2 vols. Kavyalva Publ Mysore, 1957–72.

_______, *The Quest After Perfection*, Kavyalaya Pub., Mysore, 1952.

HINTIKKA, JAAKKO, *Knowledge and Belief: an introduction to the logic of the two notions,* Cornell, Univ. Press, Ithaca, 1962.

HUME, DAVID, *Enquiries Concerning Human Understanding and Concerning the Principles of Morals*, Clarendon Press, Oxford, 1975.

_______, *Hume on Religion* (selected writings, with Intro. by Richard Wollheim), Collins, Fontana, London, 1963.

HUSSERL, EDMUND, *Cartesian Meditations*, (Dorian Cairns, tr.) Martinus Nijhoff, The Hague, 1970.

_______, *Ideas, (Ideen*), (Vol. I, W. R. Boyce Gibson, tr.) Allen and Unwin, London, 1931.

_______, *Logical Investigations*, 2 vols. (J. N. Findlay, tr.) RKP, London, 1970.

_______, *The Idea of Phenomenology,* (W. P. Alston & G. Nakhnikian trs.) Martinus Nijhoff, The Hague, 1969.
-see also under Mohanty, and Pivčević.

HUTCHINGS, PATRICK, *Kant on Absolute Value,* George Allen and Unwin,

London, 1972.
INDICH, WILLIAM M., *Consciousness in Advaita Vedānta,* MB, Delhi, 1980.
INGALLS, D. H. H., *Materials for the Study of Navya-nyāya Logic*, Harvard Oriental Works, vol. 40, Camb. Mass, 1951.
———, 'Śaṃkara's Arguments against the Buddhists', *PEW* vol. III, no. 4, Jan. 1954, pp. 291–306.
JAINI, PADMANABH, *The Jain Path of Purification*, MB, Delhi, 1979.
———, 'The Vaibhāṣika theory of words and meaning', *BSOAS* 22 (1959); 95–107
IYER, SUBRAMANIA, K. A., 'Bhartṛhari on Dhvani', *ABORI*, XLV1, I-IV, 1966, pp. 49–65.
JAMES, WILLIAM, *Pragmatisim* (NY 1907; re: Longmans, Green & Co., Harlow, Essex, 1949; also in *The Works of William James* (see next item).
———, *The Meaning of Truth*: *a sequel to 'Pragmatism'*, (NY 1909; Ch. 2 in:) -*The Works of William James*, Harvard University Press, Mass. Camb., 1970. (See also Ayer.)
———, *Varieties of Religious Experience*, Fontana, 1979.
JAYATILLEKE, K. N., *Early Buddhist Theory of Knowledge,* Allen and Unwin, London, 1963.
JHA, GANGANATHA, *Pūrva-Mīmāṃsā in its Sources*, BHU, (1942—with bibliography by Umesha Mehta), Varanasi, 1964. (I)
———, *The Prābhākara School of Pūrva Mīmāṃsā*, MB, Delhi, 1978.
———, 'Influence of Mīmāṃsā on legal and other branches of literature', in G. Jha (I) chp. XXXIII, p. 323 ff.
———, Original Commentary on *Jaimini Sūtra* (see under Jaimini)
JHA, RAMACHANDRA, *The Vedānta and the Buddhist Concept of Reality as interpreted by Śaṅkara and Nāgārjuna,* Firma K. L. Mukhopadhyay, Calcutta, 1973.
JHA, V. N., 'Naiyāyikas Concept of Pada and Vākya' in S. D. Joshi* (ed.) *Sentence-Meaning*, pp. 85–94.
———, 'The Structure of Śābda-bodha' (unpublished paper) by courtesy of author, CASS, Poona, 1980.
JOACHIM, H. H., *The Nature of Truth* , OUP, 1939.
de JONG, J. W., 'Mādhyamika', *JIP*, Vol.1, no. 1, 1971.
JOSHI, R. V., 'Validity of Knowledge in Indian Logic' in Dandekar,* Sharma, *et al* (eds.), *Sanskrit and Indological Studies*, V. Raghavan felic. volume, pp. 175–191.
JOSHI, S. D., 'Bhartṛhari's concept of Pratibhā: A theory of the Nature of Language Acquisition', in *Some Aspects of Indo-Iranian Literacy and Cultural Traditions.* Ajanta Publications, Delhi, 1977, pp. 71–76.
———, 'The Mīmāṃsā Theory of Verbal Denotation', in *Vishveshvarananda Indological Journal*, XII, no. I and II March-Sept. 1974, pp. 139–144.
———, *Patañjali's Vyākaraṇa—Mahābhāṣya, Samarthānika on P.2.1.1*, (ed. tr. with notes) CASS, No.3, Univ. of Poona, Poona, 1968.
———, (ed.) *Proceedings of the Winter Institute on Ancient Indian theories of Sentence-Meaning* (held in 1979, March, CASS) University of Poona, Pune, 1980.
———, 'Two Methods of Interpreting Pāṇini', CASS Publication Class A, No. 5, Poona, Univ. of Poona, 1965.
———, *The Sphoṭanirṇaya of Kauṇḍa Bhaṭṭa* (*Sphoṭa: Distinctive, and Significative Levels of Language*), edited with introduction, text, trans. notes,

Chp. XIV of *Vaiyākaraṇa-bhūṣaṇasāra*, Univ. of Poona, Poona, 1967.
_______, 'Word-integrity and Syntactic analysis', CASS, Class A, No.20, Univ. of Poona, Poona, 1968.
KANE, P. V., *History of Dharmaśāstras* (various) 5 vols. B.O.R.I. 1962–7.
_______, *History of Sanskrit Poetics*, Banaras, 1942.
KANT, IMMANUEL, *Critique of Pure Reason (1787)* (Norman Kemp Smith, tr.) MacMillan, St. Martin's Press, 1970.
_______, *Groundwork of the Metaphysics of Morals*, (H.J.Paton, tr.) Harper and Row, New York, 1964
_______, *Prolegomena to Any Future Metaphysics*, (P. G. Lucas, tr.) Manchester, 1953. (see also Strawson; Hutchings).
_______, *Religion within the Bounds of Reason*, (T. N. Greene and Hoyt H. Hudson, trs) reissued: Harper and Row, NY, 1960.
KAPALI SASTRY, T. V., 'Sphoṭa and the Spoken word', in *Sri Aurobindo Mandir* (India), vol. 15, Aug. 1945, pp. 29–43.
KATZ, STEVEN T., (ed.), *Mysticism and Philosophical Analysis*, OUP, Oxford, 1978.
KAVIRAJA, GOPINATH, *Aspects of Indian Thought*, The Univ. of Burdwan, Burdwan, 1966.
_______, 'The Doctrine of Pratibhā in Indian Philosophy', in his *Aspects of Indian Thought*.
_______, *Gleanings from the History and Bibliography of the Nyāya-Vaiśeṣika Literature*, K. L. Mukhopadhyaya, Calcutta, 1961.
_______, 'The Viewpoint of Nyāya-Vaiśeṣika philosophy' in *The Prince of Wales Saraswati Bhavana Studies*, Vol. I, pt. 1, Benaras, 1922, p. 27–45.
KEITH, A. B., *Indian Logic and Atomism*, The Clarendon Press, Oxford, 1921.
_______, *The Karma Mīmāṃsā*, Oriental Books, Reprint, Delhi, 1978.
KESARCODI-WATSON, IAN, 'Śruti and Philosophy' [authored under Ian Watson], *Numen* (Leiden), 1972, XIX; 204–215.
_______, 'Hindu Metaphysics and its Philosophies—*Śruti* and *Darśana*', *IPQ* (Fordham), Dec. 1978; XVIII, no. 4; pp. 413–432.
_______, *Eastern Spirituality*, Agam Prakashan, Delhi, 1976.
_______, *Studies in Hindu Wisdom*, Allied Publications, Delhi, 1981.
_______, 'Are There Real Things? Borrowings from Nāgārjuna', *JIP* 5, 1978, pp. 371–383.
KIELHORN, FRANZ, 'The Authorities on Grammar quoted in the *Mahābhāṣya*' (1887) with text of Pāṇini's *sūtras* in Staal* (ed.) *RSG*. pp. 106–134. Also see Patañjali, *Vyākaraṇa-Mahābhāṣya*.
KIERKEGAARD, SØREN, *Philosophical Fragments*, (D. F. Swenson, tr.) 2nd edn. Princeton Univ. Press, Princeton, 1962.
_______, *On Authority and Revelation*, (Walter Lowrie, tr.) Harper & Row, New York, 1955.
KIPARSKY P., and STAAL, J. F., 'Syntactic and Semantic Relations in Pāṇini', *Foundations of Language*, 5 (1969), pp. 83–117
KLOSTERMAIER, KLAUS, 'Man Carries the Power of All Things in his Mouth', Jacob Boehme's Ideas on Word and Language', in *Revelation in Indian Thought*, Coward* and Sivaraman (eds), 1977, pp. 87–98.
_______, 'The Creative Function of the Word', in Coward* (ed.) *Language in Indian Philosophy and Religion*, pp 5–18.
KOSAMBI, D. D., *The Culture and civilization of ancient India in historical outline*, RKP, London, 1965.

KRISHNANMOORTY, K., (I) *Dhvanyāloka and its critics*, Kavyalaya Publishers, Mysore, 1967.

———, (II): *Studies in Indian Aesthetics and Criticism*, D. V. K. Murty, Mysore, 1979.

KRISHNA, WARRIER A. G., 'Gauḍapāda and Śaṅkara (A Study in Contrast)', in *ABORI*, Golden Jubilee volume, XLXIII-XLIX, 1968, pp. 179-186.

KROY, MOSHE, Review of *Philosophy East/Philosophy West*, B. A. Sharfstein (ed.), (Blackwell, Oxford), in *AJP*, Vol 59, No 1, March 1981, pp 115-118.

KUHN, THOMAS, S., *The Structure of Scientific Revolution*, 2nd edn. The University of Chicago Press, Chicago, 1970.

KUNJUNNI RAJA, *Indian Theories of Meaning*, ALRS, Madras, 1969.

———, 'The Role of Tātparya in understanding Sentence-Meaning', in S.D. Joshi* (ed.) *Sentence-Meaning*, pp. 95-100.

KUNHAN RAJA, 'In defence of Mīmāṃsā', *Adyar Library Bulletin?*

———, *'Bhagavadgītā and the Mīmāṃsā'*, *Adyar Library Bulletin*, (Madras), 10, 1946, pp. 9-22.

———, *Some Fundamental Problems in Indian Philosophy*, MB, Delhi, 1974.

KUPPUSWAMI, SASTRI, *A Primer of Indian Logic (According to Annaṃbhaṭṭa's Tarkasaṃgraha)*, The Kuppuswami Sastri Research Institute, Madras, 1961.

LAKATOS, IMRE, 'Falsification and the Methodology of Scientific Research Programmes', in Lakatos and Musgrave* (eds) pp. 91-196.

LEGGETT, TREVOR, *Śaṅkara on the Yogasūtra: The Vivaraṇa sub-commentary to Vyāsabhāṣya on the Yogasūtras* (2 parts), RKP, 1980.

LEVI-STRAUSS, CLAUDE, *Structural Anthropology*, tr. Jacobson, Schoepf and Layton, 2 vols. Basic Books Inc. London, 1963, 1972.

LOCKE, JOHN, *An Essay Concerning Human Understanding*, Clarendon Press, Oxford 1894.

LOSKII (LOSKY), N. O., *The Intuitive Basis of Knowledge*; an epistemological inquiry, tr. N. A. Duddington, MacMillan, London, 1919.

LYONS, JOHN, *Introduction to Theoretical Linguistics*, CUP, 1968.

———, *Semantics*, 2 vols. CUP, 1977.

MCKEON, R., *Selections from Medieval Philosophers,* Vol. 1, Charles Scribner & Son, New York, 1929.

MACDONNELL, A. A., *A History of Sanskrit Literature* (1899), MB, Delhi, 1976.

———, *Vedic Mythology* (1898), MB, Delhi (1974).

MAHADEVAN, T.M.P., *Gauḍapāda: A Study in Early Vedānta,* Univ of Madras, Madras, 1975.

———, *The Philosophy of Advaita*, (with special reference to Bharatitirtha-vidyaranya) Compton Russell, Element (Salisbury), 1977.

———, (Gen. Editor) *Word-Index to the Brahmasūtrabhāṣya*, 2 parts, Centre for Advanced Study in Philosophy Series 17, Univ. of Madras, 1973

MAINKAR, T. G., *A Comparative Study of the Commentaries on the Bhagavadgita*, MB, Delhi, 1969.

———, *Some Poetical Aspects of the ṚgVedic Repetitions*, Univ. of Poona, Poona, 1966.

———, *Sāṃkhyakārikā of Īśvarakṛṣṇa, with Gauḍapādabhāṣya* (trans. and notes), Oriental Book Agency, Poona, 1972.

MAITRA, S. K., *Fundamental Questions of Indian Metaphysics and Logic*, 2nd edn. Univ. of Calcutta, Calcutta, 1974.

———, *Madhva Logic* (Jayathīrtha*), Calcutta University, Calcutta, 1936.

_______, 'Truth and Error', in Murty* and Rao (eds.) 1970, pp. 179–293.

MALKANI, G. R., *Vedāntic Epistemology*, The Indian Institute of Philosophy, Amalmer, 1958.

MARLEAU-PONTY, *The Phenomenology of Perception*, tr. Colin Smith, Humanities Press, New York, 1962.

MASSON, J.M. and MASSON, T. C., 'The Study of Mysticism: A Criticism of W.T. Stace', *JIP*. vol. 4, 1976, pp. 109–125.

MATILAL, BIMAL KRISHNA, *Epistemology, Logic and Grammar in Indian Philosophical Analysis*, [= ELG] Mouton; The Hague-Paris, 1971. See also review of *ELG* by John W Yolton, in *JIP*. 2 (1974) pp. 373–383;

_______, *The Navya-nyāya Doctrine of Negation: The Semantics and Ontology of Negative Statements in Navya-nyāya Philosophy* [= *NND*]; Harvard Oriental Series, 46. Harvard Univ. Press, Camb. Mass. 1968. (Review by J. N. Mohanty, in *JIP*, no 1, 1971, pp 197–211.)

_______, 'Indian Theorists on the Nature of the Sentence (*vākya*)', in *Foundations of Language*, 2, 1966, pp. 377–393.

_______, 'Indian Theories of Knowledge and Truth' (Review article on *Gaṅgeśa's Theory of Truth* by J. N. Mohanty*), in *PEW*, No.18, 1968 pp. 321–333.

_______, 'The Intensional Character of *Lakṣaṇa* and *Saṁkara* in Navyanyāya', *Indo-Iranian Journal* (Leiden), vol. 8, 1964–5, pp. 85–95.

_______, 'Jagadīśa's Classification of Grammatical Categories', in *Sanskrit and Indological Studies*, Dr. J. Raghaven Felicitation Volume, Dandekar* *et al.* (eds) pp. 221–229.

_______, *The Logical Illumination of Indian Mysticism*, Inaugural lecture at Oxford, 5 May, 1977. (re) Oxford University Press, New Delhi, 1978.

_______, *Nyāya-Vaiśeṣika*, fasc. 2 vol. 6: A History of Indian Literature (ed. Jan Gonda), Otto Harrossowitz, Wiesbaden, 1977.

_______, *Logic, Language and Reality in Indian Philosophical Analysis*, MB., 1985.

MATTHEWS, P. H., *Morphology*, Cambridge University Press, Camb. 1974.

MAYEDA, SENGAKU, *A Thousand Teachings: The Upadeśasāhasrī of Śaṅkara*, (trans. with intro, and notes) University of Tokyo Press, Tokyo, 1979.

MAZUMDAR, P., *Philosophy of Language, An Indian Approach*, Sanskrit Pustak Bhandar, Calcutta, 1977.

MEDAWAR, P., *Induction and Intuition in Scientific Thought*, Methuen, London, 1969.

MEHTA, J.L. (ed.) *Language and Reality* and other Papers, (Proceedings of 2nd All India Seminar, BHU, Varanasi, 1968.

_______, *et al*, (eds.) *Vedānta and Buddhism and other papers*, (Proc. of 3rd All India Seminar, 1966) BHU, Varanasi, 1968.

MEHTA MAHESH, 'Ineffability Reconsidered', in Coward (ed.) *Language in Indian Philosophy and Religion*, pp. 63–82.

MESTHENE, E. G., *How Language Makes Us Know*, Martinus Nijhoff, The Hague, 1964.

MILL, J. S., *A System of Logic: ratiocinative and inductive*, 2 vols. Longmans Green and Co., London, 1906.

MILLER, JEANINE, *The Vedas—Harmony, Meditation and Fulfilment*; B.I. Publications, New Delhi, 1976.

MISRA. G., *Analytical Studies in Indian Philosophical Problems 'Śaṅkara's doctrine of adhyāsa'*, *IPQ* (Poona), Vol II, No. 3, 1975.

MITCHELL, BASIL, (ed.) *The Philosophy of Religion*, OUP, London, 1971. (see also under Flew)

MOHANTY, J.N. (JITENDRANATHA), *Gaṅgeśa's Theory of Truth prāmāṇya(jñapti)vāda* (txt, trans. notes, with Intro) Centre of Advanced Study in Philosophy, Viśva-bharati, Santiniketan, 1966.

_______, 'Indian Theories of Truth: Thoughts on their framework', *PEW*, vol. XXX, no. 4, Oct. 1980.

_______, 'Language and Reality', in Mehta* (ed.), *Language and Reality and other papers*, pp. 1-17

_______, 'On the Nature of the Prāmāṇya Theory', *Our Heritage*, (Calcutta, no. 8, 1960, pp. 43-47.)

_______, 'Prāmāṇya and Workability: Response to Potter', *JIP*, Vol 12, No. 4, Dec. 1984, pp 329-338.

_______, 'Nyāya Theory of Doubt', reprinted in his *Phenomenlogy and Ontology*, Martinus Nijhoff, The Hague, 1970.

_______, 'Indian Philosophy Between Tradition and Modernity', in Pappu* & Puligandla (eds), 1982, pp 233-252).

_______, 'Philosophy as Reflection on Experience', in N. K. Devaraja (ed.) *Indian Philosophy Today,* MB, Delhi, 1975, pp 169-185.

_______, 'Phenomenology and Existentialism: Encounter with Indian Philosophy',*IPQ* (Fordham) vol. XII, no. 4, Dec. 1972, pp. 485-511.

_______, *Phenomenology & Indian Philosophy,' Proceedings of the XI International Congress of Philosophy,* Brussels, 1953, (XIII, pp. 255-262.)

_______, *Phenomenology and Ontology*, Martinus Nijhoff, The Hague, 1970.

_______, (ed.) *Readings on Edmund Husserl's Logical Investigations*, Martinus Nijhoff, The Hague, 1971. (also see under Husserl).

_______, 'Subject and Person: Eastern and Western Modes of Thinking about Man', *IPQ* (Fordham) vol. XX, no. 3, Sept. 1978, pp. 266-273.

_______, 'Understanding Some Ontological Differences in Indian Philosophy', *JIP*, 8, 1980, pp. 205-217.

_______, *Edmund Husserl's Theory of Menaing,* 2nd ed. The Hague, Martinus Nijhoff, 1969.

_______, 'Husserl's Thesis of the Ideality of Meaning', in above, p. 76-82

_______, 'Frege's Context Principle and Indian Semantics', paper presented at International Philosophy Conference, Jadavpur, 1983.

_______, 'Kalidas Bhattacharyya as a Metaphysician', in Banerjee* and Mohanty (eds), 1978, Preface.

MOHANTY, SUBHODH K., 'Śaṅkara's Autobiography: A Philosopher's Excavation', *IPQ* (Poona), III, 3., 1981, pp. 401-410.

MOGHE,S. G., 'Śaṅkarācārya and Pūrva Mīmāṃsā', *The Mysore Orientalist*, IV, 2, Sept. 1971, pp 79-80.

MONTAGUE, WILLIAM P., *The Ways of Knowing*, Allen and Unwin, London, 1962.

MOORE, C. A., and RADHAKRISHNAN, S., *A Source Book of Indian Philosophy*, Princeton University Press, 1957.

MOORE, G. E., *Philosophical Studies*, RKP, London, 1922.

MOWRER, HOBART, O., 'The Psychologist Looks at Language', in *Readings in the Psychology of Language*, L. A. Jakabovitis and Miron (eds), Prentice-Hall, New Jersey, 1967.

MUKERJI, A. K., 'The Epistemological Realism of Śaṅkara', *Philosophical Quarterly* (Calcutta), vol. 34. no 5, 1961, pp 183-185.

MÜLLER, MAX, *The Six Systems of Indian Philosophy*, Longmans, Green, London, 1928.
_______, *The Vedas*, Indological Book House, Delhi, 1969.
MURTI, T.R.V., *The Central Philosophy of Buddhism*, George Allen and Unwin, London, (1960) 1974.
_______, 'Some Comments on the Philosophy of Language in the Indian Context', *JIP* 2, 1974, pp 321-331. (a version of Presential Address, *Proc. 37 Indian Philosophical Congress*, Chandigarh, 1963.
_______, 'Vedānta and Buddhism', in Mehta, J.L. *et al*, (eds) *Vedānta and Buddhism*, Prod 3rd All-India Seminar, 1966, BHU, Varanasi 1968, pp. 63-82. -*The Collected Papers of T. R. V. Murti*, see Coward: *Studies in Indian Thought* (1983), also see, Coward and Sivaraman.
MURTY, K. SATCIDANANDA, *Revelation and Reason in Advaita Vedānta*, Andhra University, Waltair, 1959; re: MB, Delhi, 1974.
_______, AND RAMAKRISHNA RAO, K., (eds) *Current Trends in Indian Philosophy*, Andhra University Press, Asian Publishing House, Waltair, 1972.
MUSGRAVE, ALAN, and LAKATOS IMRE, (eds) *Criticism and the Growth of Knowledge*. CUP, 1974.
NAGARAJA RAO, *Epistemology of Dvaita Vedānta*, The Theosophical Pub. House, 1972.
_______, 'Problems relating to Verbal Testimony with special reference to Dvaita Vedānta', *Poona Orientalist*, vol 2 no 4, 1937-8, pp 212-226.
NAGATOMI, MASATOSHI, '*Mānasa-Pratyakṣa*: A connundrum in the Buddhist *Pramāṇa* System', in M. Nagatomi, B. K. Matilal, J. M. Masson, and E. Dimock, (eds) *Sanskrit and Indian Studies*, D. Reidel and Co., 1979, pp 243-260.
NAKAMURA, HAJIME, *A History of Early Vedānta Philosophy*, MB, Delhi, 1983.
_______, 'Conflict between Traditionalism and Rationalism: A Problem with Śaṅkara', *PEW* vol 16, no2, pp. 157-162.
_______, *Religions and Philosophies of India, A Survey of Bibliographical Notes*, Hokuseido Press (*Eastern Institute). Tokyo 1974.
_______, 'Notes on Śaṅkara's *Yogasūtrabhāṣyavivaraṇa* I', *Journal of Indian Buddhist Studies*, vol XXV no 1, 1976.
_______, 'Bhartṛhari and the Scholar', *Indo-Iranian Journal*, vol. 4, 1960, pp. 282-305.
NAYAK, G., 'A reappraisal of the Vedānta of Śaṅkaracharya', *IPQ* (Poona), New Series, vol 1. no 1, pp 65-66.
OGDEN, C.K. and RICHARDS, I. A., *The Meaning of Meaning*, (with essay by Malinowski) Harcourt, Brace, and World, New York, 1959.
PALSULE, G. B., 'Some views of Pāṇini and his followers on Object Language and Meta language', CASS, (monograph) Class A, no. 36, Univ. of Poona, Poona, 1970.
PANDEY, K. C., *Abhinavagupta: an historical and philosophical study*, 2nd edn. Varanasi, 1963.
_______, *Indian Aesthetics*, Varanasi, 1959.
_______, 'Abinavgupta's Theory of Meaning', *New Antiquity* 5, 1943, pp 241-248.
PANDEYA, R. C., *The Problem of Meaning in Indian Philosophy*, MB, Delhi, 1963.
_______, 'Metaphysical Foundations of Buddhist Theory of Knowlegde', in *Proc. of Indian Philosophical Congress*, Patna, 1968, pp 147-165.

PANDIT, M. P., *Mystic Approach to the Vedas and the Upanishad*, Ganesh and Co., Madras, 1974.

PANIKKAR, RAIMUNDO, *The Vedic Experience Mantramañjarī, An Anthology of the Vedas for Modern Man and Contemporary Celebrations*, (with the collaboration of N. Shanta, M. A. R. Rogers, B. Baumer, M. Bidoli) University of California Press, Berkeley, LA, 1977.

———, 'Words and Terms', *Archivio di Filosopia*, Instituto di Studi Filosofici, Roma, 1980, pp. 117–133.

———, 'Texture of a Text', *Point of Contact*, New York, II,I, April-May 1978, pp 51–64.

PAPPU, RAMA RAO and PULIGANDLA, R., (eds) *Indian Philosophy: Past and Present*, Delhi, 1982.

PARKINSON, G.H.R., (ed.) *The Theory of Meaning*, OUP, London, 1968.

PASSMORE, JOHN, *Philosophical Reasoning*, Basic Books, New York, 1968.

PEGIS, ANTON, C., (ed.) *Basic Writings of St. Thomas Aquinas. Summa Theologica*, Third Article, Random House, N. Y., 1945.

PEIRCE, C. S., in Douglas Greenlee: *Peirce's Concept of Sign*, Mouton, The Hague, 1973. (See also Ayer)

PIAGET, JEAN, *Psychology and Epistemology: Towards a Theory of Knowledge*. The Viking Press, New York, 1971.

PIVČEVIĆ, EDO, *Husserl and Phenomenology*, Hutchinson Univ. Lib., London, 1970.

PLATO, *Dialogues: Sophist, Phaedo, Phaedrus, Meno, Theaetetus*, (B. Jowett, tr.) Sphere Books, 1970.

———, *Republic, Timaeus*, (H. D. P. Lee, tr.) Penguin Books, 1965.

———, *Plato's Epistemology*, G. Matthews, Faber and Faber, London, 1972.

POLANYI, MICHAEL, *Personal Knowledge: Towards a Post-Critical Philosophy*, Univ. of Chicago, Chicago, 1958.

POJMAN, L. P., 'Rationality and Religious Belief', *Religious Studies*, vol. 15, no.l 2, June 1979, pp. 159–172.

POPPER, KARL, *Conjectures and Refutations: The Growth of Scientific Knowledge*, RKP, 1965, 1969. (See also Lakatos and Musgrave (eds), 1974)

———, *The Logic of Scientific Discovery*, Hutchinson, London, 1968

POTTER, KARL H., 'Prāmāṇya as Meaning Divorced from Truth-Conditions', paper at International Philosophy Conf. Jadavpur 1983.

———,'Some Thoughts on Nyāya Concept of Meaning', *JIP*, vol. 3, 1975, pp. 209–216.

———, 'Does Indian Epistemology Concern Justified True Belief?', *JIP*, vol 12, no 4, Dec 1984, pp 307–328.

———, 'Toward a Conceptual Scheme for Indian Epistemologies', in Mohanty and Banerjee (eds) *Self, Knowledge and Freedom* , pp. 17–30

———, *Presuppositions of India's Philosophies*, Prentice-Hall, N.J. 1964. -see also *Encyclopedia of Indian philosophies*; and Raghunātha Śiromaṇi.

PRASAD, JWALA, *History of Indian Epistemology*, pub. by Munshiram Manoharlal, Delhi, 1958.

PRICE, H.H.,*Belief*, George, Allen & Unwin, London, 1969.

PULIGANDLA, R., and RAMA RAO PAPPU (eds)(see Pappu).

PUTNAM, HILARY, 'The Meaning of 'Meaning'', *Mind, Language and Reality*, Vol. 2 (CUP, 1975).

QUINE, W.V.O., *Word and Object*, M. I. T. Press, Cambridge: Mass. 1960.

———, *From a Logical Point of View: Logico-Philosophical Essays*, Harper

Torch, 1963; Camb. Mass. 1964.
_______, 'Dispositional Theory of meaning', paper at International Philosophy Conference, Jadavpur, 1983.
_______, 'Mind and Verbal Disposition', in Guttenplan* (ed.) *Mind and Language*, pp. 83 ff.
RADHAKRISHNAN SARVEPALLI, *The Principal Upaniṣads** (trans. notes).
_______, and MUIRHEAD, (eds) *Contemporary Indian Philosophy*, A&U, London, 1966. (Also see C. A. Moore.)
RAGHAVAN, V. *Sanskrit and Indological Studies*, Felicitation volume presented to V. Raghaven, Dandekar* *et al.* (eds).
RAJU, P. T., *Lectures on Comparative Philosophy*, Univ. of Poona, Poona, 1970.
RAMANA MAHARISHI, *The Collected Works of Ramana Maharshi*, (A. Osborne, ed) Rider and Co., London, 1959.
RAMASVAMI, V.A. 'Bhartṛhari: A Pre-Śaṅkara Advaitin', *IXth All-India Oriental Conference, Proc. and Transactions*. Dec. 1937; pp. 548–562.
RAMACHANDRAN, T. P., *The Concept of Vyāvahārika*, University of Madras, 1980.
RAMSEY, IAN, *Religious Language*, SCM, London, 1967.
RANADE, R. D., *A Constructive Survey of Upanishadic Philosophy*, Bharatiya Vidya Bhavan Bombay, 1968.
_______, *Essays and Reflections*, Bharatiya Vidya Bhavan, Bombay, 1964.
_______, *Vedānta – The Culmination of Indian Thought*, Bharatiya Vidya Bhavan, Chowpatty, Bombay, 1970.
_______, and BELVALKAR, S. K., *History of Indian Philosophy, The Creative Period,* Oriental Reprints, New Delhi, 1974.
RANDLE, H. N., *Fragments from Dinnaga*, Royal Asiatic Society, London, 1926.
RANGANATHANANDA, SWAMI, *The Message of the Upaniṣads,* Bhartiya Vidya, Bhavan, Bombay, 1971.
_______, 'Vedānta and Modern Science' (being correspondence between Sir Julian Huxley and the author), Bharatiya Vidya Bhavan, Bombay, 1971.
READINGS IN SEMANTICS, F. Zabeeh, F. D. Klemke, and Arthur Jacobson (eds), Univ. of Illinois Press, Urbana-Chicago London, 1974.
RESCHER, NICHOLAS, *Cognitive Systematization*, Basil Blackwell, Oxford, 1979.
RENOU, LOUIS, *The Civilization of Ancient India*, Susil Gupta, Calcutta, 1959.
_______, *The Destiny of the Vedas in India*, MB, Delhi, 1965.
_______, (ed). *Hinduism* (Great Religions of modern man series), Washington Square Press, N. Y., 1972.
_______, *Indian Literature*, Walker and Co., N. Y., 1964.
_______, *Vedic India*, tr. Philip Spratt, Indological Book House, Varanasi, 1971.
RESCHER. NICHOLOS, *Studies in the Theory of Knowledge*, American Philosophical Quarterly Monograph Series 4, 1970.
RICOEUR, P., *History and Truth*, (C. Kelbley, tr.) Northwestern Univ. Press, Evanston, 1965.
_______, *The Rule of Metaphor*, (R. Czerny, tr.) Univ. of Toronto Press, Toronto, 1977.
ROBINSON, RICHARD H., 'Did Nāgārjuna Really Refute all Philosophical Views', Mehta* (ed) (1968), pp 1–12.
ROCHER, R., 'The Concept of Verbal Root in Indian Grammar' (on Pāṇini 1.3.1), *Foundations of Language*, 5, 1969, pp. 73–82.
RORTY, RICHARD, *Philosophy and the Mirror of Nature*, Princeton University

Press, Princeton, 1979.
RUEGG, DAVID SEYFORT, *The Literature of the Mādhyamika School of Philosophy in India*, Otto Harrassowitz, Weisbaden, 1981.
———, *Contributions a l'histoire de la philosophie linguistique Indienne*, Paris, 1959.
RUNES, DIGOBERT, *Dictionary of Philosophy*, Philosophical Library, Inc., N. Y., 1960.
RUSSELL, BERTRAND, *An Inquiry into Meaning and Truth*, A&U, 5th imp. 1956.
———,'Common-Sense Inference', in *Science and Perception in Human Knowledge, its scoper and limits*, Clarion Books (& Simon & Schuster), N.Y. 1948.
———, 'On Denoting', in *RS*.
———, *Basic Writings*, (Robert E. Egner and Lester E. Denonn, eds), A&U, London, 1961
RYLE, GILBERT, *The Concept of Mind*, Barnes and Noble, NY, 1949.
SANTAYANA, GEORGE, *Scepticism and animal faith*, N. Y., 1955.
SATPRAKASHANANDA SWAMI, *Methods of Knowledge—according to Advaita Vedanta*, Advaita Ashrama, Calcutta 1974.
SARMA, ANJANEYA, *Citsukha's Contribution to Advaita*, Kavyalaya Publishers, Mysore, 1974.
SASTRI, GAURINATH, *History of Classical Sanskrit Literature,* MB, Delhi, 1974.
———, *A Study in the Dialectics of Sphoṭa*, MB, 1980.
———, *The Philosophy of Word and Meaning*: Some Indian Approaches with reference to Bhartrhari. Government of West Bengal, Sanskrit College, Calcutta, 1959.
SASTRI, MARKANDEYA C., *Sureśvara's Contribution to Advaita*, Vemur, Andhra Pradesh, 1973?.
SASTRI, PASHUPATINATH, *Introduction to Pūrva Mīmāṃsā*, Ashok Nath Bhattacharya, Calcutta, 1923.
SASTRI, P. S., 'The Ideal Content of a Sentence', *Calcutta Review*, June 19576, pp. 239–56.
SAUSSURE, de F., *Cours de linguistic gênérale*, (Wade Buskin, tr.): *Course in General Linguistics*, Fontana, Collins, Glasgow, 1974.
SEN, AMARTYA and WILLIAMS, BERNARD, (eds) *Utilitarianism and Beyond* , CUP, 1982.
SEN, P. D., 'Pramāṇa Śivaḥ (on Udayana's Theism)', *Proc. Indian Philosophical Congress, 57th session*, 1971, pp 52–63
SENGUPTA, BRATINDRA KUMAR, *A Critique on the Vivaraṇa School*, Firma K.L. Mukhopadhyaya, Calcutta, 1959.
SEARLE, JOHN R., *Speech Acts: An Essay in the Philosophy of Language*, CUP, 1969
———, *Intentionality: An Essay in the Philosophy of Mind*, CUP, 1983.
———, 'Literal Meaning' (reprinted) in *The Philosopher's Annual* Vol II, Boyer/Grim/Sanders (eds), Blackwell, Oxford, 1979, pp. 155–272.
SELLARS, WILFRED, 'Language as Thought and as Communication', *Philosophy and Phenomenological Research*, 29, 1969, pp 506–527.
SINHA, DEBABRATA, *The Metaphysic of Experience in Advaita Vedānta—a phenomenological approach*, MB, Delhi, 1983.
———, 'Cognitive Language in Vedanta', in Mohanty* and Banerjee, (eds)

pp.213-228.
SHARMA, ARVIND, 'Śaṅkara's Attitude to Scriptural Authority as Revealed by his Gloss on Brahmasūtra 1.1.3', *JIP*, vol 10, 1982, pp 179-186.
SHARMA, B.N.K., *The Brahmasūtras and their Principal Commentaries*, 2 vols. Bharatiya Vidya Bhavan, Bombay, 1974.
SHARMA, DHIRENDRA, *Differential Theory of Meaning in Indian Logic*, (includes trans. of *Apohasiddhi* of Ratnakīrti), Mouton, The Hague, 1969.
_______, *The Negative Dialectics* (in Indian Philosophy) Sterling Publishers, New Delhi, 1974.
SHARMA, P.S. *Anthology of Kumārilabhaṭṭa's Works*, MB, Delhi, 1980.
SHARPE, ERIC J., 'Some Problems of Method in the Study of Religion', *Religion*, Spring, 1971, no 2. pp 1-14.
SHASTRI, D. N., The Philosophy of Nyāya-Vaiśeṣika and its Conflict with the Buddhist Dignāga School, Agra University, Agra, 1964.
SINARI, R., 'The Phenomenological Attitude in the Śaṅkara Vedānta', *PEW*, vol. 2 July 1972, pp 281-290.
SINHA, JADUNATH, *Indian Realism*, RKP, 1938.
SIVARAMAN, K., 'The Word as a Category of Revelation' in Coward* and Sivaraman (eds) *Revelation in Indian Thought*, 1977, pp 45-64.
_______, 'The Śaiva and the Grammarian Perspective on Language', in Coward* (ed.) *Language. . .* (1976), pp 19-32.
SMART, NINIAN, *Doctrine and Argument in Indian Philosophy*. (Muirhead Library of Philosophy) A&U, London, 1964; Humanities Press, NJ, 1969.
_______, *Reasons and Faiths*, SCM, London, 1959.
_______, 'Some remarks on Apauruṣeya Śruti', IAHR paper, Sydney, 1985.
SMITH, DANIEL H., *The Smith Āgama Collection: Sanskrit Books and Manuscripts relating to Pāñcarātra Studies* (a descriptive catalogue), Syracuse University, Syracuse, 1978.
SMITH, MORTON, 'From Ritual to Philosophy in India', *JIP*, 4, 1978, pp181-197.
SMITH, WILFRED CANTWELL, *The Meaning and End of Religion* (Foreword by J. Hick), Harper and Row, New York, 1978.
SMET, R., 'Language and Philosophy in India', *Proc. XII International Congress of Philosophy*, Firenze, 1960, 10, pp47-54.
SPRUNG, MERVYN, (ed.) *The Problem of Two Truths in Buddhism and Vedānta*, D. Reidel & Co. Dordrecht, and Boston, 1973.
SPRINIVASA CHARI S. M., *Advaita and Viśiṣṭadvaita*, MB, Delhi, 1976
SRINIVASACHARI,P.N., *The Philosophy of Viśiṣṭadvaita*, A.L.R.S., No.39, 1978.
SRINIVASA RAO, 'Anātman anirvacanīyakhyāti and Advaita – A re-examination', *PEW*, vol. 26, 1 Jan, 1976, pp. 71-74.
STAAL, J. FRITS, *Advaita and Neoplatonism*, Univ. of Madras, 1961.
_______, 'Linguistics in South Asia' in *Current Trends in Linguistics*, Vol. 5, Thomas A Sebeok, ed., 1969, Mouton, pp. 499-531,
_______, *Nambudiri Veda Recitation*, The Hague, 1961.
_______, 'Philosophy and Language', in *Essays in Philosophy presented to Dr. T. M. P. Mahadevan*, C. T. K. Chari* (ed.) (Madras) pp. 10-25
_______, (ed.) *A Reader on the Sanskrit Grammarians* (*RSG*), M.I.T. Press, Mass, 1972.
_______, 'Ṛgveda 10.71 on the Origin of Language', in *Revelation in Indian Thought*, Coward* and Sivaraman (eds), PP 3-14.
_______, *Word Order in Sanskrit and Universal Grammar*, Foundations of

Language (Supplemenatry Series, Vo.5) D. Reidel, Dordrecht, 1967

STCHERBATSKY, TH., *Buddhist Logic* (2 vols); (Vol 1 inc tr. of *Pramāṇa-samuccaya* (in part), p. 461F), Mouton, Graven-Hage.1958; Dover, NY, 1962.

STRAWSON, P. F., 'Knowledge and Truth', *IPQ* (Poona), April, 1976 vol III, pp. 273–282.

———, 'Identifying reference and truth-value', re. *RS*, pp. 194–216.

———, *Logico-Linguistic Papers*, Methuen, 1974 (1st 1971) 'Meaning and Truth', pp 170–189.

———, 'On Referring', re: *RS* pp 1–27

———, *Individuals*, Methuen, London, 1959.

———, *Subject and Predicate in Logic and Grammar*, Methuen London, 1974

STRENG, FREDERICK, *Emptiness: a study in religion and meaning*, Abingdon Press, New York, 1967.

SUBRAMANIA IYER, K. A., 'Bhartṛhari on Dhvani', *ABORI*. vol.XLVI, 1965, pp. 49–65.

———, *The Vākapadīya of Bhartṛhari with the Vṛtti*, under Bhartṛhari.*

———, 'The Doctrine of Sphoṭa', *Journal of the Ganganatha Jha Research Institute*, vol. 5, pt.2; Feb.1948, pp. 121–147.

———, 'The Point of View of the Vaiyākaraṇa's', re: in *A Reader in the Sanskrit Grammarians*, J. F. Staal*, (ed.), pp. 393–400.

———, 'Bhartṛhari on Vyākaraṇa as a means of attaining mokṣa', *Adyar Library Bulletin*, Adyar, no. 28, 1964, pp. 112–131.

———, 'Pratibhā as the Meaning of a Sentence', *All India Oriental Conference, Proceedings and Transactions*, vol. 10,1941, pp. 326–332.

———,(tr.) *Sphoṭasiddhi of Maṇḍana Miśra*, DCPR, Poona, 1966.

SUNDARAM, P. K., *Advaita Epistemology* – with Special reference to *Iṣṭasiddhi*, University of Madras, Madras, 1968.

———, 'Advaita and the Problem of Religious Language', *Annals of Oriental Research*, Marad University, 1975, pp 145–155.

SURYANARAYANA SASTRI, S. S., 'A note on marks determinative of purport (*Tātparya-liṅga*)', *Madras University Journal*, vol. 2, 1929, pp. 128–129.

———, (ed. tr.) *The Sāṅkhyakārikā of Īśvarakṛṣṇa*, Univ. of Madras, Madras, 1973.

TABER, JOHN, *Transformative Philosophy A Study of Śaṅkara, Fichte, and Heidegger*, The University Press of Hawaii, Honolulu, 1983.

———, 'Reason, Revelation and Idealism in Śaṅkara', *JIP*, vol 9, no. 3, 1981, pp 283–307.

———, 'Review of Halbfass, *Kumārila and Śaṅkara*', *PEW*, XXXV no 3, 1985, pp 311–314.

———, 'Review of Octmar Gächter*, (1983), PEW XXXV no 2, 1985, pp 215–217.

TACHIKAWA, MUSASHI, *The Structure of the World in Udayana's Realism: a study of Lakaṣaṇāvalī and the Kiraṇāvalī*, D. Reidel & Co, Dordrecht, SCI 4, 1981.

TAGORE, RABINDRANATH, *Upanishad in the eyes of R. Tagore* (anthology comp. by A. K. Mukherji), Dasgupta, Calcutta, 1975.

TARSKI, ALFRED, 'The Semantic Conception of Truth', *Philosophy and Phenomenological Research*, IV, 3, 1944, pp. 321–75; re: in *RS*.

TAYLOR, C. M., 'Theories of Meaning', (Dawes Hicks lecture) *Proc. of the British Academy*, vol LXV!, OUP, 1980.

THADANI, N. V., *The Secret of the Sacred Book of the Hindus*, Bharati Research Institute, Delhi, 1952.

THAKUR, SHIVESH C., 'Conjecture and Criticism in Religious Belief', *Religious Studies* (Cambridge) March 1979, vol. 15, no. 1, pp. 71-78.

_______, *Religion and Rational Choice*, Library of Philosophy and Religion, Macmillan, London, 1981.

TILAKASIRI, J., 'Abhinavgupta – A Literary Critic and Commentator (An Assessment)', *ABORI*, XLVII, 1966, pp 1-10.

TIWARI, KAPIL N., *Dimensions of Renunciation in Advaita Vedānta*, MB, 1977.

ULLMAN, S., *The Principles of Semantics*, 1963.

UPADHYAYA, K. N., *Early Buddhism and the Bhagavadgītā*, MB, Delhi 1971.

VEEZINATHAN, N., 'The Problem of Method in Advaita', *Indian Philosophical Annual*, vol 4, 1968, pp 232-239.

WHITEHEAD, A. N., *Adventure of Ideas*, Macmillan, NY, 1933; 1942.

_______, and RUSSELL B., *Principia Mathematica*, CUP, 1929.

WINTERNITZ, M., *A History of Indian Literature*, (parts I and II), Oriental Reprints, New Delhi, 1979.

WITTGENSTEIN, LUDWIG, *Tractatus Logico-Philosophicus* (Intro. by Bertrand Russell, (trs. Pears, D.F. and McGuinness, B.F.) The Humanities Press, N. J., 1961.

_______, *Philosophical Investigations* (*PI*) (tr. G. E. M. Anscombe), Blackwell, Oxford, 1953.

_______, *The Blue and Brown Books*, preliminary studies for the 'Philosophical Investigations', Harper and Row, New York, 1965.

WOTERSTORFF, NICHOLOS, *Reason within the bounds of Religion*, William Eerdmans Publ., 1976.

ZABEEH, F., *et al* (eds) *Readings in Semantics.* *

ZIFF, PAUL, *Semantic Analysis*, Cornell Univ. Press, N. Y., 1964.

NAME INDEX

The following name index includes references to a few texts only in instances where the author is unknown or uncertain, or inconsequential. Specific references to texts relevant to the proper names occur in the chapter notes, with details and reference to further or other works, editions, etc., in the Bibliography (Appendix B). (The numbers refer to pages.)
The subject index is given separately under General Index.

GENERAL INDEX

The following is a combined Sanskrit and English subject index. Sanskrit terms are italicised and, in some cases, followed by their approximate English equivalents (added in parentheses). Roman alphabetical ordering is followed throughout. This index is not intended to be exhaustive. (* = *qv*; numbers refer to pages.)